University of Edinburgh
30150 024904788

Nazi Rule and the Soviet Offensive in Eastern Germany, 1944–1945

THE DARKEST HOUR

Nazi Rule and the Soviet Offensive in Eastern Germany, 1944–1945

THE DARKEST HOUR

Alastair Noble

2 4 6 8 10 9 7 5 3 1

First published 2009 in Great Britain by
SUSSEX ACADEMIC PRESS
PO Box 139
Eastbourne BN24 9BP

and in the United States of America by
SUSSEX ACADEMIC PRESS
920 NE 58th Ave Suite 300
Portland, Oregon 97213-3786

British Library Cataloguing in Publication Data
A CIP catalogue record for this book is available from the British Library.

Library of Congress Cataloging-in-Publication Data
Noble, Alastair.
Nazi rule and the Soviet offensive in Eastern Germany, 1944–1945 : the darkest hour / Alastair Noble.
p. cm.
Revision of the author's thesis (Ph.D.)—University of Leeds, 1999.
Includes bibliographical references and index.
ISBN 978-1-84519-285-3 (hbk. : alk. paper)
1. World War, 1939–1945—Propaganda. 2. World War, 1939–1945—Germany (East) 3. World War, 1939–1945—Psychological aspects. 4. World War, 1939–1945—Campaigns—Eastern Front. 5. Nazi propaganda—Germany (East) I. Title.
D810.P7G3596 2008
940.53′431—dc22

2008010883

Typeset and designed by SAP, Brighton & Eastbourne.
Printed by TJ International, Padstow, Cornwall.
This book is printed on acid-free paper.

Contents

Acknowledgments vii
Abbreviations and Glossary ix
List of Illustrations xii
Maps xiv–xix

Introduction 1

PART I A Faraway Land

CHAPTER 1
Come the *Gauleiters*, 1933–1939 17

CHAPTER 2
An Oasis of Tranquillity? The German East, 1939–1944 33

CHAPTER 3
Enjoy the War, the Peace will be Dire 44

PART II The War Comes Home: Eastern Germany July 1944–January 1945

CHAPTER 4
A Deep Anxiety over the Fate of East Prussia 73

CHAPTER 5
A Unique, Improvised Exertion: *Ostwallbau*, 1944 95

CHAPTER 6
Confronting Catastrophe: The October Invasion of East Prussia and the Launch of the *Volkssturm* 128

CHAPTER 7
A Stay of Execution 161

PART III Endgame: Eastern Germany 1945

CHAPTER 8
The Deluge **191**

CHAPTER 9
Our Brave Fortresses in the East **218**

Conclusion **242**

Notes 245
Bibliography 332
Index 356

Acknowledgments

This book constitutes a much remodelled version of a PhD thesis submitted to the University of Leeds in February 1999 entitled *Propaganda, Morale and Flight. The Eastern Provinces of the Third Reich, summer 1944 to spring 1945*. My interest in an 'unknown Germany' east of the Oder was triggered by a chance schoolboy encounter with a geography book in a Scottish public library. The enduring fascination has led to this study of the final chaotic months of Nazi rule in Germany's eastern provinces. Too frequently this period has been neglected and scholars have directed their attention to the suffering endured by eastern Germans at the hands of the Red Army and the new Polish regime. Their misery often started months or years before.

During the preparation of the thesis and book I have received advice and assistance from numerous sources. Prior to starting my research in Germany I received welcome suggestions from Professor Michael Burleigh, Dr Theo J. Schulte, Mr Ted Harrison and Professor A. J. Nicholls. Whilst in Germany a number of archivists and other staff were particularly helpful. In this respect I would like to thank Dr Ringsdorf, Frau Hubb and Herr Hufnagl at the Bundesarchiv-Lastenausgleichsarchiv for being so accommodating on my two visits to Bayreuth. Similarly, I would like to express my gratitude to Dr Ritter and Herr Lange at the Bundesarchiv Berlin, Dr Schulz at the Deutschlandhaus Berlin, Frau Bühring at the Brandenburgisches Landeshauptarchiv in Potsdam, Frau Hanske at the Vorpommersches Landesarchiv in Greifswald and Frau Renz at the archive section of the Bibliothek für Zeitgeschichte in Stuttgart. Thanks must also be extended to the staffs of:

Brotherton Library, University of Leeds
Bundesarchiv-Militärarchiv, Freiburg
Geheimes Staatarchiv Preußischer Kulturbesitz, Berlin-Dahlem
German Historical Institute Library, London
Imperial War Museum, London
Institut für Zeitgeschichte, Munich
National Library of Scotland, Edinburgh
The National Archives, Kew.

Valuable assistance was forthcoming from Professor Peter Wende, Director of the German Historical Institute, Mr Peter Simkins, Senior Historian at the Imperial War Museum and Mr Neil Plummer, Modern History librarian at the Brotherton Library.

I would also like to acknowledge Dr Craig Gibson, Dr Martin Longden, Mr Philip Buss, Dr Klaus Schmider and Anne Overell for their advice at various stages. Likewise, my thanks are extended to my PhD supervisor at the University of Leeds Dr Geoff Waddington for his detailed comments on my research. Following my PhD, I also received considerable assistance and encouragement from the late Professor John Erickson FBA, my external examiner. Professor Erickson, the foremost western historian of the Eastern Front, was a wonderful source of information, inspiration and advice. Thanks for financial assistance must be extended to the School of History at the University of Leeds for a three-year Postgraduate studentship, the German Historical Institute for a Postgraduate scholarship and the Royal Historical Society for a research support grant. I am also most grateful to Mr Anthony Grahame of Sussex Academic Press and Dr Keith Hamilton of Foreign and Commonwealth Office Historians for their help and advice with the final manuscript.

At this point I must also mention the financial support and continual encouragement which was provided by my parents James and Irene throughout my years at university. My appreciation is also expressed to my in-laws John and Julia Rogers for their assistance during my research. Finally, I must take the opportunity to my wife Sarah for her willing and unstinting support in so many aspects of the production of this book. Sarah and our wonderful daughters Katie and Gemma have had to put up with a great deal over a long period.

It should be noted that the opinions and interpretations expressed in this book are purely personal and do not in any way represent the official position of the Foreign and Commonwealth Office.

Dr Alastair Noble
February 2008

Abbreviations and Glossary

Alter Kämpfer	'Old Fighter', National Socialist parlance for those who had joined the Party prior to 30 January 1933.
ARD	*Arbeitsgemeinschaft der öffentlich-rechtlichen Rundfunkanstalten der Bundesrepublik Deutschland* (Consortium of public-law broadcasting institutions of the Federal Republic of Germany).
Asoziale	'community aliens' or antisocial elements (National Socialist racial term).
BAB	Bundesarchiv Berlin.
BA-LA	Bundesarchiv – Lastenausgleichsarchiv, Bayreuth.
BA-MA	Bundesarchiv – Militärarchiv, Freiburg.
BBC	British Broadcasting Corporation.
BdM	*Bund deutscher Mädel* (Hitler Youth girls' organisation).
BDO	*Bund Deutscher Offiziere* (League of German Officers).
BfZ	Bibliothek für Zeitgeschichte, Stuttgart.
BLHA	Brandenburgisches Landeshauptarchiv, Potsdam.
Bundestag	present-day German Parliament.
Bürgermeister	mayor.
DAF	*Deutsche Arbeitsfront* (German Labour Front).
DBFP	*Documents on British Foreign Policy 1919–1939*.
DDP	*Deutsche Demokratische Partei* (German Democratic Party).
DNB	*Deutsches Nachrichten Bureau* (German news agency).
DNVP	*Deutschnationale Volkspartei* (German National People's Party).
DVP	*Deutsche Volkspartei* (German People's Party).
EHQ	*European History Quarterly*.
Endsieg	final victory (National Socialist propaganda promise).
Freikorps	Right-wing volunteer paramilitary units, formed after the November Revolution of 1918.
Gau	Nazi Party administrative region.
Gauleiter	Head(s) of Party regional administration.
Gendarmerie	Police constabulary in non-urban areas.
Gestapo	*Geheime Staatspolizei* (Secret State Police).
GH	*German History*.

GSA — *Generalstaatsanwalt* (Chief Public Prosecutor).
GStA — Geheimes Staatsanwalt Preußischer Kulturbesitz, Berlin.
Herrenvolk — master race (National Socialist racial term).
HJ — *Hitlerjugend* (Hitler Youth).
HMSO — Her Majesty's Stationery Office.
IfZ — Institut für Zeitgeschichte, Munich.
IWM — Imperial War Museum.
JCH — *Journal of Contemporary History.*
JMH — *Journal of Modern History.*
Junker — Prussian landowner (squire).
Kaiserreich — German Empire (1871–1918).
KAZ — *Königsberger Allgemeine Zeitung.*
KPD — *Kommunistische Partei Deutschlands* (German Communist Party).
Kriegsmarine — navy.
Küstenwacht — coastal guard.
Landrat — Head of state administration at district level.
Landsturm — militia.
Landtag — Land Parliament (e.g. Prussian *Landtag*).
Landwacht — rural guard.
Landwehr — territorial army.
NA-US — National Archives of the United States, Records of Headquarters German High Command.
NCO — Non-commissioned officer.
NKFD — *Nationalkomitee Freies Deutschland* (National Committee for Free Germany).
NKVD — Soviet People's Commissariat of Internal Affairs.
NSDAP — *Nationalsozialistische Deutsche Arbeiterpartei* (National Socialist German Workers' Party).
NSF — *Nationalsozialistische Frauenschaft* (National Socialist Women's Group).
NSFO — *Nationalsozialistischer Führungs-Offizier* (National Socialist Leadership Officer).
NSKK — *Nationalsozialistisches Kraftfahr-Korps* (National Socialist Motor Corps).
NSV — *Nationalsozialistische Volkswohlfahrt* (National Socialist People's Welfare Organisation).
Oberbürgermeister — Lord Mayor.
Oberpräsident — Governor.
OKH — *Oberkommando des Heeres* (Army High Command).
OKW — *Oberkommando der Wehrmacht* (High Command of the Armed Forces).
OLG — *Oberlandesgericht* (Higher Provincial Court).
Ost-Dok. — *Ost-Dokumentation.*
OT — *Organisation Todt* (Reich construction organisation involved in the building of air fields and fortifications).

OZ	*Oberschlesische Zeitung.*
PomZ	*Pommersche Zeitung.*
PWE	Political Warfare Executive.
PZ	*Preußische Zeitung.*
RAF	Royal Air Force.
Reichstag	pre-1945 German Parliament.
Regierungspräsident	Government President, head of State regional administration, controlling a government region (*Regierungsbezirk*).
RM	*Reichsmark.*
RMVuP	*Reichsministerium für Volksaufklärung und Propaganda* (Reich Ministry for Public Enlightenment and Propaganda).
RPA(Ä)	*Reichspropagandaamt (-ämter)* (local propaganda office).
RSHA	*Reichssicherheitshauptamt* (Reich Security Main Office).
RVK	*Reichsverteidigungskommissar (e)* (Reich Defence Commissar).
SA	*Sturmabteilung* (National Socialist Storm Troop, paramilitary organisation).
SD	*Sicherheitsdienst* (Security Service).
SH	*Social History.*
SOE	Special Operations Executive.
SPD	*Sozialdemokratische Partei Deutschlands* (Social Democratic Party).
SS	*Schutzstaffeln* (police and security apparatus commanded by Heinrich Himmler).
Stadtwacht	town guard.
SZ	*Schlesische Tageszeitung.*
TBJG	*Die Tagebücher von Joseph Goebbels, Teil II, Diktate 1941–1945, 15 Bände.*
TNA	The National Archives, Kew.
USAAF	United States Army Air Force.
Untermensch	subhuman life (National Socialist racial term).
VB	*Völkischer Beobachter.*
Vergeltungswaffe (n)	revenge weapon (National Socialist propaganda).
VfZ	*Vierteljahreshefte für Zeitgeschichte.*
völkisch	racial-nationalist.
Volksdeutsche	ethnic German.
Volksgemeinschaft	'National Community' – Nazi social idea implying a harmonious society devoid of class conflict and class differences.
Volksgenosse (n)	'National Comrade(s)', Nazi term for ordinary German citizens.
Volksgrenadier	People's Grenadier.
VPLA	Vorpommersches Landesarchiv, Greifswald.
WiH	*War in History.*
W&S	*War and Society.*
Wehrkreis	'Defence District', regional unit of *Wehrmacht* administration.
ZDF	*Zweites Deutsches Fernsehen* (Second German Television).
Zentrum	Catholic Centre Party.

List of Illustrations

Cover illustration: Swearing-in the *Volkssturm* and demanding desperate resistance. *Gauleiter* Karl Hanke in *Festung* Breslau, February 1945. (Bundesarchiv Bild 183-1989-1120-502)

Illustrations between pages 120 and 125:
Hitler in Breslau. The *Führer* arrives in the *Jahrhunderthalle* for a speech to a mass audience of officer cadets on 20 November 1943. Behind him (from left), Field Marshal Wilhelm Keitel, *Reichsführer-SS* Heinrich Himmler, Field Marshal Erhard Milch of the *Luftwaffe* and SA Chief of Staff Wilhelm Schepmann. (Ullstein Bild 00046100)

An East Prussian gateway to the east. The Queen Louise Bridge over the River Memel at Tilsit. It was blown up by the retreating *Wehrmacht* in October 1944. (Bundesarchiv B 145 Bild-PO17308)

A symbol of German victory in East Prussia. The Tannenberg memorial at Hohenstein was dynamited by the withdrawing *Wehrmacht* in January 1945. (Bundesarchiv Bild 146-2004-0008)

Defending the *Heimat*. Mass participation in the digging of fortifications in East Prussia, August 1944. (Ullstein Bild 00661957)

Dicing with a death-trap. *Gauleiter* Erich Koch in a one-man-bunker, part of the East Prussian defences, autumn 1944. (Ullstein Bild 00662395)

The People Rise Up. *Reichsführer-SS* Himmler proclaims the formation of the *Volkssturm* at the Marwitz barracks, Bartenstein, East Prussia, 18 October 1944. (Bundesarchiv Bild 146-1987-128-10)

Propaganda image of the East Prussian *Volkssturm*, December 1944. Christmas post is distributed in a cellar bunker. (Bundesarchiv Bild 183-J28377)

Boys doing a man's job. Hitler Youth serving with the *Volkssturm* in the defence of Pyritz, Pomerania, February 1945. (Bundesarchiv Bild 183-J28536)

Defending the Oder Front. A *Volkssturm* position at Frankfurt an der Oder, February 1945. (Bundesarchiv Bild 183-J28787)

The misery of flight. A seemingly endless trek near Braunsberg, East Prussia, January/February 1945. (Bundesarchiv Bild 146-1976-072-09)

Leaving East Prussia. Refugees attempting to board the *FSS Wedel* at Pillau, 1945. (Bundesarchiv Bild 146-1972-093-65)

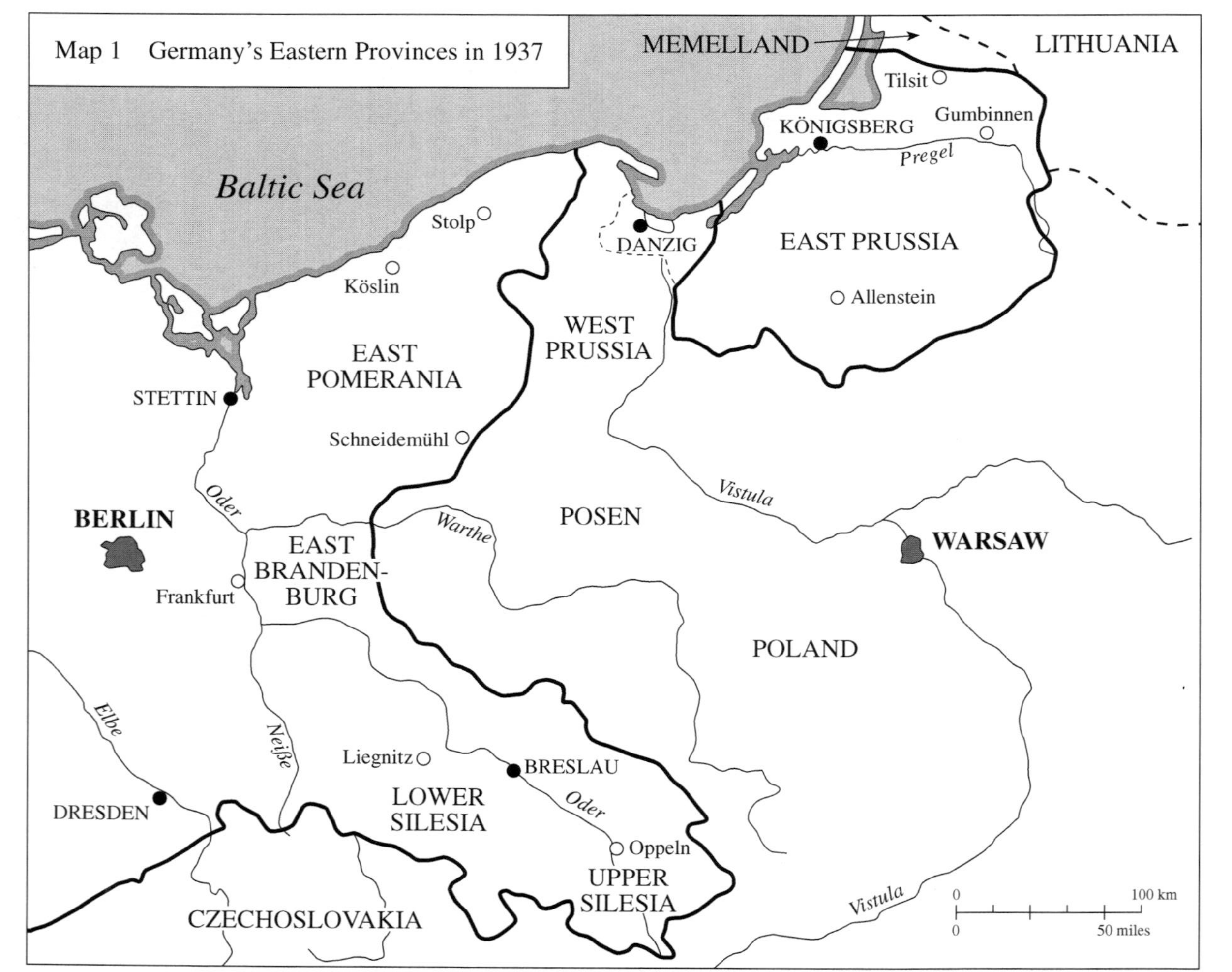

Map 1 Germany's Eastern Provinces in 1937

Map 2 Pomerania, Brandenburg and Silesia east of the Oder–Neiße line: 1937 frontiers

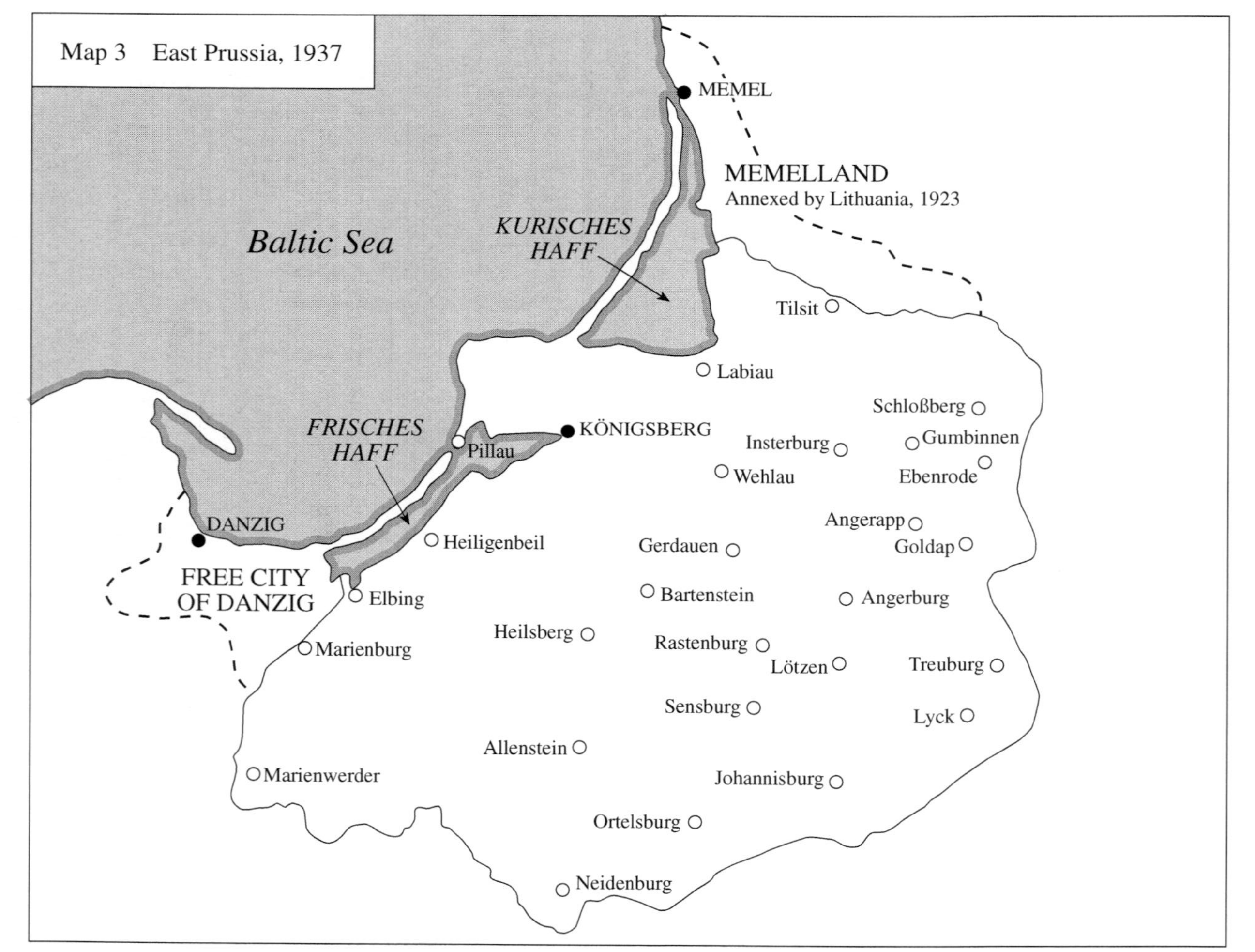
Map 3 East Prussia, 1937
Baltic Sea
MEMEL
MEMELLAND
Annexed by Lithuania, 1923
KURISCHES HAFF
FRISCHES HAFF
Tilsit
Labiau
Schloßberg
KÖNIGSBERG
Pillau
Insterburg
Gumbinnen
Wehlau
Ebenrode
DANZIG
FREE CITY OF DANZIG
Heiligenbeil
Gerdauen
Angerapp
Goldap
Elbing
Bartenstein
Angerburg
Heilsberg
Rastenburg
Marienburg
Lötzen
Treuburg
Sensburg
Lyck
Allenstein
Marienwerder
Johannisburg
Ortelsburg
Neidenburg

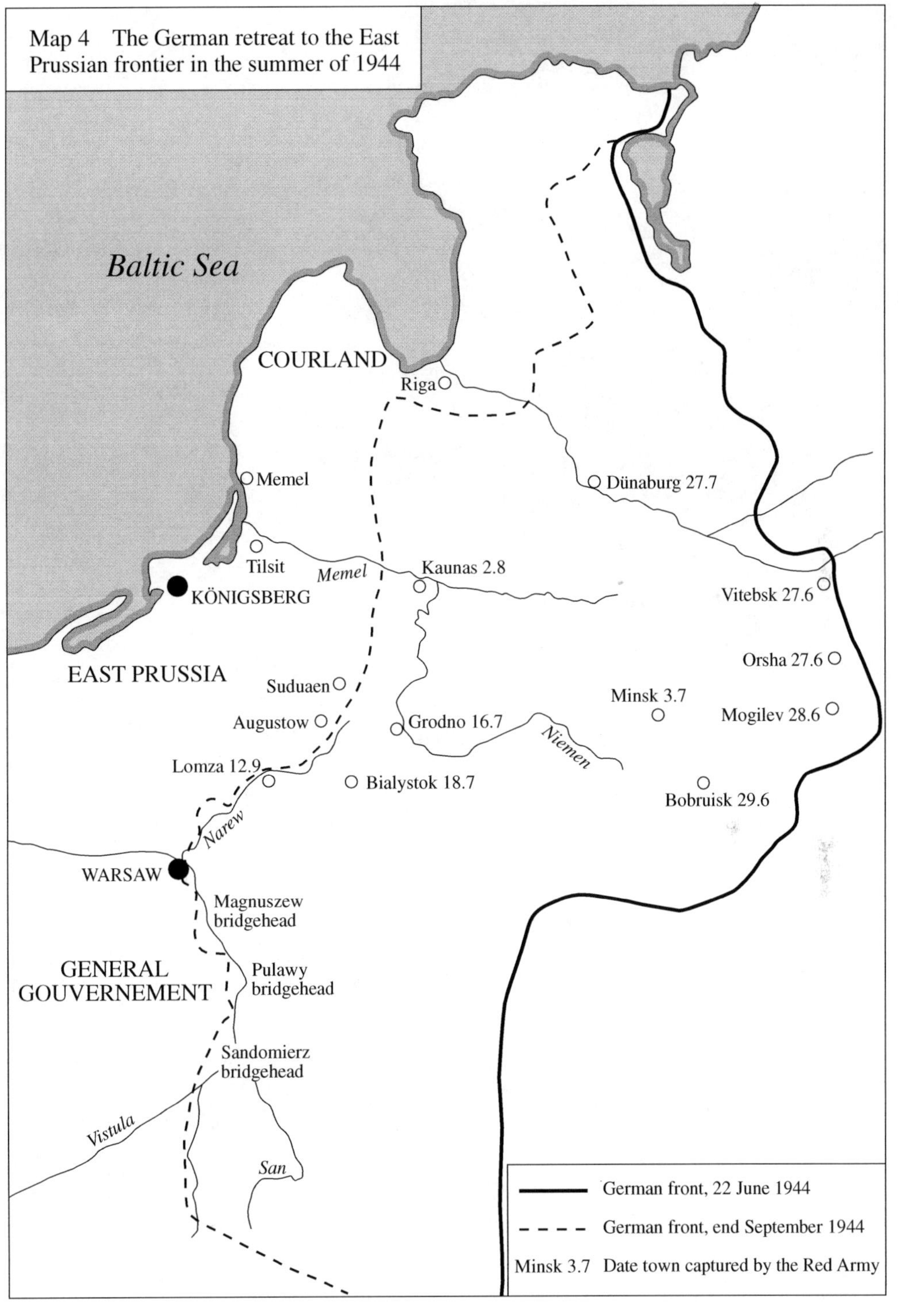
Map 4 The German retreat to the East Prussian frontier in the summer of 1944
Baltic Sea
COURLAND
Riga
Memel
Dünaburg 27.7
Tilsit
Memel
Kaunas 2.8
KÖNIGSBERG
Vitebsk 27.6
EAST PRUSSIA
Orsha 27.6
Suduaen
Minsk 3.7
Augustow
Grodno 16.7
Mogilev 28.6
Niemen
Lomza 12.9
Bialystok 18.7
Bobruisk 29.6
Narew
WARSAW
Magnuszew bridgehead
GENERAL GOUVERNEMENT
Pulawy bridgehead
Sandomierz bridgehead
Vistula
San
German front, 22 June 1944
German front, end September 1944
Minsk 3.7 Date town captured by the Red Army

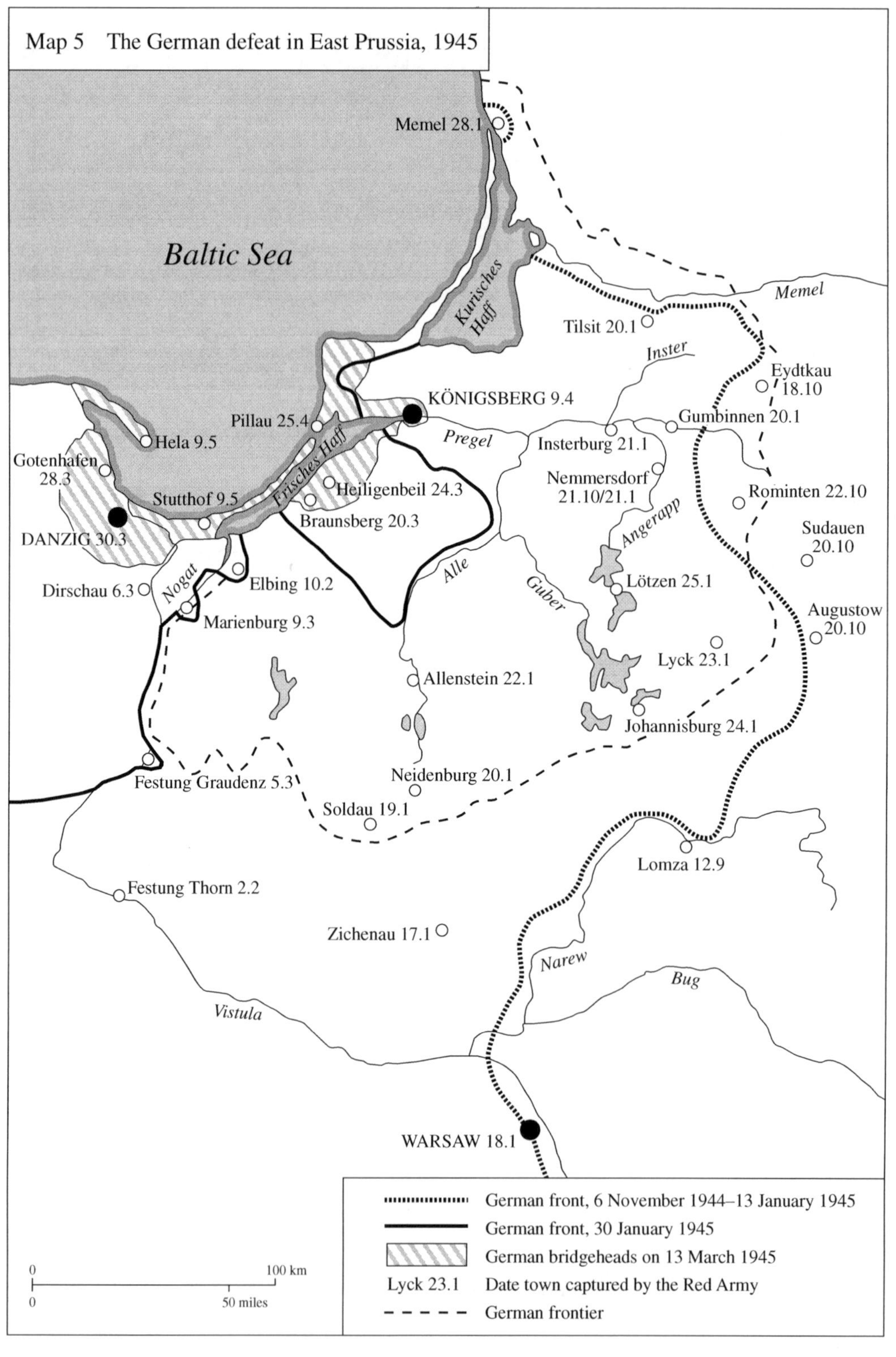
Map 5 The German defeat in East Prussia, 1945
Baltic Sea
Memel 28.1
Kurisches Haff
Memel
Tilsit 20.1
Inster
Eydtkau 18.10
KÖNIGSBERG 9.4
Gumbinnen 20.1
Pillau 25.4
Hela 9.5
Pregel
Insterburg 21.1
Gotenhafen 28.3
Frisches Haff
Nemmersdorf 21.10/21.1
Heiligenbeil 24.3
Rominten 22.10
Stutthof 9.5
Braunsberg 20.3
Angerapp
Sudauen 20.10
DANZIG 30.3
Alle
Elbing 10.2
Lötzen 25.1
Dirschau 6.3
Nogat
Guber
Augustow 20.10
Marienburg 9.3
Lyck 23.1
Allenstein 22.1
Johannisburg 24.1
Neidenburg 20.1
Festung Graudenz 5.3
Soldau 19.1
Lomza 12.9
Festung Thorn 2.2
Zichenau 17.1
Narew
Bug
Vistula
WARSAW 18.1
German front, 6 November 1944–13 January 1945
German front, 30 January 1945
German bridgeheads on 13 March 1945
Lyck 23.1 Date town captured by the Red Army
German frontier
0 100 km
0 50 miles

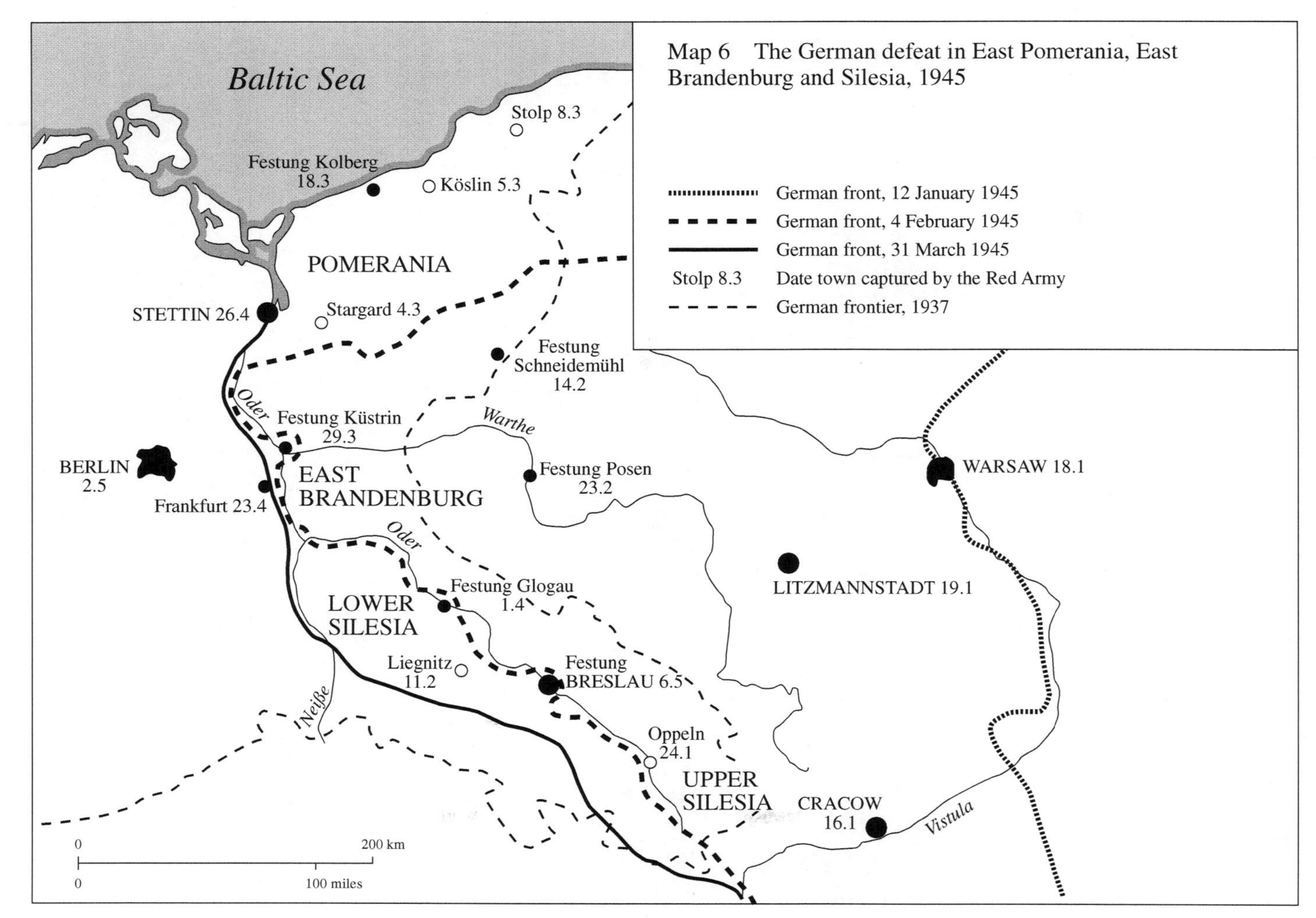

Map 6 The German defeat in East Pomerania, East Brandenburg and Silesia, 1945

Introduction

The closing years of the twentieth century witnessed the return of the term 'ethnic cleansing' to the political stage. Most notably this phrase was used in conjunction with the bloody excesses seen in the former Yugoslavia and Rwanda and relayed into western homes via nightly news bulletins. Ethnic cleansing had contemporary resonance. The media showed an interest in investigating previous sightings. Precedents could be cited such as the shifting of peoples during the Balkan Wars of 1912–1913 and the misery surrounding the exchange in minority populations between Greece and Turkey in 1922–1923. The Nazi–Soviet Pact of 1939 led to centuries-old German communities in the Baltic and Balkans 'coming home' to Hitler's Reich, or more accurately to farms seized from their owners in western Poland or to grotty temporary accommodation. More recent was the bloodshed accompanying the partition of British India and the creation of independent India and Pakistan in 1947. Even greater notoriety was reserved for the Turkish massacres of the Armenians in 1915 as details of this crime became better known in the west. Most infamous of all was the Third Reich's attempt to exterminate European Jewry.

However, some grim episodes appear to have been swept under the carpet. The British and North American attitudes to the flight and expulsion of the Germans from their homes in eastern Germany and central and south-east Europe in 1944–1949 falls into this category. This forced mass migration scarcely merited footnote status in many accounts of the war and its immediate aftermath. The neglect of their suffering led the expellees to constitute one of the groups of forgotten victims of the Second World War. Only in the Federal Republic was their ordeal officially acknowledged and most work on their fate was undertaken by German scholars.

Two-thirds of the 12 million surviving expellees had settled in the Federal Republic by 1950. Expellees comprised almost one-sixth of the West German population. The *de facto* annexation of Germany's eastern provinces by Poland and the Soviet Union, a process which spanned the period before, during and after the Potsdam Conference of 17 July–2 August 1945, was a lasting consequence of the Third Reich's defeat.[1] Germans from these regions provided the bulk of the expellee influx. They came from the pre-war German provinces east of the rivers Oder and Western Neisse, Poland and Danzig and numbered 5.2 million in the Federal Republic by 1950, about 65 per cent of the total expellee figure.[2] After overcoming initial hardships the expellees gradually integrated into their new surroundings and shared in the Federal Republic's growing economic prosperity, their tenacity being widely viewed as one of the motors in the economic miracle which arose from the ashes of *Jahr Null* (Year Zero).

Expellees in the eastern zone, around four million in 1950, were encouraged to remain silent and to refrain from political activities related to their plight. Citizens of the new German Democratic Republic were told that they too were victims of Nazism and 1945 marked their liberation. These were key constituents of the founding myths of the East German state – an identity fastened to an official ideology of anti-Fascism. East Berlin's relationship with Warsaw was cloaked in socialist fraternity and rubber-stamped by the Görlitz Agreement signed on 22 July 1950 which confirmed the Oder–Neisse frontier. Behind the scenes, leading Communist politicians such as the GDR's first president, Wilhelm Pieck, a native of Guben on the Oder, were reluctant to accept the territorial settlement as enduring. During the years of the Warsaw Pact disputes continued between the two states, often over economic and trade issues. Privately, the sentiments expressed by the protagonists showed that the racial stereotypes and prejudices of the past would not go away even under Moscow's tutelage. The longstanding personal animosity between Poland's Communist leader Wladyslaw Gomulka and his East German counterpart Walter Ulbricht epitomised this tension.[3]

Thoughts of the old homelands, now behind the Iron Curtain, were not extinguished among the expellees. In the Federal Republic, regular mass gatherings and a plethora of newspapers, newsletters and memorabilia devoted to the lost provinces illustrated this nostalgic yearning. In recent years fresh opportunities have become available as a result of rapid technological and political change. The onset of the Information Age has led to a multitude of Internet websites pertaining to expellee organisations, their publications and the lands they left behind. Moreover, the collapse of Soviet Communism in 1991 has allowed hundreds of thousands of Germans to finally see their *Heimat* once more as 'nostalgia tourists'.

Cold War Clashes

Neither the post-1949 Federal government, West German academics nor the vociferous expellee groups accepted the Oder–Neisse line as a permanent frontier. The Federal government was pledged to the frontiers of 1937 and official publications described the eastern provinces as 'presently under Polish or Russian administration' or 'under alien administration'. Post-war West German literature on this subject was heavily influenced by Cold War exigencies, bitterness emanating from the loss of German territory and a lingering resentment at the brutal treatment frequently endured by German civilians at the hands of the invading Red Army and the new Polish occupation authorities. These studies emphasised Germany's historic right to the lands passed to the Soviets and those provisionally handed over to the Poles at Potsdam in 1945 and stressed their prosperity and cultural achievements under German rule. They echoed the demands made for the peaceful return of the eastern provinces on the lines of the Charter of the German Expellees (1950) which renounced both revenge and retaliation. Critical expellee pamphlets together with publications from the Göttingen

Research Committee and the Johann-Gottfried-Herder Research Council in Marburg were at the forefront of this campaign.[4]

Simultaneously, these tracts highlighted post-war mismanagement of agrarian and industrial resources. Expellee material blamed Polish idleness for transforming once bountiful lands into economic deserts. For instance, German scholars stressed that even with possession of Pomerania, the richest potato growing soil in Europe, the Poles imported potatoes from the Soviet zone of Germany.[5] The conservative, avidly anti-Communist governments of the early Federal Republic embraced the irredentist mood. Beyond the Oder, a picture of wanton neglect[6] was portrayed where the Polish authorities demolished damaged and even hitherto intact former German properties to provide bricks for the rebuilding of Warsaw's Old Town,[7] the remnants of which had been systematically razed to the ground by the Germans during the final months of their occupation – the period between the brutal suppression of the Warsaw Rising (1 August–2 October 1944) and the Red Army's capture of the ruins on 17 January 1945.[8] Only in 1970, following the advent of Chancellor Willy Brandt's *Ostpolitik*, did Bonn recognise the Oder–Neisse frontier. Prior to this, as a leading British scholar remarked:

> Many of the German refugees and expellees from the East would not, or simply could not, accept the loss of their ancestral homelands as history's last word . . . In the 1950s this was still a burning issue in West German politics. No major German party would dare publicly to declare the territory to the east of the Oder–Neisse for lost, whatever the private conviction of this or that politician might be.[9]

Another commentator, pointing to the reality of the permanent and irrevocable nature of the territorial settlement, has noted that 'the [Chancellor Konrad] Adenauer government and assorted refugee organisations simply cried out periodically as an amputated man might express "ghost pains" in the limb he no longer had'.[10] Indeed, in the midst of the social, economic and political integration of the refugees during the 1950s, Chancellor Adenauer's government soothed the demands of the expellee lobby by documenting their recent suffering. In publishing these excesses Adenauer aimed to embarrass German Communists who supported the Soviet and East German advocation of the Oder–Neisse frontier and to satisfy the nationalist SPD-led opposition.[11]

Between 1951 and 1961 a historical commission appointed by the Federal Ministry for Expellees (from 1954 the Federal Ministry for Expellees, Refugees and War Victims) collated written and oral testimony from those who had endured flight and expulsion. The research project was entitled *Dokumentation der Vertreibung der Deutschen aus Ost-Mitteleuropa* (The Documentation of the Expulsion of the Germans from Eastern-Central-Europe). Five multi-part volumes of these testimonies replete with commentary were published by the Federal government detailing the expulsions of the Germans from east of the Oder–Neisse line, Hungary, Romania, Czechoslovakia and Yugoslavia. The editor, Theodor Schieder, and leading Ministry officials hoped that the publication of an English translation would have wide ramifications. They wanted greater support in Britain, and more importantly in the United States, for a revised frontier settlement in the east more favourable to Germany and recognition of the repercussions arising for Germany from the Western Allies' actions at Potsdam. The volumes were never best-sellers, even in West Germany, although those involved in this undertaking included prominent members of three generations of historians. Individual accounts emanating from the series and repeatedly reprinted in paperback were much more popular.[12]

The preparation of the Expulsion Documents ran parallel with an effort by the *Bundesarchiv*, supported by other research institutions and expellee groups, to record German settlement and administration east of the Oder–Neisse line and German communities in eastern-central and south-eastern Europe. Prominent among this vast amount of material were reports by local government officials on events and developments in these areas concentrating on the period between 1930 and 1947. These extensive holdings comprise the *Ost-Dokumentation* and are now located in the *Bundesarchiv Lastenausgleichsarchiv* in Bayreuth.

Both the Expulsion Documents and the *Ost-Dokumentation* are invaluable sources to the researcher of the German East. This partly arises because of the paucity of contemporary sources due to the destruction of sensitive material by the retreating Germans, damage in battle, fire raising by Red Army soldiers and the spiriting away of files to Moscow. Certain reservations must be outlined. The compilers of the Expulsion Documents were influenced by contemporary concerns and the national political aspiration for a favourable revision of the Oder-Neisse frontier.[13] Moreover, despite the editorial committee's claim that the documents were not meant to 'promote mere sentiments of self pity,'[14] somewhat understandably a catalogue of atrocities and outrages at the hands of the Soviets and the Poles is the result. These documents also tended to treat the fate of the Germans between 1944 and 1949 in isolation. The editors rarely considered the atrocities committed by the German authorities further east after 1939 as a backdrop to the attitude and behaviour of Soviet and Polish troops when they invaded the Reich. Furthermore, the vast majority of reports were submitted in the 1950s, a decade or more after the events in question and the time lapse throws into doubt the veracity of some statements. Even sympathetic German scholars observed that the *Ost-Dokumentation* contained contradictions and errors, and required critical analysis and comparison with other sources.[15] Unsurprisingly, correspondents displayed no desire to admit complicity in the unsavoury aspects of daily life in the Third Reich. Any mention of Jewish suffering tended to be confined to the final phase of the war when wretched columns of emaciated Jews evacuated from camps were encountered on the snowy roads. Even these remarks were all too frequently laced with anti-Semitic prejudices.[16]

One key objective of the editors of the Expulsion Documents was to ascertain the number of victims of flight and expulsion. They initially claimed that 1.6 million Germans from Reich territory east of the Oder and Neisse and at least 400,000 Germans from the pre-1939 Free City of Danzig and Poland had perished. The Expulsion Documents also emphasised that German losses 'under Russo-Polish government' were more than three times greater than those inflicted during the full-scale flight which had commenced throughout the eastern territories from January 1945. However, more recent studies have cast doubt on German estimates of the number of victims, noting that 400,000 have been documented and estimating that the entire number was around 600,000.[17]

The German literary onslaught and German casualty estimates were disputed by the Warsaw government's *Zachodnia Agencja Prasowa* (Western Press Agency). Polish authors were encouraged by the Communist authorities to substantiate Poland's historic claims to the 'recovered Western territories' dating back to the Piast dynasty. They pointed to the strategic dangers to Poland and the possibility of internal destabilisation from any German presence east of the Oder. Moreover, the Poles stressed that one-sixth of their countrymen had died during the German occupation and asserted that expulsion was the only means to preclude the possibility of German aggression in the future.[18] More positively, the Polish press stressed the impressive economic progress in the western territories which had been achieved, in stark contrast they claimed to a period of decline prior to 1939 and in the face of immense destruction by the retreating Germans in 1945.[19] Polish writers protested that German statistics concerning flight and expulsion were wrong and they attributed German civilian losses during the flight to the NSDAP's (*Nationalsozialistisches Deutsche Arbeiterpartei*, National Socialist German Workers' Party) national and local leadership. The Nazis were accused of prolonging a lost war and driving women, children and elderly eastern Germans onto the roads in a last-gasp, unplanned evacuation in the depths of winter. The Poles labelled the expulsions 'resettlement' and emphasised that prior to their arrival more than half the Germans had already left the eastern provinces.[20] The struggle for international sympathy was conducted via the pages of books, press articles and academic journals such as in the pages of the *American Journal of International Law* during 1964–1965.[21]

Academic interest in the flight and expulsion waned during the 1960s as the expellees peacefully integrated into West German society. By this stage the right-wing expellee vote had already been swept up by the mainstream Christian Democratic Union (CDU) and the Bavarian Christian Social Union (CSU). Significantly less polemical material appeared during the 1970s and early 1980s as the era of *Ostpolitik* witnessed a measurable reduction in the tensions between Bonn and Warsaw.[22] Nevertheless, there remained 'a largely, isolated stream of so-called *Vertriebenenliteratur*, or expellee literature, that was all too often focused on individual fates and marred by politically distorted memories and polemics.' By 1990, it is estimated that some 5,000 German language works could be found on the expulsions.[23]

A changed political and intellectual climate emerged following the appointment of Helmut Kohl as Chancellor at the head of a CDU-led coalition government in October 1982. Conservative historians exploited the opportunities afforded by political contests and evocative anniversaries to reappraise the Nazi regime and the impact of its legacy on contemporary Germany. This *Tendenzwende* (change of direction) involved a political and intellectual shift to the right and arose from conservative intellectuals attacking liberal trends which had been in the ascendancy since the 1960s. On 8 May 1985, Kohl and US President Ronald Reagan visited the Bitburg military cemetery where SS troops were buried. That same morning they had visited the site of Bergen-Belsen concentration camp. This provoked controversy over the issue of failing to distinguish between the perpetrators and victims of Nazi crimes. Together with the growing confidence of conservative commentators, the incident was instrumental in exposing the differing interpretations of the Nazi past within the historical profession. This erupted into a public row, the *Historikerstreit* ('historians' dispute'), conducted on the pages of German newspapers and magazines which peaked prior to the January 1987 *Bundestag* election.[24]

Andreas Hillgruber, the respected conservative foreign policy historian, played a prominent role in the *Historikerstreit* because of his slim volume: *Zweierlei Untergang: Die Zerschlagung des Deutschen Reiches und das Ende des europäischen Judentums* ('Two Forms of Downfall: The Destruction of the German Reich and the End of European Jewry') published in 1986.[25] His claim that 'both catastrophes . . . belong together' was seized upon by his critics.[26] In his first essay on 'The Collapse of the East in 1944–45 as a Problem of German National History and of European History', Hillgruber, born in Angerburg, East Prussia, lapsed into language similar to that pedalled by Nazi propagandists during the closing stages of the war.[27] Sir Ian Kershaw, the leading British historian of the Third Reich, contended that 'The most charitable reading would suggest that the emotion of the native East Prussian has in this instance triumphed over the cool and rational assessment of the professional historian.'[28] At the crux of the first essay was Hillgruber's plea for historians to empathise with the plight of eastern Germans during the final war winter:

> They must identify with what was actually happening to the German population in the east and with the desperate and costly efforts of the eastern army and the German navy to defend the population of eastern Germany from the orgy of revenge of the Red Army – mass rape, wanton murder and arbitrary deportations – and to keep open in the final phase of the war an escape route to the west for eastern Germans, either by land or by sea.[29]

This argument seemed to suggest that the continued suffering and murder of Jews, concentration camp inmates, forced labourers and opponents of the regime could be condoned as long as Bolshevism did not engulf the Reich. Eastern German lives were, according to this reasoning, more valuable than the lives of the victims of Nazism. Hillgruber also claimed that the dismemberment of Germany was another tragedy for Europe and argued that the German Reich had fulfilled an essentially civilising and christianising role in the east for centuries.[30] Hillgruber has been criticised for failing to mention that the Third Reich unleashed a 'war of ideologies' of unprecedented cruelty against the Soviet Union in June 1941 and of ignoring the criminal orders issued in this respect.[31] Although Hillgruber did admit that the Soviet 'orgy of revenge' was a response to the crimes committed by all branches of the German authorities in occupied Russia from 1941 to 1944,[32] this was indeed 'a "rogue" article among his massive list of publications'.[33]

In his extensive writings, the American lawyer Alfred Maurice de Zayas has championed the cause of the expellees and expressed similar views to Hillgruber on their suffering.[34] De Zayas considers the expellees to be 'forgotten victims' and outside of Germany his assessment is accurate. The interpretations forwarded by de Zayas and by the German military historian Joachim Hoffmann, have found favour among expellee circles and in the expellee press. Rather than concentrating on any revenge factor, they stress the active encouragement of the Soviet authorities in the bestial events of 1944–1945 and cite virulent propaganda, emotive Orders of the Day and arrangements for the transfer of people and plunder from Germany to the Soviet Union.[35] It was only when the resultant orgy of destruction threatened a collapse in discipline and impairment of the combat capacity of the Red Army that strict orders were issued to counter such behaviour.[36]

The counter-accusation that the fanatical German defence of eastern cities in 1945 only resulted in additional suffering and destruction has also been made. This challenged the heroic image of dogged German defence put forward by the commandants of Königsberg and Breslau when they published their memoirs following their release from Soviet captivity in 1955.[37] Erhard Lucas-Busemann, a native of eastern Pomerania, detailed the civilian casualties and destruction inflicted on Königsberg and Breslau. He attributed much of the blame for this carnage to the actions of not only the Nazi but also the military authorities. In addition, Lucas-Busemann pointed to Nazi crimes in both cities and sought to highlight the greater support for National Socialism in the eastern territories during the final Weimar elections.[38]

Twenty-First Century Interpretations

Weighty new contributions by Norman Davies and Anthony Beevor have significantly augmented the limited English language material on the fate of the eastern Germans in 1945. Davies' *Microcosm: Portrait of a Central European City*, co-written with his former researcher Roger Moorhouse, charts the history of Wroclaw, a city which under various guises has passed under Polish, Bohemian, Austrian, Prussian, German and, since 1945, again Polish rule. It is as German Breslau that the city is introduced – fires sweeping through the rubble-strewn streets as the besieged garrison fights a futile battle against the Red Army in 1945.[39] Desperate German resistance and, even more so, Soviet brutality constitute the core content of Antony Beevor's *Berlin* – a grim chronicle of the murder and rape which accompanied the Red Army advance to the Reich's capital.[40] Beevor and his researchers have uncovered a long list of excesses and violations, leading to the conclusion that freed concentration camp prisoners and former slave labourers of the Third Reich frequently shared the same grisly fate as their old German masters at the hands of the Soviets. Beevor, already well known for his best-selling military history *Stalingrad*, received extensive media exposure on account of his new revelations. Both in Britain and Germany this coverage was generally favourable.[41] However, claims that Beevor had written the definitive book on the subject must be treated with due caution, for the new century has witnessed a growing willingness by prominent German writers to document and analyse the wartime suffering of their fellow countrymen.

While Jörg Friedrich and W.G. Sebald have focused on the impact of enemy air attacks,[42] others have concentrated on the misery arising from flight and expulsion. In an examination of Germany's turbulent history, *Im Krebsgang* (Crabwalk) by Günter

Grass, the Danzig-born Nobel laureate, explored the sinking of the refugee-laden liner *Wilhelm Gustloff* by a Soviet submarine in the Baltic on 30 January 1945. This historical novel, acclaimed as the best work by Grass since *The Tin Drum,* received considerable media attention.[43] Television and magazines have also brought the issues to the attention of a mainstream audience. K. Erik Franzen's book *Die Vertriebenen: Hitlers letzte Opfer* appeared alongside an ARD documentary series on the subject.[44] Guido Knopp has produced a lavishly illustrated volume, *Die große Flucht*, unfortunately without footnotes and a bibliography, to accompany his latest documentary series on ZDF.[45] The monthly history magazine *Damals* devoted an entire issue to flight and expulsion, under the heading 'Also a German catastrophe'.[46] At the same time, *Spiegelbuchverlag*, the publishing arm of the weekly news magazine *Der Spiegel*, followed up a serialisation and special edition on the expulsions with the publication of *Die Flucht*, a book claiming to provide 'a shocking picture of the mass expulsion, the painful consequences of which reach into our own times'.[47]

Political Repercussions

The expulsions and questions relating to Germany's post-1945 frontiers have also remained politically sensitive. Some are still contemporary political issues and have generated considerable media interest since reunification in 1990. Three controversies come to mind. First there was the unease over Chancellor Kohl's delay in acknowledging the Oder–Neisse frontier with Poland during the reunification process. Secondly, there is the ongoing saga of the Benes Decrees and the tensions these still provoke in German–Czech relations. Finally, Europe's attention has also been drawn to the protracted negotiations over the future of Kaliningrad (Königsberg), in the post-Soviet world a Russian territory stranded far from the Russian mainland.

It has been said of Chancellor Kohl's attitude to the Oder–Neisse line that, 'Again and again . . . he allowed uncertainty and doubt and misunderstanding to arise around the issue.' In 1985, Kohl's address to Silesian expellees had concerned his Foreign Minister Hans-Dietrich Genscher; the Chancellor's appearance with his host, the revisionist Silesian leader Herbert Hupka, being duly exploited by the Communist authorities in Poland and the Soviet Union as an example of West German revanchism. Kohl's actions in early 1990 when he initially refused to recognise the frontier caused anxiety in Warsaw, where there were fears that the frontier treaties concluded with East Germany and West Germany in 1950 and 1970 respectively would be discarded by the new unified German state. Indeed, Kohl had reaffirmed the 1970 treaty on his November 1989 visit to Warsaw. His behaviour has been viewed as purely political, arising from a desire not to offend nationalist-minded voters prior to the December 1990 election. Kohl later claimed that the international criticism of his actions showed the extreme right and the most entrenched figures in expellee circles of the price of the 'unification of Germans between Oder and Rhine'.[48] Finally, a frontier treaty with Poland was signed by the respective foreign ministers in Warsaw on 14 November 1990 and ratified by the *Bundestag* on 18 October 1991.[49] In 1995, to mark the 50th anniversary of the war's end, leading members of the Federal government emphasised the fate of the eastern Germans, and significantly, for the first time, the Polish government issued a message of regret.[50]

The media spotlight has also turned on the fate of the three million Sudeten Germans stripped of their citizenship and property and summarily expelled from Czechoslovakia in 1945 under decrees issued by President Eduard Benes.[51] German and Austrian right-wing politicians called for the scrapping of the Benes Decrees as a precondition for the Czech Republic's admission to the European Union (EU), demands which alarmed Czechs fearful of wealthy Germans returning and reclaiming their property if the decrees were lifted. Czech President Vaclav Havel's 1995 denouncement of the 'ethnic cleansing' of the Germans and description of the deportations as 'immoral' proved unpopular among his fellow countrymen. However, even he rejected restitution claims, asserting that he was 'not prepared to let new storms wreak havoc in the area of property rights' which ultimately questioned 'the very ground in which the post-war order of Europe had been built'.[52] The best that could be achieved, after two years of wrangling, was the signing of a mutual declaration on the Sudetenland in January 1997. Germany apologised for the suffering inflicted on the Czechs during the Nazi wartime occupation while the Czechs expressed their regret over the 'excesses' that accompanied the expulsions.[53]

Across the border, where many Sudeten expellees found a political home in the Bavarian Christian Social Union (CSU), the revival of interest in the issue predictably soon involved the Party's leader Edmund Stoiber, the Bavarian Prime Minster and defeated CDU/CSU candidate for the Chancellorship at the September 2002 elections. Matters came to a head in January 2002 when Milos Zeman, the Czech Prime Minister, accused the Sudeten Germans of being 'Hitler's Fifth Column' and said they were lucky not to have been shot as traitors. Stoiber, with a wife of Sudeten origin and a track record supporting the refugees' cause, responded that the expulsion 'was and remains a blatant injustice' and attacked Zeman for 'raising the prejudices of the past'.[54] Since the collapse of Communism, Czech courts have upheld the validity of the Benes Decrees and on 24 April 2002, the Czech Parliament voted unanimously against repeal.[55] Thus, at the time of writing, despite the Czech Republic's admission into the EU, these 60 year-old racially motivated laws based on the expropriation of property and ethnic cleansing remain in force.

Finally, 2002 also saw the resolution of the long-running saga of access to Kaliningrad, as Königsberg district was renamed in July 1946 in honour of the recently deceased Soviet President Mikhail Kalinin. The Kaliningrad Oblast's post-war 'redevelopment' consisted of its repopulation by one million new citizens forcibly directed to the region from throughout the Soviet Empire,[56] the attempted erasure of the region's German heritage, the construction of particularly ugly examples of Soviet architecture[57] and the criss-crossing of the land with military installations.[58] As the anchorage of the Red Navy's Baltic Red Banner Fleet (at Baltiysk, formerly Pillau) and the headquarters of the 11th Guards Army (in Kaliningrad), it was sealed off from the outside world by the Soviets until 1991.[59] The break-up of the Soviet Union, and the enlargement of the EU led to renewed fears of isolation, this time from the Russian

Federation. A visiting British journalist was forcefully told by a Russian inhabitant in 1992 '"We lost 20 million people and we got this strip of land in return." If the Germans say "Give us back this land" we will say "return to us our victims"'.[60] Yet, no Russian leader could afford to give up Kaliningrad, particularly President Vladimir Putin, whose wife was born in the city. The events marking Kaliningrad's 750th anniversary in July 2005 stressed Russia limited historical role in the city's rich past. Kaliningrad had emerged from a time-warp beset with social and economic decay, and there were attempts in the 1990s to give the area 'special economic status', leading to talk of 'The Hong Kong of the Baltic'. Instead, the post-Soviet period has been characterised by mounting crime, illegal arms sales and environmental scares arising from the rusting and leaking hulks of the Baltic Fleet.

Historic Königsberg, city of the Teutonic Knights, Prussian coronations and home of the eighteenth-century philosopher Immanuel Kant, had become as Kaliningrad by 2001, 'a centre of organised crime' where more than half of income came from what was euphemistically called 'informal activities'.[61] After months of haggling, the conclusion of a deal between President Putin and the EU in November 2002 ensured access for Kaliningraders to mainland Russia upon EU enlargement. Moscow's initial rejection of visa requirements was overcome by EU insistence due to fears of possible illegal immigrants, crime, health and drug problems. Eventually, it was agreed that the two new member states, Poland and Lithuania, surrounding the enclave would issue all Kaliningrad residents with multiple-entry transit documentation.[62] Perhaps, the possibility of some form of stability will mean that the grim Soviet era and chaotic post-Cold War period in the region's recent past can now be consigned to history.

At the very time of writing a fresh controversy blew up leading to renewed tension between Germany and her new European Union partners. The proposal by the *Bund der Vertriebenen* to build a Centre Against Expulsions to be sited alongside Berlin's new Holocaust Memorial led to a predictably cold response in Poland and the Czech Republic. With the Memorial, the *Bund der Vertriebenen* (BdV) aimed to show 'that the German people also suffered terribly as a result of being expelled' and sought to commemorate Germany's own 'victims of ethnic cleansing'. A joint appeal by leading Polish and Czech politicians against the scheme claimed that it created 'mistrust among neighbours and cannot be in the interest of our countries'. The suggested site led to charges that this was an attempt to 'weigh up the suffering of one group against another.' Some Polish protests took a cruder form. The news magazine *Wprost* depicted Erika Steinbach, the CDU MP and President of the *Bund der Vertriebenen*, who as a small child had fled from West Prussia with her mother, dressed in a black SS uniform and straddling Chancellor Gerhard Schröder. Opposing the scheme, Schröder and Polish Prime Minister Leszek Miller cobbled together a compromise and proposed a centre, overseen by the Council of Europe, to commemorate European exiles. Sarajevo, Geneva and Strasbourg were put forward as possible locations.[63] Nevertheless, a privately-funded temporary exhibition entitled 'Forced Paths', covering 600 square metres in a central Berlin museum, was opened by the BfV in August 2006 and Steinbach received the backing of her Party's leader, the new German Chancellor Angela Merkel, to set up a permanent Centre against Expulsions in Berlin.[64]

Chancellor Schröder had emphasised his opposition to the restitution of German ancestral property in Poland, a cause championed by the Prussian Trust organisation, when he attended the 60th anniversary commemoration of the Warsaw Rising held at the beginning of August 2004. The Prussian Trust, a claims society founded in 2003 by Rudi Pawelka, a retired police officer born in Breslau in 1940 and Head of the *Landmannschaft Schlesien* (Silesian Association), planned to use the European Court of Human Rights in Strasbourg as a forum to obtain the return of lost property from Poland and the Czech Republic. In response, Schröder assured his Warsaw audience that 'Germany opposes restitution claims that would turn history on its head.'[65] Nevertheless, among the nationalist Right in Poland a near hysterical mood prevailed leading to massive counter-claims for compensation arising from wartime suffering and damage. Despite these sentiments, the Polish government emphatically rejected the demands of members of the *Seym* (Polish Parliament) that it should seek compensation.[66] Schröder and Polish Prime Minister Marek Belka agreed to set up a joint German–Polish legal team in late September 2004 to fight compensation claims by ethnic Germans and both governments agreed not to support claims by individuals in either country.[67]

Nevertheless, the disputes over the exhibition and compensation claims remained a major issue when new Polish Prime Minister Jaroslaw Kaczynski[68] visited Germany at the end of October 2006. Kaczynski, a conservative nationalist, highlighted 'misunderstandings' which undermined bilateral relations. Although the government in Berlin had renounced restitution claims, Warsaw remained sceptical leading Kaczynski to remark that, 'It makes no sense to remain silent over what causes us in Poland concern'. On the 'Forced Paths' exhibition, Kaczynski had commented that the expulsions were 'sad, even tragic,' but added, 'It has to be clear who were the victims and who were the perpetrators.'[69] The disputes rumble on.

Eastern Germany 1944–45: The Evidence

The above brief summary illustrates a range of issues emanating from the repercussions of flight, expulsion and the sentimental interest in these developments arising from the fact that so many Germans originated from beyond the frontiers of the Federal Republic. These observations provide a contemporary introduction to this book which is primarily concerned with assessing the mood in eastern Germany during the final months of the war. Certain parameters need to be outlined. The area of research is confined to districts east of the Oder which were within the Reich's frontiers of 1937 and were inhabited overwhelmingly by Germans. Thus, East Prussia, eastern Pomerania, east Brandenburg and Silesia generally comprise the geographical remit of this study and discussion of the territories incorporated into Germany following the defeat of Poland in 1939 is limited. In Part I the setting and major characters are introduced, before the narrative turns to discussing the effect of the war in the eastern provinces. However, emphasis is placed in subsequent parts on the period commencing with the arrival of the Red Army at the gates of East Prussia in July 1944 and concluding with the withdrawal of the German authorities from January 1945. This book is not a survey of Soviet and Polish occupation policy in eastern Germany.

In addition to the aforementioned *Ost-Dokumentation*, a number of contemporary reports form the archival basis of this study. Nazi leaders had witnessed the revolutionary events of November 1918 and were anxious to avoid a repeat, encouraging official organs to monitor morale. Security service, propaganda and judicial reports fall into this category. In defining 'morale' the Nazis differentiated between *Stimmung* (mood) and *Haltung* (bearing or behaviour). A bad mood and a pessimistic view of the future could coexist with unchanged behaviour as Germans continued to work for victory. As a result of this the propagandists were more concerned with fluctuations in *Haltung*, while the relatively minor importance ascribed to the more immediate and superficial characteristics of *Stimmung* resulted in often frank reporting.[70] The SD's *Meldungen aus dem Reich* (Reports from the Reich) and later *Berichte zu Inlandsfragen* (Reports on Internal Questions) were compiled weekly from September 1939 until the summer of 1944. These reports were edited by *SS Gruppenführer* Otto Ohlendorf and emanated from information submitted by tens of thousands of SD agents and informants nationwide. One historian notes that the reports 'were characterised by their uncommon honesty' and adds that Ohlendorf aimed to 'influence opinion at the highest level with objective assessments which knew no favourites'.[71] Naturally, this aim ran contrary to the ambitions of various Nazi luminaries. Propaganda Minister Joseph Goebbels had the circulation of these 'defeatist' reports reduced before Martin Bormann, head of the Party Chancellery and Hitler's secretary, and Dr Robert Ley, head of the German Labour Front, banned Party and Labour Front personnel from assisting the SD in this undertaking from the summer of 1944.[72]

The weekly activity reports compiled by the Propaganda Ministry from information provided by Regional Propaganda Leaders were less outspoken than the SD reports. The major reservation with this source is that the authors were senior Party figures remote from the masses. Moreover, for career reasons they were sensitive to the feelings of their superior Goebbels and attempted to put a positive gloss on most major issues. This does not, however, imply that these reports were purely sycophantic, and grumblings about the military situation and Party initiatives which originated from this collection are cited in the following chapters. Similar observations are appropriate for the reports submitted to the Reich Ministry of Justice by the *Oberlandesgerichtspräsidenten* and *Generalstaatsanwälte*. These were prepared at three-monthly intervals, and, although the authors regularly extolled the achievements of the Party and state authorities, criticisms were raised. As will be shown, reports from senior east German judicial figures during the second half of the war remarked upon food shortages, the loss of manpower to the military, excessive Party demands on staff and the plundering of German homes by the *Wehrmacht*. In dealing with contemporary accounts the bitter rivalries existing between officials and departments in competing Party and state structures, the motivation of the author and the date of the document always have to be considered.

Meanwhile, newspapers were reduced to the role of mouthpieces of Party propaganda, highlighting individual acts of heroism at the fighting fronts and pointing to favourable historical precedents in an attempt to obscure the military setbacks and territorial losses. It has frequently been possible to compare these official sources with clandestine accounts, letters and post-war testimonies. Occasionally, such as in the reporting of conditions endured by non-German labour building fortifications, SD reports were more critical than most *Ost-Dokumentation* sources. A particularly interesting gamut of opinions is found in the *Sammlung Sterz*, a collection of letters in the archive of the *Bibliothek für Zeitgeschichte* in Stuttgart. The sentiments expressed range from an unyielding confidence in Hitler to a level of downright defeatism which could have imperilled the life of the writer. Another worthwhile source is the weekly reports of the British Political Warfare Executive on German propaganda available at The National Archives, Kew. These are extremely valuable in assessing the rhetoric of the Third Reich. Compiled from a variety of sources these reports frequently cited leading eastern German Party figures and quoted the contents of broadcasts and newspapers from this part of the Reich.[73]

Much of what follows concentrates on the fear of Soviet occupation and the efforts of Nazi propagandists to stir Germans to ever greater efforts by exploiting this anxiety. Initially, this took the form of promises that the Red Army would not tread on German soil. As the military situation deteriorated, refugees were told that their homes would be recaptured and civilians in encircled cities were encouraged to believe that relief was forthcoming. At a practical level the Party authorities attempted to boost morale by instilling a sense of participation in total war through mass mobilisation for fortification building and local defence forces. The eastern provinces were at the forefront of both of these developments, discussed in depth in Part II.

This book also illustrates the regime's growing readiness to resort to coercion against fellow German *Volksgenossen* (National Comrades) as propaganda was rendered impotent by military reality. This was particularly true in the eastern provinces where, as is highlighted in Part III, notorious Nazi leaders were preoccupied with saving their own skins and oblivious to the misery of their fellow Germans in 1945. The suffering endured by eastern Germans prior to Soviet occupation is in stark contrast to the heroic images evoked in propaganda. In the end, the repercussions of brutal Nazi expansionism led to the demise of seven centuries of German settlement east of the Oder. The grumblings of the interwar period were eclipsed after 1945. A sense of loss, engendered by flight and expulsion from cherished homelands, led to a nostalgic yearning for an idyllic and all too often mythical past.

PART I

A Faraway Land

CHAPTER 1

Come the Gauleiters, 1933–1939

Studies by German scholars on the history, development and eventual loss of German lands east of the Oder have been shrouded in sentimentality and heavily motivated by political agendas. Richard Bessel outlined the prevailing arguments before and after the Second World War:

> During the 1920s and 1930s a vast literature documenting their social and, especially, their economic condition was published, mainly to stress the harmful effects of the post-war borders and to justify regional claims for subsidies and preferential treatment. After the Second World War the emphasis in the literature about the former eastern German territories changed considerably, focusing less upon their disadvantaged position and more upon the extent to which they formed an integral part of the German social and economic whole. Both approaches were influenced greatly by contemporary political concerns.[1]

An Economic Backwater

The eastern territories lost inhabitants on account of internal migration and remained the most economically backward and poorest part of Germany during the inter-war period. These long-term trends were visible long before the 'Diktat' of Versailles and the propagation of the 'bleeding frontier' myth. The industrial revolution, which had commenced in western and central Germany during the middle of the nineteenth century, made little impact. Although there were a few industrial regions, most notably the Upper Silesian coal basin, development was often retarded by the lack of readily available natural resources and the considerable distance to major markets in the west. The eastern lands became a significant source of labour for industry in western and central Germany. Internal emigration largely cancelled out natural increases in population. Between 1840 and 1925, 2,559,300 people left East Prussia, Pomerania and Silesia.[2] This haemorrhaging of manpower continued during the latter period of the Weimar Republic and throughout the peacetime years of the Third Reich.[3] One historian has described the eastern provinces as a 'labour reservoir for the industrially advanced West'.[4]

The twin attractions of better wages and a higher standard of living in the Ruhr and Berlin were a draw for easterners. Few job opportunities existed outside of poorly paid agricultural employment. The proportion of the population engaged in agriculture and forestry exceeded both Prussian and Reich figures. The 1925 census illustrated that around 30 per cent of the German population worked in the agricultural sector. In the eastern provinces the figures ranged from 36 per cent in Lower Silesia to almost 61 per cent in the border province of Posen-West Prussia.[5] These percentages had significantly reduced by the time of the census of May 1939, but still remained higher than the national average.[6] Meanwhile, the Weimar era also witnessed a decline in farm prices and land values and a steady increase in farmers' debts. As a larger percentage of the region's workforce was employed in low-paid and increasingly insecure occupations, this had a detrimental effect on the economy. Statistics indicate that employees in all sectors earned considerably less than the national average prior to 1914, during the era of the Weimar Republic and throughout the pre-war National Socialist years. By 1936 *per capita* income levels were still less than two-thirds of the national average in Posen-West Prussia and, at the upper level, amounted to 82 per cent of the national figure in Pomerania. Similarly, the lower income levels were not compensated by lower prices for foodstuffs and manufactured goods.[7] Housing was more expensive and of a poorer quality in eastern cities and the cramped conditions had an adverse impact on health.[8] Nevertheless, after 1945 eastern scholars chose to emphasise the magnitude of the loss of rich agricultural lands in the east which had provided a surplus and had contributed to Germany being self sufficient for almost 75 per cent of its food between the wars.[9] In reality, inter-war eastern Germany remained an underdeveloped agricultural hinterland which failed to pay its share of the national tax burden.[10]

Inter-war logic reasoned that only a revision of the punitive terms of the Treaty of Versailles could produce an economic upturn. Most of both Posen and West Prussia was given to the new Polish state, the latter creating the Polish Corridor to the Baltic Sea. Danzig was designated a Free City under the administration of the League of Nations. The Memelland in the north of East Prussia was detached from East Prussia and came under League of Nations jurisdiction before being seized by Lithuania in 1923. Plebiscites, based on the principle of national self-determination, were held in disputed frontier districts. The overwhelming votes in 1920 in favour of Germany in the Allenstein district of south East Prussia and in the former West Prussian district of Marienwerder were accepted by the victorious Allied powers.[11]

Elsewhere, the Allied governments seemed more concerned with securing the economic and territorial viability of the new Polish state than in responding to the wishes of eastern electorates. The result of the March 1921 plebiscite in eastern Upper Silesia, which took place in the midst of a civil war between irregular German and Polish forces, was disregarded despite 60 per cent of voters expressing their wish to remain German citizens. Thus, numerous pits, blast furnaces and zinc foundries were lost by Germany as most of this industrial region was awarded to Poland. The break up of Upper Silesia as a single entity caused severe structural problems and economic and administrative disputes.[12] A similar insensitivity was displayed when the East Prussian railway junction of Soldau was given to Poland against the wishes of most inhabitants and in the absence of a plebiscite.[13] The new territorial arrangements separated East Prussia from the rest of the Reich. Road and rail links with the province now passed through the Polish Corridor. More than 40 years after Versailles one German historian bitterly complained that 'Poland received her industrial region and her access to the Baltic at the expense of that country which the creators of the Polish state were anxious to cripple economically and keep in subjection.'[14]

No Weimar government accepted these eastern territorial realignments as binding. Relations between Berlin and Warsaw were fraught with difficulties. There were frequent altercations over the treatment of the German minority in Poland and trade and tariff disputes. Aggressive German revisionism in the aftermath of Hitler's appointment as Chancellor (30 January 1933) led to the very real possibility that Poland would launch a preventative war. This danger was only averted because Poland's allies showed no enthusiasm for the prospect while, at the same time, the Nazis adopted a softer diplomatic line, ascertaining that both states and peoples had a right to exist and, moreover, shared a common antipathy to Soviet Communism.[15] Economic relations did improve after the signing of the German–Polish Non-Aggression Pact of January 1934. Until April 1939, when Hitler demanded the return of the Free City of Danzig and an extra-territorial road and railway across the Corridor to East Prussia, Poland seemed to get along better with Nazi Germany than she had with the Weimar Republic.[16]

The territorial alterations of 1919 reversed the pre-1914 government-backed policy of 'Germanisation' in Prussia's Polish provinces. Around 2,100,000 Germans lived within the frontiers of the resurrected Polish state. Two-thirds were located in the former German lands where the presence of the former masters was not welcomed by the new authorities. Estimates suggest that some 750,000 had emigrated to Germany by 1929.[17] Around 400,000 of these new arrivals settled in the eastern provinces, where, at least initially, they often required substantial financial assistance. Moreover, their resentments 'helped to provide a reservoir of right-wing and anti-Polish sentiment'.[18]

The impact of the new frontiers and changed political circumstances only exacerbated the region's economic malaise. The inauguration of trade fairs in Breslau and Königsberg to exhibit eastern German products were attempts to put a brave face on the situation.[19] German ports no longer constituted the only entry point into eastern Europe. Business with Bolshevik Russia virtually dried up. The two states no longer shared a common border. Customs barriers and tariffs suffocated trade with the plethora of newly established central and eastern European states. In east Brandenburg the loss of the former hinterland of Posen was lamented. The area was reduced to a border district, the agrarian sector declined and after 1930 economic activity in some localities was said to have come to a standstill.[20] In isolated East Prussia a British visitor to Marienburg, home of the imposing seat of the Teutonic Order, observed the depressed economic position in 1929: 'Outward appearances, however, are misleading: the town carries a heavy load and makes sacrifices in the hope that its patriotism will one day be rewarded; but in the hearts of the people there is extreme bitterness.'[21]

The Polish Corridor was the most widely resented of all the Versailles provisions. The distress seemed to flow more from the isolation of East Prussia, the creation of the

Corridor exemplifying the threat from Poland, than from the loss of most of the West Prussian lands. One British visitor argued:

> In conversations with Germans . . . the impression has slowly gathered shape that East Prussia rather than the actual "Corridor" is the matter of most concern to the patriotic German heart . . . It was the unanimous opinion of all these Germans that the enforced separation of East Prussia was indefensible on what were claimed to be the larger grounds of national sentiment and historic association and tradition. . . . The impression gained was that sentiment, rather than any economic or political reason, was of more importance in determining the attitude of the German race to the "Corridor" problem.[22]

East Prussia was the only German province to endure enemy occupation during the First World War. The province's sentimental place in German hearts arose latterly from the sacrifices rendered to ensure its preservation in 1914–1915. East Prussia was inextricably linked to the personage of Field Marshal Paul von Beneckendorff und Hindenburg, elected President of the Republic in 1925. The reputations of Hindenburg and his Chief of Staff, Erich von Ludendorff, were founded on their role in the defence of East Prussia against the Tsar's armies, exemplified by their stunning victory at Tannenberg. From 1927 Hindenburg was master of Gut Neudeck, his family's former East Prussian estate, purchased for him by German industrialists. Tannenberg was a patriotic rallying point during the Weimar Republic and was fully exploited by the Nazis. The image evoked of the Russian invader and the portrayal of East Prussia had great symbolic importance.

A Legacy of War

By adopting the Schlieffen Plan and leaving only ten divisions in East Prussia, the German General Staff exposed the province to great danger from the 'Russian Steamroller' in 1914. Only in the spring of 1915 were the Russians finally pushed out of East Prussia.[23] Three major German military successes are discernible. The German victory at Tannenberg (25–30 August 1914) over General Samsonov's Narew Army occurred in the vicinity of the battle of 1410 when the Poles had crushed the Teutonic Order. The second invading Russian army, General von Rennenkampf's Niemen Army, was soon defeated at the Battle of the Masurian Lakes (7–14 September) and the Russians were driven back to the frontier. After Russian counterstrokes, a period of stalemate ensued. German forces, weakened by the withdrawal of two corps to bolster the defence of Silesia but supported by indigenous *Landwehr* and *Landsturm* militia, then moved back to positions along the River Angerapp and the Masurian Lakes. The third important encounter (7–12 February 1915) was christened the 'Winter Battle in Masuria' by the Kaiser and deemed by some participants to have been a more successful operation than Tannenberg.[24] German accounts stressed the relatively modest losses suffered by the *Ostheer*. One East Prussian source estimated the German dead from the three major aforementioned battles at 10,000, while another observed that almost 28,000 Germans were buried in the East Prussian earth.[25] Accurate figures for Russian losses during the campaign are also difficult to fathom. There is widespread agreement that over 90,000 Russian prisoners were taken at Tannenberg and the total number captured during the September and February battles in the Masurian Lakes approached this figure.[26]

German accounts used emotive language to describe Russian atrocities and the extensive material damage inflicted on the province. The Kaiser saw with his own eyes the impact of the battles in Masuria and proclaimed at Lyck on 17 February 1915:

> My joy over this glorious success is diminished by the sight of the district, once so flourishing, which for weeks has been in the enemy's hands. Void of all human feeling he has in his senseless rage during his flight burnt or destroyed almost to the last house and the last barn. Our beautiful Masurian land is waste.
>
> Irrecoverable has been the loss, but I know I am in agreement with every German when I vow that everything in human power will be done to cause new and fresh life to rise from the ruins.[27]

As early as January 1915, the *Oberpräsident* of East Prussia, Adolph von Batocki, asked officials to gather together testimony from East Prussian refugees describing their experiences during the Russian invasion. The formation of a Provincial Commission for Wartime History, at Batocki's instigation and under his chairmanship, to investigate the invasion was announced on 28 September 1915. Over the next two years they produced five volumes covering major incidents based on selected official and private reports.[28] Approximately 1,500 inhabitants died in enemy hands during the occupation. Although civilians never fired on Russian troops, the suspicious invaders condemned around 350 as spies or agents. Moreover, 13,700 innocent civilians including, more than 6,500 women and children, were deported to Russia.[29] Around 5,400 never returned. Meanwhile, 39 towns and 1,900 villages were damaged. More than 40,000 buildings were destroyed and around 60,000 damaged during the occupation. The Russians also killed or seized substantial numbers of horses and cattle.[30] The southern East Prussian town of Neidenburg, which dated from the times of the Teutonic Knights, was burnt to the ground by the Russians on 22 August 1914. The fire could be seen at Hohenstein, 20 kilometres to the north, where most of Neidenburg's citizens had fled.[31]

The men of the Russian Imperial Army often came to similar conclusions to the soldiers of the Red Army three decades later in their impressions of East Prussia. One told a reporter, 'Germany is a fine country, no comparison with our poor villages – stone houses, brick houses, three storeys, fine carpets, gramophones.'[32] However, even Russian accounts admitted that German villages had been ransacked, livestock slaughtered and that Russian soldiers had acquired watches, rings and other jewellery from the German dead and looted East Prussian homes.[33] This rather contradicted earlier Russian claims that, 'We were forbidden under pain of death to molest peaceable inhabitants or to take what is not ours. We faithfully obeyed the order.'[34]

When Russian troops crossed the East Prussian frontier, the native population embarked on sudden flight, blocking the roads and obstructing German forces. During August and September 1914 perhaps one-third of the population fled in an attempt to escape from the enemy, particularly the feared Cossack cavalry. Some refugees crossed the Vistula to the security of West Prussia. Others headed north to the Baltic coast. A large number returned home after the summer victories but had to be evacuated again when the German Eighth Army retreated to winter positions during October. At the end of 1914, 350,000 East Prussians were accommodated in the Reich's interior. These included over 100,000 refugees housed in royal palaces, barracks, camps and empty factories in Berlin. The circumstances for mass population movement were certainly more favourable than those confronted three decades later. The refugees took to the roads in summer and autumn and were a novel phenomenon, earning the sympathy of the nation at the outset of war. Their far more numerous successors in 1944–1945 fled in winter to a land exhausted by six years of war and devastated by air attack.[35]

As the border districts were cleared of Russian troops from February 1915, only key personnel were initially allowed to return to commence rebuilding the infrastructure and dwellings. The majority of refugees were allowed to go home from 1916 and returnees continued to flow back until the war's end.[36] Indeed, as the British blockade took hold, exemplified by the harrowing 'turnip winter' of 1916–1917, children from western German cities and Berlin were actually sent to East Prussia.[37] Government resources, private initiatives and sponsorship (*Patenschaft*)[38] from other German cities to East Prussian towns and districts were ploughed into the reconstruction programme, which was half completed by the war's end. [39] A British observer, travelling through south East Prussia a decade later, commented that, 'The town of Osterode was wrecked by shell fire and then burned; the town has been reconstructed, but from the lack of style in the buildings I think hurriedly.'[40]

The Russian invasion and occupation made a deep impression on East Prussians, and indeed on all Germans. The sudden departure of the frontier inhabitants indicated a preordained decision to avoid the anticipated brutalities of Russian rule. Russian behaviour was profoundly shocking and the destruction of German Protestant churches appeared to illustrate the barbarity of the 'ungodly Asiatic foe'. German propagandists used the Russian incursion into East Prussia to underline the defensive character of the war and to invoke a startling vision of the invader from the steppe. In an 'Appeal to the Cultural World', a manifesto of German intellectuals of October 1914 claimed that 'the blood of women and children slaughtered by the Russian hordes soaked the earth in the east.'[41] As with reports of German atrocities in Belgium, many of the rumours which spread about Russian actions were overstated and excesses were the exception rather than the norm. Nevertheless, the hatred felt by East Prussians and German troops for the Cossacks was later described by Hindenburg: 'It was only against the Cossacks that our men could not contain their rage. They were considered the authors of all the bestial brutalities under which the people and country of East Prussia had suffered so cruelly.'[42]

Hindenburg and Ludendorff were lauded by a grateful nation as the heroes who had transformed a potentially disastrous situation into an unquestionable triumph of German arms. These victories laid the foundations for the mythical status that both enjoyed in later years. Hindenburg was afforded the freedom of Königsberg and was given an honorary doctorate by the city's Albertina University[43] shortly after Tannenberg. Public buildings were named in his honour throughout the province. His portrait hung in the homes of grateful East Prussians and a film of his exploits in the province *Ostpreußen und sein Hindenburg* (1917) entertained audiences throughout Germany.[44] The Albertina University also conferred an honorary doctorate of medicine on Ludendorff in August 1921 and thousands of students flying monarchist banners held a torchlight procession. According to the diploma Ludendorff was, among other things, 'the liberator, who with an iron hand cleared our East Prussian homeland from plundering and burning Russian hordes'.[45]

The Tannenberg myth promulgated during the Weimar Republic fulfilled a number of roles. Dennis Showalter argues that 'the Weimar Republic needed heroes; its critics required focal points for nostalgia. Tannenberg was one of the few points of common agreement.'[46] Moreover, the old Tsarist foe no longer inhabited the political stage and could not be slighted. The commemoration of Tannenberg signified the continued commitment of the Weimar Republic and the Prussian government to exposed East Prussia. This palliative helped to soothe the feelings of nationalistic East Prussians, the self-appointed guardians of the Reich's eastern frontier.[47] According to one recent study, Tannenberg performed a similar symbolic role in inter-war Germany to that of Verdun in France and Gettysburg in the United States.[48]

The tenth anniversary celebration in 1924 was an impressive spectacle as Hindenburg, Ludendorff, Field Marshal von Mackensen and General von Seeckt, Commander-in-Chief of the *Reichswehr*, were in attendance. A crowd of 100,000 gathered on the battlefield and 30,000 former soldiers and younger members of patriotic associations were reviewed by the military dignitaries. Hindenburg also had the honour of striking the first foundation stone of what was to become the Tannenberg memorial.[49] The funding and building of this war memorial on the site of the battlefield was orchestrated by veterans' associations and other representatives of the nationalist Right. The imposing memorial unveiled on 18 September 1927[50] covered around 40 acres and consisted of eight large towers, 70 feet high, placed in a circle and connected by a 20-foot high wall. At the centre of the vast enclosed courtyard was the burial site of the remains of 20 German soldiers. Following his death at Neudeck on 2 August 1934, Hindenburg's body was buried within the memorial, with full National Socialist pomp, on 7 August 1934, with an estimated 200,000 mourners in attendance.[51] The memorial was soon dedicated the Reich War Memorial by the Nazis. In Hitler's presence a service, broadcast nationally, was held on 2 October 1935 when Hindenburg's body was moved from the Feldherrn Tower and reburied in a new vault in the Middle Tower.[52] During the Third Reich a wave of popular histories evoked Tannenberg to celebrate the valiant deeds of the province's German defenders and to illustrate the danger of 'Asiatic hordes' running amok.[53] Furthermore, the precedent of 1914–1915 was exploited by the Nazis in 1944–1945 when they stressed that the Red Army would be halted and defeated on the German frontier. A sizeable percentage of the East Prussian population exhibited a similar misguided faith.

The Rise of the Nazis

In marked contrast to the heroic image of Tannenberg and the actions of the paramilitary *Freikorps* in frontier conflicts with the Poles, most notably in Upper Silesia in 1920–1921, everyday life in the eastern provinces during the Weimar Republic was characterised by lingering economic misery. This was exemplified by the hyperinflation which peaked in 1923 and wiped out savings and pensions. Then at the end of the decade eastern Germany felt the impact of the Depression and subsequent worldwide trade slump. Politically, the overwhelmingly Protestant lands east of the Oder, replete with their *Junker* hegemony and dependence on agriculture, were bastions of social deference and rural conservatism. Richard Bessel argues that during the Weimar era 'regional economic and social structures, rather than the fears and resentments engendered by the "bleeding frontier" were most important in determining patterns of political support in the East.'[54] The social and economic sectors of society most likely to support Weimar democracy were thin on the ground in eastern Germany. On the other hand, those groups considered particularly susceptible to right-wing rhetoric were to be found in abundance.[55]

The NSDAP arrived relatively late on the east German political scene and only built up their organisation from 1926. Despite the challenge posed by indigenous *völkisch* groups, the party soon gained a greater percentage of the vote in the eastern provinces than it enjoyed nationally, during the wave of *Reichstag*, provincial *Landtag* and Presidential elections of 1930–33. Three general observations can be made on electoral politics east of the Oder. First, throughout the 1920s, the conservative DNVP (*Deutschnationale Volkspartei*, German National People's Party) polled consistently higher than in the rest of the country. Secondly, the 'respectable' Weimar coalition parties – the DVP (*Deutsche Volkspartei*, German People's Party), DDP (*Deutsche Demokratische Partei*, German Democratic Party) and *Zentrum* (Catholic Centre Party) – were weaker than elsewhere in Germany. Thirdly, the parties of the Left, the SPD (*Sozialdemokratische Partei Deutschlands*, Social Democratic Party) and KPD (*Kommunistische Partei Deutschlands*, German Communist Party), gained marginally less support than at national level because of the smaller proportion of industrial workers. Upper Silesia, overwhelmingly Roman Catholic and with a large working class, was the major exception to these trends.[56]

Weimar administrations attempted to address the economic ills of the eastern provinces. Throughout the 1920s substantial subsidies and spending on new infrastructure were approved by the national and Prussian governments in an attempt to shore up the agrarian sector. President Hindenburg, encouraged by his *Junker* neighbours, agreed to new measures ostensibly designed to rescue East Prussian agriculture. However, the prevailing economic conditions and inherent structural problems of the eastern provinces combined to render these sustained initiatives useless. Politically such measures were also ineffective. The majority of the agrarian population believed, not unreasonably, that any benefits were being siphoned off by large landowners. Bessel observes that 'As a piece of economic and political bribery, the *Osthilfe* failed almost completely. The government fell into further disrepute, the roles of traditional interest groups were undermined, and conventional political solutions appeared increasingly inadequate.'[57] Similar government-backed schemes to encourage migration to the eastern border districts were condemned as ill-advised state interference in agriculture.

Through its participation in Weimar coalitions, the DNVP was identified with these government failures. The economic measures backed by the DNVP at national level appeared to enrich the estate owners and punish small farmers.[58] This growing resentment, the hostility felt by wide sections of the population to the so-called 'Marxist parties' and 'weak' Weimar democracy provided a fertile constituency for the NSDAP at the outset of the Depression.

In the aftermath of the failed Munich Putsch (November 1923), the Nazis embarked on the road to power by 'legal' means. The first members in eastern Germany drifted into the Party from various *völkisch* splinter groups. Many were former *Freikorps* fighters with experience of irregular warfare in the Baltic and Upper Silesia. The growth of the Party was sporadic and was punctuated by internal disputes at local level often involving the SA (*Sturmabteilung*, National Socialist Storm Troop), the Party's paramilitary organisation and its most visible manifestation on the streets.[59] Support for the NSDAP transcended social and class barriers to an extent unknown in Weimar politics. A number of affiliated organisations spawned by the Party spread the propaganda message among professional and economic interest groups. Crucial to holding this unwieldy structure together was Hitler, the charismatic leader and focus of all loyalty. The Nazis were devoid of detailed policies to alleviate the economic misery but their propaganda was effective in identifying the sources of Germany's misfortune, namely, Versailles, Reparations, the Republic, Jewry and Marxism.[60] The promise of national renewal and the expectation of uncompromising measures against the Left seemed to be particularly enticing in the German East. The NSDAP's local Farmers' Leader in Königsberg/Neumark, east Brandenburg recounted that Hitler and the Party offered salvation against the escalating threat from left-wing radicalism. He recalled the packed meetings in Küstrin addressed by prominent Party speakers, such as Wilhelm Kube, the local *Gauleiter* and a *Reichstag* deputy.[61]

Outside Upper Silesia, the Nazis captured almost half the eastern German vote at the July 1932 *Reichstag* election. Nevertheless, the disappointment emanating from the failure to secure a decisive victory at the polls and the Party's exclusion from the new government, following Hitler's rejection of a Cabinet post, led to an upsurge in SA inspired violence against political opponents and the state authorities. The SA seemed to be beyond Party control, a sign that many in the movement had lost patience with the tactics of 'legality'. This alienated a percentage of the Party's 'respectable' supporters, as did the savage attacks on Chancellor Franz von Papen's aristocratic administration, dubbed the 'Cabinet of Barons', and the Party's apparent support for Communist-led strikes. The November 1932 *Reichstag* election witnessed a decline in NSDAP support, most notably in East Prussia. The Party and the SA were disintegrating, the former experiencing a huge drop in income and the latter fearing mass defection to the KPD. Concurrently, Papen's successor as Chancellor, the *Reichswehr* general Kurt von Schleicher, attempted to split the NSDAP and gain some form of popular legitimacy by entering into clandestine talks with Gregor Strasser, Hitler's right-hand man.

Strasser resigned his Party offices on 8 December 1932. However, the manner of his departure ensured that Hitler nipped any potential secession in the bud with a series of emotional performances which appealed to the loyalty of senior Party figures. Schleicher's failure to split the NSDAP contributed to his downfall and finally on 30 January 1933 the call went out to Hitler to assume the office of Chancellor. Suddenly the Party was transformed 'into a rapidly growing organisation enjoying the spoils of power'.[62] In East Prussia, Pomerania, Lower Silesia and in the Posen–West Prussia border province Nazi support broke the 50 per cent barrier in the March 1933 *Reichstag* election. With the state machine at their disposal and through murder, assault, arrest and other threats, the Nazis made it impossible for their opponents to wage effective campaigns.

The first months of National Socialist rule were characterised by a violent 'Revolution from Below' with the burgeoning SA at the forefront. This was a time to repay old scores and provided the opportunity for Party and SA leaders to sample the spoils of victory by acquiring senior positions within the state structure in their respective provinces.[63] Other political groupings were declared illegal or coerced into dissolution while professional organisations and interest groups were 'co-ordinated' with their Nazi counterparts. For some in the movement this was still not enough. However, the all-encompassing 'Second Revolution', viewed by SA commander Ernst Röhm and many of his followers as essential to sweep away the traditional elites, was neutralised by the Blood Purge ('Night of the Long Knives') of 30 June 1934. The utterances of SA leaders and conservative critics, gave Hitler and his inner circle the pretext of defending the state when they unleashed a nationwide murder spree, eliminating opponents from within the Party, SA, *Reichswehr* and conservative elites. Gregor Strasser, Röhm and Schleicher headed the list of those slain, estimated at between 85 and 200.[64]

The Characters

At this juncture it is helpful to look at the leading figures in the Party east of the Oder. Primarily, this focuses on the *Gauleiter*, often trusted *alte Kämpfer* (old fighters from the Party's earliest days) and viewed by Hitler as his personal agents in the field. During the war most were elevated to the status of *Reichsverteidigungskommissar* (RVK or Reich Defence Commissioner), deriving their authority from orders issued by Hitler in September 1939 and November 1942. In this capacity they were responsible for areas corresponding to military districts and authorised to commandeer all Party and state resources for the defence of their *Gau*.[65]

The eastern *Gauleiter* can be characterised collectively by their arrogance, avarice and brutality. The longest-serving and most infamous member of this little group was Erich Koch, *Gauleiter* of East Prussia between 1928 and 1945. Koch was born in the Ruhr town of Elberfeld in 1896, fought on the Eastern Front during the war, served with the *Freikorps* in Upper Silesia and was jailed by the French during the Ruhr occupation in 1923. He joined the Nazi Party in 1922. His political activity led to dismissal from employment as a railway official in 1926. Koch, a stocky and moustached figure, rose rapidly in the Party. Appointed Deputy *Gauleiter* of the Ruhr in

1927, he was named *Gauleiter* of East Prussia on 1 October 1928. Party propaganda alleged that he took over the most difficult post the movement could confer. Koch was said to have led a reactionary province to National Socialism and fully understood the foreign policy situation arising from East Prussia's territorial separation from the Reich. Koch seemingly appreciated the additional complications resulting from the provocative posture of the Poles and the Bolshevik threat.[66] In reality Koch took over a strife-ridden little group, but as the NSDAP gained adherents from other *völkisch* sects, and as a consequence of growing disenchantment with the DNVP, membership numbers soon took off.[67]

Politically, Koch was closely linked with Gregor Strasser's 'Socialist' wing of the Party which aimed to convert workers to the nationalist cause by making them feel part of the nation. Koch utilised his friendship with Strasser, the Party's organisational supremo, to assert his authority against the SA prior to 1933.[68] After the assumption of power Koch was appointed *Oberpräsident* of East Prussia (June 1933). The following month he gave a glimpse of his intentions to a mass meeting of party officials: 'Who cares about Berlin? Here in East Prussia I'm the one who gives the orders!'[69] Koch was a law unto himself. He remained in contact with the discredited Gregor Strasser and defied Hitler and Goebbels by stating that 1933 was only the first stage of the German revolution. On the first anniversary of the 'seizure of power' Koch publicly praised Ernst Röhm's demands to maintain the revolutionary spirit of earlier years.[70] In East Prussia, Koch's closeness to Strasser provoked rumours of his arrest by the SS on the 'Night of the Long Knives'. However, Koch, well aware of the danger, took the precaution of spending 30 June 1934 on board a visiting Dutch minesweeper in Pillau harbour.[71]

Koch's reputation for graft was notorious even in Nazi circles. This culminated in December 1935 when Koch was accused of embezzling money collected for the Party's Winter Relief Fund. Coming on the back of numerous other infringements, this should have led to his downfall. SS *Gruppenführer* Erich von dem Bach Zelewski, the chief of the Königsberg Gestapo and infamous for his later role in the suppression of the Warsaw Rising (1944), was suspicious of Koch's 'Socialism' and loathed his corrupt administration. A report on the malpractice and criminality of leading Party functionaries was prepared by the Königsberg city councillor Paul Wolff and forwarded to Hitler in October 1935. The *Reichsführer SS* Heinrich Himmler appeared in Königsberg to support Bach Zelewski against Koch. During this 'Oberpräsidentenkrise' Koch was deposed as *Oberpräsident*, arrested by the SS and taken to Berlin. A later account by Wolff suggested that Koch was handed over to the SS for execution at Lichterfelde barracks. However, a surprising intervention by Hitler on 22 December 1935 led to Koch's rehabilitation and reinstatement. Wolff was dismissed and Bach Zelewski was transferred to Breslau. It has been rumoured that Koch deposited incriminating documents abroad detailing Nazi abuses and threatened their release should any harm befall him.[72]

This apparent scare did not alter Koch's demeanour. He still behaved like a colonial viceroy and surrounded himself with a coterie of advisers drawn from younger, ambitious elements in the civil service and Party. This 'Königsberg Circle' evolved, at the latest, in the aftermath of the September 1930 *Reichstag* election. Most of the members of this leadership clique served with Koch until 1945. Ostensibly, they advocated 'Prussian Socialism' incorporating the virtues of simplicity, modesty and incorruptibility in contrast to the class interests represented by the old governing and agrarian elites.[73] Party literature stressed Koch's achievements. After a few weeks of his energetic leadership East Prussia was said to have become the first *Gau* in the Reich to eliminate unemployment.[74] Koch also stimulated interest in the *Deutsche Ostmesse* held annually in Königsberg and East Prussia was said to have become the centre of what the Nazis termed 'the great north-eastern European economic area'.[75] These boasts were not altogether unfounded. Dietrich Orlow notes that 'The *Gauleiter* was able to secure for his *Gau* economic aid in the form of subsidies and privileges that aroused nothing but envy in a visiting Bavarian dignitary.'[76] Nevertheless, as Koch refused to follow orders which did not directly emanate from Hitler, he was constantly in conflict with various Party bodies. Particularly bitter were the disputes with the Reich Food Estate headed by Walther Darré. Their office of agricultural policy (*Amt für Agrarpolitik*, AfA) acted as a pressure group for farmers rather than converting them, as Koch envisaged, to fully-fledged National Socialists. When he had the AfA's chief provincial official arrested and flung out of the Party, Darré refused any further communication with Koch.[77]

Koch's corruption and arbitrary rule was exemplified by the establishment of the 'Erich Koch Stiftung' (Erich Koch Foundation) in 1934. This was a 'front' organisation designed to camouflage Koch's predatory attacks on the province's economy for the benefit of himself and his cronies. Koch, an undoubted anti-Semite, took the opportunity to take over Jewish businesses and confiscate the wealth of others deemed enemies of the state. Lies and threats were used in order to intimidate individuals into signing over their businesses to the 'foundation'. The Königsberg Gestapo arrested more stubborn proprietors. The reincorporation of the Memelland in March 1939 led to the territory's textile mills falling into the clutches of the 'foundation'. The scale of this operation mushroomed during the war years. Opportunities for further growth arose when the district of Zichenau was incorporated into East Prussia after the victory over Poland. Eventually the 'foundation' consisted of 121 businesses, ranging from factories to hotels. This huge conglomerate was valued at RM 331 million by 1945.[78]

After Koch, the longest serving *Gauleiter* east of the Oder was Franz Schwede-Coburg in Pomerania. Schwede-Coburg was the fourth *Gauleiter* in this *Gau*. He was appointed in the aftermath of the Röhm Purge when his predecessor, Wilhelm Karpenstein, was dismissed for being too weak in his dealings with the SA. Karpenstein had allowed an unauthorised concentration camp to be erected near Stettin. The intervention of the Prussian Interior Minister, Hermann Göring, led to the camp's closure, Karpenstein's expulsion from the Party and his detention for two years.[79] Franz Schwede was born in 1888 in Memel. Prior to and during the World War he served in the *Kriegsmarine* as an engineer. After the war he settled in Coburg, Bavaria. In 1922 he was appointed machine master at the town's electricity works. Later that year he co-founded the NSDAP branch in Coburg and by Christmas 1923 he had been promoted to local leader. Schwede's political career prospered as Nazi support grew. He was elected a member of the Bavarian *Landtag* in September 1930 and from August 1931 was Deputy *Bürgermeister* of Coburg. The Nazi assumption of power led to Schwede's appointment as *Bürgermeister* of Coburg in March 1933 and in June 1934 he became governor of Lower Bavaria and the Upper Palatinate. Schwede was in this post for scarcely seven weeks when suddenly on 22 July 1934 he was installed as *Gauleiter* and *Oberpräsident* of Pomerania. Schwede, who was honoured by Coburg and allowed to insert the town's name in his surname, was assigned to 'strengthen the political unity of the [Pomeranian] *Gau* as a whole'.[80]

The Silesian *Gau* had a similarly troubled history. During the *Kampfzeit* (the Party term for the 'period of struggle' prior to 1933) there were numerous disputes between the Party hierarchy under *Gauleiter* Helmut Brückner and the SA in addition to schisms within the latter organisation.[81] There were also violent confrontations with the authorities and political rivals. This came to a head with the notorious Potempa incident in August 1932 when a group of drunken SA men brutally killed an unemployed Polish labourer with Communist sympathies.[82] Both Brückner and Edmund Heines, the sadistic Silesian SA commander from mid-1931 and creator of one of the earliest makeshift concentration camps after the 'seizure of power', were swept away during 1934. Heines, who had joined Röhm at Bad Wiessee near Munich, was found by a furious Hitler in bed with a male companion. He was taken to Munich and shot on 30 June 1934.[83] Brückner, who had participated in the arrests and murders in Silesia, despite having strong reservations about the scale of the bloodshed, was dismissed as *Gauleiter* and *Oberpräsident* in December 1934, arrested for a period and eventually found employment at the Heinkel aircraft factory in Rostock.[84]

His replacement, Joseph Wagner, already *Gauleiter* of South Westphalia, was a known opponent of the SA. He enjoyed the then influential patronage of Göring, leading to his appointment as *Reichskommissar* for Prices in 1936. Wagner's star, however, did not shine for long. On religious and racial issues his opinions soon diverged from the path pursued by Hitler. Wagner's Roman Catholicism, once an asset in winning over sceptical Westphalians and Silesians to the regime, was now complicated by his feelings about the treatment meted out by the German occupation authorities to his Polish fellow believers in 1939. Wagner made little secret of his rejection of brutal SS actions in the occupied eastern territories. He was opposed to SS resettlement and Germanisation programmes and deployed the tactical argument that industry and the war economy needed Polish labour. Moreover, in Berlin and at the *Oberpräsidium* in Breslau, Wagner displayed a marked preference for key people without Party affiliation and who were passively opposed to the regime.[85] Intrigues against Wagner centred around two men. One was Udo von Woyrsch, a Nazi *Reichstag* member, the SS and police chief of the province and the commander of an *Einsatzgruppe* which indulged in a three week killing frenzy at the start of the Polish campaign. The other was Wagner's ambitious Deputy *Gauleiter* Fritz Bracht, a notorious anti-semite who enjoyed Himmler's patronage.

Himmler and Martin Bormann, Hitler's Secretary and by now the key figure in the Office of the Deputy *Führer*, Rudolf Hess, were receptive listeners to Bracht, who wanted his superior's job and plotted accordingly. They doubted that Wagner's allegiance to the movement could remain unaffected by his devout Catholicism. This impression was bolstered when Wagner allowed his wife to oppose the marriage of their pregnant daughter to an atheist SS officer. Furthermore, rumours, probably emanating from Bracht, circulated indicating that Wagner was a member of the 'Catholic Action' resistance group and had divulged secret information. The Party authorities under Hess repeatedly placed Wagner on the list of *Gauleiter* recommended for replacement and demanded that he choose between Westphalia and Silesia. Wagner opted for the latter; in Breslau he was both *Gauleiter* and *Oberpräsident* whereas Alfred Meyer, the *Gauleiter* of North Westphalia, was *Oberpräsident* for all Westphalia.[86]

However, it would be the pretext provided by the incorporation of annexed Polish territory into the Silesian *Gau* that ultimately sealed Wagner's fate. Hitler was determined to split this overlarge *Gau*, now with a population of seven and a half million, and send Wagner back to Westphalia. In April 1940, Hitler proposed that one half went to Bracht, while the other was to be given to Karl Hanke, the former Under-Secretary at the Propaganda Ministry, 'after the war'. Despite attempts by Göring to delay the issue, Hitler insisted on Wagner's dismissal following the victory over France. Fritz Dietlof von der Schulenburg, the *Regierungspräsident* in Breslau, saw the writing on the wall and reported for *Wehrmacht* service on 17 May 1940. He realised that Wagner's removal was imminent and would not provide political support for Bracht. Wagner, deemed to be 'overloaded' by Hitler, was given until September to hand over the administration of Silesia to Bracht and was effectively sidelined. Whilst on leave from the *Wehrmacht* prior to Christmas, von der Schulenburg was told by Wilhelm Stuckart, State Secretary in the Interior Ministry, that Hitler had personally ordered the division of Silesia. On 20 December 1940, Prussian law created the provinces of Lower and Upper Silesia, governed from Breslau and Kattowitz respectively, although numerous institutions remained all-Silesian bodies. Hitler's decree of 27 January 1941 led to the division of the *Parteigau* and the appointment of Hanke and Bracht as *Gauleiter*. They started work in this capacity on 9 February and during the first week of April, at solemn ceremonies in Breslau and Kattowitz, Wilhelm Frick, the Interior Minister, swore both men into their new role as *Oberpräsident*.[87]

Hanke has been described as 'cynically arrogant in the exercise of power, and given to turgid hyperbole'.[88] Born in 1903, he was a Protestant Lower Silesian who was involved with the *Freikorps* and Black *Reichswehr* before joining the Party in 1928.[89] Starting out as an apprentice miller, Hanke progressed to a senior teaching position at a Berlin trade school but his NSDAP activity led to his dismissal. Thereafter he was engaged in full-time Party work in Berlin. Hanke was a favourite of Goebbels and became his personal adjutant in 1932. The following year Goebbels appointed him as his special assistant at the new Propaganda Ministry and in December 1937 Hanke became Under-Secretary at the Ministry. Hanke also enjoyed the high regard of Albert Speer, an old Berlin Party colleague, Hitler's architect and later Armaments Minister, and the Baltic German Alfred Rosenberg, the self-proclaimed ideologue of the movement.[90] As the Propaganda Minister's trusted right-hand man, he witnessed his frequent dalliances with young secretaries and actresses which belied Goebbels' public image as the father of the Reich's first family. However, Goebbels' infatuation with the Czech actress Lida Baarova caused Hanke to take Magda Goebbels' part and he gradually fell in love with her.

In early August 1939 following Magda's reconciliation with her husband at Hitler's insistence, Hanke left the Propaganda Ministry to join the *Wehrmacht*. He participated in both the Polish and French campaigns, serving in the latter as a lieutenant under General Erwin Rommel. Hanke also reported to Hitler his extremely unfavourable impression of Red Army units encountered at the demarcation line in Poland.[91] Evidently Hanke's distinguished military record and his chivalrous behaviour towards Magda impressed Hitler, who wanted to find him a new role, with the result that he leapfrogged over a number of notable rivals in his appointment as *Gauleiter*. Hanke, who joined the SS in 1934, was also favoured by Himmler who bestowed on him an honorary rank of *Obergruppenführer* in the *Waffen-SS* in 1944. In contrast, Bormann, a persistent barrier to Hanke's further advancement, was unimpressed, describing him as 'no speaker' and 'very weak'.[92]

Scandal was also present within the higher Party circles in *Gau* Brandenburg or Kurmark. This *Gau* was created from the Potsdam and Frankfurt an der Oder administrative districts and enlarged in 1938 with the addition of the Meseritz district from the former border province Posen–West Prussia. The *Gauleiter* until 1936 was a former journalist Wilhelm Kube, born in Glogau, Silesia, in 1887 and previously a member of the DNVP and *völkisch* groups. In Breslau, Kube was a founding member of the nationalist, anti-Semitic *Deutscher Bismarckbund*. In 1928, he was appointed *Gauleiter* of the 'Ostmark' which comprised the Frankfurt an der Oder *Reichstag* electoral district. His realm was enlarged and he was appointed *Oberpräsident* when the 'Ostmark' was fused to Brandenburg west of the Oder in 1933. Kube was prominent after the 'seizure of power', involving himself in disputes with the Prussian bureaucracy over Party intervention in government appointments. Kube revelled in his own importance. He ordered that church bells should be rung when he toured the province and children stand to attention when he visited their communities. Inappropriately, Kube publicly praised Röhm's loyalty immediately prior to the 30 June 1934 but it was his personal life which led to his downfall.[93] When he made his secretary pregnant, Kube instigated divorce proceedings against his wife. *Reichsleiter* Walter Buch, the NSDAP's chief judge, frowned upon this scandal but Hitler did not intervene. However, Kube sought revenge against Buch. In April 1936, Kube issued a proclamation, purporting to come from a Berlin Jew, accusing Frau Buch of having Jewish origins. As a result of this accusation against Buch, Kube was forced to resign and spent a short spell in a concentration camp. The appointment of his replacement, Emil Stürtz, the deputy *Gauleiter* of south Westphalia, in August 1936 received little coverage as the country's attention was then fixed on the Berlin Olympics.[94] Born in 1892, Stürtz had been a sailor in the World War. He was a metalworker and driver in civilian life and joined the Party in 1925. Five years later he was elected as a *Reichstag* deputy. A year after his appointment as *Gauleiter* of Kurmark, Stürtz was named *Oberpräsident* of Brandenburg.[95] Stürtz, a friend of Speer, remained *Gauleiter* and *Oberpräsident* of Kurmark (Brandenburg) until 1945.

These were the men who ran the Nazi movement and increasingly directed the state machinery in eastern Germany. They were representatives of a regime committed to the dismantling of the territorial settlement imposed by Versailles and to the attainment of *Lebensraum* (living space) in the East. Nevertheless, there was no wild excitement among Germans when the *Wehrmacht* invaded Poland on 1 September 1939 and the regime made every effort to camouflage its intentions. When troops disembarked at Pillau and Königsberg, after sea journeys from the Reich, East Prussians were encouraged to believe that they had arrived to participate in celebrations marking the 25th anniversary of the Battle of Tannenberg.[96] However, the festivities planned for 27 August, with the *Führer* in attendance, were abruptly cancelled on the evening of 25 August 'owing to the tense situation'.[97] The crisis stoked up by the Germans over Danzig and the Corridor was about to reach its climax. The military plans drafted weeks before to attack Poland by 1 September were now set in motion.

CHAPTER 2

An Oasis of Tranquillity? The German East, 1939–1944

The Enemy in the East: Anti-Bolshevik Propaganda

The Polish campaign of September 1939 provided the *Wehrmacht* with a rapid and relatively bloodless victory.[1] Prostrate Poland was carved up by the Nazis and Soviets in accordance with the secret additional protocol of their Non-Aggression Pact, signed in Moscow in the early hours of 24 August 1939. However, the major crusade in the East, directed against the real ideological foe, the Soviet Union, ultimately led to the demise of the Germany's historic eastern provinces and centuries of German settlement.

Anti-Bolshevism was a major component of Nazi rhetoric as the propagandists attempted to restructure values in order to create a new Nazified society or 'fighting community'. The overriding goal was the mobilisation of the population for war and the maintenance of commitment during the conflict.[2] This propaganda emphasised the superiority of 'Germanness' and correspondingly highlighted the racially inferior inhabitants of the eastern states, who could be afforded no pity. Nazi propagandists merged ideological and racial prejudices to produce a vivid picture of the enemy in their attacks on the Soviet Union. Moscow was the nerve centre of a Jewish-Bolshevik world conspiracy. Moreover, in Nazi eyes Communism meant misery and backwardness; a regressive philosophy, derided by Hitler as 'the most primitive basic form of shaping peoples and nations'.[3]

This invective against Moscow and its German lackeys [the KPD] was only tempered for a short spell in late 1932 for political expediency and during the period August 1939–June 1941, the duration of the mutually beneficial Non-Aggression Pact. The aversion to Communism, both internally and externally, was most conspicuous in the orientation of Nazi violence and the outpourings of Nazi propaganda during the *Kampfzeit* and the pre-war dictatorship. This was cranked up to new levels following the invasion of the Soviet Union on 22 June 1941. The vilification of the Soviet state and its Slav and Jewish inhabitants was highlighted in the most emotive ideological and racial language. Fiendish stereotypes such as the evil Jewish Bolshevik Commissar and the barbarous Slav *Untermenschen* were demonised in films, newsreels, radio programmes, exhibitions, newspapers and quasi-academic studies. This rhetoric only served to reinforce anti-Bolshevik and anti-Russian prejudices existing among substantial sections of the German population.[4] The Nazis exploited deep-rooted anxieties grounded in the conduct of the Tsar's armies in East Prussia and the sensationalist reporting in the press of stories from former Germans POWs, White Russians and Baltic German refugees telling of tortures and other atrocities committed by the Reds during the Russian Civil War (1918–1920). The disproportionately high numbers of Jews within the Bolshevik Party's senior leadership was seized upon by the Nazis as providing further evidence of the danger that this alien creed posed to German Christian values. Closer to home, the disorders arising from Moscow-inspired KPD insurrections throughout Germany in the period 1919–1923 were recounted.

Anti-Communist rhetoric had peaked during the first months of Nazi rule in 1933 and during 1935–1937. The latter upsurge was partly a response to the Seventh Comintern Congress in Moscow in 1935. This was the scene of virulent attacks on National Socialism as the representatives of international Communism endorsed the creation of 'Popular Fronts' to combat Fascism; an issue sharpened by the outbreak of the Spanish Civil War a year later. Bitter invective against Communism was a staple ingredient of the NSDAP's annual *Reichsparteitag* at Nuremberg during these years. Germans were thus confronted with a bolt from the blue in August 1939 when Foreign Minister Joachim von Ribbentrop returned to Königsberg following the conclusion of his successful negotiations in Moscow. Political, strategic and economic considerations overcame ideological prejudices to produce a volte-face in diplomatic relations with the Soviet Union. The improvement in relations led to parallels being drawn by the propagandists and by Ribbentrop himself, with Chancellor Otto von Bismarck's relatively cordial relations with Russia in the late nineteenth century.[5] The public remained unconvinced of the pact's durability. Despite protestations to the contrary, Goebbels was unable to convince even the Party faithful that this was not a short-term tactical manoeuvre. Privately, Goebbels considered it to be a temporary measure and instructed the German press to avoid slipping into Bolshevik terminology and not to report on life in Russia. Furthermore, despite the issuing of guidelines to the contrary, some old films with an anti-Bolshevik message were still screened which added to public distrust.[6] The abatement of rabid anti-Bolshevik propaganda did not dispel worries about the Soviet Union. Soviet territorial and economic demands, submitted when the *Wehrmacht* was preoccupied in western Europe during the summer of 1940, made Germans increasingly uneasy. The Baltic States, Bessarabia and Bukovina fell under Moscow's rule.[7] Meanwhile, accounts of German troop movements from west to east, in the aftermath of the defeat of France, fuelled further rumours of a clash, despite attempts by the propagandists to avoid any discussion of Bolshevism.[8] Similarly, rumours that around 400,000 workers were building an East Wall to combat Soviet expansionism suggested, that in the perception of the *Volk*, the German–Soviet relationship was not so calm.[9]

Barbarossa

Nevertheless, the sudden attack on the Soviet Union after a near two-year enforced lull in anti-Bolshevik invective presented German propagandists with a new challenge. Unlike previous campaigns, the military assault was not preceded by a fierce media barrage, as the exigencies of military secrecy ruled this out.[10] Operation Barbarossa, launched in the early morning of 22 June 1941, signalled the beginning of a merciless ideological war of annihilation. The Nazi regime claimed that the Soviets were making preparations for an invasion and stressed that Barbarossa was a defensive measure taken by Germany on behalf of all Europe.[11] The shortlived Non-Aggression Pact was dismissed as a strategic necessity and Hitler and the leadership proclaimed their relief at being able to speak freely once more.[12]

As had been the case with the Polish campaign, East Prussia was a launch pad for the invasion of the Soviet Union. During the weeks leading up to the attack five armies assembled in the province.[13] East Prussia resembled a military camp and this naturally provoked lively discussion. When rumours spread throughout the country, the German media gave the impression that the invasion of Britain was forthcoming and that the story of the movement of troops to the East was simply an elaborate ruse.[14] As Soviet economic deliveries continued until the hour of the German onslaught, stories spread that the *Wehrmacht* intended to simply pass through Russian territory *en route* to British interests in the Middle East. Nevertheless, the scale of the preparations resulted in a growing conviction that war with the Soviet Union was unavoidable. The strength of the *Wehrmacht* apparently convinced the population that the province was not seriously threatened and nobody thought that the events of 1914–1915 would be repeated.[15] The President of the *Oberlandesgericht* (OLG) for East Prussia, Dr Max Dräger, visiting the frontier district of Sudauen (Suwalki) on 19 and 20 June 1941, noted that any layman could ascertain that an attack was imminent. He observed that 'troops of all types, aeroplanes and munitions lay in immense quantities on the border'.[16] Some precautionary measures were taken to protect civilians. From 18 June, the *Nationalsozialistische Volkswohlfahrt* (National Socialist People's Welfare Organisation, NSV) evacuated the majority of women and children from Memel.[17] After 22 June 1941 the front steadily moved east far from the province's borders. However, unlike earlier land campaigns, no knock out blow was delivered. The spectacle of the parade by regiments of the First East Prussian Infantry Division in Königsberg on 24 September 1940, in honour of the victory over France, was never repeated.[18]

Although East Prussian towns were not subjected to any sustained artillery fire, Soviet bombers were deployed over the province and attacked Königsberg on three occasions between 22 and 24 June. The first attack was the heaviest and completely surprised the defenders as the Soviets flew in over the Baltic at great height. Military targets and war industries were untouched while damage in residential areas was limited. The OLG President, Dr Dräger, reported that 19 civilians had perished during the three attacks and a number had been wounded. Over 100 bombs were dropped on Königsberg.[19] In Memel there was heavy damage in the old town leading to the deaths of 23 civilians, 15 POWs and a few soldiers. A Soviet raid on Gumbinnen on 23 June resulted in the deaths of four soldiers and 11 civilians. Casualties arising from air attacks were also reported from Ebenrode, Tilsit, Sudauen and Lyck. Goebbels, who dubbed the raids 'little fleabites' and insisted that 22 out of the 43 Red Air Force attackers had been downed over Tilsit, also noted that 'things in East Prussia had got a little out of hand, with air-raid precautions, evacuation etc.'[20] The local authorities played this down and maintained that the population was displaying a calm and sensible attitude.[21]

The Wartime Role of the Eastern Provinces

As the battlefront shifted east it is generally perceived that the war had little impact in eastern Germany. The Pomeranian-born historian Erich Murawski described the remoteness of his home province from the conflict:

> The province, excepting the city of Stettin and its surroundings, received only little sense of the rigours of war. Admittedly, at the end of August 1939 eastern Pomerania and other eastern parts of the Reich had become a German [troop] assembly area but then, as a result of the immediate and sweeping success of the German troops, the front moved unexpectedly quickly away from the eastern border of Pomerania and shifted far to the East.[22]

There are dissenting voices. Christian Tilitzki believes that it is mistaken to describe conditions for the East Prussian judicial authorities as an 'oasis of tranquillity' in contrast to western and central Germany which were seriously affected by the air war. He argues that:

> The province was not only an assembly area and supply nerve-centre for the military operations in the East. Soviet air raids, the dropping of agents by parachute as well as Polish and Soviet partisans in their sphere of responsibility certainly gave the judicial officials in the annexed territories a daily wartime routine, already long before the *Ostwallbau* and the bombing of Königsberg.[23]

East Prussia became the heart of the German war machine following the invasion of the Soviet Union. The province housed Hitler's most famous wartime headquarters, the *Wolfsschanze* (Wolf's Lair), located amidst forests and lakes, eight kilometres east of Rastenburg. The *Organisation Todt* (OT) commenced construction under the guise of a chemical factory and the well-camouflaged facility, which included barracks, bunkers and an air strip, was occupied by Hitler and his large retinue from June 1941. This secluded spot was Hitler's home for most of the next three and a half years. The occupants of the Wolf's Lair avoided external attack and its exact location remained unknown to the Allied powers. However, with this complex in the vicinity, Rastenburg's hotels enjoyed an upsurge in business and the town acquired more than provincial significance. The armed forces, government departments and important personages such as *Reichsmarschall* Hermann Göring, Himmler, Ribbentrop and Hans Lammers, head of the *Reichskanzlei*, had extensive facilities in the environs of the *Führerhauptquartier*. These incomers had the opportunity to pursue their activities in a deceptively calm environment.[24]

Although the fighting was hundreds of miles away, East Prussia retained important support and supply functions. Recruits were trained at the province's numerous barracks and at the training areas in Arys and Stablack. New units were constantly in the course of formation and concurrently a significant proportion of the escalating casualties arrived in the province's military hospitals. Supplies were sent from East Prussian ports for Army Group North, dug in on the outskirts of Leningrad from September 1941 until January 1944. Nevertheless, in 1941 the regime attempted to maintain a veneer of normality in the eastern provinces. Trade shows such as Breslau's *Süd-Ost Messe* and Königsberg's *Ostmesse* were still staged. The latter was held two months late, in October. This was a time when, in the minds of German economic officials, the notion of expansion and exploitation in the East appeared to open up unlimited possibilities.[25] Contemporary publications emphasised East Prussia's enhanced role. The restrictive frontiers of Versailles had been blown away, the Corridor and the Memelland, symbols of East Prussia's misery and German humiliation were long forgotten. The opportunity for East Prussia to act as the land bridge between the Baltic and the Black seas lay ahead – 'the border province of East Prussia had become the heartland of the entire East'. So said a travel guide for the province in 1942.[26]

Gauleiter at War, 1939–1944

The war brought immense opportunities for Koch and his cronies to participate in the plundering of the conquered east. Following the defeat of Poland, the addition of Zichenau (Ciechanow) to the south and Sudauen (Suwalki) to the east increased the population of East Prussia by around one million. Scarcely 15,000 of the new inhabitants were German.[27] These backward lands were governed by Koch's trusted lieutenants. They were encouraged to promote 'colonisation work', but few Germans sought to follow them. Girls from the *Bund Deutscher Mädel* (Hitler Youth girls' organisation, BdM) went to these annexed areas to assist the *Volksdeutsche,* the supposed sturdy race of German colonisers, on the land and to promote German culture. Contact with reality, however, only showed that these racially categorised Germans farmed and lived in a strikingly similar manner to their Polish neighbours.[28]

The treatment of Poles varied in the annexed territories, often as a result of the whims of individual *Gauleiter*. In Danzig–West Prussia, the fiefdom of *Gauleiter* Albert Forster, and in east Upper Silesia, many Poles were simply registered as Germans, gaining some material benefit but at the expense of being subject to German military service, an increasingly unappetising prospect as the war dragged on. In the Warthegau, an enlarged version of the old Prussian province of Posen and the domain of *Gauleiter* Arthur Greiser, a favourite of Himmler, Poles were flung off their farms to make way for *Volksdeutsche* from the Baltic States and the Balkans who had 'come home to the Reich' under the terms of the Nazi–Soviet Pact.[29] In a brutal flurry of ethnic cleansing Poles and Jews were dumped into the cesspit that was the *General Gouvernement*. This comprised the rump of Poland and was governed from Cracow. The indigenous Polish population received brutal treatment from the various arms of the Nazi state machine. Poles had their radios confiscated, their schools and newspapers closed and were subjected to a racially discriminative rationing system. Rations failed to reach subsistence levels but were considerably better than those allocated to their Jewish fellow-countrymen, herded into ghettos. Hitler's former lawyer Hans Frank, the Governor-General in Cracow, made his feelings abundantly clear to German officials in late November 1939: 'We won't waste much time on the Jews. It's great to get to grips with the Jewish race at last. The more that die the better; hitting them represents a victory for our Reich. The Jews should feel that we've arrived.'[30] In Greiser's Warthegau over 160,000 Jews were pushed into the Litzmannstadt (Lodz) ghetto. The horrific attrition rate reduced their value to the German war economy and the ghetto was finally cleared in the summer of 1944 when those remaining were sent to their deaths at Auschwitz.

Poland's Nazi and Soviet occupiers embarked on policies designed to wipe out the Polish intelligentsia, the kernel of Polish nationhood and national resistance against despotism. West of the demarcation line, the Germans rounded up academics, teachers, doctors, engineers, officers and priests for mass execution or onward transmission to concentration camps to be worked to death. In the east, the NKVD (Soviet secret police) indulged in the mass shooting of more than 20,000 captured Polish officers and the deportation of entire communities to Siberia.

In the Polish lands appended to East Prussia, Poles were subjected to draconian sentences passed by newly installed Special Courts. Minor offences were punishable by death; this summary 'justice' was motivated by the prevailing racial and ideological factors.[31] Rather than producing subservience, partisan bands consisting of the remnants of defeated Polish formations sprang up within months. Hiding in the extensive forests, they ventured out to raid isolated German settlements both in the incorporated territories and in the southern fringes of East Prussia proper.

The invasion of the Soviet Union resulted in Koch's area of jurisdiction increasing enormously. On 15 August 1941 he was appointed head of the civilian government in the newly annexed Bialystok district, where the varied population approaching 1.4 million included only 2,000 recognised *Volksdeutsche*. East Prussian officials were seconded to the key positions in the administration while simultaneously retaining their posts back home. A regime featuring arbitrary justice and deportations to the Reich for slave labour soon followed. Unsurprisingly, this again provoked widespread partisan activity. At the same time, more than 130,000 Jews from these former Polish lands were herded into ghettos. Their number steadily declined on account of malnutrition, indiscriminate German violence and deportations to the extermination camps. The last remaining ghetto, in Bialystok, was dismantled from mid-August 1943 when approximately 25,000 Jews were sent to the Treblinka and other extermination and work camps. Only 300–400 Bialystok Jews survived the war.[32]

It was Koch's appointment as *Reichskommissar Ukraine* that earned him greatest infamy. Koch arrived in Ukraine in August 1941. His new role was announced in the Party press later in the year and was formalised on 9 May 1942. The *Völkischer Beobachter* applauded the appointment of Koch and his Party colleagues to leading positions in the East: 'With them the Reich knows that the conquered eastern territories are in the best hands.'[33] Koch was said to have a major role in securing both the future of the Reich and Europe as he confronted a task of the greatest magnitude in attempting to undo the pernicious effect of 25 years of Bolshevik rule.[34] In reality, Koch's appointment was an unmitigated disaster on all fronts. His greatest talent remained in the realm of personal enrichment. The vast residence that Koch acquired through government money at Groß Friedrichsburg in Königsberg's western suburbs was now insufficient for his needs.[35] A palace was seized from the Polish Prince Czartorisky in Zichenau and completely remodelled to Koch's specifications.[36] East Prussian architects and builders were ordered by Koch to design and construct a palace for him at Tsuman, the hunting estate of the famed Polish Radziwill landowning magnates outside Rowno (Rüwne, Polish, Rovno, Russian, Rivne, Ukrainian), the provincial Ukrainian town Hitler had designated as the capital of Koch's new fiefdom. Renovation work, using the most expensive materials, was undertaken at the quarters of Koch's minions in Rowno and Kiev. When news of this extravagance filtered back to East Prussia it caused some to remark that Koch was behaving like an Indian Maharaja. Nobody spoke anymore about the old National Socialist ideals of simplicity and plainness.[37]

Koch's conduct in the Ukraine alienated the local population and infuriated other leading Nazis. His oldest cronies were given senior posts. For instance, the veteran East Prussian Nazi, Waldemar Magunia, a former master baker and President of Königsberg's trade corporation became *Generalkommissar* in Kiev.[38] Many Ukrainians were favourably inclined towards Germany, on account of the famine of 1932–33 induced by the repercussions of forced Soviet collectivisation. Goodwill was also extended to the Germans in the formerly Polish-governed western part of the Ukraine where 21 months of Soviet rule following the Nazi–Soviet Pact had featured mass arrests, executions and deportations to the Russian interior.[39] Indeed, as the *Wehrmacht* advanced, the NKVD eliminated all political prisoners and other inmates serving sentences in excess of ten years.[40] But Koch did his best to dispel the fanciful notion held by the various Ukrainian nationalist movements that Ukrainian resentment against Moscow and Bolshevism would be embraced by the invading power. Upon his arrival in Rowno, Koch made his position clear to his staff, 'Gentlemen, I am known as a brutal dog; for that reason I have been appointed *Reichskommissar* for the Ukraine. There is no free Ukraine. We must aim at making the Ukrainians work for Germany and not at making the people happy.'[41] Germany had embarked on a war of extermination involving the slaughter of Jews and Communists and the starvation of millions of 'superfluous eaters'. In Koch's estimation, the Ukrainians, whom he notoriously dubbed 'natives' and 'niggers', fell into the latter category. As Koch reminded a German audience in Kiev on 5 March 1943, 'The lowliest German worker is racially and biologically a thousand times more valuable than the population here.'[42] Koch sought to destroy Ukrainian national identity. Racial prerogatives coupled with a determination to ruthlessly exploit economic resources precluded compromise. Koch admitted that his objective was 'to suck from the Ukraine all the goods that we can get hold of'.[43] Paul Dargel, the 40-year-old former timber-merchant from Elbing and Koch's permanent representative in the Ukraine, underlined Nazi intentions: 'We want to annihilate the Ukrainians . . . we want to get rid of this rabble.'[44]

Koch was criticised in leading Nazi circles for failing to procure sufficient produce and labour from Ukraine. These complaints reached a crescendo on 6 August 1942 at a conference in Berlin's Air Ministry where even Göring, his old mentor, ridiculed Koch's efforts to seize Ukrainian manpower. He belittled the half-million Ukrainians sent to the Reich compared to the nearly two million foreign workers already brought to Germany by Fritz Sauckel, the Reich's Plenipotentiary for Labour Force Deployment.[45] Thereafter, Koch assiduously reported to Hitler detailing the amounts of foodstuffs, livestock, textiles and chemicals that had been extracted from the Ukraine and sent back to the Reich. He did not tell his *Führer* of the value of the commodities returned surreptitiously to Germany by his appointees and other branches of the occupation authorities, but the figures were certainly vast.[46] Goebbels regularly despaired at Koch's treatment of an initially friendly population and the visiting Albert Speer was dumbfounded at his cultural vandalism in Kiev.[47] Koch, who tended to spend more time in Königsberg than in Rowno, paid little attention to his nominal superior Alfred Rosenberg, the Minister for the Occupied Eastern Territories, a Baltic German born in Reval (Tallinn) who had studied in Riga and Moscow.[48] In March 1943, Rosenberg observed that among growing numbers of Nazi leaders the name Koch was viewed with contempt. He added that there was increasing despair and a growing feeling of rancour throughout Ukraine.[49]

Rosenberg's complaints about Koch led to them both being finally summoned to see Hitler on 19 May 1943, where the *Führer* indicated his favour for Koch's purely colonial and exploitative form of rule in preference to Rosenberg's desire to win over the minority peoples, especially the Ukrainians, to the German cause. Hitler attacked Rosenberg's 'sentimentality' and repeated the need to maintain the flow of Ukrainian labour and food to the Reich.[50] But wide swathes of Ukraine were under partisan rule. Rosenberg was informed by officials, such as *Generalkommissar* Ernst Leyser of Zhitomir, that the partisans were taking most of the Ukrainian harvest and livestock. German Agricultural Leaders were frequently unable to operate and withdrew to their former Soviet tractor depots, guarded as strongpoints by German police units.[51] However, Koch's bloody stint in the Ukraine was concluded by the Soviet advance during the winter of 1943–1944. During this period Koch's initiatives and interference only impeded *Wehrmacht* operations. The accusations of defeatism that he levelled against the leadership of Army Group South in the Ukraine were later repeated with more serious repercussions during the final months in East Prussia.[52]

The SS did not think much of Koch but they had few qualms about his brutal actions which contributed to the 'destruction of 700 cities and towns and 28,000 villages and the deaths of nearly seven million people, including virtually all Jews'.[53] The SS, keen to increase its influence and widen its economic interests, was more concerned at Koch's 'political gangsterism' both in the Ukraine and in East Prussia. The chief of the SS and Police in Königsberg, *SS Gruppenführer* Georg Elbrecht, observed that the National Socialist *Führerprinzip* (leadership principle) depended on the characteristics of the leaders and Koch was an 'ingenious bum'. His abuse of the *Führerprinzip* was unrivalled throughout the Reich.[54]

Publicly, as the war turned against Germany Koch toed the Party line and extolled the idea of *Endsieg*. In a Christmas 1943 address to war orphans in Königsberg he said, 'We celebrate the fifth war Christmas – nobody can foretell how many times this will happen again – we must not ask when will peace come but when will victory come.'[55] Similarly, Koch's New Year message to the Ukraine for 1944 ignored the disastrous military situation in this theatre of the war. The retreat was explained as part of the *Führer's* strategy and the front was said to have been stabilised because of the shorter front line. The task for the German occupiers of Ukraine remained the same – 'to provide supplies for the Front and Homeland'.[56]

The other eastern *Gauleiter* were less prominent during the war but still gathered immense power in their RVK capacity. Schwede-Coburg denuded Pomerania of capable administrators who were sent to the *Wehrmacht* or to the occupied territories. The remaining *Landräte* were responsible for the administration of two or even three rural districts concurrently. In post-war accounts these hard-pressed officials regularly bemoaned the scale of their workload by 1944, when their staff had been savagely pruned and insufficient petrol was available for them to oversee their vast areas of jurisdiction adequately.[57] Schwede-Coburg boasted of his achievement in getting all sections of Pomeranian society working together at an immense tempo to propel the province forward. However, in addition to his hatred of Jews, Schwede-Coburg displayed a pronounced distaste for the aristocracy, the officer corps, the Prussian spirit and Christianity. Wide circles of the middle classes as well as former members of the organised working class were hostile to him. As Murawski remarks, Schwede-Coburg's period as *Gauleiter* was compared to the unpleasant period of rule by Swedish troops (Schwedischen Soldateska) during the Thirty Years War and described as 'the second Swedish era in Pomerania'.[58]

Schwede-Coburg's private life led to him being placed under SD surveillance, as he 'preferred the charms of his secretary to those of his wife'. Knowledge of his intimate circumstances compromised his position against Himmler and Bormann.[59] However, Hitler placed far greater trust in the *Gauleiter* cohort in comparison with other functionaries; a trait rooted in his gratitude to certain *Gauleiter* for their service in the Nazi movement's earlier leaner years. Thus Koch was praised for having won over reactionary East Prussia[60] while Schwede had conquered 'Red Coburg'. Despite the Party Chancellery suspecting Schwede-Coburg of all sorts of corruption, Hitler still held him in high regard during the war years and seriously considered him as Adolf Wagner's successor for the plum post of *Gauleiter* and Minister-President in Munich and Upper Bavaria in the summer of 1942.[61] Schwede-Coburg made a number of wartime suggestions illustrating his brutal thinking and his antipathy to the military. For instance, as the numbers of condemned prisoners continued to rise, Schwede-Coburg suggested to Bormann that hanging, which was less labour intensive than the guillotine, should be the fate of looters.[62] Schwede-Coburg also attempted to interfere in the military realm during March 1943 but his request to have control over draft exemptions in his *Gau* was flatly rejected.[63] Subsequent chapters will vindicate Murawski's pithy verdict that 'Schwede-Coburg remained to the end a man of empty words and insufficient actions.'[64] Despite Germany's defeats Schwede-Coburg also proclaimed his faith in *Endsieg*. In October 1943 he stressed to an audience in Stettin: 'The present topical question of how long the war will last must be answered: The war will last until it is crowned with a German victory.'[65]

Similarly, visitors to Lower Silesia, leading local officials in the province and the general public tended to be unimpressed by Karl Hanke. The *Gauleiter* and his leading officials abused their positions and Hanke increasingly devalued local government by issuing instructions solely through his *Kreisleiter*.[66] When Speer was appointed Armaments Minister in February 1942, following Dr Fritz Todt's death in an air crash, he earmarked Hanke for the post of Plenipotentiary for Labour Force Deployment, responsible for the task of procuring labour from throughout German occupied Europe. Pointing to Hanke's inexperience as a *Gauleiter* and motivated by the considerations of internal power politics, Bormann secured Hitler's agreement to veto the appointment. Fritz Sauckel, the veteran *Gauleiter* of Thuringia, eventually got the job and his actions in this new capacity led to his conviction and execution at Nuremberg. Some interpretations have highlighted Sauckel's *alte Kämpfer* pedigree, age and greater clout in the *Gauleiter* fraternity and have argued that these were the key determinants in the decision.[67] However, Hitler still rated Hanke highly and included him in a Party delegation sent to Italy in October 1942 to participate in the festivities commemorating the 20th anniversary of the Fascist 'March on Rome'.[68]

Eighteen months later, in March 1944, Bormann played an instrumental role in another snub. On this occasion, Speer suggested Hanke's appointment to the key post of Head of the Fighter Production Programme, a role awarded instead to Speer's deputy *Hauptabteilungsleiter* Karl Otto Saur, a conduit for Himmler.[69] Apparently, Hitler did not want to overburden the *Gauleiter* with other duties outside their area of jurisdiction. This reasoning crumbles in the face of the *Gauleiter* and ministerial roles performed by Goebbels and Sauckel and the *Reichskommissar* posts held by Koch and Hinrich Lohse in the east.[70] More credible is the argument that Bormann did not want Speer's appointee to occupy a powerful position considered vital to any turnaround of Germany's wartime fortunes.

During the final years of the war Hanke also played host to the leaders of the regime when they travelled to Breslau to make important speeches. Breslau was doubly attractive in this respect as it remained a refuge from air attack and offered a magnificant auditorium – the Jahrhunderthalle (Centenary Hall). It was here that Hitler made his last major public speech to a mass audience. On 20 November 1943, he addressed a gathering of officer cadets, estimated at 10,000 by Goebbels and 20,000 in official reports.[71] Goebbels also delivered a major speech at the same venue on 8 July 1944. Alarmed by the Red Army's rapid advance to the Reich's borders, he stressed that Germany was engaged in a life or death struggle. Goebbels noted approvingly that around 50,000 people had gathered in the environs of the Jahrhunderthalle and another 150,000 Silesians had heard the speech broadcast over the *Drahtfunk* (loudspeaker) system. He praised Hanke for his charming reception, friendly introductory speech and enjoyable company and concluded that the old conflict over Magda was now history.[72]

This then was the highest echelon of the Nazi Party at war. For them the war meant a continuation of the constant round of intrigue, corruption, power struggles and turf wars, but they were now armed with greater powers and playing for higher stakes.

Trying to live in the midst of this chaos were ordinary eastern Germans but for them the war was the harbinger of numerous new, and all too frequently tragic, experiences.

CHAPTER 3

Enjoy the War, The Peace will be Dire

Despite the near absence of air attack and the distance from the battlefront, the war had a profound impact on everyday life in eastern Germany. The composition of the population altered dramatically. The largest outflow consisted of approximately one and a half million eastern German men called up by the military, a higher percentage of men being recruited from these mainly agrarian areas than from more industrialised regions. It was considered easier to replace agricultural workers with foreigners than to substitute foreign labour for skilled workmen in industry.[1] This was counterbalanced by a varied and enormous influx into the eastern provinces. Industrial enterprises, their workers and civilians were evacuated from the air raid threatened western and central regions of the Reich. Entire schools were transferred east as the raids became heavier. Meanwhile, Germany's early victories led to the capture of vast numbers of POWs. Many were interned in camps throughout the eastern provinces. Foreign workers comprised another group of incomers, lured to Germany by the promise of a living wage or through compulsion as their native lands were forced to fulfil labour quotas for the Reich. By autumn 1943, almost four million Polish and Soviet citizens were working in Germany and their numbers increased during the following year, by which time foreign workers from all over Europe made up approximately one quarter of the German labour force.[2] The war also placed fresh demands on the authorities. State bodies, already heavily Nazified in staff and sentiment prior to 1939, saw their role and authority diminished by the massive conscription of personnel and the Party's efforts to be at the vanguard of all aspects of the war on the Home Front.

Luftschutzkeller Deutschlands: Evacuees

Evacuation matters became a major part of *Gauleiter* workload during the war. In their role as RVKs they planned and initiated evacuations. As early as the summer of 1939, sections of the population had been evacuated from frontier zones in the West to the interior of Baden and Palatinate. The Party's *Kreisleiter* led the evacuation, organised accommodation and then arranged the homecoming following the victorious campaign in France.[3] Similarly, the Memel NSV evacuated most women and children from the town during the days immediately before Barbarossa. Thereafter, the threat to Reich territory from the ground disappeared until the summer of 1944. Increasingly, the real danger came from the air and the evacuation of cities threatened by bombing became a major component of the RVK's role. Following the RAF's retaliatory strikes on Berlin in September 1940, a response to *Luftwaffe* attacks on London, Hitler agreed to *Nationalsozialistische Volkswohlfahrt* (NSV, National Socialist People's Welfare Organisation) proposals to send children up to the age of 14 from Berlin and Hamburg to Brandenburg, Upper Austria, Saxony, Thüringia, Upper Bavaria, Silesia, the Sudetengau and the Warthegau. The Nazi authorities shrouded this measure with the suggestive epithet 'Kinderlandverschickung' and avoided the words billeting or evacuation. Rather, they emphasised the opportunity to provide a higher level of care and welfare during wartime. The NSV placed the younger children with families or in homes while the welfare of older children fell within the remit of the *Hitlerjugend* (HJ, Hitler Youth). In designated camps classes of older children, far from family influences, were to be subjected to intensified Nazi indoctrination. However, the Party was determined to erase any impression of forced evacuation and perpetuate the voluntary nature of the decision. Indeed, when the evacuation of entire classes was attempted in the Rhineland in the summer of 1940, less than one-sixth of the eligible children were sent away.[4]

By 1942, the increased danger of air attack meant that sections of the population had already been evacuated from threatened cities in the west. Early that year, the Interior Ministry worked on a general evacuation scheme to restrain unilateral measures by individual RVKs. However, some *Gau* authorities had already produced Mobilisation Plans for post-raid Party deployment. The plan for Cologne featured detailed objectives including the salvaging of cultural materials, the protection of the Party structure and measures to combat espionage and sabotage. The various Party bodies had their own specific roles in the evacuation plans. For instance, the welfare of evacuees was entrusted to the NSV, their transport was organised by the *Nationalsozialistische Kraftfahr-Korps* (NSKK, National Socialist Motor Corps) and care of the homeless was the remit of the *Nationalsozialistische Frauenschaft* (NSF, National Socialist Women's Group).[5]

From July 1943, the growing number of regions threatened by ever heavier air attack led to the Interior Ministry inaugurating a general scheme setting quotas for the distribution of civilians from cities in the north west and Berlin (*Entsendegaue*) to specified reception districts (*Aufnahmegaue*). Evacuees from *Gau* Köln–Aachen were sent to Lower Silesia and evacuees from South Westphalia were accommodated in Pomerania. Berlin evacuees were earmarked for East Prussia and Brandenburg but were soon to be found throughout the eastern provinces. Towards the end of the war, the threat of enemy occupation necessitated vast increases in the quotas imposed on the *Gaue* of the rapidly diminishing Reich.[6] Party organs attempted to undertake state duties at every turn. The NSV was responsible for the accommodation of the evacuees, selected suitable quarters and then directed the *Bürgermeistern* or *Landräten* to requisition them.

Moreover, to prevent wild flight from the threatened cities, instructions and declarations on evacuation issues were only to be broadcast by the *Gau* propaganda authorities. Unsurprisingly, as Peter Hüttenberger illustrated in *Gau* Baden, where 'no less than 139 circulars' were issued in nine months, the attempt to provide evacuees with everyday items was soon swamped by NSV bureaucracy.[7] New arrivals in eastern Germany faced similar obstacles.

By early 1944, around 825,000 evacuees were accommodated in eastern Germany. Some 450,000 were placed in Silesia, 200,000 in East Prussia, 100,000 in east Pomerania and 75,000 in east Brandenburg[8] but numbers fluctuated from province to province during the remainder of the year. Further dislocation arose from internal evacuation within the eastern provinces as civilians left bombed or air raid threatened cities for rural districts. This process had already began in earnest in Stettin after the firestorm raids on Hamburg between 24 July and 2 August 1943. From August 1943, 107,000 civilians were evacuated from the city, but by the first week of October over one-third of these had returned. Indeed, for evacuees from Stettin it could be more dangerous to leave the city. When on 9 October 1943 the United States Army Air Force (USAAF) attacked the Arado aircraft plant at Anklam, south west of the city, around 700 perished. Many of the casualties were evacuated Stettin schoolchildren.[9]

Nazi propaganda painted an idyllic picture of newcomers from the West enthusiastically embracing the rigours of rural life. For instance, city women apparently adapted to heavy harvest work in Elchniederung, East Prussia, because of their positive attitude.[10] This appeared to substantiate the regime's manufactured new consensus – the *Volksgemeinschaft*. In reality, social, cultural, religious and regional differences remained. Ian Kershaw observes that in Bavaria evacuees would not join in hard farm work. In rural districts resentment against the incomers was accentuated by the 'decadent idleness of the "ladies" of the town' and frequent disputes in the remaining poorly provisioned shops.[11] Similar scenarios were also encountered in the eastern provinces.

The aforementioned RAF attacks on Hamburg and British warnings that a similar fate would befall Berlin, led to the partial evacuation of the capital in early August 1943. 'When Berlin experiences such an attack as Hamburg has had, then we will have peace' and 'Enjoy the war, the peace will be dire' were utterances heard by the SD from fearful inhabitants of Frankfurt an der Oder.[12] Throughout the Reich the view was heard that enemy air forces could attack Berlin with impunity and the government would give up and leave the city. This illustrated the enemy's strength and Germany's weakness, and was viewed as the beginning of the end.[13] The influx of infants, their mothers and schoolchildren from Berlin into east Brandenburg during the second half of 1943 transformed the evacuation trickle into a flood. The *Landrat* of Königsberg/Neumark (population May 1939, 98,247) reported in December 1943 that around 16,000 evacuees and air raid victims were located in his country district, including 13,000 Berliners. Further NSV transports made numerical registration impossible as officials were preoccupied finding long-term accommodation for these families.[14] Other officials expressed their concern as the Battle of Berlin (November 1943–March 1944) peaked. In Züllichau, the accommodation and care of the Berliners became increasingly difficult, particularly the procurement of stoves and household effects.[15] Similarly, the *Oberbürgermeister* of Landsberg an der Warthe noted that his town was housing 4,354 persons, mainly from Berlin, and no more could be accommodated. Most were staying with relatives, but numbers fluctuated during the winter of 1943–1944 as some returned to Berlin while others fled the city following particularly heavy raids. Numbers continued to spiral and by early January 1945 almost 12,000 evacuees, bombed out civilians and foreigners were in Landsberg, a figure which corresponded to roughly one-quarter of the town's pre-war population.[16]

By the end of 1944 over 153,000 German incomers were quartered in east Brandenburg (including the Oder towns of Frankfurt, Guben and Forst). This included almost 105,000 Berliners and equated to nearly 20 per cent of the pre-war population.[17] Even after the final Soviet winter offensive commenced on 12 January 1945 the influx from the West continued. The final transport of western evacuees arrived in Landsberg on 28 January at the very time locals were making preparations for their own flight. Some post-war testimonies highlighted the unwillingness of the local population to accommodate evacuees and suggested that this only subsided due to the prudence displayed by active senior local officials.[18]

The air raid victims and evacuees became the best propagandists for the effectiveness of Allied bombing by leaving their home cities and disseminating stories of their own experiences. One million Hamburgers spread across the Reich in the aftermath of the July 1943 firestorm raids were the clearest manifestation of this. The British Special Operations Executive (SOE) received information from the Committee of Underground Warfare in Poland on the arrival of Hamburgers in *Gau* Danzig–West Prussia in September and October 1943. The new arrivals were to be isolated from the local population as they were 'spreading defeatism and anti-Nazi views'. A propaganda van which greeted them at Bromberg station was mobbed during a welcome speech. In general, it was noted that the evacuees were 'depressed and apathetic' and had 'received a very cold welcome from the German settlers'.[19]

The SD also picked up numerous other complaints and rumours. Lower Silesians believed that leading Party and ministerial officials in Berlin had been allocated official transportation to remove their furniture from the city whereas ordinary Berliners were only allowed to take hand luggage. Likewise, senior officials were seemingly able to leave the capital, although workers apparently had to stay.[20] In the meantime, the virtual absence of air attack led Lower Silesia to be dubbed *Luftschutzkeller Deutschlands* (Germany's Air Raid Shelter) making it an attractive site for relocated industry, including much of Berlin's electrical and instrument manufacturing sector.[21] This influx of industry demonstrated Lower Silesia's increased significance to the German war effort. Krupp, Siemens, Borsig, AEG and Arado were major corporations with plants in the province. Local officials hoped that their continued presence would help the province prosper after the war.[22] Government offices also arrived from Berlin. The Foreign Ministry, Finance Ministry and other state ministries were evacuated to health resorts in the Riesengebirge.

In late September 1943, the OLG President in Breslau noted that, despite the military reversals and worries regarding air attacks, locals and evacuees displayed a determination to hold out (*durchhalten*) until the *Endsieg*. Admittedly, although the new arrivals were initially unpopular due to their complaints about shortages, he insisted that these difficulties had been resolved.[23] The incomers no longer had ready access to radio, cinema, baths and toilets but children had more freedom in their new surroundings. Nevertheless, some evacuees found life in their new environment so unappealing that they returned home without authorisation.[24] Richard Spreu, *Landrat* of Habelschwerdt on the Sudeten frontier, recounted that evacuees came predominantly from Hamburg, Berlin and the Rhineland. He commented that 'The quality of the evacuees was so different that the reporter can say with good conscience that the female evacuees from Berlin were the most hard working and best [but] those from the Rhineland were the worst in every respect.'[25] This same correspondent also noted that the morals of the evacuees made a particularly bad impression in the locality of Bad Landeck, where a military hospital with 1,000 beds had been built but 'just as many expectant women from the air-raid endangered areas were accommodated there'.[26]

Entire schools were transported east in the *Kinderlandverschickung*. Teachers, their families and pupils arrived in Pomerania from Bochum, Hagen and Berlin. Dr Otto Kleinschmidt, the Pomeranian official charged with school relocation, stressed the co-operation he received from the local authorities, Party bodies, the NSV and the HJ. He considered that difficulties were only encountered because of the continually changing and unforeseeable conditions. Between June and September 1944, on Schwede-Coburg's order, the schoolchildren were accommodated in Baltic coastal resorts. For children whose families accompanied them to Pomerania this summer schooling was optional. Moreover, as the designated Baltic resorts were in the vicinity of Swinemünde, an important port threatened by air attack, many parents possibly recalled the aforementioned raid on Anklam, and chose to keep their children by their side. Despite a shortage of teaching space, teachers and material, this stay by the sea was reported to have been a healthy experience. However, the influx into the province from further east during the final months of 1944 led to the transformation of schoolrooms into makeshift military hospitals or refugee accommodation. There was a significant decline in teaching prior to Christmas 1944 and many schools closed altogether. Older pupils and teachers were also drafted into fortification building or other tasks to assist the *Wehrmacht*, although admittedly the same was expected of local teachers and pupils.[27]

A number of Pomeranian testimonies emphasised that detailed criticism of the relationship between the incomers and the local population was rare.[28] The *Generalstaatsanwalt* (GSA) in Stettin did mention in late September 1943 that the reception of evacuees in rural districts led to friction and he was receiving an increasing amount of information from his local officials on this subject but this was not disclosed in subsequent submissions.[29]

In contrast, the Königsberg judicial authorities underlined the strained relationship between native East Prussians and Berliners. There was already a sense of uneasiness within the province due to new air raid protection measures, but the arrival of the Berliners and their stories of recent unfortunate personal experiences launched damaging rumours. In Lyck, the Berliners quickly made themselves as unpopular as possible. They had assumed that local farmers lived in abundance and demanded foodstuffs from them. Incomers were said to have complained that the Berlin *Gauleitung* had sent them to live in this barren land bereft of cinemas, theatres and concerts. It was said that the Berliners boasted that they had previously been richly supplied with fruit, chocolate and coffee. This caused unease among the indigenous population and a belief that East Prussia was disadvantaged compared to other parts of the Reich. Perhaps alluding to the capital's left-wing reputation and the lack of enthusiasm shown by its citizens at the outset of the war, a certain 'Berlin mentality' was apparently noticeable among the evacuees. Occasionally Berliners blamed East Prussia for the war, asserting that the province should have been handed over to Poland and thereby the conflict would have been avoided. Berliners were said to be lucky with their hosts:

> The opinion of a senior paymaster, born in Upper Bavaria, appears accurate as he has frequently observed the manner of the Berliners in East Prussia and declared that the Berliners were best suited to quiet and somewhat dull East Prussia; had one attempted to evacuate them to Bavaria this would have already long ago given rise to murder.[30]

The demanding and unreasonable behaviour of Berliners lost them sympathy in Allenstein where they were treated 'with a certain mistrust and scarcely concealed aversion'.[31] In Memel, the arrival of large numbers of Hamburgers and Berliners initially had a detrimental effect on the public mood but those initiating or spreading malicious horror stories had 'their games stopped by the Gestapo'.[32] In late November 1943 OLG President Dräger in Königsberg noted that the evacuees were not embracing the simple lifestyle prevalent in the province. Above all, the incomers were disappointed to find that food was not plentiful. Berliners also complained more and attributed the political discipline of locals to their stupidity and limited horizons. Berlin youths did not use the German greeting (Heil Hitler! and the outstretched right hand) and were apathetic to HJ activities. Dräger feared that after the November terror raids on Berlin, East Prussia would be flooded with evacuees to the detriment of the hitherto firm standing displayed by the local population.[33]

These complaints continued into 1944. Berlin women, lauded in earlier Lower Silesian testimony, were criticised by East Prussian rural dwellers, shopkeepers and officials for presumptuous and intolerable behaviour. They were reproached for their unreasonable demands concerning accommodation and provisions, accused of hoarding scarce commodities to send back to Berlin and criticised for complaining about the monotony of East Prussian life. Party propaganda claimed that the new arrivals helped on farms[34] but often, when there was a heavy demand for agricultural labour, the evacuees refused. Indeed, locals were often too busy cultivating to entertain the new arrivals and simply wanted them to muck in. Moreover, female evacuees from Berlin were blamed for an increasing number of wartime offences, particularly the escalation of cases involving illegal contact with POWs. They were also condemned for failing to control their children, whose penchant for playing with matches caused numerous fires and considerable property damage across East Prussia.[35] Koch was still demanding that evacuees in East Prussia participate in agricultural work in April 1944. In an appeal, published on 15 April, he emphasised that, 'As *Gauleiter* of this province, I have considered it my foremost duty to mitigate in every respect the fate of evacuees from other *Gaue*. In return, I now demand of everyone whom the Party and State authorities consider fit that he should work as an auxiliary worker in the countryside.'[36]

This sudden migration placed great strain on officialdom and the railways. Moreover, families were separated because of evacuation arrangements. For instance, a married man from Bremen moved with the relocated Focke-Wulf aeroplane factory to Sorau, east Brandenburg while his school age children were sent to Saxony and his wife and small children were evacuated to Bavaria.[37] Many evacuees arrived in the eastern provinces devoid of possessions as they were only allowed or able to take limited luggage with them. Thus household goods and bedding were left behind. Before 1943 air raid victims could expect to have some of their destroyed property replaced, but, as their numbers mushroomed and precious resources were directed to the armaments industry, it was impossible to meet basic needs. Even when evacuees had appropriate ration coupons they found it difficult to procure clothes and shoes. Shops were either empty or their proprietors refused to sell to incomers, their meagre stocks being allocated to the local population. Complaints highlighting the lack of suitable accommodation and absence of facilities were a feature of evacuees' letters home.[38] When the authorities imposed compulsory billeting, the so-called 'better circles of the population', attempted to evade taking in evacuees or claimed that they had limited space. Rumours spread in Königsberg in the late summer of 1943 that the homes of leading Party officials were exempted from being occupied by evacuees.[39] Further unease emanated over communal cooking facilities. In some areas communal kitchens and shared accommodation was provided, sometimes with radios, but the women still desired their own space. Evacuees did not want to be housed in camps or barracks or treated like beggars or vagabonds. They remarked that the south and east of the Reich would soon face similar air attacks and worried that they had 'fallen out of the frying pan into the fire'.[40]

Both locals and new arrivals faced daily material difficulties. The SD's correspondents observed that procuring women's clothes and bedding in Breslau, Königsberg and Stettin was very difficult. Warm clothing was almost unobtainable. Despite attempts to give air raid victims priority, in Königsberg and Memel it was virtually impossible to supply them with clothing, underwear and hosiery. In Königsberg these problems were attributed to business closures in line with total war measures. In Stettin there was a shortage of bedding and clothing for children and infants; the latter groups particularly significant as they made up a large proportion of the influx. The monthly reports produced by the statistical office in Pomerania for the pricing authorities in Berlin detailed the cost and availability of consumer goods.[41] Availability was grouped into four categories – good supply, sufficient supply, shortage and finally, considerable shortage or not distributed. Clothing, bedding and general household items were listed under the two latter headings.[42] The Pomeranian authorities admitted that it was increasingly difficult to meet even the most pressing demands for clothing. In Stettin the finger was pointed at incomers who scoured the city's shops for goods. The limited supply of bedding meant that the needs of air raid victims could only be partially catered for. Shoes, particularly children's footwear, were another scarce commodity, exacerbated by the poor quality of shoemaking – some two-thirds of shoes being deemed deficient.[43] At the height of the winter of 1943–1944 there was a pronounced lack of winter coats, under garments, scarves, hats and socks for men and insufficient supplies of winter coats, outer clothing, underwear and stockings for women. In most communities children's clothes were unobtainable. Meanwhile, the supply of household goods for bombed out evacuees was scarcer than ever. Despite the rising population of Pomeranian rural districts, the quotas were steadily reduced.[44]

Other problems also emerged. The availability of clothing was adversely affected by the destruction of warehouses in air raids on Stettin. Moreover, Pomeranians were angered at the high price for goods from the occupied territories and the *General Gouvernement*.[45] Elsewhere, reports from Frankfurt an der Oder stated that the diminishing supply of textiles to stores led to the requirements of air raid victims only being met because of restrictions imposed on everyone else. It was impossible to meet the demands of air raid victims for shoes and in Brieg, Lower Silesia, the allocation of footwear failed even to cover the pressing needs of local expectant mothers.[46] Nevertheless, the authorities were ever alert to the possibility of privileges being abused. In east Brandenburg, attempts to give Hamburgers an advance to purchase clothing and bedding was exploited, there being no checks that the beneficiaries were from the city. Some who claimed these benefits reportedly vanished only to reappear in a neighbouring district to repeat the racket.[47] The Lower Silesian SD also reported that new arrivals from the West were attempting to obtain additional suits at the expense of locals.[48]

Material difficulties worsened in 1944. There was a lack of simple household items, stoves and furniture. The East Prussian NSV advised that attempts to give evacuees the use of household items had proved impossible as locals were already enduring considerable shortages themselves. Breslau reported that the allocation was totally unsatisfactory and sought approval for special deliveries to meet the needs of evacuees. During December 1943, as an additional 1,000 consumers per day arrived in Lower Silesia, even the most urgent demands for household and cooking utensils could not be met. However, it was popularly perceived in East Prussia and Lower Silesia that the *Wehrmacht* and Party authorities could obtain bountiful supplies. But other incomers experienced the shortages. An SD report cited a military hospital in Insterburg, East Prussia where the wounded were sharing cutlery. It was not exceptional for four disabled soldiers to share a set of utensils.[49]

Food was not abundant. But despite the unavailability of some imported items, Germans who had not fallen foul of the regime faced no threat of starvation. Healthy dietary levels were maintained and the desperate shortages associated with 1916–1918 were avoided. In mid-December 1943 and mid-January 1944 supplies of meat, sausage, bread, potatoes, milk and cheese in Pomerania were apparently adequate but evacuees apparently 'familiar with a plentiful supply of vegetables' were dismayed at shortages in this sector.[50] Shortages were obscured by reducing entitlements and then claiming that sufficient supplies were available to meet the new smaller allocations. Ration reduction and a growing recourse to replacement products such as 'Kaffee und Tee Ersatzmittel' were increasingly conspicuous. Finally, in mid-March 1944, the impact of the poor harvest of 1943 was felt as the vegetable ration was cut.[51]

Similar difficulties existed elsewhere in the Reich. In late November 1943 the SD reported that many shops had not stocked potatoes for four weeks. This had led to bad feeling and widespread bitterness towards the officials deemed responsible. Serious worries were expressed about the forthcoming winter and recollections of the 'turnip winter' of 1916–1917 remained vivid.[52] In Frankfurt an der Oder most of the population had not been supplied with potatoes for weeks in early November 1943 leading to scenes of distraught women on the roads.[53] The Breslau SD advised in early November that in Liegnitz, where many consumers had already waited eight weeks for potatoes, housewives stormed every small delivery. In Sagen, wide circles of the population had not received their ration for weeks because traders had only received half or sometimes only one quarter of the area's minimum consumption.[54] The subsequent cutting of the potato ration and the shortage of fruit and vegetables in Lower Silesia, coupled with bad news from the fighting fronts, caused the public mood to sink periodically according to judicial accounts.[55] Sometimes, however, rural inhabitants exploited the situation. An official from Schönlanke, Pomerania recounted that city dwellers came to the area prepared to pay excessive amounts for foodstuffs such as poultry which was not rationed.[56] In Stolp, Pomerania, profiteers were demanding up to 200 RM for a goose, 40 RM for poultry and 60 RM for a duck.[57] A particularly crass example of exploitation arising from the shortage of potatoes was reported from Frankfurt an der Oder. Here a farmer had demanded 50 RM from a townswoman for one pound of potatoes.[58]

In contrast, GSA Szelinski in Königsberg insisted that: 'The nutritional situation in East Prussia, considering that we are living in the fifth year of wartime, cannot at all be described as bad.'[59] Deliveries to the *Wehrmacht* apparently accounted for the shortage of vegetables. At the same time a considerable volume of all types of goods was smuggled into East Prussia from the incorporated territories by civilians, German officials, businessmen and military personnel.[60] As shortages began to bite, not all Germans believed that they were being treated fairly. Rumours, attributed by the authorities to 'British broadcast propaganda', spread telling of extra 'diplomatic' rations said to be enjoyed by Ministers, *Gauleiter*, *Kreisleiter* and even by Party members.[61] Indeed, the well connected and those engaged in black market activities could still procure luxury items. A Königsberg student recalled that one senior German Red Cross official, with high Party rank, attempted to proposition her in exchange for travel documentation. Even in August 1944 he had stocks of brandy, cigars, liqueur chocolates, cakes and coffee to tempt her with.[62]

In straitened economic circumstances the relationship between evacuees and their hosts was rarely smooth. Individual and local circumstances were significant. For city dwellers, the shock of air attack, with the possible attendant devastating effect on relatives, friends and possessions, was compounded by transplantation to an alien land and different lifestyle. In contrast, the indigenous population rarely considered them as distressed fellow German racial comrades, but more immediately viewed evacuees as rivals for scarce commodities. They were an unwelcome intrusion into hitherto sedate rural life. The authorities had to coerce country people into housing evacuees; sometimes locals exploited the situation and charged them excessive rents.[63] Incomers were criticised as workshy and accused of acting in an insensitive, offensive manner. Likewise, they were perceived to be the source of malicious or defeatist rumours which threatened the posture of the stolid indigenous population. There was no uniform evacuee experience in the East. Rather, it is noticeable that no amount of propaganda could eradicate the day to day difficulties emanating from unhappiness, resentment and shortages.

'Not so Bad as They are Portrayed': Foreign Workers and POWs

The disdain exhibited towards many eastern Germans to their evacuated fellow countrymen can be compared with their relationship with foreign workers and POWs. The regime's racial rhetoric had long attacked these groups, with particularly vicious invective being reserved for Poles and Russians. Russian POWs were at the bottom of the Nazi hierarchy of foreign labour. To reinforce this idea, images of wretched 'subhuman' Russian POWs were a regular component of newsreel content as the *Wehrmacht* advanced towards Moscow in 1941. Many succumbed at the outset, perishing from starvation and disease during the autumn and winter of 1941 – the victims of an officially sanctioned policy of neglect. The survivors were subjected to the most draconian legislation, received least food, minimal clothing and were often directed to the hardest forms of labour, in damp infested underground factories and quarries, producing correspondingly horrendous mortality rates. No consideration or kindness was to be extended to these 'racial inferiors'. As a result some 3.3 million of the 5.7 million Red Army soldiers captured during the war were dead by 1945 – a 57.5 per cent attrition rate.[64] In the eastern provinces perceived racial defects were sometimes blurred by wartime realities in the form of scarcity of labour and everyday encounters. Moreover, these arrivals from the East included a vast influx of men into a largely female society. Harsh punishments awaited those who transgressed the line between *Herrenvolk* and *Untermenschen.* However, this did not stop sections of the population once more behaving in sharp contrast to the regime's racial invective.

The importance of foreign workers to the German economy was outlined by Ulrich Herbert: 'By the summer of 1944, 46 per cent of all agricultural workers and a third of the workers in mining, the metal industry, chemicals and construction were foreigners. Foreign forced labour had become the backbone of the German war economy.'[65] In eastern Germany most foreign workers and POWs were engaged in agriculture, although they also comprised a substantial proportion of the labour force in major industrial concerns such as the Schichau shipyards in East Prussia and the FAMO (*Fahrzeug und Motorenwerke*) tank works and Linke-Hoffmann-Busch locomotive works, both in Breslau.

Observers in east Brandenburg mentioned the predominance of POW and foreign labour in the fields. It was claimed that foreign workers were handled fairly, were not overworked, overwhelmingly had decent accommodation, were well clothed and had a better diet than many German city dwellers. Moreover, local people repeatedly contravened rules and invited foreign workers to eat at their table or treated them as friends. In general, foreign workers were said to be willing and able.[66] Similarly harmonious circumstances were outlined in post-war Pomeranian testimonies. French workers and POWs were held in particularly high regard. Libussa von Oldershausen, from Glowitz near Stolp, recalled arguing with her new husband, a *Wehrmacht* captain, when he objected to her throwing buns at French POWs on their wedding day in June 1944:

> What nonsense; we thought of them as "our" Frenchmen. At Christmas they got their roast rabbit, at Easter their painted eggs, as was only proper. They had been with us for four years by now, they had learned to understand the Pomeranian low German dialect, and had taken over all the responsible jobs from which our German men had been dragged away by the war . . . And imperceptibly, behind their own backs, so to speak, these exiles had come to take pride in their accomplishments, to identify with their duties.[67]

In Schneidemühl, Pomerania, the inmates of the POW camp were initially all French and they maintained good discipline. Russian prisoners later joined them. The town's then *Oberbürgermeister* later insisted that there were no complaints and he was certain that POWs had not encountered 'bad experiences'.[68] The former *Landrat* of Bütow, Pomerania remembered that Russian POWs were occasionally allowed to stay with their employers. Revealingly, he also alluded to the type of epidemic, arising from poor conditions, which wiped out so many Russian POWs and slave workers, in this instance a typhus outbreak in a local camp.[69]

Post-war Lower Silesian accounts highlighted the good relationship between locals and foreign workers.[70] The RAD's directives concerning the payment of foreign labour were said to have been ridiculous. Foreigners were paid a pittance and this was reportedly a regular source of disagreement.[71] POWs faced more serious problems. Despite the erection of delousing buildings in camps,[72] mortality levels remained high. In Landeshut the local authorities were worried about the high death rate arising from malnourishment in a camp for Russian POWs and called for a proper graveyard and official registration of deaths.[73] Meanwhile, in Namslau, Poles, failing to settle in to their new duties, were brutally treated.[74] Moreover, despite later denials of sabotage or disruptive action, contemporary judicial reports demonstrate that in some areas of Lower Silesia foreign workers were convicted and summarily executed for these activities.[75] In early April 1944 the OLG President in Breslau commented on the widespread criminal offences committed by foreigners. A particularly bloody deed was attributed to a group of Ukrainians who, during the course of an attempted robbery, had murdered three women. Foreigners and incomers from the West were also blamed for the 'not inconsiderable rise' in thefts and traffic accidents.[76]

Despite threats of severe punishment, relationships between POWs and German women, especially those with husbands at the front, increased. This development, strictly contrary to the regime's racial tenets, caused the GSA in Stettin to note on 29 September 1943 that 'Up to now there is no observable decrease in the shameless behaviour of women and girls in contact with POWs.'[77] The OLG President in Breslau bemoaned the fact that most Germans did not comprehend the need for severe punishment in these instances. He cited the case of French POWs who in their leisure time were allowed to visit guest houses and cinemas in civilian clothing. While instances of sexual intercourse with French prisoners were punishable by heavy prison sentences, there was confusion among the population because social contact with civilian workers from the West was not prohibited and they were even allowed to marry.[78] Nevertheless, confusion or not the OLG President noted in August 1944 that criminal offences committed by foreigners and contact between German women and POWs remained widespread.[79]

Foreign labour was crucial to the functioning of the East Prussian agrarian economy. Antipathy to the Germans among the Poles of Sudauen, Zichenau and Bialystok was more marked following Stalingrad. To the Polish population this defeat signified a change in Germany's war fortunes. In Sudauen and Bialystok, Poles were not seduced by the anti-Communist content of German propaganda which followed the announcement of the discovery of the bodies of thousands of Polish officers at Katyn in April 1943.[80] Poles observed that the Germans did not treat them any differently than the Soviets. Meanwhile, the German authorities were concerned at the circulation of enemy propaganda pamphlets and the increasing number of ambushes carried out by well-armed Polish bands. German businesses, police, *Volksdeutsche* and collaborators were attacked and railway lines were cut. Occasional incidents occurred within the pre-war East Prussian frontiers. On the evening of 15–16 August 1943, a band of Poles raided the home of a deputy forest master in Johannisburg district, killing him, his wife and two of their children. After this attack the band proceeded to the village of Mittenheide where eight inhabitants were killed, buildings set alight and weapons and ammunition stolen.[81] The isolated rural population also faced the risk of encountering escaped foreign workers and POWs. Attempted robberies, resulting in fatalities, were reported from Insterburg and Lyck districts. On account of the danger these foreigners posed to the local population, particularly in time of air attack, the authorities reported the energetic efforts to develop the *Landwacht*, *Stadtwacht* and *Küstenwacht* to combat this threat.[82]

The East Prussian authorities also observed disturbing trends in the relationship with foreigners. There were clear parallels with Silesian accounts. The cases of forbidden contact with POWs mostly involved sexual intercourse with French prisoners. Again, the judiciary claimed that confusion played a significant part in these developments. A considerable rise in such offences arose when French POWs were given leave from their workplaces. The population knew that contact with civilian foreign workers from the West did not involve the threat of punishment but when Germans read that French prisoners were also granted leisure time this produced uncertainty. Some POWs wore civilian clothing when they ventured out, while others, attired in military uniforms, sported civilian armbands. In late June 1943, OLG President Dräger expressed the viewpoint that it should be made clear to the population through press and radio that contact with POWs was forbidden and criminal. However, subsequent judicial reports to Berlin still maintained that Party propaganda had been unsuccessful in enlightening the population on the different categories of Frenchmen.[83]

Criminal cases involving East Prussian women and girls increased during the war. Most conspicuous was the steady growth in offences involving relationships with

POWs and foreign workers from the East. An 'epidemic spread of these offences' occurred, which threatened the racial purity of German blood and adversely affected the discipline and attitude of foreigners. One senior prosecutor ventured the opinion that many women no longer considered these sexual offences worthy of disgust but rather a feminine peccadilo.[84] Party officials believed that a growing number of *Neugeburten* (babies) were conceived during such relationships. Despite staff shortages and other wartime priorities, the *Gau* authorities, assisted by the head of Königsberg University's Racial Biology Institute, considered it essential to discover the ancestry of children when there was a possibility that the father was of foreign, gypsy or *asozial* origin.[85]

Eastern workers and POWs were subject to barbaric strictures in any dealings with German women. Decrees issued by the *Reichssicherheitshauptamt* (RSHA, Reich Security Main Office) in Berlin in 1940 rendered intimate sexual contact between German women and Polish men a capital crime. Polish workers were to be publicly hanged and German women were to be sent to jail or concentration camp. From at least the end of 1941 the authorities began to order abortions in cases of pregnancy. Sexual intercourse was also prohibited between German males and Polish females. The RSHA decreed that German males were to receive a three-month sentence in a concentration camp. Polish females were to be detained for up to 21 days if they had been seduced by their superior. Otherwise, they were to be sentenced to an unspecified spell in a women's concentration camp. Similar rules governed Russian workers in the Reich after June 1941. The number of public executions of Polish and Russian workers charged with sexual offences declined after mid-1943. However, the total number of executions of eastern workers and Soviet POWs for this offence continued to rise. By 1944 two or three execution orders a day were being issued by the RSHA against Russian workers accused of sexual intercourse with German women.[86]

The judicial authorities were also worried that the numerous incidences of contact between German women and girls with Russians and Poles had a negative effect on morale. They were said to be better informed about military and political events than their German masters, because of clandestine listening to foreign radio. This accentuated German unease at the increasingly unfavourable military situation.[87] The local propaganda authorities were also concerned at these alarming developments and sought to initiate their own *Gau*-wide propaganda programme. The Propaganda Office in Königsberg argued that this effort was necessary because East Prussia was the most easterly province of the Reich and had a duty to act as a bulwark against Bolshevik agitation. Due to the province's location, the risk from subversive propaganda was deemed greater and unskilled eastern farm labourers were considered conscious or sometimes involuntary carriers of this agitation. The East Prussian propagandists wanted to target women and old men in the countryside with this campaign, involving posters, pictures and leaflet drops illustrating Bolshevik atrocities. Seemingly, these groups did not read newspapers and were particularly susceptible to agitation from their Russian workers whom they declared were 'not so bad as they are portrayed'. The campaign aimed to avert the spread of these subversive views and avoid the creation of an unexpected breeding ground for Bolshevism.[88]

SD reports compiled during late 1943 and early 1944 demonstrated that as the war turned against Germany fear of foreign workers and POWs increased. Russian POWs were described as lazy, gullible and violent. In Oels, Lower Silesia, locals were apparently critical of the inadequate supervision of Russian prisoners, allowed to remain inactive for 15 minutes or more without their German guards saying a word; this apparently explained their corresponding lack of work.[89] The Breslau SD reported that some Soviet POWs said that they no longer wanted to work as the war was in its final three months. They had seemingly heard these sentiments from French co-workers.[90] The presence of growing numbers of foreigners in the Reich produced rising anxiety. The Breslau SD claimed that women dared not leave their homes unaccompanied in the evenings or walk along secluded paths during the day.[91]

The German security services were anxious to gauge the mood of foreign workers and ascertain their attitude towards Germany. In East Prussia the police found a growing sympathy for Communism as it was believed that the Bolsheviks would soon be in the province.[92] Generally the authorities noticed growing anti-German sentiments among eastern workers and asserted that many exhibited a fanatical hatred of Germany. In Stettin, a propaganda brochure with a picture of Hitler had been distributed among the eastern workers. Their hatred had been expressed by them using pins to gouge out the *Führer*'s eyes. One eastern worker had stated that the time would also come to pull the eyes out of the living Hitler. The Gestapo was investigating the affair.[93] The SD reported in February 1944 that 7,000 letters from eastern workers in Stettin had been censored. Most expressed hatred for everything German and demanded revenge.[94]

During the final stages of the war the Nazi authorities and many ordinary Germans were fearful of a rising by foreign workers to coincide with an enemy invasion. Operation Valkyrie, put into motion by the conspirators in their attempt to overthrow the Nazi regime on 20 July 1944, was a contingency plan geared to countering an uprising by foreign workers. The German press admitted that anxiety over a foreign workers' rebellion existed, but insisted that the authorities were prepared for this eventuality and cited the example of the Warsaw rising, crushed in the late summer of 1944.[95] For instance, plans were made in Pomerania to confront a Polish resistance movement in the province made up of POWs and civilian workers. Party officials were ordered to be most observant to counter any such developments. This fear had been triggered by the Gestapo's discovery of documents in the paper basket of a Neustettin dairy on 2 September 1944. These indicated the existence of a secret Polish organisation which planned to initiate a rising using weapons dropped from Allied planes.[96]

Nazi propagandists highlighted the racial defects of these foreign workers. However, in wartime eastern Germany evidence points to the authorities' concern that sections of the population were ignoring this and breaching official guidelines concerning 'strict but correct' conditions. This is not to suggest that in general foreign labour was anywhere near adequately treated. Housed in the most basic accommodation, poorly clothed and malnourished, eastern workers, Soviet POWs and Jews died like flies from epidemics and execution or were worked to death by the SS in mines, quarries and underground factories. Nevertheless, certain requirements and feelings caused ordinary Germans to risk punishment by circumventing the regime's racial tenets and treating individual foreigners more fairly. As Jill Stephenson argues, mitigating factors such as the lack of labour, desire for sexual relationships and 'humanitarian' responses gave rise to this development.[97]

In mundane, everyday life, labour of whatever racial origin was deemed a precious commodity. Foreign workers and POWs tended to be treated better in agriculture than they were in industry. Eastern workers had traditionally participated in eastern German agriculture for decades in order to compensate for the region's lack of manpower. Their presence was hardly startling and the demand for labour coupled with unavoidable personal contact helped to temper old national prejudices and break the racial barriers the regime had erected. Even Russian labourers were found to be intelligent human beings who failed to correspond to the stereotypical Bolshevik monster. As illustrated earlier, some German women gave these incomers more than a seat at the family table or a room in the home. The sexual liaisons between German women and foreigners were a major concern to the authorities. With the outflow of men to the military, there was a dearth of German men in the eastern provinces. On account of their apparent exotic or cultured background, or because of their very availability, new arrivals presented a temptation to sex-starved German women.

The seemingly decent treatment of some foreigners, is palpable in contemporary and memoir material. In the later stages of the war this may have been motivated by the desire not to further antagonise foreigners when the Red Army stood at the gates. While individual foreigners and POWs could be valued and even liked, there remained the fear of a mass rising. However, in addition to their perception of likely Soviet excesses and a mutual desire for self-preservation, the fact that so many foreigners assisted east Germans during the dark days of 1945 indicates a sense of attachment to individual Germans and their families. Although most Germans were motivated by their own daily concerns and were oblivious to the suffering of the foreigners in their midst, evidence from the eastern provinces also demonstrates that individuals from across society, ranging from farmers to young women and motivated by differing needs, sometimes took a greater interest in these incomers.

'The Terror Attacks by the Enemy'

While the human landscape of the eastern provinces underwent considerable change during wartime, until 1944 eastern Germans rarely confronted the danger from the air faced by their counterparts in western regions and Berlin. But British, American and Soviet bombers were all in action over eastern Germany prior to the war's final months. Admittedly, while eastern Germans were not bombed regularly they were not entirely spared. The aforementioned Soviet air raids on East Prussia (late June 1941)[98] petered out as the *Wehrmacht* advanced. Subsequent raids, such as the attack on Breslau on 13 November 1941 and the attacks on Königsberg in the summer of 1942, had greater propaganda value than strategic significance. They demonstrated to eastern Germans that the Soviets had not suffered the ultimate defeat promised by the Nazi leadership.[99]

Soviet attacks were stepped up in April 1943 and were directed at 'centres of the armaments industry and administration in the East Prussian area'.[100] The attacks on Königsberg on 13 April and Tilsit on 20 April, Hitler's birthday, were more noteworthy. Some 40 to 50 aircraft raided Königsberg. City centre buildings and university facilities suffered damage, but the death toll was low and the impact on war industries was minor.[101] In Tilsit there were over 100 fatalities and greater material damage.[102] Over 4,600 inhabitants were made homeless and the absence of flak and night fighters provoked local criticism. A significant amount of Army Group North's supplies passed through the town and the bridges over the River Memel had significant strategic value. The population was restless and some tried to leave. Exaggerated rumours concerning losses and damage spread throughout the province and were particularly noticeable in areas where no air attacks had yet been recorded.[103] Soviet bombers only flew around 1,000 sorties against Germany in 1943 but the attacks on East Prussia succeeded in forcing the German leadership to divert resources into the province's air defence.[104] GSA Szelinski in Königsberg identified favourable developments such as an increased interest in air raid safety measures, a general willingness to make sacrifices on behalf of air-raid victims and seemingly more understanding of the plight of west Germans.[105] There may have been understanding from afar, but as has been demonstrated this often evaporated when East Prussians encountered real evacuees on their doorsteps.

British bombers occasionally attacked eastern objectives.[106] Some 44 Lancaster bombers were sent to Danzig on 11 July 1942 but one-third of this force failed to locate their destination. The targets were the city's submarine building yards and invasion barges transferred east following the postponement of Operation Sealion (the planned German invasion of Britain in 1940). The attack had no effect on U-Boat production and did little damage.[107] Nine Lancasters undertook a similar mission on the evening of 27–28 August 1942 against nearby Gotenhafen (Gdynia). Their objective was the new German aircraft carrier, the *Graf Zeppelin*, which was seemingly in the final stages of construction. However, because of haze the seven planes reaching Gotenhafen could not locate the ship and attacked the harbour area instead.[108]

Most British attention focused on Stettin, an entry point for supplies from Sweden and an important shipbuilding and industrial centre. Stettin was a target throughout the war despite being 600 miles from England, most notably in a series of raids at the end of September 1941. The synthetic oil plant at Pölitz to the north of the city was also a regular target.[109] Nevertheless, the attacks on the evenings of 20–21 April 1943 and 5–6 January 1944 were much heavier than before, with over 300 bombers deployed on both missions.[110] Extensive damage was inflicted on the city centre, port facilities and industrial premises. The April 1943 raid claimed 586 lives, left more than 1,000 people injured and made around 25,000 homeless. Factories, shipyards, hospitals, *Wehrmacht* and police barracks and the main goods station were damaged and 13 industrial premises totally destroyed. Damage was also inflicted on gas and water installations[111] but the local armaments authorities were upbeat. They wrote that the raid had had a negligible impact on armaments manufacture, with only slight damage at the affected plants, and underlined that the damage was quickly repaired.[112] In contrast, British accounts were later to claim that 'the attack did little damage to the town proper but caused devastation in the industrial district to the south'.[113] On the ground, the authorities also tried to bolster the city's air raid protection programme, but were frustrated by the twin problems of procuring scarce labour and material to undertake this work. RAF Bomber Command picked up on the anxiety in the city, observing in a report that, 'There has been a continuous to-do about evacuation and ARP and anxious official injunctions to get a stiff upper lip ready for the attack that was bound to come.'[114]

In the January 1944 raid on Stettin, 244 were killed, over 1,000 wounded and approximately 20,000 rendered homeless. The RAF lost 16 aircraft compared to 22 the previous April. Whilst German civilian casualties were lower, damage to industry was greater and 20 industrial premises were totally destroyed. Police President Grundey recalled that motorised fire fighting appliances were sent to the city from Berlin, Halle and Rostock together with volunteer fire brigade personnel from throughout Pomerania.[115] The widespread damage to the city's business and commercial centre, port facilities and industry was compounded by the effect on public utilities, the transport system and shipping. The supply of gas, electricity and water initially broke down and the main telephone exchange suffered substantial damage.[116] A number of military installations were destroyed or damaged, the main railway station was gutted and the goods station was partly wrecked.[117] In the harbour area dock cranes collapsed, warehouses were destroyed and a training ship and numerous smaller vessels were sunk. Nevertheless, reports stressed that the fires were controlled and war industries had only suffered isolated damage.[118]

One senior female member of the RAD in Stettin wrote on 7 January 1944 that 18 bombs fell on her short street. However, that evening, gas, water and electricity had been restored. She remarked that it was amazing how rapidly order had been re-established but admitted that the city centre looked ghastly, worse than after the 20 April 1943 attack.[119] The GSA noted that despite the significant damage, in the circumstances life had quickly returned to orderly lines. He considered that 'the attitude of the population is serious but calm and optimistic'.[120] Cases of plundering were reported. After the 20 April raid, one plunderer was executed and a few other inhabitants were jailed for refusing to accommodate their bombed out fellow citizens.[121] Following the 5 January attack the GSA thought that numerous incidences of plundering had occurred. Few cases could be investigated because insufficient evidence was available although three Latvians were summarily shot for this offence.[122]

Further significant attacks on Stettin were recorded on 11 April and 13 May 1944, this time in the form of American daylight raids, while the nearby Pölitz synthetic oil plant was bombed on 29 May and 20 June 1944. Stettin again suffered extensive structural damage. The harbour and industrial installations were also attacked, with a major aero-engine works being particularly badly damaged. Police President Grundey recounted that almost 350 were killed and over 12,000 residents were rendered homeless as the result of the two attacks on the city.[123] No cases of plundering were reported.[124] One correspondent noted on 19 April that dreadful damage had been inflicted on a number of major thoroughfares. Moreover, the novelty of the American daytime raid on 11 April had unfortunately caused some inhabitants to view this attack as less serious, leading them to watch the spectacle with predictably deadly consequences.[125]

Other raids were aimed at aircraft factories transferred from the west or formed diversionary strikes on Oder towns such as Frankfurt and Küstrin while the main force raided Berlin. On 9 October 1943, the same day as the Arado works at Anklam was attacked, other formations of the USAAF raided the Focke-Wulf works at Marienburg and destroyed an FW190 assembly line. The Americans launched similar strikes against the Marienburg plant and the firm's Posen works on 9 April. Finally, on 29 May 1944 considerable damage was caused by the Americans at the Focke-Wulf factories at Posen, again, and at Sorau (East Brandenburg) as well as at industrial facilities in Schneidemühl.[126] No part of the Reich was now beyond the reach of Allied bombers, able to attack from the south, east and west. East Germans dreaded the prospect of British and American formations flying on shuttle missions from Russian airfields. The Americans, who established bases near Poltava in the Ukraine, exacerbated this anxiety by dropping propaganda leaflets outlining this intention.[127]

'The Belief in Final Victory Dwindles More and More'

The adverse developments on the Eastern Front also concerned eastern Germans. This theatre of operations consumed the lion's share of German men and material and was physically ever closer to the eastern provinces. Throughout the period from the failure of the Kursk offensive (mid-July 1943) until the Allied invasion of Europe (6 June 1944), a steady deterioration was noticeable in the German public mood. Small upswings after a rare *Führer* speech or official hints that new revenge weapons would soon be deployed could not buck this general trend. Accompanying the anxiety arising from the *Wehrmacht's* retreat from mid-July 1943 was the erosion of confidence in the *Endsieg*. This was compounded by growing scepticism about the reliability of official war reporting. Phrases such as 'shortening of the front' and 'strategic withdrawal' were widely interpreted as propaganda-speak for continued military setbacks.[128] The authorities maintained that the Red Army was racially inferior, badly led, poorly equipped and decimated by immense losses. This rhetoric was discredited by events. German propagandists no longer had victories to exploit or even stalemates to explain. The propaganda and the reality of the situation were strikingly different. Alternative sources of information gained greater credence. Foreign broadcasts, conversations with soldiers returning for increasingly infrequent furloughs and field post from relatives and friends at the front were seen by many Germans as more accurate barometers of the situation. Other factors were also detected which caused the regime anxiety. There was a genuine fear that the retreat in the East would develop into a disorganised flight to the Reich's frontier. Furthermore, there was a growing tendency to respect the Soviet leadership, the Red Army's fighting spirit and the seemingly infinite Russian manpower resources.

The loss of the Ukraine, portrayed in propaganda as Germany's future breadbasket, was greeted with dismay and foreboding. In early September 1943, the SD reported the popular sentiment that 'when the Ukraine must be given up, then the war is lost'.[129] Indeed, after Kursk the SD assessed that in north eastern Germany the mood of the population had deteriorated. Increased war-weariness was evident and 'the belief in final victory dwindles more and more'.[130] Terse statements in the *Wehrmacht* report alluding to the rapidity of the German retreat provoked dismay and doubts that the withdrawal remained orderly. With the loss of major Ukrainian cities there were worries that a 'stampede' would follow[131] and by early October there were apprehensions 'that the Russians in the foreseeable future would stand on the borders of the old Reich'.[132] Nevertheless, two months later, and despite the continued setbacks, a 'Stalingrad mood' was generally not discernible.[133] The Silesian SD reported in early January 1944 that the situation in the East was seen as very critical as 'the offensive strength of the Russians, in spite of all losses, was unbroken'.[134] Five weeks later there was a degree of optimism in Silesia because: 'Rumours over strong German troop concentrations in the *General Gouvernement* strengthen the hope of a speedy end to the defensive conduct of the war in the East.'[135] However, by April 1944, further reversals in the north and south of the Eastern Front had caused 'a type of Stalingrad mood' to descend over Germany.[136]

In East Prussia, the loss of Rovno, the base of Koch's Ukrainian fiefdom, and Lutsk, which followed the Red Army's penetration of Poland's prewar eastern frontier in early January 1944, depressed the general mood. Rumours and criticism were commonplace and East Prussians expected a simultaneous attack on Germany from both East and West in 1944.[137] Others also worried about the threat to German territory. Christabel Bielenberg, an Englishwoman married to a German working in a Graudenz (West Prussia) aircraft factory, recalled her husband's advice in autumn 1943 that she move 'as far to the west of Germany as possible' because of the Red Army's advance.[138] German soldiers on the Eastern Front seemed to comprehend the repercussions of defeat. A corporal wrote from Bobruisk (Belorussia) that 'the war must turn out well'. On the radio he had heard that the Russians planned to compensate Poland for territorial losses in the east by giving them Silesia and East Prussia.[139]

Back home there was growing mistrust with official news sources, increasingly viewed as selective, unreliable and downright depressing. In late August 1943 the SD observed popular concern at the reporting of individual or localised successes rather than any general discussion of the overall situation on the Eastern Front.[140] The language of reports was also criticised. The evacuation of Orel, Kharkov and Taganrog had been 'planned', but so had the great retreats of the previous two winters when these had in fact been most serious setbacks.[141] Many Germans believed that the Red Army was already further west than was conceded. In Pomerania, the Party's *Pommersche Zeitung* gave the impression that some Soviet units were already behind the officially admitted German frontline.[142] The terminology used by German reporters, such as 'in the area of', was a clue that the town named was already lost.[143] Silesians doubted the credibility of the *Wehrmacht* report because of the silence over the Cherkassy fighting in February 1944.[144] The repeated references to the evacuation of strong points provoked unease despite such operations being apparently conducted in an orderly manner. The grounds for these withdrawals, the so-called 'shortening of the front', 'straightening out of the front' and 'dropping-off movements' met with scepticism in Germany.[145]

Alternative sources of information about the Eastern Front were sought. The opinions outlined in soldiers' letters (fieldpost) and their thoughts when returning on leave became ever more prized as a true indicator of developments. Statements attributed to soldiers mentioned inexhaustible Russian reserves and their own corresponding lack of men and material. Losses remained high. The number of death notices appearing in the newspapers indicated that, despite the reported 'timely' withdrawals, German losses remained considerable.[146] Newspaper, newsreel and official *Wehrmacht* accounts of the fighting were questioned and some soldiers said that 'wild retreats' had actually occurred. The attitude of officers was criticised. In rear areas officers had taken up with Russian women, were engaging in drinking bouts and were active in supply rackets. Soldiers claimed that these developments adversely affected the mood at the front. This image of demoralisation on the Eastern Front led to comparisons with 1918.[147] Soldiers caused further unease by underlining the huge Soviet superiority and adding that the German front was 'dreadfully weak'. The relative manpower strength in the most favourable instances was put at 20 or 30:100.[148] The SD reports also included extracts from fieldpost and comments by doctors on the pathetic condition of the retreating troops, while soldiers themselves told of the huge casualty figures. Few reserves were available and munitions were scarce whereas the Red Army was said to be abundantly equipped. Moreover, soldiers returning to the River Dnieper in Ukraine were dismayed to find that no system of fortifications was prepared. The SD concluded that many Germans believed that the fighting spirit of the *Wehrmacht* had already been considerably weakened by the unrelenting Soviet attacks.[149]

The Red Army's advance in the northern sector of the front from January 1944 caused much anxiety in East Prussia. In March 1944, OLG President Dräger in Königsberg observed 'a certain agitation, not to be underestimated, among the population of the frontier districts'. German settlers in Zichenau were already preparing to move themselves and their possessions to more secure parts of the Reich.[150] The SD also detected this uneasiness but attributed much of this to letters and accounts of soldiers. According to the Zichenau SD, soldiers from these districts feared for the safety of their wives and children if the Bolsheviks made further advances during their absence.[151]

Despite the pessimistic tone of these soldiers' letters and depressing statements concerning events in the East, the SD still discovered some Germans who believed that the situation was surmountable. The account of a mechanic who had worked in the Soviet Union was reported by the Silesian SD in late August 1943. He accepted that the Red Army had more men and weapons but was convinced that German soldiers were better trained and anticipated a sudden successful German blow.[152] The notion was also conveyed that the Red Army was scraping the bottom of the barrel and that the Soviet Union was on the verge of starvation. Soldiers sometimes gave the impression that the enemy was nearing exhaustion and many prisoners were said to be women, youths and old men. Other soldiers contended that the Soviet advance was deceptive and predicted its collapse. They maintained that the Soviets would be unable to muster such large masses of men and material for long.[153] Some true believers at home consoled themselves with less rational thoughts. As German forces pulled back, the SD observed in late September 1943: 'A part of the population see in these German measures a strategic manoeuvre in keeping with an inspired plan of the *Führer*, who intended to gather together all forces, leading to the appropriate counter-blow in early 1944.'[154] A few *Volksgenossen* took perverse comfort that the German retreat would illustrate the danger of Bolshevism to 'neutral' European states.[155]

However, a grudging respect was forthcoming for the 'ice cold' Stalin, the Soviet military machine and the efforts of Russian workers.[156] In the Baltic coastal area the Soviet supply organisation was dubbed 'the greatest wonder of this war'.[157] In East Prussia discussions about a possible Soviet invasion led some agricultural workers to remark that 'the Soviets would surely not be as dangerous as the propaganda attempts to portray'. A worker added that it 'was impossible for the Soviets to fight as bravely and doggedly, and attack for month after month if they really had to live in such dreadful hell'.[158] The SD reported the oft-cited argument that the Russians were superior economically and numerically, and that their forces were still apparently unspent. Germans were confronting a 'terrible awakening', namely that, 'today the Russians are stronger than before'.[159]

Similar pessimism was evident in East Prussia and Silesia concerning the risk of bombing. The East Prussian SD reported in early October 1943 the widespread fear that the Allies would deploy poisonous gas.[160] Likewise, unease was forthcoming about the ramifications of close Allied co-operation. Following the meetings of Allied leaders in late November 1943 (Cairo and Teheran), Silesians worried that the USAAF would use Russian bases to attack the Upper Silesian industrial area.[161] Meanwhile, East Prussians feared that American bombers transferred to Russia would exploit the shorter flying time to German targets following recent retreats and impending withdrawals.[162]

The intensification of Party-led air raid protection measures caused many to believe that heavy attacks were imminent. In Breslau, blackout regulations were enforced despite the absence of air raids as the authorities feared the devastating consequences on the timber- built city-centre housing. The influx of transferred industries and evacuees caused the city's population to rise from a pre-war figure of 630,000 to nearly one million by early 1944.[163] In the aftermath of 'the terror attacks by the enemy on Hamburg and Berlin', the OLG President believed that the fear of air raids had been impressed by the authorities on the local population.[164] The attacks on aircraft plants in Posen and Sorau, in neighbouring Warthegau and Brandenburg, over Easter 1944 markedly illustrated the growing threat to Lower Silesia. Hanke's directive for the limited evacuation of Breslau in the spring of 1944 added to the fears. Schools were moved into the surrounding countryside. Mothers and young children resident in the city centre were shifted to rural areas. The GSA claimed that the Party's efforts had soothed initial worries concerning possible acclimatisation difficulties in the reception areas. Those remaining in Breslau volunteered or were called up by the Party to construct covered trenches, bunkers and command posts and to assist the preparations of the fire authorities.[165] The Party had initiated a similar programme in East Prussia. OLG President Dräger commented in late July 1943 that despite the recent absence of attacks the population fully understood the need to strengthen defences. By early autumn, following heavy raids in the West, East Prussians worried that they would soon suffer a similar fate, fears only substantiated by the new initiatives.[166] For the moment the attacks did not materialise, but most realised that they were on the horizon although a degree of complacency was observed and misplaced hopes that the province would avoid heavy raids were expressed.[167]

'Order' on the Home Front

In the midst of a supposed total war there was anger that, despite increasing privation, Party functionaries were shirking their duty to the Fatherland and indulging in scams at home. The Party's unpopularity was accentuated by its local role informing families of the death of relatives at the front.[168] As losses mounted, this duty became ever more onerous to explain. Moreover, their frequent assertion that fallen soldiers had been shot in the head and had died a quick death, attributed to a Party directive to sanitise losses, was soon contradicted through contact between comrades of the dead men and the bereaved families.[169] The fact that Party officials of military age were evading military service was also frowned upon. The public deemed state and Party activities not directed towards the war effort as superfluous.[170] Meanwhile, as propaganda struggled in ever more depressing circumstances there was a correspondingly greater urge to resort to coercion to maintain 'order' on the Home Front.

The focus on 'order' was reflected in the regime's increasingly strident line against those discovered making defeatist remarks; reflected by the upsurge in widely publicised death sentences passed for such offences during the war years. Himmler's appointment as Interior Minister in August 1943 was seen as indicative of tougher measures against defeatism. SD sources observed that Party members were particularly keen to silence these 'malicious windbags'.[171] Political jokes were frowned upon as they were viewed as undermining morale. *Kreisleiter* Ernst Wagner of Königsberg spoke about this in February 1944: 'Anyone who makes jokes about the *Führer*, victory or the Party insults the German people and we must protect ourselves against such insults.'[172] These sentiments were echoed in an article which appeared in the *Schlesische Tageszeitung* on 23 February 1944 and talked of, 'Philistine jokes about victory and defeat, about success and failure, are about the most miserable things imaginable in these great times.'[173] In Pomerania, the judicial authorities reported that malicious remarks were made about Schwede-Coburg and accused the Catholic clergy of listening to forbidden foreign radio.[174] Schwede-Coburg warned a Party audience in Lauenburg at the beginning of December 1943 that he 'demanded the active reaction of all Party members, particular with regard to deliberate or unintentional saboteurs of our efforts wherever they may appear'.[175]

The need to impose death sentences for uttering or spreading defeatist remarks or for listening to foreign broadcasts indicates how readily the regime resorted to terror against racial comrades when propaganda was rendered ineffective. People returned all too quickly to their old points of loyalty for reassurance. In Lower Silesia, church attendance among both denominations significantly increased during the later stages of the war.[176] The Pomeranian SD reported that the Catholic Church was increasing its cultural influence among the Catholic minority in rural areas.[177]

Death sentences were also passed for particularly crass acts of theft or deception. From Stettin in April 1944 it was reported that a 'food ration card printer' and his wife had been sentenced to death for 'stealing and receiving at least 2,000 ration cards of all kinds over a period of one year'.[178] A fortnight later the *Pommersche Zeitung* also reported that two goods station officials had received death sentences for 'continually stealing clothing and food from the Reich Railways'. Many of their fellow employees had apparently been made to attend the trial.[179]

Even German youth, prized by the regime as the nation's future, was disenchanted. The increasing wartime regimentation of HJ activities proved unattractive for many older boys who opted to explore other paths. Youth crimes, particularly cases of arson, were regularly mentioned in judicial reports. The number of groups of young people, outside the HJ, increased dramatically during the war years. At national level the youth leadership worried in 1942 that 'a serious risk of the political, moral and criminal breakdown of youth must be said to exist'.[180] The shortage of manpower during the latter stages of the war intensified demands on young people to join the military or serve in ancillary bodies. Following a general Party order in February 1943 more senior school pupils were directed to serve in their immediate home area as *Luftwaffenhelfer*. However in practice it was soon necessary to deploy them far from home. For instance, Königsberg schoolchildren, accompanied by their teachers, were sent to Hamburg, Berlin and industrial sites in central Germany to assist the *Luftwaffe* and to operate flak batteries and searchlights. Likewise, *Flakhelfer* as young as 15-years-old from throughout the Reich defended the Upper Silesian industrial region. They manned anti-aircraft guns surrounding the hydrogenation and synthetic oil plants at Heydebruck and Blechhammer. But their families soon discovered the fallacy of believing that Silesia still remained *Luftschutzkeller Deutschlands*. This was ruthlessly exposed on 7 July 1944 when waves of American Flying Fortress bombers, operating from bases in Italy, blitzed Blechhammer and the surrounding district.[181]

Despite the opportunity for dissent being stifled, it was not completely extinguished among German youth. In bomb-shattered Stettin the judicial authorities reported in November 1944 that illegal cliques with criminal and political motivations were operating in the city. Greater apprehension was expressed at the deeds and background of the 30 or so members of the political clique. This group, named 'Die Rächer' (the Avengers), met at nightfall and exploited the darkness to attack HJ patrols. Ironically, some had previously held positions in the HJ, but had been disillusioned because of personal enmities. Worryingly for the authorities most of the group's members came from orderly backgrounds. Many had fathers who were members of the Party or its affiliate organisations, sometimes with block or local leadership responsibilities.[182]

Critics and opponents of the regime both young and old could expect no mercy if apprehended and Nazi 'justice' became more brutal further east. Around 5,000–6,000 cases were heard by the Königsberg Special Court between 1939 and 1945 and roughly one-tenth of these resulted in a death sentence being imposed. In comparison,

Schleswig–Holstein, a province which displayed similar economic and social characteristics to East Prussia, had slightly fewer Special Court cases but passed one-fifth of the death sentences.[183]

The fate of mentally ill inhabitants and Jewish neighbours in the eastern provinces also tends to be forgotten in expellee accounts. As Kershaw notes, Schwede-Coburg, Koch and Greiser were quick to authorise the 'evacuations' of inmates of asylums under their remit, knowing full well the deadly repercussions of their actions.[184] The Nazi leadership was determined to make the newly annexed eastern *Gaue* (Danzig–West Prussia, Warthegau and the eastern part of Upper Silesia) *Judenrein*. The Lublin district of the *General Gouvernement* was soon earmarked as a Jewish reservation by zealous officials in the RSHA. In October 1939, several train loads of Jews were expelled from Upper Silesia, as well as from Vienna and the Protectorate of Bohemia-Moravia. Transports were dumped in Lublin where the Jews were variously ordered to build a primitive camp, driven into the countryside or simply shot. Some 500 even survived this experience and were returned home in April 1940 but their reprieve was to prove all too brief.[185]

Jews from within the Reich's 1937 frontiers were also herded onto transports bound for Lublin. Pomeranian Jews from Stettin and Schneidemühl suffered a fate in March 1940 which mirrored that of their expellee neighbours five years later. The 160 Schneidemühl Jews were not allowed to take any possessions whatsoever with them while the 1,200 Stettin Jews, whose dwellings were said to be urgently needed for war purposes, had to walk through deep snow from Lublin to outlying villages. At least 72 Stettin Jews perished, largely from exposure. These included, 'A mother who was carrying a three-year-old child in her arms, trying to protect him from the cold with her own clothes [and was] found dead, frozen in this position.'[186] This was only the beginning.

The largest Jewish community east of the Oder, and the third largest in Germany behind Berlin and Frankfurt an der Main, was found in Breslau. It numbered 30,000 when the Nazis came to power. By 1940–1941 emigration abroad had reduced this figure to 6,000–7,000. However, new arrivals from other parts of Silesia resulted in perhaps 12,000 Jews remaining in the city at the onset of Barbarossa.[187] They led a precarious existence on the margins, encountering discriminatory legislation, grounded in the Nuremberg Laws of 1935, at every turn and being allotted the most menial of tasks. Willy Israel Cohn, a retired teacher deported to his death in late 1941, still maintained in his diary that among ordinary Breslauers, 'Generally there is no hatred, rather compassion.' Indeed, it is reported that the wild excesses against Jews, their synagogues and their remaining property which characterised the nationwide *Reichskristallnacht* (Crystal Night or the Night of Broken Glass) of 9–10 November 1938 were criticised in workers' circles, by the police and even by elements in the Party and SA. Nevertheless, most observers remained apathetic to the mayhem while others exploited the situation to loot Jewish stores and homes. The city's Jews went to their deaths in batches between November 1941, when the first 2,000 were shot in the forests of Lithuania, and June 1943. Others met their end at the Theresienstadt camp in the Sudetenland, at the extermination camps in the *General Gouvernement* or in the concentration and work camps dotted around Breslau. The SS claimed that Silesia was 'cleansed' of Jews in June 1943 but this was not actually the case. For this same report noted that 50,570 stateless and foreign Jews were 'engaged in camp activity' at various locations in the Breslau area. However, in the SS mindset Jews in the camps had long ceased to constitute part of the population.[188]

The eastern provinces also housed facilities where outsiders were brought to be killed. These were in addition to the extermination camps established in the *General Gouvernement*, the huge extermination and concentration camp complex of Auschwitz-Birkenau in incorporated Upper Silesia and the Kulmhof (Chelmno) extermination facility in the Warthegau. A much smaller but similarly sinister development involved the fate of prisoners from the occupied territories in the west sent to the Reich for secret and summary trial under Hitler's notorious *Nacht und Nebel* (NN) (Night and Fog) decree of December 1941. Initially, Special Courts in western cities and Berlin tried these prisoners. However, growing Allied air attacks resulted in new Special Courts being established in Breslau and Oppeln in November 1943 and March 1944 to try cases previously earmarked for Cologne and Essen respectively. In Breslau, French NN prisoners were routinely condemned and guillotined in the city's Kletschkaustraße prison.[189]In March 1944, escaped Allied airmen from the *Stalag Luft III* camp near Sagan were also killed on Hitler's express orders. After a nationwide manhunt some 50 of the 76 escapees were shot; 27 died at the hands of the Breslau Gestapo.[190]

In addition to the numerous POW camps erected in Lower Silesia, a concentration camp was established in 1940 at Groß-Rosen, near Schweidnitz. Although it was not a systematic extermination site, the facility did hold 12,000, mainly political, prisoners by 1944. Estimates suggest that some 160,000 inmates passed through Groß Rosen, its sub-camps and nearby workcamps and perhaps 100,000 died.[191] Every bit as horrendous was the camp complex constructed at Stutthof to the east of the Vistula delta, the final destination for more than 70 per cent of its 120,000 inmates, comprising mainly Jews, Polish intellectuals, Polish partisans and Russian POWs.[192]

Propaganda and coercion had been deployed in tandem by the regime since 1933. The latter played a larger role as the war turned against Germany and was publicised rather than obscured in order that the message hit home. Germans increasingly distrusted their own propaganda. Some grew accustomed to reading between the lines to gain an accurate picture of events. But propaganda gloss could not counter the pessimism engendered by repeated military reversals, nor could it explain shortages, ration reductions and growing inequality and corruption in wartime. Despite draconian penalties for 'black listening', the BBC and Radio Moscow gained greater credence. Damaging rumours, sometimes initiated by foreign broadcasters or returning soldiers, spread and eroded confidence in the *Endsieg*.

The regime could tolerate the mood being depressed so long as basic attitudes remained unaffected and the population fulfilled their everyday functions, thus ensuring no repeat of 1918. As we have seen not only the mood but also behaviour was altering. Reading enemy tracts, listening to enemy radio, ignoring the Hitler salute and entering into prohibited relationships were manifestations of this disobedience. Nevertheless, the regime could still count on the patriotism of most Germans and the widespread dread of defeat at Soviet hands. Similarly, the majority wanted to believe that the expected Allied invasion would flounder against the Atlantic Wall and that all forces could then be turned against the Red Army. These wishes were destined to remain unfulfilled and the Red Army would soon arrive at the gates of the Reich.

PART II

The War Comes Home: Eastern Germany, July 1944–January 1945

CHAPTER 4

A Deep Anxiety over the Fate of East Prussia

Despite the misgivings exhibited by sections of the population at the continued military reversals after July 1943, the Red Army remained a distant threat to German soil. These circumstances altered dramatically during the summer months of 1944. Devastating military setbacks were reported from all the fighting fronts. Rome was given up on 4 June. Two days later the Western Allies landed in Normandy and pierced the vaunted Atlantic Wall. Paris was lost on 25 August and on 11 September 1944 the Americans gained a foothold on German soil near Aachen. Meanwhile, Germany's allies at opposite ends of the Eastern Front, Finland and Romania, sought armistice terms. It was, however, reports of the retreat from Belorussia and the Red Army's surge towards East Prussia and the River Vistula which most concerned eastern Germans. The repercussions arising from the collapse of Army Group Centre in Belorussia were felt throughout eastern Germany, but particularly in East Prussia, the first province threatened by the Soviet advance.

The Smashing of Army Group Centre

One German historian fittingly begins his book on the flight and expulsion of the Germans with the observation that 'the downfall of the German East began on Thursday 22 June 1944 . . . in an area many hundreds of kilometres from the borders of the Reich.'[1] The Red Army launched its summer offensive on the third anniversary of the German invasion of the Soviet Union. Code-named Operation *Bagration*, after the fallen hero of 1812, it aimed to destroy Army Group Centre, the last vestige of German military power in Russia. Soviet commanders also envisaged that a successful operation would cut off Army Group North in the former Baltic states, complete the liberation of Soviet territory and allow the Red Army to advance into Poland along the most direct route to Berlin.[2]

Army Group Centre's long and exposed front protruded out as a result of the vast territorial gains made by the Red Army at the expense of Army Groups North and South during the previous winter. The 'Belorussian Balcony' was inadequately defended. German units were deficient in men and material.[3] However, Army Group Centre did not expect to bear the brunt of the anticipated Soviet summer offensive. Hitler and the *Oberkommando des Heeres* (OKH, Army High Command) thought that the Red Army would attack in the south. OKH's intelligence arm *Fremde Heere Ost* (FHO), 'Foreign Armies East', was hoodwinked by elaborate Soviet deception planning. This was FHO's most serious wartime failure. The experience of the previous winter and available intelligence reports pointed to Red Army concentrations in western Ukraine. Hitler believed that the Red Army aimed to drive German forces back to the Carpathians posing a grave danger to the rear of German armies further north, opening the way to Warsaw and simultaneously have appalling consequences for Germany's allies in south-eastern Europe. FHO thought that the offensive would initially fall upon Army Group North Ukraine (part of the former Army Group South) and aim to drive towards Warsaw. Thereafter it would swing north towards the Baltic coast or attack through the Carpathians into Romania. The former was not that far-fetched as it was only a distance of 280 miles for the leading Red Army units from their positions at the sources of the Pripet to the Baltic.[4]

On the eve of the offensive Army Group Centre, under the command of Field Marshal Ernst Busch, consisted of four Armies (Third Panzer, Fourth, Ninth and Second) comprising 42 divisions (including four Hungarian). Although Army Group Centre expected to face solely diversionary attacks, Busch, prompted by the commanders of the individual armies, proposed that the three exposed northernmost armies withdraw to more secure positions in the rear. This would shorten the front and create reserves. Hitler, however, remained fixed to the concept of fortified areas. Vitebsk, Orsha, Mogilev and Bobruisk in the forward area and Slutsk, Minsk, Baranovichi and Vilnius in the rear received this designation. Hitler envisaged that these fortified areas would suck in Soviet troops who otherwise would be available to attack elsewhere. The fortified areas were to be defended to the last man. Only the *Führer* himself could authorise withdrawal. Hitler resolutely believed that the loss of these strategically or symbolically important towns would further weaken the resolve of Germany's remaining allies. Busch followed Hitler's orders to the letter and was sacked six days after the Soviet assault commenced when the *Führer* finally accepted that this was far more than a diversionary attack.[5]

However, behind German lines a number of rearward movements were initiated and warnings issued. The *Volksdeutsche* from the Ukraine, originally moved to the Bialystok district, were transferred further west to Litzmannstadt. Rumours spread in Bialystok that the district had been assigned rear area status by the military and OLG President Dräger in Königsberg admitted that East Prussia was used to a greater extent than hitherto for accommodating reserves of supplies.[6] Following the Normandy landings, Deputy *Gauleiter* Großherr of East Prussia also warned that, 'The enemy will learn that all attempts at unrest or sabotage on the part of foreign workers will be nipped in the bud.'[7] Further east, German propagandists attempted to convince Belorussians that the *Wehrmacht* was there to stay. Festivals and a celebration of the third anniversary of the 'liberation' of Minsk, featuring march-pasts, were held a week before the Soviet offensive began.[8] The Ministry of the Occupied Eastern Territories was evidently less confident of a lengthy German presence in Belorussia. An order dated 12 June 1944, concerning the abduction of juveniles to the Reich to be trained as skilled workers, revealed likely military developments:

> Army Group Centre has the intention to apprehend 40,000–50,000 youths of the ages 10 to 14 who are in the army territory and to transport them to the Reich . . . Corresponding orders were given during last year's withdrawals in the Southern Sector . . . [9]

The Soviet summer offensive was first mentioned in the *Wehrmacht* report on 23 June when there was said to be bitter fighting 'on both sides of Vitebsk'.[10] Heavily outnumbered, confronted by an enemy with a vast superiority in planes, artillery and tanks, harried by partisan operations and devoid of tactical and operational freedom, Army Group Centre was pulverised for five weeks. The Red Army sliced through the German defences. Fortified areas were encircled but still the Red Army ploughed on. A huge rupture appeared in the German front. Minsk was lost on 3 July, Vilna (Vilnius) on 13 July, Grodno (Hrodna) on 16 July, Bialystok on 18 July, Dünaburg (Daugavpils) on 27 July and Kowno (Kaunas) on 2 August. On 1 August Soviet troops reached the Baltic coast near Riga and for a few days cut the land route to Army Group North. Only the combination of losses and the wear and tear suffered by mechanised formations forced the offensive to lose impetus. Field Marshal Walter Model, Busch's replacement at Army Group Centre, in tandem with his command of Army Group North Ukraine, could not halt the Soviet juggernaut. He was engaged in a frenetic damage-limitation exercise, managing to obtain reinforcements from Army Group South Ukraine and receiving Hitler's grudging authorisation for withdrawals from some fortified areas. This could not obscure the scale of the disaster suffered by Army Group Centre. Vast moving pockets and bands of stragglers attempted to evade Soviet forces and sought the sanctuary of German lines. Between 10,000 and 15,000 men escaped from the encirclement of the Fourth Army on the River Berezina but no more than 900 reached the German front line in East Prussia.[11] German losses were enormous. Experienced Eastern Front divisions were ripped apart overnight. At Vitebsk, the 206th East Prussian Infantry Division was annihilated on 26–27 June. Some 12,000 men were lost and the division was disbanded on 18 July.[12] The foremost western historian of the conflict in the East asserted:

> When Soviet armies shattered Army Group Centre, they achieved their greatest single military success on the Eastern Front. For the German army in the East it was a catastrophe of unbelievable proportions, greater than that of Stalingrad, obliterating between twenty-five and twenty-eight divisions, 350,000 men in all.[13]

The Nazi media downplayed the disaster by emphasising the space available in the east and stressing the advantages of shorter lines. However, Germans following the daily *Wehrmacht* report realised that the Red Army was approaching the East Prussian frontier and a marked deterioration in the public mood ensued. News of the heavy fighting in Belorussia was greeted with concern throughout the Reich. As the Red Army advanced, signs of fear and panic were discernible. In eastern Germany news of the fighting strengthened the impression, already conveyed by press and radio, that Germany was now approaching the 'irrevocable highpoint of the war'.[14] Concerning developments in Belorussia, it was admitted that 'in recent days the attention of the entire population but particularly those in the eastern border areas, had turned to events on the Eastern Front.'[15] From north-eastern Germany the news regarding strong Soviet troop concentrations at Vitebsk and enemy breakthroughs increased fears of a Soviet attack towards East Prussia. Furthermore, press reports of the *Luftwaffe*'s successful raid on American airfields at Poltava and Mirgorod in the Ukraine on the night of 21–22 June only produced greater anxiety. It was felt that an insignificant number of bombers had been destroyed. There were rumours that the Americans already had 1,000 aircraft in Russia. The SD in Kattowitz detected the widespread fear that shuttle bombing posed a greater threat to the eastern provinces. Similarly, the air raid protection propaganda week held in the East Prussian border towns was viewed as a signal of likely air raids.[16]

The Red Army's unrelenting advance caused Germans to question whether it could be stopped. The SD advised that in north-eastern Germany 'the attention of the population has shifted by leaps and bounds from the events in the west to the fighting on the Eastern Front.' The Soviet advance in the Minsk area was viewed as particularly threatening. Ominously, it was observed in eastern frontier areas, where refugee treks had arrived, that there was an increase in worrying opinions.[17] The greatly superior strength of Germany's enemies was evident to Germans. Official sources maintained that there remained trust in the *Führer* but the enemy's numerical and material superiority ensured that their assaults on all fronts were successful. Only a few particularly resolute *Volksgenossen* were said to appreciate that the war had followed this course for 18 months. They declared that Germany had gone through many crises and was ready for this one. The rapid Soviet territorial gains and indications in the *Wehrmacht* report that troops had fought their way out of encirclements and back to German lines, stirred up an impression of failure by Army Group Centre's leadership. Many Germans believed that an *Ostwall* had been constructed in the conquered eastern territory. Now the question was being asked – why had this wall not been built?[18]

The speed of the Soviet advance caused East Prussians to fear imminent fighting on the province's soil. The Königsberg SD contended that the arrival of refugee treks caused anxiety. Evacuees from the west declared that they had jumped out of the frying pan into the fire and commented that it would be 'better to be buried by a bomb than fall into the hands of the Russians'. Measures enacted by the Party and public authorities, in part a plan by the Party in Allenstein to create armed formations ready for action, caused further unease. Adding to worries were reports of an alleged advance by bandits (Polish partisans) into East Prussia.[19] Rumours spread throughout Germany that East Prussia was in the throes of evacuation and that the thunder of battle could be heard in frontier districts. Many Germans believed that Königsberg and Danzig were immediately threatened. Part of the indigenous East Prussian population was said to be leaving for more secure lands behind the Vistula.[20] All sections of society asserted that preparations should be made for the repatriation of evacuated women and children. Anxious west German mothers demanded the return of their children from East Prussia.[21]

Reports on the state of the public mood made depressing reading for the regime. The population grasped the seriousness of the situation. In mid-July women were said to be particularly downcast, and one exemplified these feelings with the remark that, 'It is almost beyond my strength to listen to the *Wehrmacht* report. I must simply wait until better news comes again.'[22] Meanwhile, the Eastern Front was still placed after the West, the launch of the V-1 revenge weapons and Italy in the order of the *Wehrmacht* report.[23] A few days later in eastern Germany, 'an insidious mood of panic' gripped many *Volksgenossen*. Again women were said to be particularly affected.[24] There was growing concern at the economic consequences of the defeat. Foodstuffs, depots and important agricultural districts in the *General Gouvernement* were lost, compounding the earlier loss of the Ukraine and leading to worries regarding food supplies.[25]

Germans pondered the causes of the rapid retreat. In eastern districts, soldiers' accounts exacerbated the notion that this was no ordinary retreat but rather a collapse. It was deemed unsurprising that German positions had been overrun as it was well known that the German front was very weak. Even valiant soldiers could not hold out when confronted with such enemy superiority.[26] Whilst ordinary soldiers were not believed to have failed, there was widespread criticism of the military leadership for seemingly neglecting essential preparations and contingency measures. In German rear areas, instead of preparing trenches or drilling, the army was said to have lived off the fat of the land and enjoyed regular working hours and free time.[27]

In mid-July, the East Prussian SD observed that in many circles an increasingly pessimistic view of the present situation was already clearly noticeable and admitted that, 'a deep anxiety over the fate of East Prussia had taken hold of the population of the entire province.' Pessimists were claiming that, in the long run, this Red Army attack could not be halted. Above all, the population feared a sudden Russian incursion as it was too late to evacuate women and children.[28] The SD reported the prevailing feeling of uneasiness. Rumours emanating from eastern refugees, particularly from railwaymen's circles, put the population into a greater sense of nervousness. People could not comprehend how the breakthrough and spread of Soviet power had occurred.[29] They wondered if the front would ever stabilise.

Ironically, at the very time the rumblings from the collapse on the Eastern Front were being heard, the East Prussian Party leadership appeared to be preoccupied with lavish celebrations in honour of the 400th anniversary of Königsberg University. The participants appeared oblivious to the war. One witness, who had recently returned from the carnage and terror of Berlin, was amazed at the spectacle:

> The Rectors of all the German universities turned up in full fig; for days together there were festival recitals, torchlight processions and concerts and seats of honour were fought for as in times of profoundest peace, while the dull thudding of the Russian guns was beginning to make itself heard in the east.[30]

Seemingly the festivities, held between 6 and 9 July, were blessed by sunny weather.

Among the visiting dignitaries were the East Prussian born Minister of Economics Dr Walther Funk and the Education Minister Bernhard Rust. Eight new academic chairs were created and a substantial amount of money was promised to construct new buildings.[31] A special 400th anniversary commemorative stamp was issued and the events received national press coverage. *Das Reich* envisaged that the outlook for the future pointed to the university as a 'Prussian bulwark against Asiatic influence'.[32] These days were numbered and it does seem likely that Koch's visitors took the opportunity to remind him to ensure the timely evacuation of plundered cultural treasures housed in Königsberg.[33]

Elsewhere, the prevailing pessimistic mood enveloping East Prussia during July is outlined in correspondence between the Propaganda Office in Königsberg and the Propaganda Ministry in Berlin. This provides an indication of how seriously the regime viewed the situation and highlights the difficulties the propagandists faced in attempting to explain developments. The first indication of defeat was the appearance of retreating troops and refugee columns in the recently annexed territories and frontier districts of East Prussia. Germans were shocked at the sight of *Wehrmacht* stragglers, unkempt and often unarmed, following their ordeal in the woods and swamps of White Russia. Russian auxiliaries (*Hiwis*) and multitudes of civilians ostensibly fleeing the Red Army were interspersed with the troops and caused the local population additional distress.

Criticism was directed at the army and particularly the officer corps for losing control. Area Leader Battinat from Scharfenwiese district (Zichenau) wrote to Koch and commented on the scale of the scenes he had witnessed which he attributed to sabotage: 'Men, who had participated in the war of 1914–18 said they had seen nothing like it before.' Units or parts of units were rolling back from the front in an uninterrupted stream towards the west. Military and refugee columns were indistinguishable. Nobody appeared to be attempting to rectify the situation. No officers were spotted trying to direct the individual formations to assembly points. Vehicles were filled with animals and furniture but little in the way of military hardware. He observed few items that were needed for war. Moreover, many Russian women were riding on the vehicles. The soldiers conveyed a dilapidated and demoralised impression and Battinat believed that they could not undertake further fighting unless harsh measures were taken. Their officers passed the evenings consuming spirits. Meanwhile, the huge influx of refugees also vexed Battinat. Most of the men seemed to be armed and partially attired in German uniforms. He recommended their disarming as some refugees had already shot Poles and stolen their cattle and horses. Battinat stressed that the military influx had to be halted and the troops organised in barracks or assembly points.[34]

Similar observations were submitted to *Gauamtsleiter* (regional organisation leader) Paul Dargel by a Dr Pfafferott stationed in Bialystok. He had experienced the withdrawals from the Marne and Somme during the First World War and the return from France after the Armistice. He had also been in Rowno when the Germans pulled out earlier in the year. Dr Pfafferott believed that the attitude of the troops had been influenced by enemy superiority. However, while retreating troops always looked worn out and filthy, a picture had emerged and opinions formed which had nothing to do with a normal retreat. Dr Pfafferott attributed this as a symptom of the attitude and discipline of the troops. His previous experiences were not as depressing as the disorder he had witnessed during the first days of the retreat through Bialystok. Vehicles filled with an assortment of plunder and strange women were the norm. From a soldierly point of view their continued presence was impossible as they adversely affected discipline. He described a particularly depressing column of lorries carrying refugees, *Hiwis*, Mongolians and German soldiers which had stopped in Bialystok. In public view these soldiers cavorted with the women. Few spoke German and it was a relief that the column soon departed because lively contact with the local population seemed imminent. Even when some sort of order was established, passing lorries remained full of plunder and women. Officers were seldom seen. Furthermore, the troops displayed a hostile attitude to Party officials. Occasionally, insulting remarks such as 'Golden Pheasant' (Peacock) and 'Base-Wallah' were aimed at Pfafferott. Some troops, shattered by recent experiences, expressed defeatist opinions. One soldier declared that the SS could fight alone and that the Russians would not do anything to the workers, only to the Party bigwigs. Pfafferott insisted that officers were not encouraging their men to display the correct attitude during the retreat. The dubious mixing with neglectful, unclean *Ostvolk* had a negative effect on the troops, OT personnel and on the transportation corps of the NSKK.[35]

These Party members clearly viewed racial indiscretions with particular dismay. They worried about the impact such lurid sights and the inflammation of defeatist rumours would have on the morale of the native population. Major Kurt Dieckert, a liaison officer with the Third Panzer Army, later recalled disorganised units heading west to what they believed was the security of the East Prussian border. Vehicles were laden with plundered goods useless for the conduct of war. In addition, he detected a certain degree of malicious glee among the population at the spectacle of passing 'Golden Pheasants', distraught and shaken from their warm nests in Courland, Lithuania, White Russia and Poland. The Red Army had brought their activity to an abrupt end; now they only wanted to get back to Berlin. The endless columns of horse-drawn vehicles reminded Dieckert of the 1914–1918 war, whilst the curious sight of the *Hiwis* around evening campfires aroused the memory of war in earlier times. He noted that care was taken to ensure that the *Hiwis* were relieved of their weapons at the frontier. There was disquiet, particularly among East Prussian women, as every column was followed by crowds of White Russian women. Responding to the indignation of local females, soldiers remarked that the women worked as hard as bees, were unpretentious and had hearts of gold. They added that many German women could follow their example. Overall, Dieckert concluded that the gypsy-like picture resembled the Thirty Years War and not a modern conflict featuring tanks and aeroplanes.[36]

The SD gauged the anxiety among Germans arising from soldiers' accounts of the retreat. First-hand accounts were evidently available in East Prussia, the *General Gouvernement* and the Warthegau. Moreover, through soldiers' letters details of the defeat reverberated throughout Germany. Whilst some soldiers said that a hasty retreat had occurred, others frankly admitted that this was no retreat, rather a collapse. Rumours spread that entire regiments had gone over to the Soviets. Criticism of the military leadership and officers in general was widespread. Hitler was urged to dismiss more generals and have Field Marshal Busch shot. Officers were said to have failed their men and then disappeared with their Polish and Russian women. Troops also spoke about the enormous superiority of the enemy, the thinly manned German lines and the strength of the Red Air Force, equipped with American planes.[37]

In East Prussia, the impact of soldiers' accounts caused locals and Berlin evacuees to try to leave the province for the interior of the Reich. A hurried exodus was reported from the border districts. The railway system was congested and trains overflowed with people. Increased withdrawals were made from banks and luggage was sent from the province. The coastal towns were crowded with those trying to leave East Prussia by sea. There was also a fear that news of the Red Army's advance would precipitate an insurrection of foreign workers, particularly in areas where the few remaining German men were heavily outnumbered by incomers. There was little confidence in the authorities. East Prussians did not believe that the local leadership had made preparations for all eventualities.[38] Some tried to take out forms of insurance for the future. Investigations by the Zichenau Gestapo at the beginning of August showed that Germans were returning previously confiscated goods to Poles. Fearing Red Army excesses these Germans viewed their Polish neighbours as possible lifelines for the coming months.[39] In contrast, others spoke, somewhat whimsically, of a coming partisan war against the Soviets in the East Prussian forests.[40]

In an attempt to build a new German front, East Prussian units fighting in other sectors, border guards, training regiments, Panzer cadets and even Hitler's own guard battalion were sent east.[41] One NCO from the Pomeranian raised Twelfth Panzer Division wrote of his journey through East Prussia to the front. He enthused over the peaceful villages and the clean, neatly appointed farms, a marked contrast to Russia or the Baltic lands, and only wished that East Prussia would be spared from the war. Tellingly, the NCO admitted speaking to men from units scattered by the retreat, who reported little that was pleasant or exalting. This did not dampen morale because 'We are still full of confidence and trust the *Führer*.'[42] Soldiers made clear their desire to defend their own *Volk*. One wrote that 'The Russians are standing close to the German border and up here German soldiers are protecting Estonia, whilst our own land is in greater danger.'[43]

Meanwhile, measures were enacted to re-establish order on the frontier, reassemble the scattered military units and to register and deploy refugees. Koch demanded characteristically strident measures to stem the chaos. In Bialystok a control staff was created which consisted of police, Party and military personnel. This body was to gather together uncontrollable and wild groups, reform these units and give them a military appearance once again. Camp followers were to be separated from the troops. Plunder brought along by the eastern refugees was to be sent to assembly camps. *Wehrmacht* field police were deployed on the frontier and new units were to monitor the crossroads in rear areas. Koch recommended that the toughest men lead these teams.[44] Goebbels suggested to the *Wehrmacht* High Command that particularly vigorous judges be sent to these localities and drumhead courts martial deployed. However, he observed that Koch had already sealed the border crossings with energetic men and the 'riffraff' flowing back to East Prussia had been picked up.[45] Gradually discipline and order was restored whilst marauders received draconian punishment. It was reported from Lyck that a few deserters had been rounded up and death sentences had been passed and carried out immediately. Seemingly, this had a very favourable effect on the population.[46]

Army Group Centre established headquarters at Ortelsburg. Three German armies covered the frontiers of East Prussia. The Second Army protected the south of the province and the Fourth Army defended the central sector. Further north, the Third Panzer Army of the ultra-Nazi Colonel General Georg-Hans Reinhardt set up headquarters in Schloßberg, described by the army's diarist as an 'orderly little German city almost incomprehensible after three years on Soviet soil'.[47] The citizens of Schloßberg, anxious at the proximity of the Red Army, warmly greeted the men of the First East Prussian Infantry Division sent to bolster the defence of their homeland.[48] As supply depots were established on East Prussian soil, the men of the Third Panzer Army were urged in an Order of the Day, dated 11 July 1944, to respect the local population. A copy of this document found its way into Soviet hands and was later used for propaganda purposes because of the drastic change in behaviour it demanded:

> . . . The withdrawal of the German Army to German territory will naturally cause grave disturbance and alarm among local inhabitants. The German soldier must, therefore, by his conduct, inspire in the population of Germany that confidence in victory which accompanied him in the campaigns carried deep into enemy territory. This necessitates a radical change in all existing rules and habits. Russia's wide expanses offered the army a liberty of action for which there is no room on the territory of Germany . . . Everything that was needed could be taken wherever it was to be found . . . Many units which received additional supplies from local resources did not stop to reflect that they were living better than many people in Germany. When troops were quartered usually no attention was paid to the population; everywhere the soldier was master. The situation in German towns and villages is diametrically opposite to what has been described. The people we shall now come in contact with are our fellow countrymen whom we must respect and whom it is our duty to help.[49]

Reservists moving up to the front were addressed by Field Marshal Model. He demanded that they 'defend with their bodies the approaches to the German homeland'. They were 'to bar the enemy's access to the German *Gaue* and to keep murder, fire and plunder away from the German villages and towns, together with the seasoned fighters of the East who have shown themselves superior to the Bolsheviks in the many battles of three war years. There is no going back now!'[50]

Some Berliners Depart

The *Wehrmacht*'s much greater presence on German soil was utilised by the authorities to account for other developments. Explanations were authorised by the Propaganda Ministry to be circulated by the Party to counter rumours of an evacuation of East Prussia and to justify essential limited measures. First, the *Wehrmacht* required buildings for conversion to military hospitals. Secondly, the *Wehrmacht* needed billets for troops and facilities for military administration. Thirdly, accommodation was sought for those building fortifications on the Lithuanian side of the frontier and, finally, room had to be found for the evacuees from the east. These seemingly legitimate reasons were used to explain the removal of the Berliners from East Prussian border districts. For the time being, proposals to evacuate vulnerable members of the indigenous community to the interior of the province remained at the planning stage.[51] At the same time, broadcasts from the Soviet-sponsored NKFD (*Nationalkomitee Freies Deutschland*, National Committee for Free Germany) in Moscow attempted to reassure eastern Germans. They were advised on 13 July to stay put and to make every effort to stop the fleeing Nazis from slaughtering livestock and dismantling factories.[52]

The fate of the Berlin evacuees in East Prussia evidently concerned their *Gauleiter* Goebbels. There was disquiet in the capital at the possible fate of relatives at the hands of the Red Army. Goebbels shared this pessimism. He frequently despaired at recent developments on the Eastern Front and their repercussions for the eastern provinces. Indeed, in early July when visiting Breslau, he had been surprised to discover that Hanke and General Rudolf Koch-Erpach, the commander of the Silesian military district (*Wehrkreis* VIII), were making preparations for the eventual defence of that province. Goebbels feared that the Soviets would soon stand on the East Prussian frontier and privately acknowledged that the loss of Army Group Centre had immense consequences. He believed that this was the largest military defeat of the war, placing Stalingrad in the shade.[53]

Goebbels proposed the return of all 170,000 Berliners from East Prussia and liaised with the Dr Albert Ganzenmüller, State Secretary at the Transport Ministry, about involving the *Reichsbahn* in this operation.[54] However, Goebbels had not reckoned on Koch's intervention. Koch refused to countenance evacuation. He maintained that if all the Berliners returned home, then East Prussia would have to be evacuated too. In the interim a compromise was agreed to allow Berlin women and children in Schloßberg, Ebenrode, Memel, Heydekrug, Goldap, Lyck and Johannisburg and in parts of Lötzen and Gumbinnen districts to leave the province. In total around 55,000 people were involved at the outset.[55] Goebbels observed that Koch had secured Hitler's authorisation for the limited evacuation and diplomatically added that East Prussia would not be given up. On the contrary, Goebbels hoped that the resistance put up in this sector would act as an example to all fronts.[56] This concept would be a mainstay of Nazi propaganda concerning East Prussia during the following months, underlining the province's heroic *Frontgau* status.

The East Prussian *Gau* authorities and the Interior Ministry undertook the arrangements for the population transfer. On 14 July, after a telephone conversation with Hitler, Koch issued the following teleprinter order:

> I have ordered that the evacuated Berlin women and children from the eastern border districts of the province of East Prussia will be transported by special trains of the *Reichsbahn*. The first trains will depart today, 14 July 1944, in a westerly direction. This measure will allow for the time being 55,000 Berlin women and children to be brought to safety. Reception districts are: Halle-Merseburg, Thüringia and the Sudetenland.[57]

The ratio of Berliners sent down to the Sudetenland, *Gau* Halle-Merseburg and *Gau* Thüringia was 7:7:3.[58] Some Berliners went back to the bomb-ravaged capital. One evacuee wrote from Gumbinnen in early July that 'Probably I shall soon go home again, for the Russians are too close upon our heels here. It is hardly 200 km from here to the front'. When she returned to Berlin the writer recalled that Gumbinnen 'had become so uncomfortable . . . with the Russians about'.[59] Meanwhile, the East Prussian propaganda leader Maertins candidly admitted that local communities did not lament the departure of the Berliners. He told State Secretary Sondermann at the Ministry of Propaganda, that in Goldap, 'The Berliners, who had particularly contributed to the uneasiness of the East Prussian population, had in part left.' He later reported that Tilsit and Treuburg advised that the mood had improved since the Berliners had departed.[60] Goebbels was livid at these slurs against 'his' Berliners. He took up the matter with Maertins, and Koch was also made aware of the dispute. Maertins replied on 17 July 1944 that 'The points of criticism cited by the Minister are also fully appreciated here. It isn't that Berliners were simply railed at indiscriminately or that we are overbearing in our criticism of them. In my report about them I expressed myself very carefully and guardedly.'[61]

During the second week of July the East Prussian authorities had initiated measures to counter a mass exodus from the province. Travel restrictions were tightened to stop journeys through Elbing, Miswalde, Soldau and Deutsch Eylau and then onward into the Reich. In their desperation, travellers from East Prussia had apparently undertaken the journey to the Reich on the roofs of express trains. Meanwhile, the transport authorities also banned holiday excursions because of the growing volume of military traffic being sent east.[62] The crucial question concerned the widening of the travel restrictions to the neighbouring *Gaue* of Danzig–West Prussia and Wartheland (Warthegau). This was demanded by both the transport authorities and by Koch who realised that East Prussians were circumventing the restrictions unilaterally imposed in their province.[63]

Koch emphasised that the impact of travel restrictions limited solely to East Prussia were illusory and to make this measure effective, similar ordinances needed to be enacted immediately in the adjoining provinces. Koch cited the example of Königsbergers undertaking the 92-kilometre journey to Elbing (West Prussia) and then travelling further west. He stressed that urgent measures were required to avoid both an avalanche-like exodus from East Prussia and the mood of panic this would induce among those remaining. Nevertheless, despite Koch's protestations, after discussions among the various interested bodies at the Interior Ministry, the wider travel ban was only enforced from 15 July.[64] That same day the Party's *Völkischer Beobachter* announced that journeys over 100km could only be taken with special certification.[65] Maertins insisted that the reaction to the ban was generally favourable, it being viewed as necessary and having been accepted without complaint.[66] Party propaganda stressed that locals were content to stay. In Memel, it was claimed that 'no single person had approached [the *Kreisleiter*] to ask for a permit to leave or [to] visit an ostensibly ill aunt elsewhere'.[67] Similarly, Koch justified his actions at a mass meeting of workers when he explained that 'Women and children are still in the East Prussian frontier district, because the East Prussians know that the die has already been cast.'[68]

Although around one-third of the Berliners departed and the indigenous inhabitants were coerced into staying put, the refugee problem remained.[69] The Interior Ministry and local Party bodies tried to resolve the problem. The former issued detailed guidelines on procedures and areas of responsibility to Koch and *Generalgouverneur* Frank in Cracow. The RVK was responsible for the collection, accommodation and provision of supplies for the refugees. *Landräte*, *Oberbürgermeister*, police and labour administrators were detailed to assist the Party. The NSV was entrusted with looking after German and *Volksdeutsche* refugees. Non-German refugees, including children over the age of ten, were to be put to work immediately. The incomers were to be segregated on national grounds. Germans and *Volksdeutsche* had the possibility of accommodation in private quarters, whereas Ukrainians, White Russians and Poles were to be sent initially to assembly camps. Estonians and Latvians, with relatives in the German military, were eligible for private quarters. However, even basic camp accommodation was not guaranteed for those fleeing Lithuania. Measures were also outlined to tackle marauding and plundering elements found among the refugee influx. Vehicles, laden with plundered goods, were to be made available for other purposes. The police were to register and check the refugees, whilst the security forces also examined the health of those entering the Reich.[70]

The East Prussian authorities advised Berlin that crossing points had been established at six points on the frontier. The refugees were to be gathered in assembly camps and from there transported by rail into the Reich.[71] Foreigners deemed fit enough for work were pressed into fortification construction projects on the frontier but it was envisaged that on completion this workforce would be sent into the Reich for further deployment.[72] Meanwhile, *Volksdeutsche* from Lithuania were to be accommodated in *Gau* Danzig-West Prussia. Nevertheless, the authorities remained unconvinced that existing arrangements could cope with the scale of the refugee influx. New bodies were created in a second zone (the East Prussian border) and in a third zone (the borders of *Wehrkreise* II (Pomerania), III (Brandenburg) and VIII (Silesia)). A new structure, the so-called Albert Commission, was established, to register non-German refugees. Participants in this commission included the SD, *Wehrmacht*, Transport Ministry, Ministry of the Occupied Eastern Territories, *Gau* and public health authorities.[73] Representatives of the Albert Commission were particularly prominent beside bridges over the Vistula in *Gau* Danzig–West Prussia and at intersections on the eastern frontiers of the Warthegau and Upper Silesia. However, the ability of the Interior Ministry to implement standard guidelines via this body throughout the affected area was lost because the local commissions were subordinated to the local RVK.[74]

The final order creating the Albert Commission, issued by the Interior Ministry on 18 July, stressed that the commission's main duty was to ensure that refugees were put to work immediately. The refugees were to be assessed as families and not as individuals. Families with one member fit for work or serving with the *Wehrmacht* were not to be separated. Women and children over the age of ten were considered fit for work. It was envisaged that the latter would eventually serve as *Luftwaffe* and SS helpers. Simultaneously, it was stressed that families with members serving with the German military should, on account of political and psychological grounds, receive particular care.[75] Nevertheless, in the chaotic conditions of the high summer of 1944 some refugees still avoided security and registration checks. The SD also reported a lack of administrative coordination in East Prussia where there was a shortage of camp accommodation, food, fodder, doctors and competent officials.[76]

Ingrained racial and national prejudices caused the authorities to look on the new arrivals with mistrust. They were a fresh source of manpower – a scarce commodity by 1944. However, they were also a potential source of infection and dangerous rumours; and because of their origins and appearance doubts were expressed about their commitment to the German cause. The fear persisted that Soviet agents were within their ranks. The very sight of these strange people caused one Baltic German, who had lived in the Warthegau for more than four years, to remark that 'Cossacks serving with the *Wehrmacht* came through our area, some of them in traditional garb, and some in SS uniforms. They came with families, with horse-drawn carriages, and with camels. Suddenly the atmosphere became very tense.'[77] The authorities hoped that these Cossack, Tartar and Caucasian units, together with the notorious Kaminsky Brigade, could be located in the *General Gouvernement* to reinforce German police formations.[78] The Kaminsky Brigade soon displayed its savage reputation, earned from participation in anti-partisan operations in Russia, during the suppression of the Warsaw Rising. The riotous behaviour of these units and their camp followers continued when they entered Germany.[79]

The Nazi authorities offered these eastern incomers the most rudimentary accommodation in camps, halls and schools. Occasionally local *Landwacht* or *Stadtwacht* units were raised to guard them. These desperate people, far from home and who had backed the wrong horse in a murderous gamble, were shunted back and forth within the shrinking Third Reich. Militarily, their menfolk were considered unreliable and prone to mutiny or desertion. Members of General Vlasov's[80] Russian Liberation Army were deployed on the Oder Front in early 1945 whilst Cossacks were used in anti-partisan duties in northern Italy. By this stage, Germany's collapse was imminent. The downfall of those *Ostvolk* prepared to co-operate with Germany was sealed much earlier.

'No Blade of Grass would Grow'

Whilst these population movements were taking place in their midst, East Prussians were subjected to a sustained propaganda campaign to bolster morale and banish thoughts of flight. In tandem with travel restrictions, a direct attempt to ensure that the population remained within the province, the Party tried to buoy up the public mood and emphasised that the Soviets would not cross the frontier. They were confronting an increasingly sceptical population, worried that the fate of their province would be decided within a few weeks. Even in Königsberg, a corporal observed that the military situation was viewed as dangerous. The mood was bad and the population was restless.[81] Maertins, with Koch's approval, issued clear orders to all *Kreisleiter* concerning the direction of propaganda. The attitude of the *Heimat* would be determined by Party members and political leaders displaying resolute composure during these critical hours. Through their work and attitude they were to make clear expressions of their unconditional belief in victory and in the *Führer*. It was also emphasised that fickleness and cowardice would be countered with extreme severity. Party speakers were to underline the message of 'strength through fear'. Nothing would survive the destruction of Anglo-American plutocracy and their unnatural ally, the forces of 'Bolshevik world extermination'. Defeat would result in Germany's complete annihilation: 'No creatures would survive in Germany, no blade of grass would grow, no insects would live.' Both creeds shared the common goal of destroying Germany's cities and transforming the country into a wasteland. Millions would be wiped out, millions more would be deported to serve as slaves in Siberia and German womenfolk would be sterilised. Speakers were instructed to highlight the numerous miscalculations made by the western Allies. They had failed to realise that German resistance did not recognise the word 'capitulation'. Their continued air attacks had not destroyed the German armaments industry or exterminated the spirit of resistance of the German people.[82]

A mixture of extravagant promises and threats to malcontents characterised the remainder of the advice given to *Kreisleiter* and other Party speakers. The utmost tenacity and perseverance was demanded from all German forces in this crucial phase of the war. The course of the war would then move in Germany's favour. Germany held the trump cards for victory, not only the V1 rocket but also other weapons with more terrible consequences for its enemies. The threat to those considered overanxious or lacking political faith was made clear. Should these elements try to unsettle the excellent attitude of the East Prussian population, the Party and state would render them harmless. Those who did not maintain the correct attitude during these difficult times would perish when victory was secured. Others, who were not prepared to fight and work, as was necessary at this hour, would suffer a similar fate. A few fickle characters would not be allowed to weaken the resolve of real East Prussians. Furthermore, it was emphasised that nobody was allowed to leave their workplace. The *Kreisleiter* were to inform speakers of those who had refused to adhere to this regulation. Their cases would be highlighted by the speakers as a warning against precipitate flight. Finally, it was to be stressed that the best protection came from the *Führer* himself. He believed in East Prussian toughness. His strength and willingness to work were a pledge and example to East Prussians.[83] To bolster morale the rumour was spread that the *Führer* was based in East Prussia. This was greeted with a sigh of relief.[84] It was true that after a flying visit on 9 July for a crisis conference with Eastern Front commanders, Hitler had returned permanently to Rastenburg from the Obersalzberg at Berchtesgaden on 14 July. Goebbels, relieved that the situation in East Prussia appeared to have stabilised, was delighted that Hitler was once again in a military atmosphere and hoped that a new decisiveness would ensue.[85]

German spokesmen even pointed to the possibility of a counter-offensive and claimed that the advancing Red Army would be vulnerable to attack from the stable German flanks. State Secretary Sondermann of the Propaganda Ministry amazed foreign journalists in Berlin on 11 July with the remark: 'If the British are at present saying that the Soviet Command will shortly be using maps of East Prussia', he could only say that 'the Soviets should not destroy their maps of Smolensk too soon'.[86] Similarly,

Colonel General Guderian, Chief of Staff on the Eastern Front, claimed on 29 July that 'the present Soviet assault will not only be broken, but that the Bolshevik intruders will again be thrown out of all territories that they are now devastating so cruelly.'[87] German radio commentators stressed that resistance intensified as the Red Army neared the Reich as 'It is just at these points where the enemy was able to get within reach of the Reich frontiers, that the threatened parts of the Reich radiated a many-time increased morale, and even material strength.'[88]

The situation reports, forwarded by Maertins to Berlin, accentuated the positive. On 10 July, Maertins stressed the advantages of frontier crossing points and the onward transportation of refugees by rail. This would avoid them causing unease among the locals. Meanwhile, the native population was seemingly still quiet and trusted the regime to take all necessary measures to keep the Soviets out of East Prussia. Indeed, it was rumoured that divisions were either moving up to the front or had already arrived and that this contributed to the slowing down of the Soviet advance. Maertins commented that unfortunately a few overanxious idle women had travelled to the Reich on the grounds of visiting parents or for holidays. However, the population was apparently reassured by the clear and calm delivery of the *Wehrmacht* report and above all, by Goebbels' Breslau speech on 8 July. It was hoped that following this address the relevant measures to register the entire workforce would take place as there was disquiet that the rich were evading their duties and still employing teams of servants.[89] Maertins occasionally indicated the severity of the situation. Refugees and ill-disciplined troops were blamed for disturbing the local population. He reported that rear echelon formations had fled back to the frontier with pigs, goats, plunder and foreign women in tow. Worryingly, these units had advised the inhabitants of Eydtkau that the Soviets could not be halted and the border areas should be evacuated immediately. Maertins claimed that these troops had no military decorations and pointed to horror stories spread by OT units in Lyck as an example of cowardly rear units upsetting a hitherto calm civilian population.[90]

Maertins again criticised the baleful impact of refugees from the east and scattered military units on the mood of the East Prussian population in his 14 July report. Soldiers spreading rumours about huge German losses made a particularly bad impression. From Insterburg it was reported that the population was quieter because troops were no longer allowed to pass through the town. Meanwhile, the arrival of casualties was also observed. Numerous hospital trains arrived in Lyck and a large number of badly wounded disembarked in the town. In Insterburg three new military hospitals were soon fully occupied. More positively, despite the Soviet threat, it was reported from Ebenrode that only the upper strata of society had left the district. The *Kreisleiter* made provision for their dwellings to be seized by the authorities and opened to other members of the community.[91]

By 17 July, reports insisted that the mood of the population was calmer. The registration of men for fortification building (see chapter five) was said to be proceeding smoothly, the men deemed to be willing and enthusiastic. The instances of disorder among troops fleeing into East Prussia, which had led to Koch lambasting Model a few days earlier at the *Führerhauptquartier*, were being addressed. The activity of *Wehrmacht* patrols was having a positive effect.[92] Throughout the province the mood was described as upbeat and Maertins attributed much of this to the intensification of the propaganda effort, a viewpoint strengthened by the very favourable response to Party and *Wehrmacht* speakers. Koch himself addressed district representatives of the NSF and district propaganda leaders on 15 July, and had seemingly reassured his audience as he 'emphatically stressed that there is really no reason for any serious alarm among the population of East Prussia'. Local reports also underlined that 'both town and country know that the solid and thoroughly trained NSDAP is ready to maintain internal order'. Interestingly, the local press also felt it necessary to emphasise that there had been no repeat of August 1914, when Berlin had not appreciated the gravity of the East Prussian situation. [93]

Despite German efforts to play down the threat from the East and to dismiss reports of panic in East Prussia, propaganda organs and leading regional figures were heavily involved in a damage-limitation exercise which aimed to bolster the regime's leaders and strategy. Buschmann, military correspondent of the *Pommersche Zeitung*, admitted that, 'the fact that the Soviets are knocking at the gates of the Reich fills us with deepest bitterness and our hurt is only too natural'. However, only the leadership of the Reich knew where, and on which front, to strike back against the enemy.[94] With the march of the Red Army to the Vistula, Upper Silesia was now under threat and *Gauleiter* Bracht tried to reassure Party officials in Kattowitz on 26 July when he said: 'There should be no anxiety in our *Gau* about events at the front. Upper Silesia remains firm and ready for any sacrifice, standing behind Hitler in the knowledge that the fate of the German people is in good and strong hands.'[95] The anxiety in Lower Silesia was expressed in an editorial in the *Schlesische Tageszeitung* on 30 July which pointed to 'this obvious crisis on the Eastern Front' and added that, 'We East Germans look to the east with particular attention and the strongest emotion.'[96] The *Danziger Vorposten* tried to be more positive and told readers not to view the situation from the standpoint of 1942 when the *Wehrmacht* had reached the Volga but instead to compare the situation with maps of 1939. German forces in the east were leaning their backs against a wall – 'a wall which derives its stability from a thoroughly organised Germany, from first-rate communications and from a conscious realisation of the fact that it is now German territory which is being defended'.[97]

Back in East Prussia, Hitler's interest in the province was underlined. As the *Königsberger Allgemeine Zeitung* had loudly proclaimed on 16 July:

> We answer the *Führer's* confidence in us with our unshakable confidence in him – we do not let ourselves be shaken by anything – just as little as we did, when at the beginning of the Polish and Russian campaigns, the greedy enemy was about to stretch out his hands for our dear homeland. On the contrary, we fully realise our indebtedness for the fact that the *Führer* and the Armed Forces spared East Prussia any direct interference.[98]

Nevertheless, despite the non-German refugees being assigned to digging duties on the East Prussian frontier and the measures undertaken to gather scattered soldiers, a sense of unease was detected in the frontier districts on 20 July. Rumours still circulated that these districts should be evacuated. These caused some restlessness, but Maertins concluded that this could be remedied through immediate clarification from the authorities. Incidents were cited illustrating the composure of the population or highlighting Party actions to restore confidence. From Goldap district it was said that the thunder of the guns was audible but inhabitants were not especially anxious. Meanwhile, remarkable reports were submitted from a few districts claiming that some Berlin evacuees had stayed behind and were determined to remain in their quarters to the very end. In Treuburg district restlessness arose because of military developments in adjoining Sudauen. An address by the Deputy *Kreisleiter* seemingly had a favourable effect and the population reportedly had faith that there would be a complete evacuation in an emergency. However, signs of fear were evident elsewhere. News of a breakthrough by some Soviet tanks in Augustow region caused great anxiety in neighbouring Lyck. Soviet planes dropped leaflets over Insterburg calling on German troops to go over to the Red Army. Alarmingly, Tilsit reported that a large number of Russian POWs had escaped and were heading in an easterly direction. Moreover, Maertins' continued determination to work with the military in order to root out troops deemed guilty of spreading horror stories indicated the still delicate nature of the public mood.[99]

A letter by a woman in Deutschheide, in the south-east corner of East Prussia, dated 21 July, illustrated the still tense situation on the frontier, a marked contrast to the propagandists' bravado:

> We are ready to flee at any moment because the Russians are not far from our border. Everybody has packed, but we haven't so many trunks. It is too terrible; we were terribly nervous when we heard the thunder of the cannon from Grodno. The people didn't want to work any more, they were all too miserable. And nobody knows at all what is going to happen . . . The fugitives from Russia are supposed to be going to work here, but we shall all leave before then . . . New billetees are arriving again, and those from Berlin as well as all who are here on a visit have to leave.[100]

The intensification of propaganda, travel restrictions and draconian punishments could not smother the truth and did not reassure the population. The *Wehrmacht* had suffered a catastrophic defeat and the Red Army now stood at the gates of East Prussia. Nevertheless, the East Prussian Party authorities did not remain inactive when confronted with such adverse circumstances. As will be outlined in chapter five, they became trailblazers for the defensive measures initiated by the regime during the final months of its existence. In the meantime, a plausible explanation for the continued military reversals was provided by the events of 20 July 1944.

The 'Criminal Attack' of 20 July

Although Hitler remained closeted at headquarters and distant from his *Volk*, his name still retained strong resonance and engendered residual loyalty. Even at this stage of the war it is possible that a majority of Germans from across the social spectrum viewed Germany's salvation and the fate of the *Führer* as irrevocably linked. There was widespread shock at the assassination attempt on him by Colonel Claus Schenk Count von Stauffenberg, Chief of Staff to the Commander of the *Ersatzheer* (Reserve or

Replacement Army), at the *Wolfsschanze* on 20 July.[101] Immediately, the propaganda machine went into overdrive to explain and exploit the event. The regional Party authorities were encouraged by Berlin to hold mass rallies in order that the population could have the opportunity to express their gratitude at the *Führer*'s miraculous survival.

Maertins advised that the East Prussian population reacted with 'stunned consternation' and then with deepest shock at the 'criminal attack'. However, the fact that Hitler was only slightly injured convinced many that he would fulfil his mission. There was satisfaction that reports indicated that the 'criminals' would be dealt with straightaway.[102] Rumours, particularly circulating among military personnel, hinted that the traitors had played a part in recent defeats. There was a feeling that Germany would escape from deadly danger and a stronger belief in victory.[103] Other official evidence suggested that the assassination attempt was found to be as profoundly shocking in the eastern territories as it was elsewhere in the Reich:

> From several cities (e.g. Königsberg and Berlin) there are reports of women bursting into tears in stores and on the streets, some completely out of control. The joy at the mild outcome was extraordinarily great. Heaving a sigh of relief, the public ascertained: "Thank God, the *Führer* is alive".[104]

Pomeranians were said to be outraged and repugnant at the news. There were relieved that Hitler had escaped virtually unscathed and the conspirators were condemned. Himmler's appointment as Commander of the *Ersatzheer*, following the arrest of the deeply implicated Colonel-General Friedrich Fromm, was welcomed. It was envisaged that he would pursue energetic measures against wavering elements in the *Wehrmacht* and shirkers within rear echelon military staff. Again the opinion was raised that these traitors had engaged in sabotage on all fronts. It was hoped that their unmasking would lead to a transformation in Germany's fortunes.[105] From Breslau there were repeated requests for a public display of thanksgiving in conjunction with the *Wehrmacht* and *Luftwaffe.* Lower Silesian Propaganda Leader Schulz proposed that Hanke and Koch-Erpach should both speak and asked Berlin whether the event should be solely a Party affair or if the military should be involved.[106]

Guidelines were soon forthcoming. Following authorisation for mass rallies throughout the Reich, detailed instructions were provided for Party speakers. Certain points were to be emphasised in the treatment of 20 July:

1. That only a small reactionary clique of traitors was behind the deed;
2. that they shamelessly misused their powers of command in an effort to sabotage the Nazi victory;
3. that this camarilla, out of hatred for the movement, had sought to prevent the Nazification of the military and to hinder promotion of Nazi officers;
4. and that the military, whose loyalty had repeatedly been proven during the most difficult front conditions, remains unblemished by the attempted coup.[107]

Reports forwarded to Berlin stressed the positive impact of the *Treuekundgebungen* (thanksgiving or loyalty rallies) held throughout the Reich on 21 July. In Stettin public and military representatives reavowed their loyalty to the *Führer.*[108] Schulz reported that over 200 outdoor rallies and other events were held in Lower Silesia; some 350,000 to 400,000 people were said to be involved. The propaganda line was followed faultlessly. No damaging comments were made about the *Wehrmacht*. It was underlined that the traitorous clique was minuscule and an insult to the army. The scale of the rally in Breslau's Schloßplatz on 22 July was comparable to pre-war music and gymnastic festivals. Party members, workers and military personnel marched alongside bands or sang and carried flags and banners. Around 35,000 people took part and the mood was deemed outstanding, despite fierce rain. The speech by Koch-Erpach was enthusiastically greeted and Hanke's address made a strong impression. Hanke used the comradely 'Du' when greeting Koch-Erpach, and he stressed that through the actions of a few traitors the uniform of the German soldier had been stained. According to Schulz, the gathering in Breslau and others throughout the province proved the solidarity of the community in the face of the unsuccessful attempt on the life of the *Führer* and had strengthened the resolution 'to fight on to the final battle, as hard as it may become'.[109]

Meanwhile, the Königsberg propaganda authorities advised that prevailing circumstances made it difficult to organise thanksgiving rallies. Many political leaders were busy supervising the building of fortifications. Nevertheless, 104 demonstrations were held and 96,400 *Volksgenossen* displayed their loyalty to the *Führer*. Koch and his *Kreisleiter* addressed these gatherings. The former sent Hitler a telegram on behalf of the province. Proceedings had been concluded with a loyalty rally, attended by 10,000 people at an East Prussian factory and addressed by Robert Ley.[110]

The OLG President in Breslau reported that the 'rescue' of the *Führer* was viewed as a miracle and had strengthened 'trusting confidence' in a favourable outcome to the war under the present leadership. The swift action against traitors was greeted with satisfaction and other total war measures were welcomed. Goebbels was appointed Reich Plenipotentiary for the Mobilisation of Total War and immediately ordered activities deemed non-essential for the waging of total war to be cut to the bone. It was widely hoped that recent events would lead to the swifter deployment of new weapons which would have a decisive influence on the military situation.[111] On 10 August, the OLG President in Stettin advised that there remained 'clear anger' at the 'cowardly attack' on Hitler. Despite foreign press reports spreading stories to the contrary, the real response in Stettin could be gauged by the public thanksgiving led by Schwede-Coburg. The report concluded that 'The swift suppression of the putsch and the immediate condemnation of the leading guilty men in public trials has made a good impression here and substantially contributed to the stabilisation of the situation.'[112]

At national level the SD observed that the attempt on Hitler's life relegated discussion of the situation on the fighting fronts into the background.[113] Most Germans were relieved that the *Führer* had not fallen victim to the attack. The bond with Hitler had apparently deepened, trust in the leadership was strengthened and the weekly propaganda report recorded that the 'rescue' of the *Führer* had produced a great upsurge in the public mood. The greater powers allocated to Himmler and Goebbels were welcomed by these Germans. Himmler's likely harsh measures were considered essential, as it was envisaged that the circle of conspirators was likely to be far greater than originally disclosed. Likewise, the public were said to demand real total war measures.

Previous attempts had drifted into lethargy. Responsible *Volksgenossen* deemed travel restrictions insufficient and demanded solid, meaningful action.[114]

Letters from civilians and soldiers at the front displayed similar views. Soldiers realised that anti-Hitler remarks were dangerous; but they were not required to glorify him, or even to mention him and the attempt on his life in their letters home.[115] However, individual letters and reports on correspondence examined by the military censor, reveal that the assassination attempt was regularly discussed. An East Prussian colonel, serving with Army Group South Ukraine, wrote that God wanted the *Führer* to complete his work. The writer believed that Hitler 'looked after . . . our East Prussia'.[116] A Stettin RAD leader noted that there was outrage among the population over so much stupidity and irresponsibility.[117] Meanwhile, faith in Hitler blinded some writers to the approaching danger. An East Prussian woman remarked that the Russian advance had caused many people to leave. She lamented that it was sad for the *Führer* to see how little trust some had in him, but she believed he would use the revenge weapon at the appropriate time.[118] Even soldiers in formations recently savaged by the Red Army appeared to have welcomed Hitler's survival. The Field Post Inspection Office for the Third Panzer Army reported in August, after studying almost 45,000 letters, 'the high number of expressions of joy at the *Führer*'s deliverance, presented as a real stroke of good fortune for the German people'.[119]

The assassination attempt was viewed in wide circles as an unsuccessful repeat of the 'Stab in the Back' of November 1918. Recent defeats were attributed to the actions of the small clique of traitors. There was widespread hope that the uncovering of the plotters would act as a purifying storm and that a transformation of military fortunes would ensue.[120] From Königsberg, the SD reported that rumours had spread among the population alleging that a forthcoming coup had been spoken about in *Wehrmacht* circles for a few days. Suspicions also turned to the causes of the untimely deaths in air crashes of *Reichsminister* Dr Fritz Todt (February 1942) and General Eduard Dietl (June 1944). Popular perception linked their demise to the traitorous clique.[121] Rumours concerning leading military figures were rife, and the public wanted to know the identity of the guilty officers so that suspicion directed at innocent officers would cease.[122]

Characteristically, Ley had attempted to stoke up class conflict in a speech broadcast from a Berlin armaments plant on 22 July. Goebbels complained that Ley's outburst of hate against reactionary old elites, broadcast without his permission, created a bad impression as Ley had as ever, 'raged like an elephant in a china shop'.[123] However, the SD observed that sometimes class resentment was noticeable. The Königsberg SD reported that the wives of large landowners and officers', already criticised for evading Labour Service and maintaining servants in times of total war, were compromised in the opinion of *Volksgenossen*.[124] Official channels also picked up more critical observations. People wondered how it had been possible for Hitler to be deceived for so long. Some asked whether the situation was now so bad that these men, in close proximity to the *Führer*, could have lost their faith in victory.[125] Moreover, the SD detected an admiration for Stalin's ruthlessness as he had unceremoniously removed all unreliable officers and opponents among the intelligentsia. In Stettin these measures were considered more reliable than the hitherto tolerant line pursued by their own leadership.[126]

The Party authorities were particularly keen to associate the treachery of the perpetrators of 20 July with the collapse of Army Group Centre. 'The traitors in Minsk' were responsible for this defeat and earlier reversals and radio broadcasts by Hans Fritzsche of the Propaganda Ministry following the coup attempt bolstered this impression.[127] Then there was the belated discovery that Brigadier General Henning von Tresckow, Chief of Staff to the Second Army, had been at the forefront of a group of traitorous staff officers located at the Army Group's headquarters.[128] Moreover, the Army Group's leadership was further tainted because of the number of generals ensnared by the Red Army during the Belorussian battles and their subsequent behaviour in Soviet captivity. The capture of 21 German generals and the decision of 16 of them to sign an appeal, under the auspices of the NKFD, denouncing Hitler's direction of the German military, highlighting the magnitude of the defeat and emphasising the shortage of reserves and lack of air support, convinced the Nazi leadership that a link existed with the conspiracy.[129] Goebbels noted in his diary that the generals were captured one after the other, and, after a couple of days in Soviet captivity they were already leading lights in the NKFD. He raged that 'Stalin would soon be able to raise a regiment from the ranks of captured German generals. It is shameful and outrageous.' Bormann was anxious because NKFD pamphlets had been dropped onto Army Group Centre troops and also into East Prussia.[130] Both men were convinced that Army Group Centre had been home to a nest of traitors. Entire divisions, led by their commanders, were accused of having gone over to the Soviets.[131]

The propaganda organs of the NKFD encouraged resistance against the Nazis, broadly welcomed the attempted coup and later exploited it in broadcasts and pamphlets. However, there was no link with the conspirators.[132] Even the Nazi leadership gradually realised that insinuations concerning *Wehrmacht* officers was counter-productive. Goebbels distanced himself from those inciting class hatred and said that 'We refuse to make the events around 20 July an occasion for publicly criticising a branch of the *Wehrmacht*, a profession or a class.' Goebbels opted to condemn 'a small and unimportant group of officers and civilian misfits'.[133] Bormann later announced that Party speakers had made unjustified reproaches at the expense of the officer corps and added that, 'The generalisation of a few single cases contradicts not only previously issued orders, but, above all, the dedication and loyalty of hundreds of thousands of brave officers.'[134] Instead a new line was adopted, emphasising that 'agitation against the generals' was a product of Soviet propaganda designed to shatter the bond between troops and their officers. The large number of generals killed or wounded in the east was highlighted. Blame for defeats was attributed to NKFD personnel and émigré Jews and communists who had disguised themselves as German generals and officers to mislead the troops and sow the seeds of confusion.[135]

The impact of the upsurge in morale following the assassination attempt was brief. The defeats did not cease. Popular anxiety concerning the setbacks in the east, west and in the air re-emerged. Goebbels hoped that the defeat of the *putsch* would break down the walls between the *Wehrmacht*, the leadership and the people.[136] However, the aftermath of 20 July signalled a further incursion into *Wehrmacht* affairs by the Party and SS. Their operatives further permeated the military, most notably Himmler's appointment at the *Ersatzheer*. The army was already soiled because of its past conduct. Fresh indignities abounded. The influence of *Nationalsozialistischer Führungs-Offizieren* (NSFOs, National Socialist Leadership Officers), a system of political officers in the *Wehrmacht* established on Hitler's order in December 1943, in the indoctrination of the troops increased.[137] The German greeting was imposed in the *Wehrmacht* at the instigation of Göring and the suspension of Party membership, proscribed by the military law of 21 May 1935 for the period of military service, was revoked. Finally, senior German officers implicated in the conspiracy were drummed out of the *Wehrmacht* through a hastily created Court of Honour, presided over by Field Marshal Gerd von Rundstedt. They then suffered the humiliation of trial before the People's Court and more often than not were handed summary death sentences.

Numerous leading eastern German families were implicated in the various resistance groups. Koch remarked that he was not surprised to discover that East Prussian aristocrats had participated in the conspiracy, but was satisfied that these plotters had been strung up and their landholdings confiscated by the state.[138] The Silesian resistors included many members of the Kreisau Circle, which met at Helmuth James Count von Moltke's estate in Schweidnitz district. Almost all of them perished at the regime's hands prior to the war's conclusion. The lawyer, Hans Lukaschek, the former *Oberpräsident* of Silesia and Centre Party member, designated regional political chief by the conspirators, was one lucky survivor.[139]

Hitler's own profile again diminished once the short-term effects of 20 July wore off. Kershaw observes that, 'Hitler was never again to be at the centre of public attention . . . He had become for most a distant, shadowy figure, only seldom to be seen now in newsreels, hardly ever speaking to the nation.'[140] The events of 20 July shocked both the eastern *Gauleiter* and the population in general. The former swiftly recovered their composure and revelled in the *Wehrmacht*'s discomfort.[141] Most *Volksgenossen* initially asked how the war could be brought to a successful conclusion without the leadership of the *Führer*. The existence of the plot and its treacherous ramifications formed an effective propaganda crutch to account for the devastating military situation. The perpetrators were condemned by the majority of the population for their actions, but increasing unease was discernible at the scale of the conspiracy. More significantly, no upturn in military fortunes materialised. Germany had already suffered 2.8 million war deaths up to 20 July 1944 but now entered the bloodiest period of the conflict. Some 4.8 million German soldiers and civilians would perish during the nine and a half months from 20 July to the surrender of the Third Reich in May 1945.

As the situation steadily deteriorated, ever greater demands were placed by the Party on eastern Germans.

CHAPTER 5

A Unique, Improvised Exertion: Ostwallbau, *1944*

The *Ostwall* was a generic term for the various fortifications constructed in Germany's former eastern territories during the final months of the Second World War. In East Prussia, Pomerania, Silesia and Brandenburg around 500,000 Germans and forced foreign labourers built defences or revamped existing positions. A mainly Polish work-force was conscripted to do similar work in Danzig–West Prussia, Warthegau and in the rump of the *General Gouvernement* which remained under German occupation. As these obstacles failed to halt the Red Army's drive into eastern Germany in 1945 they have been condemned as 'one of the most desperate and in the last analysis useless efforts made during the last months of the war'.[1] Nevertheless, the *Ostwall* should not simply be dismissed as a harebrained undertaking. The scale and significance of the entire project render it worthy of more detailed study. It was one of the key developments of this period, with a lifecycle that epitomised the final months of Nazi rule in eastern Germany.

Nazi leaders at national and regional level had definite objectives when they dragooned eastern Germans into the fortification building programme. It was a calculated attempt to soothe the concerns of the population by directly involving them in the war effort and a means of displaying that, in time of crisis, the Party stood shoulder to shoulder with the *Wehrmacht* in the defence of the Reich. Crucially, the building of the *Ostwall* also provides a snapshot of the strength of the power blocs that jockeyed for position throughout the lifetime of the Third Reich.

Bulwarks in the East

The fortifications dug during 1944–1945 often bolstered earlier outdated defences. German settlement in the east had taken the form of centuries of colonisation. Principal cities were founded as fortresses. Königsberg, 'a German bulwark in the east against the Slav waves', owed its origins to a castle built by the Teutonic Order around 1255. The city's defences underwent ongoing development through the ages. The construction of an 11-kilometre fortified line with six bastions ringing the city started in 1843 and was completed in 1873. The most visible singular manifestation of Königsberg's fortifications was the fortified defensive belt further out from the city. Built between 1874 and 1882, it featured twelve sturdy, but soon militarily obsolete, forts.[2] To the west, the town of Marienburg, on the right bank of the Nogat branch of the Vistula, had been the seat of the Grand Master of the Teutonic Order between 1309 and 1457. The castle, built during the fourteenth century and restored during nineteenth century, was a military stronghold.[3] Upstream, Graudenz and Thorn, in Polish hands after 1919, were renowned bastions as were the Oder fortresses of Küstrin and Glogau further west.

The building of frontier defences commenced during the *Kaiserreich*. At the turn of the twentieth century East Prussia's fortifications were limited to the fortresses around Königsberg, the sea defences at Pillau on the Samland peninsula and the fortress of Boyen at Lötzen in the Masurian Lakes. Under the energetic direction of General Colmar Freiherr von der Goltz, a native East Prussian, the so-called 'Blockhaus Line' was built between 1904 and 1907. This line of fortified buildings and wide stretches of barbed wire was erected south of the Masurian Lakes and aimed to prevent a surprise Russian cavalry attack. Other proposals from von der Goltz, such as the building of a defensive line on the River Deime, east of Königsberg, were rejected. Instead, in the early years of the century most resources went west to shore up the fortresses of Metz and Strassburg (Strasbourg). Prior to 1914, resources were also channelled into the construction of a line of defences on the Vistula, centred on Thorn, Graudenz, Kulm and Marienburg.[4] Breslau's defences were destroyed following the French occupation in 1807. A few light positions were built in late 1914 when Russian forces posed a threat to Silesia. However, as was noted in chapter one, only East Prussia was probed by the Tsarist armies.

Throughout the inter-war period the new Polish Republic was envisaged as the greatest threat to eastern Germany and the building of new defences commenced during the Weimar era. The conditions of the Treaty of Versailles forbade the construction of new defences and fortress installations. Surreptitious German attempts to circumvent this stricture were generally frustrated until the departure of the Inter-Allied Military Control Commission in 1927. Thereafter, planners during the latter years of the Weimar Republic were quietly given the task of completing the fortification of East Prussia, the building of the Pommern and Oder positions and the construction of the Oder–Warthe fortified area, to be completed by 1942.[5]

The Nazis accelerated this programme after 1934. Defences were to be especially thick in isolated East Prussia and in Brandenburg, which formed the shortest route to Berlin in the event of a Polish attack. The East Prussian defences and the fortifications stretching from Pomerania to Upper Silesia, consisting of the *Pommernstellung* (Pomeranian position), the fortified front of the Oder–Warthe Bend and the Oder Line, were designed to exploit the natural barriers provided by lakes, rivers, marshes and swamps. Construction of the so-called 'Heilsberger Dreieck' (triangle) defences in East

Prussia had already commenced during the later years of the Weimar Republic. Covering one-third of the province, including Königsberg, and incorporating deep, camouflaged defences with machine gun positions and belts of barbed wire, these light fortifications may have proved a tricky obstacle for an invading Polish force in the 1930s. With 1,100 individual positions and stretching for almost 200 kilometres, the defences ran from the Frisches Haff west of Braunsberg, followed the river Frisching running in a south-easterly direction towards Heilsberg before veering northwards in the direction of Tapiau and finally following the River Deime to reach the Kurisches Haff near Labiau. Further fortification building continued on the East Prussian frontier until the eve of war with Poland with the construction, from west to east, of the Christburg, Hohenstein and Ortelsburger positions, the Lötzen fortified area and the Masuren Kanal positions.[6]

The extensive Oder–Obra positions in east Brandenburg featured forward defences on the rivers Netze, Warthe and Obra and covered the eastern borders of Schwerin, Meseritz and Züllichau–Schwiebus districts. Here lakes and rivers were dammed and in an emergency situation it was possible to flood wide areas. The large number of bunkers constructed in Meseritz district constituted the Tirschtiegel Riegel (position).[7] By the time of Hitler's visit to the Oder–Warthe fortified area on 30 October 1935 the first of the *Hindenburgstände* (small bunkers) had been erected and a seemingly enthusiastic *Führer* ordered the intensification and acceleration of the work. Indeed, General Otto Förster, Inspector of Engineers and Fortifications from October 1934 until 1939, received a free hand from Hitler, who perhaps cast an envious eye at the French Maginot Line, to build fortifications and an enormous connecting tunnel system. Förster's Fortress Engineers Corps was only seven battalions strong and much of their work involved the direction of labour service battalions and local civilian building firms at the construction sites.[8] A useful by-product of these 'public works' was the pumping of significant sums of government money into some of the poorest parts of Germany and the considerable cut in local unemployment, particularly when the work intensified after 1936. Some 40 construction companies alone were engaged in the work in East Prussia.[9]

With war approaching completion deadlines became more immediate. The original building time of 15 years for the Oder–Warthe defences was ultimately cut in successive stages to a mere four years. It was envisaged that the fortifications would be 110 kilometres long, three kilometres deep and capable of accommodating 35,000 troops.[10] By 1939, the Oder–Warthe Bend fortified front stretched for almost 80 kilometres but was still unfinished. The strongest sectors began at Schwerin, the confluence of the Warthe and Obra rivers, before running south along the Obra west bank to Meseritz. The line then extended southward towards the Oder, passing west of Schwiebus and reaching the Oder east of Crossen. It consisted of the main line, an advance line 10–12 kilometres in front and a third line the same distance to the rear. The central sector of the defences, some 16 kilometres long, were the strongest and most modern in the Reich, heavier even than the *Westwall*.[11] It featured a complex tunnel system designed to include an underground railway network, ultimately unfinished as the rails were never laid. The nine *Werkgruppen* (strong points) of the central sector consisted of 41 *Panzerwerke* (large bunkers) often connected by tunnel and complete with their own underground facilities and garrisons. The Oder–Warthe Bend defences had a total of 83 *Panzerwerke* and 13 *Werkgruppen*. In contrast, individual bunkers were fitted out for field troops and needed only routine maintenance. In front of the bunkers were rows of obstacles, concrete or wooden stakes dubbed 'Dragon's Teeth'. Hitler was less happy when he revisited the defences in mid-1938. He deemed the tunnel system useless and was very critical of the weaponry in the strongest *Werkgruppen* fortifications, most notably of the absence of heavy artillery. The Oder-Warthe defences were 'worthless mousetraps devoid of fire power', due to the inability of German heavy industry to deliver sufficient cupolas for gun batteries. Moreover, Hitler angrily described the fortifications as a place for 'war shirkers' and his stern post-visit memorandum of 1 July 1938 led to the curtailment of construction within days.[12]

The Pomeranian and Oder defences were longer and lighter than the fortifications of the Oder–Warthe Bend. Construction of the first bunkers on the *Pommernstellung* began in 1934. Running for 275 kilometres it began at the confluence of the rivers Netze and Warthe and thereafter exploited the natural barriers provided by a line of lakes before reaching hilly ground north of Schlochau. The defences were close to the Polish border but did not at this stage extend to the Baltic coast. There were thousands of positions but only eight *Werkgruppen* and 12 *Panzerwerke*, each with a garrison of around 35 men. To the south, in southern Brandenburg and Silesia, construction of the Oder defences on the river's west bank had started in 1927 and until 1930 most effort was expended on re-routing water obstacles to benefit the proposed fortifications. The Oder defences stretched for more than 150 kilometres from the flat area around Frankfurt to the lightly defended but hilly terrain of Upper Silesia. Construction of the first bunkers started in 1930 and although some 778 positions were finally built, no heavy works were included in this figure and the defences consisted of light bunkers, troop shelters and observation posts.[13]

Despite these measures, in Pomerania, where lines of newly constructed bunkers faced the Polish frontier, many local inhabitants remained apprehensive in 1939 and assembled their possessions, still fearing a successful Polish invasion.[14] Hitler was more confident. In conversation with the Italian Foreign Minister Count Galeazzo Ciano at the Obersalzberg on 12 August 1939, Hitler used maps to emphasise to his guest the dense fortifications in East Prussia and the 'impregnable system' of staggered defensive lines covering the approaches to Berlin from the east.[15] However, the defences remained untested. The short, victorious Polish campaign meant that they soon lost their significance. The invasion of the Soviet Union seemingly completed this process. With the Red Army hundreds of miles to the east the fortifications were effectively redundant.[16] With their *raison d'être* gone, the fixed positions were stripped of everything. Weaponry which could be removed, barbed wire and steel was cannibalised by the fighting fronts or used in the building of the Atlantic Wall. The efforts of civilian guards could not halt the dilapidation of the defensive installations dotted around the eastern frontier – the decay was only addressed in the dramatically altered circumstances of late 1944.

In the face of the continual retreats in Russia following Kursk, the Nazi leadership maintained in practice their public line that lost territory would be reconquered.[17]

Ordinary Germans were less confident. The SD reported in late August 1943 that Germans wondered why a defensive line, similar to the *Westwall*, had not been built in Russia. They envisaged that this *Ostwall* could be manned by relatively few troops and Bolshevik attacks would 'bleed to death' against this barrier.[18] The notion of an *Ostwall* utilising the obstacles provided by the Molochnaya and Dnieper rivers had been tacitly agreed by Hitler in the aftermath of the failure at Kursk and the almost simultaneous downfall of Mussolini's regime in Italy.[19] However, suitable positions were not prepared in time. Armaments Minister, Albert Speer, recalled that the *Organisation Todt* (OT) commenced fortification construction on the River Bug, then more than 100 miles behind the front, in December 1943. A furious Hitler ordered the work to be stopped immediately.[20] Colonel-General Heinz Guderian, in his capacity as Inspector General of Panzer Forces, later claimed that in January 1944 he recommended the reconditioning of existing defences on the Reich's eastern frontiers and the building of fortifications along river barriers in the German rear. According to Guderian's account, Hitler rejected the idea because of the shortage of labour available to Germany in the east. Privately, Guderian believed that Hitler was actually motivated by his fear that German generals would think only of retreat if rear defences were prepared.[21] Despite rumours in Königsberg concerning the fortification of bunker lines along the East Prussian border and the construction of a Vistula–Nogat line, a further period of inaction followed.[22]

'Comprehensive Defensive Measures'

This inertia was shattered by the events in Belorussia in the summer of 1944. Following the disintegration of Army Group Centre no significant fortified line stood between the Red Army and East Prussia. Field Marshal Model ordered General Jacob from the OKH's Engineering Section to rectify this matter but he predicted that four weeks of intensive work would be required to build the positions.[23] When Hitler returned to Rastenburg in mid-July he assembled Eastern Front commanders to assess the situation. As the Red Army juggernaut lurched towards the Reich, the Nazi leadership was forced to address the real possibility that fighting would soon take place on German soil. From July 1944, Hitler and other senior figures in the regime issued decrees pertaining to the defence of the Reich in case of invasion. Most notable were Hitler's orders concerning the exercise of command in areas of operation within the Reich of 13 July and 19 September 1944 and the powers they gave to the Party to intervene in military issues.[24]

The new orders outlined the scope of Party and *Wehrmacht* power in combat and rear areas with *Wehrmacht* jurisdiction confined to a narrow band of territory adjacent to the fighting front. Ultimately, these orders encompassed subjects such as the construction of defences, the conferring of fortress status on towns and cities, the raising of a Home Guard militia (the *Volkssturm*) and evacuation measures. The Party drafted the labour force for digging, undertook *Volkssturm* enlistment, appointing unswerving Nazis as commanders, and from December 1944 had sole powers to authorise evacuation from areas threatened by the enemy. This extension of Party authority, personified by the *Gauleiter* in his capacity as RVK, further curtailed the operational freedom of the *Wehrmacht*. This trend is discernible even prior to the 20 July attempt on Hitler's life. The army's stock was damaged by 18 months of retreat in Russia. Koch, in his role as *Reichskommissar Ukraine*, had already accused Army Group South's leadership of defeatism in December 1943.[25] As previously observed, the collapse of Army Group Centre in the summer of 1944 and the capture and subsequent conduct of German generals in Soviet capacity led the Nazi hierarchy and many ordinary Germans to conclude that something more sinister was afoot.

The decision to initiate a programme of fortification building in the provinces threatened with invasion was laid out in directives issued by Guderian, appointed Chief of Staff for the Eastern Front following the assassination attempt, and Field Marshal Wilhelm Keitel, Chief of Staff of the Armed Forces, in July 1944.[26] Although these orders were drafted on a national framework, initially they were only applicable to the eastern theatre. Later orders specifically addressed the revamping of the *Westwall*, the construction of coastal defences and the designation of fortress status on key cities and transportation centres.[27] As early as August 1944, at the instigation of Hitler and the High Command, most major eastern German cities were classified as fortresses.[28] In the case of a Red Army breakthrough these fortresses, ordered to hold out until the last, were to draw in Soviet forces and provide the Germans with time to regroup and to prepare a counter-stroke. Ultimately, this strategy was frustrated by Hitler's obstinate refusal to yield ground.

With the Red Army at the gates, the building of the eastern defences was to proceed under the auspices of the appropriate *Gauleiter* working in 'closest co-operation' with the military authorities.[29] Guderian, a native of West Prussia, demanded that eastern Germany be transformed into a fortress with deep, staggered defences. Maps were issued to the chiefs of military districts and to Party leaders outlining the proposed location of belts of defences in the German rear. From the Vistula to the old Reich, east to west, these defences were named the A, B, C and D positions. Particular emphasis was placed on the Warsaw sector and the fortification of strong points on the Vistula and Bug. Although the military authorities requested reports detailing the progress of construction work, the Party was responsible for the drafting, welfare and supervision of the labour force.[30] Guderian's attempts to procure men and material to man and equip the defences proved fruitless as the new fortress units were simply sent to the collapsing Western Front in early September.[31]

The *Gauleiter* soon exploited these directives. As RVKs they were already empowered under previous orders issued by Hitler in September 1939 and November 1942 to commandeer all Party and state resources for the defence of their *Gau*.[32] At this grave hour it is clear that Koch had Hitler's ear. His tough measures to stem the chaos on the frontier and his successful clash with Goebbels over the proposed removal of Berlin evacuees from East Prussia signified that he was again an influential player in policy formation in the east. This viewpoint was confirmed by his appointment as *Reichskommissar Ostland* in August 1944, entrusted with the organisation of fortification building in the territories of the former Baltic States remaining under German rule. Koch had already called up remaining German males in the East Prussian frontier districts on 13 July, the same day that Hitler issued his first order outlining Party and *Wehrmacht* jurisdiction in areas threatened by invasion. This new call-up for compulsory labour service supplemented the labour pool already formed by eastern refugees detained in the province. Under Party supervision they crossed into Lithuania and into Bialystok district to commence excavation work. Much to the dismay of *Generalgouverneur* Hans Frank, Koch's newly-formed *Ostwall* authorities, led by his subordinate Paul Dargel, were charged with the building of fortifications from Memel to Warsaw while the SS was responsible for the sector south of Warsaw.[33] Koch's lead was soon followed by the *Gau* authorities in Pomerania, Brandenburg, Lower and Upper Silesia, Danzig–West Prussia and Warthegau. Hitler's order to the RVKs on 1 September, specified that all resources be diverted to the building of frontier defences so they would be completed in the shortest period of time. This further accelerated the pace of construction.[34]

Koch's decision to embrace the digging programme arose from a number of factors. His fiefdom no longer extended from the Baltic to the Black Sea. The Ukraine was lost and the Soviets had already named him as a war criminal.[35] Now the Red Army threatened Koch's East Prussian power base and extravagant lifestyle. There was also popular support for the construction of defences. Indeed, many Germans wrongly assumed that an *Ostwall* had been constructed in the conquered eastern territory[36] and the events of 20 July led some more unswerving *Volksgenossen* to conclude that the 'traitorous clique' had sabotaged a defensive line.[37]

The East Prussian Party hierarchy asserted that the erection of an *Ostwall* was a responsible National Socialist initiative to protect the population and bolster the province's defences. The valuable time secured by halting the Soviet thrust could be used to collect the harvest and salvage valuable economic goods from the threatened frontier strip, a particular concern among Party and state officials in Berlin.[38] Concurrently, the *levée en masse* appeared initially to boost morale, the measure diverting attention away from worries about the Soviet advance and instilling a sense of real public participation in total mobilisation.[39] Scholars from the communist German Democratic Republic later pointed to the rigorous drafting, the imposition of manpower quotas and the use of coercion.[40] These aspects were undoubtedly present but GDR historians, bound by ideological constraints, conveniently underplayed the motivation provided by fear of a Red Army invasion. As one military historian has remarked, 'The German population worked with the idealistic hope that by means of digging duty their homeland could remain protected from Bolshevism.'[41]

In East Prussia the scope of the call-up soon extended to incorporate the entire province. Orders concerning deployment and departure were given by senior Party figures. Only the *Kreisleiter* or *Gau* medical authorities could sanction exemptions and solely in exceptional circumstances. Those who attempted to evade the directive were liable to punishment under the terms of martial law. The men were told to bring tents, waterproof clothing, bedding, crockery, saucepans and provisions for two days. Spades, shovels, hacksaws, pistols and hunting rifles were also to be brought along. Transportation for those travelling less than 30 kilometres was to be provided by horse-drawn vehicles or lorries if the latter were available. Longer journeys were to be undertaken by train. Only those deemed essential for the maintenance of the most important sectors of public life were to stay behind. Senior Party and state officials, armaments workers, police and male employees of the transportation and public utilities authorities were exempt. Likewise, bakers, butchers, grocers and dairy owners, whose services were considered necessary for the supply of the population, were not to be drafted.[42] At this stage, no indication was provided of the likely duration of service.

Gau authorities throughout the eastern provinces issued similar orders. Men between the ages of 18 and 65 were detailed to participate in the so-called *Einsatz Zielenzig* in eastern Brandenburg. Stürtz admitted to his *Kreisleiter* that the workforce faced physical labour in primitive conditions. The expected duration of the deployment was four weeks. The directive stressed the important role of the *Kreisleiter* in the operation. They were to enlist appropriate supervisory staff for the sectors under their command. Again it was stated that staff from the armaments industry, *Reichsbahn*, communications, food and supply sectors were to remain at their posts. The *Kreisleiter* were to ensure that the men were subjected to a medical examination prior to departure. Foreign workers and POWs were to be transported separately to the construction zones where they would work in segregated sectors under their regular German supervisors. As in East Prussia men were ordered to bring working clothes and shoes, blankets, crockery and cutlery, a drinks container, provisions for two days and any spades from their homes and businesses.[43]

Within a week of the start of the digging, East Prussian Propaganda Leader Maertins was advising Berlin that objectives were being attained quicker than expected. The construction of the so-called *Ostpreußenschutzstellung* (East Prussian defensive position), built around 20 kilometres in front of the province's frontier, involved between 65 and 84 per cent of the male population of the border districts. Maertins boasted that within a day of Koch's directive, work had commenced. Furthermore, he viewed the tempo of the work as astonishing. Maertins claimed that the speed and enthusiasm of the diggers resulted in surveying units having to make the greatest effort to remain ahead of the work columns. Moreover, the Party was said to have tackled potential problems straightaway. The lack of supply trains to feed the workforce caused the Party to requisition pots from throughout Germany so that meals could be cooked on site. At the same time, plentiful supplies of meat were available because of the localised slaughter of the cattle brought along by refugees flooding into the province. The shortage of doctors was addressed by the Party through the call-up of Königsberg University's medical students.[44]

Party sources were pleased with the public response to the fortification programme. Public sentiment concerning the fortification building was deemed optimistic by Party sources. Maertins maintained that the defences were not viewed solely as insurmountable barriers, but also seen as starting points for the coming German offensive. To further bolster the spirits of the German labour force, Maertins liaised with editorial staff in the major frontier towns adjacent to the construction sites and proposed the printing of a two-sided news sheet. The first side was to have a mainly political content whilst the second side was to be devoted to local and provincial issues. Publication of this news sheet commenced on 21 July. This propaganda offensive did not ignore foreign workers. Russian, Polish and Lithuanian editions soon appeared in an effort to galvanise the forced labourers to greater efforts.[45] In the *General Gouvernment* German propaganda organs, purporting to be Polish journals, insisted that it was 'political nonsense to complicate the defence of the Vistula Line and proclaimed, 'To the trenches! To the shovels! To reinforcements! For the realisation of every Polish demand quite simply depends on German success on the eastern front.'[46]

Nazi propaganda stressed the importance of the *Ostwall* and underlined the determination of East Prussians. The scale of the fortifications and the example of East Prussia to Germany, and indeed to the world, when confronted with the threat of Bolshevism received widespread coverage. Visiting Labour Leader Ley viewed what Nazi propagandists dubbed 'comprehensive defensive measures' constructed by a 'confident and enthusiastic' labour force. Ley asserted that the construction of the *Ostwall* was evidence of the fanatical will of all Germans to halt the Bolshevik onslaught.[47] Press reports underlined that the total deployment of all forces in East Prussia illustrated the impassioned will of the population to prevent the 'Bolshevik death fiend' from violating the province's sacred earth. The historical threat from the east to this symbolic province, with its proud military past, was emphasised. Already a proportionately greater number of East Prussian men and youths served with the *Wehrmacht* while those remaining were also determined to defend the province. When Koch appealed for men to participate in this 'unique, improvised exertion', hundreds of thousands had poured into assembly points with their spades. According to this standard propaganda line, all ages and professions were represented in this initiative which transcended social barriers. An oft-quoted example of the enthusiasm for the *Ostwall* concerned Königsberg University. Apparently, within three hours of the receipt of Koch's order the university closed and academics, students and staff marched to departure points. However, the East Prussian student leader privately ridiculed this press coverage. He claimed that academics had displayed no enthusiasm for the *Ostwall* and cited instances where scholars had sent their wives and children from the province.[48] The propagandists also failed to mention that men had barely any time to grab bedding. It was later admitted that organisation to feed and billet diggers only existed on paper and at first the men slept outside under blankets.[49]

The scale of the *Ostwall* was also highlighted in the regime's rhetoric. On 8 August 1944, the *Völkischer Beobachter* emphasised that 'the entire population was working hard and concentrating with total devotion on the defence of their frontier.' Within 24 hours of the commencement of digging, a continuous line, hundreds of kilometres long, was said to have been built in front of the border. Diggers carried out this task through staggered shifts and relief working.[50] The weekly newsreel said that immense columns of labourers were moving to assist in the defence of their homeland. This unique occurrence proved that Germany possessed insurmountable potential and showed that when the German people acted as one, with fanatical will, difficulties would be surmounted. Moreover, aerial views of the defensive works and the extensive trench system reinforced impressions of the scale of the construction.[51] Radio reports emphasised that there was no panic in East Prussia and that the province's male population was engaged in digging trenches under the slogan 'Do not organise but improvise'.[52] The propagandists observed that the success of the programme indicated the value of improvisation and the harmony between participating groups. There was said to be no trace of bureaucracy. Critical events at the front had not produced panic in East Prussia, but rather had been answered by the most determined feats, thereby demonstrating the will of the community and providing a glowing example for all Germans. The steadfast defence of the province was a signal of German resistance. The Red Army would pay in rivers of blood for every inch yielded until the hour of the German attack when the *Wehrmacht* would once again settle accounts.[53]

Unsurprisingly, Koch amplified his own role in the proceedings. He claimed that, without the Party's intervention, there would have been no *Frontgau* East Prussia.[54] Koch told his subordinates that the beginning of the digging coincided with calls for a new front on the Vistula which would have necessitated the surrender of East Prussia. Koch admitted to his *Kreisleiter* that psychological reasons were central to his decision to launch the digging programme. The maxim 'a good trench is still better than a bad evacuation' was quoted by Koch and he claimed that this was the reason that the 'Bolshevik hordes' did not stand on East Prussian soil.[55] The *Preußische Zeitung* insisted that Koch had acted and not talked, and claimed that, 'The whole apparatus worked without a hitch. There was not the slightest bit of red tape or conflict over competence: the button was pressed and the East Prussians enabled their *Gauleiter* immediately to tackle what the *Führer* demanded from him.'[56] From small beginnings a gigantic defensive work was created and Koch attributed this to the beneficial effects of 15 years of hard National Socialist education in the province. Koch emphasised that beyond the frontiers of the province, even within the enemy camp, the immense achievement of East Prussia was discussed.[57] Goebbels, a persistent critic of Koch's mindless brutality in the Ukraine, now saluted his newly discovered energy and 'fabulous' enthusiasm.[58]

Moreover, despite earlier clashes,[59] Model apparently praised the defences, built under Koch's 'energetic direction'. Model seemingly told Koch that the new defences had brought about the stabilisation of the Eastern Front.[60] Koch in a radio interview talked of the *Wehrmacht*'s appreciation of the fortified defence system. He clearly implied that the military had not been involved in the planning: 'Yes, not only the Command, the distinguished Field Marshal Model and his staff, but also the commanders of armies and dozens of officers commanding divisions and regiments have made comments. They were all surprised and gratified at finding such excellent fortifications.'[61]

The East Prussian Party leadership maintained that they had transformed the province into a fortress. Now, the province had passed the first acid test and a masterpiece of improvisation had been erected; a unique feat corresponding to no examples or models. The trenches, barbed wire, tank traps, bunkers, mine fields and machine gun nests ensured that every metre of soil was covered by deep defences.[62] The apparent enthusiasm for the defences was conveyed in official news agency material datelined from Königsberg. On 24 August it was asserted that:

> Digging is better than evacuating! That is the slogan with which East Prussia has rallied to build

> defence positions on its frontier. Head and brains of this East Prussian rising is *Gauleiter* Erich Koch . . .
>
> Thus National Socialist readiness for action proves itself once again here in East Prussia. The example of East Prussia furnishes new proof of the inexhaustible creative energy and willpower inherent in the German people which only need to be reawakened and directed in the right manner to make the impossible possible.[63]

The efforts of Koch and his subordinates were also explained:

> The *Gauleiter* labours night and day. He gives his orders at building site after building site and listens to reports by the *Kreisleiter*, in whose hands lies the organisation of the trenching, and makes sure of the progress of the work, samples the food of the men and asks after their children . . . The *Kreisleiter* takes over the responsibility and orders the necessary measures. The *Landesbauernführer* has prepared the necessary means for feeding the men, the NSV looks after the provisioning, the NSF has taken over the cooking, and all organisations have been set their tasks.[64]

The Nazi media claimed that the Soviets, who had been speaking about a victory parade in Königsberg, were halted at the gates of the Reich.[65] Koch received a congratulatory telegram from Guderian on 5 September expressing Hitler's thanks for the endeavours of East Prussians involved in constructing the fortifications. The Party's *Preußische Zeitung* boasted that East Prussia was setting a wartime example for the entire German nation, similar to the precedent set in 1933 when unemployment had been swiftly eliminated in the province.[66]

Special reports highlighted the valiant deeds of the *Hitlerjugend* (HJ) and Koch praised 'our splendid Hitler Youth'.[67] Reporters emphasised that these had not been easy weeks for the HJ but the boys had displayed composure, discipline and comradeship. Correspondents concluded that the HJ had understood the gravity of the situation and fulfilled their duties.[68] Similarly, Guderian eulogised the volunteer spirit of the Hitler Youth in East Prussia in a broadcast transmitted on 3 September and went on to stress the infantry's need for such brave young replacements.[69] Elsewhere, HJ diggers in Upper Silesia were also undergoing pre-military training in addition to their arduous duties in the trenches. At Gross Zeidel anti-tank trenches flooded and collapsed. Barefoot in the water, as there were not enough Wellington boots, the boys laid fascines – wiring together bundles of brushwood to be placed between freshly cut tree trunks and the wall of the trench.[70] Other HJ were even more unfortunate. The *Oberschlesische Zeitung* reported that four lads had left their workplace, which was said to be tightly guarded by the *Wehrmacht* and police, without permission. They had ventured into the forest and had perished at the hands of bandits.[71]

Press coverage also mentioned the incentives offered to the workforce. Diggers received two Marks per day, although it was stressed that 80 per cent of participants refused this money. Koch commented approvingly that 'they were working for the protection of their homeland, not for money'.[72] Sweets and soap were distributed to young workers, while their older compatriots received tobacco, schnapps, soap and shaving equipment.[73] During the duration of the entrenchment work the diggers also earned the honorary title *Wehrkamerad* (military comrade).[74] On completion of the work *Schutzwallehrenzeichen* were distributed. Typically, at one such occasion, a mass rally at Graudenz on 3 December 1944, *Gauleiter* Albert Forster of Danzig–West Prussia praised the diggers for their achievements and handed out great numbers of these decorations.[75]

Meanwhile, the propagandists also discussed the impact on the economy and the gathering of the harvest. Koch praised the Party's organisational prowess and claimed that the call-up of men in separate waves for three-week periods ensured that economic life did not collapse.[76] Disruptions were trivialised. In Königsberg's restaurants the call-up of waiters meant that diners had to fetch their own meals from the kitchens. Holiday trains no longer ran to popular Baltic seaside resorts. Many shops displayed signs advising of restrictions arising from the loss of employees to digging or harvest work. However, only the frontier districts were totally laid bare of manpower during the most threatening period between mid July and early August.[77] Koch insisted that harvest collection could take place alongside the entrenchment work. Women were not expected to participate in the latter. Instead, together with youths and POWs, they were called to bring in the harvest.[78] Longer hours were worked and tractors were sent to East Prussia from throughout Germany. Meanwhile, reports dismissed the notion that the proximity of the Bolshevik threat was an overbearing worry for the farming folk of the frontier districts. An idyllic image was evoked. In the absence of the farmer who was serving in the military and his farmhand who was engaged in entrenchment work, the farmer's wife milked the cows while their 14-year-old son gathered in the fruit.[79] Similarly, a Front Report broadcast on the radio in August claimed that 'East Prussian farmers quietly pursue their activities as if the front was hundreds of miles away. They know that they can rely on the German fighters and on those who immediately behind the lines are establishing a defence wall which will withstand even the biggest mass assault by the enemy.'[80]

As Allied forces probed Germany's western frontier and fieldworks were dug in the western *Gaue*, more propaganda underlining the example of East Prussia was circulated. A wireless feature programme of 16 September again extolled the virtues of improvisation and an East Prussian official was quoted saying, 'All the work centres round the trench. Nothing is organised; there is no office, no paper plans, we just dig.' The method of working at the site was also outlined: 'The *Wehrmacht* investigates the ground and gives instructions on how to proceed. Then we have a handful of German overseers, servicemen of the First World War and of this war. The *Gauleiter* has ordered us to build the way soldiers would like, just as if we ourselves had to defend the position tomorrow.'[81]

The *Wehrmacht* was also press-ganged into articulating their gratitude for the new positions.[82] After the Germans had parried the Red Army's thrust into East Prussia in October 1944, Colonel General Reinhardt, Model's successor as commander of Army Group Centre, was interviewed by Günther Heysing of the *Völkischer Beobachter*. Reinhardt diplomatically praised the deep defences. They had provided his troops with cover from Soviet fire and armour and acted as assembly points prior to counter-strokes. The Red Army was forced to charge at a continuous German line or at well-camouflaged machine gun nests. Reinhardt thanked East Prussians for their hard work, which had spared many German casualties.[83] Throughout the East Prussian frontier districts senior personnel from Army Group Centre attended ceremonies to mark the completion of the defences and praised the Party and population for their endeavours. During October these events coincided with the swearing-in of the East Prussian *Volkssturm* battalions. Maertins appealed to the Propaganda Ministry to request the presence of reporters from the news bureaux and major newspapers at these public functions.[84] Headlines such as 'The *Wehrmacht* thanks the East Prussian workers' stressed the close co-operation between the front and the homeland. When the diggers returned to Lötzen they were addressed by representatives of the Party and *Wehrmacht* in the town's market place. Two long-standing themes were repeatedly stressed. First, there was the customary eulogy to the varied ages and backgrounds of the diggers. Secondly, it was emphasised that the defences had a political value in addition to their military importance. The construction of the *Ostpreußenschutzstellung* showed the *Wehrmacht* and the Party working together to strengthen the bond between the front and the homeland.[85]

However, the continual rhetoric extolling the heroic achievements in East Prussia did not always have the desired effect. The SD reported from western Germany that developments in the province only highlighted the immediate threat to the German frontier.[86] Even leading Nazis had their private reservations. Goebbels observed on 2 August that the defences covering East Prussia on the Lithuanian side of the frontier had been pierced.[87] Two days later he noted that fighting was taking place on the thinly manned 'Koch Line' and commented that defensive lines had no purpose when they were devoid of troops and weapons.[88] Later a second *Ostpreußenschutzstellung* was built on the frontier with Lithuania.[89] A Party official from Goldap recorded his role at the *Ostpreußenschutzstellung* in Lithuania and Sudauen and noted that the *Wehrmacht* and OT further refined the positions. The Party officials were then deployed in Goldap district at the *Ostpreußengrenzstellung.*[90]

Toiling Under the Summer Sun

Propaganda promises relating to the construction and effectiveness of the new defences did not translate into reality. Huge discrepancies ensued which had a detrimental impact on the morale of the workforce and their perceptions of the defences. In the background lurked strained relationships and administrative rivalries between the Party, *Wehrmacht* and residual civilian authorities.

A varied labour force was involved in the numerous defensive projects undertaken in eastern Germany. The nature of the defences and the status, gender and age of the diggers varied greatly. The number of participants also fluctuated from season to season, peaking during the late summer of 1944. Thereafter, the completion of the work, the apparent reduction of the Soviet threat and the deteriorating weather conditions led to many labourers being discharged. The workforce involved in the construction of the East Prussian defences was estimated at around 200,000 in contemporary Party reports. They were divided into three sectors. Similar numbers of Germans and foreigners were said to be involved.[91] The building of the *Pommernwall*, in eastern Pomerania, running from the Baltic coast, around Schneidemühl and joining the

Brandenburg defences, commenced on 10 August and also required a substantial labour force. Schwede-Coburg reported in October that 400 kilometres of defences had been dug by 135,000 labourers, 100,000 of whom were women and youths.[92] An official from Lauenburg, in the extreme north-east of the province, recounted that 90 per cent of the draftees were women and girls.[93] Indeed, a multitude of overwhelmingly women workers, toiling under the summer sun, was observed by a passing railway traveller: 'Somewhere between Schlawe and Stolp we passed masses of people, mostly women, armed with spades and shovels. For miles and miles, as far as the eye could see they were digging a deep trench.'[94] Other aspects of the work involved the construction of thousands of log machine gun bunkers with a concrete facade and open to the rear.[95]

The *Ostwall* in Lower Silesia was constructed in the immediate vicinity of the former frontier with Poland.[96] It was christened *Unternehmen Bartold* (Operation Bartold) by Hanke, in respect of a mythical 13th century German coloniser of Silesia, when Silesians had defended themselves against Mongolian invaders.[97] Work commenced in early August. Hanke announced the new initiative in the midst of a large Party parade in the courtyard of Namslau castle.[98] Hanke toured the excavation sites to drum up enthusiasm for the programme and the regional newspaper, the *Schlesische Tageszeitung* proudly informed readers on 20 August that, 'For two weeks an army has been digging entrenchments with pick and spade along the border of *Gau* Niederschlesien.'[99] By mid-September, the SS estimated that 102,000 people were involved. This total was made up of 32,000 German men, 7,000 German women, 24,000 HJ, 7,000 from the BdM, 18,000 foreign male workers and 14,000 foreign female workers.[100] Concurrently, Hitler's decision to confer fortress status on Breslau led to construction commencing on two rings of defences around the city. The outer ring was to be around 120 kilometres long and able to accommodate five divisions. Initially, a workforce of 20,000 was called up from throughout Silesia.[101] Behind the new defences, constructed in the *General Gouvernement* and Warthegau by an overwhelmingly *Volksdeutsche* and Polish labour force, the old fortifications in Brandenburg were spruced up.[102] A mixed German and foreign labour force was deployed at the aforementioned *Einsatz Zielenzig* along the eastern frontier of Schwerin, Meseritz and Züllichau. Members of the HJ and BdM, foreign workers and POWs comprised a substantial proportion of the workforce.[103] Some 40,513 Brandenburgers were called up in early August and 18,000 diggers were active in Züllichau alone.[104]

It appears from the remaining sources that East Prussian diggers were somewhat less critical of conditions than their counterparts elsewhere in the eastern territories. A number of factors perhaps explain this. Due to its geographical location, East Prussia was most immediately threatened by the Red Army and this perhaps focused minds on the task at hand. More technical staff were also available to assist construction because of the proximity of the front. In addition, bitter memories of the Russian invasion and occupation of 1914–1915 remained vivid and acted as a further spur to the German workforce. Finally, German women were not mobilised to undertake entrenchment work in East Prussia. On the other hand, the East Prussian workforce was exposed to physical danger. The digging was sometimes disrupted by Red Air Force activity while a backdrop was provided by the continual growling of artillery duels at the front. Occasionally, workers were shelled or surprised by Red Army tank spearheads.[105]

The Party authorities were aware from propaganda activity reports that there was unease at civilian labour being deployed in threatened frontier districts.[106] While the propagandists emphasised the virtues of improvisation and rapid registration, the inevitable shortcomings were soon encountered. The workforce was allocated construction sectors and split into groups. The local Party authorities established headquarters, ostensibly to manage the work. Everywhere, the lack of planning was manifest. There was a shortage of spades. Heavy work was done by hand and the use of machinery was rare. Difficulties transporting workers and materials arose from the shortage of lorries and petrol.[107]

The feeding of the diggers was entrusted to the NSV which set up field kitchens for this purpose. The East Prussian NSV leader Erich Post claimed that food was provided at 473 locations and around 200,000 diggers were receiving hot and cold food daily. He boasted on 5 September that during the 52 days of the so-called K[och]-Action around 10.4 million portions of hot food, 20.8 million portions of cold food and 20.8 million portions of coffee had been dispensed.[108] Nevertheless, complaints about the lack of food, especially hot food, were picked up in SD and propaganda reports. The authorities attributed this to the inability to make sufficient preparations and to transportation difficulties. The SD noted that a lack of food resulted in a corresponding decline in the appetite for work. No uniform system of ration cards was drawn up and no regular feeding arrangements were finalised for the large percentage of diggers who came to the construction sites on Sundays by special trains. Some brought their own food, others were fed by the NSV and a third category received additional ration coupons for the day. The SD also pointed to insufficient water supplies at eastern construction sites and the long marches to these sites endured by the workforce.[109]

Privately, the Nazi authorities realised that there was a lack of adequate accommodation for the labour force but maintained that this was unavoidable because of the improvised nature of the enterprise.[110] Many East Prussian diggers slept under canvas. Elsewhere the sudden influx of vast numbers of outsiders into sleepy localities led to considerable difficulties. Groß Wartenberg district in Lower Silesia had 27,800 inhabitants but overnight had to accommodate around 28,000 HJ and BdM diggers. The then *Landrat*, Detlev von Reinersdorff-Paczenski, provided quarters for 80 girls in his house, but noted that the lack of sufficient washing facilities caused some girls to wash in the garden pond. As insufficient toilets were available, many girls resorted to nature, but fortunately this did not provoke sickness epidemics.[111]

The workforce tended to be quartered in villages within the digging area. Billets included private houses, halls, schools, barns and stables. Floors and straw mattresses served as beds. In Lower Silesia the school holidays were extended, and when reopened, the schools only catered for younger pupils.[112] Teachers and older pupils were called up for *Bartold*. The HJ were often housed in special camps. Whilst they dug trenches, the BdM undertook cooking, washing and cleaning duties in the camps.[113] One Berlin HJ leader recalled being sent to Meseritz, Brandenburg where his group was accommodated in the barns and haylofts of neighbouring farms. Their work was well arranged and the BdM organised sufficient feeding.[114] On the other hand, a Lower Silesian *Landrat* remembered that the primitive washing and toilet facilities in HJ camps led to repeated cases of dysentery throughout the summer. He claimed that this caused a shortfall of labour and necessitated the mobilisation of the NSF and other Party formations.[115]

The Party hierarchy gave sanitary and welfare provision a low priority and consequently contagious diseases were commonplace. Schwede-Coburg admitted privately that Pomeranian diggers endured unhealthy conditions.[116] One Pomeranian *Landrat*, von Wuthenau of the Netzekreis, lamented that the cramped, unhygienic circumstances led to diphtheria and scarlet fever claiming the lives of many women and girls.[117] Meanwhile, amputees, tuberculosis sufferers and severe diabetics were called up in East Prussia.[118] This seemingly indiscriminate drafting caused public concern and practical problems.[119] SD reports attributed this to insufficient medical checks on the fitness of the conscripted men. The lack of available doctors and the need for immediate departure to the construction areas were blamed.[120] In addition to accidents and acute sickness, it was evident that, as time moved on, more diggers were diagnosed unfit for work as a result of old physical complaints and the strain of unaccustomed heavy work.[121] Those citing ill health as a reason for being unable to work included many women now mobilised for the first time. They received little sympathy from the regime. The *Schlesische Tageszeitung* pointed to 'incorrigible shirkers' and added 'Just at present they are eagerly hunting for certificates. By what diseases are they not now suddenly tortured!'[122]

A medical service for East Prussian diggers was established and the *Gau* Doctors' Leader was placed at the helm. Civilian doctors, HJ doctors and the SA's Group Tannenberg were involved. In addition, around 370 medical students from Königsberg University were distributed among the various construction sectors and border hospitals. The authorities observed that most sick diggers, when treated, were able to return to work. They insisted that the mortality level had not exceeded normal levels.[123] However, an SD report disclosed that at many fortification construction sites on Germany's frontiers there was a shortage of doctors and medicines. This was aggravated by the lack of transportation and petrol which made it difficult for doctors to reach patients in the extensive building sites.[124]

Various sops were offered to distract attention from the rigorous camp regimes, cheerless work and poor accommodation. Daily diggers from Breslau received bread, meat and fat coupons and two or three cigarettes as a reward for putting in an 18-hour day. This included rail travel to and from the vicinity of the deployment area and a march of more than two hours to and from the construction site in all weathers.[125] Additional allocations of cigarettes, tobacco and alcohol also varied widely. The SD observed that the workforce on the eastern frontier was better catered for and these perks even extended to foreign labour.[126] Vehicles laden with additional canned foods and soap were seen heading to Pomeranian building sites.[127] *Kreisleiter* Siegfried Schug of Stargard–Saatzig–Pyritz, a decorated Party veteran, claimed that the workers in his sector of the *Pommernwall* were the best fed and provisioned in Germany. He highlighted the tobacco, sweets, candy and fruit that they received for their hard work.[128]

Pomeranian reports also commented on competitions to find the tidiest billets. Furthermore, *Wehrmacht* musicians and actors from the Stettin city theatre entertained the diggers.[129] In late summer the workers swam in nearby lakes. The outdoor life and work led to Schug remarking approvingly as to how tanned and healthy the conscripted female office workers now looked.[130] Around the same time, the *Pommersche Zeitung* reported the visit of *Reichsfrauenschaftsführerin* Scholtz Klink to a digging site in the province 'where women though digging hard soil were radiant with humour'.[131]

Foreign labourers and POWs endured poorer conditions than their German counterparts. Post-war accounts said the bare minimum about non-German labour. Lithuanian labourers and French POWs were occasionally commended for their efforts.[132] The attitude of the Poles, threatened with court martial if caught attempting to evade digging duties, was also apparently influenced by the prospect of additional rations and their traditional hatred of the Russians.[133] In the incorporated territories of Danzig–West Prussia and Warthegau Polish labourers received extra meat, bread and fat allowances.[134]

One Lower Silesian official maintained that Poles and even Jews deployed in the Militsch–Trachenberg sector were accommodated as well as was possible at the time.[135] A Pomeranian source spoke highly of loyal foreign workers. They caused no difficulties but also received sympathetic treatment from unarmed German supervisory staff. This explained why they were not attacked at night by their charges.[136] However, a substantial part of the initially willing Polish workforce in the Lomza (Zichenau) sector in East Prussia was alienated in early August when their *Wehrmacht* Pioneer Corps overseers were replaced by crude Party supervisors.[137] Another report from Zichenau mentioned that Poles suffering from bloody diarrhoea were seized from hospital isolation by a local Party deputy section leader and whipped. Some later died and the infection spread to others.[138] The SD condemned the Party's failings during the registration of Poles in the *General Gouvernement*. These measures were ineffective as many Poles did not register, while others fled from the digging sectors or displayed little effort on site. In Czestochowa, too few Poles registered to work on the fortifications in late July so the Germans simply resorted to the proven policy of roundups. The SD conceded that generally the treatment of Poles had been incorrect. The maxim of 'hard but correct' treatment was recommended. The SD proposed that incentives, reasonable feeding and better accommodation would improve the performance of Polish workers.[139]

The Party received further criticism for conscripting women workers, failing to meet promises regarding the duration of the digging and for the behaviour of its functionaries. The decision to register older and sickly women as well as mothers with young children caused widespread anger in Pomerania and Silesia. In Pomerania, the NSF rarely overcame the *Kreisleiter* authorities to gain women exemption from digging.[140] Bereft of men, the Party remorselessly trawled the province for any warm body capable of wielding a spade.

One complaint was submitted to Goebbels by O. Sattelberg, a Berliner whose 50-year-old wife, presently in menopause, had moved to be with her mother in Greifenberg, Pomerania. She had then been drafted to work on the *Pommernwall* in

Schlawe district. Sattelberg underlined that old and sick women were undertaking excavation work in Pomerania, whereas Koch publicly stated that no German women were performing digging duties in East Prussia. He condemned the ruthless mobilisation of women to the age of 55, regardless of their disposition. Moreover, the women received no information on the conclusion of service. Sattelberg worried that undertaking this work against medical recommendations would have severe consequences for his wife. He called for the Pomeranian Party authorities to be as responsible as their East Prussian counterparts. Sattelberg also made detailed criticisms of the primitive accommodation. The toilets and washing area were completely open on one side and the foreign workforce could view these German women. The food was generally insufficient. Only bread was plentiful. This caused the writer to wonder if this arose from negligence or criminality. The length of the deployment period had made the women increasingly depressed. Even younger and fitter women endured cramps caused by the physical exertions and pressures. Hopes that the work would last four weeks were dashed when the women were told to have warm clothes sent to them. This led to rumours that their next assignment would be to collect the potato harvest.[141]

These criticisms were commonplace. A letter written from Stolp, Pomerania spoke of an unbroken, seven-hour working day, after which the women were 'kaputt'. The author recounted sarcastically that women were deemed to be the upholders of the German nation.[142] This unease was compounded by the knowledge that these respected, older women were forced to stay in unhygienic mass quarters.[143] In late October, one Hitler Youth noted with relief that at least he and his newly arrived comrades did not have to meet the norms set for women workers.[144] Similarly, in the *General Gouvernement* a visiting Swedish reporter wrote that Polish boys over 12 had to dig and remove two cubic metres of earth, women 3½ cubic metres and men 4½ cubic metres daily.[145] Back in Pomerania, morale steadily dropped as the digging continued into autumn. There was a lack of suitable clothing for the inclement weather. Stettin women, deployed in the Neustettin sector, were granted leave to return home to collect waterproof clothing. In particularly pressing instances they were given supplementary clothing coupons. Morale in this sector was also adversely affected by news of the two major air raids on Stettin in late August. Worries about the fate of relatives resulted in some women being granted leave to return to Stettin, although abuses of these privileges equated to desertion.[146] The Pomeranian judicial authorities admitted that the enlistment of women over 50 was seen as harsh, but insisted that 'all in all the population was willingly complying with the heavy demands of the time'.[147]

Deputy *Gauleiter* Simon, subordinated by Schwede-Coburg to command the civilian workforce, maintained that if the entire labour force had undergone medical examinations, the project would have been delayed. Simon claimed that medical officials were constantly checking hygiene in the communal quarters and added that doctor–patient ratios in some areas of the province equated to 1:15,000, whereas it was 1:3,000 for those constructing the *Pommernwall*. Sick beds had been set aside for diggers in the camps and at local hospitals. Pointedly, he differentiated between those with psychological heart problems and those with real heart defects. He also asserted that the Party authorities monitored the amount and quality of rations. Bad food was removed immediately. Simon advised that women between the ages of 21 and 55 had originally been called up but the age limit had been altered to 50 after around three weeks. Sick women were sent home straightaway or received lighter work such as peeling vegetables. From the beginning a six-hour working day was enforced and the authorities claimed to be trying to cut travel time and give the women more time for relaxation. Simon contended that women over 50, mothers with three or more unattended children and women whose withdrawal was recommended by doctors, were released. Likewise, women were discharged to undertake seasonal work. Simon concluded that the mobilisation of female labour arose because, in contrast to East Prussia, no workers were conscripted from the armaments and agricultural sectors.[148] Simon downplayed the conditions in an editorial in the *Pommersche Zeitung* which said of the Pomeranian diggers, 'They all realise that everyone must make a small sacrifice – either go cold on straw all night, simply because there are not enough blankets, or get sore feet from marching, or contract some other little ailment. Is all that real sacrifice?'[149]

In Lower Silesia it seems that the *Gau* authorities came to the conclusion that the deployment of German women was more trouble than it was worth. The *Schlesische Tageszeitung* announced on 3 September: 'The time for improvisations and occasional inconveniences is now over and therefore the *Gauleiter* has decreed that all German women and girls should, for reasons of health and physical suitability and despite their brilliant efforts, be removed from direct entrenchment work and join the armament industry instead, unless the *Unternehmen Bartold* requires them for assistance and the production of fascines.'[150] Nevertheless, even in mid-November it was admitted that women still made up 8 per cent of the labour force at the entrenchment sites of Lower Silesia. While the men continued to dig and lay defences these women were still binding the fascines together.[151]

During the autumn the most important complaint, namely the cessation of digging duties, was addressed throughout the eastern territories. The numbers participating steadily declined. German women comprised a significant percentage of those stood down. The foreign workforce tended to remain on site.[152] For instance, around Neustettin (Pomerania) the women workers were discharged from October and men were released because of illness, or sometimes stood down for the meantime. By the year-end, only a few supervisors, watching over foreign workers, remained.[153] Elsewhere work continued on a reduced but nonetheless significant scale. *Regierungspräsident* Refardt in Frankfurt an der Oder declared on 6 December that large numbers of diggers were still accommodated in barns and camps throughout Züllichau, Schwerin and Meseritz districts, and that work would continue for the time being.[154] In East Prussia a 45,000-strong workforce was still engaged in November 1944. As weather conditions deteriorated, they were deployed reinforcing coastal defences, attempting to upgrade Königsberg's obsolete fortifications and constructing obstacles in areas where natural barriers were rendered redundant because of the freezing conditions. Great effort was expended constructing an anti-tank ditch behind the frozen Masurian Canal in East Prussia. This new position was completed in 15 days by 6,000 labourers but the solid earth and lack of equipment hampered work around Königsberg.[155] Similarly, it was practically impossible to excavate earth frozen 'as hard as rock' in Pomerania.[156]

Moreover, the high-handed, thoughtless attitude of Party officials led to tension and alienated many initially favourably predisposed to the work. From Upper Silesia it was reported in early October that:

> Bitterness was particularly aroused by the totally unsuitable male supervisory staff who apparently had the nerve to drive up to the site in automobiles and then walk along without picking up a shovel; instead they not only controlled those who were working, men and women, in some cases elderly, but also screamed at them in quite an inappropriate tone of command . . . [157]

The behaviour of *Kreisleiter* Heuer of Angerapp (East Prussia) so enraged an unnamed OT leader, who was in the area to co-ordinate the construction of field works, that he contacted the SD. The conduct of Heuer and his cohorts brought the Party great discredit among the civilian population. They consumed schnapps and sparkling wines in abundance and appropriated food from the communal kitchen. Heuer welcomed the 'best drinking mates' in East Prussia to his gatherings and the entire company was regularly '*besoffen*' (sloshed). Some Party officials were drunk almost every day. Significantly, the drunken officials were failing to use the German greeting, much to this informant's disappointment. He concluded that at a time of immediate danger, these Party officials were setting a bad example and distressing decent elements in the local administration and the civilian population. Instead of contributing to the objective of 'throwing back the Bolsheviks', their 'disgraceful Russian-like behaviour' compared most unfavourably with the tough conditions endured by soldiers at the front.[158]

By virtue of their actions, Party officials in East Prussia appeared to comprehend the gravity of the military situation. Great bouts of drinking and gorging were the order of the day at construction sites near Memel. Female typists and office helpers were involved in veritable orgies with senior staff. Everyone was living by the maxim 'Enjoy the war, the peace will be dreadful'.[159] Food and drink earmarked for the diggers was regularly siphoned-off by Party officials. Diggers near Memel frequently failed to receive tobacco rations although this commodity was available in abundance in the supply camps.[160] Similar developments were observed in the Namslau sector of *Bartold*. The leadership and female staff partied, exploiting the extensive alcohol stocks. Moreover, they also acquired large quantities of scarce items such as fruit and stockings which were generally unavailable.[161] The SD criticised the laziness of Party supervisory staff and their inappropriate behaviour towards their own countrymen. Widespread drinking, a lack of effort and instances of dereliction of duty were also observed.[162]

There is evidence that even in East Prussia some of those conscripted to dig tried to evade this duty. A letter sent from the province in late July told how many elderly soldiers of the World War ran away from the fortification sites because of the proximity of the front and the intensity of the work. Police had to fetch them back.[163] Firms in Königsberg had to prove to Party officials that their employees had been released from service on the *Ostwall*[164] and those failing to dig had to report to their local Party group. It was made clear that, 'Anyone who does not obey must expect the well-known consequences'.[165]

SD reports also mentioned the issue of discipline and the punishments meted out by special courts established in the vicinity of the field works. In East Prussia sentences lacked uniformity. The public was aware that punishments ranged from small fines and short terms of imprisonment to death sentences.[166] The Lower Silesian judicial authorities established special courts at Glogau and Oels to deal with those refusing to undertake digging. However, apart from a few exceptions, the population adhered to the appeal for diggers and the new bodies were hardly troubled at the beginning. Revealingly, a sign of the waning enthusiasm was noticeable by early December when the imprisonment of several offenders was reported.[167]

Germans labourers soon questioned the effectiveness of such hastily built defences. There was criticism of this 'pathetic system of trenches' after the failure of the much-heralded Atlantic Wall to deter the western allies landing in France.[168] The publicity highlighting the construction of field works received widespread criticism. Skilled workers had laboured for years on the Atlantic Wall but it had been overcome, whereas the new defences often only consisted of a few trenches and were thus easier to pierce. Moreover, the newsreel had given the impression that the throwing up of trenches only placed something different in the enemy's path.[169] Dismay grew during August when the Red Army brushed aside unmanned fortifications built in Lithuania.[170] Although some participants viewed their work with pride, others mocked: 'These ditches will hold up the enemy for one hour and two minutes: one hour to get over the laughing fits the Russian soldiers will have when they first notice them and two minutes to get across.'[171]

An editorial in the *Pommersche Zeitung* in mid-September conceded the limitations of the defences in the passage: 'The fact that the war cannot possibly be won this way is obvious and everyone knows it, but what matters is that we should delay the enemy.'[172]

In addition, the fact that positions were being constructed far behind the front line contradicted the official view that the Red Army would be halted at the East Prussian frontier and on the Vistula causing anxiety among those living in front of the defences. A quarter of the population of Pomerania, a pre-war figure of 625,000, lived in districts in front of the *Pommernwall*.[173] The then *Landrat* of Saatzig later noted that 'this aroused in the eastern Pomeranian population a sense of the steadily approaching danger to the soil of the homeland'.[174] Similarly, a former Lower Silesian *Landrat* later remarked that participation in *Bartold* signalled the immediate threat to the province.[175] Hanke hardly dispelled these fears when he told Lower Silesian diggers that they might soon be occupying the trenches that they had dug: 'One thing is certain: these fortifications which we have built will one day, if necessary, be manned by ourselves, changing the spade for a rifle and defending the frontier together with our soldiers.'[176]

Contemporary accounts and post-war testimonies also illustrate the scale of friction between the Party and *Wehrmacht*. There is little evidence of a good working relationship being forged. Both started out with differing aspirations. The Party was concerned with the propaganda value of the fortifications, hoping that they would calm the worries of local inhabitants and consolidate the idea of *Endsieg*.[177] The possible military value was of secondary importance. On the other hand, the *Wehrmacht* sought well-sited, solid and habitable positions and the co-operation of the local Party authorities. Guderian ambiguously remarked in his memoirs that 'a few *Gauleiter* were also helpful; if their excessive zeal led on occasion to friction, their desire to make themselves useful must be acknowledged nevertheless.'[178]

Schwede-Coburg decreed that the digging of the *Pommernwall* should cease on the *Gau* border and not go one inch further, whatever the military considerations.[179] This behaviour only reinforced the belief that every *Gauleiter* wanted his own East or West Wall.[180] Moreover, the location of defences was frequently determined by political rather than strategic considerations. The *Wehrmacht* complained that the actions of Koch and *Gauleiter* Fritz Bracht of Upper Silesia exemplified this trend. For psychological and internal political grounds Koch demanded that efforts to defend Königsberg be concentrated further from the city with the upgrading of the 190-kilometre long Heilsberg–Deime position. However, a *Wehrmacht* directive had ordered the bolstering of the 87-kilometre long Frisching Canal position. Ultimately, neither line was completed when the Red Army appeared in late January 1945 and both were swiftly breached. Similarly, the military wanted to fortify Oppeln. Again psychologically adverse factors were cited and Bracht vetoed the proposal, claiming that the B1 and B2 defences covered Upper Silesia. When the Red Army broke through at Czestochowa in mid-January 1945 the road to Oppeln lay wide open and the city fell shortly afterwards.[181]

Locally the *Kreisleiter* were scarcely more obliging. The recommendations of *Wehrmacht* pioneer staff or wounded ex-officers detailed to the construction sites in an advisory capacity were regularly ignored. *Kreisleiter* Feldmann in Memel rejected the advice of a Pioneer officer assigned to his sector of the *Ostwall*. Soldiers passing through the area remarked that they would never occupy such fortifications.[182] *Kreisleiter* Grau, in charge of a sector north-east of Memel, said that there was no obligation to follow the suggestions of *Wehrmacht* officers concerning the location of the lines.[183] These disputes only complicated the lives of diggers. Meanwhile, a Pomeranian account noted that the plans of the military staff were initially unsuccessful and trenches were dug on two or three occasions. This duplication of effort eroded morale among the workforce.[184]

The SD reported that numerous submissions had been received from all frontier areas identifying organisational, tactical and technical difficulties and shortages as well as questioning the fortifications' military value. In East Prussia disputes arose between the building authorities and Army Group Centre. Responsibility for the area of *Wehrkreis* I (the military district which roughly equated to East Prussia) was delegated to the Party. The Army Group was designated authority in areas beyond the province's frontiers, within the vicinity of the border defences and around bridgeheads. There were also arguments over tactical questions. Officers bemoaned the lack of understanding exhibited by their older counterparts, often veterans of the First World War. These problems were exacerbated because of regular personnel changes and a lack of vehicles for observation purposes.[185] The sudden mobilisation for fortification building also led to the workforce initially experiencing days of idleness on account of the Party's inability to fix the line of defences or to secure adequate technical assistance. Trenches followed the wrong course, were the wrong depth and width and were bereft of views or fields of fire. Later, the military ordered long stretches of trenches to be filled in. Thus, thousands of hours of labour were lost, materials wasted, soil damaged and trust in the construction leadership shattered.[186]

Trenches flooded because they had been dug in river valleys or because no attention was paid to drainage or water table levels. Some trenches remained unoccupied because of the danger of collapse or of the water freezing. In the sandy soil of Pomerania one supervisor had insisted that the workforce constructed trenches with straight sides. These collapsed as soon as it rained.[187] Moreover, there were insufficient minefields in front of the lines and camouflage was neglected. In open ground, the white, sandy topsoil made camouflaging the positions difficult. From the air and on the ground they were visible for kilometres. Similarly, when lines followed routes through forest clearings good camouflage was needed but was often lacking.[188] Furthermore, questions were raised about the security of these unoccupied, rear defences. Worries were expressed that they would be utilised by partisans and paratroops as they were ideal for shelter and defence. Suspicious elements could move for kilometres along the trench system undetected.[189] Preventative measures, such as the deployment of *Volkssturm* units to secure these positions, were eventually taken.

There were also complaints from the *Wehrmacht* that some aspects of the fortifications were downright dangerous. In East Prussia the one-man portable prefabricated concrete bunkers, constructed by the notorious 'Fire Brigade General' Fiedler at his Metgethen cement factory, came in for particular criticism. They comprised most of the thousands of bunkers which sprang up throughout the frontier areas and were christened Koch Pots (*Koch Töpfe*) by the troops. Badly sited, their construction was deficient and they posed great danger to their occupiers as they 'consisted of concrete tubes which were partially sunk in the earth and furnished with two machine-guns each. Escape from the pots was impossible when battle commenced, and the concrete broke up on the first hit from artillery, which was profoundly discouraging.'[190] Diggers dubbed them 'Mouse Traps' and pitied the troops who would be under the concrete covers designed to provide protection against tanks. Later, the covers were removed but these concrete holes permitted no escape when the enemy employed grenades and flamethrowers in close-quarters fighting. Erected in great numbers and at great cost, these bunkers largely remained unused.[191] One officer told the war reporter Günther Heysing that the hastily thrown up trenches, positions and *Koch Töpfe* were not recorded on any maps. Nobody knew where they lay, so they remained unused or provided shelter for the enemy.[192]

Despite Party claims to the contrary, evidence suggests that throughout the eastern provinces a growing number of businesses were closed or severely curtailed because of the *Ostwall*. The Gustav Drengwitz chemical factory in Insterburg, East Prussia was one such business. At the end of July, 250 men, largely from the firm and town's maintenance services, were ordered to undertake digging duty on the Lithuanian side of the frontier. Production came to a virtual standstill. Only a handful of senior personnel, older workers and POWs remained. The absence of the mass of the workforce was lamented when Soviet bombers attacked the plant and few fit men were available to fight the flames.[193] Similarly, Dr Hoffmann-Rothe, the *Oberbürgermeister* of Glogau,

Lower Silesia recalled that two days per week all business and public bodies closed as everyone had to participate in the digging.[194]

In Pomerania the withdrawal of such a large proportion of the labour force damaged the economy and caused much ill feeling. Administrative bodies and government departments had their staffs slashed.[195] For instance, as all available workers in Schneidemühl were engaged in entrenchment work, the local hospital administration, already missing numerous key workers because of military call-ups, fell into disorder.[196] Pomeranian reports submitted to the Reich Ministry of Justice tended to echo these themes but put a positive perspective on the participation of their officials. Some county courts lost up to three-quarters of their staff. Nevertheless, the OLG President in Stettin concluded that, as these measures were in the interest of a successful defence of the Reich's eastern frontier, a temporary standstill in the administration of justice could be allowed.[197] Later he visited his officials digging at Neustettin and was impressed with the excellent example they set by their participation.[198]

Once Pomeranian employees were released for the so-called *Sondereinsatz-Ost* (Special Deployment – East) it proved very difficult to get them back. When the President of the Stettin District Court requested the return of court attendants, a representative of the *Kreisleitung* Greater Stettin noted that their discharge could only be granted on grounds of importance for the war effort. The Party argued that police officials could fill their role during *Sondergericht* (special court) hearings and these urgent requests for the discharge of employees from the *Osteinsatz* proved fruitless. Finally, the OLG President wrote to the Party authorities recommending the prompt release of these men but there is no indication as to the outcome of this request.[199]

Lower Silesian judicial reports exhibit a similar superficial enthusiasm for the idea of field works combined with a realisation of the detrimental effect on staffing levels. This fresh demand for manpower intensified the difficulties arising from Goebbels' post 20 July 1944 total war measures which aimed to direct men remaining in the shrunken civilian sector into the military or armaments production. Initially, the participation of Lower Silesian judicial officials in *Bartold* and in the preparation of defences around some of the province's cities was confined to Sundays. However, the Party demanded that those fit to dig should do so on working days.[200] The OLG President in Breslau mentioned the large number of public officials involved in *Bartold* and complained that obtaining their release was difficult. Variations within the province were evident and the Breslau Party authorities, supervising the construction of defences around the city, were especially guilty. Some judicial staff had been engaged in *Bartold* since early August, while the others were called to the construction sites twice weekly. This caused 'not insignificant inconvenience', but was bearable as long as the two-day limit was not exceeded. However, occasionally in some district court areas, officials had been called up for four days digging per week. Naturally, this disrupted court business, especially as during the four months from 1 August some 62 per cent of judicial officials were lost to the *Wehrmacht* or armaments industry. The OLG President concluded in early December that for many Lower Silesian employees Sunday entrenchment work was on top of Party responsibilities, air raid protection duties and *Volkssturm* training. These demands bordered on the impossible for some individuals.[201]

Furthermore, despite Party promises to the contrary, the sudden conscription for *Ostwallbau* also had a pernicious effect on the gathering of the harvest and on armaments manufacture. Although some accounts indicate that the rural population was virtually untouched by mobilisation for the *Ostwall* and that diggers were overwhelmingly drawn from towns,[202] it would be misleading to suggest that the agricultural sector was unaffected. In East Prussia a 'grotesque' scenario arose. Farmers and labourers were deployed digging trenches while *Wehrmacht* detachments assisted women, children and POWs with the harvest. The lull in the fighting during late August and early September resulted in the men of the First East Prussian Infantry Division being seconded to this task. An officer's diary recounted that despite this intensive activity his sector of the frontier still resembled a picture of tranquility.[203] Meanwhile, the Pomeranian potato crop was only rescued because the weather was favourable and a significant proportion of the workforce and pack animals were redirected to the fields.[204]

The detrimental effect of the demand for diggers was felt within the armaments industry. This sector was already concerned that more and more men were being conscripted by the armed forces. The manpower shortage was considerably aggravated by the demands of the Party authorities. The Frankfurt an der Oder Armaments Command remarked that during the July–September period there had been a considerable reduction in the availability of labour because of this duty.[205] The Armaments Command in Liegnitz, Lower Silesia recorded on 12 August that the RVK had ordered armaments firms to release workers. Over the next few days repeated requests from the Party demanding additional manpower were received. Initially, claims against these withdrawals were successful.[206] However, the intensification of fortification building during mid-September meant that the armaments industry could not remain unaffected. It is evident that skilled workers were taken and their immediate return was demanded. *Bartold*, according to these Liegnitz officials, caused 'considerable disturbance'. More men were taken than initially requested. Some factories were denuded of all apprentices and forced to operate without numerous skilled workers.[207]

The Breslau Armaments Command was also involved in exchanges with *Bartold* staff in respect of encroachments into the armaments sector and had little luck procuring exemptions.[208] Similarly, the Armaments Inspectorate in the city observed that *Bartold* resulted in 'considerable aggravation' over manpower and bemoaned that the project had been initiated without adequate guidelines concerning enlistment from the armaments industry. Moreover, the drafting of miners for *Bartold* had an adverse effect on Silesian coal production and the withdrawal of so many skilled workers led to decline in manufacturing and military orders being turned down.[209]

The deficiencies besetting the *Ostwall* were evident weeks and months before the new or remodelled defences faced their ultimate examination by the Red Army in January 1945. Proponents of the *Ostwall* later argued that it prevented a fatal collapse of the Eastern Front, revived military and moral resistance, stopped the entire East Prussian population from falling into Soviet hands in 1944 and allowed the harvest to be collected.[210] Alternatively, it can be argued that if the *Ostwall* provided any breathing space it was for an odious regime to continue killing; for as we shall see the period

Hitler in Breslau. The *Führer* arrives in the *Jahrhunderthalle* for a speech to a mass audience of officer cadets on 20 November 1943. Behind him (from left), Field Marshal Wilhelm Keitel, *Reichsführer-SS* Heinrich Himmler, Field Marshall Erhard Milch of the *Luftwaffe* and SA Chief of Staff Wilhelm Schepmann. (Ullstein Bild 00046100)

An East Prussian gateway to the east. The Queen Louise Bridge over the River Memel at Tilsit. It was blown up by the retreating *Wehrmacht* in October 1944. (Bundesarchiv B 145 Bild-PO17308)

Defending the *Heimat*. Mass participation in the digging of fortifications in East Prussia, August 1944. (Ullstein Bild 00661957)

A symbol of German victory in East Prussia. The Tannenberg memorial at Hohenstein was dynamited by the withdrawing *Wehrmacht* in January 1945. (Bundesarchiv Bild 146-2004-0008)

Dicing with a death-trap. *Gauleiter* Erich Koch in a one-man-bunker, part of the East Prussian defences, autumn 1944. (Ullstein Bild 00662395)

The People Rise Up. *Reichsführer-SS* Himmler proclaims the formation of the *Volkssturm* at the Marwitz barracks, Bartenstein, East Prussia, 18 October 1944. (Bundesarchiv Bild 146-1987-128-10)

Propaganda image of the East Prussian *Volkssturm*, December 1944. Christmas post is distributed in a cellar bunker. (Bundesarchiv Bild 183-J28377)

Boys doing a man's job. Hitler Youth serving with the *Volkssturm* in the defence of Pyritz, Pomerania, February 1945. (Bundesarchiv Bild 183-J28536)

Defending the Oder Front. A *Volkssturm* position at Frankfurt an der Oder, February 1945. (Bundesarchiv Bild 183-J28787)

The misery of flight. A seemingly endless trek near Braunsberg, East Prussia, January/February 1945. (Bundesarchiv Bild 146-1976-072-09)

Leaving East Prussia. Refugees attempting to board the *FSS Wedel* at Pillau, 1945. (Bundesarchiv Bild 146-1972-093-65)

between July 1944 and January 1945 was not fully exploited to rescue people and possessions from the eastern provinces. However, these conflicting suggestions give the *Ostwall* far greater military significance than it deserved. The *Ostwall* could never be an impregnable military barrier. It was constructed at the dawn of the sixth year of the war. The *Ostwall* was a pale imitation of the Atlantic Wall and *Westwall*. By the summer of 1944 insufficient concrete and steel was available to build solid or continuous lines of defence in the east. Moreover, the transportation network was retarded by the impact of air attack and beset by the shortage of fuel. There was a dearth of fit manpower to build and man positions and a lack of weaponry and material to fortify them. However, the achievements of the diggers in the eastern provinces were lauded across Germany and provided rare crumbs of comfort against a backdrop of disastrous military developments. The western German press highlighted East Prussians 'armed with spades and picks, going to build a wall' to galvanise their own labour force to undertake similar work in an effort to halt the Anglo-American advance. The example of East Prussia 'proved to the enemy that he will not find a war-weary and desperate nation but a fighting community determined to make the utmost effort and willing to defend its soil with the last drop of blood'.[211]

From another standpoint, the mobilisation for excavation work can be viewed as a means of social control.[212] Nazi leaders were mindful of the precedent of November 1918. The increasing burdens heaped on Germans on the Home Front such as a 60-hour working week, air raid protection duties, Party-led digging and *Volkssturm* service further stifled the opportunity for dissent against a regime already buttressed by a pervasive secret police system with a wide body of informants. The building of the *Ostwall* does, however, illustrate the supremacy of the Party at the end of the Third Reich. The *Wehrmacht* wanted defensive positions but the Party hijacked their construction. It was not an especially difficult manoeuvre. The *Wehrmacht* was now employed operationally on German soil and subjected to the whims and machinations of antagonistic RVKs, backed because of their sound Nazi credentials by Hitler. The Party leaders, empowered to utilise any means to protect their domains, did not appreciate the retreating *Wehrmacht* trespassing on their patch. Their initiation and direction of fortification building served a number of purposes. Ostensibly, it exemplified the assistance provided by the Party to the *Wehrmacht* and illustrated the unity of purpose between *Front und Heimat*. In reality, it curtailed the army's freedom of action and illustrated the powerlessness of the *Wehrmacht* vis-à-vis the Party. Concurrently, state officials were allocated no meaningful role in the project.

Finally, and perhaps most importantly, the *Ostwall* served a propaganda function. It tapped into the goodwill of the eastern German population, their patriotism, their determination to defend their *Heimat* and their fear of Soviet Communism, carried on the bayonets of the Red Army. The building of an *Ostwall* was to inspire faith in the ability of Hitler's Party to carry out necessary and competent measures to protect the eastern territories and reinforce the idea of *Endsieg*. It was also hoped that the defences would provide a psychological boost to the front-line troops, the determination of the *Heimat*, in contrast to 1918, spurring the troops to achieve a military miracle and keep the Soviets out of East Prussia. Nevertheless, the sudden conscription of a sizeable proportion of the civilian population aroused unease and rumour. This hurriedly announced building programme could be viewed as a responsible precautionary measure but it also indicated the gravity of the military situation. The construction of rear defences hundreds of kilometres behind the frontline signified that the East Prussian and Vistula fronts would not be held. Moreover, public faith in fortifications had been damaged by the experience of the Atlantic Wall. Millions of tonnes of concrete and steel and millions of man-hours had been poured into this enterprise but to no avail. Sceptics pointed to newsreel footage which illustrated the technology of war. Both diggers and observers wondered how puny trenches could halt massed Red Army tank formations.

This grim foreboding was compounded by the reality faced at the construction sites. The Party rejoiced in its ability to mobilise the population overnight and stressed the advantages of improvisation and will over staid, bureaucratic practices. However, hasty call-ups simply disrupted all branches of economic life and resulted in initial periods of enforced idleness. The Party's organisational ineptitude was ruthlessly exposed. At the sites, the headstrong behaviour of Party figures contributed to a transformation in the mood of what was initially, by and large, an enthusiastic workforce. Dismay arose from the lack of planning, inadequate supervision and the Party's refusal to liaise productively with competent military personnel. Many labourers should not have been called up. The absence of medical checks at registration resulted in patently unfit citizens being sent to do long hours of arduous work. Subsequent injuries and illnesses were predictable. The lack of suitable accommodation and the insecurity arising from indefinite digging periods worsened matters. The desire to return home as the weather deteriorated was apparent. Any brief period of enthusiasm soon evaporated when the everyday drudgery of primitive entrenchment work was faced. The *Ostwall* was a significant development during the final phase of Nazi rule in eastern Germany and a largely negative experience for those involved, months before the fortifications were swept aside by the Red Army.

CHAPTER 6

Confronting Catastrophe: The October Invasion of East Prussia and the Launch of the Volkssturm

Between the late summer of 1944 and mid-January 1945 the German political leadership, military hierarchy and ordinary citizens awaited the resumption of the Soviet offensive. Officially, the regime stuck rigidly to the *Endsieg* motif. To buttress spirits commentators declared that German forces deployed on the shortened Eastern Front had never been stronger and maintained that the Bolsheviks would never set foot on German soil. Both of these claims were soon exposed as false. During October 1944 the Red Army made its first unsuccessful attempt to envelop East Prussia. This assault led to instances of last-minute evacuation and German civilians falling for the first time into the clutches of the Red Army. Following this battle, German propagandists attempted to exploit the short lived military success and highlighted Russian atrocities as a foretaste of a Soviet occupation of Europe.

'The Russians Haven't Far to Go'

Panic had gripped eastern German communities in early August. *Gauleiter* Greiser forbade the evacuation of Germans from Litzmannstadt as anxiety spread following the Red Army's advance to the Vistula and the outbreak of the Warsaw Rising. Greiser attempted to reassure Germans by visiting the city and proclaiming that 'The events in Warsaw of which we have heard will not take place in the Wartheland. This should be understood, especially by certain Poles'.[1] Panic evacuation was also reported from Silesia. In Lower Silesia there was a surge in demand for furniture vans.[2] A neutral observer noted that Germans feared 'that the Russian breakthrough, particularly to Upper Silesia, was only a question of weeks'.[3]

Letters which were written by eastern Germans and came into the hands of the

British Political Warfare Executive show that even in the summer of 1944 suicide was already considered as an option to any form of existence under Soviet rule. An old woman writing from Insterburg heard the Red Army's guns in the distance and feared that 'we old people will be dispersed in all directions or suffer an odious death. . . . All listen and whisper "What now?" Father asked what I shall do when we are torn apart . . . [He said] we have still time to take our lives, but that I would not do. God gave us our lives and let Him take them.'[4] In Breslau in mid-July, another woman took a different viewpoint: 'The Russians haven't far to go now to the German frontier. If it gets very bad, there will be nothing left for us but the gas tap. We won't let ourselves be deported [to Russia]. Many are of my opinion.'[5]

As Germany entered a sixth year of war the Propaganda Ministry made every effort to encourage desperate German resistance. Werner Naumann, State Secretary in the Propaganda Ministry, made the Party's position clear to Germans in a speech at Danzig on 1 September 1944, the fifth anniversary of the outbreak of the war which had led to the city's return to the Reich. He insisted that there would be no repeat of November 1918 as 'There is no one in the homeland who fails us and no one at the Front who harbours any thought of defeat.'[6] The war was not lost even if the enemy crossed the Reich's frontier as history showed that decisive battles had been fought and won on German soil – Teutoburger Wald, Liegnitz and more latterly Tannenberg – were worthy examples of this happy phenomenon.[7] The Third Reich would not succumb in the closing months of 1944 but instead was systematically throttled by cautious foes with overwhelming forces at their disposal. The pressure was soon exerted again on the East Prussian front.

The Soviet Invasion of East Prussia, October 1944

The Soviet summer offensive was halted just short of the East Prussian frontier.[8] A temporary lull in the fighting ensued. Soviet aircraft attacked border towns, railway installations, trains and military columns but, considering the proximity of the front, enemy air activity was limited,[9] leading to a false sense of security in the province. Colonel Mendrzyk, Quartermaster of the Third Panzer Army, recalled that most Party and state officials still believed that the Soviet threat was temporary and would be countered when the long-anticipated new revenge weapons were deployed.[10] During this period many of those hastily evacuated under the thunder of Red Army guns from Memel and Ebenrode at the beginning of August returned to their homes. The Chief of Staff of the Third Panzer Army, Major General Burkhart Müller-Hillebrand, stood by the road bridge over the River Memel at Tilsit on 6 September and watched evacuated Memellanders streaming home. He was astonished that the question of evacuation was the affair of the RVK and that Koch had approved the return of the evacuees.[11] Men were sent back to the Memelland by the authorities to salvage the harvest. Women and children returned voluntarily, as did some Memel towndwellers. The rye and potato crops were harvested. Occasionally people commented that they would have to leave again, but hoped to be able to return for the spring sowing.[12]

During September the rural economy returned to normality. People seemingly forgot the danger on their doorstep and grew accustomed to nearby artillery duels.[13] The *Wehrmacht* did not share this confidence. One official recalled an officer advising him that the army deemed the Memelland an evacuation area and civilians should be ready to leave their homes within hours.[14] Further south, a similar scenario arose in Ebenrode district. Following the stabilisation of the front, many inhabitants concluded that there was no immediate danger. Some returned, but left their belongings in their evacuation district. Women with families said that they did not want to be parted from their husbands who were digging defences.[15]

The judicial authorities in Königsberg observed that evacuees returned when the situation calmed down and noted that 'even evacuees from other parts of the Reich had not complied with the evacuation request, preferring to remain in East Prussia.' Their trust in the strength of the Eastern Front was deemed praiseworthy as the frontier population had witnessed distressing scenes of *Wehrmacht* indiscipline during the summer.[16] However, the East Prussian population was living behind a dam which was not strong enough to halt the 'Red Flood' growing from day to day and hour to hour.[17] Only the military leadership and a handful of local officials appreciated the danger and their attempts to undertake responsible evacuation measures were frustrated by Koch.

Koch was determined to ensure that although the *Wehrmacht* had retreated into East Prussia they would not become 'masters of the house'. He insisted that civilians could only be evacuated from a narrow strip of land ten kilometres behind the German front line and ordered local officials to remain in this area. Major General Erich Dethleffsen, Chief of Staff of the Fourth Army, asserted that Koch's actions put the military under great strain, hampering activity by ensuring that the army did not have sole authority in the battle area.[18] The long-running dispute over the evacuation of non-combatants was a major bone of contention. The *Wehrmacht* leadership argued for the removal of civilians from areas adjacent to the fighting and not solely from the slim band of territory behind the front. Previous experience had demonstrated the rapid speed of advancing Soviet mechanised formations. Late evacuation from the likely scene of fighting would lead to an 'extraordinary difficult situation for the civilian population', causing refugee columns to block the roads and impede *Wehrmacht* operations.[19]

Senior military figures expected a swift resumption of Red Army offensive operations. Müller-Hillebrand recalled that it was accepted that the Germans would once again confront considerable enemy superiority.[20] General Friedrich Hoßbach, commander of the Fourth Army, later asserted that the leaders of Army Group Centre and its three component armies realised that the assault would recommence when the Red Army overcame its state of exhaustion and replenished its formations by constructing efficient supply lines through devastated Belorussia.[21] Furthermore, Hoßbach had grave reservations about the immobility and inexperience of his newly acquired *Volksgrenadier* divisions. He was even more scathing about so-called security divisions made up from aged men and totally lacking in artillery and modern weapons. Only his police formations had less fighting value. Hoßbach concluded that the Fourth Army had insufficient forces to cover its broad front even during the lull in operations. Therefore, his command could only view with anxiety the absence of reserves for the forthcoming decisive struggle for East Prussia.[22] During August, Hoßbach requested the immediate evacuation of the districts east of the Masurian Lakes. Koch, however, interpreted this as a sign of 'defeatism' and vetoed the proposal.[23] Dethleffsen recounted that, 'the *Reichsverteidigungskommissar* repeatedly rejected evacuation from the eastern part of the province with the remark that every evacuation would weaken the morale of the civilian population and also that of the troops.'[24]

Koch refused to accept evacuation because this contradicted the regime's promise of final victory. Among the indigenous population only non-combatants from the frontier towns were allowed to leave. This was explained under the guise of air raid protection measures. Evacuees were initially sent to reception districts elsewhere in the province. Dr Wander, the then *Bürgermeister* of Insterburg, recalled commencing evacuation planning in early August. However, the Königsberg authorities were more concerned with removing valuable industrial machinery from the Insterburg area in case of a possible Red Army breakthrough. They based their proposals on a possible incursion which they claimed would be swiftly eliminated. The *Oberpräsidium* forwarded around 150 strictly secret letters to Insterburg which were stored in a strongbox and were only to be passed to leading local firms when the code word *'Zitronenfalter'* was activated. These letters were never distributed. Dr Wander considered the proposals unworkable in view of the paucity of transportation and the likely lack of time.[25] He also remembered that:

> Any preparation for evacuation in the case of the immediate approach of the enemy was forbidden. Such attempts were designated "defeatist" and threatened with proceedings before the Special Court . . . Preparations for the departure of the population on the approach of the enemy were neither permitted nor affected. The *Gauleiter* continually declared that not only the *Wehrmacht* but above all, from now on, all groups of men would dig their claws into their home soil and no enemy would be able to force their way further into the province.[26]

However, on 5 October the Red Army attacked the thinly manned lines of the Third Panzer Army covering Memelland.[27] By 10 October Soviet forces had reached the Baltic north and south of Memel. The town was surrounded, but the garrison, comprising the remnants of three divisions, withstood air and artillery attack until their withdrawal was finally sanctioned on 28 January 1945. Concurrently, Army Group North was cut off from East Prussia and withdrew into the Courland peninsula of northern Latvia.[28] By 10 October, the Red Army also stood along the northern side of the River Memel. The rapid Red Army advance produced harrowing scenes. Guy Sajer, an Alsatian serving in the *Großdeutschland* division, which eventually fell back on Memel, later outlined his impressions:

> [The rural inhabitants] had still been living a more or less normal life until four or five days earlier, although they had realised that their danger might become imminent at any time. Now, for the last two days, old men, women and children had been desperately digging out the trenches, gun pits and anti-tank ditches which were to stop the waves of enemy tanks. [A] pathetic and heroic effort before the infernal débâcle which would sweep them into the flux of terrorised civilians.[29]

The hopes of the returning Memellanders had been cruelly betrayed. Now they were forced to leave their farms forever. The Party authorities exacerbated their distress by issuing evacuation orders too late. This became a common feature throughout eastern Germany over the following months. The leadership of the Third Panzer Army realised that a Soviet breakthrough could not be prevented by 6 October and recommended that Koch order the immediate evacuation of the Memelland. However, Müller-Hillebrand was enraged when he saw the population peacefully working on the land when he flew over the region the next day.[30]

Radio announcements ordered all women to leave the town of Memel on 7 October. Civilian officials exempted from service in the *Volkssturm*, the new Home Guard discussed later in this chapter, were allowed to accompany them. Escape was possible by boat over the Kurische Haff, a salt water lagoon, or by foot or cart along the Kurische Nehrung, the narrow strip of land joining Memel to the Samland peninsula west of Königsberg.[31] In the days that followed, the remaining men were gathered together and, wearing their Sunday best, were allocated weapons, put onto lorries and thrown against the Red Army. Unsurprisingly, the Memel *Volkssturm* suffered considerable losses.[32] The cutting of the Memel–Heydekrug–Tilsit road following the Red Army's capture of Heydekrug on 10 October had deadly consequences for the rural population, already flung into disorderly flight at short notice. Contemporary estimates indicated that 3,000 inhabitants stayed behind in Heydekrug, 8–10,000 cattle were lost and the entire harvest fell into enemy hands.[33] Refugees were relocated throughout East Prussia. Some settled with their surviving livestock in the Elchniederung, Labiau and Samland districts, only to be forced to flee again in January. Town dwellers were sent initially to Osterode district then later re-evacuated to Saxony or Pomerania during November.[34] One former Memel official later wrote that, 'the losses of the Memelland civilian population were undoubtedly enormous.'[35] Tanks rolled over the refugee columns and crushed carts, horses and people. Germans were murdered, women raped and possessions plundered. Some abandoned their carts, horses and livestock and fled to the coast east of Heydekrug to be rescued by small boats which ferried them across the Kurisches Haff. Some 30,000 people, almost one-third of the population, fell into Soviet hands. Many had mistakenly stayed behind expecting a repeat of August's false alarm.[36]

The major Soviet assault was launched by the Third Belorussian Front between Sudauen and the River Memel on 16 October. The accompanying heavy air raid on Gumbinnen compounded the effect of the attack. Soviet artillery and armoured units pierced German defences and advanced across the frontier. German reports highlighted the vast material superiority enjoyed by the enemy and the huge volume of firepower assembled for the assault on East Prussia: 'Even seasoned campaigners, who have been through a great deal, searched their memory for a similar massing of strength . . . Never had the enemy employed aircraft in such numbers.'[37] The losses suffered by the First East Prussian Infantry Division during the first day of fighting were their heaviest ever. Despite determined resistance, Eydtkau, Goldap and Ebenrode were given up. After reaching the outskirts of Gumbinnen and crossing the River Angerapp, the offensive lost impetus and the arrival of Panzer reinforcements led to the recovery of some territory. Goldap was retaken on 5 November, but the Red Army had established a foothold on German soil by occupying a sizeable slice of East Prussia. Schirwindt, Eydtkau, Ebenrode, Trakehnen and the Rominten Heide were lost. Tilsit and Gumbinnen, already reduced to ruins, were within Russian artillery range.

Despite the psychological shock of Soviet forces penetrating East Prussia the German media soon proclaimed the campaign as a defensive success. Nevertheless, propaganda reports had already indicated that the deterioration of the German position in the Baltic had provoked anxiety back in Königsberg. It was feared that this would lead to easier operating conditions for the Soviet Baltic Fleet and expose the coastline to invasion. Apparently, elsewhere in the Reich wide circles of the population still thought that the forces protecting East Prussia and the Warthegau would be able to drive back the Bolsheviks. However, this optimism was tempered in eastern regions. Eastern Germans hoped that the border would be defended, but considered that the possibility of further evacuation from frontier districts might arise. This impression arose from the leaking of directives concerning the removal of supplies and an alleged instruction by the *Wehrmacht* to give no more armaments' orders to East Prussian firms. Moreover, officers suggested that there was neither the time nor the means to implement punctual evacuation.[38] The commencement of the Soviet offensives in the Baltic and against East Prussia, the subsequent loss of territory and the isolation of Army Group North produced dismay. This expressly contradicted a promise recently made in an address by Koch that land would no longer be given up. While the powers of resistance exhibited by German troops convinced many *Volksgenossen* that a deep breakthrough would be thwarted, others remembered Hitler stressing in 1941, in his justification for *Barbarossa*, that invading Red Army motorised units would be very difficult to stop on the good East Prussian roads.[39]

The Germans conceded that the Red Army had advanced into East Prussia and revealed that a tank group had reached the vicinity of Angerapp.[40] These admissions and upbeat Soviet communiqués, which admittedly also mentioned fierce German resistance and staggered defences, led some British newspapers to speculate that the evacuation of Königsberg had begun.[41] Meanwhile, Goebbels was outraged to observe a 'serious psychological mistake' in the *Wehrmacht* report when the phrase 'breaking-off movement' was used in connection with the East Prussian fighting. He contended that 'the East Prussian population are extraordinarily indignant over this'. Such terms were not to be used to describe actions on German soil.[42]

National and provincial newspapers underlined the vast forces invested by the enemy in this operation, but equally stressed their immense losses. Analogies were drawn with 1914 to lift spirits. Reports repeatedly highlighted the fanaticism displayed by German defenders and cited examples of individual heroism and the valour of small battle groups in their determination to drive the enemy out of the province. On 28 October, the *Völkischer Beobachter* claimed that a turnaround in military fortunes had occurred and reported that Red Army Guards' formations had been encircled and destroyed: 'Standing motionless on the battlefield south of Gumbinnen are dozens of enemy tanks, including many "Josef Stalins" and T34s, shot to pieces. Hundreds of dead Bolsheviks also lie there.' A Red Army bridgehead over the river Angerapp at Nemmersdorf was smashed, the enemy had been conclusively thrown back and the initiative was regained. The reporter mentioned that in 1914 a similarly decisive German attack had been launched in this sector.[43] The sight of burning German towns and farms had, it seemed, produced similar fire in the hearts of German soldiers. A Grenadier apparently claimed that the enemy did not want Russian troops to make comparisons between the 'miserable huts in the "Soviet Paradise" and our beautiful, clean villages'. The Russians wanted to 'exterminate, destroy, level-out, proletarianise and wipe out all Germans'. The spirit of the defenders, even those of a weaker disposition, was said to have increased three-fold because they were now protecting the *Heimat*, German villages and German civilians.[44]

In Königsberg, the *Preußische Zeitung* and *Königsberger Allgemeine Zeitung* admitted that bitter frontier fighting was taking place, but attempted to bolster the resolve of readers by pointing out parallels with events 30 years earlier. The military correspondent of the *Preußische Zeitung* acknowledged that Soviet forces were stronger than their Tsarist predecessors, but insisted that the numbers of tanks knocked out meant that within five days two full strength Red Army tank corps had melted away. German forces were also said to be stronger than in 1914, being boosted by newly formed *Volksgrenadier* divisions and the thick frontier defences. Furthermore, the province's woods, lakes, rivers and swamps provided natural defensive terrain. Reassuringly, the Soviets still stood to the east of these natural barriers and an awareness of the precedent of 1914 fortified the defenders.[45] Although German forces had been 'pushed back a few kilometres', the defensive front remained unbroken and Soviet losses were huge.[46] The German soldier knew that 'he was fighting for the fate of his homeland'.[47] On 30 October, the press advised that the Soviets had lost four-fifths of their attacking forces and were reduced to comparatively localised thrusts as 'our troops, fighting at the height of their fanaticism on home soil, have for the moment won the upper hand over the Bolshevik human and material masses.'[48] Newspapers reported that prisoners disclosed Moscow's plan for a rapid breakthrough which would have opened up East Prussia as far as the Vistula and brought about the collapse of the Eastern Front. Instead, the Soviets had made minimal advances and hundreds of their tanks and thousands of their dead littered the battlefield.[49]

After a three-day battle the Germans recaptured Goldap. The town was reduced to ruins as cellars were converted into bunkers and houses served as small fortresses. The interiors of houses presented a desolate sight and the German reports stated that Red Army plundering could be explained by avarice. This arose from the humiliation of seeing products emanating from a higher culture that Soviet citizens would never be allowed to enjoy. In the evenings lorries had rolled east filled with furniture, pianos, crystal, porcelain, foodstuffs and alcohol. Prisoners reported that these items were distributed among senior Soviet officers.[50] One local *Volkssturmmann* later recalled the scene in front of the smoking local government offices. Destroyed Russian weaponry, plunder, dead horses and disfigured Russian corpses produced a dreadful picture.[51] Major Dieckert, battalion commander in the town prior to the war, remarked that new building after 1918 had left Goldap looking tidy and clean. Now churches were burnt out, the town centre resembled a rubbish heap and the various barracks were wrecked. Dieckert's own home lay in rubble and he left the town with sadness.[52] The battlefront now settled along the eastern fringe of and shells continued to fall on the town.

Activity on the East Prussian front remained limited until 13 January 1945. The Red Army occupied an area 100 miles broad and 25 miles deep.[53] However, Dieckert later contended that, 'in spite of the breakthrough in the East Prussian frontier districts, all in all this was still a defensive success.'[54] Nazi propagandists endorsed this viewpoint. They highlighted reports in *The Times* and communiqués issued by the Soviet news agency Tass describing the frenzied resistance offered by the German defenders.[55] General Chernyakhovsky, the commander of the Third Belorussian Front, explained that the Germans had prevented a breakthrough by deploying vast numbers of tanks and mobile artillery, and above all by exploiting the cover provided by countless well-camouflaged defensive lines. Moscow sources also apparently remarked that the Germans converted every village and crossroads into a bastion, replete with concrete bunkers and wide minefields.[56] Privately, Goebbels noted that for the first time the Soviets admitted that German troops had displayed furious resistance.[57] He also observed with satisfaction the depressing effect of the German successes at Arnhem, Warsaw and in East Prussia on British politicians and the 'war weary' English population.[58] Indeed, as late as the beginning of 1945, German leaders still harboured hopes of a possible breakdown of the Allied coalition and figures such as Goebbels called for Ribbentrop's dismissal because of his failure to engineer such a split.

The military leadership was also encouraged to emphasise this significant defensive success. Colonel General Reinhardt, interviewed by Günther Heysing of the *Völkischer Beobachter*, outlined the build up of Soviet armies south of East Prussia and the danger of an attack towards Danzig. Reinhardt also stressed their clear intention to advance on Königsberg, but observed that the tenacity exhibited by his officers and men had prevented the Soviets from occupying the city.[59] Similarly, the NSFO for the Fourth Army produced a propaganda pamphlet entitled *The Border Battle for East Prussia, 1944*. This consisted of accounts by war reporters, extracts from *Wehrmacht* reports, German and overseas newspapers, congratulatory messages sent to Hoßbach and details of Soviet losses. Colonel General Gotthard Heinrici, a native of Gumbinnen and former Fourth Army commander, told Hoßbach that 'the whole world watched the battle on East Prussia's border with suspense.' Colonel General Walter Weiss, commander of the neighbouring Second Army, praised Hoßbach for the 'outstanding military success of your brave Fourth Army'. The sheer scale of enemy forces was also stressed. The Soviets had reportedly committed five armies with between 37 and 40 divisions and around 1,500 tanks to this offensive. However, the heavily outnumbered Fourth Army, strengthened by the Hermann Göring Panzer Corps and the Fifth Panzer Division, claimed to have destroyed two-thirds of them. Interestingly, the relatively low number of captives, less than 1,200, convinced Hitler that the Red Army relied on its artillery strength to compensate for hugely understrength divisions.[60] Perhaps this development fuelled thoughts that the long-awaited Soviet manpower shortage really was developing and partially explains Hitler's subsequent decisions to denude the East Prussian and Vistula sectors of highly regarded units during the following months.

Significantly, German propagandists did not claim that the battle for East Prussia was over. As in the summer, they emphasised that German counter measures had proved successful. Nevertheless, anxiety at the occupation of German territory, the chaotic attempt to enact full-scale evacuation in the midst of battle and the discovery of Soviet atrocities outweighed any comfort arising from the temporary stemming of the Red tide.

Time to Leave

Various plans for the evacuation of East Prussia had been prepared before and during the war. Pre-war measures were influenced by the experience of 1914 and concentrated on moving men of military age and important economic goods from the border districts to the province's interior. However, the feared Polish incursion into Neidenburg and Ortelsburg never materialised.[61] Similar plans involving evacuation zones were drawn up by the Königsberg civil authorities in conjunction with the military and *Reichsbahn* in October 1943. Routes for civilian treks were established to avoid collisions with the *Wehrmacht*. These plans went out of the window as the withdrawal from the Ukraine and the return of Koch and his subordinate, Paul Dargel, ensured that evacuation decisions would henceforth be a strictly Party matter.[62]

The then *Regierungspräsident* in Königsberg, Paul Hoffmann, recalled that exact evacuation plans had been prepared prior to the summer of 1944. However, Koch and Dargel argued that it would be impossible to issue such detailed plans and expect the contents to remain secret within the ranks of leading Party and state officials. They feared that evacuation measures would provoke panic throughout Germany and start an uncontrollable exodus from East Prussia. They hoped that the Red Army would be halted on the frontier or soon thereafter and argued that it would be unwise to order evacuation from unaffected areas. The original plan was deposited in a safe. Improvised evacuations of the areas adjacent to the front were initiated instead but these took no account of the speed of modern motorised warfare.[63]

Evacuation was only to commence by order of the *Kreisleiter* with Dargel's approval. Only a few officials such as Dr Rhode, *Regierungspräsident* of Gumbinnen, and Dr Wander in Insterburg succeeded in circumventing these procedures. Frequently, the issuing of evacuation orders and the arrival of the Red Army were virtually simultaneous. Orderly evacuation was thus impossible and panic spread. In the midst of this confusion, hastily assembled treks from the districts of Treuburg, Goldap, Angerapp, Gumbinnen, Schloßberg and Ebenrode set off in mid-October 1944 in a westerly direction. A district Propaganda Leader in *Gau* Danzig-West Prussia detailed the complaints made by refugees from Gumbinnen reaching his province. Only one train had been commandeered to evacuate civilians from the district and no allowance had been made for people taking minimal hand baggage with them. 'Catastrophic conditions' were experienced on the journey. Civilians were left to facilitate their own departure and often had to leave all their belongings behind. Their agony was further compounded shortly before the Red Army's breakthrough when the *Wehrmacht* requisitioned all the best horses.[64] *Gauleiter* Albert Forster of Danzig-West Prussia was furious. For weeks he had proposed the evacuation of the East Prussian frontier districts and housing the inhabitants in his *Gau*. Koch had categorically rejected this idea. Forster was now faced with a sudden influx and had the greatest difficulty in finding the most basic accommodation for them.[65] He condemned the attitude of the East Prussian Party authorities but Dargel, acting for Koch, said his province would never be evacuated and retorted that instead Danzigers would flee into East Prussia. Forster criticised the disorganisation in East Prussia and demanded that Koch be held responsible. The refugees had received no assistance from the authorities. Some had only heard about the Soviet threat from retreating German troops. Bereft of possessions the refugees arrived in the early winter without heavy coats or shoes. The Danzig authorities noted that: 'They make extraordinarily disparaging remarks over the crass differences between the statements of *Gauleiter* Koch in the press and on the radio, and the actual situation.'[66]

In Goldap the ringing of church bells and bugle calls signalled the beginning of the evacuation.[67] Elsewhere no warnings were given and the Red Army announced its arrival with shellfire. Disputes flared up between Königsberg and the local authorities. *Landrat* Paul Uschdraweit of Angerapp recalled being advised of the sighting of Soviet tanks. In line with recent directives he sought the approval of Deputy *Kreisleiter* Kaiser to initiate evacuation proceedings. Kaiser explained that Koch had given the sharpest orders against such unauthorised behaviour. Uschdraweit, upon hearing further alarming reports concerning the proximity of Soviet forces, authorised evacuation in the most threatened locality. When Uschdraweit called for more extensive measures on account of the lack of German defenders, Kaiser concurred. In a subsequent telephone conversation overheard by Uschdraweit, Dargel condemned Kaiser's actions. Kaiser explained that east of the river Angerapp there was already complete disintegration and that all roads were 'hopelessly blocked'. Angerapp was undefended and the Red Army was no more than four kilometres away. Dargel insisted that he had received no news of this breakthrough and commented that the Angerapp authorities had gone crazy with fear. He ordered that the people be chased back and a few shot. To deter the Soviets, Dargel recommended that women boil water and throw this from windows over the Red Army and he warned Kaiser that it was his responsibility to stop this unauthorised flight. Eventually it seems that the intervention of the local SD led Himmler to give the order for evacuation.[68]

The Party authorities were responsible for providing food and accommodation for the refugees through the NSV. Nevertheless, *Landrat* Uschdraweit asserted that state officials carried out the entire evacuation. Heated clashes arose with the Party over the use of scarce lorries to evacuate civilians stranded by the roadsides. In Angerapp the *Ostwall* authorities wanted vehicles to salvage their extensive alcohol stores.[69] In contrast, a senior official in Gerdauen remarked that the accommodation of 20,000 evacuees from Gumbinnen, often in quarters previously occupied by Berliners, and their onward movement to Osterode district in late November proceeded smoothly. This testimony also contradicts David Irving's observation that refugees streamed past the *Wolfsschanze*. Instead, they were diverted through Gerdauen along narrow streets, through fields and over hills. This was to avoid blocking the roads next to headquarters and was implemented ostensibly at the *Wehrmacht*'s behest. Further suffering arose from this diversion, although warm food and hot drinks were provided by field kitchens to passing treks.[70]

Reports submitted by one SS officer, a Dr Stahl, whose Alt-Wüsterwitz estate south of Gumbinnen had been occupied by the Red Army for three days in October, outlined the scale of material losses and the difficulties encountered during evacuation. Most of his farm buildings and cottages had been burnt out and much of his grain was lost. The local farmers' leader had pressed for the evacuation of valuable commodities, but this was repeatedly rejected by the *Kreisleiter* as unnecessary. Goods, possessions and livestock fell into Soviet hands as farmers could only take along the horses pulling their carts. Stahl contended that the rural population was critical of the lack of planning and the absence of able leadership. They asserted that the Party should have been guided by the precedent of 1914 and lamented the loss of irreplaceable breeding animals. Stahl agreed with the Ministry of Food and Agriculture that there was a 'Koch problem'.[71]

Half measures such as moving inhabitants from one part of a district to another were justified by the authorities as a way of demonstrating of the temporary nature of evacuation.[72] Moreover, fear of the Red Army only heightened when the population learnt from passing treks and troops about atrocities in Nemmersdorf, Großwaltersdorf and Goldap.[73] Letters from the front testified to the ferocity of the autumn fighting and the suffering of the civilian population. By this stage in the war, months of continuous retreat had weakened the belief in final victory among officers and men. Few, however, envisaged the totality of the approaching collapse. The miserable columns of refugees, shattered villages and untended cattle all had a profound effect on *Wehrmacht* personnel. One NCO wrote bleakly on the retreat of his flak artillery unit into East Prussia and the misery of the local inhabitants forced into panic flight. He could only hope that the entire war would soon end.[74]

During November a great migration was finally sanctioned in East Prussia. Noncombatants, inhabiting a belt of territory 30 kilometres behind the front, were now evacuated. Around 600,000 people, roughly one-quarter of the province's population, were moved. Whilst rural inhabitants and their livestock tended to be relocated to the interior and western districts of East Prussia, town dwellers, the elderly, the sick and women with small children were sent to Saxony, Thuringia and Pomerania.[75] RPA Maertins made a report to Berlin asserting that inhabitants from the threatened districts had been evacuated to reception areas by rail or in treks under NSV supervision. The towns of Memel, Heydekrug and Tilsit, their rural environs and the districts of Elchniederung, Schloßberg, Ebenrode, Gumbinnen, Angerapp and Goldap had been cleared of civilians. Partial measures were initiated in Treuburg while a 'loosening-up' of economic activity commenced in Lyck, Angerburg, Insterburg and Gerdauen districts. Only a fraction of the population in the Lötzen fortified district was moved. The evacuation of the rural population was co-ordinated by the Party's Farmers' Association which arranged overnight quarters and fodder for the cattle of those *en route* to the west of the province. Meanwhile, the NSV assumed responsibility for the provisioning of evacuated town dwellers at intermediate railway stations. Maertins insisted that the evacuation was orderly and proceeded without panic.[76] Despite the strain on the population, many were said to be optimistic that the *Wehrmacht* would reconquer the frontier districts.[77]

In reality, however, the evacuation did not proceed so smoothly. One NCO commented on the misery of witnessing civilians aimlessly struggling on the roads for weeks.[78] OLG President Dräger was similarly affected when he visited the evacuated Tilsit and Ragnit districts in mid-November. Here he reported a scene of abandoned farms, herds of untended cattle wandering the fields and stray dogs searching for food.[79] The Insterburg surgeon Count von Lehndorff recalled the 'neglected cows standing . . . hardly able to move, with dried-up udders and prominent backbones, threatening and complaining. And when the first snow fell they collapsed, silently, one after another.'[80]

An economic evacuation was initiated in order to salvage machinery, goods and foodstuffs from the evacuated and threatened districts. Reception districts were established in the west of the province as Koch insisted that valuable economic resources were not to leave East Prussia. Braunsberg and Mohrungen were the designated reception districts for Tilsit and Insterburg respectively. One business moved to Braunsberg was a clog factory owned by the *Gauleiter*'s brother. A local official later reported that Koch angrily rejected his brother's proposal to shift the business to the Rhineland. This official condemned the economic evacuation as a 'complete failure' and observed that in 1945 wagons laden with goods fell entirely into Soviet hands near Braunsberg.[81] Bakers, butchers and other small concerns were closed in Insterburg and transferred to Mohnungen. Insterburg's schools closed on 20 October and their equipment and files were moved. Large factories were partly or totally dismantled. Machinery and important parts were transferred into the interior. Relocation was a tiring exercise. Gymnastics halls, garages and barns were requisitioned, but accommodation in these small communities remained insufficient and new building was duly authorised. Due to lack of time and material this process was still incomplete when the Red Army overran the province.[82]

Despite evacuation measures and the regime's emphasis on Soviet atrocities, civilians still returned to threatened areas during the lull in the fighting. Police resources were not available to deter women with children returning to Angerapp. It was later claimed by *Landrat* von Wuthenau that some made ten journeys from western and central Germany to collect possessions.[83] *Bürgermeister* Dr Wander believed that some Insterburgers had to be evacuated on three occasions. Following the October incursion old people and women with children were loaded onto packed trains bound for Mohrungen and Saxony. As the front remained quiet, a few managed to return home. They were motivated by rumours concerning new weapons and the strength of the Eastern Front, distaste for life in their new quarters and a desire to access food and fuel stores from their own homes.[84] The authorities deemed these journeys to be an unnecessary burden on the railways. The constant comings and goings also created difficulties in the distribution of ration cards but despite the risk for the travellers these movements were not halted.

'Blind, Destructive Fury'

Soviet troops exploded into an orgy of revenge when they crossed the East Prussian frontier. News of these excesses spread to adjoining districts triggering panic and flight. The bodies of 65 civilians were discovered in various recaptured localities in the south of Gumbinnen district between the rivers Angerapp and Rominte. In Nemmersdorf, 26 corpses were found and 20 bodies from an intercepted refugee trek were discovered on the outskirts of the village. A further 15 charred bodies of civilians were found at Dr Stahl's aforementioned estate of Alt-Wüsterwitz, ten kilometres south of Gumbinnen. The third major discovery was made in Goldap where the *Wehrmacht* found ten bodies. These comprised of six civilians, three of whom were senior Nazi officials, including the deputy *Kreisleiter* of Insterburg, and four *Wehrmacht* prisoners.[85]

The events in Nemmersdorf became a byword for Soviet atrocities. The Red Army occupied the village for less than 48 hours (20–22 October), but left behind them the bodies of victims ranging from babies to octogenarians.[86] Evidence of these atrocities was used by the defence at Nuremberg and at post-war tribunals set up under the auspices of the Western Powers. The victims had perished by various brutal means. General Werner Kreipe, the *Luftwaffe* Chief of Staff, visited the Hermann Göring Panzer Corps fighting in Gumbinnen. In Nemmersdorf, on 23 October, he observed the bodies of women and children who had been shot and crucified on barn doors. Kreipe ordered that photographs be taken as evidence.[87] An officer, Dr Heinrich Amberger, later recalled that an entire trek of refugees had been crushed by Russian tanks. Women and children had been squashed flat, and Amberger also discovered the bodies of murdered civilians on roadsides and in farmyards. Some had been shot at close range while others had been battered to death with shovels and rifle butts. Amberger maintained that he saw no surviving German civilians in the recaptured territory.[88] Karl Potrek, a Königsberg civilian drafted into the *Volkssturm* and sent to Nemmersdorf, substantiated this claim. He observed a number of hideous sights. A naked woman was found crucified on a barn door. Some victims had been shot in the back of the neck, but most perished more brutally. Babies had their heads smashed in and the corpse of an 84-year-old woman was found minus half her head, which had been sliced off by an axe or a spade.[89]

German officers maintained that these were the most harrowing sights they had ever witnessed. Captain Emil Herminghaus reported that the frightful scenes showed the German people what awaited them should they fall into Soviet hands. The women-folk of Nemmersdorf, including several nuns, had been herded together then raped and abused prior to being killed.[90] Similar sentiments were later expressed by Dethleffsen whose army had recaptured the affected areas. He recounted that the last minute nature of evacuation had given civilians scarcely half an hour to gather together their most valuable possessions. He alleged that many hundreds of Germans perished and that the Russians had shot 50 French POWs. Dethleffsen blamed Koch for these deaths as he had ignored numerous evacuation requests from the military.[91] In turn Koch attempted to reassure his own frightened female staff after Nemmersdorf with the promise, 'That's as far as they'll be allowed to get. We can stop them here.'[92]

German propagandists exploited the rape and brutal murder of German civilians. The Reich Press authorities ordered newspapers to emphasise that Bolshevik terror was not directed solely at major landowners and industrialists but against ordinary Germans. Indeed, the Bolsheviks were said to be intent on massacring every single German and transforming the country into one huge graveyard.[93] The atrocities were reported in gruesome detail with graphic pictures of the murdered civilians appearing in newsreels and newspapers. The newsreel commentator proclaimed that, 'no restraint is placed upon Bolshevik soldiers and this has resulted once again in women being raped, old men beaten to death and children murdered. The whole countryside is ravaged by death.' Echoing the theme of the threat posed by rampaging Bolshevism to western European civilisation, the commentator concluded that 'this testimony of brutal bestiality may be the last warning to Europe.'[94] The German news service emphasised that 'The Bolshevik object was not merely to kill everything German, but to torture their victims beyond description.'[95] Soviet troops were said to have orders to murder all Germans and the killings were attributed to 'Jewish commissars'.[96] Rudimentary propaganda slogans were daubed on East Prussian walls promising 'revenge for Nemmersdorf'. Some of these slogans can be seen to this day on surviving buildings.[97]

The authorities rushed correspondents, academics and doctors from neutral nations and occupied territories to the scene. They were formed into an International Commission for the Investigation of Bolshevik Crimes and charged with investigating the atrocities. Buried bodies were hastily exhumed and examined. The *Völkischer Beobachter* featured the headline 'Fearful Crimes in Nemmersdorf: The Fury of the Bolshevik Beasts'. The report claimed that almost the entire population had been promptly evacuated, but a sudden Red Army tank breakthrough had led to a few villagers being taken by surprise. This detailed account described the brutalities inflicted on murdered German women and children. These atrocities finally disproved any notions that the Bolsheviks were 'not so bad' and provided an ample illustration of Soviet methods to Britain and America. Soon it was prophesised that the treacherous policies of the 'plutocracies' would rebound on them and the 'Bolshevik rabble' would pour down their roads.[98]

Nazi commentators stressed that Bolshevik behaviour in Germany was no different to their conduct elsewhere in Europe. It was 'a blessing for the people of Europe that the Bolsheviks had been flung back by German tanks in the area south of Gumbinnen'.[99] Captions accompanying a front page *Völkischer Beobachter* photograph of murdered children advised that this was a terrible warning of the consequences if German defences and fighting spirit flagged.[100] The *Preußische Zeitung* indignantly reported the Soviet slur that German troops had shot civilians and had then photographed the corpses. These accusations only demonstrated the depravity of the Soviet leadership.[101] The *Völkischer Beobachter* quoted statements by *Wehrmacht* and *Volkssturm* personnel given to the International Commission. Germans surprised by the sudden Bolshevik advance had been murdered or carried away to Siberia. One NCO reportedly remarked that although during four years of soldiering he had encountered dreadful sights on the battlefield, his experience of Nemmersdorf had affected him most deeply. Moreover, Soviet cultural vandalism was also highlighted as churches were used as billets or munitions stores and religious symbols were smashed. The International Commission had made a number of findings. Bolshevik troops had killed German civilians regardless of age or sex in localities where no resistance was offered. In almost all cases young women had been raped prior to their death and children shot at close range. In addition to gunshot wounds, stab wounds and injuries inflicted by axes and spades were observed on the bodies. Those shot had been killed by small calibre weapons 'used exclusively by officers and commissars in the Red Army'. The plundering and destruction was indiscriminate and the Commission insisted that Soviet conduct contradicted the norms of international law and outraged human decency.[102]

The Nazi press commended reports appearing in newspapers in occupied or neutral states. Journalists witnessing the 'blood bath in Nemmersdorf' had apparently become convinced of the 'gruesome murderous system of Soviet subhumanity'. A Norwegian reported the 'blind destructive fury' of the Soviets and described the bayoneting and stabbing of women and children. This writer noted that the same fate had befallen French POWs and named one victim. He also spoke to Soviet prisoners who, having been told by their own commissars of the poor conditions in Germany, had subsequently been shocked at the prosperity of the East Prussian frontier community. More credence can perhaps be given to an article in the *Geneva Courier* on 7 November. Their special correspondent wrote that prisoners had been mutilated and executed, and that the rural population had been exterminated. French POWs had been similarly treated. This experience had provided the author with an 'insight into the terrible methods of the Bolsheviks.' He had been left with an impression which 'exceeded the most vivid phantasy' and spared his readers the most dreadful details. Similarly, a Spanish journalist reported that mutilation seemed to be a Soviet sport.[103]

Evidence suggests that this intensification of 'strength through fear' propaganda did not produce the desired result. Instead, the sensational coverage transformed fear of the Red Army into outbreaks of panic. These reports, when substantiated by stories of Soviet excesses transmitted by refugees and military personnel, contributed to the high number of suicides prior to Red Army occupation in 1945.[104] Other factors weakened the effect of this propaganda campaign. The SD advised that the population considered Soviet behaviour unsurprising because of German crimes committed on enemy soil. Moreover, Nazi condemnation of the murder of a few East Prussians was viewed as ridiculous on account of the previous conduct of the Germans in Russia and the value of human life in Nazi Germany.[105]

The sections of the weekly propaganda reports on the response to the atrocities and the accompanying media coverage noted that among women the news triggered 'certain feelings of fear'. Others were more cynical and believed that the coverage was driven by propaganda considerations. Seemingly, their confidence in the press and radio had been shattered by the 'apparent failure' of the Atlantic Wall. People repeatedly asked how civilians had fallen into Soviet hands and questioned whether timely evacuation had been sanctioned by the responsible authorities. In Danzig and Stettin many inhabitants could not understand why 'unreliable' Estonians and Latvians were led back to safety in Germany, 'while our own "People's Comrades" were left to the Bolsheviks'.[106]

The Propaganda Ministry was eager to dispel widespread criticism of late evacuation. On 7 November, the Ministry issued a rebuttal to be disseminated orally by its agents. This stressed that the area immediately behind the front had obviously been evacuated. Difficulties had arisen because of a surprise breakthrough on a narrow front deep into the German rear. Moreover, the victims in Nemmersdorf were deemed to be groups of stragglers from isolated farms rather than villagers. Despite the sudden Soviet incursion, the propagandists underlined the effectiveness of Party measures such as the deployment of the *Volkssturm*. However, the significance of the East Prussian potato and turnip crops, which were mostly still in the ground, to the feeding of the Reich was also highlighted. The able bodied, including childless women workers, were required to remain as long as possible in areas behind the front to collect this harvest. The propagandists justified this decision by arguing that 'the higher necessity of personal duty to the German people had to be placed above the security of the individual. This hard but essential maxim applies today not only for soldiers at the front, but for everyone.'[107]

Maertins admitted that 'regrettably' a number of people from Memel district and the area south of Gumbinnen had been bestially murdered when their treks were surprised by sudden Soviet breakthroughs.[108] Within East Prussia a dispute over responsibility for events in Nemmersdorf erupted between the Party and state authorities. Dr Rhode in Gumbinnen had agreed with the military leadership and recommended an urgent evacuation prior to the October invasion. Dargel, however, angrily rejected Rhode's appeal for evacuation following the commencement of the attack. Rhode eventually issued appropriate orders without the consent of Königsberg. Despite these facts, Dargel attempted to place the blame for civilian losses on Rhode and to secure his removal on grounds of age. This manoeuvre was frustrated by the sudden appearance in East Prussia of Dr Stuckart, State Secretary of the Interior Ministry. Official records substantiated Rhode's version of events. Stuckart advised Himmler that Rhode was worthy of decoration rather than dismissal.[109]

On the other side, the Red Army was subjected to sustained propaganda as it entered East Prussia. Army newspapers described the province as 'The Homeland of the German Military Clique' and 'The Most Important Pillar of Hitler-Fascism'.[110] *The Times* Moscow correspondent noted that the *Red Star* newspaper predicted that every German town would share the fate of the frontier town of Schirwindt, now reduced to ruins.[111] As Soviet reinforcements flowed into East Prussia they encountered large notice boards bearing inscriptions such as 'Here accursed Germany begins' and 'You are entering the wild beast's lair'.[112] German interrogations of Soviet prisoners indicated that no restrictions had been placed on their conduct. Red Army officers advised that German civilians were 'fair game' and that women could be raped. Severe punishment was threatened for plundering in Lithuania, but in Germany officers and men were unfettered. When the civilian population appeared unfriendly to the Red Army they were to be killed. One soldier apparently asked his deputy battalion commander if he could accost German women and received the reply, 'Why not?' Another prisoner testimony described Soviet officers bringing two German women to dinner. Following the meal the women were raped and then shot. Their bodies were flung into a latrine.

On another occasion when two German men protested their Communist allegiances they were summarily shot because 'only in Russia were there proper Communists'.[113] A Red Army colonel disclosed the order given by his divisional commander:

> We are marching into East Prussia. The following rights are granted to Red Army officers and men: 1. The extermination of any Germans. 2. The plundering of property. 3. The raping of women. 4. The burning of German treasures. 5. The soldiers of the Russian Liberation [Vlasov] Army are not to be taken prisoner. Any bullet for them is wasted. They are to be killed and trampled underfoot.[114]

Another divisional commander told his troops that this was the opportunity 'to take revenge on the Germans'.[115] Similar sentiments were contained in pamphlets and army newspapers. Writers such as Ilya Ehrenburg reminded the Red Army of German atrocities, arguing that 'the Germans are not people' and repeating the slogan 'death to the Germans'.[116] A number of studies contend that the hate propaganda of Ehrenburg, sanctioned by the Soviet leadership, incited the Red Army to indulge in the most violent excesses. De Zayas has dubbed Ehrenburg 'The Soviet Julius Streicher'.[117] The front line newspapers of the Third Belorussian Front urged the Red Army finally 'to destroy the wounded German beast' and reminded the troops that the fate of thousands of their fellow countrymen who still toiled in Fascist slavery lay in their hands. The theme of personal revenge was also stressed. Hiding in Germany were the Germans who had 'murdered your children, raped your wives, fiancées and sisters, shot your mothers and fathers'. Troops were to go forward with 'indelible hate against the enemy' and advance into the 'beast's lair to punish the Fascist criminals'.[118]

One Soviet pamphlet entitled *Forwards to the Destruction of the Enemy* came into the possession of the Third Panzer Army. This described East Prussia as the 'stronghold of German Fascism' where land was divided between great estate owners and 'kulaks' (rich peasants). East Prussia's role as a bridgehead for the German 'push to the East', its numerous fortifications and thick network of railways was highlighted. The province was also condemned as the breeding ground of Fascism and the role of Koch and other East Prussian Party functionaries in the Ukraine was underlined. The large number of German generals and officers originating from the province was equally emphasised. The article also outlined German atrocities such as the systematic starvation of Red Army prisoners and the withholding of medical care from Russian wounded, sick and slave labourers. Significantly, the troops were reminded of the recent discovery of Majdanek extermination camp near Lublin. The 'hour for the settlement of accounts' was approaching and the destruction of the 'Fascist nest of snakes' in East Prussia would speed up the Soviet Union's conclusive victory.[119]

The large volume of pamphlets, newspapers and military orders encouraged the Red Army to behave in a pitiless manner when they stepped on German soil. The hour of revenge for years of merciless German occupation had arrived. The brutal treatment of German civilians, the destruction of property and the plundering of clothing, furniture and valuables was not discouraged. However, whether propaganda and orders sanctioning brutality can fully account for the murders in Memel and Gumbinnen is debatable. Red Army personnel had witnessed the scenes of sufficient German crimes.

These included extermination and concentration camps, deportations, mass graves and the sight of miserable Russian civilians and the dreadful tales they told. In the Ukraine and Belorussia the Red Army had encountered the devastation caused by German scorched earth tactics. Cities were destroyed and empty, factories and dams were dynamited and railway lines systematically ripped to shreds. The propagandists wanted the memories of German excesses to remain fresh among the men of the Red Army. They were mindful that the men were weary, fighting far from home and no longer engaged in the liberation of Russian lands. Motivation for the continuation of a brutal struggle had to be provided. Some were already primed. They had been liberated from Nazi captivity, dragged into the service of the Red Army and had their own agenda of revenge. Others knew that their families had been murdered or carried away to Germany. The Third Reich unleashed an unforgiving war of ideology against the Soviet Union. The Red Army confronted the consequences of this barbarity between the Volga and the Vistula. Soviet propagandists further inflamed the passions of the Red Army when it reached the Reich.

'People to Arms': the *Volkssturm*

On 18 October 1944, at the same time as the Red Army was crossing the East Prussian frontier, the NSDAP announced the formation of the *Volkssturm*. This Home Guard organisation ultimately became a national programme at the behest of the Party leadership with the aim of incorporating all men between the ages of 16 and 60 previously exempted from military service on account of reserved occupations or ill-health. At this critical juncture they were deemed capable of bearing arms. The *Volkssturm* was a Party army motivated by Martin Bormann's political ambitions. It has been described by the German military historian Franz Seidler as, 'a product of the power mania and rival viewpoints, a piece of absurd theatre at the end of the Second World War'[120] and by one historian of the Party as, 'the last and most naive attempt by the Nazis to create a military force controlled solely by the NSDAP'.[121]

Other commentators had different agendas. In 1962, General Hans Kissel, the *Volkssturm* Chief of Staff, asserted that it was a viable military instrument. He claimed that the *Volkssturm* was a territorial militia modelled on nineteenth- and twentieth-century resistance organisations. As examples Kissel cited the defenders of Kolberg in 1807, the British Home Guard of 1940 and Russian factory militia units rushed to the Leningrad front line in 1941. Kissel also had contemporary concerns. He called for the West German *Bundeswehr* to be organised on a militia basis and campaigned nationally on this platform, arguing that the *Volkssturm* provided an ideal model.[122]

In marked contrast, the historian Klaus Mammach from the GDR suggested that the *Volkssturm* performed a pacification role against dissent in order to prevent a repeat of Germany's internal collapse in 1918. In a study later published in West Germany, Mammach argued that weekly *Volkssturm* sessions provided further opportunity for Party observation and made additional demands on individuals. Thus the *Volkssturm* was a form of political control. The regime certainly attempted to delay imminent defeat by deploying the *Volkssturm* at the front, but, according to this interpretation, class considerations in the rear had greater significance. Mammach admitted that overall the *Volkssturm* had negligible fighting value, but believed that any additional time it gained was to be used by the ruling classes of 'Fascist German Imperialism' to split the Allied coalition by portraying Germany as the 'bulwark against Bolshevism in Europe'. On a practical level he contended that the great industrialists and bankers were given time to transfer capital and property assets to the west. Moreover, this account maintained that the existence of the *Volkssturm* deterred millions of foreign workers and POWs from launching mass uprisings. Mammach also commented on the *Volkssturm*'s military performance, again basing his findings on class factors rather on reactions to the nature and conduct of the respective foes confronting the *Wehrmacht* and *Volkssturm* on the Eastern and Western fronts. He asserted that in the industrial Ruhr the working class effectively sabotaged the *Volkssturm* whereas in eastern districts rural landowners provided the nucleus of units resulting in some detachments 'even having considerable military significance'.[123]

More recently, in a comprehensive study, the American military historian David Yelton has claimed that the launch of the *Volkssturm* was part of a coherent German strategy for victory which still existed in 1944. The *Volkssturm* was to consist of fanatical battalions with a spiritual allegiance to the Nazi regime, grounded in their binding oath to defend the homeland and to remain loyal to the *Führer* and the Party. It was to form a substantial part of Germany's defence, manning trenches and fortified zones and bolstering fortress garrisons so as to inflict huge losses on the enemy and to bleed them white. The resulting bloody stalemate, a repeat of the trench conflict of the First World War, would erode Allied morale beyond toleration. According to this interpretation, if the Reich could win this race for time and exploit Allied war-weariness, then Germany's deployment of fresh weapons such as rockets, new jet fighter aircraft and a new fleet of U-Boats would force the members of the Allied coalition, viewed in Nazi eyes as a fragile and unnatural alliance, to enter into separate peace negotiations.[124]

Nevertheless, the dominant viewpoint maintains that at this late stage of the war the *Volkssturm* was hardly a practical military proposition. The German military had suffered vast material losses during the summer of 1944 and the *Volkssturm* subsequently lacked weapons, equipment, uniforms and training. The *Volkssturm* was a misplaced and desperate gamble, an attempt to substitute 'elan and fanaticism for military skill and equipment'.[125] In eastern Germany, boys in short trousers and old men with a few antiquated rifles were 'now to stop the assault of the largest army in world history'.[126]

Although the idea of a Party militia was not new, this was 'the last and most naive attempt by the Nazis to create a military force controlled solely by the NSDAP'.[127] The adherence of Ernst Röhm and others in the paramilitary SA leadership to this idea had contributed to their demise in the 'Night of the Long Knives' on 30 June 1934. In their wartime RVK capacity, the *Gauleiter* in Baden, Swabia, Hesse–Nassau, East Hanover and Schleswig–Holstein attempted to register and conscript men in 1943 and 1944. But Himmler sought to maintain the SS's monopoly of internal security and blocked these initiatives while Bormann did not want an ambitious *Gauleiter* to promote a successful regional scheme into a national movement and thereby mount a challenge to the authority of the Party Chancellery.[128] Elsewhere, in the incorporated territory of the Warthegau, the domain of *Gauleiter* Arthur Greiser, the military authorities commenced the training of all remaining fit German men to undertake internal security duties, the so-called 'Grolmann Aktion', from the beginning of 1944.[129] Meanwhile, Major General Adolf Heusinger, in the Operations Department of the High Command, proposed a Home Defence Force in 1943, but Hitler deemed this unnecessary.[130] Guderian warmed to this suggestion in the late summer of 1944. As was noted in the previous chapter the fortress battalions he had earmarked for the eastern fortifications had been sent to man the West Wall in early September. Guderian now advocated the formation of a Home Guard in the eastern provinces and liaised with Wilhelm Schepmann, the SA's Chief of Staff. As Guderian recalled:

> I was interested in this idea of setting up units, led by officers and consisting of men in the eastern territories capable of active service but hitherto exempted from the Army because of being employed in reserved occupations; these units would only be called out in the event of a Russian breakthrough. I took my proposal to Hitler and suggested that the SA, so far as it could produce reliable men, be entrusted with the task of setting up this force.[131]

Party authorities proposed grander schemes than a localised *Landsturm*. Within the Propaganda Ministry there had been disappointment at Koch's limited proposal in early July for the creation of a defensive force in East Prussia under Party auspices. Lemke of the Ministry's staff asked on 13 July, 'Why only the Party and why only in East Prussia? Do we want to wait for a still greater catastrophe? Now the moment has come when the spirit of the War of Liberation of 1813–1814 must become accepted.' Lemke considered that it was too late to organise compulsory measures and suggested that 'an appeal to the Party membership, an impassioned call by the *Führer* to the idealism and love for the Fatherland held by the entire nation would be enough, for in a few days hundreds of thousands would rally around the flag and erect a dam in the East.'[132]

Koch made more ambitious proposals to Bormann two months later. For Koch the calling up of a *Landsturm* marked 'the beginning of a hallowed People's War' utilising all forces to gain the decisive victory and he hoped that 'a revolution in the area of military leadership would follow'. With local leadership the population would stand solidly together to protect the *Heimat*. Koch pointed to earlier resistance to Napoleon and highlighted the roles of Uwe Nettelbeck at Kolberg in 1807 and Andreas Hofer in the Tyrol in 1809 to bolster his argument for local defensive forces on a national basis. Koch firmly rejected the idea of a *Landsturm* operating under the auspices of the regional *Wehrkreis* and emphasised that the battalions could only be led by respected local Party figures with an unrivalled confidence in victory. The role once played by the priest, the lord of the manor and mayor was now to be assumed by the *Ortsgruppenleiter*.[133]

Guderian's idea of the formation of *Landsturm* detachments in frontier districts metamorphosised following Bormann's discussions with Hitler into a Reich-wide *Volkssturm*. Hitler's directive ordering the formation of this new force, renamed the *Volkssturm* on his instruction, was issued on 25 September but only received press publicity following the public launch on 18 October, the anniversary of the Battle of Leipzig (1813). Hitler prefaced the order by admitting that after five years of the hardest fighting the enemy now stood on or close to the German frontier. These foes sought to smash the Reich and to destroy the German people and social order. Due to setbacks and the treachery of her allies, Hitler stated that, as in the autumn of 1939, Germany stood alone. Now he ordered the full deployment of all Germans to confront 'the total destructive will of our International Jewish enemy'. Himmler, in his role as commander of the Replacement Army, was to oversee the military organisation, training and arming of the *Volkssturm*. Members of the *Volkssturm*, irrespective of rank, were to provide their own clothing and equipment. Political and organisational matters fell to Bormann's Party Chancellery operating through the *Gauleiter*. The *Gauleiter* were to raise formations in their own *Gau* and appoint the most capable leaders from the Party, SA, SS, NSKK and HJ as commanders.[134] Schepmann was named as *Volkssturm* Inspector-General, with special responsibility for training in shooting, an area of sustained SA training activity since 1939. It was anticipated that *Volkssturm* battalions would only operate in their own *Gau* to seal off enemy breakthroughs. The first inkling that battalions would be deployed further afield was provided by Goebbels. In his capacity as *Gauleiter* of Berlin, he swore in the capital's *Volkssturm* on 12 November and said that some units could be thrown into the breach if a crisis developed at the front.[135]

The formation of the *Volkssturm* was indicative of the process whereby the vesting of ever greater powers in the Party accelerated after 20 July 1944. This reflected Hitler's growing tendency to place his faith in trusted 'Old Fighters' who had joined the NSDAP prior to January 1933. Bormann fully understood the dimensions of his political victory. On 26 September, he sent a circular to all *Gauleiter* concerning the setting up of the *Volkssturm*. He underlined the *Führer*'s faith in the spirit of the Party and Hitler's loss of confidence in hitherto accepted military methods:

> Once again the Führer has demonstrated his boundless confidence in his Gauleiter. We want to show ourselves worthy of this new proof of trust . . . .Our unrivalled devotion to our people and our task, our determination and our energy must rouse everyone who has become weary. This is to say: we are not to raise new units of the Armed Forces according to an order and a blue-print, but we are to appeal to fellow Germans in the homeland who are fit for armed service. Each one of them must be inspired politically, must be moved in his heart and mind, so that he follows the call to arms willingly and gladly.[136]

The *Volkssturm* was to be raised in four waves:

1. Men aged 20 to 60 engaged in occupations deemed non-essential to the war effort. They could be mobilised for duty for six weeks anywhere in their home *Gau*.
2. Men aged 20 to 60 engaged in essential war industries, communications and transportation precluding their inclusion in the first wave. They were only to serve in their home *Kreis* (district).
3. HJ not yet called up; including the remaining men from the 1925–1927 recruiting classes.

4. Those considered incapable of undertaking active combat missions but able to perform guard or rear area security duties.[137]

The men of the second wave lacked military training and were generally younger than those in the first who were frequently First World War veterans and had an average age of 52. The first wave could also be deployed outside their local areas. In theory four million men were eligible for the *Volkssturm* and the first wave alone comprised 1.2 million men formed into 1,850 battalions.[138]

Following the drafting of these regulations and the creation of a vast Party bureaucracy to oversee the project, the launch of the new force was accompanied by a frenzied propaganda offensive. Posters called for volunteers and makeshift recruiting offices were established for registration purposes. In East Prussia, the creation of *Volkssturm* units predated the rest of the Reich and Koch championed the principle of voluntary service. Koch told his *Kreisleiter* that the impulse behind the new force should be a spontaneous desire to volunteer, itself arising from a willingness to defend the cherished *Heimat*. The basis of the *Volkssturm*, in common with earlier alleged NSDAP achievements, did not arise from military call ups or the issuing of draft papers but from spontaneity and improvisation. Nevertheless, Koch did not rule out compulsion. Ominously, he stated that if individuals wilfully failed to comply with the new measures Special Court or drumhead court martial proceedings would follow.[139] Party files, occupancy and rationing records were consulted to identify men eligible for service. Similarly, in Stettin, the local knowledge of NSDAP Block Leaders was exploited to enlist the appropriate men.[140] Throughout Germany, those declining to volunteer were pressed into service.

Himmler launched the *Volkssturm* on 18 October when he reviewed 13 companies of the East Prussian *Volkssturm* at the Marwitz barracks in Bartenstein and made a speech relayed over German radio. The East Prussian NSDAP created a ritual Party spectacle. Hallowed Party flags and standards were placed in prominent positions. Important personages from the Party and army were present, although Bormann was absent despite the proximity of the *Führerhauptquartier*.[141] The radio announcer proclaimed, 'Across this border land of forests and lakes, sweeps like a hurricane the cry from town to town, from village to village: "People, arise; the enemy stands on your border!"'[142]After repeated choruses of 'Volk ans Gewehr' ('People to Arms') and the reading of Hitler's decree over the radio, Himmler, flanked by Keitel, Guderian and Koch, spoke. He evoked parallels between Germany's position in 1944 and Prussia's seemingly hopeless situation in 1813 when the *Landsturm* was formed in the face of a sceptical military leadership. Himmler heaped praise on those fanatical freedom fighters whose spirit of resistance had culminated in the glorious victory over the French at Leipzig. It was 'essential that Germans supported the *Wehrmacht* through the establishment of the *Volkssturm*' in order for a similar change in military fortunes to occur.[143]

Himmler's appeal for desperate resistance was followed by a short reply from Koch, who reported that tens of thousands had enrolled into the East Prussian *Volkssturm*. Koch requested that Himmler inform the *Führer* that they were ready for action and would 'fight to the final round against the bestial enemy'.[144] *Volkssturm* propaganda peaked with the publication of Hitler's appeal on 18 October and the national swearing-in ceremonies on Sunday 12 November. The Party merged the ceremony with the annual commemoration for the 'martyrs' of the Munich Putsch of 9 November 1923 in an attempt to provide a form of spiritual legitimisation for the new undertaking.[145] Bormann envisaged the *Volkssturm* as a classless band of fighting men. The *Volkssturm* was to be an all-encompassing movement with men of all professions, businesses, classes and ranks standing side by side. He scolded the representatives of organisations proposing to raise their own detachments and dismissed the idea of a 'bakers' *Volkssturm*' as nonsense.[146] Nevertheless, reams of directives and circulars emanated from the Party Chancellery covering the status of all conceivable groups in the *Volkssturm* ranging from convicted homosexuals to the members of former royal houses.[147]

In East Prussia, after correspondence with the Bishop of Ermland, Deputy *Gauleiter* Großherr confirmed to the district Party offices on 13 October that, 'priests of both confessions are not to be called up for the *Volkssturm*'.[148] A flying *Volkssturm* was also contemplated in East Prussia where the local National Socialist Flying Corps leader, Ewald Oppermann, was allowed to form a *Volkssturm* Night Attack Squadron consisting of training planes and sporting machines. The chronic shortage of fuel which beset the Third Reich by this stage of the war meant that this scheme never took off. But at least those involved were able to avoid the drudgery and the likely dangers of *Volkssturm* service in the province.[149]

Throughout Germany on 12 November addresses by the attending *Gauleiter* or *Kreisleiter* were followed by the men swearing an oath of allegiance to Hitler. They vowed to fight bravely and to die rather than surrender their freedom and the future of their race. Koch swore in deputations from 20 battalions at Nemmersdorf, 'where Bolshevik subhumanity had performed in a sadistic manner' during their two-day occupation of the village.[150] German military newspapers applauded the new force and the Party distributed pamphlets to *Volkssturm* officers containing propaganda material to be disseminated among the men. The weekly *Wehrmacht* newspaper *Der Politische Soldat* published a special *Volkssturm* edition. A weekly newspaper, *Der Dienstappell*, was issued to company commanders, and a special *Volkssturm* issue of the series entitled *Rustzeug für die Propaganda in der Ortsgruppe* was produced. This propaganda propagated a number of key themes. Fear propaganda was interspersed with appeals for heroic resistance. The men of the *Volkssturm* were urged to fight fanatically and never surrender. They were fighting for the preservation of their families, the German people and the European continent. Extermination would follow capitulation. The *Volkssturm,* aided by German womenfolk and the strength emanating from improvisation and willpower, would exploit any tactic to defend every house, every ditch, every bush and every clump of trees.[151]

Slogans such as 'The *Volkssturm* fights for the Life and Freedom of Greater Germany' and 'The People Rise Up, the Storm Breaks Loose' were repeated to instil enthusiasm for the new venture. A postage stamp with the inscription 'The People Rise Up' featured three generations of German males advancing to confront the foe. By late 1944 Nazi propaganda offered Germans the stark choice of victory or death. This spirit was epitomised by Veit Harlan's colour film *Kolberg*. Shot at vast expense during this period, it was Goebbels' interpretation of the heroism of the defenders of the besieged Baltic port in 1807 and designed to encourage contemporary Germans to hold out, exhaust their enemies and attain final victory.[152]

Propaganda reports for late October and November indicate that the *Volkssturm* and the accompanying media fanfare inspired few Germans. They asked how the *Volkssturm* could be armed overnight. For instance, East Prussians had been advised that recent military reversals were attributable to a shortage of ammunition and heavy weapons. Therefore they deduced that insufficient arms would be available for the *Volkssturm*.[153] Pessimists, who formed the majority of the population, viewed the calling up of 'lame and crippled men' as a desperate measure indicative of Germany's military weakness. Concerns were also expressed about the nature of the new force, leading to comments that it resembled the partisan formations previously condemned by the German authorities throughout occupied Europe. There was no standard *Volkssturm* uniform and the men sported only an identifying armband with the words 'Deutscher Volkssturm-Wehrmacht'. The authorities stated that this minimal identification was permitted under the terms of The Hague Convention of 1907. However, rumours soon spread from East Prussia that this was not the case and it was accurately discerned that captured *Volkssturm* personnel suffered a frightful fate at Soviet hands. Many Germans ridiculed the notion that antiquated small arms could be deployed against enemy tanks and bombers. They viewed the *Volkssturm* as a 'purely propaganda operation' which was not taken seriously by Germany's friends or foes. Soldiers did not expect much from the *Volkssturm*, although a section of the population believed that it would act as an internal security organ against rebellious foreign workers or enemy paratroops. Propaganda reports stressed that the integration of all men into the *Volkssturm* regardless of standing or profession was one aspect of the entire enterprise initially greeted favourably. Soon, however, complaints arose that directors, lawyers and specialists were being exempted from service or placed in the second wave. Nevertheless, national reports indicated the positive impact and scale of the swearing-in ceremonies, particularly in Brandenburg and in Danzig where *Volkssturm* Inspector-General Schepmann took the salute. First World War veterans were said to be enthusiastic at having the opportunity to serve the nation again. Set against this, they felt slighted when Party leaders, bereft of military experience, were appointed to lead units.[154]

Jokes soon sprang up. The *Volkssturm* was described as a 'casserole' – old meat and green vegetables.[155] One East Prussian observer described the *Volkssturm* as 'men with sporting rifles and artificial legs'.[156] German radio dubbed these jokers 'inoffensive clowns' and saved their anger for the 'most dangerous types' who declared that they were 'going to draw up their wills before it was too late'.[157] On 2 October, Koch ordered that the men of the East Prussian *Volkssturm* were to receive training with all available weapons within four weeks so that they could be deployed against the enemy without risk to themselves or their comrades.[158] The *Volkssturm* first saw action on 7 October on the outskirts of Memel. Two companies in civilian clothes and with green armbands helped secure a sector threatened by a sudden Soviet incursion until the *Wehrmacht* units appeared to stabilise the situation. The poorly armed companies suffered high losses for their efforts.[159] Following the Red Army's drive towards Memel and their probing of German defences to the south-east of the province, on 10 October, Koch ordered that the first 39 battalions of the *Volkssturm* occupy the defensive positions. Each battalion consisted of four companies of 100–150 men. From the first wave, a battalion from Heinrichswalde and two from Tilsit were told to occupy the Memelstellung within three days and a further 21 battalions were to man other defences by 15 October. The remaining 15 battalions of the second wave were to follow them into the fortifications by 20 October. As well as being split into two groups North and South,[160] the East Prussian *Volkssturm* battalions were either deemed to be *Einsatzbereitschaft* (familiar with weapons and with combat experience) or *Standbereitschaft* (essentially labour battalions, still not fully armed and with orders to fortify towns and villages). Physical fitness was given a low priority as Koch placed the emphasis on discipline. He emphasised that battalion commanders should have combat experience and strong leadership personalities, being 'convinced National Socialists and fanatical Hitler followers' who would inspire their soldiers.[161] By the end of October, Koch called for an additional 85 *Volkssturm* battalions. He also ordered that the construction of fortifications was to cease by 30 November and the battalions were to reach a level of training whereby they could effectively man the defences. A three-week rota system was to operate, half the battalion would be in the defences while the other half would be stood down. Every man participating in this active service was to receive a winter coat, full uniform and warm underwear.[162]

Although some *Volkssturm* battalions first saw action in East Prussia during October, elsewhere the *Volkssturm* was spared from fighting until 1945. This time was used to engage in rudimentary training while attempts were made to scrape together weapons and clothing. *Volkssturm* activity was restricted to rear area security duties and participation in the building of additional defences. Units operating on a rota basis also occupied sectors of the completed field works and this was a regular feature of *Volkssturm* activity throughout eastern Germany.

East Prussian SA units had drilled throughout the summer and weapons training was a feature of life in the camps accommodating men building fortifications.[163] The East Prussian *Volkssturm* was at the forefront of a national movement. On 13 November, in a speech broadcast from Königsberg, Koch told German radio listeners that, 'I am proud of the fact that the *Volkssturm* was born here in East Prussia, was accepted by the *Führer* and is now sweeping over the whole of Germany like an avalanche.'[164] The East Prussian *Volkssturm* was Koch's private army. Characteristically both he and Dargel boasted to Bormann about the actions and bravery of the new units while simultaneously downplaying the *Wehrmacht*'s efforts. According to these claims, East Prussian *Volkssturm* units were in the thick of the heavy October fighting, repulsing enemy breakthroughs and manning defence lines. At first battalions patrolled and secured the roads behind the front against a sudden Red Army thrust and in the Gumbinnen–Goldap area 1,675 *Volkssturm* men were already deployed by 20 October. Four days later, on 24 October, 4,500 *Volkssturm* men in total were operating in the Gumbinnen–Angerapp and Treuburg sectors and reporting described some lively contact with the enemy. Further north, in the now surrounded port of Memel, the *Volkssturm* were involved in security patrols in the town and the safeguarding of those digging trenches. In Tilsit, by this time a front-line town under enemy artillery fire, two *Volkssturm* battalions were engaged in rear area security duties and completing the evacuation of the town.[165]

Similarly, the propagandists claimed that seven East Prussian *Volkssturm* battalions were in action immediately following the 18 October proclamation. They had earned merit for their role in the successful defence of Gumbinnen and Treuburg.[166] Slogans authorised by the Propaganda Ministry for oral dissemination by their agents stressed that 'Not only the *Ostwall* but also the *Volkssturm* had seen its significance fully proved in East Prussia.'[167] RPA Maertins compiled a report on the 'People's War in East Prussia' for distribution to the foreign press. He produced a glowing testimony stressing the leadership, bravery and effectiveness of the *Volkssturm* and underlined the close relationship with the *Wehrmacht*. In Angerapp and Treuburg men who were apparently enthusiastic and possessed valuable local knowledge occupied positions which ran through their own farms. Maertins particularly praised the demeanour of First World War veterans who manned their positions with 'unshakeable calm'. He contended that all Soviet incursions had been repulsed and that the fortification of villages in the rear made deep enemy breakthroughs impossible. Maertins acknowledged 'a few insignificant misunderstandings', but maintained that the co-operation between the *Wehrmacht* and the *Volkssturm* had apparently had a 'very favourable effect on the morale of the troops'. The *Wehrmacht* behaved in a comradely manner with experienced front line officers and NCOs overseeing training courses on the use of modern weapons such as the *Panzerfaust* and *Panzerschreck* and instruction on close quarter fighting against tanks. Maertins stressed that Colonel General Reinhardt reinforced this impression when he addressed the swearing-in ceremony of the *Volkssturm* in Insterburg. In Koch's presence, Reinhardt had used 'deeply sensitive words' to describe the relationship between the *Wehrmacht* and the *Volkssturm*.[168] Nazi propagandists wanted to emphasise to the forces that the *Volkssturm* was in the thick of the fighting and had indeed suffered losses. The military newspaper *Front und Heimat* claimed that 21 men had been lost out of the first 1,000 *Volkssturm* men deployed in East Prussia.[169]

Senior military figures voiced their support for Koch's actions despite widespread contempt for the man and his methods. Reinhardt did indeed make ostensibly supportive remarks when interviewed by the reporter Heysing. He mentioned that the *Volkssturm* had already seen action, and added that, although only partially equipped and armed, and pushed into the front line at a depressing stage of the battle, the units had displayed commendable steadfastness. The theme of historical parallels was again highlighted when Reinhardt asserted that the East Prussian *Volkssturm* had 'proved to be the valiant sons of the old East Prussian soldier race that so often in our history have experienced assault from the enemy in the east'.[170] Colonel General Ferdinand Schörner, the Nazi commander of Army Group North, also congratulated Koch. In a teleprinter message Schörner sent comradely greetings on behalf of his troops to the East Prussian *Volkssturm*. He added that 'The example of East Prussia and the great determination to fight for the homeland filled the soldiers of the Northern Front with admiration.' The men of Army Group North stood in closest solidarity with the men of Koch's *Volkssturm* to defend East Prussia in a 'fanatical struggle against the hated enemy of our homeland'.[171] However, this was a false veneer of unity as following Koch's appointment as *Reichskommissar* for what remained of the Ostland in August 1944, according to staff gossip the pair clashed violently in Riga and Koch reportedly never ventured within earshot of Schörner again.[172]

Behind the propaganda smokescreen, the real East Prussian *Volkssturm* was a sickly beast. By late November it comprised approximately 80,000 men serving in around 90 battalions 'under arms or under the spade'. Koch told Bormann that some were in barracks, but most were occupying positions. The second wave was deployed digging additional defences.[173] Half of the remaining fit men in East Prussia were in the *Volkssturm*.[174] However, the call up of indigenous men for the *Volkssturm*, their continued deployment together with foreign workers in the building of defences and the loss of the frontier districts had a detrimental effect on the East Prussian agrarian economy. This led to a sharp decline in the production of dairy produce and a corresponding reduction in rations.[175]

The East Prussian *Volkssturm* was ill-prepared to confront the Red Army. It was inadequately armed and equipped, almost completely untrained and led by Party functionaries who had been chosen for their political zeal. In reality, the first deployment was far from painless. The Goldap battalion which had been involved in hard fighting defending the Rominte position had needed to be reformed and reinforced south of Angerapp. The battalion, consisting of 400 men in four companies, had been comprised of men over 45 dressed in civilian clothing and equipped with unreliable Russian rifles. By 23 October, according to one account, it had 'lost 76 men through death and wounds. The wounded that fell into Russian hands were probably shot as partisans for fighting without uniforms.'[176] At the same time, contact with a company from the Angerapp battalion was lost altogether.[177]

Advised of the real situation by unfortunate participants, *Wehrmacht* officers and local officials privately expressed their misgivings and anger. An NCO wrote that armed 'with flintlocks' the *Volkssturm* would 'get nowhere' against Soviet tanks.[178] Major Dieckert recounted a conversation with an outraged estate administrator who fought with the Angerapp battalion at Nemmersdorf and had been provided with an Italian rifle with five bullets.[179] This ammunition was of Dutch or Belgian origin. One-tenth of the men received a *Panzerfaust* but many more were completely unarmed. Lacking direction, the Angerapp *Volkssturm* disintegrated into disorderly flight when confronted by the Soviets. Some were killed and many more were wounded or declared missing. The shattered remnants of this force returned to the town with devastating tales of their experiences.[180]

The sight of children marching alongside feeble old men shocked even Eastern Front veterans. Guy Sajer, serving in the *Großdeutschland* division, refitting at Litzmannstadt in the Warthegau, later commented: 'Were the authorities going to stop the Red Army with them? The comparison seemed tragic and ludicrous.'[181] Heysing recalled one officer remarking that 'the *Volkssturm* has neither weapons nor means of communications; no field kitchens, no uniforms and no leaders. We lack manpower for our infantry regiments but they form the *Volkssturm*. It is absolute madness . . . alone they are only cannon fodder.'[182] General Hoßbach observed that the *Volkssturm* displayed all the characteristics of improvisation and was unsuitable for combat. However, it did provide an organised workforce for building rear defences. At lower levels he asserted that the *Wehrmacht–Volkssturm* relationship was good – difficulties only arose from Koch's behaviour.[183] Similarly, Colonel Lassen, Chief of Staff of the Twenty-Eighth Army Corps in besieged Memel, said that the local *Volkssturm* had no combat value but was useful for digging and salvage work.[184]

Military sources stressed that because of Koch they had no influence in the operation of the *Volkssturm*.[185] Koch was determined that the *Volkssturm* would not be integrated into the *Wehrmacht*.[186] *Volkssturm* deployment was a Party matter. The *Wehrmacht* was sometimes unaware of the whereabouts of units, forcing officers to ask around or send dispatches in order to discover the appropriate details.[187] When *Volkssturm* battalions were located, their commanders, often the local *Kreisleiter*, exploited the authority given to them by Koch and forced the *Wehrmacht* to allow them to defend their own sectors of the front.[188]

The East Prussian *Volkssturm* was armed from stocks of captured weapons from Party stores and by the collection or seizure of weapons from individuals.[189] The first units to face the Red Army were mostly clad in Party or SA uniforms with brown-grey or grey-green overcoats.[190] However, one veteran Nazi remarked that the men preferred to wear different uniforms as they correctly feared inhumane treatment if they fell into Soviet hands. This caused many *Volkssturmmänner* to try to join the *Wehrmacht*.[191] As it was impossible to arm and equip the *Volkssturm* solely from available German resources, other avenues had to be explored. Koch was at the forefront when he attempted to place orders for vast quantities of goods, including 25,000 pairs of boots and 200,000 metres of material for uniforms, from the Italian black market at prices ranging from three to ten times the normal rate. Yelton observes that purchases were even to be made from anti-German partisans! Albert Speer's Armaments Staff Italy was able to thwart this endeavour. Despite orders being placed with more reputable Italian manufacturers transport difficulties and currency shortages meant that the equipping of the *Volkssturm* underwent no considerable improvement.[192]

The propaganda image of a well-armed volunteer force was belied by reality. The Replacement Army provided the East Prussian *Volkssturm* with only 1,000 *Panzerfäuste* but Koch attached little importance to the glaring shortages in weapons and equipment. He argued that the fighting quality of the *Volkssturm* was not a question of weaponry but one of leadership.[193] Considerable unease resulted from rumours spread in East Prussia that inadequately armed units had faced the Red Army.[194] The *Gau* authorities knew that men of the *Volkssturm* age hitherto resident in frontier districts had accompanied treks to the West. However, they had frequently failed to return home for *Volkssturm* service. Men taking this unauthorised leave were considered guilty of desertion and the *Kreisleiter* in the reception districts were instructed to send them back immediately.[195] While Koch and his cohorts placed little emphasis on the quality of training or equipment, discipline and coercion were another matter altogether. Party officials who concealed weapons were threatened with the 'harshest Party punishment'. Koch stated that indiscipline was a sign of bad leadership which was intolerable in such serious times.[196]

Koch advised Bormann that the scale of the *Volkssturm* led to 'small disciplinary offences' which necessitated the sitting of a Special Court to administer appropriate sentences. He cited a case from Memel where a committed Jehovah's Witness had refused to swear the oath of allegiance and had been placed before a Party Special Court, sentenced to death and shot. Koch considered that the case had been correctly handled, but advocated the creation of a judicial framework with the *Gauleiter* as the ultimate authority to judge offenders from the *Volkssturm*.[197] Koch's call for simpler procedures and tougher sentences subsequently led to the creation of a disciplinary hierarchy with the *Gauleiter* at the helm and, beneath him, battalion and then company commanders.[198] They would pass countless summary sentences in early 1945.

Elsewhere in eastern Germany the proclamation of the *Volkssturm* was accompanied by arbitrary *Gauleiter* actions and an outpouring of patriotic propaganda. In mid-September the SS reported that Hanke planned to form a *Heimatschutz* (home defence force) with 200,000 members to defend Lower Silesia. Hanke intended to equip the force with heavy weapons obtained from Krupp's Breslau plant and ammunition from local *Wehrmacht* stocks. Training courses were already taking place at Breslau–Markstadt. Hanke had personally ordered the local leader of the textiles industry, Dr Winkler, to undertake duties in support of the Bartold digging programme. His first assignment was to procure 200,000 uniforms from the local textile industry within four weeks. Furthermore, only half of the *Wehrmacht* orders placed in the province would now be delivered and the remainder would be requisitioned for local use. Some 30,000 woollen blankets had been requisitioned and 10,000 pairs of boots ordered for Bartold. Stocks of miners' and industrial clothing and footwear were also requisitioned by the Party to boost its holdings.[199] Hanke's encroachments into the economy to furnish *Unternehmen Bartold* and *Heimatschutz* enraged the Economics Minister. Dr Funk wrote to Hanke making his feelings clear on this 'unpleasant matter'. He condemned Hanke's high-handed and unauthorised requisitioning of textiles as it made disciplined control of economic production impossible.[200] Dr Lammers, Head of the Reich Chancellery, was alerted and a *Reichskanzlei* file note recorded that a meeting between Dr Funk and Hanke was planned but apparently had not taken place. On the contrary, Hanke was involved in new encroachments.[201]

Hanke sought to clad the Lower Silesian *Volkssturm* in light brown Party uniforms to provide a visible sign of the responsibility of the NSDAP for the defence of the Reich. He obtained 10,000 brown uniforms, 2,500 of them from *Organisation Todt* (OT) stores. This requisition led to a clash between Hanke and Xaver Dorsch, the head of the OT. Hanke defended his conduct by arguing that his *Volkssturm* operated day and night in 'bandit infested territories' and therefore had a more pressing need for brown uniforms than building workers at their concrete mixers.[202] Similar disputes arose in Upper Silesia where the Party attempted to appropriate 80,000 OT uniforms.[203] Other sources of uniforms were also exploited. *Gauleiter* Bracht boasted to Bormann that Upper Silesian women had voluntarily handed in the uniforms of dead husbands and sons to local Party offices for the use of the *Volkssturm*.[204] The German population of Upper Silesia hoped that the *Volkssturm* would perform an effective role against Polish partisan forces.[205]

A happier occasion for Hanke was a mass rally held at Breslau Schloßplatz on 20 October which was said to have involved 20,000 *Volkssturmmänner* and 80,000 civilians. In accordance with the theme of a national uprising involving all Germans, groups from outside the Party encompassing all sections of society had paraded. RPA Dr Schulz emphasised the enthusiasm of the occasion, in contrast with the disciplined and sombre inspection by Himmler in East Prussia. Hanke's speech, relayed throughout the city by the public address system, was applauded by his listeners. The familiar theme of the precedent of 1813 was repeated and Dr Schulz believed that the demonstration had a favourable effect on delegates from outside Breslau. He was convinced that this spectacle provided the greatest boost to morale that year.[206]

Nevertheless, the deficiencies of the Lower Silesian *Volkssturm* corresponded to the national pattern. There was unease that the new detachments were placed under NSDAP leadership rather than under the command of experienced military personnel.[207] Familiar problems arose in the provision of weapons and uniforms. The Habelschwerdt battalion had German, Dutch, Danish and Russian weapons. The only common feature was the lack of ammunition. Although officers received uniforms, more than half the men were still in civilian clothing as late as February 1945.[208] The former *Landrat* of Landeshut, Dr Otto Fiebrantz, recalled that, 'the superficial training of the *Volkssturm* was a catastrophe.' When *Panzerfaust* training was offered, a number of participants were injured and many declined the opportunity of a test fire even under *Wehrmacht* supervision.[209] However, there is not complete uniformity of opinion on the condition of the Lower Silesian *Volkssturm*. Whereas the former *Landrat* of Groß Wartenberg, Detlev von Reinersdorff-Paczenski, claimed that each company of 150 men received five rifles,[210] a different scenario was apparently enacted in neighbouring Namslau. Uniquely, the then *Landrat*, Dr Ernst Heinrich, later repeatedly maintained that the arming of the *Volkssturm* in frontier districts was 'not as bad as portrayed in the post-war period'. He recalled that the battalions in Namslau and Brieg were equipped with rifles and also possessed machine guns and mortars. In contrast, however, he viewed the Lauban *Volkssturm* as very poorly equipped and not combat-worthy.[211]

A radio report on 21 October described the swearing-in of the Upper Silesian *Volkssturm*: 'In the big square of a town in Upper Silesia the first battalions of the *Volkssturm* in Upper Silesia are lined up, wearing their field-grey uniforms . . . A squad of miners in their black working clothes has fallen in, the hewer at the side of his foreman. Behind the field-grey *Volkssturm* battalions thousands of people are massed.'[212] Silesian metal workers said that they expected to be away from their homes for some time on *Volkssturm* duty but said that their workshops would be carried on by their wives. *Gauleiter* Bracht remarked, 'I know that I speak in the name of all comrades of the *Volkssturm* when I say that we men of Upper Silesia are proud and happy to man the defence works which we have built ourselves.'[213] Reports indicated that the *Volkssturm* battalions were bound for 'the rear of the deeply echeloned protective positions' built by the local population and that they would improve and guard these defences against a surprise enemy attack.[214]

Prior to Christmas 1944, around 40 Silesian *Volkssturm* battalions had moved into the positions built on the province's Polish frontier. A four-week rota system operated and training with weapons, mainly of Italian origin, was also provided. Most participants were accommodated in nearby communities.[215] Concurrently, the Soviets sought to further deflate *Volkssturm* morale. One pamphlet dropped on Lower Silesia in December included a cruel cartoon of hunchbacks, the lame and babies in prams parading by a headless officer supported by Himmler. This was accompanied by a poem lampooning the 'tank driving grandad' and 'the squirt with the pistol'. The Russians promised that Himmler's levy would not save Hitler's Reich.[216]

In East Brandenburg difficulties were also encountered. All officers and NCOs for the *Volkssturm* in Landsberg were chosen by the Party with the assistance of the local SA leader, a badly wounded First World War veteran. Military training took place on Sunday mornings, but was hindered by the onset of winter and the fact that most participants had only civilian clothes. None had fired a *Panzerfaust* prior to being deployed against the Russians in January. Officers attended a special ten-day training course at a Landsberg barracks in late December.[217] Former *Landrat* and *Kreisleiter* Hauk of Züllichau–Schwiebus later admitted that the entire male population under 60 was called up for *Volkssturm* service. The men were placed in front of two military doctors and directed towards the appropriate draft. Even men with serious injuries were incorporated on the grounds that they could guard public buildings and watch over prisoners.[218] The lack of weapons and equipment led to the deployment of only one battalion of the Züllichau–Schwiebus *Volkssturm* against the Russians. Barely armed, this battalion saw action in the Meseritz fortified zone during late January, but was 'steamrollered by Russian tanks' and suffered horrendous losses.[219] The losses suffered by more than 30 Brandenburg *Volkssturm* battalions in the vicinity of the Oder during 1945 outweighed any apparent benefits. *Regierungspräsident* Refardt of Frankfurt an der Oder later condemned the Party's thoughtless deployment of so many valuable and completely ill-prepared men and laid the blame for this 'insanity' on *Gauleiter* Stürtz.[220]

The Pomeranian Party authorities expressed their high hopes in the *Volkssturm.* During October 1944 Schwede-Coburg addressed a training course for *Volkssturm* commanders in the Stettin area. To stormy applause from these Party members he made the absurd claim that by the beginning of 1945 the *Volkssturm* would be able to defend Germany on the East Prussian frontier while the entire *Wehrmacht* fought in the West.[221] The *Gau* authorities advised Berlin that 50 Pomeranian *Volkssturm* battalions were available. This statement amazed leading officers of *Wehrkreis* II in Stettin. They knew that no single *Volkssturm* battalion was ready for combat on account of the shortage of weapons and equipment.[222]

Events in Pomerania followed a familiar format. Bad feeling arose because the leading positions were distributed among Party functionaries as political reliability was considered more important than military experience in the selection of officers. The shortage of weapons, equipment and uniforms and the inadequacy of the training also provoked adverse comments.[223] One former official observed that experienced officers from famous Prussian military families were excluded from the *Volkssturm* by the Party authorities.[224] Others viewed the formation of the *Volkssturm* as another effort by

Schwede-Coburg to eliminate the remnants of orderly administration. All organisational matters now lay in the hands of the Party. Meanwhile, the population greeted the formation of the *Volkssturm* with a 'resigned shaking of heads', frequently finding it difficult to conceal their derision. Every half fit man had been called up long ago. Only the old and sick remained.[225]

Party weapons stocks in Pomerania were woefully inadequate. In Naugard district only 10 per cent of the men had rifles. These were of five or six different calibres and only five cartridges of ammunition were provided.[226] The former *Kreisleiter* of Stargard–Saatzig, Siegfried Schug, later confessed that the lack of weapons and equipment led to high losses in early 1945.[227] The former *Landrat* of this district observed that when the condition of *Volkssturm* equipment became known it was impossible not to be depressed. Machine guns and anti-tank weapons were not forthcoming and only every second or third man possessed a firearm of varying origin and calibre.[228] In Bütow district, French and German ammunition was distributed for Belgian and Dutch rifles.[229] In neighbouring Rummelsburg only a fraction of the men were armed. In 1945 they were merged with other units and thrown against the Red Army. By this stage the Rummelsburg *Volkssturm* was 'all over the place'.[230]

Schwede-Coburg suggested that *Wehrmacht* officials, auxiliaries and officers serving on the Home Front should surrender their uniforms to the *Volkssturm*. His unrealistic proposals were motivated more by his running feud with the *Wehrmacht* 'in smart uniforms with long boots pursuing their bureaucratic activity' rather than by any concern about the welfare of *Volkssturmmänner*.[231] A few men were attired in SA or old military uniforms, but the majority wore civilian clothing and were distinguishable only by their armbands.[232] Training was similarly slipshod. Admittedly a number of men had previous experience with weapons in their capacity as auxiliary policemen and foresters. However, they generally lacked knowledge of newer weapons such as the *Panzerfaust*.[233] Training was limited to two hours on a Sunday morning.[234] Due to the shortage of *Panzerfäuste*, little training was available with this weapon and few *Volkssturmmänner* were familiar with it.[235] On the rare occasions when men were given *Panzerfaust* training the results could be disastrous. For instance, at a *Volkssturm* course on anti-tank fighting run by the SS in Lauenburg two men perished.[236]

From mid-December, 15 battalions from the first wave of the Pomeranian *Volkssturm* manned the *Pommernwall* and the *Festung* Schneidemühl fortifications. Schwede-Coburg advised Bormann that accommodation and rations had been procured without *Wehrmacht* assistance. The men were deployed for a 14-day period and received military training. Winter clothing was also provided on site but was returned at the end of the deployment period and passed on to the next batch of men.[237] These Party soldiers did not impress the *Wehrkreis* II staff. General Werner Kienitz, the then Commander, later observed that 'the thought that a poorly armed mass levy of old men and boys would turn around the fate of Germany in the struggle against massed Soviet tank armies was totally unprofessional not to say criminal. This material was unsuitable.'[238] Another officer, Major Klaus Schaubert, added that the *Volkssturm* served an essentially propaganda function in an attempt completely to distort the strength and superiority of the Red Army. Germans were to believe that

Russian tanks would be halted by roadblocks, a few poorly armed men and sheaves of grand-sounding directives.[239]

The Nazi hierarchy were aware of the miserable state of *Volkssturm* equipment. Bormann, Himmler, Goebbels and Funk initiated the *Volksopfer* (People's Offering) appealing for textiles, uniforms, steel helmets, shoes, tents, rucksacks, cutlery and binoculars for the *Volkssturm* and *Wehrmacht*. This initiative, organised by Party functionaries at local level, initially ran from 7 to 28 January but was extended to 11 February 1945. The *Volksopfer* decrees included the provision that the clothing of dead soldiers and civilians be handed in by their relatives. Official sources claimed that the population considered it to be a 'meaningful sacrifice'.[240] Germans were encouraged in this endeavour by Hitler's directive authorising the death penalty for those deemed guilty of stealing or concealing items. However, in the eastern provinces, much of the *Volksopfer* collection was looted by retreating German troops or more likely fell into the hands of the advancing Soviets. This explains the drop in the total amount collected nationally from 80,000 to 60,000 tons.[241] Elsewhere, the population condemned the 'large scale fraud' arising from Party officials selling goods donated for the *Volksopfer* to desperate refugees who had fled from the eastern provinces.[242]

The *Volkssturm* was a victory for Party bureaucracy. It demonstrated the strength of the Party in the ongoing power struggle during the final stage of the Third Reich. The *Volkssturm* was also an attempt to buoy up the public mood and provide a focus of distraction from the depressing military situation. However, this 'feel good factor' had a short shelf life. The Party's boasts of the power of improvisation and the strength of the National Socialist spirit could not compensate for the catalogue of deficiencies detailed in the previous pages. Any initial enthusiasm rapidly waned. As Seidler concludes, the 'People's Levy' always remained a 'military paper tiger',[243] a judgment largely substantiated in the maelstrom of 1945.

CHAPTER 7

A Stay of Execution

No Longer 'Germany's Air Raid Shelter'

The realisation that the tide of war now brushed eastern Germany was not solely illustrated by the deteriorating situation on the Eastern Front. The second half of 1944 also heralded a growing threat to eastern German towns and cities from the air forces of the three major Allied powers. Soviet planes bombed East Prussian border towns, German supply depots and railway facilities in the province. They also attacked Breslau in early October. The RAF launched the heaviest assaults on eastern targets with devastating attacks on Stettin and Königsberg during late August. The same British formations also mined the Baltic, in the vicinity of Danzig and Königsberg, and together with the USAAF attempted to destroy the vital synthetic oil producing plant at Pölitz near Stettin. At the same time, American aircraft, based in southern Italy, were deployed attacking Upper Silesian oil and transportation installations.

The Soviet raids on East Prussia during the summer and autumn of 1944 were of a greater intensity than hitherto. They encountered little opposition from *Luftwaffe* fighters and stretched the air raid protection services to the limit. The heaviest raids were directed at Tilsit, Insterburg, Ebenrode and Gumbinnen. Whilst the Party authorities refused to issue evacuation orders for the indigenous population on account of the proximity of the Red Army, the impact of air attacks resulted in the removal of women, children and elderly inhabitants from these towns.

Tilsit, a key railway junction for the supply of Army Group North, by this time pressed back against the Baltic, was repeatedly attacked during the final week of July and the final week of August. Soviet reports highlighted the damage done to the German railway system at Tilsit. They claimed that German troop trains were hit and ammunition and fuel dumps blown up. Numerous fires had been started and were visible for many miles.[1] Nazi Party reports asserted that around 150 Soviet aircraft were involved in the night raids of 25–26 and 26–27 July but military reports numbered the attackers at around half this number.[2] Casualties were moderate, but there was extensive damage to the railway system and munitions trains in the shunting station.

Numerous large fires were started in the town centre and barracks, hospitals and the electricity works suffered damage.[3] The attacks in late August further aggravated the situation. Between 23 and 27 August, 815 buildings were totally destroyed and 400 buildings were badly or moderately damaged.[4] Party authorities estimated that the 300 Soviet planes dropped 3,500 bombs during the evening of 26 August. They admitted that there were large fires and initially estimated that 12,000 Tilsiters had been rendered homeless, around one-quarter of the town's population.[5] Other estimates were even higher. The NSV claimed that in the aftermath of this raid they found accommodation for 23,000 inhabitants and had distributed around 244,000 portions of hot food and 480,000 portions of cold food and coffee.[6]

A resident of Ragnit, around five miles east of Tilsit, recalled columns of soldiers and refugees from 'heavily bomb-shattered' Tilsit passing by. Evenings were largely spent in the cellar. The fighting on the Eastern Front was audible and following the nights of air attack the deterioration in conditions was evident everywhere. Windows were boarded up and scarcely any tradesmen were available to undertake repairs. Businesses were closed three days per week.[7] This same correspondent noted that after the July raids Tilsit was 'heavily battered'. Great agitation was noticeable among women and children, business had come to a standstill and there was no interest in work.[8] Little time now elapsed between the sirens sounding and the dropping of the first bombs. The front was so close and Soviet planes only faced a short flight to bomb Tilsit. Witnesses recalled fire storms raging in the devastated town centre. Parts of the famous cellulose factory, by the River Memel, were destroyed. Both gas and water supplies were cut and the gas and electricity works suffered extensive damage.[9] In order to raise the mood of those remaining in the ruined town, additional quantities of alcohol were distributed. This only produced noisy evening excesses at a time when the remaining inhabitants had hardly any sleep and according to one witness contributed to a rapid deterioration in the moral attitude of the remaining women in Tilsit.[10]

Inadequate precautions were taken in Tilsit against air raids. Shelters consisted of camouflaged splinter trenches, although Russian POWs and Polish labourers later shored them up with concrete. Large concrete bunkers were not built. Initially, no evacuation measures were enforced and the Party sought to prevent the population leaving Tilsit. However, more cautious citizens moved their families to the local countryside or to other towns within the province. Others left the town in the late afternoon and this resulted in arterial roads being blocked by pedestrians with suitcases and prams.[11] A senior police official recalled great bitterness at the attempts to force the population to stay in the face of escalating danger. This was attributed to the decisions of the authorities in Berlin and Königsberg. Certification from the police was required to purchase a train ticket. This simply heightened panic and failed in its objective of preventing an exodus. The population evaded these restrictions by walking to a station in a neighbouring town, where controls had not been arranged, and purchasing an appropriate ticket. The erection of roadblocks also proved ineffective and was not feasible for any length of time. By the time the authorities approved evacuation measures, many inhabitants had already left. The departure of the remaining women and children, in reserved trains, did not proceed smoothly. This only increased bad feeling among the population. Evacuation was permitted far too late leading to chaotic scenes.[12] Further damage was inflicted on Tilsit when it experienced renewed air attacks on 11 and 13 October. These raids necessitated the acceleration of evacuation measures. Within a week the Red Army stood on the opposite bank of the River Memel and for the three months prior to its capture by the Soviets on 20 January 1945 the town was subjected to artillery bombardment. A fraction of the pre-war population was in Tilsit when the Soviet shelling commenced and they quickly left.[13]

Insterburg, another important rail junction, also suffered at the hands of the Red Air Force.[14] The largest Soviet raid took place on the evening of 27 July. According to a military report, the town centre, railway station and a foreign workers camp were hit. There were 30 large fires. Railway buildings and rolling stock were damaged and a munitions train exploded.[15] The chief of the town's fire service later put the death toll at 120. He recalled encountering 120 fires of varying intensity. The town's industrial district was the focus of the attack and the Gustav Drengwitz chemical factory was badly affected.[16] This company had built bunkers and shelters and the workforce had received air raid protection training. However, when the raid occurred, most workers were digging defences in Lithuania. The factory owner had also been assigned to this task. The local Party authorities telephoned and advised him that the premises had been burnt down. He praised the heroic efforts of POWs, employed at the factory, for dealing with dozens of fire bombs.[17] Until the days immediately preceding the Soviet occupation on 21 January 1945, no raids of a comparable scale were launched against Insterburg. On isolated occasions, most notably on 23 December, bombs were dropped on the town but further damage was negligible. This was fortunate because the air raid protection authorities were continually weakened as personnel were called-up by the army.[18] A partial evacuation of the town was implemented at the behest of local state authorities and against the will of Koch. This arose from the Red Army's advance during October to within 25 miles of Insterburg and was not initiated on account of the air raids.[19]

Gumbinnen, around 15 miles east of Insterburg, was even more immediately threatened by the Red Army's advance. From July alarms became more frequent as Soviet planes regularly flew overhead and occasionally scattered bombs over the town. Women and children were evacuated in early August as a precautionary measure. Limitations were placed on the amount of luggage to be taken but evacuees believed that the inconvenience would be short-lived. One woman recalled that it was not foreseen that they would never see their home town again.[20] The evacuees were resettled within the province. Gumbinnen was spared until the early evening of 16 October. Then, according to one post-war account, around 800 fire and high-explosive bombs were dropped and the town was enveloped in a sea of flames and reduced to rubble. Structures not destroyed by the high explosive bombs were consumed by fire. Despite all the local fire brigades being summoned to the scene, little could be salvaged and 16 people were killed. Radio Moscow proclaimed that 'the entire town and railway station were enveloped in flames'. In view of the aerial threat and the Red Army's advance, all remaining civilians were evacuated from 20 October. A further devastating attack followed two days later.[21] The Red Air Force was virtually unchallenged over the East

Prussian frontier districts prior to the January offensive. However, no more heavy raids were launched. Instead, Soviet air activity was largely confined to probing attacks, reconnaissance activity and the dropping of agents behind German lines.

Silesia was also a target for the Red Air Force. Breslau, untouched for almost three years, was attacked on the evening of 7 October. The raid was aimed at the rail yards at Brockau in the south of the city and claimed 69 lives.[22] Military reports noted that although four factories, 55 buildings and a few *Wehrmacht* installations had been hit, the transportation system was not fractured.[23] Instances of plundering arose and one offender was condemned by the Special Court and executed.[24] Eastern cities such as Breslau, Königsberg and Danzig did not feel the full impact of the Red Air Force until the critical weeks of early 1945. For the time being, contemporary letters indicate that among eastern Germans there remained a far greater fear of the destructive powers of the British and American Air Forces than of their Soviet counterpart.[25]

The raids launched by the RAF on Stettin and Königsberg in late August 1944 were hugely destructive. The RAF maintained that these distant targets were chosen in order to disrupt German communications with the Eastern Front in an effort to support the Red Army's advance. As we have seen, Stettin had been a regular RAF target since 1940. Königsberg had hitherto been a Soviet target. However, on the evening of 9 April 1944 Bomber Command had dropped mines into the Baltic off Pillau in an attempt to block the sea channel to Königsberg.[26] The RAF despatched 461 bombers (five lost) to Stettin, 600 miles distant, on the night of 16–17 August and 403 bombers (23 lost) on the evening of 29–30 August.[27]

Stettin's historic old town, as well as numerous industrial concerns and the harbour facilities, were obliterated by the two raids. Numerous ships were sunk. After the first raid an initial Party report noted 'extraordinary high losses' in the old town.[28] Police President Grundey concurred and later recalled that the attack claimed 1,150 lives, including 78 children, five policemen and 33 soldiers. The death toll arising from the second raid was marginally less. The Police President noted that there were 1,033 fatalities, including 64 children, 13 policemen and 20 soldiers.[29] Both the Police President and the Party put the number made homeless by the first attack at around 50,000 and the former considered that 60,000 suffered this fate following the second raid.[30] The GSA in Stettin observed that at least 100,000 were made homeless as a result of 'two heavy terror attacks on the densely populated residential area'.[31] Some 3,077 residential buildings were totally destroyed, 1,565 badly damaged and 2,653 lightly damaged.[32] Huge quantities of foodstuffs were destroyed as bombs damaged the slaughterhouse, a major dairy and a sugar refinery.[33] The Party did not escape the carnage. The *Gau* building, home to the Propaganda Office, was totally destroyed in the second attack.[34]

The attack on 16 August was aimed at the port and industrial areas. However, Party reports immediately claimed that because of heavy flak defences the attackers dropped their bombs on Stettin's old town,[35] which, together with the port installations and the administrative area, were chiefly affected. In the narrow old town streets phosphorous bombs caused countless blazes to break out simultaneously and the firestorm produced a dreadful roar. Seas of flame blocked the streets and exacerbated the difficulties confronting rescuers. Hundreds crowded into the cellars under the old town hall and adjoining buildings or sought salvation in the tunnels beneath the castle. At least 1,850 people were rescued from the old town and from the cellars and tunnels under the castle. The historic heart of Stettin, on the west bank of the Oder, was ripped out. Major thoroughfares were reduced to rubble. Public buildings, schools, churches and hospitals were destroyed or badly damaged. In the harbour district, east of the river, warehouses and a grain silo were burnt down. Ships, fishing boats and barges amounting to around 27,000 gross register tons were sunk or badly damaged.[36] Numerous industrial premises, including important parts of the Stettiner Oder-Werke, were destroyed or heavily damaged, resulting in a subsequent fall in production.[37]

The raid on 29 August affected parts of the city which had previously escaped damage. In the industrial northern part of the city a number of shipyards and industrial concerns were destroyed. German reports intercepted by the British indicated that the Stettiner Oder-Werke East dockyard, a submarine repair facility, had been heavily hit. The 4th U-Boat flotilla reported that the the upper decks of some vessels were damaged and listed various parts of the dockyard which had been put out of action. Elsewhere in Stettin, the heat was so intense that the steel supports of the bridge, which formed part of the main road north from the city, buckled, and thus cut the route. The bombs devastated working-class districts and this accounts for the higher number rendered homeless. The harbour district received negligible additional punishment. Most of the 31,000 gross register tons of shipping sunk or damaged was located further down the river.[38]

The raids caused concern at the highest level. Goebbels repeatedly worried that negligible RAF losses indicated that the British were applying new tricks against the German defenders.[39] Contemporary reports indicated that German defences were weak. *The Times* reported that 'At Stettin the enemy appeared to be caught completely unawares, for the ground defences were only moderate and very few fighters were over the target.'[40] Goebbels noted that the second attack had 'fairly devastated' Stettin but was somewhat reassured because at least this time the RAF had suffered heavier losses. Moreover, despite Stettin's plight, he consoled himself that Schwede-Coburg was an 'energetic personality' who was already coping with situation.[41]

However, among Stettiners, rumours abounded regarding the conduct of Schwede-Coburg. Wide sections of the community passed on, with satisfaction, a rumour that Schwede had been taken to task by Göring and Goebbels and later arrested on account of the insufficient air raid protection measures. Remarkably, the location of the *Gauleiter*'s command bunker was also mentioned. Some rumour-mongers were jailed for six months or one year, and the sentences received publicity in the Party's *Pommersche Zeitung*. Moreover, despite the deployment of the entire police force and thousands of soldiers to assist the emergency and maintenance services, it appears that plundering was widespread. The level of confusion arising from such heavy raids led to few offenders being caught.[42]

The two RAF raids on Königsberg by relatively small numbers of bombers, resulted in the devastation of the city five months before the start of the Soviet siege. Königsberg was a 1,900-mile round trip for the Lancasters of No. 5 Bomber Group. The first raid was launched on the evening of 26–27 August by 174 bombers (four lost) and the devastating second attack three nights later involved 189 bombers (15 lost).[43] The low rate of aircraft lost in the first raid, despite the immensely challenging nature of the mission, can possibly be explained by the fact that many of the attacking force failed to find Königsberg. Nevertheless, the secret diary of the German High Command judged that the first raid on 26 August was centred on the north and north-eastern parts of the city. It produced numerous large fires, but had no adverse impact on war industries.[44] German accounts insisted that on both occasions the RAF violated Swedish airspace and tended to grossly overestimate the numbers of British bombers participating in the second raid on 29 August.[45] There were legitimate military targets in the northern part of the city, but they remained unscathed. It is because of this and the city centre being hit by a few stray bombs that the first raid has not attracted the same degree of notoriety as that associated with the second. However, it is estimated that 1,000 still perished, five per cent of buildings were destroyed and 10,000 people were rendered homeless.[46] In a letter written the following morning, a corporal claimed that one third of the city had burnt down, described the scene as terrible and wondered what the evening would bring.[47] Another witness remembered that the sky over the north of the city had turned red and recalled smelling what he thought was phosphorous or magnesium.[48]

East Prussian newspapers attempted to bolster morale following the first raid. The Party's *Preußische Zeitung* featured a sketch of a chain of civilians passing buckets of water to douse the flames with the caption 'Against British terror – the fighting people's community'.[49] Other articles constantly stressed that the British had infringed Swedish air space and that this terror raid against civilians in residential areas was motivated by the British wish to support Bolshevism. It was admitted that there had been considerable fire damage in the northern outer districts of the city. Nevertheless, the role played by *Gauleiter* and Party was lauded. Koch had taken personal charge of the situation, visited the afflicted districts and given out direct orders. Energetic air raid protection measures were said to have ensured that casualties were relatively low. The actions of the Party's NSV were mentioned before those of the Red Cross in the provision of care for the bombed out. Moreover, reports stressed the determination of those who had suffered during the raid and their unbroken faith in victory. The attack had been successfully confronted and the smooth functioning of the emergency services and Party formations was highlighted. The notion of a 'fighting community', with the NSDAP at the forefront, was nurtured. It was maintained that the bombing had only strengthened the attitude of the population and reinforced the bonds of comradeship.[50]

Koch also took the opportunity to address an appeal to Königsbergers. He condemned the 'cruel and barbaric enemy' which had inflicted terror on innocent women and children. Equally, to stiffen morale he pointed to the danger of death faced every day by German troops on all fronts. Furthermore, he also reflected on the suffering endured by other large German cities from air attack. This served to emphasise that the enemy would not break German resistance. The public was to assist the authorities in every way possible, follow orders and maintain their composure. Persons who had suffered loss or damage were promised provisions. Concurrently, Koch also warned against plundering which was punishable by death. Nobody was to leave the city without permission and employees were to report to their workplaces. Koch concluded that 'victory or annihilation lie in our hands' and proclaimed that 'Enemy terror bombing cannot shatter our fanatical belief in victory. Harder than the stone destroyed in the bombing terror, is the will of 80 million Germans in victory.'[51]

The will of the Königsberg population was certainly tested on the night of 29–30 August 1944. Sirens droned and the radio announced the approach of a strong attacking force over the Danziger Bight. Although a Mandrel Screen (jamming apparatus) concealed the objective for much of the way, the distance to the target meant that the Germans were able to plot the progress of the bombers and provide strong opposition over Königsberg. Despite this heavy German fighter opposition, *en route* and over the city itself, a 'brilliant attack . . . wrought tremendous havoc in Königsberg'.[52] *The Times* claimed that the attackers had 'completely outwitted' *Luftwaffe* fighter packs on their way to Königsberg.[53] One historian contends that '[this attack] lay the foundations for the fire-storm raids on Darmstadt, Brunswick, Heilbronn, and finally Dresden'.[54] From Insterburg, 50 miles distant, it was possible to 'see the fiery glow rising into the night sky'.[55]

Low cloud over the target led to a 20-minute delay in commencing the attack which had been set for 1.07 am on the morning of 30 August. When the marker aircraft found a break in the clouds the Master Bomber allowed the attack to start. The final bombs were dropped at 1.52 am. On account of the distance to the target and the extra fuel required, bomb loads were lighter and 491 tons of bombs were dropped on Königsberg, 137 tons of High Explosive bombs and 354 tons of incendiaries of the small but destructive four pounds type. While new marking and bombing techniques ensured that a raid by minor forces could achieve major results,[56] the attack was costly for Bomber Command. Some 175 machines out of the 189 all-Lancaster force despatched attacked the target and 15 planes and crew were lost – 7.9 per cent of the force deployed – a rate which was more than double the average, 3.7 per cent, for major night raids on Germany in August 1944.[57]

Entries in the German military diary and Goebbels' diary illustrate that the scale of the raid was immediately appreciated. The centre-points of the attack were the port area, old town, city centre and western districts. Extensive fires in the city centre and considerable damage to housing and hospitals were reported.[58] Goebbels stated that the raid would have a particularly bad effect in Königsberg which had hitherto been spared from such attacks. He also extended his sympathy to Koch already burdened with so many other problems and now encountering this in his *Gauhauptstadt*.[59] A telephone conversation with Koch provided a fairly shocking picture of the situation. Koch confirmed that most of the city centre was obliterated.[60]

Initial RAF reconnaissance obtained from photographs taken on the morning of 2 September highlighted damage 'concentrated mainly in the town centre and extending into the docks area in the South-west'.[61] It was noted that:

> Damage to business and residential property is very heavy, particularly in the closely built-up area around the castle where the State theatre has been burnt down, a road bridge over the Schlossteich destroyed, and the Post Office and Reichsbank damaged. The castle itself has been gutted with the exception of one tower.[62]

The report also stressed that railway installations had been hit, 44 warehouses on the banks of the River Pregel had been destroyed and parts of the Waggonfabrik Steinfurt AG rolling stock works were damaged.[63] However, the Immediate Assessment of Results produced by Air Staff Intelligence on 5 September adopted a triumphant tone and celebrated Königsberg's passing:

> 1,900 miles, 176 aircraft, 485 tons of bombs, 16 minutes and 400 acres of devastation. This calls, and without apology, for yet another misquotation of the Prime Minister's famous epigram: "Never has so much destruction been wrought by so few aircraft, at so great a distance in so short a time". Königsberg, the capital of East Prussia, the greatest port in Eastern Germany, and the base for nearly 50 enemy divisions is no more. Königsberg, the administrative centre of that province of Germany which has been the most malignant breeding ground of the arrogant military caste, a town which has stood unchanged for 600 years has, to the benefit of mankind, been wiped-out over-night.[64]

The report underlined the assistance rendered to the Soviets by the attack: 'Königsberg may have been just another strategical target to Bomber Command, though a large and important one at that – it was a tactical target of the Russians of absolutely first-class importance.'[65] The RAF estimated that 41 per cent of all buildings and 20 per cent of industrial buildings had been destroyed, 134,000 Königsbergers had been made homeless and another 61,000 had their homes damaged.[66] Some 420 tons of bombs, 86 per cent of the bomb load, had fallen on the built-up administrative area of the city. The RAF estimated that between 1,100 and 2,200 had been killed and a similar number had suffered serious injury but caution was placed on the accuracy of these figures as the fires had been so extensive.[67] The RAF's Assessment Report of 24 September concluded:

> Damage in Königsberg resulting from the recent raids is severe. Fire appears to have been the primary agent, and the effects spread roughly in a SW-NE direction across the town. The devastation is for the most part concentrated in the old centre, known as the Inner Town which forms a medieval nucleus of the Hanseatic type. There the proportion of built up area which has been destroyed is high – in the fully built up zones it amounts to 65% whilst areas of the Outer Town immediately surrounding the core are only slightly less affected.[68]

On the ground the German authorities tried to ascertain the damage. OLG President Dräger noted on 9 September that the city centre had been the focal point of the attacks and the area destroyed was three kilometres wide. Some 840 bodies had been recovered while a further 1,000 were under the debris. Initially, it was thought that between 130,000–150,000 people had lost their homes, roughly half of the city's remaining inhabitants.[69] Similarly, on 5 September, Erich Post, the East Prussian NSV leader reported that 117,520 people had been evacuated from their city into the neighbouring countryside.[70] At the end of October, the repercussions of the raids still occupied a large section of the OLG President's report to Berlin. He mentioned that half the city's homes had been lost and 120,000 inhabitants had been moved to the countryside. In the meantime, a large proportion of this exodus had been transported on to Saxony.[71]

However, post-war accounts argue that even these figures were too low. Fritz Gause, the city's postwar historian, asserted that the attacks were directed against residential and business areas. He contended that the numbers buried in the rubble, suffocated in air raid shelters or devoured by the firestorm would never be ascertained. Gause settled for an estimate of 4,200 killed and missing and 200,000 homeless.[72] The studies by Major Dieckert, General Lasch and Edgar Lass all quote figures similar to those suggested by the city's *Oberbürgermeister*, Dr Will, following his release from Soviet captivity in 1955. Will maintained that the second attack was directed at the densely populated area, with its narrow streets, within the city walls. He fixed the death toll at almost 2,400, the homeless at approximately 150,000 and believed that almost half of the city's buildings were never restored.[73]

Contemporary accounts outlined the magnitude of the devastation. Over 90 per cent of the outlets selling food, textiles, shoes, glass and porcelain were destroyed. Around 60 per cent of storage space was lost because of the destruction of numerous warehouses. The majority of public buildings were reduced to rubble. Moreover, the railway offices, stock exchange and five major banks centred around the Steindamm, the main business district of the city, were levelled to the ground. The commercial damage was matched by the cultural losses. A notable casualty was the Dom (cathedral) located on the Kneiphof, an island in the River Pregel. This Gothic structure, dating from the early sixteenth century, was burnt out. A similar fate befell the adjoining old university building. The Schloß (castle), which contained the District Court, offices and various museum collections, suffered extensive damage. The Schloßkirche (Castle Church), the coronation church for Prussian kings, also fell victim to the fire. As the university and most of its institutes were destroyed, studies were suspended and the students re-directed into war-related activities.[74] It was a far cry from the pomp and promises surrounding the 400th anniversary celebrations in early July, a mere eight weeks before.

Industrial districts on both sides of the Pregel, the harbour area, the famous Schichau shipyard and the main railway station remained untouched.[75] However, fires raged on for days in cordoned-off areas within the city centre.[76] Count Hans von Lehndorff remembered the scene:

> Three days later it was possible to travel to the town. Everything was smoking and charring under a radiant September sky. A road had been cleared for traffic through the unimaginable sea of ruins, and on either side of it, lay the iron skeletons that had come down as whirling firebrands.[77]

All sections of the population were shattered by the experience of the raid and its appalling impact on the city's rich historic heritage. One observer recalled that the explosions of the bombs seemed endless. An inferno sprang up which engulfed the area between the North Station and the Main Station in the south.[78] The scale of the disaster totally overwhelmed the authorities on the night of the bombing.[79] Rescuers were stretched to the limit. Everyone pitched in. French workers from the Schichau shipyard were among those driving emergency vehicles into stricken districts. An accompanying writer, viewing the immense seas of flames, was drawn to make comparisons with the eruption of Vesuvius and Dante's inferno.[80] In the city centre, the

Kneiphof island was completely cut off as all five bridges over the Pregel were destroyed. A number of Königsbergers attempted to escape from the flames, jumped into the river and drowned.[81] As would be the case in the aftermath of the raids on Dresden and the later atomic explosions, the intensity of the firestorm caused debris to be swept into the air and dispersed far and wide. Charred papers and packaging passed by one witness as he stood on his balcony and viewed the burning city.[82] A similar sight was experienced by an estate owner 25 miles from the city. As he rode around his property, he observed that papers and pages from books covered his fields.[83]

In common with other victims of heavy raids, Königsbergers expressed disappointment that their suffering did not receive greater national recognition. British sources observed: 'Instead to judge from the lack of comments in the Press and on the wireless it has left the enemy speechless.'[84] German propaganda followed the usual format, with the focus being on the vilification of the enemy for its 'sadistic terror attacks' carried out by the 'Barbaric gangsters of the air'.[85] Laconic radio reports downplayed the extent of the disaster to the rest of the Reich and talked of 'great destruction in residential quarters'.[86] The scale of the human tragedy was ignored. At local level serious technical difficulties hampered the dissemination of propaganda material. The damage inflicted on newspaper offices and printers resulted in the suspension of publication of Königsberg's three daily titles and their temporary replacement by an emergency news sheet.[87] The second issue, dated 1 September 1944, featured a proclamation by Koch in which he stressed that military targets had not been the enemy's objective. He condemned the murderous raid which had taken place when the Bolshevik foe stood on the province's frontier. Relief measures were outlined, such as the reissuing of ration cards to those who had lost their original documents. Moreover, Koch also promised that the city's menfolk deployed constructing defences would be called back immediately. Once more it was emphasised that Königsberg had endured the same terror that other great German cities had already suffered for years.[88] Indeed, a stick of bombs landed on Koch's Groß Friedrichsburg estate. Supervising the cleaning up he seethed, '*That* won't be allowed to happen again.'[89]

Similar sentiments were conveyed in an article entitled 'The People's Community is Stronger than Terror Bombing' which was published in the *Preußische Zeitung* on 5 September. Königsberg had now fallen victim to the 'murderous lust' of the 'British air pirates'. The authorities emphasised that the priority was to restore order and get the economy functioning again. Milk and water supplies were being distributed while telephone and gas services were being restored. In the absence of shops, purchases could be made from traders operating with wheelbarrows.[90] The Party hierarchy played a central role in the subsequent mass funeral. On Sunday 10 September, the bodies of 1,044 victims including 35 children, were cremated. Koch, his deputy Ferdinand Großherr and Königsberg's *Kreisleiter* Ernst Wagner were present. The latter thanked Koch for the welfare measures which accounted for the extremely low number of 'murdered children'. Koch also addressed the gathering and attacked the enemy for their insane, hate-filled actions which had left so many East Prussians dead and reduced Königsberg to a field of rubble. Nevertheless, the report concluded that from the feeling of standing together, united in grief, there flowed a stronger sense of confidence.[91]

Propaganda 'spin' could not alter the reality that now confronted Königsbergers in their daily lives. The authorities were suddenly faced with a huge number of homeless people requiring food, accommodation and clothing. The NSV claimed that around 505,000 portions of hot food, 1,150,000 portions of cold food and 265,000 portions of coffee had been distributed. Moreover, substantial quantities of tobacco, and goods from military stores were handed out.[92] Party organisations provided shelter, coffee and words of encouragement. They were self-appointed relievers of suffering, but they themselves had brought about the circumstances which led to Königsberg's demise.[93] Those involved in measures to alleviate the situation worked hard. One young woman, whose home had been partly destroyed by the bombing, recalled seeing citizens in chain formation passing buckets of water in an effort to extinguish the fires. This was hot, strenuous and thirsty work.[94] Meanwhile, female students assigned to dispense hot soup had to remain at their posts for four days before being permitted to return home.[95]

While national newspapers later mentioned that Königsberg was the victim of cultural barbarians,[96] local reports attempted to highlight the city's recovery. Gradually normality was restored and this was said to illustrate the victory of order over Allied destruction. Columns of workers, organised by the OT, were involved in reconstruction. Rubble was utilised as building material.[97] The cleaning-up process was partially successful and services were restored. One observer noted:

> Some small roads were closed forever, but the big ones were cleared, leaving the rubble at the side, often covering all the pavements. We had water and electricity, shops were open, trams and trains were running . . . We even had post, with the post-women delivering letters every day.[98]

Accounts show that in Königsberg, as elsewhere in Germany, despite the destruction, morale recovered. Those staying in the city tried to resume their daily lives and re-establish a routine. Indeed, some of the city's suburbs remained virtually untouched by war until the beginning of the beginning of the Soviet siege at the end of January 1945 and armaments were still manufactured locally for the garrison during this struggle. Those evacuated to central Germany hoped to come back and sometimes made short trips home in the weeks before the Red Army avalanche engulfed the province to check property or recover possessions.

Despite the efforts of the administration and the population the scale of the devastation could not be disguised. A forestry official, visiting the city on official business in early January, was shocked at the 'completely destroyed' city centre and noted that ruins and rubble stretched as far as the eye could see. The once pulsating business sector of the liveliest city in eastern Germany was totally obliterated.[99] The authorities downplayed the impact of the air raids on East Prussia. The GSA in Königsberg insisted that 'The air raids have, in contrast to developments on the Eastern Front, apart from the first shock, had no important consequences on the mood and attitude of the population.'[100] Meanwhile, Maertins sent a teletype message to Berlin urgently requesting new pictures of the *Führer* and Dr Goebbels for the propaganda office's new premises. However, the reply from Berlin illustrated the state of the Third Reich by November 1944. The Propaganda Ministry advised that it had no more portraits at its disposal as they had all been distributed to other bombed out departments.[101]

The protestations of the regime were to no avail. The bombing of Königsberg symbolised the city's downfall. Temporary bridges and emergency accommodation were stopgap measures. Gause considered that 'Königsberg as a living organism was paralysed following these two August nights. What followed was a fight to the death without hope of a favourable outcome.'[102] One account argued that 'the heart of our homeland was broken'.[103] Nazi propaganda enjoyed some success in the realm of apportioning blame. Some 25 years later the East Prussian expellee newspaper echoed the same sentiments as 1944. It emphasised that cultural treasures, accumulated over 700 years, had gone up in smoke and that the attacks had simply been aimed at the residential areas of a defenceless city. Meanwhile, industrial installations by the Pregel, factories, shipyards and the railway network 'had been spared for the Asiatic bands'.[104]

The attacks caused considerable suffering, administrative dislocation and shattering symbolic damage. Rudimentary recovery was achieved among the ruins. Ironically, the evacuation of bombed out civilians to Saxony proved to be a blessing in disguise in view of Königsberg's tribulations over the next few months and years. The city's heritage may have disappeared overnight but the raids had a limited impact on the German war machine. Königsberg's rail and harbour installations continued to function and it retained its key role in the supply and reinforcement of the Eastern Front. Unlike Bomber Command's raids on Stettin in 1944 there were no reports of shipping being sunk or damaged. In contrast, an RAF reconnaissance report, using photographs taken over the city on 15 September 1944, noted that 'the dockyard facilities are engaged to full capacity especially for the re-armament of vessels. The berths in the area Naval Base to Schichau are all occupied, often with two ships moored abreast. The floating docks are all in use.'[105] The impact on the fortification programme was minimal too as this was already being scaled down from the heady levels experienced between mid-July and early August. As we have seen, the *Wehrmacht* had already propped up Army Group Centre. September 1944 was a quiet month on the East Prussian front as Soviet efforts were directed against the *Wehrmacht* in the Balkan and Baltic theatres. Königsberg's military capabilities were unscathed by the attacks. The barracks and ring of forts were hardly touched. Bomber Command undoubtedly disfigured Königsberg in August 1944 but it did not knock the city out of the war. That task was completed by the artillery of the Red Army in April 1945.

Allied bombers were also directed against the Pölitz oil plant, north of Stettin, and at similar hydrogenation works within Upper Silesia. The attacks were overwhelmingly undertaken by the USAAF which had given these sources of precious fuel a priority status. Such targets were heavily defended by flak and fighters and the Germans attempted elaborate deception measures to lure the bombers into dropping their incendiaries into surrounding countryside. The raids, which increased in scale and intensity during the latter half of 1944, were part of the American effort to cut the lifeblood of the German military machine.[106]

No area of the Reich remained immune from bombing. It was no longer a question of the 'bombed' and 'unbombed'. By the dawn of 1945 only Dresden, Breslau and

Danzig among major German cities had avoided devastation from air attack. However, the hour of their downfall was approaching. The almost daily attacks on Upper Silesia, were by December 1944 reminiscent of earlier sustained Allied campaigns against the Ruhr and Berlin, although the suffering inflicted on the civilian population was milder in comparison. One historian has contended that 'the city street became the battlefield on which a steadily increasing number of Germans fought their nightly struggle for survival'.[107] A growing number of town and city dwellers in eastern Germany were now involved in this battle. As a result, a further displacement of the population arose. By the end of 1944 rationing statistics indicate that the population of Stettin had fallen by almost 38 per cent from 382,984 in 1939 to 238,116. In Königsberg numbers declined by more than 32 per cent from 372,164 in 1939 to 252,752. Corresponding increases were reported from rural districts in the eastern provinces.[108]

The regime's propagandists insisted that the Allied fliers were 'murderers', 'pirates' and 'barbarians'. The rhetoric emphasised that all sections of German society suffered together, producing a *Volksgemeinschaft* bonded together by sacrifice; sharing similar privations to those endured by frontline soldiers. This was a heroic image but a distinctly unappealing reality as Germany entered the sixth year of war. The destruction visited on German cities exemplified the emptiness of the regime's rhetoric and the powerlessness of the *Luftwaffe*. Allied air armadas flew unmolested from one end of the Reich to the other. A Stettiner who witnessed the attacks on his city during 1944 reckoned that it was no longer a question of the *Luftwaffe* acting as a defensive factor against the enemy air forces. Rather, the Allies simply planned the systematic destruction of one part of the city after another.[109] Before the Soviets launched their January 1945 offensive, Königsberg, Stettin, Tilsit and Gumbinnen were already fields of rubble. Centuries of cultural development vanished in a matter of minutes under the bombs.

Before the Storm

Nazi propagandists did not attempt to deny the prospect of a major Soviet offensive on the Eastern Front over the winter of 1944–1945. In an effort to reassure the population, the regime's rhetoric concentrated on emphasising German defensive preparations, shorter lines and apparent Soviet weaknesses. Newspapers exuded confidence that a Red Army offensive would be repelled, and the military also expressed positive opinions when liaising with local officials. In the aftermath of the October fighting, East Prussia was reported to be a hive of activity in keeping with the spirit of total war. The roads were said to be busy as refugee columns moved westwards from the frontier districts and tanks headed east. The *Volkssturm* undertook duties in the rear, the Hitler Youth were deployed reinforcing the fortifications systems and youths on labour service gathered the turnip crop. Eastern Front veterans taught local farmers how to use rifles, hand grenades and *Panzerfäuste*. Every dwelling housed refugees and a friendly atmosphere seemingly prevailed. Although the winter was approaching, hearts were warmer and the entire East Prussian *Gau* was bound together to overcome the demands of this fateful hour.[110] A front-page article in *Das Reich* emphasised that the East Prussian population had reacted positively during October. The stabilisation of the front signalled the end of the first battle for East Prussia. This demonstrated to the Soviets that their attacks on German soil lacked penetration, and it was underlined that German forces on all fronts were daily becoming more concentrated.[111]

Reports from war correspondents in East Prussia highlighted the positive mood and determination of the German defenders. The value of the *Ostwall* and the *Volkssturm* in halting numerically and materially superior enemy forces was continually emphasised in their despatches. The defences had already blunted Red Army attacks during August and October leading to enormous enemy losses.[112] The Propaganda Ministry also ordered the dissemination of oral propaganda to combat the kind of criticism of defensive positions which had been prevalent since the Atlantic Wall had failed to stop the Allied invasion in June 1944. This had led to many people placing too little value on the building of frontier defences. However, during the Soviet autumn offensive 'not only the *Ostwall* but also the *Volkssturm* had seen its significance fully proved'. The propaganda slogans claimed that the frontier defences had won Germany time to regroup and regain freedom of action which would ultimately result in the repulsion of the enemy from the Reich's borders.[113]

East Prussian newspapers said that the province had been transformed into a fortress as the *Volkssturm*, in addition to receiving anti-tank combat training from the *Wehrmacht*, undertook further work to consolidate established positions. Trenches, bunkers and tank traps were dug or strengthened. It was repeatedly stressed during this lull in fighting that every town and village was being converted into a fortress surrounded by trenches, belts of barbed wire, tank traps and camouflaged strongpoints.[114] Koch told representatives from a locally raised *Volksgrenadier* division that in 'Fortress East Prussia' the entire population was prepared to take an active part in the defence against any Bolshevik breakthrough. Koch also claimed that more than 100,000 *Volkssturmmänner* were deployed at the front or in the rear, where their presence ensured that younger soldiers could be released for front-line duties. He concluded that East Prussia bravely awaited the approaching winter campaign.[115]

The press also reported brutal Soviet orders and localised German successes in East Prussia. The Red Army had been ordered to 'kill off the wounded Fascist beast in his lair' but once again individual German achievements were underlined and it was emphasised that German preparations ensured that they would not be 'killed off' in East Prussia.[116] Publicly, and sometimes privately, the *Wehrmacht* put on a brave face. Colonel-General Reinhardt told a *Volkssturm* swearing-in ceremony at Insterburg's stadium that the front was stable.[117] In mid-December, Reinhardt's counterpart at Army Group A, Colonel General Josef Harpe, advised the commander of the Silesian military district that the *Wehrmacht* remained strong enough to protect Germany's borders. Therefore, the conversion of Breslau into a fortress was not considered particularly urgent.[118]

In December 1944, propaganda concentrated on events in the west and the struggle for Hungary. There was very little coverage of the East Prussian and Polish sectors of the Eastern Front. The few reports mentioned the German defence in depth and the confidence of the troops following the defeat of the October offensive against East Prussia. A broadcast of 'A tour of the Eastern Front' on 9 December did, however, concede that, 'For the time being forces are still only being concentrated on the likely new focal points in East Prussia and on the southern sector of the Eastern Front, where the protective wall in front of Silesia has been erected.'[119] East Prussian officials recounted positive briefings from Army Group Centre officers. Dr Victor von Poser, *Landrat* of Ortelsburg, had the Army Group's headquarters in his district and frequently met staff officers. They provided a confident assessment of the situation which appeared to be borne out by the peacefulness of the Narew front and the absence of enemy air raids. Over Christmas the chamber orchestra of the Berlin Philharmonic played for the staff. An optimistic mood prevailed even when the headquarters moved back to Wartenburg in Allenstein district at the beginning of January.[120] The Army Group liaison officer with the local administration remained upbeat, repeatedly assuring one Allenstein official that the formation had never been so strong or better dug in.[121]

The propagandists also attempted to identify heartening signs of Soviet weakness. They pointed to partisan activity in the Ukraine, the challenge posed by the Vlasov movement and mass desertions in the East Prussian sector. Party propagandists were told to distribute details of a Ukrainian uprising in late October which had forced the Soviets to deploy NKVD troops and to highlight the ongoing anti-Soviet partisan campaign. Moreover, German propagandists exploited a radio report by Alexander Werth, Moscow correspondent of *The Times*, which appeared to endorse the success of German scorched earth tactics. Werth had said that the rebuilding of Kiev's industry would take years as almost the entire population had departed, mostly to Germany. The lack of able workers led to little activity in the mining sector in the Ukraine and an inability to rebuild the destroyed electricity system.[122] Goebbels took comfort from the upsurge in partisan activity in the Soviet rear, particularly in the Ukraine, recalling how extraordinarily dangerous this had been for Germany earlier in the war. He hoped that this, together with German demolitions, would cause the Soviets transportation difficulties over the winter.[123]

German propaganda claimed that the resistance in the Soviet rear illuminated the significance of General Vlasov's leadership of the Russian struggle for freedom from Bolshevik terror.[124] However, Goebbels believed that the German people could not accept this new sustained propaganda and, bearing in mind that the Russians had been labelled subhuman for years, said that a decision had to be made as to whether they were 'swamp people' or 'ideal figures'. Goebbels, echoing Hitler's lack of enthusiasm for the whole scheme, declared that Vlasov propaganda was better directed at Soviet troops than at Germans.[125] Indeed, Vlasov's 'Committee for the Liberation of the Peoples in Russia' was launched in Prague in November 1944 but the whole enterprise was rendered impotent, embroiled as it was in disputes involving the SS, *Wehrmacht* and *Reichsleiter* Alfred Rosenberg's *Ostministerium*. Nazi propaganda also predicted a sudden Soviet military collapse, claiming that the Red Army was only held together by draconian measures. A captured document was cited which reported that desertions had dramatically risen following the stabilisation of the East Prussian front. During the first fortnight of November, 240 men from one division alone were shot for this offence. In future in any unit where a single case of desertion was reported ten men were to be shot.[126] German propagandists tried to highlight demoralisation among members of the various minority peoples making up much of the Red Army. The new recruits, seized during recent offensives, allowed the Soviets to advance and according to one radio report, 'Without its masses of booty soldiers, the Soviet army would today be compelled to stop its attack, and, at the expense of production, recruit an army from the masses of armaments workers.'[127] Throughout the closing months of 1944 Goebbels received reports from various sources on the condition of the Soviet Union. On 23 October, he stated that in Moscow it was estimated that losses of seven million had been sustained to date, but he correctly believed the true figure to be far higher.[128]

The problem with Goebbels' information was that much of it came from old Party comrades, either visiting or on leave from the Eastern Front, or from Red Army prisoners anxious to appease their German interrogators. Goebbels sought evidence to prove that the Red Army was 'war weary'. The composition of prisoners seemed to substantiate this notion. They were either very young or very old and most originated from areas recently under German occupation. Goebbels wrote that Soviet troops were of the 'worst class' and that it was only their material superiority which enabled them to stand opposite to the Germans on the battlefield. He hoped that the Bolsheviks had finally reached the end of their manpower resources.[129] Christmas visits by Berlin *Kreisleiter* to East Prussia led Goebbels to observe that German troops in the province were upbeat and convinced that they would repulse the imminent Soviet offensive. German troops in the Warsaw sector were also said to be optimistic.[130] Nevertheless, privately Goebbels feared what was approaching. Initially, he thought that Stalin would celebrate the anniversary of the Bolshevik Revolution by launching his attack on 7 November 1944. Thereafter, he regularly speculated on the likely launch date.[131]

Furthermore, despite his public confidence in the strength of the Eastern Front, Goebbels was sometimes privately unconvinced about the state of German defences and the depth of Soviet difficulties. He realised that defensive lines were very thinly manned.[132] Moreover, he also admitted that a report on life in the Soviet Union submitted by a German officer who had escaped from Soviet captivity was 'too optimistic'. This account claimed that the Soviet population was exhausted and that the regime relied solely on terror to continue the conflict. Goebbels confessed that very strong Red Army troop concentrations were massing for an attack over the Christmas period.[133] When it did not materialise he thought that 'Stalin is purposely giving us a chance so that our defences in the West shall not be weakened so much.'[134] Divisional commanders from the front visiting Berlin over Christmas maintained that the line was extremely strong, but then admitted that petrol was in short supply and that the new *Volksgrenadier* divisions were third and fourth-rate. They also predicted that in the 'unlikely' event of a successful Soviet breakthrough German morale could shatter.[135]

Propaganda reports appeared to indicate a similarly fluctuating mood in East Prussia. In early December the view was heard that the Russians were unable to begin the planned offensive because of growing demoralisation among their troops. This led to comparisons being made with 1917.[136] Three weeks later it was reported from 'the eastern part of the Reich' that the population hoped that their entrenchment work would assist 'our troops to withstand a new onslaught'.[137] This apparent repetition of the regime's propaganda tenets was contradicted by evidence of the disappointing response of East Prussians to the weekly newsreel. When this was shown at the end of the programme half the audience made sure that they left the cinema after the main film.[138]

Privately, officers told both the reporter Günther Heysing and *Bürgermeister* Wander of Insterburg that an offensive was imminent and the front was grossly undermanned.[139] Fortunately the Red Air Force was less evident at the onset of winter.[140] However, the Soviets retained overwhelming air superiority. The *Luftwaffe* was bereft of fuel. It undertook isolated reconnaissance missions but was unable to interfere in the Soviet build up by attacking their major railway junctions.[141] From decrypted messages, British codebreakers found out that *Kriegsmarine* vessels operating in the eastern Baltic were not receiving adequate fighter cover from *Luftflotte* 6 as it anticipated a Soviet thrust at East Prussia and had to conserve fuel stocks.[142] Similarly, despite naval requests, no air reconnaissance was undertaken by the *Luftwaffe* over the eastern Baltic in November 1944.[143]

Ordinary soldiers confronted a fourth war winter on the Eastern Front. Whilst mud and sludge caused similar problems to those encountered in Russia, one East Prussian soldier was consoled that empty steppe was rare in his home province.[144] Conditions still remained grim, however. A soldier occupying an advanced position east of Gumbinnen complained that he was leading a 'dog's life'. He was unable to wash and shave. For weeks he had been expected to remain outside in the freezing cold for 15 hours every day, snatching a few hours sleep in primitive winter quarters in which there was no stove.[145] Rations were insufficient and troops could not simply seize foodstuffs from the local population as they had done in Russia. Nevertheless, despite official warnings to the contrary, the herds of cattle wandering behind German lines proved a temptation and were sometimes killed and butchered by the troops.[146] Another account was relayed by refugees on their return to Königsberg from Tilsit where they had collected additional clothing and linen. In Tilsit they were amazed to see that in one house German soldiers had stripped down a freshly slaughtered pig on a couch and smashed a sideboard to pieces for firewood when sufficient chopped wood was available in the cellar.[147]

Local judicial authorities and the SS commented angrily at the behaviour of soldiers in the East Prussian evacuation zone. The judiciary reported that German soldiers had gone on the rampage during the evacuation of Ostenburg (Zichenau district).[148] Later it was observed in Ragnit district that *Wehrmacht* and *Volkssturm* personnel had plundered most properties. The damage presented a 'terrible sight'.[149] The SS complained that troops had been stationed in the east for years and did not seem to understand that they were now on German soil defending German values. Wooden buildings close to the front were stripped down. Boarding and panelling was torn away, floorboards ripped out, beams sawn out and hatches, windows and doors taken. This wood was either used in bunkers or for burning, whilst trees in nearby woods were either untouched or had been felled wastefully. Valuables had disappeared from homes and furniture was destroyed or removed. The SS claimed that waste and squandering on a scale unparalleled since the beginning of the eastern campaign had occurred. Considering the losses to property suffered through bombing, Germany could scarcely afford to lose more because of the arbitrariness and indiscipline displayed by *Wehrmacht* units.[150] The Deputy Chief of the General Staff, General Walther Wenck, received these SS complaints. On 28 December, he promised that sharp directives would be issued to combat such behaviour and that the perpetrators would be punished.[151] However, German troops were to remain in these areas for barely three more weeks.

The final period of German rule in East Prussia also witnessed an upsurge in partisan activity involving instances of murder, fire raising and robbery, attributed to Soviet agents dropped into the province. Some were former German POWs with Soviet training who joined this scheme simply to escape Russia. Upon landing they reported voluntarily to the local military authorities.[152] *Oberforstmeister* Kramer of Elchwald, east of Insterburg, remembered that a man reported to him purporting to be a German lieutenant. He had been assigned to a partisan group by his Soviet captors but at a favourable moment had killed his companions. After further enquiries it was established that this initially fantastic account was indeed true.[153] However, a number of post-war testimonies emphasised the scale of the partisan problem. *Forstmeister* Hartwig of Memelwalde recalled that following clashes with these Soviet agents and the discovery of their camp, he concluded that they had been observing German troop movements and communicating the details by radio. The agents were supplied with German rations, identity and rail passes and wore German uniforms.[154]

Colonel von Bredow, then with the *Gendarmerie*, maintained that Soviet agents were almost exclusively former German POWs and frequently originated from areas forcibly incorporated into the Reich such as western Poland (Danzig–West Prussia, Warthegau, eastern Upper Silesia) and Alsace-Lorraine. Bredow stressed that sabotage troops in German uniforms played an important role supporting the Soviet advance by issuing false orders and sowing confusion in the German rear.[155] The Germans enacted measures to counter the threat. The Bialystok *Gendarmerie* was transferred to the affected area and a headquarters was established in Angerburg to co-ordinate operations and liaise with the *Luftwaffe* which monitored all flights over the province. Losses were negligible with the exception of a major clash with a strong partisan group west of Nordenburg (Gerdauen district) in early November. Bredow claimed that prior to 20 January 1945 some 200 partisans were arrested or 'put out of action'.[156] Similarly, prior to Christmas 1944, 87 agents were reportedly dropped by parachute on the Lötzen fortified area. They caused little damage, but their activities provoked anxiety among the population.[157]

All the time, East Prussians were kept in the dark about the true gravity of the situation. When German reconnaissance aircraft discovered the scale of the Soviet build up opposite East Prussia, their findings were not disclosed to a home audience but were disseminated for foreign consumption: 'Photographs taken despite extremely strong fighter and AA defences show strong concentrations of enemy artillery forces which are considerably greater than the artillery employed in the first battle . . . The Kremlin has made available for the new offensive a fleet of about 1,350 aircraft.'[158] A number of potentially shattering symbolic blows also occurred in the utmost secrecy. Preparations for the evacuation of the Hindenburg coffins and the demolition of the Tannenberg monument were made in early October.[159] Likewise, Hitler's final departure from Rastenburg on 20 November was shrouded in secrecy. Despite suffering from the side effects of injuries sustained on 20 July, the *Führer* had remained at headquarters. Hitler apparently dismissed the idea of leaving, noting that 'the East Prussians would say I was leaving them to the Russians, and they'd be right. However secret we kept it, they'd still find out. The wretched people have already had one taste of Russian terror in 1914 and 1915. I want to spare them a second dose.'[160]

Bormann continued to press Hitler to evacuate headquarters on account of the proximity of Soviet armour and initiated appropriate preparations himself. However, he admitted that Hitler's presence composed the population and inspired the military to greater efforts.[161] Goebbels had criticised the atmosphere and remoteness of Rastenburg. He maintained that the eternal bunker lifestyle at headquarters had caused a further deterioration in Hitler's health and argued that Germany was now fighting a multi-front war which the *Führer* could only control politically and militarily from Berlin – Goebbels' own *Gau.*[162] The sickly *Führer* did not visit the troops nor did he intervene in the successful operations of the Fourth Army during the autumn fighting.[163] Still, his mood further deteriorated when he was advised of Red Army atrocities. 'They aren't human', he ranted, 'They're the beasts of the Asiatic steppes. The war I am fighting against them is a fight for the dignity of European man. No price is too high for victory.'[164]

Despite the ongoing reinforcement of the Wolf Lair's defences,[165] Hitler and his entourage knew they were finally leaving East Prussia. Hitler travelled to Berlin for throat surgery on 20 November before heading west to direct the Ardennes offensive. Following Hitler's departure from East Prussia the province's defence took on secondary importance. In the eastern theatre his major concern appeared to be the mineral resources of Hungary and the retention of Budapest. Unknown to East Prussians, their *Führer* weakened the province's defences to pursue these objectives. In December, as the lion's share of tank production rolled westwards, Army Group Centre was forced to give up four Panzer divisions for service in Hungary.[166] Heysing privately observed that 'this conclusively sealed the fate of East Prussia', and one General Staff officer told him that 'they'll come too late for Budapest and in East Prussia they are irreplaceable'.[167]

Meanwhile the judicial authorities were privately fearful for East Prussia's future. OLG President Dräger in Königsberg, in common with numerous military figures, anticipated a Red Army attack along the right-bank of the Vistula in an attempt to reach the Baltic and cut off the province. He advised that it was 'hardly possible to evacuate the one and a half to two million East Prussians over the [Vistula] bridges at Graudenz and Dirschau'. Instead, as in 1939, East Prussia would have to hold out as a besieged fortress until relief arrived from the Reich. This required supplies of foodstuffs, weapons and ammunition. Despite this gloomy scenario, Dräger took heart from the fact that so few inhabitants had left the province.[168] In reality, however, travel restrictions, Party and police surveillance, difficulties with ration cards in other provinces, the demands of 60 (and even 72)-hour weeks, conscription for fortification building, harvest work and the discipline demanded by the *Volkssturm* effectively precluded the opportunity for free movement. Meanwhile, the judicial authorities were keen to remove records to Pomerania and files were moved from East Prussia to Stolp.[169] As the situation became more critical after October some 'important but seldom used' files were transferred to Flatow and Schneidemühl districts.[170]

The first East Prussian refugee treks arrived in Pomerania during November. Most were quartered for a night or two before travelling further west. The OLG President in Stettin reported the scramble for accommodation but maintained that the authorities were doing their utmost to care for the refugees in the cold conditions.[171] The lack of manpower and resources aggravated efforts to alleviate the suffering of refugees on the snowy roads. Elderly police struggled to direct the onslaught of vehicles. The NSV attempted to set up feeding points along the main highways. These were located in guest houses and schools closed since the autumn but were too few to offer adequate relief.[172]

The *Wehrmacht* also made heavier demands in Pomerania, particularly in the Schneidemühl fortified area. The increased military presence exacerbated the shortage of accommodation and put pressure on farmers due to the requisitioning of many of the remaining horses.[173] The *Wehrmacht* frequently engaged in unauthorised requisitions of foodstuffs, fuel, vehicles and petrol as had previously been the norm in occupied enemy territories. Fragments of various military formations arrived and demanded accommodation and rations from local authorities. *Wehrmacht* and SS representatives were increasingly evident searching for quarters and sites for ammunition depots and food stores to be prepared in case of retreat. The authorities could not satisfy these demands because of the lack of suitable facilities.[174]

Pomeranian judicial authorities also reported a number of disturbing sentiments which pointed to the failure of the atrocity propaganda campaign to mould opinion. Because of the actions of 'weak or malicious characters' disparaging criticism was becoming more frequent. Recurrent statements such as 'Germany has lost the war', 'a further spillage of blood is pointless' and 'the Bolsheviks are certainly not as bad as they are portrayed in our propaganda' were heard.[175] In contrast, the OLG President in Breslau seemed more optimistic in early December. He reported that fears felt during the late summer had subsided and the population now exhibited 'greater confidence and hope in a favourable outcome to the war'. Lower Silesians were apparently appreciative that the leadership was doing everything possible to strengthen defences and forge new weapons to repulse the enemy. The experience of 1918 and an understanding of the enemy's desire to destroy Germany caused the population to stand together and reject capitulation.[176]

Two issues did provoke uneasiness in Lower Silesia. One was the demand on time and the adverse effect on the civilian economy arising from Party-led initiatives and activities such as *Bartold* and the *Volkssturm*. The other concerned evacuation preparations undertaken by the state authorities in early November in areas east of the Oder in the 'fortresses' of Breslau and Glogau and in some districts west of the Oder. Despite all attempts to keep this development secret, information leaked out. The OLG

President insisted that subsequent anxiety was temporary and not serious.[177] In public, Hanke was upbeat. In public pronouncements he said that the Red Army would never set foot in Silesia or alternatively proclaimed that the River Oder would serve as an inpenetrable barrier. The propagandists underlined the historical parallels dating back centuries by claiming that Silesians acting alone had defeated the Mongols at the bloody battle of Wahlstatt (near Liegnitz) in 1241.[178] Visiting Goebbels at the end of 1944, Hanke reassured his former superior of his firm conviction that the new fortifications in Lower Silesia would lead to the defeat of the imminent Soviet offensive.[179] Privately, Hanke took a graver view of the situation. A few months earlier, as a 'precautionary' measure, Hanke had secretly moved his most valuable possessions to his Upper Bavarian chalet.[180]

In hindsight, it is evident that eastern Germany was facing a catastrophe. Nazi propaganda refused to countenance this but tacitly admitted the possibility by stressing that it would be better to die than live under enemy rule. The likely fate of the eastern provinces should Germany lose the war was only mentioned in an effort to bolster resistance. Newspapers reported that Churchill, Roosevelt and Stalin had agreed that the Soviet Union would acquire East Prussia. However, it was emphasised that this was a pipedream. All Germans were united in defending this province which had been of decisive significance in German history for more than 700 years.[181] Indeed, Churchill advised the House of Commons on 15 December that Poland had been offered territories to the north and west, including Danzig and those parts of East Prussia west and south of Königsberg.[182] The Allies had yet to fix Poland's western frontier. Of more interest to German propagandists were the disputes over the 'Polish Question' and the opportunity this presented to exploit differences between the participants in this 'unnatural' enemy coalition. German commentators, such as Hans Fritzsche, portrayed Churchill's speech as signalling Britain's 'final surrender' to Moscow on the Polish question.[183] Fritzsche did mention that Poland, which would lose its lands beyond the Curzon Line to the Soviets, would be 'over-amply compensated with territories of the Reich' and warned listeners that the Poles would not need to deal with a mixed German–Polish population in the new territory as 'the Germans would be killed off by the million'. For the moment, German propaganda only told the home audience that East Prussia and Danzig had been offered to the Poles; but material for abroad mentioned Stettin and a Polish frontier on the Oder.[184]

To gauge the mood of the civilian population and their military defenders at this critical juncture it is possible to compare official sources, the accounts of senior *Wehrmacht* personnel and the thoughts of ordinary Germans. One SD report submitted to General Hoßbach on 28 December discussed the sentiments being expressed in the south-eastern part of East Prussia. The German population were said to be avidly following the battles in the west, and were confident that the greater deployment of new weapons in 1945 would lead to a decrease in enemy bombing. Some dissenters doubted the value of the Ardennes offensive, but their views were dismissed as insignificant. Statements emanating from *Wehrmacht* circles convinced many that there would be no more Soviet breakthroughs, a sentiment strengthened by rumours that 'secret weapons' had recently been unloaded in Lyck. Koch had seemingly boosted morale during his Christmas travels through the province. He claimed that Sudauen would soon be retaken and that the *Volkssturm* would be stood down after the spring sowing, enabling men to return home. In contrast, rumours emanating from the Polish minority talked of the Ardennes offensive as a 'propaganda trick' and claimed that East Prussian industry was decimated. There were also further signs of disturbing *Wehrmacht* behaviour. A member of the Nemmersdorf *Gendarmerie*, whose dwelling was undamaged during the two-day Red Army occupation, had recently been away from his home for a few days. He returned to discover that his house had been ransacked and soiled by German troops.[185]

The authorities also monitored the response to New Year radio addresses by Hitler and Goebbels. It was Hitler's first national speech since the early hours of 21 July 1944. During this period Himmler had become increasingly prominent as the leading public face of the regime, leading to speculation over Hitler's health and authority. Both Hitler and Goebbels proclaimed that 1945 would be the decisive year of the war and forecast a change in Germany's fortunes. The propaganda authorities were heartened that Hitler's speech dispelled doubts and rumours blamed on enemy agitation.[186] Goebbels, drawing on reports from his subordinates nationwide, enthused that Hitler's speech had created a sensation and had made a 'deep impression across the entire population'. It had given 'the broad masses great hopes for the future'.[187] Propaganda Leader Maertins had reported rumours in East Prussia that the *Führer* was sick or even dead. However, his broadcast had raised confidence, particularly as he had indicated that Germany would resume the offensive in 1945. Unease was expressed by a section of the population over the lack of information concerning the haul of prisoners and captured material in the west. Others were comforted by the thought that the Ardennes operation was still ongoing.[188]

In Breslau, Propaganda Leader Dr Schulz advised that 'the announcement of the *Führer*'s speech was received with great joy'. Failure, uncertainty and doubt were confronted with the words of the *Führer* bolstered by his belief and confidence in victory. There was renewed concern, however, over the lack of attention given to military developments in the speech. This was tempered by gratitude that Hitler had spoken again, had praised the German people for their efforts to date and had promised new forces in 1945. Goebbels' speech, coming so soon after his Christmas address, was overshadowed by Hitler's broadcast and considered badly timed.[189] In Stettin, Propaganda Leader Popp observed that the attitude of the Pomeranian population was flawless despite recent heavy burdens. The announcement of Hitler's speech had come as a surprise and people had awaited it with great excitement. His calmness and determination inspired hopes of further 'military successes'. On the other hand, the speech had encountered practical problems in Pomerania as so many air raid victims had no radios and could not even hear the address.[190]

Hitler's words did not reassure the military hierarchy. Guderian dismissed Hitler's claim made at his western headquarters that the Eastern Front possessed more reserves than ever before with the famous retort: 'The Eastern Front is like a house of cards. If the front is broken through at one point all the rest will collapse.'[191] Colonel-General Josef Harpe suggested in early January that his Army Group A be withdrawn to the so-called 'Hubertus Line' immediately behind the Vistula. This was to reduce the devastating impact of the opening Red Army artillery barrage, shorten the front and create reserves to mount counter attacks.[192] Harpe's Chief of Staff, Lieutenant General von Xylander, concluded that it would take the Red Army six days to advance to the Silesian frontier. He advocated that the *Wehrmacht* should beat a tactical retreat back to either the A1 defences in central Poland or to the defences on the Silesian border and head-off the Soviets there. Xylander's plan, code-named *Schlittenfahrt* (sleigh ride), aimed to safeguard Upper Silesian industry, ensuring thereby that the enemy did not enter Silesia and gaining time for a political solution to be brokered. However, by this stage Xylander's idea was probably untenable. Despite alarming intelligence reports concerning Red Army concentrations in its Vistula bridgeheads, Hitler ordered German troops to fight where they stood and rejected *Schlittenfahrt*.[193] Further north Reinhardt had thought that his forces could stop the Red Army if they remained intact.[194] The removal of divisions to Hungary led him to request that the Fourth and Second Armies be withdrawn from the Narew to the East Prussian border, a request Hitler also dismissed.[195]

The military leadership was gravely concerned about the repercussions of the Ardennes offensive, launched on 16 December, and the decision to leave Army Group North in the Courland peninsula. Reinhardt was sceptical about the Ardennes operation, but hoped that following a heavy blow more forces would be transferred to the Eastern Front. He remarked that the success of this operation would determine the fate of East Prussia.[196] Hoßbach later claimed that Fourth Army headquarters was completely surprised by the offensive in the West. He asserted that this action removed the last prospect of strengthening the East Prussian front before the Red Army began the decisive attack.[197] Hitler repeatedly rejected Guderian's pleas for the evacuation of Army Group North.[198] The *Führer* maintained that the navy needed Libau's port facilities to control the eastern Baltic and implied that this strip of land would be the starting point for a future German offensive.[199] Reinhardt was fully aware that Koch was a millstone around his neck and their ideas on the province's defence differed, but on the other hand, he hoped that Koch's close connections at headquarters could be exploited to plead for more forces to defend East Prussia.[200] General Otto Lasch, the commander of *Wehrkreis* I, incorporating Fortress Königsberg, was viewed as a mediator between Reinhardt and Koch and attempted to represent military interests.[201] He realised that even Koch endorsed his frequently stated view that the troops be evacuated from Courland to provide reserves for Army Group Centre. Lasch hoped that Koch would influence Hitler, but, although he apparently tried, this floundered when confronted by Hitler's rigid attitude.[202]

Lasch's position was particularly awkward. The proximity of the front made it logical for East Prussia to fall under the jurisdiction of Army Group Centre. Instead the *Wehrkreis* fell within Himmler's domain in his capacity as commander of the Replacement Army, headquartered in distant Berlin. As Lasch attempted to form and train new formations and construct rear defences, he became embroiled in a bureaucratic morass. For instance, the responsibility for POW labour was taken from the military authorities and transferred to the senior SS and police leader for East Prussia.

Meanwhile, POW guards remained under military jurisdiction.[203] Koch also intervened in purely military matters when, with Hitler's authority, he checked the activities of officers, NCOs and men in rear districts.[204] Guderian later noted in his memoirs that Koch 'could not do enough to bring the generals into disrepute'.[205] Lasch mentioned this intrusion to Himmler when they met at Posen on 5 November 1944 when the latter made a speech celebrating the fifth anniversary of the foundation of the Warthegau. He realised that Himmler and Koch 'were not the best of friends'. Himmler said they should meet again so Lasch could report his views and he could intercede. However, Lasch never got the opportunity to speak with Himmler again.[206]

The military also faced climatic and manpower problems. German defences exploited the natural barriers offered by lakes, streams and marshes, but these were rendered invalid by the freezing winter conditions. Frozen lakes lengthened the front and provided landing sites for enemy parachutists. Hoßbach, whose front sector was the most affected, tried various techniques to prevent an ice covering from forming. These included depositing wagons and agricultural machinery laden with stone on a frozen lake near Goldap. Furthermore, the weather caused other difficulties as the snow caused trenches and barriers to sink and rendered mines ineffective.[207] Concurrently, the lack of manpower and the fear of abduction by enemy scouting parties became a cause for concern during the long, dark nights. In late December, Reinhardt and Hoßbach noted the large number of missing men and decided that manpower should not be sprinkled thinly along advanced positions during the evenings. Instead men were to be grouped together or the positions were to be evacuated.[208]

As the anticipated Red Army offensive failed to materialise over Christmas, Party propagandists announced that invasion was impossible. Major Dieckert remarked that the *Wehrmacht* was conscious of its own weakness, but, as the front remained quiet, the state of great suspense was accepted as the norm and a spirit of lethargy took over.[209] General Dethleffsen realised that the Soviets were preparing to resume the attack, and the Fourth Army deplored Koch's decision to evacuate only part of the civilian population outside East Prussia and leave most in the west of the province. The army repeatedly warned that East Prussia could be cut off and recommended that only civilians building defences or assisting the troops should stay behind.[210] Colonel General Erhard Raus, the Austrian commander of the Third Panzer Army, later told his American captors that 'the morale of the troops was excellent and they faced the coming events with confidence'.[211] However, at the time Raus complained that he had not seen German planes in the air for weeks and that his own car had been sprayed with machine gun and rocket fire on a visit to the front.[212] In the *General Gouvernement*, the *Krakauer Zeitung* was uncannily accurate about impending Soviet operations from their Vistula bridgeheads. An article on 24 December 1944 stated: 'One can also make guesses about the aims of the offensive. The Bolsheviks imagine it as follows: roll back the Vistula front, thrust into Upper Silesia and the Warthegau, march into Berlin.'[213] Koch's Christmas message to East Prussian soldiers underlined the significance of the challenge facing Germany and to their home province: 'We all know that this battle – which is a matter of "To be, or not to be"- must and will give us only one outcome, victory, if we are to preserve our nation, our freedom, our daily bread, our living space and a secure future for our children.'[214]

Various unofficial sources indicate the contrasting moods during these final weeks of German rule. In towns adjacent to the front a grim picture emerges. The journalist Günther Heysing, who recalled pleasant memories of Tilsit in 1937, was confronted seven years later by a field of ruins. Civilians were evacuated and soldiers inhabited the cellars.[215] The town's famous Memel bridges were blown up by the *Wehrmacht* – 'an eternally unforgettable moment' according to one witness.[216] An NSV official described Insterburg as a 'fairly dead town'. Street scenes there and in Rastenburg were dominated by soldiers and military vehicles.[217]

The interior of East Prussia appears to have presented a different picture to the younger generation. One 12-year-old boy recalled the trek from Treuburg to Sensburg in October. In this beautiful landscape he spent his final late autumn and early winter in the province. Although worries strained the nerves of adults, youngsters found the new surroundings exciting. He recalled the peaceful lakes, sufficient food and shops remaining open. Only the sight of soldiers and passing military columns intruded into this peaceful environment.[218] Similarly, Heysing noted that in Erben (Ortelsburg district) that the full impact of the war was still to be felt. He was impressed by the wonderful landscape and tranquillity of Masuria. It seemed that the wartime restrictions had made little impact on rural life. Mountains of cakes and real coffee were a feature of birthday celebrations at the school house where military reporters were billeted.[219]

Most accounts testify that the final war Christmas was a melancholy affair. Eleonore Burgsdorff, the stepdaughter of Count von Schwerin, recalled her last Christmas at his Wildenhoff (Preußisch Eylau) estate. The prisoners working on the estate sang carols in the courtyard of the great house and exchanged gifts – pieces of wool to knit clothes. Burgsdorff sensed the terror of the Russian prisoners at the prospect of 'liberation' by the Red Army, 'We all recognised that we were living on a volcano. Our Russians knew that for them the coming of the Red Army meant death.'[220] Some East Prussian evacuees returned home and attended church services with the military.[221] Similarly, Libussa von Oldershausen recalled the service at Glowitz (Stolp, Pomerania) and the predominance of women in the congregation:

> In the old days, men and women sat on different sides of the aisle. But now that the flood of refugees had brought us so many more women, and there were so few men, this principle had been abandoned; women now occupied places denied them for time immemorial.[222]

Members of the East Prussian *Volkssturm* were photographed with their *Panzerfäuste* beside Christmas trees. Older East Prussians recounted the legendary victory at Tannenberg and the actions of Hindenburg and Ludendorff. Others remained convinced that Hitler would never give up East Prussia or consoled themselves that the Russians had come and gone in 1914, would do the same again and nothing much would change. However, some recalled the more recent sightings of refugee columns from the Baltic States and the Memelland. Despite the Party warning against 'defeatist evacuation preparations' they had picked up much practical knowledge from the experience.[223] Heysing remembered previous war Christmases all over Europe and, despite the decorations and candles in the Erben teacher's house, concluded that the 'atmosphere was never so subdued and sombre than in this year'.[224] Similarly, the author Arno Surminski, then a 10-year-old boy, recalled that a Saxon unit was quartered in his village over the last war Christmas. Frequently they exclaimed 'My God, get out of here, it's getting quite bad.'[225]

The authorities found it increasingly difficult to provide the basic necessities. Evacuees returning to their homes in East Prussia over Christmas reported the shortage of potatoes and, more critically, heating fuel in their new quarters. Coal deliveries failed to arrive and evacuees returned in December 1944 with boxes to collect coal and firewood from their old homes.[226] Overcrowding in reception districts was blamed for this problem. The *Landrat* of Schloßberg observed on 2 January 1945 that in Wehlau district there were 24,000 evacuees. This influx had increased the district's population by almost 50 per cent. Moreover, *Wehrmacht* units, construction battalions and evacuated factories also arrived. Potatoes and heating fuel were in scarce supply.[227] A Königsberg nurse recounted that the weather was 'bitterly cold', but the coal shortage meant that wards were barely heated. She also noted that the hospital was 'short of medical supplies and received parcels with paper bandages, which were hard and painful on the wounds'.[228]

Moreover, rations became ever more meagre. Bread rations were cut in October 1944 while around the same time beer production was wound down and the ersatz coffee ration reduced. Sugar supplies for bakeries ceased. Other than the cinema, a medium particularly dear to Goebbels, little entertainment remained. Cultural activities were cut to the bone in line with the post 20 July Total War measures. Theatres closed and orchestras disbanded as actors and musicians were directed to the factories or front.[229] German propaganda justified the closure of schools and theatres on the grounds of total war with the claim that such facilities would not exist in Germany if the enemy had their way.[230] However, Rebentisch asserts that total war measures were a failure which at best delayed defeat by a few weeks. Some structures, such as the Justice Ministry, had already been cut to the bone – only 127 out of its 4,020 male employees born since 1906 were fit for military service on 1 August 1944.[231] At the same time Bormann fought a determined action to maintain the Party cadre. As soon as gaps appeared in the corps of Political Leaders from enlistments to the *Wehrmacht*, he made sure that the vacancies were filled immediately. Whilst critical of the state bureaucracy, he claimed that the Party apparatus played a key role on the Home Front.[232] During the final months of the war so many orders were issued by the Party Chancellery that in practice it became ever more difficult to impose its will on the situation and was described by Goebbels as a 'Paper Chancellery'.[233] In the midst of this central authority in Berlin gradually broke down under the continual air attacks and evacuated departments were preoccupied searching for and salvaging charred records.

The mood of impending collapse can be detected even among Party members. The young Königsberg Jew Michael Wieck noticed 'an unmistakable change in the attitude of our tormentors'. Some were friendlier and others anxious.[234] An Aryan youth who had been drafted into a construction detachment following the closure of his school dutifully travelled across East Prussia from the coastal resort of Cranz to his home town of Lyck to restart work after his Christmas holiday. The cheerless sight of a near empty town, closed shops and a deserted family home greeted him. He would be in the area for only three more weeks.[235] Further south in Johannisburg, a New Year visitor observed that almost the entire population had made preparations for departure and noted that 'cases were packed and stood ready. One was conscious that the hour approached when the frightful message to take flight would be given.'[236] Likewise, a Breslau priest commented that everyone was conscious that 1945 would be the most decisive and also the worst year for the German East.[237]

In Danzig, *Gauleiter* Forster worried about the reliability of the *Volkssturm* in his *Gau*. He told the *Kreisstabsführer* that the Party's most important task for 1945 was to summon sufficient energy 'to inculcate the will to resist, courage and above all fanaticism' into the men of the *Volkssturm*'.[238] Similarly, in his New Year instructions to local Party leaders he called upon them 'not to weaken, not to lose their nerve, to think only of the greatness of Germany and of the duties imposed by the sacrifice of those who died for the Fatherland and for the people'.[239]

The Party leadership still refused to heed the warnings and initiate mass evacuation. In late-December transport specialists in Berlin advised Hanke of plans they had quietly drafted for the evacuation of Breslau. These envisaged the removal of 200,000 sick, elderly and frail inhabitants from the city. To Major General Johannes Krause, the fortress commandant, Hanke expressed doubts about the availability of sufficient transportation, adding that if he commenced this operation in times of 'deepest calm' the *Führer* would have him shot.[240] Paul Dargel, Koch's leading subordinate, was similarly stubborn, proclaiming on 11 January 1945 that 'East Prussia will be held. An evacuation is not in question.'[241] *SS-Obergruppenführer* Wilhelm Koppe inspecting fortifications in the *General Gouvernement* in early-January talked of soldiers manning the defences laughing at the failure of the Soviets to attack, which they attributed to the strength of the German positions. Koppe promised that the defensive network would be extended in 1945 and 'no power on earth would be able to storm it'.[242] Hitler remained convinced that some further territory could still be lost, 'In the east I can still lose land' and moreover, was more interested in the Hungarian sector than East Prussia.[243] Goebbels, after a conversation with his *Führer* at the beginning of January, stressed that while a mass Soviet attack on East Prussia would 'certainly not be pleasant' it would allow still considerable tank forces tied up in the middle of the Eastern Front [in Poland] to be transferred for relief operations at Budapest, recently encircled by the Red Army.[244]

On 12 January, State Secretary Werner Naumann of the Propaganda Ministry appeared in Posen where he addressed a large German audience. He described the situation in rose-tinted terms, repeating the theme of much recent rhetoric that 'the Eastern Front had never been so strong as it is now', speaking of 'wonder weapons' and new armies and prophesising Final Victory in the near future. *Gauleiter* Arthur Greiser concurred and added that not one square foot of the Warthegau's soil would be given up. That evening at his Mariensee estate outside Posen, Greiser held a small reception. Here he impressed on his guests the optimism spread by Naumann – the Bolshevik flood would bleed to death before the Warthegau's frontier and there suffer decisive defeat. Greiser was grateful to Naumann for making it clear to all Germans in the Warthegau that as they were protected by the resolute will of the *Führer*, Bolshevik soldiery would never set foot in their province.[245] This absurd pretence was about to be swept away.

The growl from the East had already reached a crescendo on 12 January. Early that morning the Red Army erupted from its Vistula bridgehead at Sandomierz in central Poland and tore into Army Group A. East Prussia was given a day's respite before a similar storm broke. By 20 January, the *Gauleitung* in Posen had issued evacuation orders for all districts in the Warthegau and Greiser's bags were packed. The end of the German East was nigh.

PART III

Endgame: East Germany 1945

CHAPTER 8

The Deluge

The early months of 1945 saw the disintegration of the German East. By the time of the Third Reich's unconditional surrender on 7 May 1945 German authority east of the Oder was restricted to isolated strips of territory, namely Courland and the Hela peninsula in the Gulf of Danzig.[1] For almost four months, from 12 January, the German military endured unrelenting defeat. German cities were reduced to ruins, fields left untended and the surviving populace scattered far and wide. The *Herrenvolk* had suffered the decisive defeat in their *Drang nach Osten*.

'The Long-Awaited Bolshevik Winter Offensive'

At this stage in the narrative it is pertinent to return to the military situation at the dawn of 1945. On the key East Prussian and Vistula sectors of the Eastern Front, Army Groups Centre and A confronted four Soviet fronts. The Red Army had established a staggering superiority in men and material. In central Poland, Army Group A faced the might of Marshal Zhukov's First Belorussian Front and Marshal Konev's First Ukranian Front. The ratio of Red Army superiority was more than 5:1 in manpower and tanks, 7:1 in artillery and 17:1 in aircraft.[2] Further north the situation was marginally less depressing from a German perspective. Army Group Centre defending East Prussia faced General Chernyakovsky's Third Belorussian Front and Marshal Rokossovsky's considerably reinforced Second Belorussian Front. The combined strength of these commands gave the Red Army a near threefold superiority in manpower, an almost fivefold advantage in tanks and six times as many aircraft.[3]

The ensuing carnage from mid-January 1945 can be summarised on a north to south basis. After initially determined German resistance in the Schloßberg–Ebenrode sector in the days after 13 January, the front cracked and Chernyakovsky's forces stormed into the heart of East Prussia, surrounding Königsberg on 30 January. Concurrently, the right wing of Rokossovsky's front, attacking from the south, cut the Königsberg–Berlin railway line on 23 January and four days later reached the Frisches Haff at Tolkemit to sever East Prussia from the Reich. To Hitler's fury, General

Hoßbach's Fourth Army, which faced encirclement, gave up the Lötzen fortified area and headed west in an attempt to reach the rivers Nogat and Vistula.[4] In the bitter late January snows their repeated efforts to break through to Marienburg and Elbing were blocked. Hitler forbade further attempts. Reinhardt was dismissed on 26 January and Hoßbach four days later for their role in the 'Lötzen "treachery"'.[5] Koch played a critical role in this decision by sending Bormann a teleprinter message accusing the Fourth Army of attempting to flee East Prussia. Koch promised to defend the province with his *Volkssturm*.[6] Front Reports made clear the German intention to hold East Prussia to the last: 'East Prussia is a Fortress . . . It has to fulfil its task as [an] outpost of the Reich with steadfastness and sacrifice . . . Greater things are at stake than villages, towns or a Province.'[7]

As a direct response to the calamitous events on the Eastern Front, Hitler and the High Command ordered the reorganisation of army groups on 25 January. This resulted in Army Group Centre being renamed Army Group North. Command was passed to an Austrian, Colonel-General Dr Lothar Rendulic. Rendulic, latterly in Norway, had been on Latvian soil for less than a day as commander of Army Group Courland before he received an urgent radio order to proceed to East Prussia. Within a day Rendulic claimed that he had warned Koch that he alone would issue orders for the defence of the province, leading a shaken Koch to reportedly proclaim, 'I can but assure you that I stand totally behind you.'[8] Meanwhile, General Friedrich-Wilhelm Müller took over the shattered Fourth Army at that stage being pushed back towards Heiligenbeil. German forces in East Prussia were fragmented into three district entities – the Heiligenbeil cauldron, Königsberg fortress and the remnants of the Third Panzer Army in the Samland peninsula. A significant localised success was achieved on 20 February when German forces broke the first siege of Königsberg and reopened communications with Samland and the port of Pillau.[9]

This small military success, however, was merely a stay of execution. The Third Belorussian Front, under a new commander Marshal Vasilevsky, following Chernyakhovsky's death from wounds at Mehlsack on 18 February, embarked on the methodical liquidation of the East Prussian pockets. The 19 assorted divisions in the Heiligenbeil cauldron were smashed between 13 and 28 March and perhaps 140,000 men were killed or captured.[10] The final onslaught against Königsberg commenced on 6 April and involved a major artillery bombardment, massive air attack and eight concurrent assaults on the German defences, manned according to inflated Soviet figures by '130,000 fanatical Fascists ready to fight to the last bullet'.[11] German forces actually numbered less than one-third of this figure and Königsberg was quickly cut off from its Samland lifeline. The defenders were split into pockets and coherent command became impossible. The Commandant, General Otto Lasch, was forced to surrender on 9 April and around 35,000 German officers and men marched with him into captivity.[12] On 13 April the Third Belorussian Front attacked the remnants of German forces in Samland. The German defenders, numbering around 65,000, fought a determined rearguard action against overwhelming odds in order to facilitate the evacuation of soldiers and civilians from Pillau. The last units attempting to cling on to East Prussian soil were finally eliminated on 27 April.[13]

Further south the Red Army swiftly ejected the Germans from Poland. The First Belorussian Front commenced the offensive from the Magnuszew and Pulawy bridgeheads on 14 January and immediately made deep incisions through German defences shattered by the initial artillery bombardment. Army Group A's withdrawal from the ruins of Warsaw, completed by 17 January, resulted in renewed accusations of military treachery by Hitler and the replacement of Harpe, cast into the role of scapegoat, by General Ferdinand Schörner. Litzmannstadt fell intact to the Red Army on 18 January and Posen was reached two days later. No orderly German defensive front existed. Red Army tank spearheads raced across the frozen Polish plains. In late-January Zhukov's forces closed in on the Pomeranian and Brandenburg frontiers. Konev's First Ukrainian Front had already crossed the Silesian frontier at Namslau on 20 January, eight days after the breakout from Sandomierz. Konev's formations soon established bridgeheads on the River Oder's west bank north and south of Breslau. In the final week of January they captured the prized Upper Silesian industrial district intact.[14]

Zhukov's armies entered southern Pomerania on 26 January. Three days later they drove into Brandenburg, brushed aside German defences and surged towards the Oder. On 31 January, the First Belorussian Front established its first bridgeheads on the Oder's west bank. Zhukov's forces spent more than two months on the Oder infuriating some of his subordinates, such as General Vasili Chuikov, the victor of Stalingrad, who believed that the weak German forces covering Berlin could have been overcome and the city captured in February at a lower cost to the Red Army. This was the backdrop to a bitter postwar dispute between Chuikov, commander of the 62nd Army (later Eighth Guards Army) and Zhukov, whom he accused of meekly submitting to Stalin's directive to concentrate on the threat emanating from German forces in Pomerania and Silesia. The decision followed Stalin's telephone call on 6 February to Zhukov, then conferring with his army commanders. Their discussions on an advance to Berlin were scuppered by the Supreme Commander's intervention. The Chief of Staff of the Red Army, General S.M. Shtemenko, deemed the delay on the Oder to have arisen from military considerations and not from political machinations on the part of Stalin.[15] This time was used to expand bridgeheads, strengthen units, bring up supplies and eliminate German forces at Küstrin, the historic fortress town at the confluence of the Oder and the Warthe. The final offensive against Berlin, less than 40 miles distant, began on 16 April.

Chuikov viewed Berlin as the nerve centre of a Nazi state which would disintegrate following the city's capture. At the beginning of February, Zhukov seemed to agree and called for the First Belorussian Front to make a rapid forward movement to take Berlin on 15–16 February.[16] At this point the vacillating *Vozhd* intervened. Stalin had already reminded Zhukov on 25 January that when his First Belorussian Front reached the Oder it would be 150 kilometres from the flank of Rokossovsky's Second Belorussian Front. Fearing a German counter-attack from Pomerania against Zhukov's right flank, Stalin told him to wait until Rokossovsky completed his operations in East Prussia and got his troops over the Vistula. Zhukov, however, successfully appealed to Stalin to reconsider so that the Germans would not be given a breathing space to adequately man the Oder–Warthe defences at Meseritz.[17]

In his memoirs Chuikov lambasted the Supreme Command's 'excessive caution' lest German forces strike south from Pomerania.[18] He was sceptical about the possibility of a serious German counter-blow and asserted that the advance into the province and then turning towards Gdynia and Danzig, 'was what you might call advancing with a backward turn', and needed the same forces and material as any advance on Berlin.[19]

Zhukov underlined the looming threat from Pomerania when he chided Chuikov in his memoirs. He observed that, 'with a thrust from the north the enemy would have been able to break through our flanks, cut us off at the Oder River and thus place the troops around Berlin in a precarious position'.[20] Zhukov contended that the shortage of men, lack of tanks and stubborn German defence combined to ensure that 'neither the First Ukrainian Front [Konev's command to the south] nor the First Belorussian Front was in a condition to carry out the Berlin operation in February 1945'.[21] Tens of thousands of troops were also tied up in the Red Army's rear reducing German strongpoints such as Posen. Nevertheless, many of Zhukov's divisions were soon heading towards the Baltic while Konev's forces cleared large tracks of Silesia. By 16 April, when the Red Army launched the assault on Berlin, the Germans, despite dwindling resources, had managed to address their defensive deficiencies before Berlin to a limited degree.

Entrusted with the defence of Pomerania and the approaches to Berlin was a new German command, the grandly titled Army Group Vistula led by the *Reichsführer-SS* himself, Heinrich Himmler. Hitler's order for the formation of Army Group Vistula on 21 January 1945 also conferred on Himmler responsibility for the organisation of national defence on German soil behind the Eastern Front. Army Group Vistula was a ragtag outfit. It comprised the shattered remnants of the Ninth Army, the Second Army and the recently formed Eleventh SS Panzer Army, renamed the Third Panzer Army on 24 February. An assortment of scratch formations and *Volkssturm* detachments from throughout the Reich increased the manpower of Army Group Vistula on the Oder and Pomeranian balcony to perhaps 450,000 by mid-February.[22] The reshuffling and reorganisation of remaining German forces was completed with the renaming of Army Group A as Centre, responsible for a fighting front reaching from Silesia to Slovakia.

Significantly, Germany's new commanders, Rendulic, Himmler and Schörner, were chosen primarily for their ideological and political reliability. They were renowned for their ruthless attitude towards men found moving behind German lines without correct papers. Acting on their encouragement, field police, roving SS detachments and drumhead courts martial gave short shrift to 'shirkers'. The bodies of these unfortunates swayed from trees, lamp-posts and bridge parapets bedecked with placards with inscriptions such as: 'I am a deserter and have declined to defend German women and children.'[23] Even hardened *Waffen-SS* commanders such as the Belgian Leon Degrelle were disturbed by the sight of the hanged youths. He saw their stiffened corpses dangling from the bridge between Altdamm and Stettin and lamented their 'momentary weakness'.[24] Further south, on a front visit to Frankfurt an der Oder, Goebbels and his Press spokesman Wilfred von Oven saw the bodies of German soldiers in full uniform hanging from the girders of the bridge over the Oder clearly marked with the inscription 'I am a deserter'. Von Oven noted that this type of example was favoured by the local SS commander *Obersturmbannführer* Otto Skorzeny, famed as Mussolini's rescuer from captivity in September 1943, and he observed that 7,000 stragglers had reported in to Skorzeny's staff during the previous eight days.[25] Senior officials fared no better, and in an effort to convince ordinary soldiers that harsh measures transcended all barriers, their punishments received wide publicity.

The chaos which accompanied the German withdrawal from Bromberg (West Prussia) had brutal repercussions. *Kreisleiter* Rampf ordered the evacuation of the city on 21 January without permission from *Gauleiter* Forster. On 30 January, Berlin announced the fate of the city's leadership. SS *Standartenführer* von Salisch, the Police Director in Bromberg was disgraced and then shot for cowardice and neglect of duty after leaving the city. *Kreisleiter* Rampf, Government-President Kühn and Mayor Ernst of Bromberg, were reportedly forced to witness von Salisch's execution then stripped of their rank and flung into punishment battalions to be 'deployed in difficult and dangerous duties'. On 10 February, in an order to the officers of Army Group Vistula calling for 'fanaticism' and 'burning flames of hate' against Bolshevism, Himmler underlined the Bromberg sentences and reported the execution of a Colonel von Hassenstein, accused of evacuating a secure position without order.[26] Meanwhile, Kurt Flöter, *Kreisleiter* of Königsberg/Neumark (Brandenburg), was condemned by a court at Schwedt on 5 February and hanged for desertion and cowardice. He had left his *Volkssturm* battalion at the front and reportedly rushed to an SS command post at Schwedt. Here he foolishly proclaimed to Skorzeny, 'All is lost at Königsberg'.[27]

Himmler had a few weeks command experience in Alsace and his two-month tenure at Army Group Vistula left senior *Wehrmacht* figures incredulous. The Reich's chief executioner clutched at ever-more unlikely straws as his stock plummeted in Hitler's eyes on account of his inability to halt the Red tide. A telegram to one of his detractors, Guderian, described the thawing of the Oder ice as 'a gift from fate' and stressed that in these hours 'the weather is our ally', a sign that the 'Lord God had not forgotten his brave German *Volk*'.[28] Himmler also expressed a grudging admiration for the hated Bolshevik foe and sent his subordinates at Army Group Vistula a study of the successful Soviet defence of Leningrad to illustrate the 'brutal, ice-cold' opponent that they faced. In view of this they could not cut deals or complain. Rather it was a time to be firm and steadfast in their protection of the women and children of the German *Volk* against this latest assault from the East and Himmler claimed that their forefathers had fought off hundreds of similar incursions by the Avars, Mongols, Turks and Tartars.[29]

During February and March activity centred on the flanks. Zhukov's northern flank in eastern Pomerania was particularly exposed. Rokossovsky's units further east were attempting to cross the Vistula and meeting fierce resistance at Graudenz and Marienburg, investing East Prussia and blocking German breakouts. German concentrations in East Pomerania and Lower Silesia caused Stalin to fear that leading formations on the Oder could be trapped by enemy pincers striking simultaneously from north and south. The First Belorussian Front's operations were further hindered by the withdrawal of forces to pacify the encircled fortresses of Schneidemühl and Posen which only surrendered on 14 and 23 February respectively.[30] However, the Germans lacked the men and material to launch a rapid, converging attack from Pomerania and Silesia. The Sixth SS Panzer Army, blunted after its exertions in the Ardennes, was refitting prior to deployment in Hungary. Similarly, Guderian's pleas for a withdrawal from Courland and the transfer of units from Yugoslavia, Italy and Norway to create effective counter-attacking forces were rejected by Hitler.[31] Operation *Sonnenwende* (Solstice) was launched on 15 February south of Stargard by the Eleventh SS Panzer Army in an attempt to recapture southern Pomerania. After initial successes, such as the freeing of the encircled Arnswalde garrison, the offensive fizzled out. This was due to heavy German losses and the incapacitation of General Walther Wenck, entrusted at Guderian's behest, with the direction of the operation, but injured in a car accident as he returned from briefing Hitler in Berlin on 17 February.[32]

The Red Army soon embarked on the reduction of Pomerania.[33] The Second Belorussian Front commenced a five-day attack on 10 February and returned to the offensive on 24 February. Zhukov's tanks also headed north on 1 March, confounding German intelligence reports predicting a thrust towards Berlin. The Red Army, with the First Polish Army in the vanguard, reached the Baltic coast west of Kolberg on 4 March. German forces were shattered into fragments. The Soviets then veered east and captured Köslin and Stolp on 5 and 8 March respectively. Meanwhile, frenzied attacks by Rokossovsky's forces throughout the previous month led to the final elimination of the Vistula fortress of Graudenz (5 March) and Marienburg (8 March) on the Nogat. They then pressed on towards Danzig and Gotenhafen defended by the German Second Army and harbouring more than one million refugees. The Red Army soon ruptured this pocket to capture Gotenhafen on 26 March and Danzig four days later. German forces escaping this maelstrom clung on to tiny shards of land on the Hela Peninsula and to the marshy meadowland of the Vistula delta until the war's end, dodging the Red Air Force and succeeding, with the assistance of local fishermen and the *Kriegsmarine*, in securing the evacuation of all accompanying civilians and some troops.[34]

To the west, groups of *Wehrmacht* and *Volkssturm* put up dogged resistance to cover the withdrawal of soldiers and civilians by sea, most notably during the two-week siege of Kolberg and also from Dievenow to nearby Wollin island.[35] Throughout March Zhukov's forces closed in on Stettin which had been declared a fortress on 22 February.[36] The Germans lost Pyritz and Stargard during the first four days of March. Stettin's port facilities were under direct artillery fire from late March. The city eventually fell without a fight on 26 April when the fortress garrison and remaining civilians left in a north-westerly direction, all major bridges and industrial installations having already been blown up.[37]

Further south the First Belorussian Front's attention focused on Küstrin, the old Prussian fortress at the junction of the rivers Oder and Warthe. Küstrin's capture by the Fifth Shock Army was prematurely announced by Moscow in early February, when the town had been completely encircled. The significance of the town was illustrated in a Radio Moscow report on 12 March which again incorrectly proclaimed that, 'The town and fortress of Küstrin has been captured – the most important transportation junction and the strongest base of the Fascists on the Oder which covered the entrance to Berlin.'[38] The final Soviet onslaught on the town commenced on 22 March. Küstrin was defended by *Wehrmacht*, *Volkssturm* and police detachments under the ideologically reliable commandant, SS Lieutenant-General Heinz-Friedrich Reinefarth, most recently prominent in his role in the bloody pacification of the Warsaw Rising. In an attempt to relieve the encircled garrison and thereby delay Russian offensive preparations against Berlin, five divisions of the Ninth Army launched an attack in a northerly direction from Frankfurt. Concurrently, Himmler, whose reputation had been tarnished by the defeats in East Pomerania, was replaced on 20 March as commander of Army Group Vistula by Colonel-General Gotthard Heinrici, a doughty defensive fighter. The slaughter of German infantry on the outskirts of Küstrin caused Heinrici to condemn the offensive as 'a massacre'.[39] Meanwhile, Guderian's attempt to defend General Theodor Busse, a native of Frankfurt an der Oder, and his Ninth Army against Hitler's furious accusations of cowardice had led to Guderian's dismissal from the post of Chief of the General Staff on 29 March. By the end of the month Küstrin was cleared of German troops, although Reinefarth and around 1,500 men managed to break through to German lines. The defence and attempted relief of Küstrin incurred German losses of 20,000 men killed, wounded or captured.[40]

In the Silesian theatre of operations, from late January the thunder of Red Army guns could be heard in Breslau from the direction of Oels, 20 miles to the west.[41] However, Soviet thrusts were parried as Breslau's defenders were bolstered by troops transferred from the West and retreating units falling back from the Vistula. The First Ukrainian Front resumed the offensive on 8 February and quickly overran Liegnitz district. Glogau was surrounded by the Red Army on 12 February and Breslau suffered the same fate three days later. Glogau held out until 3 April.[42] By this stage more than 90 per cent of the town was destroyed. More than half of the 4,000 remaining civilians and 6,000 strong garrison perished.[43] With the exception of localised German successes at Lauban and Striegau during early March, the front in Lower Silesia remained virtually static until the war's end. Sudeten foothill districts remained in German hands and administrative departments from Breslau were transferred to Hirschberg and Waldenburg. Breslau's garrison encompassed regular troops, replacement and emergency units, stragglers entering the city, *Luftwaffe*, SS and police detachments and *Volkssturm* battalions from throughout Silesia.[44]

During late February and March the Red Army made moderate gains to the south and west of Breslau, but, despite a threefold numerical advantage, the decisive breakthrough remained elusive. A massive air and artillery attack over Easter caused 10,000 deaths and the destruction of churches and cultural buildings. Subsequent Soviet gains in the west led to the capture of Gandau airport in early April, vital for continued *Luftwaffe* supply operations. Although the *Wehrmacht* report claimed that the Soviet assaults had come to grief against the steadfastness of the garrison,[45] the fortress's days were numbered thereafter, despite the ad hoc efforts detailed in the next chapter to prepare a new landing strip. The *Wehrmacht* report maintained that Soviet breakthroughs had been repulsed by valiant defenders and Major Mohr's regiment was selected for praise on 6 April on account of its unshakable steadfastness during the toughest defensive fighting and for its determined counterattacks.[46] Frenzied Red

Army bombardments with artillery of all calibre, sometimes supported by tanks, and assaults against the west of the city went on throughout April.[47] However, when Breslau finally surrendered on 6 May, the Germans still held the city centre. The cost of withstanding a 78-day siege was enormous. Some 20,000 civilians and 6,000 German soldiers perished and more than 70 per cent of the city's buildings were destroyed during the siege and by subsequent Soviet fire-raising in the days after the city's capture.[48]

The defeat suffered by the *Ostheer* between the Vistula and the Oder was total. The Soviet 'High Command headquarters' (STAVKA) believed that during January the Germans lost 400,000 men.[49] These men could not be adequately replaced. Racial considerations and concerns regarding reliability on the battlefield no longer remained a barrier to combat service for the Reich. Various hastily assembled units were deployed – simply *Kanonenfutter* to give the leaders of the Third Reich a few more hours or days at the helm. Scandinavian, French, Dutch and Belgian SS volunteers were prominent in Pomerania while units of Vlasov's 'Russian Liberation Army' saw service on the Oder. The manpower of other branches of the German military was combed out and *Luftwaffe* personnel and sailors were sent to the front. In addition to declining manpower resources, the chronic fuel shortage resulted in the immobilisation of tanks and the grounding of fighters.[50] The *Reichsbahn* made heroic efforts to transport troops eastwards, but this increasingly required to be conducted at night to evade enemy aircraft. Improvisation was now more than ever the watchword. German war industries did not have the raw materials to provide sufficient weapons and ammunition for the continuation of effective defensive fighting. The loss of Upper Silesia, on top of the incapacitation of the Ruhr by Allied bombing, was the final nail in the coffin.

'Die Russe Kommt': Flight from the Red Army

More than five million eastern German civilians fled from the Red Army during January 1945. Various interpretations have been suggested to account for this sudden migration. The Polish scholar Stanislaw Schimitzek claimed that German propaganda had produced a 'psychotic fear of the Red Army' and this provoked unnecessary flight.[51] Alternatively, the British academic Elizabeth Wiskemann argued that the Germans were well aware of earlier *Wehrmacht* and SS crimes in Russia and were terrified of Soviet retribution.[52] In contrast, the East Prussian born journalist Arno Surminski asserted that eastern Germans had 'scarcely a hunch' of German crimes. Surminski described the flight as a 'purely German matter' and contended that by delaying evacuation until the last minute, the German leadership exacerbated civilian suffering.[53]

What can be discerned is that prior to the arrival of the Red Army, there were a number of shared experiences. The *Kreisleiter* were responsible for issuing local evacuation orders following confirmation from the appropriate *Gau* authorities. Accommodation and care of evacuees was the responsibility of the NSV. In Pomerania, Danzig–West Prussia and the Warthegau, codewords were issued to initiate evacuation. However, the ability of the German authorities to reduce human suffering was adversely affected by the shortage of transportation and the lack of manpower due to the call up of all remaining able bodied men for *Volkssturm* service. Zealous Party officials often aggravated civilian suffering by proclaiming until the final critical hours that talk of evacuation was defeatist and they frequently obstructed those making a timely departure.[54] When evacuation orders were eventually issued they were often couched in optimistic terms emphasising that this was a temporary measure as any Soviet occupation would be a brief affair.[55] German propagandists insisted that despite the freezing weather German refugees retained their discipline, a marked contrast to the scenes witnessed in France in 1940.[56]

The late evacuation orders and the shortage of trains and lorries forced many civilians into moving by foot, pulling sledges and prams piled high with belongings, or into covered wagons drawn by horses or oxen. The wagon columns, described as 'treks' and strikingly similar to the vehicles used in Boer migrations during the 1830s, were slow moving affairs. As the military had requisitioned the best horses, weakened beasts pulled hurriedly packed and overloaded wagons. At the behest of the *Wehrmacht*, major roads were given over to military transportation and the treks struggled along icebound minor roads and tracks. These soon became blocked because of accidents and the volume of traffic. As a result, refugee columns strayed into the midst of fighting and were brutally shunted aside by leading Red Army tank units. German news broadcasts attempted to portray the efficient control of the roads by the military but in doing so only indicated the chaos and confusion of the treks. In East Prussia, it was claimed that, 'Energetic and resolute officers made sure that no traffic jams occurred, that the endless flood of suffering German humanity hit so hard by fate was able to move on. Officers seized the reins of carts drawn by bolting horses, brought distracted motorists to their senses and got almost inextricably mixed masses of vehicles and people going again in no time.'[57] However, despite their post-war protestations to the contrary, the indifference displayed by *Wehrmacht* commanders to the plight of German civilians has come in for sharp criticism in recent years. Their orders hindered the movement of treks, leading to the claim that they, along with the Party leadership, shared much of the blame for German suffering. As the German historian Heinrich Schwendemann has observed, all too often the writers of post-war military memoirs sought to build up the myth that they had only pursued a hopeless war on their own territory out of a determination to rescue eastern Germans from the vengeance of the Red Army.[58]

However, the refugees' most immediate enemy was the cold. Following the cutting of the land connection with East Prussia, the only escape route from the beleaguered province was from the ports of Pillau or Danzig. The latter could only be reached by travelling along the Frisches Nehrung, a narrow strip of land lacking proper roads. To get on to the Nehrung the treks had to go over the frozen Frisches Haff lagoon where the weight of the wagons and the level of traffic caused the ice road to collapse plunging refugees, horses and carts into the frozen water. To add to their misery the only decent road on the Nehrung was reserved for *Wehrmacht* traffic only, thus forcing the refugees to chance their luck on the ice.[59] The refugee columns negotiating this precarious route also faced attacks by Soviet aircraft. On the Haff and the Nehrung babies froze to death, exhausted civilians collapsed and expired, and the bodies of those overcome by hopelessness hung from trees. There was no time to bury the dead.[60] Those who reached Pillau or the Gulf of Danzig still faced overcrowding, shortages of food, fuel and water and aerial bombardment.

For the refugees getting a place on the naval vessels operating a shuttle service in the Baltic under *Kriegsmarine* direction, the onward journey to the Reich or Denmark could be equally dangerous. Soviet submarines and aircraft sank numerous ships resulting in more than 20,000 fatalities. The former 'Strength through Joy' liner *Wilhelm Gustloff* was torpedoed on 30 January and only 838 of her 6,000 passengers survived. A similar fate befell the transport ship *Steuben* laden with 3,000 wounded soldiers. Only 300 survived her sinking on 9 February. Another enormous loss of life arose from the sinking of the freighter *Goya* on 16 April. The ship had been carrying more than 6,000 passengers and a mere 183 were plucked from the Baltic. Despite these horrendous losses it is estimated that during the course of this four-month naval evacuation, christened 'Operation Hannibal' by the *Kriegsmarine,* more than two million German civilians and soldiers escaped the Soviets from Pomeranian, East and West Prussian ports.[61] However, not all found salvation west of the Oder. Thousands of Silesian refugees perished in the Anglo-American bombing of Dresden (13–15 February 1945) where the death toll has been put at 35–40,000 although estimates as high as 200,000 have been suggested. Lesser known is the fate of the Pomeranian port of Swinemünde, the destination for thousands of eastern Germans rescued by the *Kriegsmarine*. An American raid on the town on 12 March 1945 was a devastating 'attack of cold precision' leading to the 'Dresden of the North' in which between 9,000 and 23,000 perished, the majority of them civilians.[62] In the chaotic circumstances of these terrible times casualty estimates often vary widely.

Prevarication and chronic disorganisation characterised the evacuation of Lower Silesia and East Brandenburg. The first indication of the approaching danger was the mention of familiar towns in the *Wehrmacht* report and the haunting appearance of bedraggled treks of ethnic Germans from the *General Gouvernement* and Warthegau.[63] The then *Oberbürgermeister* of Glogau, Dr Hoffmann-Rothe, believed that the sight of these endless refugee treks shattered belief in victory and rendered propaganda powerless. Feeding points and temporary quarters were established, but on an eight-mile stretch of road leading into the town 72 bodies were discovered.[64] The Party had attempted to conceal the danger. In mid-January *Kreisleiter* Fischer told state and Party officials in Namslau that the military situation was not alarming enough to publicise the emergency evacuation plan.[65] Refugees from neighbouring Kreuzburg were halted in Namslau and ordered to return home. A disturbing sign was the cancellation of the regular train timetable from 17 January. When local women with children tried to leave they were placated by Party officials and told to stay. The *Kreisleiter* proclaimed on the morning of 19 January that Namslau was secure, the very day that the Red Army crossed the Silesian frontier. Early that same afternoon he made a loudspeaker announcement in the town centre, telling the population to remain at their workplaces or in their homes. However, by mid-afternoon the news that three Red Army tanks had been sighted two miles from Namslau caused the official evacuation order to be issued. People were urged to salvage what they could. By 21 January, Namslau and surrounding villages were practically deserted. Town dwellers were sent westwards by train to Landeshut which was completely unprepared for their arrival because of the NSV's lack of planning. Between two and three per cent of the population, mainly elderly citizens, remained and on the morning of 22 January the Red Army entered the town.[66]

Soviet spearheads also neared the *Gauhauptstadt* of Breslau[67] and on the evening of 18 January the city was bombed by the Red Air Force. The attack was aimed at rail centres, particularly the Brockau goods yard, although scattered bombs caused damage across the city.[68] Elements of the Breslau *Volkssturm* had been placed in the Bartold defences and in the positions around the city after the 14 January *Volkssturm* mobilisation order for eastern Germany. Within days, men of the first and second echelons were also active in the city establishing checkpoints at bridges, railway stations, crossroads and squares.[69] Startled onlookers going about their daily business realised with grim foreboding that the war had come to Breslau. The change in mood was observed by a Lauban farmer in Breslau for a *Volkssturm* NCO training course. He noted that the city appeared calm on 17 January but three days later all Breslau seemed to be in the throes of departure.[70] The schoolboy Horst Gleiss journeyed into the city centre on the morning of Saturday 20 January to get a winter coat but instead saw the columns of Silesian peasants with all they owned stacked on their carts which trudged along the congested streets. Long herds of pigs, sheep, horses and other livestock were led along the roads. Military hardware and lorries full of infantry rolled through the streets. Crowds congregated around the public loudspeakers for the latest news and to hear evacuation directives.[71]

The pitiful treks meandered through the centre of Breslau in the direction of Schweidnitz.[72] Old men and adolescents led carts pulled by exhausted animals. Breslauers looked on anxiously at the unbroken columns of refugees, ethnic Germans and fellow Silesians from districts east of the Oder, where evacuation was permitted from 20 January. Refugees from the *General Gouvernement* and the Warthegau had already been on the frozen roads for three to four days when they reached Breslau and the NSV set up field kitchens to feed them but no billets were provided.[73] Nevertheless, hundreds perished from cold and hunger. In the evenings trucks were sent out to collect the frozen bodies of those who had perished within the city limits and to deposit the corpses in the mortuary. Many of the dead were children.[74] The gravity of the situation was further illustrated as sappers prepared the steel supports on Breslau's bridges for the attachment of explosive charges – some 40 bridges over the Oder and the Oder's channels were readied in this respect.[75] Meanwhile, military police established checkpoints on these bridges or at crossroads to pluck *Wehrmacht* deserters or men eligible for *Volkssturm* service from the refugee columns. One witness recalled at this time seeing the lifeless body of a soldier hanging from the Hundsfelder Bridge. He had been found hiding in a trek and condemned.[76] As well as seizing any able-bodied man to participate in the city's defence, the military authorities were assisted by the arrival of the Hamburg-raised 269th Infantry Division from Alsace. But German countermeasures could only delay the inevitable. Further Red Army offensive operations were launched across Lower Silesia from 8 February and three armies of Konev's First Ukrainian Front encircled Breslau on 15 February, despite frenzied attempts by the German 17th Army to maintain contact with the city.[77]

The crucial questions now confronting Hanke and the German military related to the nature of the defence of the city and the possibilities of evacuation. When he proclaimed that Breslau would be defended as a fortress on 21 January, directing all men to remain at their posts and ordering the immediate evacuation of women and children, Hanke effectively sealed the city's fate. Alluding to his own military experience as adjutant to Field Marshal Rommel, Hanke demanded that Breslau's garrison honour Rommel's spirit in a determined defence of the city. All resources were to be directed into this effort. Hanke coined the frequently repeated phrase 'He who fears an honourable death will die in shame' to sum up the resistance. The human and material costs did not concern him and he ultimately ignored the pleas claimed to have been made by the visiting Albert Speer, in their last meeting on 22 January, to spare the city from destruction.[78] Hanke's reported comments did not bode well for the future. He pledged that he would never allow the recently refurbished party headquarters to fall into Russian hands and would 'rather burn it down'. Moreover, he 'didn't give a damn for Breslau if it were about to fall into the enemy's hands'.[79]

The *Schlesische Tageszeitung*, the Party's local daily newspaper, portrayed the evacuation as a smooth operation with HJ and BdM assisting at railway stations to move luggage, look after children and help the sick.[80] Despite Party claims to the contrary, the sudden exodus of 700,000 inhabitants from Breslau and its environs was never likely to be an orderly affair.[81] A German Home Service broadcast on 25 January claimed that 'in the past few days roughly 300,000 people have left the town'.[82] There were insufficient trains, buses and lorries available and panic gripped the masses thronging the railway stations. Some 60 to 70 children were trampled to death at the main railway station in the commotion.[83] At this point the Party callously ordered women and children to take to the snowbound roads and leave Breslau by foot in order to avoid 'hours of pointless waiting at Breslau's railway stations'. Only women in work and without children were to remain at their posts.[84] From the evening of 20 January the *Drahlfunk* (public loudspeaker system) wailed out the directive across the city's streets and squares: 'Women and children leave the city immediately in the direction of Opperau and Kanth.'[85] They assembled in the southern suburbs and then proceeded towards Opperau and Kanth, some 15 miles to the west, where onward transportation was to be provided. On the evening of 20–21 January, anywhere between 60,000 and 100,000 predominantly women and children embarked on what has been variously described as the 'Todesmarsch der Breslauer Frauen' and the 'Kanth Todesmarsch', which claimed an estimated 18,000 lives.[86]

One woman wrote to her mother describing conditions on the journey. Suddenly parted from her husband, who had been called up for the *Volkssturm*, she recounted the gathering of fearful women and crying children. Minus 20 degree temperatures soon took their toll. Women began collapsing in the deep snow on the outskirts of Breslau and discarded luggage littered the route. The bodies of dead children lay in one village market place. Her efforts to obtain shelter and milk for her baby proved fruitless. All accommodation was full. Struggling on with a frozen arm and frostbitten feet she reached a Dominican convent where milk was heated for the children. Unfortunately it was too late for her motionless four-month-old daughter Gabi.[87] It is reasonable to attribute responsibility for these needless deaths to Hanke because of his decision to veto evacuation proposals a month before.[88] In this bitterly cold weather, one labourer at the *Unternehmen Bartold* digging site near Lohbrück recalled that it was often too cold to work. Tools broke when they made contact with the frozen earth. In temperatures of minus 15 degrees this witness recalled the shattering picture of passing refugee treks from Breslau in the days after 20 January.[89] In Breslau itself the frozen ground and the lack of manpower made it difficult to keep up with the rising number of burials.[90]

News of the 'death march' filtered back to Breslau as some survivors opted to stagger back to the threatened city. Remaining civilians were confronted with contradictory pressures and emotions such as fear of the Red Army, the promptings of Hanke's cohorts, their affection for the *Heimat* and the terror of flight in winter.[91] Many asserted that in Breslau they had shelter, food and fuel whereas if they left the city they risked death from hunger or cold.[92] During the three weeks prior to encirclement on 15 February the Party authorities, through a mixture of appeals and threats, tried to rid the city of non-combatants whose presence would hinder defensive efforts. Local Party leaders advised that only those employed in essential war work or capable of fighting would receive rations and from 1 February ration cards had to be stamped by the Party *Ortsgruppe*.[93] In another effort to make evacuation less unappealing the *Schlesische Tageszeitung*, given out for free in large numbers, printed a series of reports of Soviet atrocities in Silesia.[94] The authorities also made it clear that entire housing blocks were to be dynamited to aid defensive fighting.[95] A local Breslau radio broadcast on 7 February warned that evacuees of German nationality returning to the city to fetch belongings would be picked up by the security patrols at the stations and in the streets. Those returning without permission would have their names taken and would then be marched out of the city by foot.[96]

Among those forced to leave Breslau were Russian workers from the Linke-Hoffmann engineering works. Rag clad, they were sent onto the snowbound roads on 25 January and marched in the direction of Cottbus.[97] However, on the following day an attempt to force men classified under the fourth levy of the *Volkssturm* (unfit for combat) to depart by foot on a 170-kilometre, 12-day march to Hoyerswerda, Saxony was frustrated by their reluctance to leave due to their knowledge of the Kanth affair.[98] Ilse Braun, the sister of Hitler's mistress Eva, was one woman who had got out of Breslau physically unscathed. But she was distraught at what she had just witnessed. At dinner in the Reich Chancellery on the evening of 21 January, Eva seemed to suggest that Ilse could return to Breslau after a short break. In response, Ilse described the refugees trudging through the snow and attacked Hitler for leading Germany to this disaster. Eva was disgusted at her sister's lack of gratitude to the *Führer* who had even offered to house her in the Berghof at Berschtesgaden. Ilse deserved to be put up against a wall and shot.[99] Hanke ensured that his secretary Eva Arlt, her sister and her nephews were taken out of harm's way by arranging their evacuation to Hain in the Riesengebirge where they were quartered in the house 'Martha', already home to part of the Foreign Ministry evacuated from Berlin.[100]

The arduous times ahead for Breslau were evident from Major General Krause's proclamation of 27 January calling up men, women and children over 10 to fully contribute in the preparations for the forthcoming battle.[101] Krause himself played little further part in the proceedings. Finally succumbing to ill health, he was replaced as commandant by Major General Hans von Ahlfen, an experienced officer who had lost an arm in battle, on 1 February.[102] Meanwhile, on the ground the feverish preparations for defence were led by Party functionaries who ordered civilians, including women, to assist in the building of barricades. Streets were sealed and corner properties blown up by the SS and *Wehrmacht* to provide the 'favourable fighting area' demanded by Hanke. Rubble and redundant trams formed obstacles, most noticeably in the centre and south of the city.[103] Nevertheless, General Ferdinand Schörner, the avowedly Nazi commander of Army Group A (then Centre)[104] from 17 January, which had overall responsibility for the defence of Breslau, was unimpressed and described the situation to a young officer: 'It is a military pigsty! It is so bad that I considered having the commanding general of the fortress staff court-martialed. The Russians are almost there, and the city cannot hope to defend itself in its present state.'[105] When the young officer arrived in Breslau to galvanise the city's defence he quickly agreed with his superior's bleak assessment: 'Schörner had been right: the place was a military mess. All the staff people were handicapped or old, and they had no idea how to fight or how to defend a big city.'[106]

At first the Germans expected the Red Army to attack the north and east of the city and civilians were moved to the southern suburbs on 10 February. However, when Soviet attacks were launched against the south and west of Breslau ruthless relocation measures were enacted by the *Waffen-SS* in the south of the city from 28 February. Residents were sometimes given as little as 20 minutes to leave their homes. The Nazi authorities maintained that only 80,000 civilians remained in the besieged city to avoid criticism of their organisation of the evacuation but the real figure was probably double this.[107] Breslau's administrative importance was also reduced by evacuation to the west. The *Oberpräsidium* of Lower Silesia was moved to Hirschberg and other city bodies were relocated to Waldenburg. The university was hurriedly evacuated to Dresden on 22 January. In an open letter of 6 February, Hanke called on Breslau's student body to return to defend their city, evoking romantic echoes of the role played by Breslau's students in the War of Liberation against Napoleon.[108]

In Brandenburg *Gauleiter* Emil Stürtz forbade precautionary evacuation despite the avalanche of refugees entering the province from the east. Stürtz was critical of the *Wehrmacht*'s continued retreat which he blamed for triggering-off the unauthorised exodus of the population when evacuation remained unnecessary.[109] One arrival was *Gauleiter* Greiser from the Warthegau. He had fled Posen before the Red Army surrounded the city, following an order from Hitler to report to Berlin and undertake new duties under Himmler's direction. When Greiser landed in Frankfurt an der Oder he was told that Hitler now wanted Posen defended as a fortress.[110] Greiser was berated by an angry Stürtz for leaving his threatened *Gau* for the security of the rear.[111] After a short stay in a Landsberg hotel, Greiser, under Himmler's protection, proceeded to the spa of Carlsbad in the Sudetenland to take a cure for his 'old gall bladder complaint'.[112]

Other arrivals in Brandenburg were in a poorer condition. Refugees who had died from cold and hunger were buried in mass graves.[113] One observer in Küstrin heard people explaining that they were not supposed to leave but did not want to fall into Russian hands. They wondered why they had not been told the truth about the situation earlier.[114] Nevertheless, Sturtz's conduct was fully condoned by the Party leadership. During these critical January days the visiting Ley praised Stürtz for his optimistic mood; Goebbels too, was impressed by Stürtz's relative confidence.[115] However, Stürtz's entrenched stance against evacuation endangered the province's inhabitants. Stürtz twice rejected appeals from *Kreisleiter* Hauk of Zullichau–Schweibus for the evacuation of the district despite the proximity of Red Army tanks and some localities coming under enemy artillery bombardment. On 27 January, Stürtz threatened Hauk with court martial should he enact evacuation measures. The following day Stürtz rejected evacuation on the grounds that reinforcements were moving into the area. Civilians discovered that no tickets could be purchased for westward railway journeys. Those who took to the roads were stopped by military police and ordered to return home. The evacuation order was finally given on 29 January. As a result of this delayed departure, at least one trek was overrun and fired upon by Red Army tanks resulting in heavy casualties.[116]

Similarly harrowing scenes were witnessed in Pomerania. Treks from East Prussia, the Warthegau and the *General Gouvernement* flooded into the province from mid-January. A number of accounts testify to the misery in the snow. Already in December 1944, when evacuee trains from East Prussia halted in Deutsch Krone, the corpses of dead children were placed in paper coffins, loaded on to lorries and taken to the town crematorium.[117] Later, Pastor Otto Gehrke remembered seeing a train with open goods wagons halted at a signal east of Stolp. When the train finally moved off, the railway workers discovered a row of bundles on the embankment. These were the bodies of 30 children, the victims of cold or hunger on the journey. Gehrke buried the bodies in the village cemetery.[118] Likewise, Countess Libussa von Oldershausen observed the arrival of a freight train full of dishevelled refugees into Stolp railway station. The bodies of frozen children were gathered together on the platform.[119] Refugees arriving in Stolp complained bitterly that the NSV displayed little interest in their plight. Many of these Party officials had already 'scarpered'.[120] Moreover, refugees soon realised that Pomerania was unlikely to be their final destination. Countess Marion von Dönhoff, after a 14-day trek from East Prussia, arrived at Varzin in Rummelsberg district, the home of the Bismarck family. Here she was surprised to find that the Bismarck archive was being packed up for evacuation. The hope of peacefulness behind the Vistula was a fallacy. Pomerania would not provide salvation. Von Dönhoff recalled that Pomeranian homes remained occupied, although the local population rightly feared that they too would be leaving within days.[121]

The Party authorities in Pomerania were also worried that the refugees from further east were spreading harmful stories of their experiences. The military correspondent Buschmann of the *Pommersche Zeitung* observed on 23 January that refugees would be accepted in the province. However, while 'Some of them may exaggerate their experiences, nobody minds this, but it is irresponsible if we dramatise matters and spread rumours the only purpose of which is to create unrest among the population.'[122] A week later, Buschmann admitted that the columns of refugees entering Pomerania meant that 'the situation is strained as never before'. But he warned of the dangers arising from rumours and enemy propaganda and called on Pomeranians 'not [to] lose our nerve when a stream of refugees passes us'.[123]

During December 1944 the Pomeranian Party authorities had issued secret directives to initiate possible evacuation of districts east of the *Pommernwall.* Ultimate authority for evacuation and the salvaging of economic resources was designated to the *Kreisleiter* on 12 December.[124] Reception districts further west but within the province and east of the Oder were assigned. Three codewords were to signify the different stages of evacuation. 'Rain' meant that the population should commence preparing their trek vehicles and luggage for departure. 'Hail' signified that all important business and military facilities were to be brought to a standstill and, so far as was still possible, important agricultural and industrial machinery was to be repatriated. Finally, 'snow' was to lead to the immediate evacuation of the population by train, truck, trek or, in the most desperate scenario, by foot.[125] The idea of sending the elderly, women and children, weighed down with luggage, into the snow and temperatures of minus 15 degrees was condemned by a former *Landrat* as 'complete insanity'.[126] Moreover, in December it had been envisaged that full-scale evacuation orders would be issued when the front was within 25 kilometres of the threatened district, but by January the enemy advance had caused this to be reduced to a mere 15 kilometres.[127]

On the morning of 21 January, the codeword 'hail' was issued in all eastern Pomeranian frontier districts. At this juncture, a conference of eastern Pomeranian *Kreisleiter, Landräte* and *Bürgermeister* was held at Falkenburg (Dramburg district) chaired by Schwede-Coburg. Although Red Army tanks were approaching Schneidemühl, it was decided that evacuation should not commence. One *Landrat* recalled that Schwede-Coburg was most concerned that valuable military supplies and economic resources should not fall into Soviet hands; if necessary these were to be destroyed.[128] Requests from the *Landräte* for full evacuation were rejected by senior figures from the *Oberpräsidium. Regierungspräsident* Eckardt deemed that this was not yet necessary. Eckardt criticised and threatened *Landräte* and *Bürgermeister* who failed to obey Party directives unconditionally. One witness concluded that the *Oberpräsidium* in Stettin had not learned anything from the unfortunate earlier experiences of East Prussian refugees. Schwede-Coburg remarked that the Soviets posed a temporary danger and ventured that short occupation of the frontier districts may ensue, although preparations were being made for a counter offensive and the encirclement of enemy forces.[129] Significantly, the threatening figure of Heinrich Himmler had now moved into Schwede-Coburg's domain in his capacity as commander of Army Group Vistula. Himmler's special train 'Steiermark' pulled into Deutsch Krone on 22 January.[130]

Perhaps Himmler's ominous presence partially accounts for Schwede-Coburg's conduct in Schönlanke, 20 km south-west of Schneidemühl, on 25 January. Still attired in civilian clothes, Schwede warned Party officials that 'Schönlanke will not be evacuated, we will stop the Russians on the [River] Netze. Those who speak of evacuation will be locked up'.[131] He told his listeners to 'hold-out' and curtly rejected a plea from the *Landrat*'s wife to provide railway wagons for the evacuation of infants from the local maternity home. The next day Red Army tanks reached Schönlanke railway station and babies and staff left the town in open lorries under artillery fire. Some 41 out of 100 children perished in temperatures of minus 20 degrees. The remainder of the population departed on foot and their town was finally captured by the Red Army on 28 January. On 26 January, in the market place of Schloppe, 15 kilometres north-west of Schönlanke and also in front of the *Pommernwall*, Schwede told townspeople that 'no danger existed' and ordered those ready to depart to unpack their luggage as any evacuation was prohibited. He claimed that only 'rogue' Soviet tanks had been spotted in the vicinity of the town and they did not constitute the harbinger of a Red Army attack. Moreover, he insisted that German troops had knocked out these vehicles. Three days later Red Army tanks were in Schloppe. Schwede's trips to Schönlanke and Schloppe were his first and only attempts to make a personal intervention at the front and he hurriedly returned to Stettin, destined never to venture east of the Oder again.[132]

Despite his fighting talk, Schwede-Coburg was criticised by the visiting Ley as being tired and preoccupied with evacuation rather than with defence.[133] In mid-January Schwede-Coburg ordered officials to remain in towns under enemy bombardment and then to fight their way out or attach themselves to *Wehrmacht* detachments. Himmler then forbade any civilian or military evacuation. Civilian officials in *Wehrkreis* II were ordered to remain at their posts under pain of death.[134] Himmler's decision to prohibit the further westward movement of East and West Prussian treks led to more than one million Germans falling into Soviet hands.[135] Schwede-Coburg also voiced his concern at the 'unworthy behaviour' of leading Party figures whose families were sent to rear areas. Local Party and state officials were encouraged to display 'exemplary behaviour'. National Socialist leaders had to live within the *Volksgemeinschaft* and share their joys and sorrows. Rather than awarding themselves special privileges, Party leaders were to display a willingness to fight, and if necessary die, so that Germany would live.[136]

The conduct of the local Pomeranian Party leadership hardly corresponded to this heroic ideal. Party officials in Schönlanke made a timely getaway before the arrival of the Red Army, leaving the local population and schoolchildren evacuated from Bochum earlier in the war to their fate.[137] The official evacuation order for Schneidemühl was given as Soviet shells fell on the station. The lack of transportation meant that many of those who left Schneidemühl by foot in the direction of Deutsch Krone perished from cold, exhaustion or at the Soviet hands.[138] A similar story unfolded in Neustettin which was occupied by the Red Army on 28 February. Although the Red Army had stood scarcely 15 kilometres from the town for four weeks, the *Gau* authorities in Stettin refused to countenance 'premature' evacuation until 26 February. The ringing of church bells signified the issue of the evacuation order, but little transportation was available and the remaining inhabitants of Neustettin left the town on foot carrying hand baggage. The *Kreisleiter* had departed earlier.[139] Party officials in Stolp rejected requests for travel authorisation to allow women and children to leave. They said that this would provoke panic and that there was no danger.[140] On the outskirts of Köslin police posts were erected to prevent civilians departing.[141] Party leaders did not exhibit a standard form of behaviour during these critical days. A few behaved responsibly and tried to initiate orderly evacuation measures. Others ordered civilians to remain at gunpoint and even ignored directives from Stettin to initiate evacuation. Some die-hards opted for suicide in their desperation. Despite being entrusted with the care of the population, others simply got drunk and fled to the rear.[142]

Typical of the turmoil of these days is the example of developments in Pyritz district south of Stettin. This was initially envisaged as a reception district for localities east of the *Pommernwall*, but was directly threatened itself by the Red Army from late January and became a battleground for six weeks thereafter.[143] When *Bürgermeister* Otto Floret of Pyritz telephoned the *Gauleitung* in Stettin to advise that Soviet tanks stood 11 kilometres from the town he was told: 'The present situation is a totally temporary condition. Pyritz is not an evacuation district rather [it is] a reception district!'[144] Eventually a frantic evacuation of the overcrowded town was conducted under Red Army artillery fire. Floret blamed this delay on Schwede-Coburg as local Party leaders had done their best in the circumstances.[145] One former official remarked bitterly after the war that 'The RVK and his responsible officials failed. They alone bear responsibility for the misery which afflicted our brothers and sisters in the east.'[146]

The Party authorities were equally stubborn in East Prussia over the issue of evacuation orders, the direction of flight treks and the allocation of reception districts. Once again they proved unequal to the demands of the moment. In Neidenburg people were going about their daily business on 18 January when suddenly the news broke that the Red Army had occupied nearby Soldau. The *Landrat*, aware of the Soviet breakthrough had already proposed evacuation, but *Gauamtsleiter* Paul Dargel in Königsberg rejected this idea. The Red Army advanced into Neidenburg on 20 January. Late evacuation orders caused most treks to fall into Soviet hands.[147] This fate also befell 20,000 people in Rastenburg.[148] When a doctor suggested to Dargel on 19 January that the hospitals in Allenstein and Wartenburg should be evacuated, he was told that if he continued to speak of evacuation he would be shot in Allenstein market place.[149] Authorisation to leave the town was only given when the Russians stood five kilometres away. Allenstein fell on 22 January.[150]

Party officials left their charges in the lurch and made their escape. A camp of HJ employed in an East Prussian shipyard woke up one February morning to find that 'all our superiors had run off. You could already hear the artillery fire.'[151] As the Soviets closed in on Königsberg, both OLG President Dräger and GSA Szelinski left by car for Pillau in order to reach the Reich. Koch telephoned news of these unauthorised departures to the Interior Ministry. When the two officials arrived in Berlin they were arrested and imprisoned. Neither outlived the Third Reich.[152] Some *Kreisleiter* perished commanding *Volkssturm* battalions. This was the fate of Karl Makinn in Labiau and Walter Schulz in Ortelsburg. Others simply fled. *Kreisleiter* Heuer of Angerapp vanished from the battlefield and reappeared in Danzig. *Kreisleiter* Schulz of Rastenburg fled over the Frisches Haff, but drowned when his car fell through the ice.[153]

Party officials in Cranz used the last remaining vehicles to facilitate their escape. Police, Red Cross and even *Volkssturm* personnel also left.[154] The wounded were hurriedly moved from place to place prior to embarkation from Pillau.[155] In Königsberg they were stacked on to hospital trains or lay in hospitals enduring air raids. Meanwhile, numerous prominent doctors were allowed to depart including senior members of Königsberg University's medical faculty, the recipients of professorial chairs at the university's 400th birthday celebrations six short months before and the holders of high military rank.[156] The SS reported that there was outrage among the garrison that doctors and military hospital personnel had left. The soldiers apparently demanded that they, together with officers from ammunition dumps who had also fled, be shot.[157]

Koch remained a major obstacle to orderly evacuation. He offered only empty slogans urging East Prussians to 'Fight like Indians',[158] 'to sink their claws into their native earth', 'to defend their farms to the last'. Königsberg Castle was 'the Alcazar of East Prussia' and would be defended to the death.[159] But like Hanke, Koch displayed a peculiarly touching concern for the welfare of his domestic staff. On 21 January, he burst into the office of his secretary Lise-Lotte Küssner at Groß Friedrichsburg and startled her with the sudden instruction, 'You must go – quickly tonight', and added, 'Take the rest of the village people'. When Küssner responded that such a departure was treason and placards signed by Koch stated this, the *Gauleiter* reportedly replied, 'No, no – that means nothing – just go.' Küssner's little convoy stayed one step ahead of the Soviets and eventually reached the River Elbe in late April.[160]

Despite the influx of refugees from the surrounding countryside, Königsbergers were repeatedly told over the radio to remain in the city.[161] However, a dramatic volte-face ensued when the Red Army crashed through the flimsy Deime Line and from 26 January probed the city's outer defences. General Lasch, commandant of Königsberg, observed that the city was 'full to the brim', but reports of a likely enemy breakthrough caused Dargel, acting on Koch's instructions, to broadcast an order over the city's loudspeaker system for civilians to leave their homes and journey to Pillau. Predictably the road was soon choked with columns of civilians moving by foot, bicycle or cart, women with prams and military support services heading for the Samland where no provision had been made for their arrival.[162] Königsberg was surrounded by the Red Army on 30 January 1945. Had the Soviets appreciated the weakness of the garrison and not made the mistaken assumption that the Germans had undertaken sufficient defensive preparations, they could have stormed the city there and then.[163]

Lasch made feverish attempts to restore discipline and form new units from the stragglers flooding into the city. A former *Bürgermeister* of Königsberg, Gustav Makowka, recalled that mobs plundered city centre shops stealing butter, fat, hams and sausages. Groups of soldiers ransacked empty houses looking for alcohol and tobacco. Unwanted items of clothing and books littered the streets.[164] Similarly, Erich Zehran, then President of the city's Finance Department, remembered returning home after a night on *Volkssturm* duty to find his home looted and soiled.[165] Makowka asserted that 20,000 deserters were apprehended and sent back to the front. On Lasch's order, to set an example, a few were publicly shot and their executions publicised in the fortress newspaper.[166] Evidently Lasch's efforts to re-impose discipline were successful as his forces were able to participate in the attack commencing on 19 February which ended the first siege and re-established land communications with the Samland.[167]

On 28 January, Koch and most of his acolytes left Königsberg. The *Gauleiter* made only four flying visits to his *Gauhauptstadt* thereafter.[168] Koch attempted to conceal his departure and his reports to Berlin gave the impression that he had remained in the city.[169] Nevertheless, Goebbels soon realised that something was amiss when Koch contacted him from Pillau appealing for foodstuffs to be sent to the port, while Deputy *Gauleiter* Großherr in Königsberg reported that the garrison intended to defend every house and every street. Großherr advised that most prominent people had 'done a bolt' and Goebbels considered that this was an unspoken reproach directed at Koch.[170] The *Gauleitung* building, guarded by two members of the *Volkssturm*, was empty. Offices and rooms were open and files, some doused in petrol, were scattered around. The conference hall was littered with files, forms, ammunition and *Panzerfäuste*. The *Volkssturm* had been given orders to torch the building rather than allow it to fall into Soviet hands.[171] The departure of the *Gauleiter* and other senior figures caused bitterness in the city. The SS advised that Soviet leaflets dropped on the city asserting that Koch was the first *Volkssturmmann* to leave Königsberg provoked 'great discussion',[172] although Party directives, leaflets and radio reports tried to give the impression that Koch had remained.

Koch established his headquarters in a luxurious Pillau hotel. However, when this was bombed on 6 February he moved to a house at Neutief naval air base on the Frisches Nehrung opposite Pillau. Here he operated behind barbed wire and watchtowers.[173] Koch asserted that he was *Gauleiter* not solely of Königsberg but of all East Prussia and could lead the refugee relief measures more effectively from Neutief.[174] In contrast to the suffering of East Prussian refugees, Koch continued to live well and arranged for the best liqueurs and spirits from the prestigious Park Hotel in Königsberg, an 'Erich Koch Foundation' concern, to be sent to Neutief.[175] In addition to his rare visits to Königsberg, Koch twice flew into the Heiligenbeil pocket by Fieseler Storch and also appeared in Berlin. On 24 March, he told Goebbels that the troops fighting in the Heiligenbeil pocket were desperately short of supplies and recommended their transfer to the Samland. However, he provided a positive impression of the 'comprehensive defence measures' enacted in Königsberg and made the grossly exaggerated claim that the Red Army had already suffered one million fatalities in East Prussia.[176] Koch's arrogance was undiminished. He suddenly appeared in Königsberg's broadcasting house on 25 February and delivered a eulogy of his 'achievements'.[177] Koch said that the sight of thousands of refugees crossing the frozen Frisches Haff under Soviet air attack was the most terrible experience of his life. However, he managed to sicken this Party and military audience by telling them that as some refugees were 'behaving like animals' he had 'made the hardest decision of his life' and given the *Wehrmacht* the order to shoot unruly flight columns crossing the Frisches Haff. This statement outraged most listeners and Koch was reportedly heckled. The majority of officers in the affected area refused to follow this order.[178]

During the initial period of the 'fortress Königsberg' era Party power effectively lay in the hands of *Kreisleiter* Ernst Wagner, the commander of the city *Volkssturm.*[179] General Lasch countersigned numerous orders drafted by Wagner concerning the civilian population and *Volkssturm.* After the war he praised Wagner for doing his duty and submitting to military authority during their period together.[180] Both wanted all able-bodied men in the city under arms.[181] Wagner's effective working relationship with Lasch was described by the reporter Günther Heysing as a Party–*Wehrmacht* relationship corresponding to the heroic model of the newly released propaganda film *Kolberg*; 'General Lasch and *Kreisleiter* Wagner in common with the historic duo Gneisenau and Nettlebeck work together without petty jealousy.'[182] One front-page *Völkischer Beobachter* article on 'The Spirit of Königsberg . . . an example for the entire nation' was essentially a copy of Wagner's appeal to the fortress garrison.[183] This coverage and the impression it made in Berlin infuriated Koch. The final straw was a telegram sent from Wagner to Hanke in Breslau. This exchange between 'fortresses' received heavy press coverage. Wagner informed Hanke of the Königsberg slogan for the 'struggle against the inhuman enemy from the East': 'Vengeance is our virtue, hate is our duty!' Europe and the world watched the fighting as both fortresses were transformed into 'mass graves for the Soviet hordes'. Wagner asserted that 'the hour before the sun rises is always the darkest', but promised that German forces would soon go over to the attack and 'sweep the Bolshevik hordes out of Germany'.[184] Wagner realised that Koch would never forgive him for this action and turned 'chalk white' when the telegram was broadcast on national radio on 1 March.[185]

Koch swiftly demoted Wagner and re-imposed his own authority following the restoration of land communications with the Samland. Großherr, 'Fire Brigade General' Fiedler and 12 other *Kreisleiter* were sent into Königsberg on 28 February; the city was divided into fifteen sectors and Wagner's area of authority was thus much diminished.[186] Koch condemned the *Wehrmacht* leadership as weak, lacking will and treacherous. The turmoil engineered by Koch destroyed the working relationship between the army and the Party. This produced the most oppressive atmosphere of mistrust which was worse even than that in Breslau.[187] In February, Lasch had apparently told his superiors that he wished to be relieved from his post because of Koch's growing interference.[188] Subsequently, in the midst of a series of accusations, Koch told Goebbels that Lasch's name was most appropriate (in German 'lasch' equates to 'limp').[189] However, Goebbels observed that the jealous Koch had demoted Wagner and wrecked Party–*Wehrmacht* co-operation: 'He [Koch] is now using in Königsberg the methods which did him so little credit in the Ukraine.'[190] Nevertheless, Koch retained enough influence for his telegram to the *Führerhauptquartier* following the surrender of Königsberg to initiate the proceedings which led to Lasch being sentenced to death *in absentia* for treachery and his family being arrested.[191]

The 'Failure' of the Military

Party criticism of the *Wehrmacht* was not confined to Königsberg. There was widespread disquiet at the army's failure to occupy defensive lines.[192] The collapse of the German front was followed by ravaged units scurrying pell-mell to the west. This shattered the illusion that prepared positions would be occupied by troops engaged in an orderly withdrawal from the front. For those who had laboured long and hard digging trenches and building bunkers there was bitterness that their work had been in vain. The

Wehrmacht admitted in February 1945 that the Red Army had overran these positions very quickly but maintained that the defences constructed under military auspices were generally well built. In contrast, the fortresses, with the exception of Thorn in the Warthegau, which actually fell almost immediately, were deemed to be poorly constructed as a lack of resources had led to the neglect of the outer defensive rings. Ironically, the interior defences of fortresses such as Königsberg and Breslau were able to stave off repeated Soviet assaults over the following months. Earlier, the A, B and C defences in Poland, bound together by switch lines and intermediate positions to combat enemy flank attacks, and the East Prussian fortifications, were unable to fulfil this task due to the absence of reserves. Numerous intermediate positions were undefended.[193] For sophisticated defences such as those of the Oder–Warthe Bend fortified front there was insufficient technical support and a lack of equipment and troops with specialised training to operate the defensive installations. Moreover, because of neglect many of the latter were no longer fit for use.[194]

It is unlikely that any defensive positions constructed by the Germans at this stage could have halted a Red Army assault for any length of time. The experiences encountered during the construction of the *Ostwall* illustrated the paucity of the nation's remaining human and material resources. Guderian recalled the 'impossibility of supplying the garrisons and the weapons needed to man the fortifications'.[195] The *Wehrmacht* had insufficient men for the front without attempting to find divisions and equipment for rear defences, and military district commanders had no authority over other sources of potential manpower such as the *Volkssturm*, *Kriegsmarine*, *Luftwaffe* and *Waffen-SS* formations. The few men that could be found were of the poorest quality. Otto Skorzeny later confessed that he had 'no fancy ideas' about the pioneer and depot battalions he found at Schwedt at the end of January for the men 'were mainly elderly invalids, all the good men having been sent to the front-line long before.'[196]

Throughout eastern Germany the mobilisation of the first echelon of the *Volkssturm* was ordered on 14 January and 176 combat battalions from this first levy, around 90,000 men, were placed in fortifications in eastern Germany.[197] It has been estimated in one recent study that as many as 650,000 *Volkssturm* men may have fought on the Eastern Front.[198] Any *Volkssturm* success was often dependent on timely reinforcement by the *Wehrmacht* or *Waffen-SS*. When these barely trained *Volkssturm* detachments were deployed, they were heavily outnumbered and lacked heavy weapons. For instance, a consignment of guns earmarked for the *Volkssturm* in the B1 positions were still in their rail carriage when the Red Army overran the positions.[199] The numbers pushed into front-line service comprised only a fraction of the men who fell within the parameters of the four *Volkssturm* levies. Frequently battalions were not flung into combat on account of the wretched state of their arms, equipment and training or because of the poor physical condition of the men.[200] Otherwise, the results could be deadly.

One *Volkssturm* man from Labiau, East Prussia recalled encountering the Red Army on the snow covered landscape. The men of the Labiau battalion, armed with Italian rifles and given 15 cartridges, were wearing civilian clothing and were visible for miles whereas enemy troops were well armed and clad in camouflaged snow suits. *Volkssturm* casualty rates in East Prussia were sometimes as high as 70–80 per cent and the province's losses amounted to nearly one-quarter of *Volkssturm* losses nationally.[201] Among the many German dead was the battalion commander, *Kreisleiter* Karl Makinn, a decorated First World War veteran.[202] The old men and boys were soon engulfed by the Soviet tide. Meanwhile, the Lower Silesian *Volkssturm* lacked weaponry and ammunition to delay the Red Army and after a short spell of fighting the border defences were broken at numerous points.[203] The rapid Red Army advance into Pomerania surprised *Volkssturm* defenders and many of the 60 battalions hastily deployed were savaged in attacks from the flanks and from the rear.[204]

Significant numbers of *Volkssturm* battalions were deployed to shore up the Oder front and to augment the garrisons of Königsberg and Breslau. So called 'elite' *Volkssturm* units were sent from throughout Germany and Austria to bolster the Oder and southern Pomeranian fronts in late January 1945 and deployed immediately. One historian dubbed them barely trained 'cannon fodder'. When they received modern weapons they could not operate them. Nevertheless, despite the privations and the losses, some of these formations manned their positions on the west-bank of the Oder for two and a half months.[205] Skorzeny recalled that a battalion from Hamburg contained 'fine specimens . . . full of enthusiasm'. Their weapons and equipment were 'excellent', due in his opinion, to the efforts of their RVK, Karl Kaufmann. Skorzeny added the pithy remark, 'The Königsberg [Neumark] battalion were worse off.'[206] Conditions were worst in the Küstrin sector where police detachments apprehended 254 *Wehrmacht* and *Volkssturm* deserters on 10 and 11 March alone and immediately sent them back to their units. A Luneburg *Volkssturm* battalion was particularly demoralised and elements of two companies led by their officers had left Küstrin and tried to march in a westerly direction.[207] The *Volkssturm* suffered horrendous losses in encircled Küstrin. Only 118 out of the initial 900 *Volkssturm* men survived to reach German lines.[208] However, at Pyritz in southern Pomerania, the *Volkssturm* battalion assisted other auxiliary units in warding-off determined attacks by the 12th Guards Tank Corps during the first week of February. The *Volkssturm* helped to regain parts of the town, destroyed over 20 Soviet tanks and inflicted heavy losses on the enemy. For a further month the link with eastern Pomerania was preserved and time was gained to bolster positions along the Oder.[209]

Volkssturm battalions from throughout East Prussia and Lower Silesia participated in the defence of Königsberg and Breslau respectively. Some 10,000 *Volkssturm* men were active in Königsberg. On occasions they fought well and contributed to localised successes such as the recapture of Neuhausen airfield, the retaking of the suburb of Metgethen and the operation which reopened contact with forces in Samland. The Königsberg *Volkssturm* faced draconian discipline from their own side and received brutal treatment from the Red Army when the city surrendered. *Kreisleiter* Ernst Wagner, commander of the Königsberg *Volkssturm*, told his men that for better or worse they were now bound to the fate of the city. He emphasised that retreat was pointless and constituted a crime. Every *Volkssturmman* was to be prepared to give his life not only to preserve the freedom of the city but also for the survival of Königsberg's women and children.[210] One veteran Nazi later claimed that over 2,000 *Volkssturm* and Party officials fell into Soviet hands on their entry into Königsberg on 10 April. Many suffered a gruesome fate, with the execution of *Volkssturm* as partisans and the murder of German wounded being widely reported.[211]

Concurrently, 38 *Volkssturm* battalions, comprising of 15,000 men, contributed to the 11-week defence of Breslau.[212] The leader of the Breslau *Volkssturm*, *SS-Obergruppenführer* Otto Herzog, forged good relations with the *Wehrmacht*. Battalions were occasionally placed under *Wehrmacht* command and were frequently sent to quieter sectors of the defence perimeter or to their home localities. Fitter men with more military training were placed in the 26 combat battalions of the Breslau *Volkssturm*, while 10 battalions of older, less fit men assisted with communications and supplies and in the building of additional defences. Two battalions were formed from the ranks of the HJ. Despite the heavy Soviet attacks, particularly in early April, *Volkssturm* morale never collapsed and the tenacity of the Breslau *Volkssturm* was highlighted in reports from the city until the very end.[213]

Some of the most fervent *Volkssturm* fighters were found among the ranks of the HJ, although they only constituted a small proportion of battalions deployed in the east. For these boys, indoctrinated in the schools of the Third Reich, service in the *Volkssturm* finally provided the chance to actually face the hated Jewish-Bolshevik enemy. Many rose to the occasion. The last Nazi newsreels showed Hitler and Goebbels decorating boy soldiers for knocking-out Soviet tanks.[214] The role of the *Hitlerjugend* and the fanaticism of some units is one aspect of the siege of Breslau that is fairly well known. The eager boys of the HJ reinforced the depleted ranks of the *Volkssturm*. Riding to their positions on bicycles, with a *Panzerfaust* over their shoulder, they were renowned for their tank-busting prowess. The exploits of the HJ were highlighted in *Wehrmacht* reports in April as the Soviets attempted to drive into the city from the south and the west following their successes at the beginning of the month. The boys of the Hitler Youth Regimental Group commanded by the local HJ Leader Herbert Hirsch fought in the bitter battle for the south of the city. Numbering around 1,000 and split into two battalions they recaptured the Rüttgers plant and Pöpelwitz station. Some boys used catapults to fire grenades at the Soviets but the fighting around the railway embankment which encompassed the city's southern defences claimed the lives of half the boys.[215] In the encircled fortress of Schneidemühl, the bravery of 14- and 15-year-old NCO cadets distressed regular officers. Major Karl Günther von Hase, the fortress operations officer, later recalled, 'It was terrible. They tried so hard to be brave. Whenever we needed volunteers for a patrol or a dangerous counter-attack, those teenagers put themselves forward. We had to get back lost ground – so we used them.'[216]

The regime's propaganda was keen to highlight instances of individual heroism in the *Volkssturm* to illustrate that apparently hopeless situations could be mastered by fanaticism. In Königsberg, *Volkssturm* battalion leader Ernst Tiburzy was feted and awarded the Knight's Cross for knocking out five Soviet T-34 tanks using a *Panzerfaust.* He was also applauded for shooting a platoon leader for cowardice. In Hindenburg, Upper Silesia, Hitler Youth Günther Nowak reportedly did even better and destroyed nine tanks.[217] A Silesian broadcast for *Volkssturm* men on 1 February insisted that the *Panzerfaust* was a simple weapon to use. Inexperienced men were to consult with 'battle-hardened comrades' or to read the instructions carefully. Above all, panic was to be avoided. It was stressed, 'If our homeland is at stake, there must be no tank fright.'[218]

There is dispute over the practical implications of the mobilisation of the *Volkssturm* in eastern Germany during early 1945. The *Volkssturm* directed refugee treks, led herds of cattle and salvaged valuable commodities from the environs of the front. The valour of two Pomeranian battalions contributing to the defence of Kolberg helped facilitate the naval evacuation of around 75,000 soldiers and civilians.[219] On the other hand, the seizure of manpower from treks often further retarded evacuation efforts. Completely bereft of fit men, treks moved at a snail's pace and were more likely to be caught by the rapidly moving front, with appalling results for the refugees. Following the collapse in the Warthegau, German officials candidly admitted that *Volkssturm* men would have been more usefully deployed remaining with their families and leading refugee treks to the old Reich.[220] On balance, it is fair to conclude that the interests of eastern Germans may have been better served if the menfolk had stayed with the treks.

As positions were undefended or swiftly occupied, some eastern Germans later attributed this to the *Wehrmacht*'s lack of competence and bravery. *Kreisleiter* Schug recalled that Stargard, Pomerania was 'swarming with staff officers and generals', but that there was a complete absence of troops fit for combat. The roads were kept open for the eastward movement of the military, but columns of *Wehrmacht* vehicles travelled to the west 'laden with ridiculous junk'.[221] In Züllichau, Brandenburg a few retreating *Wehrmacht* units were sighted. Although Züllichau was a garrison town, defences were unmanned.[222] The *Gendarmerie* commander in Frankfurt an der Oder, Lieutenant-Colonel Kahl, remarked that the cold weather eliminated natural barriers, enabling Soviet tanks to roll over frozen lakes, marshes and rivers. He added that the defences in his district were occupied by a few SA, police, *Volkssturm* and HJ units and unsurprisingly 'were overrun by the Asiatic hordes almost without a shot'. Kahl concluded that the descriptions of Soviet atrocities conveyed by isolated groups of German troops fighting their way through to German lines also had a detrimental impact on the defenders and believed that it was astonishing that the Oder front held until 16 April.[223]

Confusion also took hold. Seidler comments that the Tirschtiegel Riegel (barrier), the most easterly defences built in Brandenburg during the 1930s and strengthened in 1944, should have been manned by 25 *Volkssturm* battalions. However, it fell without a fight as the available weaponry for the garrison was dispatched to the Party authorities in Pomerania and the defences were barely manned.[224] Apparently, the retreating troops of the Ninth Army received no orders to occupy these Oder–Warthe positions, which Kissel maintained was the strongest barrier in the Reich and impregnable if sufficiently manned and supplied. In addition to new weapons not arriving for possible defenders, anti-tank barriers such as those on the Meseritz–Pieske road through the defences, remained open allowing Soviet tanks to advance in the midst of startled *Volkssturm* detachments.[225] Chuikov later wrote that any German defenders encountered in eastern Brandenburg were unfamiliar with the permanent fortifications and were not able to make full use of them.[226] Concurrently, it is clear that military discipline collapsed in certain sectors despite the activities of the notorious field police and the spectacle of public executions. *Wehrmacht* behaviour on German soil shocked onlookers. The authorities were extremely concerned at the morale of German forces in Brandenburg. A *Bürgermeister* in Meseritz district reported on 28 January that 100 soldiers had left their positions. Some had said that the Bolsheviks had broken through and they could not endure the war any longer.[227] Almost three weeks later an SS observer in the Frankfurt an der Oder sector described German forces as disorganised and lacking equipment, in particular anti-tank weapons. The demoralised troops frequently fled when Red Army tanks were sighted. With the apparent exception of units rushed in from the west and reserve formations, the prevailing view was that the war was lost. The positions on the Vistula, Warthe and Obra had failed to halt the Soviets and soldiers questioned why the Oder defences should be any more successful. Groups of soldiers fled westwards and plundered civilian property.[228]

During operations in the Küstrin area, Goebbels noted that German soldiers were described by their officers as 'weary and worn out' and reluctant to advance. Humiliatingly, some Germans were asking officers from Vlasov units and recent captives from the Red Army how German prisoners would be treated by the Soviets.[229] Meanwhile, Silesian refugees observed soldiers looting empty houses before the Red Army had crossed the Oder. These repeated occurrences were viewed by the Silesians with 'deep outrage' and articulated to the authorities in Saxon reception districts.[230] Similar scenes were witnessed by a judicial official returning on a short visit to the front line around the Upper Silesian town of Cosel. In the court building, occupied by men of a Silesian unit, the cellar was forced open and official and private property had disappeared. Numerous empty dwellings in the town had been searched by troops and ransacked. Order was restored when police units arrived in Cosel and shot a few soldiers and civilians for plundering.[231]

This was eastern Germany in the throes of collapse. Naturally, the Nazi authorities did not take any of the blame although adverse rumours about frozen children, chaos on the snowy roads and thoughtless Party conduct swirled around the Reich. On 15 February, the German news agency DNB denied that the refugees from the eastern provinces had suffered from exhaustion and exposure arising from Party callousness during the evacuation: 'Official investigations by the competent authorities have shown that the positively ridiculous rumours about the alleged losses of the refugees were either fantastic exaggeration or complete inventions.'[232]

Absolute military defeat, the disintegration of Nazi 'order' and the hell of mass flight in winter characterised a period when the whirlwind of war swept away centuries of German settlement east of the Oder. The war was lost and survival was paramount. However, the Nazi leadership was ambivalent about the welfare of individuals and indeed about the fate of Germany. To prolong the regime they demanded that Germans fight to the death, a heroic resistance to be recorded in the annals of history, and a marked contrast to the humiliation and shame of November 1918. The internal foes of the Third Reich were not to survive the *Götterdämmerung* and the machinery of death rolled until the end. To sustain this resistance the standard mixture of propaganda and terror was dispensed, with the former losing all touch with reality as the latter became ever more prevalent and 'German on German' focused.

CHAPTER 9

Our Brave Fortresses in the East

'Beat the Red Dog'

As the noose tightened around the Third Reich German propagandists confronted an increasingly uncompromising military reality. Their operational area east of the Oder constantly diminished until it comprised only the environs of the fortress cities. Here German propaganda was faced with the corrosive effect of Soviet invective and had to confront the misery of soldiers and civilians fighting a desperate daily battle for survival in appalling conditions and against overwhelming odds.

Soviet propaganda highlighted Germany's hopeless military position, promised just treatment on surrender and triggered or accentuated detrimental rumours about the actions of Party leaders. German troops were constantly urged to desert by loud-speaker and leaflet propaganda. Representatives of the NKFD and the BDO, including recent deserters and priests, broadcast appeals stressing that Germany was beaten and soldiers should consider their own survival. Following the isolation of Breslau, some seven different Free Germany Committee leaflets and eleven different Red Army pamphlets were dropped on the city on one day.[1] The official German line was also challenged by clandestine underground pamphlets such as *Der Freiheitskämpfer* (Freedom Fighter), the organ of the communist 'Freedom Movement' which had been in existence in Breslau since the summer of 1944. This pamphlet summarised the real military situation and the futility of further fighting, high-lighted the behaviour of local 'little Hitlers' and promised that the day of reckoning with the 'Nazi criminals' was near.[2]

Through the scrutiny of German military reports and Soviet propaganda, some informed Königsbergers, a minority, could ascertain the futility of their situation at the beginning of April 1945 – they were marooned on a distant island far from German lines. They knew that the Red Army was on the Oder, Danzig had fallen and German forces in East Prussia were being methodically eliminated. More ominously as the surgeon Lehndorff wrote, 'The Russians have dropped leaflets telling us that we may celebrate Easter, but after that it's all up with us.'[3] Soviet propaganda against

Königsberg peaked on the evening of 5 April when loudspeakers announced that 'tonight is your last chance to come over to us . . . Tomorrow morning at eight o'clock the offensive will begin . . . Think of Stalingrad . . . Early tomorrow the great death begins.'[4]

At national level German propagandists emphasised the stout defence of the eastern fortresses against a bestial invader. 'Whisper propaganda' authorised by the Propaganda Ministry and disseminated on the home front by decorated soldiers and trusted agents stressed vast Soviet losses which raised the possibility of a successful German counter-attack.[5] This appeal for heroic resistance and fear propaganda merged to comprise the mainstay of Nazi rhetoric during the regime's final weeks. Soldiers and civilians were portrayed as united against Bolshevism and prepared to lay down their lives and accept any material sacrifice to perpetuate the struggle. This was a nation united in will and in suffering. During January newspapers stressed that the Allied powers had the common aim of annihilating Germany[6] and would make no distinction among her people. German propagandists seized on the Morgenthau Plan for post-war Germany and the Allied demand for unconditional surrender as providing sufficient reasons to continue the struggle. The propaganda concerning Bolshevik atrocities was substantiated by the experiences of refugees. Capitulation was not an option as life would be intolerable under Soviet slavery. However, despite their sympathy for the refugees and a willingness, especially in eastern districts, to defend the Fatherland, most Germans did not want to go down with the sinking ship and did not want their towns and cities obliterated in a futile prolongation of the war.

The propagandists repeated that 'the justice of history' would guarantee Germany's final victory. Historical parallels such as Rome's plight when Hannibal was at the gates, the desperate position of Frederick the Great during the Seven Years War, the plight of the NSDAP in late 1932, the difficulties facing the British in 1940 and the Soviets in 1941 were cited to illustrate that 'no crisis was insurmountable'.[7] However, with the exception of the most committed Nazi zealots and the most indoctrinated HJ, self-preservation was paramount. As the historian Marlis Steinert contends, 'The increasingly desperate military situation sapped the strength and undermined the institutions of the Third Reich. Since propaganda could not arrest this trend the regime abandoned veiled terror for naked terror.'[8] In eastern Germany soldiers and civilians were trapped between military and Party terror and a horror of the Red Army.

Shrill Nazi rhetoric still attempted to put a positive slant on the daily setbacks. German propaganda initially attempted to downplay the Soviet threat. The military reporter Buschmann, writing in the *Pommersche Zeitung* on 15 January 1945, admitted the 'gravity of the present situation' but still deemed the [Soviet winter] offensive as 'an action to relieve the Anglo-Americans who are in difficulties in the West'.[9] As Red Army spearheads probed the Warthegau, a leading article in the *Ostdeutscher Beobachter*, published in Posen on 18 January, could still make the reassuring claim: 'The situation is not such as to cause particular alarm, for this is not the first onslaught of the Huns which has been brought to nothing at the frontier of Germany.'[10]

Even the removal of the Hindenburg coffins and the dynamiting of the Tannenberg memorial on 21 January could be explained. The Soviets found only rubble, but the propagandists promised that when German forces liberated the area the memorial would be rebuilt.[11] Similar fighting talk characterised Günther Heysing's East Prussian dispatches for the *Völkischer Beobachter*. He reported that the bravery and sacrifices of German soldiers had prevented the province from being submerged by the enormous Soviet attack.[12] While the news of East Prussia's isolation from the Reich was depressing, readers were reminded that the province had previously been detached from the Reich and barely defended during the Polish Corridor era. The Russians were at the gates of Königsberg, but all sections of the *Volk* were united in their determination to defend their *Gau*. Men served in the *Volkssturm* while women and girls nursed the wounded, cleared snow, dragged ammunition and food containers through the streets and dug trenches. This was the *Volkskrieg* in East Prussia in January 1945.[13]

Walter Mertinett, an SS reporter, admitted that Königsberg presented a depressing sight under grey skies, with dirty brown snow on the streets and ruined houses all around. However, the city was also a hive of activity as everyone worked unstintingly to bring up supplies and bolster defences. Great War veterans were fighting shoulder to shoulder with the HJ to preserve their homeland's freedom. Mertinett claimed that in the struggle for Königsberg the stronger German nerve would prevail. The German defenders were determined not to fail their fallen comrades and would never surrender the city.[14] Heysing's final report on 3 April 1945 emphasised the spirit of the defenders and maintained that the German people could view the 'fighters on the [River] Pregel with pride'.[15] Privately, Heysing had already advised Goebbels seven weeks earlier that the troops in East Prussia had suffered extraordinarily heavy losses with 'very depressing consequences for morale'.[16]

Within Königsberg, *Kreisleiter* Wagner encouraged the *Volkssturm* to fight alongside the *Wehrmacht* to preserve the city's freedom and the lives of women and children.[17] Banners draped over major thoroughfares proclaimed 'We will be victorious', 'The Sun will not set over us' and 'Beat the Red dog'.[18] The military also attempted to boost spirits. One witness recalled a speaker from the NSFO claiming at the end of February that hundreds of German tanks had arrived at Pillau and that, assisted by new weapons, they would advance together with a second force from Breslau into the Russian rear and meet near Warsaw. The speaker insisted that 'This was the *Führer*'s long cherished plan to let the Russians in, the more surely to destroy them.'[19] Similarly, General Friedrich William Müller, the commander in the Samland, visited Königsberg on 2 April. He promised military and Party leaders that a great attack would soon drive the Soviets out of East Prussia. General Lasch recalled that Müller's recent experience of the annihilation of his Fourth Army in the Heiligenbeil cauldron had not shattered his illusions. Müller added that Lasch had insufficient belief in Königsberg's defensive capabilities and told him that he would soon be replaced by a much stronger character. The watching *Oberbürgermeister* Will later reflected that Müller's remarks were lies designed to whip up the 'defensive will' among the military leadership and noted sadly that Lasch had been forced to transfer the valuable First East Prussian Division to the Samland during March.[20]

Königsbergers also hoped that a 'Himmler Army' would soon be deployed.[21]

Rumours spread that the Russians had underestimated German forces in Königsberg and that enemy morale had correspondingly deteriorated. A relief army was said to be advancing from Stettin to Stolp towards Danzig and East Prussia. Moreover, 500,000 Vlasov troops were rumoured to have escaped encirclement at Warsaw and were approaching East Prussia, while German units previously overrun by the Red Army at Insterburg and Tilsit were said to have amalgamated and were moving closer to Königsberg.[22] This was truly wishful thinking.

Morale improved in Königsberg following the reconnection of the land route with Pillau in late February. The SS noted that Königsbergers were pleased to see well armed troops and felt more secure as numerous prominent officials had now returned. Many inhabitants apparently rejected evacuation, believing that the city was now secure. The march of the victorious units through the city accompanied by military bands had made a most favourable impression.[23] The authorities emphasised that normal life continued to function. Radio Königsberg still broadcast and the city orchestra held concerts in cinemas and military hospitals.[24] The *Preußische Zeitung* was published into March and featured a staple content highlighting valiant military actions, Red Army losses and Soviet atrocities in the province. A few copies of the *Festung Königsberg*, a propaganda sheet for 'workers, soldiers and *Volkssturm* men', were also printed.[25] From February the film *Kolberg* was shown, but artillery bombardments and air raids sometimes interrupted performances.[26] In late February limited postal communication with the Reich was re-established and the banks reopened. This latter development had 'spread a great wave of reassurance' and few inhabitants realised Königsberg's precarious state of isolation.[27] On Easter Sunday, 1 April 1945, Königsbergers took advantage of the fine spring weather to undertake reconnaissance trips into the suburbs: 'Women pushed their prams through the parks. They could forget that they were living in the final phase of a long lost war. But it was the last calm before the storm.'[28]

The *Schlesische Tageszeitung*, the daily Party newspaper in Breslau, and the national press underlined the heroic resistance offered by the encircled garrison of Breslau and *Gauleiter* Hanke's defiance. The Propaganda Ministry urged the German press to highlight the city's bravery; and when specific landmarks were mentioned their association with famous Germans or their role in Breslau's history was to be illustrated.[29] Reports in late January stressed that Breslau was ready and armed, a city of men standing united against the Soviets. Prophetically, it was claimed that even when the beautiful city was reduced to rubble the defenders would fight on in the ruins. The Germans would resist at any price. Improvisation was again the watchword, but there was said to be no sense of desperation and cool heads prevailed.[30] One report emphasised that the front line could now be reached by tram. This upbeat article by a *Volkssturm* reporter noted that soldiers had previously travelled for days and marched for hours to reach their posts, but were now able to travel on tram line 11. However, in case readers interpreted this as an example of Germany's military plight, the article concluded with the promise that 'Ivan' would find Breslau 'a tough nut to crack'.[31] Concurrently, Hanke was lauded for overseeing a psychological transformation of Breslau and its overnight conversion into a fortress. Hanke had anticipated enemy attempts to cut the city's transport links by ordering the evacuation of non-combatants. This operation had been successfully completed within a 'few bitter cold days and nights'. The misery and loss of life that this had entailed was glossed over.[32]

As Breslau awaited the inevitable onslaught, the strange atmosphere was captured by the young officer Siegfried Knappe. Journeying through Breslau on the evening of 12 February, towards the headquarters of the 609 Division in the south of the city, he observed: 'Cattle and sheep wandered in the main thoroughfares, and refugees and carts and horse-drawn vehicles were camping everywhere. The military police were having trouble keeping the streets open for military traffic. I was stopped and asked for identification by civil defence men [*Volkssturm*] at every barricade in spite of the Army Corps flag on my car.'[33]

At the end of January, Goebbels had got the impression from Hanke that life continued in Breslau in a more or less orderly fashion although Soviet artillery occasionally hit the city. Even when the city was surrounded the effort was made to maintain a sense of normality.[34] The number of tram lines were reduced from more than ten to three but the Party believed that even this reduced service provided psychological assurance, for so long as the trams ran things could not be so bad.[35] Travelling to von Ahlfen's underground headquarters on 14 February, Knappe described the city as an 'eerie sight' where 'Streetcars were running on streets that were empty of people. Bursts of artillery fire exploded here and there. Herds of cattle lowed as heavy artillery shells from big railroad guns exploded every five minutes or so.'[36] The public mood sank when von Ahlfen announced on 16 February that Breslau was surrounded.[37]

To bolster spirits and prove that Breslau was holding out, an address by Hanke was broadcast on national radio on 3 March. The *Völkischer Beobachter* reported that Hanke described the conscientious attitude of the men and women in Breslau and their unshakeable faith in the Reich and the *Führer*. Hanke praised the Eastern Front veterans, the reliable *Volkssturm* and the brave HJ who epitomised Germany's future. In line with the theme of historical precedents, Hanke spoke about Breslau's role in 1813 and the successful resistance of German Silesian colonisers against the Mongols in 1241. Finally, Hanke thanked the inhabitants of other German *Gaue* for the assistance they had given to Silesian evacuees and promised that the men of '*Festung* Breslau' would not waver during future testing days and would fight on so long as they had a grain of energy.[38] Hanke was also profiled in *Das Reich*. Here he was portrayed as the tireless defender of Breslau successfully exhorting the defenders to greater efforts with inspiring speeches and directives. His slogan, 'He who fears an honourable death will die in shame', had become known throughout the Reich.[39]

Hanke was a hive of activity and resourcefulness in his attempts to find new methods to strengthen the Breslau forces and frustrate the enemy. Soviet propaganda aimed at weakening the garrison's spirit of resistance was unsuccessful for 'Here the spirit of the German [Monte] Cassino fighter lives and acts.'[40] The Nazi hierarchy appreciated Hanke's resistance. When Hanke was unable to attend the annual *Gauleiter* gathering to commemorate the launch of the Party's Programme of 1920, Hitler remarked with admiration on 24 February 1945, 'Hanke is a devil of a fellow . . . He's a Silesian himself.'[41] Broadcasts on 30 March depicted the grim reality of 'life in the battling city of Breslau' and underlined that '*Gauleiter* Hanke is the force which has made Breslau's population what it is today'.[42] On 12 April, the *Führer* awarded Hanke the Golden Cross of the German Order. Hanke had 'become a brilliant example of loyal sacrifice and the fulfilment of duty . . . in the struggle for the future of our race'.[43] On 29 April, in Hitler's last will and political testament Hanke received a more tangible award when he was appointed *Reichsführer-SS* and chief of the German police, in succession to the discredited Heinrich Himmler, dismissed upon the discovery of his clandestine attempts to parley with the Western Allies via the Swedish Count Folke Bernadotte. Hanke never had the opportunity to assume his new office.

Goebbels was most impressed by Hanke's conduct, particularly as his political skills had been honed in Goebbels's own 'Berlin school'. He noted approvingly that Hitler, drawing on the 'Kolberg' analogy, dubbed Hanke 'the Nettelbeck of this war'. Goebbels wrote that Hanke fully deserved this praise from Hitler and observed that in contrast to Breslau, Cologne had shamefully capitulated within an hour.[44] Goebbels repeatedly contrasted Hanke's determination to stay in Breslau with Greiser's shameful conduct at Posen.[45] Hanke's old friend Speer also sent his greetings. Speer later claimed that during their last meeting on 22 January he had asked Hanke to spare Breslau and initially thought that this request had been successful. However, Speer underestimated Hanke's determination to fight to the end and to destroy the city rather than surrender it to the Soviets. In a final teletype message on 14 April, Speer still wished Hanke a friendly farewell, praised his defence of Breslau and remarked that 'One day your achievements will receive the recognition reserved to only a few very real heroes in Germany's history. At this time, when a whole leadership has failed the people, you stand as a shining example and by your conduct bear witness, loud and clear, against these others.' Speer concluded: 'But I do not pity you: you are going towards a fine and worthy end of your life.'[46]

The propaganda unit in Brandenburg commented on the reception of Hanke's speech on 3 March. The population were said to have welcomed his on the spot description of the situation and admired the defenders of Breslau for their apparent readiness to die. Hanke's thanks for the care provided for Silesian refugees in other *Gaue* also made a positive impression. Brandenburgers did not, however, appreciate a speech by their own *Gauleiter* in Küstrin broadcast on 4 March. They commented that Stürtz should not have spoken as his address only weakened the impact of Hanke's speech. Stürtz was accused of falsely suggesting that he was participating in the defence of Küstrin. However, greetings addressed to him by commandant Reinefarth clearly indicated that Stürtz was only visiting the town.[47]

Meanwhile, Hanke's rhetoric was greeted less favourably within Breslau. One listener noted that the address followed the same format as Goebbels' much criticised 28 February speech when the latter had promised 'either victory or death'. Hanke and Goebbels praised the stoic, heroic posture of the German people, but this correspondent commented that Germans secretly loathed Hitler's 'bandit politics' and that life in Breslau was ever more depressing and hopeless.[48] Rumours also spread during the final week of February that Hanke had fled to the spa of Carlsbad.[49] The *Schlesische Tageszeitung* emphasised that contrary to enemy claims Hanke remained in the city.[50] The young officer Siegfried Knappe was one man who did get out. From a Ju-52 transport plane he viewed the large city surrounded by a pearl-like string of burning villages.[51]

Hanke did crave greater security. He transferred his headquarters from Liebigs Hill to the Sandinsel at the heart of Breslau where he established headquarters in the cellars of the university library. As the historian Christopher Duffy observes, 'He wanted to blow up the library so that the rubble would provide additional overhead cover, and he was deterred from burning the 550,000 books only by the fear that the flames would spread to the whole of the island.'[52] More accurate rumours spread concerning Hanke's relationship with the city's military commanders. The first commander, Major-General Johannes Krause, soon succumbed to ill health and was replaced by Major-General Hans von Ahlfen on 1 February 1945.[53] Although von Ahlfen countersigned numerous announcements with Hanke and was seen by some to be a pliable tool of the *Gauleiter*,[54] the two soon clashed over military matters. Hanke wanted to use two battalions of 'grounded' parachutists to spearhead a breakout attempt. In contrast, von Ahlfen, insisted that numerous divisions were needed to create and defend a corridor to the 17th Army of Schörner's Army Group Centre. They also disagreed over the location of a new runway. Gandau airport, to the west of the city, was subjected to Russian artillery fire and Hitler's headquarters ordered the construction of a new landing strip on 15 February. Aeroplanes could only land in the evenings and craters from shelling and bombing already littered Gandau's runway by mid-February.[55]

Von Ahlfen commenced construction of a landing strip at Friesenwiese to the east of the city, but, although this was a tactically sound position, the ground was too soft for heavy aircraft. Hanke adhered to Berlin's preference for a landing strip in the city centre and this was constructed in the heavily built up Scheitniger Stern area. Von Ahlfen was undermined by his honest but depressing reports of the military situation and critical messages sent by Hanke to Bormann in Berlin through a radio operated by naval personnel.[56] These provoked dismay in Berlin, angered Schörner and led to von Ahlfen's dismissal. Von Ahlfen was replaced by his old friend Lieutenant-General Hermann Niehoff on 5 March. Schörner warned Niehoff to work closely and cordially with Hanke. Even more ominously Schörner told Niehoff that should he surrender Breslau he would be sentenced to death and his family held accountable for his actions.[57]

In early March, following Schörner's recapture of Lauban and Striegau, the hope of relief somewhat raised spirits in Breslau. Schörner optimistically reported to Goebbels that he planned to liberate the city within a few weeks and told Niehoff that this operation would be mounted in a matter of days. Niehoff repeated this promise on his arrival in Breslau.[58]

From the Zobtenberg, south-west of Breslau, German observers could view the fiery glow from the city. But Schörner's potential relief force was soon diverted to defensive tasks as growing Soviet pressure on the small portion of Upper Silesia remaining under German control resulted in the striking formations of Colonel-General Walther Nehring's 24th Panzer Corps being sent south.[59] Moreover, on at least one occasion the Soviets attempted to trick Breslau civilians into believing that relief was imminent by broadcasting over the *Deutschlandsender* radio frequency on 2 March the instruction that the population were to proceed to the city's southern suburbs. However, they found that the streets in this direction were blocked by German troops and were sent back to their cellars. Later the Red Army launched massive artillery and bombing attacks on the area where the civilians had been told to assemble.[60]

As no relief expedition was launched in mid-March, thereafter Breslau was doomed.[61] Schörner's final mention of his attention to break the siege was contained in a report to Hitler on 30 March.[62] The issue was not raised again. The Red Army's Easter assault, encompassing a massive air and artillery bombardment, culminated in the loss of Gandau, Breslau's lifeline on 1 April. However, despite these Soviet gains in the west of the city they were unable to press home their advantage and drive into the city centre. Breslau's sole military purpose was to tie down more than 100,000 Soviet soldiers and prevent their deployment elsewhere.[63] For the propagandists other means had to be used to encourage the continuation of the struggle. One leaflet, issued on 16 April, consisted of extracts taken from the daily *Wehrmacht* report concerning the siege. This was to give the defenders a sense of pride at their achievement and it was promised that the fortress would be held 'until the turning point'.[64] Similarly, a report was broadcast over national radio on 20 April and appeared in the *Schlesische Tageszeitung* under the title 'The Wonder of Breslau'. This emphasised the length of the siege and the example set by the defenders. German hearts could withstand the Russian attacks even if stone and iron could not. Although one part of the city after another had sunk into rubble, the men fought on so that the fortress could remain in German hands. On Adolf Hitler's 56th and final birthday Breslau symbolised Germany's will to resist.[65] In the fortress it was toasted with champagne and Niehoff himself distributed chocolate to the working women and children of the city.[66]

German Women 'Do not have it Good'

German propagandists also pointed to Soviet atrocities to justify the continuation of the struggle and to extinguish persistent rumours that the Russians had behaved decently in occupied German territory. 'Whisper propaganda' directives emphasised that the Bolsheviks had committed immense crimes. Rare instances of proper Soviet behaviour were only designed to make Germans waver in their attitude towards Bolshevism. It was said that this sinister trick had already been played on the *Volksdeutsche* in Romania where after three weeks of reasonable behaviour in most districts, the Soviets had suddenly commenced the deportation of 500,000 Siebenbürger Saxons to Russia.[67] A few Germans overrun by Soviet tank spearheads still maintained that they had been left undisturbed. German propagandists claimed that this was because Soviet tank formations were not in a secure enough military position to initiate massacres and it was left to the next echelon to carry out dreadful attacks on the defenceless civilian population. All accounts from towns and villages recaptured following counter-attacks described bestial Soviet actions which were said to be part of a plan, apparently approved by Marshal Zhukov, to systematically exterminate the German race. The old, the sick and children were shot. Women and girls were violated and then brutally murdered. Men and youths fit for work were mistreated and then deported to the Russian interior.[68]

Brutal orders were issued to incite the men of the Red Army as they marched into Germany. Prior to the launch of the 13 January offensive General Chernyakovsky had instructed the men of his Third Belorussian Front to kill the Fascists and reduce their country to a wasteland. This was in revenge for the killing of Soviet soldiers and German destruction in Russia: 'The land of the Fascists must be laid waste, just as they had despoiled our land. The fascists must die, just as our soldiers had died.'[69] Indeed, for their role in the issue of directives from 3 February 1945 ordering the 'deportation of peaceful German inhabitants to slavery in the Soviet Union' Zhukov, Konev, Rokossovsky and Chernyakovsky have been accused of a crime against humanity similar to that which earned Alfred Rosenberg and Fritz Sauckel death sentences at Nuremberg.[70]

The German public was informed in a radio broadcast on 8 February that the High Command and other relevant authorities had already collected nine volumes of reliable eyewitness reports of 'Soviet savagery' from the eastern provinces.[71] The vicious orders issued by Red Army commanders at the dawn of the Vistula–Oder operation were highlighted by Guderian on 6 March. In an address to German and remaining foreign press representatives in Berlin he outlined Soviet atrocities in the eastern provinces. Eyewitness and documentary sources provided evidence of the excesses and the image of atrocities against defenceless civilians. This was said by Guderian to burn deep in the hearts of German soldiers. However, Guderian dismissed Soviet accusations of German mass graves and gas chambers as a sick fantasy.[72] Soviet propagandists also fired up the Red Army. A typical polemic by Ilya Ehrenburg raged against East Prussia:

> Now justice has come to this land. We find ourselves in the homeland of Erich Koch, the Governor of the Ukraine – that says it all. We have repeated it often enough – the judgement arrives! Now it is there.[73]

Ehrenburg made a similar attack on Pomerania shortly afterwards:

> We forget nothing. We march through Pomerania but before our eyes lies destroyed, bleeding White Russia . . . Before Königsberg, before Breslau and before Schneidemühl we think of the ruins of Voronezh and Stalingrad. Men of the Red Army, who are at this moment storming German cities, do not forget how in Leningrad mothers took their dead children away on little sledges. Berlin has still not paid us for the agony of Leningrad.[74]

Behind the Soviet front-lines 'revenge meetings' were convened where Political Officers reminded the troops of the scale of German atrocities and the need to get even.[75] In the recaptured Königsberg suburb of Metgethen and in the Silesian towns of Lauban and Striegau the Germans viewed the excesses of revenge-filled Soviet soldiery, plied with alcohol plundered from captured stores.[76] The German authorities in Königsberg swiftly disseminated details of Soviet atrocities in Metgethen. *Kreisleiter* Wagner produced a memorandum entitled 'Revenge for Metgethen' and Heysing wrote an account in the *Preußische Zeitung* on 25 February which featured a foreword by Koch.[77] Numerous hideous acts had been committed. Some 32 civilians were murdered when the tennis court where they were gathered was blown up by an electrically operated mine. Corpses lay everywhere and all the houses had been looted. Particularly horrific were the bodies of women with ropes around their necks who had been tied together and dragged to their death. Dead women lay in trenches and manure pits, their bodies showing evidence of sexual assault. All women between the ages of 14 and 65 had been raped and even those outside this age group had frequently suffered the same fate. One 16-year-old girl had been raped on eighteen occasions during one night.[78] The SS reported that all German men between 16 and 60 had been deported.[79]

The reporter Heysing saw a refugee train which had been halted at Metgethen and ransacked by the Soviets. Bodies and belongings were scattered all around. Nearby he met an old man searching for his daughter. He had hidden her in the loft when the Red Army had suddenly entered Metgethen. However, his other children had unwittingly divulged their sister's hiding place to the Red Army soldiers and she had not been seen since.[80] The Germans also captured Soviet letters admitting that terrible deeds had taken place. One wrote that 'the women do not have it good' and said that they were repeatedly raped and did not survive this ordeal. Soviet soldiers observed the relative prosperity of the province and promised to send more plunder home when they captured Königsberg.[81] Even the Communist Party and the Red Army command began to urge restraint. On 9 February, an editorial in the army newspaper *Red Star* warned that the old dictum 'An eye for an eye, a tooth for a tooth' was not to be taken at face value. 'If the Germans marauded, and publicly raped our women, it does not mean that we must do the same.' The men were to preserve 'their own personal dignity' and 'remember that every breach of military discipline only weakens the victorious Red Army'.[82] Rokossovsky ordered his men to concentrate their 'hatred at fighting the enemy on the battlefield' and emphasised the punishment for 'looting, violence, unnecessary arson and destruction' but still indiscipline remained rampant.[83] However, according to von Lehndorff, German reports of the atrocities which aimed to inspire desperate resistance were not fully understood as Königsbergers could not comprehend that these incidents had actually occurred in their own city's suburbs.[84] Meanwhile, as a means of motivating German troops at the beginning of March, the German newsreel quoted *Kreisleiter* Wagner stating that soldiers were being led past the bodies of raped and mutilated German women.[85]

Soviet observers were shocked at what they witnessed with their own eyes. When Vasily Grossman, the special correspondent of *Red Star*, entered Schwerin an der Warthe at the beginning of February he wrote, 'Everything is on fire. Looting is in full swing . . . We enter a house, there is a puddle of blood on the floor and in it an old man shot by the looters.'[86] General Chuikov, whose memoirs highlighted instances of individual heroism during the advance to the Oder, conceded to Grossman that 'there is a certain amount of looting going on'.[87] Chuikov added, 'We've stopped feeding our men. Our food isn't tasty enough for them any longer. Transport drivers are driving around in carriages, playing accordians, like Makhno's army.'[88] A Red Army major told Alexander Werth, the Moscow correspondent of the *Sunday Times*, that ordinary Soviet soldiers were 'sex-starved'. Discounting similar events throughout eastern Europe, he claimed that 'the looting and raping in a big way did not start until our troops got to

Germany'. He concluded by saying that 'it was a nasty business' and 'the record of the Kazakhs and other Asiatic troops was particularly bad'.[89]

Stalin and his NKVD chief Lavrenty Beria were well aware that all German women remaining behind faced gang rape at the hands of the Red Army.[90] However, Stalin trivialised the Red Army's excesses across eastern Europe. He teased the Yugoslav Communist Milovan Djilas in a meeting with the remark, 'Can't he understand it if a soldier who has crossed thousands of kilometres through blood and fire and death has fun with a woman or takes some trifle?'[91] As Stalin and his leading officials in Moscow eyed up the ports, factories, mines and industrial equipment to be found in eastern Germany, they were more concerned with the effect of arson and destruction than with the rapes and the murders.

In Silesia it became clear that the Soviets and the Poles were rounding up German men. Best known was the order issued by the Soviet commander in Oels on 12 February for all German men between the ages of 17 and 50 to report within 48 hours to undertake labour service in rear areas. The men were told to bring with them full winter clothing and boots, bedding, cooking utensils and cutlery and provisions for at least two weeks. Germans failing to respond to this directive were threatened with Soviet court martial.[92] One month later this order was reproduced on the front page of the *Völkischer Beobachter* and it was made clear that the men of Oels were bound for Siberian slavery.[93]

The propagandists also utilised the fear factor arising from the sights confronting German units when they retook Lauban and Striegau. The unsigned report in the Party records by an official who had spoken to survivors makes horrific reading. One Lauban woman who had been repeatedly raped and had had a broomstick forced into her genitalia had since died. In a nearby village 29 out of 30 women had been raped, often between fifteen and thirty times. The thirtieth woman had escaped rape by falsely claiming that a rash on her thigh arose from syphilis. Elsewhere a Red Army captain had reportedly given naked German women anti-syphilis injections in order that he could rape them. In one Lauban house where two women had been sexually attacked and then murdered, two German men were also found drowned in the bathtub. Six nuns in a Lauban convent were raped at gunpoint. In the destroyed house of the local vet the badly mutilated bodies of two men and two women were found. The two women had been sexually assaulted and their clothing and stockings had been torn. Together with the men they had then been brutally murdered by bayoneting to the face. In one village two sisters were so badly assaulted by the Russians that they hanged themselves. The correspondent considered this especially tragic as both were veteran Party members who had participated with distinction on the *Unternehmen Bartold* fortification programme.[94]

Retaken Striegau was a 'totally destroyed, dead town'.[95] The occupation had lasted four weeks but only 56 surviving inhabitants were found. They were wandering aimlessly around the ruins, 'psychologically broken by the atrocities committed by Konev's troops'. Around 6,000 Germans were in the town at the start of the occupation. The remainder were now dead or had been expelled by forced marches. In the houses and streets German officials discovered the bodies of nearly 200 civilians.[96]

Newspapers reported that 'Civilian life in the town appears to be dead.' A wounded woman who had lost her husband and child said that her husband 'was a cripple whose artificial leg had caused him pain so he took it off. The Soviets beat him over the stump of his leg long enough to make it bleed profusely, and then they killed him and his child.' The same report quoted the evidence of several women which said that 'these murderous bandits assaulted a girl like ferocious animals and then wiped the floor of the room with her dead body'.[97]

Grossman also recorded the horrifying treatment meted out to German women. In Schwerin an der Warthe, 'women's screams are heard from open windows'. He observed: 'An educated German whose wife has received "new visitors" – Red Army soldiers – is explaining with expressive gestures and broken Russian words, that she has already been raped by ten men today. The lady is present.'[98] The Red Army's conduct after the capture of Gotenhafen at the end of March caused profound shock even among the higher echelon of the Soviet military. Long words tried to cover up the terrible scenes witnessed by Soviet observers in the port where, 'The number of extraordinary events is growing, as well as immoral phenomena and military crimes . . . under the slogan of revenge, some officers and soldiers commit outrages and looting instead of honestly and selflessly fulfilling their duty to their Motherland.'[99] Even former prisoners of the Germans had to fight off the lust of the Red Army and their camp followers. Grossman recalled that in Schwerin some Soviet girls hid in the correspondents' room but 'during the night, we are woken by screams: one of the correspondents couldn't resist the temptation. A noisy discussion ensues, then order is re-established.'[100]

Finally, with the Red Army poised to launch the decisive operation to capture Berlin, Ilya Ehrenburg's rabid anti-German propaganda was stopped. On 14 April 1945, *Pravda* published an article by G.F. Alexandrov, the main ideologist of the Central Committee, with the headline 'Comrade Ehrenburg is Over-simplifying'. Alexandrov was critical of Ehrenburg's line on the German people, reminding readers of Stalin's maxim from his famous February 1942 speech, 'Hitlers come and go but the German people and the German State remain.' Ehrenburg's hate propaganda against the Germans was no longer useful and was stopped forthwith.[101]

German newspapers highlighted the visit by Dr Goebbels to Lauban on 8 March. That same evening Goebbels addressed a mass rally in Görlitz town hall.[102] Goebbels was accompanied into Lauban by Schörner and both addressed the troops in the town's battle-damaged marketplace. Goebbels emphasised the historic duty of the soldiers to answer the appeals of German women and children for protection and he inspired them with the example of Frederick the Great who had fought numerous battles in this area.[103] The newsreel commentator noted that every dwelling in Lauban exhibited signs of Soviet atrocities and stressed that the rape and murder of old women provided 'clear reasons why these hordes from the Steppes must be resisted'.[104] This same message was repeated at Görlitz. His speech was relayed over German radio and recorded for the newsreel. There the cameraman captured the image of an audience which epitomised the united German *Volk* defending European Christian values. Soldiers, *Volkssturm* men, women, Hitler Youths and armaments workers listened together. Next to women occupying important wartime jobs stood mothers who had 'endured the rage and atrocities of Bolshevik soldiery' and 'still had the image of their children tortured to death before their eyes'. Goebbels stressed that the German spirit of resistance was becoming harder and more bitter from day to day as the troops were enraged at Soviet atrocities and determined to exact revenge. He added that 'the hour of capitulation would never come' and that there was 'no historical example that a people had lost unless it gave itself up for lost'. Germans were to claw themselves into their earth and Goebbels proclaimed that the power of German hearts and steadfastness would overcome the enemy's material strength. German revenge was often brutal. In the Striegau sector there were reports that German soldiers had killed Soviet prisoners with spades.[105]

German propaganda also provided a form of justification for harsh Soviet occupation. When *Wehrmacht* units were bypassed by the Red Army's surge to the Oder, German radio broadcasts encouraged the idea of an impending partisan war behind Soviet lines. A radio report broadcast on 9 February to Europe mentioned, 'many German nests of resistance dispersed over the Warthegau which [will] carry out a bloody guerrilla war, highly unpleasant for the Soviets'.[106] *Red Star* was still warning Soviet soldiers in March 1945 that every German town was a potential 'nest of snakes'. Scores of German agents had allegedly been left behind by the retreating Nazis. Troops were not to be taken in by 'white flags and obsequious smiles'.[107] Soviet conduct was also influenced by their paranoid vision that behind every bush and in every ditch there lurked a member of the *Werwolf*, with his *Panzerfaust* at the ready, arms caches in the forests and sly German civilians providing shelter. This was a fallacy – for the shadowy Nazi resistance movement, set up from October 1944 on Himmler's instruction by *SS-Obergruppenführer* Hans-Adolf Prützmann, an old adversary of Koch in East Prussia and in the Ukraine, was a truly tiny affair. Like the *Volkssturm*, but on a much smaller scale, the *Werwolf* was hamstrung by a shortage of equipment and beset by organisational schisms, even within the parent SS organisation. The repeated calls for no repeat of the post-1918 collaboration with the Allies proved receptive only to a fraction of the youth of the Third Reich schooled in the ideological tenets of Nazism. *Werwolf* propaganda was stronger than *Werwolf* actions.

Despite calls from Goebbels and other propagandists, most notably the broadcasts from 1 April 1945 on the new Radio *Werwolf*, for bitter guerrilla resistance and a handful of attacks in the West, including the murder of the American appointed *Oberbürgermeister* of Aachen, Franz Oppenhoff, in March 1945, mentions of the *Werwolf* in the East are few and far between.[108] Sometimes they relate to eccentrics holed up in the woods.[109] The discovery of groups of Volkssturm stragglers hiding in the East Prussian forests led the NKVD to dramatically report that 'German bands up to 1,000 strong' were operating in the rear of the Second Belorussian Front, ambushing Soviet units and supply columns. NKVD sweeps through the forests apparently liquidated this threat to Soviet security.[110] Nevertheless, even in September 1945 one civilian wrote that the Soviets were rounding up teenagers in Königsberg – the word 'Werwolf' incriminating them as all were deemed to be former leaders of the organisation.[111] After May 1945, the existence of the *Werwolf* gave the Soviets and the Poles a pretext to accelerate their efforts to rid the eastern provinces of remaining Germans.

'An Indescribable Test of Nerve'

As the Reich collapsed, the gulf between propaganda myth and grim reality was well illustrated by events in Frankfurt an der Oder. The *Völkischer Beobachter* reported in early February that the garrison, assisted by the *Luftwaffe*, had successfully resisted a Red Army attack. During this action the civilians were said to have remained calm. Mothers and children had been evacuated from one district, but everyone had continued their work. Furthermore, the town's menfolk were seemingly determined to fulfil their duty and stop the Soviet advance.[112] By mid-March an SS correspondent in Frankfurt painted a radically different picture in a confidential report and bitterly criticised the entire fortress concept. Most Frankfurters were convinced that, after the conquest of Küstrin, Soviet forces would mass against their town which would suffer the same destruction as Posen and Graudenz. The idea of declaring towns to be fortresses was dismissed as pointless by soldiers and civilians on account of the high losses. Both towns and garrisons rapidly perished. To act as 'breakwaters' fortresses required manpower, military material and foodstuffs. Moreover, the 'knowledge of certain death' had a pernicious effect on the encircled defenders.[113]

Kreisleiter Körner of Küstrin explained the misery of fortress life in a memorandum to Bormann in early April. Körner insisted that a desire to fight until the last bullet could not compensate for the inadequacy of manpower, weapons and ammunition. To act as a fortress Körner reckoned that around 60,000 men and a corresponding level of equipment were required in Küstrin. Instead, during the course of the two-month struggle the garrison had shrunk from over 12,000 men to scarcely one-tenth of that number. The garrison had received minimal assistance from the outside and had endured continual artillery bombardments and attacks from waves of enemy planes. The lack of heavy weapons and the absence of German fighters meant that aircraft of the Red Air Force could operate unchallenged over the town. Conditions worsened following the breakdown of the gas, electricity and water supply and the collapse of the sewage system. Despite the superhuman efforts of the doctors, the wounded received little relief. There was no radio or newspapers for the troops and few letters got through. In Körner's opinion the men had faced an 'indescribable test of nerve'.[114] The high casualties and artillery and air attacks on the fortress cities undermined the morale of defenders.

Similarly, the absence of German planes over Königsberg allowed the Soviets to bomb and strafe at will. *Panzerfäuste* were available but useless against planes.[115] A corporal wrote from Königsberg that his 'nerves had completely gone to shreds' and that on many days 'morale reached zero'.[116] One woman wrote, 'Hell is boiling over and we find ourselves in its cauldron.'[117] In the midst of the Soviet storming of Königsberg, a telegram sent by Fortress Commandant Lasch reported that as a result of constant air and artillery attack the entire city was almost completed destroyed. The considerable personnel and material losses caused fighting spirit among the troops to sink.[118] Indeed, during the final massive Soviet assault on Königsberg, *Wehrmacht* morale collapsed entirely and individual soldiers, apathetic and indifferent, attempted to mingle with civilians in cellars. Lasch conceded that at many points in the city desperate women tried to snatch weapons from the soldiers and hung white sheets from windows in an 'attempt to end the horror'.[119]

Sabotage and enemy infiltration also concerned the German authorities. Bormann ordered careful checks on the wearers of *Wehrmacht*, OT and Party uniform. In Königsberg there were regular reports of turncoat Seydlitz units wearing German uniforms being parachuted into the city to undermine morale, gather intelligence, undertake sabotage and guide Red Army units. Some Seydlitz units were said to have attacked their former comrades, but other Germans voluntarily reported to the German authorities. The paranoia this caused resulted in numerous soldiers and civilians being arrested for lack of identification; sometimes those rounded up were shot. Hitler genuinely feared that if Stalin captured Königsberg he would install a puppet German regime in the historic Prussian Coronation City.[120] The Soviets made every effort to sow disaffection in German ranks at Königsberg. Marshal Ivan Bagramyan, the commander of the First Baltic Front, recalled a meeting on 4 April with 79 members of the Free Germany Committee brought up to the Königsberg area in an effort to convince the garrison that further fighting was pointless. Later in the midst of the assault on the city two groups from the Free Germany Committee infiltrated the city centre and spread copies of Marshal Vasilevsky's appeal calling for the garrison's surrender.[121]

Matters were no better on the coast. The material conditions endured by hundreds of thousands of East Prussian refugees in the Samland coastal towns were particularly miserable. These villages and resorts were ill-prepared for this sudden mass influx. Food was insufficient, accommodation lacking and the embarkation ports were under constant Soviet air attack. A visiting medical commission in mid-March complained that available quarters in Peyse, Fischhausen, Neuhäuser and Rauschen were over-crowded and dirty and warned that if action was not taken large-scale deaths of women and children could be expected. The lack of food, particularly the shortage of baby milk, was a major problem.[122] In Samland, the lack of land, resources and preparation meant that supplies for the refugees could never be sufficient. Improvised measures such as the establishment of field kitchens and the baking of bread in field ovens failed to meet their basic needs.[123] When supplies were available, the Party authorities sometimes denied desperate German refugees relief. One aircraft hangar at Neutief, on the Frisches Nehrung opposite Pillau, was full of clothing and linen assembled from manufacturers throughout the province but armed Party functionaries refused to distribute these much needed items to frozen fellow-countrymen. Ultimately, the hangar was bombed by the Red Air Force and its valuable contents destroyed.[124] Rumours of conditions on the coast even led to Königsberg women and children refusing to leave the city.[125]

The reporter Günther Heysing recalled that Pillau was crowded with refugees and wounded and he concluded that 'compared to these conditions Königsberg is indeed an oasis'. Heysing entered Pillau's old citadel and observed that the floors were covered with wounded from the Heiligenbeil cauldron. He later recalled 'the bestial stink of blood and pus' as in the dull light doctors in dirty white coats bustled around trying to save the lives of those who had survived the freezing journey across the Frisches Haff.[126] The number of deaths in Pillau necessitated the creation of a new cemetery. Meanwhile, there were distressing scenes at the harbour as refugees attempted to board boats. Only women and children were permitted to leave. People 'behaved like animals' and in the panic women dropped their children in the water to stop them being crushed by the throng. Some soldiers said they had only got on to ships to bring their families on board while others dressed as women in a desperate attempt to escape the province.[127]

The rapid Soviet advance caused great difficulties for the food distribution system and the shortage of transportation for salvaging materials led to stores being captured intact by the enemy. Nationally, a further reduction in rations was announced on 25 January. Eight weeks of rations were now to last the consumer nine weeks and allocation was disrupted by the chaotic transport situation.[128] However, in outposts such as Königsberg, Breslau and Görlitz, horses, cattle and pigs accompanying the refugees were slaughtered. Hunger was not a major problem in Königsberg and Breslau. In Königsberg each person received one-quarter of a kilogram of horse meat per week. Ration cards were issued on a weekly basis entitling the holder to almost two and a half kilograms of bread, 125 grams of clarified butter and a few other foodstuffs. Small quantities of alcohol, cigarettes or cigars were issued occasionally.[129] The cellars of those who had left the city were systematically reopened by *Volkssturm* and Party detachments and the preserved foodstuffs found therein were made available in the shops.[130] The Party also ordered searches of empty homes to locate heating fuel. In mid-March the SS reported that the lack of coal meant that weapons and ammunition production in the city would only be possible for another fortnight.[131] Königsberg did have limited electricity until the last days, gas was available on an hourly basis and the rediscovery of 80 springs from old plans provided a water supply.[132]

Despite claims to the contrary Breslau was never a 'starving city'.[133] Breslau's military commandants noted that because of the city's reputation as 'Germany's air-raid shelter' plentiful reserves of supplies of all kinds had been accumulated. These included five million eggs, 16,000 pigs and 150,000 frozen rabbits in the city's cold-storage depots. These were further supplemented by the slaughter of horses, cattle and pigs accompanying the refugees entering the city. The rationing system ensured that Germans were well fed and provided with alcohol and cigarettes. Some 600,000 cigarettes per day were produced at the AVIATIK factory during the fortress era.[134] Breslau's water and electricity supply was less reliable, but only fuel and ammunition required to be flown in. Siebel-Achenbach observes that in accordance 'with the exaggerated buoyancy of the leadership and as a way of pacifying the population already generous rations were sporadically increased'.[135] One such instance occurred after the devastating Easter air raids and the renewed Soviet attacks on 8 April. On that day Hanke opened the clothing stores in order to deter the threat to public order arising from the growing desperation and hopelessness among the population. During interruptions in the Soviet artillery fire Breslauers gathered at stores and cellar shops to be fitted out in their new clothes.[136] These items proved to be invaluable as barter for foodstuffs following Breslau's surrender.[137] Post was flown into Gandau. After the loss of the airfield post and some war materials were dropped into the city by German planes.[138] Thousands of wounded were also flown out of the city for better treatment during February and March.[139]

Conditions varied across the city. The water supply to homes ceased to function at the beginning of February and men and women went to numerous wells across Breslau in the early morning to collect water for the day ahead. The gas supply hardly functioned after late January but this was compensated by the coal stocks in the heavily depopulated city. Throughout the siege the electricity works at Scheibenweg continued to function meaning that the north and east of the city had lighting, whereas from the beginning of the siege districts in the south and west of the city were in complete darkness.[140]

Various improvised methods were used to prolong the struggle and produce weapons in the fortresses. In Königsberg, carpentry workshops anti-personnel mines were made from wood. The necessary explosive ammunition was obtained from torpedoes and sea mines found at the naval stores in Peyse and Pillau.[141] In Königsberg, the explosive content for artillery shells was extracted from old grenades found in the forts while in Breslau the filling was removed from unexploded Soviet bombs to serve this purpose.[142] Armoured vehicles were repaired by Königsberg's Schichau works and at FAMO (Fahrzeug- und Motorenwerke Breslau GmbH). SS reports noted that the Schichau works produced 65,000 grenade cases in the six weeks from the beginning of February while 130 grenade launchers were manufactured at the Ostland factory.[143] However, this improvisation could not solve the lack of heavy weapons and artillery ammunition in Königsberg. These shortages, combined with the dismal news of the Heiligenbeil fighting and the non-appearance of revenge weapons, further depressed troop morale during the second half of March.[144] FAMO's most famous achievement was an armoured train fitted with anti-aircraft and machine-guns which was in service from 20 March.[145] Nevertheless, despite this improvisation, in Breslau as in the other fortresses, it is evident that German defensive efforts were hindered by the lack of weapons and ammunition. Ever more powerless, Breslau's defenders awaited their fate. Exasperated, they observed Red Army troop movements and offensive preparations going on without disruption as they were rationed to a few artillery rounds per day or were forbidden from firing until the Soviet attack commenced.[146]

The news from all fronts was ever bleaker. The western Allies advanced into western and central Germany during March and April. Meanwhile, other fortresses in the east offered 'steadfast' and 'valiant' resistance but eventually succumbed to the numerically superior Soviets. Schneidemühl, Posen, Graudenz, Küstrin and Danzig were all lost. Glogau, downstream on the Oder, was reduced to a shell and had its garrison decimated in the course of a six-week siege prior to surrender on 2 April.[147] *Festung* Königsberg, its garrison pulverised by a Red Army artillery bombardment, was stormed by infantry and surrendered on 9 April.

The constant artillery shelling and the Easter air raids transformed Breslau into a wasteland. The heroic, almost glamorous portrait of fortress life pedaled by Nazi propagandists bore no semblance to the miserable struggle for survival waged every day. The damage to the city centre was recalled by a member of the *Volkssturm*: 'Cathedral Island was now a dreadful sight – the towers of the cathedral and the Sandkirche had been reduced to burnt-out stumps.' The human cost could also be seen as 'Large white bundles lay on the Holtei Hill. This was where many of the dead who had been killed over Easter were being buried.'[148]

There was also a huge difference between the propaganda myth of fortress life and the grim reality of the daily struggle for survival in Breslau. Out of desperation at their plight or to avoid confronting the Red Army, whose excesses were highlighted by German propaganda or gleamed from rumours and conversations with soldiers and refugees, many Breslauers opted for suicide. This did not contradict the regime's propaganda tenets as during the closing months of the war suicide was portrayed as a valid alternative to the impossibility of life under Red rule.

'Talking of Cyanide'

Few Germans were seduced by the prospect of final victory or heroic death by 1945. The misery of life in eastern Germany under the final months of Nazi rule has tended to be overlooked by the attention paid to the violence accompanying the arrival of the Red Army, life and death under Soviet and Polish occupation and the ordeal of expulsion. During the final weeks of German rule, atrocity propaganda, rumours and conversations with passing soldiers and refugees induced a sense of terror about the future. The daily reality of fortress life was equally disturbing and led thousands of eastern Germans to commit suicide out of desperation at their daily plight or to avoid confronting the Red Army.

The Nazi leadership did not view suicide as dishonourable and made it clear that this was more favourable than Soviet captivity – the individual's right to life was minimal, the future of the *Volk* was paramount.[149] One observer in Königsberg noted in his diary on 28 January that, 'Wherever you listen, you hear people talking of cyanide, which the chemists are distributing liberally, in any quantity asked for. The question as to whether one ought to have recourse to it is not debated; only the necessary amount is discussed, and this in a casual, nonchalant way, as if it was a matter of food.'[150] It seemed that more Germans were perishing by their own hand than were dying through the actions of enemy forces. Party liaison officer Schelsky reported that although 108 people were killed by aircraft and artillery fire in Königsberg during the first 14 days of the siege, during the same period a further 120 had committed suicide.[151] The former *Bürgermeister* Makowka recalled frequent instances of prominent people committing suicide, with gassing often the preferred option.[152]

The Protestant Pastor Ernst Hornig mentioned the growing number of suicides as refugees passed through Breslau when the Red Army approached in late January.[153] A fellow clergyman, Father Paul Peikert, blamed Party terror and the pressure to leave the city for a spate of suicides at this time. He counted around 60 suicides, 'particularly among circles of the intelligentsia without religious faith' who had been mentally broken by their plight. Peikert cited the gassing of a secondary school teacher's family to emphasise this point.[154] On 13 March, in response to war-weariness and the Party's ruthless conscription of civilians to construct the city centre runway, he noted an 'alarming increase' in suicides to between 100 and 120 per day.[155] Another clerical source maintained that after the Easter air raids on Breslau desperate people packed into air raid shelters and cellars repeatedly exclaimed 'Where can we go for safety? This side of the Oder isn't safe, and the other side isn't safe either. The best thing to do is drown oneself in the Oder!'[156] No accurate statistics are available for the total number of suicides during the siege. Hornig estimated that there were between 2,000 and 3,000 suicides during the fortress era, but admitted that the true number could never be known and was possibly greater.[157]

In Schlawe, Pomerania, the Russian advance in late February produced 'fear and desperation' and led 'countless people' to commit suicide.[158] Entire families killed themselves rather than fall into Soviet hands. This was particularly noticeable among the traditional *Junker* elite who realised the danger they faced at Soviet hands as 'class enemies'. Some 29 of these great landowners, their relatives or families opted to commit suicide. Countess Sibylle Bismarck, the widowed 81-year-old occupant of Varzin, was one who took her own life. On the arrival of the Red Army in Pomerania, 66 *Junkers* and their dependents were murdered and more died later of hunger or in Soviet captivity.[159] Later Polish accounts insisted that German civilians were tremendously shocked at the true state of the war which only struck them when Soviet forces threatened their towns. They maintained that this disappointment drove Germans to suicide, with 500 Germans committing suicide in Schönlanke, 600 in Lauenburg and 1,000 in Stolp immediately before the Red Army's arrival.[160] However, some Germans could not endure the terror and humiliation of Soviet occupation and this must explain some of the suicides. Indeed, the Soviet commandant of Lauenburg despaired that it was 'absolutely impossible to stop the violence'.[161]

Nazi Crimes Against Foreigners, Prisoners and Jews

Substantial numbers of foreigners were also to be found in the beleaguered fortresses and in the diminishing areas under German control. There is little evidence that they offered any concerted resistance to their German masters in Königsberg. The surgeon von Lehndorff noted immediately before the siege that it, 'seemed odd that the aliens, far outnumbering other men, hadn't taken things into their own hands long ago'.[162] In reality there were around 100,000 German civilians in the city and 15,000 foreigners and POWs. Gause noted that the presence of so many non-Germans, mostly Frenchmen, 'never led to political difficulties'. He added that the prisoners wanted their freedom, but feared their Soviet liberators more than their German guards. Thus, he concluded that some 'European comradeship' appeared in view of 'the threatening danger from the east'.[163] Other reports were less sanguine. The SS observed that Polish workers in Königsberg awaited the arrival of the Red Army, generally doubted the stories of Soviet atrocities and anticipated an independent Polish state.[164]

For Breslau, estimates of the number of foreigners range from 3,000 to more than 7,300 and by 20 March SS sources reported that 2,600 had perished from sickness or wounds.[165] Dozens were shot for plundering and possessing 'enemy agitation material'. For instance, on 2 February, five foreigners were found guilty of both charges and summarily executed.[166] On 8 February, the *Schlesische Tageszeitung* announced that two Poles had been shot for plundering and involuntary manslaughter; two days later it was reported that six Polish and two Ukrainian plunderers had suffered the same fate.[167] Foreigners were also executed in Lower Silesia for more serious crimes. The SS reported that they 'had shot by order of court martial 25 French workers in Hirschberg for making preparations for high treason and planning an uprising in the Protectorate [Bohemia-Moravia]'.[168]

A handful of accounts mention the plight of concentration camp and other prisoners during the final weeks. It has been estimated that more than 200,000 prisoners perished in the terrible death marches which followed Nazi attempts to evacuate the camps prior to the arrival of the advancing Allies.[169] These groups had lowest priority for rail or motorised transportation and were forced on to the roads accompanied by SS guards instructed to shoot the sick, stragglers and those trying to escape. Himmler gave evacuation orders for the Groß Rosen concentration camp south of Liegnitz. A state of flux ensued as around 75,000 prisoners in the main camp and network of satellite camps were marched westwards; one witness later recalled emaciated, rag clad women prisoners were driven forward by whip and pistol wielding female guards.[170] Around 1,600 *Nacht und Nebel* prisoners from France, the Netherlands and Belgium, previously mentioned in chapter three, were transferred from local jails to Silesian concentration camps during the final months of 1944. Many perished in Groß Rosen prior to its evacuation. One-third of a column of 446 NN inmates setting out on foot from Kattowitz on 22 January were dead within six days. The survivors staggered towards the hell of Buchenwald in central Germany.[171] Elsewhere, the *Kreisleiter* of Neumarkt (Lower Silesia), Ernst Dickmann, ordered the SS to shoot 93 passing prisoners from the Dyhernfurth (I.G. Farben) work camp in the town's slaughter house. As Norman Davies speculates, it is likely that the Dyhernfurth inmates were shot because of their work in the production of the nerve agent Tabun.[172]

Horrific mortality rates abounded. Some 700 prisoners from Brieg jail departed on foot for Glatz but only around 300 reached their destination.[173] Prisoners also perished in the Pomeranian snow. For instance, 138 male and female prisoners set out from Schneidemühl, but only 57 of their number stumbled into Stargard. The judicial authorities reported the tribulations encountered on another prisoner march from Schneidemühl when 'many prisoners froze to death, nine were shot on the journey and some escaped into the darkness'.[174] Some prisoners did not even make it on to the roads. In line with the precedent established in the *General Gouvernement* in July 1944 it was decided that if prison inmates, numbering around 35,000 across eastern Germany, could not be evacuated then they should be liquidated. On 30 January 1945, after consultation between Stürtz and Chief Public Prosecutor Kurt Walter Hanssen, an SS and Police Commando from Frankfurt an der Oder entered Sonnenberg Prison. They divided the prisoners into two categories – 'Useful Inmates' and 'the Rest'. Around 800, mostly foreign prisoners were shot straightaway while the remaining 150 were marched in a westward direction towards Berlin.[175]

Surviving Jews also envisaged that Nazi defeat would signal their demise. Rumours spread in Königsberg that no Jews would be allowed to fall into Soviet hands alive. Nevertheless, the half-Jewish Michael Wieck noted that the local SA man was seen less and less as worries about his own life took priority over Party directives.[176] However,

500–700 Jews from the Schichau works, predominantly young women, girls and old men, did meet a horrific end. They were marched through Königsberg accompanied by Gestapo officials. *En route*, soldiers witnessed Jews collapsing in the snow from exhaustion and then being shot in the nape of the neck by their overseers. When the survivors reached the Samland coast they were murdered and their corpses flung into the sea. The bodies of the dead Jews, identifiable because of the yellow star on their clothing, were later washed up on the shore and buried by German POWs under Russian supervision.[177]

NAZI CRIMES AGAINST THE *VOLKSGEMEINSCHAFT*

Lawlessness and overt political gangsterism held the upper hand in the Third Reich until the very end. It has even been suggested that during the final weeks of the war German civilians hated the German authorities more than they feared the Red Army.[178] The demolition of German property by the *Wehrmacht*, the compulsion to participate in construction projects under enemy fire and widely publicised threats and executions contributed to this development.

The demolition of property by the *Wehrmacht*, SS and Party was most evident in Breslau. Suburban apartment blocks were dynamited as were buildings along the Kaiserstrasse, the site of the besieged city's new runway. Inhabitants were forced out of their homes and only allowed to take a few possessions. Their homes and contents were then blown up. During the course of the siege civilians made frequent moves from flat to flat and cellar to cellar as inhabitable accommodation became scarcer.[179] Increasingly savage measures were also enacted to ensure compliance with Party orders. The most brutal military discipline was now applied to civilians. In Breslau on 7 March women, boys over the age of 10 and girls over 12 were ordered to register at Party offices for labour service. The directive emphasised that civilians evading registration and work, identified by their failure to produce a stamped labour card, would be treated similarly to deserting soldiers, court martialled and shot. In instances where the order was ignored by youngsters, their parents or guardians were threatened with the death penalty.[180] The ambivalence of Party officials sitting securely in their bunkers but unashamedly deploying civilians as slave labourers in the danger zone was fully illustrated by the runway construction which commenced during the final week of March. This was dubbed the *Blutbahn* (runway of blood) and three shifts of workers ensured constant activity. The Soviets soon realised German intentions from the movement of people and the extensive demolitions. As thousands of foreigners, women and children toiled shifting rubble, they were strafed by low flying aircraft of the Red Air Force. Some 3,000 labourers were killed and their bodies were buried in mass graves nearby.[181]

Anger at the Party's ruthless conduct provoked fatal bomb attacks on the Gneisenau and Elbing Party premises in Breslau on the evening of 29 March.[182] In Königsberg, the Party authorities forced women to build barricades and dig trenches.[183] Lasch described this enterprise as 'pointless' and condemned Koch's order for the building of a runway at the Paradeplatz as wasteful of manpower and in any case 'totally unnecessary' as no planes were available.[184] Men were 'bitter and outraged' when they witnessed women and girls being forced to undertake salvage and building work whilst being threatened by armed Party supervisors.[185]

The Party authorities also exploited the situation to settle old scores and punish any signs of wavering. Hanke displayed particular ruthlessness. On 29 January, he ordered the execution of one persistent critic, Dr Spielhagen, *Bürgermeister* (Deputy Mayor) of Breslau. At 6 a.m., by the statue of the Prussian King Frederick William III in front of the city hall, Spielhagen was shot by *Volkssturm* firing-squad. He had apparently objected to Breslau being declared a fortress and Hanke used this as a pretext to condemn him, without any kind of trial, for cowardice. This sentence was widely publicised for deterrent effect and officially Spielhagen was accused of leaving Breslau without permission to look for a new post in Berlin. Spielhagen had indeed evacuated his family from Breslau to Berlin but fatefully had returned to the city alone on 26 January.[186] According to one source, Spielhagen's corpse was taken in an open truck to the Oder and flung into the river from a bridge.[187] The execution of Dr Felix Sommer, head of Lower Silesia's agrarian office, received similar coverage. Sommer had transferred some of his office to Görlitz without informing Hanke and this unauthorised departure led to his condemnation by a court martial for 'cowardice and neglect of duty'.[188]

The establishment of drumhead courts martial in line with Justice Minister Dr Thierack's directive of 15 February was announced in the *Schlesische Tageszeitung* two days later. This directive aimed to combat unwillingness to fight, sabotage, cowardice and defeatism in provinces threatened by the enemy and to act against anyone accused of endangering the war effort. These roving courts martial were empowered to pass summary death sentences.[189] However, soldiers and civilians were condemned in Breslau before and after this ordinance for theft of food, plundering, passing on enemy leaflets and listening to enemy radio. One 16-year-old Linke-Hoffmann worker who said that Hitler would lose the war, was denounced by a fanatical colleague and summarily shot.[190] A letter from the 'Front Breslau' noted that the *Schlesische Tageszeitung* was proclaiming death sentences every day.[191] On 27 April 1945, an estimated 1,500 civilians (mainly women) waving white flags besieged Party offices and pelted military command posts with stones in the Breslau suburbs of Zimpel, Carlowitz and Bischofswalde as they called for an end to the hopeless struggle. Some 100 were arrested and 17 alleged 'ringleaders' were executed by the SD.[192] At least 264 executions occurred in the city's Kletschkaustrasse prison during the fortress period, and shortly before the end of the siege on 6 May the Nazis shot the last batch of 31 political prisoners.[193]

In East Prussia executions also continued until the final days. In Pillau, Koch directed an SS court martial to shoot recalcitrant Party members, *Volkssturm* men and ordinary civilians.[194] Likewise, in Königsberg executions of deserters by firing-squad were still taking place at the north railway station as late as 7 and 8 April. After a particularly messy execution of two deserters, signs were placed on the corpses with the inscription 'We were cowards and died as a result'.[195] According to Soviet information obtained from captured Germans, 22 death sentences were carried out in the Silesian town of Neisse alone during the second half of March.[196] In Stolp, Pomerania, on the order of drumhead courts martial numerous deserters were shot in a wood near the town. A junior lawyer was hanged from a tree in the town cemetery for hiding an SS deserter.[197] Countess Libussa von Oldershausen recounted that the byways of eastern Pomerania resembled 'Gallows Row'. The bodies of the victims of German Flying Courts Martial and German field police murdered by the Soviets swung side by side from the trees.[198]

In the midst of this final wave of terror the Party leadership plotted their escapes. As his deputy Großherr and *Kreisleiter* Wagner were killed in Königsberg on 9 April,[199] Koch prepared his departure. He left East Prussia on 23 April on the icebreaker *Ostpreussen* which sailed to Denmark with prominent Party members and Koch's Mercedes also on board. For four years Koch managed to evade capture and lived with forged papers and under a false name, Rolf Berger, in a village near Kaltenkirchen, north of Hamburg. Working as a day labourer, he found time to go to the gatherings of East Prussian refugees where he would claim that the *Ostpreussen*, with Koch on board, had been bombed and sunk by the Soviets. This foolhardy conduct backfired. He was recognised by an army officer from Königsberg and he was soon sitting in a Hamburg police cell.[200]

After Koch's arrest in May 1949 the Polish and Soviet governments requested his extradition from the British occupation authorities. Koch was handed over to the Poles in January 1950. A sickly Koch, attended by nurses and alleging maltreatment and assaults by other prisoners in Warsaw's Mokotow jail, finally stood trial in Warsaw in 1958 for the murder of 300,000 Poles including 200,000 Jews in the Polish districts annexed to East Prussia. The Soviets also held him responsible for the deaths of four million Ukrainians but did not seem to want to give his victims publicity and did not press for him to face charges in this connection. Koch was sentenced to death in March 1959 but this was commuted to life imprisonment in March 1960 on account of his poor health. He remained in a Polish prison at Barczewo (formerly Wartenburg, East Prussia) until his death at the age of 90 on 12 November 1986. Koch had been isolated from the other inmates but was generally well treated. His cell was filled with books purchased from money sent from abroad and he was allowed to receive visitors.[201]

Gauleiter Emil Stürtz of Brandenburg was captured by the Soviets in 1945 and although his subsequent fate remains uncertain it is thought that he died in captivity.[202] The SS reported on 21 March 1945, that Schwede-Coburg together with Party and provincial officials had left Stettin.[203] As Schwede tried to remain one step ahead of the Red Army he occupied five different headquarters prior to his departure from Rügen Island on 4 May accompanied by his family and Party colleagues. Schwede was arrested in 1945 and placed before the Bielefeld denazification court in early 1948 where he received a ten-year prison sentence and had his wealth confiscated. Later that year this sentence was reduced and the confiscation order overturned. A further court appearance followed in Coburg in early 1951 where he was convicted of 52 counts of causing physical injury and charges of intimidation. This led to another ten-year sentence. Again he did not serve the full prison term. A final court appearance in Munich during July 1953 led to Schwede being categorised as a major Nazi offender and the imposition of a two-year labour camp sentence. Schwede died as a pensioner in Coburg on 19 October 1960. The Pomeranian expellee newspaper observed his passing with a 20-word obituary hidden on an inside page.[204]

Armed with the knowledge of Hitler's suicide and the Red Army's capture of Berlin, a clerical delegation visited the Breslau fortress headquarters in the basement of the university library on 4 May to implore General Niehoff to surrender. Despite his apprehension at the threat still posed to him from Schörner and Hanke, Niehoff extended feelers to the Soviets for a ceasefire. For some this proved to be the last straw. SS units barricaded themselves into the *Jahrhunderthalle* while the *Volkssturm* commander, *Obergruppenführer* Herzog, committed suicide. Hanke raged at defeatism but the new *Reichsführer-SS* opted to leave the arrangements for capitulation to Niehoff and planned his own escape. Hanke made a most flamboyant departure when he commandeered General Niehoff's Fieseler-Storch and was flown out of Breslau on the evening of 5 May. This may have been the only plane ever to take off from the Kaiserstrasse runway whose construction had involved so much bloodshed. Niehoff was left to negotiate surrender terms the following day. Hanke's plane ultimately reached German occupied territory in the Sudetenland but thereafter his fate is open to speculation. The most plausible scenario is that he attempted to reach Bavaria via Czechoslovakia but was killed by Czech partisans.[205]

Hitler committed suicide in his last headquarters, a bunker under the Reich Chancellery in Berlin, on 30 April 1945. The *Gauleiter* on the fringes of this study did not outlive their *Führer* by long. As the Red Army advanced into Upper Silesia, Goebbels noted on 24 January 1945, that Fritz Bracht had suffered a severe heart attack and was in a military hospital at Neisse.[206] Bracht committed suicide in May although the exact circumstances remain unclear.[207] Arthur Greiser was handed over by the Americans to the Poles after the war and sentenced to death for his crimes in the Warthegau. He was paraded through the streets of Poznan (Posen) in a cage and publicly hanged on 22 July 1946.[208] Despite his promises to fight until victory or death in Danzig, Albert Forster escaped by sea from the flaming port at the end of March 1945. Captured by the British in May 1945, Forster was handed over to Poland in August 1946 and after a trial in Gdansk (Danzig) in April 1948, sentenced to death. He was hanged in Warsaw's central Mokotow prison in February 1952.[209]

For all the rhetoric of final victory and fighting to the bitter end the Nazi leadership failed eastern Germans in their most desperate hour and left them to their fate at the hands of the Red Army. No eastern *Gauleiter* died heroically in a *Festung*. Self-preservation proved to be a far stronger emotion than any mythical duty to the *Volk*.

Conclusion

The chaos of the flight and the suffering and terror in the fortress cities exemplified the final stage of Nazi misrule in Germany's eastern provinces. Power was vested in the *Gauleiter* in their role as *Reichsverteidigungskommissare*. They acted in cahoots with Army Group commanders such as Himmler, Schörner and Rendulic whose occupation of these key military positions arose from their apparent political reliability.[1] Together their actions deepened the misery of the civilian population and the pain they endured during these final weeks of the war has only been obscured because of subsequent suffering under Soviet and Polish occupation.

Bearing in mind the traits exhibited prior to 1945 by prominent Party figures east of the Oder, their actions during the final months were all too predictable. Prestige and personal enrichment had long been priorities for Nazi luminaries and so it continued until the final days of the war. The major change was the regime's growing use of terror as a weapon to ensure compliance. Prior to the war, the veiled threat of a Gestapo visit or a spell in a concentration camp had existed, but naked terror was overwhelmingly directed at the regime's political foes and those excluded from the *Volksgemeinschaft* on racial grounds. However, in 1945 it is evident in the eastern provinces, and indeed throughout the Reich, that, in an effort to delay the demise of the Third Reich and to maintain their own comfortable lifestyles, Party leaders presided over an escalation of violence directed at any seemingly recalcitrant German regardless of racial characteristics or previous political loyalty. Likewise, the actions of eastern *Gauleiter* in 1945, for instance Hanke's role in the 'Kanth death march' and the construction of the Kaiserstrasse air strip in Breslau, illustrated the worthlessness that the regime now also placed on German lives.

That these *Gauleiter* could routinely wield life or death powers is indicative of the growing responsibilities bestowed on the Party by Hitler, often obtained following Bormann's relentless machinations. This development is particularly noticeable during the latter stages of the war when, as propaganda claims became increasingly fanciful and more Germans accepted the likelihood of defeat, the Party undertook the twin duties of bolstering morale and monitoring behaviour. The elite and cadres of the Party now constituted the main audience for the output of Goebbels and his cohorts. The Party was also the main beneficiary of the failed 20 July 1944 coup attempt. Subsequent Party interference in military matters had predictably dire consequences for the eastern provinces. The *Ostwall*, the *Volkssturm* and repeated attempts to undermine *Wehrmacht* commanders, notably in East Prussia and Breslau, all fall into this category.

It should not be forgotten that Hitler, and to a lesser degree the Party, had once been genuinely popular east of the Oder. Prior to 1933, among eastern German voters, to a greater degree than at national level, Hitler was successful projecting his image as a source of order confronting imminent Marxist insurrection. Nazi electoral gains were secured against a backdrop of SA inspired violence. Nevertheless, not all Nazi actions were welcomed. Growing Party radicalism in late 1932 provoked a significant loss of support for the NSDAP from 'respectable' nationalists at the November election. Similarly, despite repeated complaints at the economic impact of the Versailles 'Diktat' and calls for a redrawing of the frontier, no enthusiasm greeted the invasion of Poland which offered an opportunity to nullify the bitter territorial losses of 1918–1919. The swift victory over Poland was greeted with widespread relief. For five years, by virtue of the considerably lower level of air attack than elsewhere in the Reich, the war seemed distant from the eastern provinces. The major upheaval involved the composition of the population and from this two important planks of the regime's racial strictures were challenged. First, although evacuees from western Germany and Berlin were fellow members of the *Volksgemeinschaft*, this did not deter resentment between the incomers and their hosts. Secondly, the treatment of foreign workers and POWs in the largely agricultural eastern provinces frequently circumvented Nazi tenets. As has been illustrated, this could lead to mutual respect, humane treatment, and, most alarmingly in a state based on rigid racial hierarchies, sexual relationships. To a degree this can be explained by economic exigencies overriding racial rhetoric. Evacuees were rivals for scarce commodities and constituted a burden on the local economy. On the other hand, foreigners and POWs were a source of the labour required to maintain the agrarian economy.

Nazi invective also failed to allay fears concerning the course of the war. The upbeat reporting of localised successes and heroic individual actions could not conceal the scale of the retreat in Russia. Foreign broadcasts, soldiers' letters and rumours were increasingly viewed as more reliable than official publications or broadcasts by all but the staunchest Party members. Concurrently, the image of the Soviet foe was transformed. Actual contact with Russian workers and POWs on the Home Front had already weakened the impact of 'subhuman Asiatic' propaganda. There was also a grudging respect for the fighting qualities of the Russian soldier and a degree of admiration for the Soviet system for producing seemingly abundant quantities of military hardware. Unlike previous foes, the Red Army did not succumb to *Blitzkrieg* and instead pushed towards the Reich.

The scale of the defeat in Russia was clear to all eastern Germans following the collapse of Army Group Centre during June and July 1944. The war had arrived at the gates of the eastern provinces and this feeling was reinforced by heavy Allied air raids during the second half of 1944. To divert public attention from the gravity of the situation the Party authorities exploited the building of the *Ostwall* and the decision to raise the *Volkssturm*. A degree of enthusiasm greeted the former project but this quickly dissipated on account of Party bullying and bureaucracy, the shortage of materials and machinery and a growing realisation of the futility of such defences. The launch of the *Volkssturm* signalled Germany's military weakness and the lack of weapons, uniforms and training ensured that it rarely offered effective resistance to the invading Red Army. The *Ostwall* and the *Volkssturm* were hardly triumphs of 'will' and 'improvisation', but short-term measures to pacify widespread fears by digging and drilling. A third lamentable Party intervention arose over the issue of evacuation. As evacuation was incompatible with *Endsieg*, the Party, acting on Hitler's authority contained in orders issued from July 1944, blocked proposals from the military for the prompt withdrawal of civilians. Thus a hasty departure by foot, cart or in an open railway wagon under Soviet shellfire in the midst of a freezing January was the lot of millions of eastern Germans. Moreover, evacuation soon gave way to wild flight when the regime's earlier propaganda concerning Bolshevik atrocities was substantiated by the testimonies of passing refugees.

During the final months of the war, the Party's callous indifference to the plight of the eastern German population caused it to become ever more detested. The Party had always been significantly less popular than the *Führer* himself. However, now even the 'Hitler myth', so carefully crafted by Goebbels and still able to bolster morale as late as July 1944, slid into irrelevance as eastern Germans were plunged into a battle for survival. The regime's propaganda claims became ever more fantastic and unpalatable. Eastern Germans wanted to believe in counter-attacks and the *Wehrmacht*'s re-occupation of their homelands. However, only the most fanatical believed that the *Führer* could now pull a most unlikely victory out of the bag. The rhetoric of the Party press and newsreels was sharply contradicted by daily examples of German military powerlessness such as the continued defeats on the ground and the Allied control of the air. Propaganda emphasising Soviet atrocities may have stiffened German military resistance in the east in 1945, but among civilians it contributed to panic flight and the spate of suicides.

The Nazis were paranoid that flight treks were riddled with Soviet agents. The Soviets exhibited a morbid fear that under every bush lurked a member of a nascent German resistance movement. Eastern Germans found themselves confronting terror from all directions in 1945. On one side, there were cruel Nazi Party orders, drumhead courts martial and roving SS detachments, willing to hang teenagers from trees on the pretext of failing the Fatherland. On the other side there was the revengeful Red Army, further intoxicated by indoctrination and alcohol. Behind the Red Army's first wave followed a brutal second echelon, freshly released from German captivity. Thereafter, when Soviet power was established remaining Germans had to reckon on the chilling presence of the NKVD – an organisation programmed to arrest, deport or kill the real or imagined categories of 'enemies' it unmasked. The defeat of the Third Reich did not bring an end to suffering in eastern Germany. It simply marked the end of the first chapter.

{{ Notes }}

Introduction

1 At the Potsdam Conference it was agreed in principle that northern East Prussia should be transferred to the Soviet Union. However, while the Conference eventually agreed that the southern portion of East Prussia, eastern Pomerania, east Brandenburg and Silesia were to be passed on the provisional basis to Poland, compensation of sorts for the loss of her eastern territories to the Soviet Union, the problem of Poland's western frontier was not resolved. The Communist-led Warsaw government demanded the line of the rivers Oder and Western Neisse. This incorporated much of Pomerania, Lower Silesia and east Brandenburg that the western Allies had never envisaged passing permanently to Polish administration. To legitimise these claims the Poles commenced on the 'wild' expulsions of the remaining Germans from the most contentious districts, including Breslau, Stettin and the communities immediately east of the rivers. The fact that the territorial agreement made at Potsdam regarding the German-Polish frontier was provisional was repeated by western statesmen in the weeks and months following the conference. These included statements by President Harry S. Truman, Secretary of State James Byrnes, Under-Secretary of State Sumner Welles, former Prime Minister Winston Churchill and Foreign Secretary Ernest Bevin. Final settlement was to be decided upon at a peace conference through a peace settlement. This never happened but in the interim the Poles exploited the key factor – possession of the disputed lands. See The National Archives, Kew (TNA), FO 371/50867, report on the Tripartite Conference of Berlin and Protocol of the Proceedings of the Berlin Conference; R. Butler and M. Pelly (eds.), *Documents on British Policy Overseas, Series I, Volume I, The Conference at Potsdam July–September 1945* (London: HMSO, 1984); A.M. de Zayas, *Nemesis at Potsdam: The Anglo-Americans and the Expulsion of the Germans Revised Edition* (London: Routledge and Kegan Paul paperback, 1979), pp. 156–164.

2 R.G. Moeller, *War Stories: The Search for a Usable Past in the Federal Republic of Germany* (London: University of California Press, 2003), pp. 3, 201–202. The remaining expellees mainly came from German communities in Czechoslovakia (mainly concentrated in the Sudetenland), Hungary, Romania and Yugoslavia.

3 Ibid., pp. 18–19; *Spiegel Special, Der Flucht der Deutschen*, 2002; D. Selvage, 'The Treaty of Warsaw: The Warsaw Pact Context' in D.C. Geyer and B. Schäfer (eds.), *American Detente and Ostpolitik, 1969–1972*, German Historical Institute Washington DC, Supplement 1 (2003), pp. 67–79.

4 See for instance J. Freiherr von Braun, *Germany's Eastern Territories: A Manual and Book of Reference dealing with the regions east of the Oder and the Neisse* (Göttingen: Göttingen Research Committee, 1957); Göttingen Research Committee (ed.), *Eastern Germany: A Handbook:*

Volume II, History (Würzburg: Holzner Verlag, 1963). Prominent among the studies emanating from the Johann-Gottfried-Herder Research Council was a series of books entitled *Ostdeutschland unter fremder Verwaltung* (Frankfurt: Alfred Metzner Verlag, 1955–67) which included volumes on East Prussia, East Pomerania, Danzig-West Prussia, East Brandenburg and Lower Silesia. A good illustrated overview is provided by K. Pagel (ed.), *The German East* (Berlin: Konrad Lemmer Verlag, 1954). An interesting contemporary account of the refugee groups, personalities and friction is contained in E. Wiskemann, *Germany's Eastern Neighbours* (London: Oxford University Press, 1956), pp. 179–209. The polemics of the late 1950s are summarised in R.F. Leslie, 'Germano-Polish Relations in the Light of Current Publications in the English Language', *German Life and Letters*, Volume XV, 1961–1962, pp. 129–139.

5 P.H. Seraphim, *Die Deutschen Ostgebiete: Ein Handbuch. Band I. Die Wirtschaft Ostdeutschlands vor und nach dem Zweiten Weltkrieg* (Stuttgart: Brentano-Verlag, 1952), p. 104.

6 It was noted in an otherwise balanced article in *The Times* on 1 April 1954 that Küstrin had 'been deliberately left to decay' and 'Polish planners have not yet done very much for the ports of Stettin and Danzig'. A similar article three years later on the Polish sector of East Prussia highlighted economic stagnation, failed collective farms and empty roads. *The Times*, 20 June 1957.

7 Press and Information Office of the Federal Government, *Germany Reports* (Wiesbaden: Franz Steiner Verlag, 1961), pp. 187–188. This official source estimated that some 700,000 Germans still remained in Poland in July 1960.

8 J.K.M. Hanson, *The Civilian Population and the Warsaw Uprising of 1944* (Cambridge: Cambridge University Press, 1982), pp. 83–87, 257; N. Davies, *Rising '44 'The Battle for Warsaw'* (London: Macmillan, 2003), pp. 248–253; 437; G. Bruce, *The Warsaw Uprising 1 August–2 October 1944* (London: Granada Publishing Limited, 1972), pp. 205–206.

9 T. Garton Ash, *In Europe's Name: Germany and the Divided Continent* (London: Vintage, 1994), p. 227.

10 P.H. Merkl, 'The German Search for Identity', in G. Smith, W.E. Paterson and P.H. Merkl (eds.), *Developments in West German Politics* (Basingstoke: Macmillan, 1989), pp. 6–21.

11 A.J. Nicholls, 'The Post-War Problems of the Germans', *EHQ*, Volume 17, 1987, pp. 101–107.

12 On the eastern provinces see T. Schieder (ed.), *Dokumentation der Vertreibung der Deutschen aus Ost-mitteleuropa. Band 1. Die Vertreibung der Deutschen Bevölkerung aus den Gebieten östlich der Oder-Neisse* (Bonn, Bundesministerium für Vertriebene, 1953) (Hereinafter Schieder ed., *Dokumentation*). This was soon translated into English as T. Schieder (ed.), *Documents on the Expulsion of the Germans from Eastern-Central Europe. Volume 1. The Expulsion of the German Population from the Territories East of the Oder-Neisse Line* (Bonn: Federal Ministry for Expellees, Refugees and War Victims, 1958) (Hereinafter Schieder (ed.), *Expulsion Documents*). Among the participating historians were Hans Rothfels, Werner Conze, Martin Broszat and Hans-Ulrich Wehler. See M. Beer, 'Im Spannungsfeld von Politik und Zeitgeschichte', *VfZ*,Volume 46, 1998, pp. 345–389. Other publications resulting from these accounts include the diary of the Pomeranian housewife Käthe von Norman, *Ein Tagebuch aus Pommern 1945–1946* (Munich: Deutscher Taschenbuch Verlag, 1977), and the journal of an East Prussian surgeon, Count Hans von Lehndorff, *Bericht aus Ost-und Westpreussen* translated into English as *East Prussian Diary: A Journal of Faith 1945–1947* (London: Oswald Woolf, 1963). By the mid-1960s, 235,000 copies of Lehndorff's journal were in print in West Germany. See Moeller, *War Stories*, pp. 62, 84, 180.

13 Beer, 'Im Spannungsfeld von Politik und Zeitgeschichte', pp. 347–349; Moeller, *War Stories*, pp. 56–58. Many of those involved in the project also had strong links with the pre-war eastern German academic community. Rothfels, Schieder and Conze had taught or studied at the University of Königsberg, Peter Rassow had taught at the University of Breslau and Adolf Diestelkamp had been director of the Prussian state archive in Stettin.

14 Leslie, 'Germano-Polish Relations', *German Life and Letters*, p. 131.

15 E. Murawski, *Die Eroberung Pommerns durch die Rote Armee* (Boppard: Harald Boldt Verlag, 1969), p. 17.

16 Moeller, *War Stories*, pp. 74–82.

17 Schieder (ed.), *Expulsion Documents*, pp. 122–124; The Ministry of Expellees, Refugees and War Victims later claimed that German losses through expulsion from the eastern areas of the German Reich were 1,212,000. See *Facts Concerning the Problem of the German Expellees and Refugees* (Bonn: Federal Ministry for Expellees, Refugees and War Victims, 1960), p. 2. For more recent figures see R. Overmans, 'Personelle Verluste der deutschen Bevölkerung durch Flucht und Vertreibung', *Dzieje Najnowsze*, 1994, Number 2, pp. 55–66, quoted in P. Ther, 'The Integration of the Expellees in Germany and Poland after World War II: A Historical Reassessment', *Slavic Review*, Volume 55, Number 4, pp. 779–805.

18 Polish rejoinders include: Board of Directors of the Western Institute, *Polish Western Territories* (Poznan: Western Press Agency, 1959); A. Lesniewski (ed.), *Western Frontier of Poland: Documents, Statements, Opinions* (Warsaw: Western Press Agency, 1965); B. Wiewiora, *Polish–German Frontier from the Standpoint of International Law* (Poznan and Warsaw: Western Press Agency, 1959).

19 On battle damage and the effect of German demolitions in the vicinity of the Oder see I. Rutkiewicz, *The Odra* (Warsaw: Interpress Publishers, 1977), pp. 18–22; Leslie, 'Germano-Polish Relations', *German Life and Letters*, pp. 135–136.

20 A rebuttal of German statistics and a sustained attack on the actions of the Nazi authorities is contained in S. Schimitzek, *Truth or Conjecture? German Civilian War Losses in the East* (Warsaw: Western Press Agency, 1966). The German figures for civilian losses are also disputed by Norman Davies, the prominent British-born historian of Poland, in *God's Playground: A History of Poland. Volume II, 1795 to the Present* (Oxford: Oxford University Press, 1981), pp. 563–565.

21 de Zayas, *Nemesis at Potsdam*, p. 128.

22 See, for instance, the balanced account, W. Benz (ed.), *Die Vertreibung der Deutschen aus dem Osten. Ursachen, Ereignisse, Folgen* (Frankfurt: Fischer Taschenbuch Verlag, 1985). The numerous works by the East Prussian born Countess Marion von Dönhoff and the Pomeranian born Count Christian von Krockow also fall into this category.

23 R.D. Müller and G. Ueberschär, *Hitler's War in the East 1941–1945: A Critical Assessment* (Oxford: Berghahn Books, 1997), pp. 351–352.

24 The *Historikerstreit* arose from criticism of the work and comments of a 'new revisionist trend' personified by Ernst Nolte, accused of 'relativising' the Third Reich, the neo-conservative Michael Stürmer, who complained that Germans were 'obsessed with their guilt' and the late Andreas Hillgruber (see below). At the forefront of their accusers was the left-wing philosopher Jürgen Habermas. See R.J. Evans, *In Hitler's Shadow* (London: I.B. Tauris and Co Ltd, 1989); J. Habermas, *The New Conservatism: Cultural Criticism and the Historians' Debate* (Cambridge: Polity Press, 1989); C.S. Maier, *The Unmasterable Past, History, Holocaust and German National Identity* (London: Harvard University Press, 1988).

25 A. Hillgruber, *Zweierlei Untergang: Die Zerschlagung des Deutschen Reiches und das Ende des europäischen Judentums* (Berlin: Siedler, 1986).
26 Evans, *In Hitler's Shadow*, p. 49.
27 O. Bartov, *Murder in our Midst. The Holocaust, Industrial Killing and Representation* (Oxford: Oxford University Press, 1996), pp. 73, 76.
28 I. Kershaw, *The Nazi Dictatorship: Problems and Perspectives of Interpretation. Second Edition* (London: Edward Arnold, 1989), pp. 180–181.
29 Hillgruber, *Zweierlei Untergang*, pp. 24–25.
30 Ibid., pp. 73–74.
31 Bartov, *Murder in our Midst*, p. 75.
32 Hillgruber, *Zweierlei Untergang*, p. 21.
33 Kershaw, *The Nazi Dictatorship. Second Edition*, pp. 178–179.
34 See, for instance, two of the main works by Alfred Maurice de Zayas, *Nemesis at Potsdam*; *The German Expellees: Victims in War and Peace* (New York: St. Martin's Press, 1993).
35 J. Hoffmann, *Stalins Vernichtungskrieg 1941–1945* (Munich: Verlag für Wehrwissenschaften, 1995), pp. 251–272.
36 German sources sometimes attribute the failure of the Red Army to take Berlin in February 1945 to a complete breakdown of discipline which accompanied its entry into eastern Germany. See K.F. Grau, *Silesian Inferno. War Crimes of the Red Army on its March into Silesia in 1945* (Cologne: Centre of Information and Documentary Evidence, West, 1970), pp. 10–11, 124–125. A revisionist account written by the military historian Christopher Duffy claims that the Russians were guilty of 'cruelty on a scale which far exceeds that which might have been expected from men who had been brutalised in a pitiless war'. He also maintained that German commanders did not have to be Hitler die-hards or in the SS to realise that they were 'fighting a "just" war, motivated by the mission to save the millions of refugee civilians'. C. Duffy, *Red Storm on the Reich. The Soviet March on Germany 1945* (London: Routledge, 1991), pp. 275–276. One recent study suggests that at Stalin's behest the Red Army was involved in an early form of ethnic cleansing in a [successful] attempt to facilitate the westward movement of Poland. Moreover, this account claims that by mid-1944 the Red Army was war-weary and that propaganda conveyed by newspapers and political officers played a key role in forming the mood and attitude of soldiers when they crossed the German border. See M. Zeidler, *Kriegsende im Osten. Die Rote Armee und die Besetzung Deutschlands östlich von Oder und Neiße 1944/45* (Munich: R. Oldenbourg Verlag, 1996). This issue is covered in more detail in Part III.
37 General Lasch, *So fiel Königsberg* (Stuttgart: Motorbuch Verlag, 1994); General von Ahlfen and General Niehoff, *So kämpfte Breslau 1945. Verteidigung and Untergang von Schlesiens Hauptstadt* (Stuttgart: Motorbuch Verlag, 1994). These memoirs were first published in 1958 and 1960 respectively.
38 E. Lucas-Busemann, *So fielen Königsberg und Breslau* (Berlin: Aufbau Taschenbuch Verlag, 1994). There have been especially bitter disputes over the siege of Breslau, a city virtually undamaged by air attack before 1945. Within the besieged city the fortress newspaper *Schlesische Tageszeitung* (hereafter *ST*) heralded 'The Wonder of Breslau' on 21 April 1945. These sentiments were echoed when the last fortress commandant, General Niehoff, wrote a series of reports for *Welt am Sonntag* in early 1956. The continuation of resistance was criticised in J. Konrad, 'Das Ende von Breslau', *VfZ*, Volume 4, 1956, pp. 387–390; E. Hornig, *Breslau 1945. Erlebnisse in der eingeschlossen Stadt* (Würzburg: Bergstadtverlag Wilhelm Gottlieb Korn, 1986), pp. 236–240, 249–251; P. Peikert, *'Festung Breslau' in*

den Berichten eines Pfarrers. 22. Januar bis 6. Mai 1945 (edited by K. Jonca and A. Konieczny) (East Berlin: Union Verlag, 1968) For critical Polish interpretations of post-war German historiography on the siege of Breslau see R. Majewski and T. Sozanska, *Die Schlacht um Breslau Januar–Mai 1945* (East Berlin: Union Verlag, 1979), pp. v–vi.

39 N. Davies and R. Moorhouse, *Microcosm: Portrait of a Central European City* (London: Jonathan Cape, 2002).

40 A. Beevor, *Berlin: The Downfall 1945* (London: Viking, 2002).

41 Ibid., Beevor, a former cavalry officer and writer with numerous influential contacts, received widespread praise in Britain for *Berlin*. In Germany, however, he was criticised in *Der Spiegel* by Joachim Fest, the respected biographer of Hitler, for producing a 'patchwork history'. Fest claimed that Beevor was 'historically and intellectually not up to the stature of his material'. See *Der Spiegel*, 28 October 2002.

42 J. Friedrich, *Der Brand – Deutschland im Bombenkrieg 1940–1945* (Berlin: List Verlag edition, 2004); W.G. Sebald, *On the Natural History of Destruction* (London: Hamish Hamilton, 2003), this was first published in Germany in 1999 as *Luftkrieg und Literatur*.

43 G. Grass, *Im Krebsgang* (Gottingen: Steidl Verlag, 2002) translated into English as *Crabwalk* (London; Faber and Faber, 2003).

44 K. Erik Franzen, *Die Vertriebenen: Hitlers letzte Opfer* (Munich: Propyläen Verlag, 2001).

45 G. Knopp, *Die große Flucht* (Munich: Ullstein Taschenverlag, 2002).

46 *Damals*, November 2002.

47 S. Aust and S. Burgdorff (eds.), *Die Flucht: Über die Vertreibung der Deutschen aus dem Osten* (Munich: DTV, 2002); *Spiegel Special, Die Flucht der Deutschen*, 2002.

48 In Moscow, however, the British Ambassador noted that, 'Kohl's refusal to affirm in public that he no longer had designs on the ex-German lands east of the Oder–Neisse line sent cold shivers down the spines of even moderate Russians and Poles.' R. Braithwaite, *Across the Moscow River: The World Turned Upside Down* (London: Yale University Press, 2002), p. 132.

49 Garton Ash, *In Europe's Name*, pp. 227–231; *Time*, 5 March 1990.

50 Statement by Chancellor Dr Helmut Kohl, speech by Kohl and speech by President Roman Herzog, Press Releases from the Embassy of the Federal Republic of Germany, London, 9 May 1995; *Daily Telegraph*, 29 April 1995; *Guardian*, 6 May 1995; *Sunday Telegraph*, 7 May 1995.

51 *Times Higher Education Supplement*, 13 October 2000. German estimates maintain that 250,000 Germans died during the expulsions from the Sudetenland while Czech historians talk of 18,889 deaths, 5,596 being classed as 'violent deaths'.

52 *Guardian*, 17 March 1995.

53 *The Times*, 5 December 1996; *Guardian*, 13 December 1996; *Independent*, 22 January 1997.

54 *Daily Telegraph*, 26 January 2002; *Guardian*, 26 February 2002.

55 *Guardian*, 25 April 2002; 29 June 2002.

56 The remaining Germans were drastically reduced from perhaps 100,000 in April 1945 to around 25,000 in 1947 by a combination of malnutrition, disease and deportations to the Soviet interior. The survivors were sent west in batches between 1947 and 1949. The impact of the new arrivals from across the Soviet Union was summarised in a report in the German news magazine *Stern* in 2004. Kaliningrad was portrayed as a 'strange, forgotten, rootless city full of incomers. No grandmother seen on the streets was born here. After the expulsion of the Germans in came Russians, White Russians, Ukrainians, Azerbaijanis and Lithuanians – many were wartime victims of the Germans forcibly resettled by Stalin.' *Stern* 8/2004.

57 The Soviet authorities made every effort to systematically erase the traces of Kaliningrad's rich Prussian past. For sure, much of the work was already done. The impact of bombing, a bitter 10-week siege and subsequent fire-raising by the Red Army meant that barely one-fifth of the city's structures were still standing at the war's end. And the destruction did not stop in 1945. German churches were still being demolished in 1976 by the atheist Soviet state. Königsberg castle, a symbol of German East Prussia, already a casualty of British bombing and Red Army arson, was blown up in 1955 and the remaining ruins were dynamited on President Brezhnev's express orders in 1967. On the vacant site, the city's masters approved the construction of a House of the Soviets. This ugly, concrete building, dubbed the 'Monster' by locals, was still incomplete when the Soviet regime collapsed in 1991. Blocks of flats, similar to those put up across the length and breadth of the Soviet Union, became an aspect of life in Kaliningrad. Statues commemorating the deeds of Soviet war heroes appeared in the city's concreted squares. See N. Taylor, *Baltic Capitals: Tallinn, Riga, Vilnius, Kaliningrad* (Chalfont St Peter, Buckinghamshire: Bradt Travel Guides UK, 2001), pp. 151–183.

58 The West German government was particularly angry in the late 1950s when they found out that the Soviets had installed intercontinental missile systems at Wehlau airfield and Tapiau to the west of Kaliningrad. See *The Times*, 29 April 1958; 29 May 1958.

59 The zone was also forbidden to non-resident Soviet citizens without the requisite permits. Kaliningrad was the embarkation port for Soviet leader Nikita Khrushchev's journeys to Britain and the US in 1956 and 1960 respectively. Soviet Antarctic expeditions also set sail from Kaliningrad in the mid-1950s, as did a large and modern trawler fleet, including refrigerator ships, which sought out rich fishing grounds across the world's oceans.

60 *Guardian*, 10 October 1992.

61 Ibid., 7 April 2001, article by Chris Patten, European Union Commissioner for External Relations.

62 Ibid., 12 November 2002. Kaliningrad also attracted more unwelcome attention in 2004 when it was revealed that Königsberg Castle was where the famed Amber Room perished. Built by German craftsmen for Peter the Great in 1717, it was later housed in the Catherine Palace outside St Petersburg but dismantled by German forces in 1941 and sent to the Reich. Stored in the Knights' Hall of the castle during the Soviet siege, it was destroyed in a fire started by the Red Army shortly after they occupied the city. See C. Scott-Clark and A. Levy, *The Amber Room* (London: Atlantic Books, 2004).

63 *Sunday Telegraph*, 31 August 2003; *Daily Telegraph*, 23 September 2003; *Sunday Times*, 28 September 2003. At the same time, German President Johannes Rau told the annual meeting of the *Bund der Vertriebenen* in Berlin in September 2003 that 'Hitler's criminal policies do not exonerate anyone who answered terrible wrongs with terrible wrongs.' Steinbach also organised a commemoration of the 60th anniversary of the Warsaw Rising in Berlin and infuriated Polish politicians by not inviting any Poles.

64 Although the exhibition attempted to portray the suffering of the Germans as one of the many mass expulsions seen in the twentieth century, the Acting Mayor of Warsaw, Kazimierz Markinkiewitz, a former Polish Prime Minister, immediately called off a visit to Berlin. See *The Times*, 10 August 2006; *Financial Times*, 11 August 2006; *Financial Times*, 12 August 2006; *Daily Telegraph*, 12 August 2006. The news magazine *Der Spiegel* also took the opportunity to criticise the BdV's claim that it was not a home for right-wing extremists by highlighting the large number of former Nazi Party members and SS men to be found among the higher strata of the BdV during the first three decades of its existence. *Der Spiegel*, 33/2006, 14 August 2006.

65 *Der Spiegel* 33/2004, 9 August 2004; *Stern* 34/2004, 12 August 2004; *Financial Times*, 17 October 2003; *Independent on Sunday*, 25 July 2004; *Guardian*, 31 July, 2 August 2004; *Independent*, 2, 3 August 2004; *Daily Telegraph*, 2 August 2004; *The Times*, 2 August 2004; *Financial Times*, 4 August 2004; *International Herald Tribune*, 7 August 2004.

66 See *Daily Telegraph*, 11, 15 September 2004; *International Herald Tribune*, 11, 13 September 2004.

67 *Daily Telegraph*, 28 September 2004; *Financial Times*, 28 September 2004.

68 Jaroslaw Kaczynski and his twin brother Lech, the Polish President, had been depicted in the German press as potatoes leading to the Polish prosecutor commencing legal proceedings.

69 *International Herald Tribune*, 30 October 2006. On the 67th anniversary of the German invasion of Poland, the Polish government announced plans to commence a project to name the more than six million Poles who perished during the war. *Guardian*, 5 September 2006.

70 G. Kirwin, 'Nazi Domestic Propaganda and Popular Response 1943–1945'. (Unpublished doctoral thesis, University of Reading, 1979), pp. 19–20.

71 J.W. Baird, *The Mythical World of Nazi War Propaganda 1939–1945* (Minneapolis, MN: University of Minnesota Press, 1974), p. 39.

72 Ibid., pp. 39–40. See also G. Kirwin, 'Nazi Domestic Propaganda', pp. 21–23. Ohlendorf also commanded an *Einsatzgruppe* (task force) in Russia entrusted with the extermination of Communists, Jews and other potential enemies of the Nazi New Order. This unit was responsible for the murder of 90,000 people in 1941–1942. In 1948 Ohlendorf was sentenced to death by an American military court. He was executed in June 1951. See R.E. Herzstein, *The War That Hitler Won: The Most Infamous Propaganda Campaign in History* (London: Hamish Hamilton, 1979), p. 375.

73 TNA, FO 898/186; 898/187.

Chapter 1 Come the Gauleiters, 1933–1939

1 R. Bessel, 'Eastern Germany as a structural problem in the Weimar Republic', *SH*, Volume 3, Number 2, 1978, pp. 199–218.

2 I.F.D. Morrow, *The Peace Settlement in the German Polish Borderlands* (London: Oxford University Press, 1936), p. 238. Some 917,400 left East Prussia, 775,900 left Pomerania and 866,000 left Silesia.

3 S. Siebel-Achenbach, *Lower Silesia from Nazi Germany to Communist Poland* (Basingstoke: Macmillan, 1994), p. 16; Bessel, 'Eastern Germany', *SH*, p. 210.

4 Bessel, 'Eastern Germany', *SH*, pp. 202–203.

5 Ibid., p. 208; Siebel-Achenbach, *Lower Silesia*, p. 15; D. Mühlberger, 'The Occupational and Social Structure of the NSDAP in the Border Province Posen–West Prussia in the early 1930s', *EHQ*, Volume 15, 1985, pp. 281–311. The percentage employed in agriculture and forestry was 55.7% in East Prussia, 50.7% in Pomerania and 43% in Upper Silesia.

6 von Braun, *Germany's Eastern Territories*, pp. 34–35. Some 28.9% of eastern Germans were employed in agriculture and forestry in May 1939.

7 Mühlberger, 'The Occupational and Social Structure', *EHQ*, p. 286. Bessel, 'Eastern Germany', *SH*, p. 209. The percentage of the national *per capita* average was 73% in East Prussia and 76% in Silesia.

8 Bessel, 'Eastern Germany', *SH*, pp. 209–210, mentions the greater proportion of small flats among the housing stock, the lower percentage of doctors and higher rates of tuberculosis and infant mortality.

9 See for instance, M. Kramer, 'Agriculture in Eastern Germany', in Pagel (ed.), *The German East*, pp. 123–135.

10 Bessel, 'Eastern Germany', *SH*, pp. 206–207.

11 In Allenstein 97.8% of voters opted to remain within Germany, in Marienwerder 92.3%. See R. Butler and J.P.T Bury (eds.), *Documents on British Foreign Policy 1919–1939. First Series. Volume X. German Affairs and Plebiscite Problems 1920* (London: HMSO, 1960), pp. 720–838.

12 A.A. Scholz, *Silesia Yesterday and Today* (The Hague: Martinus Nijhoff, 1964), pp. 35–37. On the Upper Silesia plebiscite see R. Butler and J.P.T Bury (eds.), *Documents on British Foreign Policy 1919–1939. First Series. Volume XI. Upper Silesia, Poland and the Baltic States January 1920–March 1921* (London: HMSO, 1961), pp. 1–197.

13 Sir R. Donald, *The Polish Corridor and the Consequences* (London: Thornton Butterworth Ltd, 1929), p. 16.

14 P. Barandon, 'The Effect of the Treaty of Versailles on Eastern Germany and the Neighbouring States', in Göttingen Research Committee (ed.), *Eastern Germany. A Handbook: Volume II, History*, p. 283.

15 M. Burleigh, *Germany Turns Eastwards* (London: Pan Macmillan edition, 2002), pp. 56–57.

16 R. Blanke, 'The German Minority in Inter-war Poland and German Foreign Policy – Some Reconsiderations', *JCH*, Volume 25, 1990, pp. 87–102.

17 Ibid, pp. 88–90; Barandon, 'The Effect of the Treaty of Versailles', in Göttingen (ed.), *Eastern Germany*, p. 296; Bessel, 'Eastern Germany', *SH*, p. 202. One million Germans remained in Poland at the outbreak of the Second World War, mostly located in the former Russian and Austrian parts of the state.

18 Morrow, *The Peace Settlement*, p. 239; Bessel, 'Eastern Germany', *SH*, p. 202.

19 Scholz, *Silesia*, p. 38; K. Baedeker, *Germany: A Handbook for railway travellers and motorists* (Leipzig: Karl Baedeker publishers, 1936), p. 131.

20 BA-LA, Ost-Dok. 8/708, p. 2; 8/716, p. 2.

21 Donald, *The Polish Corridor*, p. 107.

22 Morrow, *The Peace Settlement*, p. 220.

23 On the invasion of East Prussia see: N. Stone, *The Eastern Front 1914–1917* (London: Hodder and Stoughton, 1975), pp. 44–69, 92–121; D.E. Showalter, *Tannenberg: Clash of Empires* (Hamden CN: Archon Books, 1991); D.E. Showalter, 'Even Generals Wet Their Pants: The First Three Weeks in East Prussia, August 1914', *W&S*, Volume 2, Number 2, September 1984, pp. 60–86; A. Solzhenitsyn, *August 1914* (Harmondsworth, Middlesex: Penguin, 1974); *Das Ostpreußenblatt*, the newspaper of the East Prussian expellee community in West Germany, on the 50th anniversary of the invasion, 1 August 1964; 30 January 1965.

24 See for instance Marshal P. von Hindenburg, *Out of My Life* (London: Cassell and Company, 1920), p. 137 and the counter-argument by Stone, *The Eastern Front*, p. 118.

25 *Das Ostpreußenblatt*, 1 August 1964; 30 January 1965; Major K. Dieckert and General H. Großmann, *Der Kampf um Ostpreussen. Der Umfassende Dokumentarbericht über das Kriegsgeschehen in Ostpreußen* (Stuttgart; Motorbuch Verlag edition, 1995), p. 15. Norman Stone claimed that German losses were much higher and estimated that the Eighth Army had lost 100,000 men killed, missing, wounded or captured by the end of September 1914. See *The Eastern Front*, p. 69.

26 Stone, *The Eastern Front*, pp. 66, 68, 118. Total East Prussian military losses may never be ascertained. However, more than 300 students from Königsberg's Albertina University

were killed and by the winter semester of 1915/16, 880 students out of 1,299 were in military service and half of the remaining students were women. See A. Kossert, *Ostpreussen: Geschichte und Mythos* (Munich: Siedler, 2005), p. 204.

27 *The Times*, 19 February 1915; A. Kossert, *Ostpreussen: Geschichte und Mythos* (Munich: Siedler, 2005), p. 203.

28 These five reports formed the *Ostpreußischen Kriegshefte*. Professor Albert Brackmann, the then Chair of Medieval History at the University of Königsberg was the Head of the Provincial Commission, an editor of this series and a regular contributor to the *Königsberger Allgemeine Zeitung* (hereafter *KAZ*) where he covered the suffering and destruction at Russian hands. Brackmann, left Königsberg in 1922 before his work could be completed and in Berlin he became a leading light in German study of Eastern Europe (*Ostforschung*). This nationalist, conservative historian would be lauded and decorated in the Third Reich where he was proclaimed 'the worthy *Führer* of *Ostforschung*'. See Burleigh, *Germany Turns Eastwards*. Brackmann also wrote the foreword to F. Gause, *Die Russen in Ostpreußen 1914/1915* (Königsberg: Gräfe und Unzer Verlag, 1931). This long awaited book, Brackmann claimed that it was always envisaged to allow a certain time interval to elapse to ensure an objective study of historical events, appeared some 16 years after testimonies were collected and formed a chronicle of Russian indiscipline, plundering, fire-raising, atrocities and deportations (of non-combatants).

29 Russian newspapers admitted that German women had been taken prisoner and that over 100 had been seized by the Cossacks in Willenberg alone. Young and old were said to have turned upon the Russians. A 17-year-old was said to have signalled Russian movements to German forces from a belfry with a flag until the Cossacks caught her. A 70-year-old said to have lost her sons and grandsons in the war had reportedly fired at Russian troops with a machine gun from a belfry, killing and wounding 15 in the process. See *The Times*, 22 September 1914.

30 *Das Ostpreußenblatt*, 14 November 1964; Dieckert and Grossmann, *Der Kampf um Ostpreussen*, p. 14. See also Kossert, *Ostpreussen*, p. 202 for details of the deaths and deportations in various districts. Kossert also notes the catastrophic impact on agriculture. The harvest of 1914 was destroyed or carried away by the Russian and German armies. Some 135,000 horses, 250,000 cattle and 200,000 pigs were also lost.

31 Despite the excesses by Russian troops, the occupiers quickly established [short-lived] civil authorities headed by Germans, to govern Gumbinnen and Insterburg. See Kossert, *Ostpreussen*, pp. 198, 200–202.

32 *The Times*, 22 September 1914.

33 Ibid.

34 On the other hand, Russian propaganda accused the Germans of breaking military convention through 'ill use of the white flag'. This had led Russians to believe that the enemy wanted to surrender only to be 'treacherously shot at' when they approached. After two such incidents in one village 'the white flag ceased to be considered a sign of surrender'. Ibid., 29 August 1914.

35 *Das Ostpreußenblatt*, 27 March 1965.

36 Ibid.

37 Kossert, *Ostpreussen*, p. 206; see also *The Times*, 9 September 1918. It carried the headline 'Well-fed Junkerdom – Present Day Conditions in East Prussia' and said that according to a neutral visitor food supplies were ample in the east of the province but less plentiful in Königsberg. The mood was said to be 'comparatively cheerful', the population was

'placidly satisfied' and placed great hopes in Hindenburg being able to defeat the western Allies.

38 As early as September 1914 a *Kriegshilfskommission* was set up under the chairmanship of Adolph von Batocki, *Oberpräsident* of East Prussia. Following the 'Winter Battle' the concept of 'Patenschaft', the stimulus for which has been attributed to numerous individuals, became a reality. Shattered East Prussian communities received financial assistance from their counterparts further west. For instance, the town and county of Lötzen received help from Frankfurt/Main. In early September 1915, officials from Frankfurt visited Lötzen and were most impressed by the demeanour of the local population. Later that month the 'Kriegshilfsverein für den Kreis Lötzen' was founded in Frankfurt. Contributions from this body were forwarded to Lötzen between 1915 and May 1922. While reconstruction costs were met solely by the Prussian State authorities, the money collected from the sponsors in Frankfurt led to the foundation of military cemeteries or was channelled into additional social, cultural and sporting projects. See *Das Ostpreußenblatt*, 24 April 1965; M. Meyhöfer, *Das Kreis Lötzen. Ein ostpreußisches Heimatbuch* (Würzburg: Holzner Verlag, 1961), pp. 133–135. See also Kossert, *Ostpreussen*, pp. 204–207. For example Cologne provided funds for Neidenburg, Oppeln (Silesia) assisted Lyck and Hanover aided Rastenburg.

39 *Das Ostpreußenblatt*, 14 November 1964.

40 Donald, *The Polish Corridor*, p. 67.

41 *Das Ostpreußenblatt*, 24 April 1965; *Spiegel Special, 1/2004, Die Ur-Katastrophe des 20. Jahrhunderts*.

42 Hindenburg, *Out of My Life*, p. 97. Russian accounts outlined the nature of this German rage. Russian counter-propaganda alleged German atrocities and the testimony of one wounded soldier which appeared in the press described the savage events: 'We thought they were civilised, but we saw how they killed and mutilated our wounded . . . .In some places armed inhabitants offered resistance. The Cossacks did not spare them, but, on the other hand no quarter was shown to the Cossacks. The Germans cut off their hands and ears and tortured them.' See *The Times*, 29 August 1914.

43 *The Times*, 17 October 1914.

44 Kossert, *Ostpreussen*, p. 203.

45 *The Times*, 16 August 1921; 18 August 1921.

46 Showalter, *Tannenberg*, p. 347.

47 Ibid.

48 C. von Krockow, *Begegnung mit Ostpreußen* (Munich: Deutscher Taschenbuch Verlag, 1995), p. 90.

49 *The Times*, 2 September 1924; J.W. Wheeler-Bennett, *Hindenburg: The Wooden Titan* (London: Macmillan, 1967 edition), p. 245.

50 *The Times*, 19 September 1927. At the unveiling and before an audience including leading politicians, military figures and diplomats, Hindenburg took the opportunity to repudiate German responsibility for the war and challenged Germany's wartime enemies to an impartial inquiry.

51 Ibid., 8 August 1934; von Krockow, *Begegnung mit Ostpreußen*, pp. 89–90; Showalter, *Tannenberg*, p. 348; G. Ulrich (ed.), *Ostpreussen in 144 Bildern* (Leer: Verlag Gerhard Rautenberg, 1987), p. 67.

52 *The Times*, 26 September 1935; Kossert, *Ostpreussen*, pp. 212–214. 2 October 1935 was the 88th anniversary of Hindenburg's birth.

53 Showalter, *Tannenberg*, pp. 353, 406.

54 Bessel, 'Eastern Germany', *SH*, p. 214.

55 See for instance S. Baranowski's two articles, 'Continuity and contingency: agrarian elites, conservative institutions and East Elbia in modern German history', *SH*, Volume 12, 1987, pp. 285–308; 'The Sanctity of Rural Life: Protestantism, Agrarian Politics and Nazism in Pomerania during the Weimar Republic', *GH*, Volume 9, Number 1, 1991, pp. 1–22.

56 R. Bessel, *Political Violence and the Rise of Nazism: The Storm Troopers in Eastern Germany 1925–1934* (London: Yale University Press, 1984), pp. 10–12. Ermland in East Prussia, which had a mostly Catholic population, was also an exception to the general electoral trends east of the Oder due to the history of the bishopric.

57 Bessel, 'Eastern Germany', *SH*, p. 212. A *Reichstag* Inquiry into the *Osthilfe* noted the need for repeated 'reconstruction' of some failing estates, highlighted instances of absentee landlords and the squandering of public money on 'wine and women' while creditors remained unpaid, see Wheeler-Bennett, *Hindenburg*, pp. 423–424.

58 Baranowski, 'Continuity and contingency', *SH*, pp. 305–306.

59 Bessel, *Political Violence*, pp. 57–65.

60 I. Kershaw, 'Ideology, Propaganda and the Rise of the Nazi Party', in P.D. Stachura (ed.), *The Nazi Machtergreifung* (London: George Allen and Unwin, 1983), pp. 162–181. The allegedly crippling burdens placed on Germany by the Young Plan became a major constituent of Nazi propaganda after 1929.

61 BA-LA, Ost-Dok. 8/716, p. 4. At the 1932 Presidential election Hitler even gained almost 50% of the vote in Neidenburg district, adjacent to the Tannenberg memorial. Conservative newspapers chastised Neidenburg's electorate for the lack of gratitude they had shown to Hindenburg, their Great War liberator. Kossert, *Ostpreussen*, p. 260.

62 Bessel, *Political Violence*, p. 26.

63 Ibid., pp. 97–129.

64 I. Kershaw, *Hitler 1889–1936: Hubris* (London: Allen Lane, The Penguin Press, 1998), p. 517.

65 For a summary of the accumulation of *Gauleiter* authority during the war see J. Noakes, *Nazism 1919–1945. Volume 4. The German Home Front in World War II* (Exeter: University of Exeter Press, 1998), pp. 63–80. As RVKs their powers covered the realms of 'total war' measures, civil defence, evacuation and resettlement issues.

66 BAB, Akte Koch, Lebenslauf des Gauleiters Erich Koch, 25 May 1943, p. 1. This document was prepared by the Party Chancellery. See also E.G. Lass, *Die Flucht. Ostpreussen 1944/45* (Dorheim: Podzun Pallas Verlag, 1964), p. 318; K. Höffkes, *Hitlers Politische Generale. Die Gauleiter des Dritten Reiches-Ein biographisches Nachschlagewerk* (Tübingen: Grabert Verlag, 1986), pp. 183–184.

67 Bessel, *Political Violence*, pp. 15–16, 20, 22. Koch told the Party authorities in Munich in January 1930 that membership had grown from around 200 to over 8,000 and that since his arrival the number of local groups had risen from 4 to 211. See also Kossert, *Ostpreussen*, p. 260.

68 Ibid., pp. 59–60.

69 Quoted in J. Noakes, 'The Nazi Party and the Third Reich: The Myth and Reality of the One Party State', in J. Noakes ed., *Government, Party and People in Nazi Germany* (Exeter: University of Exeter Press, 1980), p. 16.

70 C. Tilitzki, *Alltag in Ostpreußen. Die geheimen Lageberichte der Königsberger Justiz 1940–1945* (Leer: Verlag Gerhard Rautenberg, 1991), pp. 13–15.

71 Ibid., p. 15; Bessel, *Political Violence*, p. 144. Other accounts suggest that Koch hid in the

Königsberg house of the evangelical Reich Bishop Ludwig Mueller during this unsettling period. G. Reitlinger, *The House Built on Sand: The Conflicts of German Policy in Russia, 1939–1945* (London: Weidenfeld and Nicolson, 1960), pp. 180–181.

72 On this episode see Lass, *Die Flucht*, p. 318; Tilitzki, *Alltag in Ostpreußen*, p. 15; Höffkes, *Hitlers Politische Generale,* pp. 184–185.

73 *Tilitzki, Alltag in Ostpreußen*, pp. 16–19.

74 Koch told Hitler on 26 July 1933 that there was no more unemployment in East Prussia. Preferential credits obtained from Göring, Prussian Minister of the Interior, led to the establishment of public works programmes which had swallowed up the rural and urban unemployed. J. Noakes, '"Viceroys of the Reich?" Gauleiters 1928–45' in A. McElligott and T. Kirk (eds.), *Working Towards the Führer: Essays in Honour of Sir Ian Kershaw* (Manchester: Manchester University Press, 2003), pp. 118–152, p. 140.

75 BAB, Akte Koch, Lebenslauf, 25 May 1943, p. 2.

76 D. Orlow, *The History of the Nazi Party 1933–1945* (London: University of Pittsburgh Press, 1973), p. 157.

77 Ibid., pp. 58–59.

78 On the 'Erich Koch Stiftung' see BA-LA, Ost-Dok. 8/524, p. 8; F. Gause, *Die Geschichte der Stadt Königsberg in Preußen. III Band. Vom Ersten Weltkrieg bis zum Untergang Königsbergs* (Cologne: Böhlau, 1996), pp. 136–137.

79 Höffkes, *Hitlers Politische Generale*, p. 169; Orlow, *The History of the Nazi Party*, pp. 123–124.

80 Murawski, *Die Eroberung Pommerns*, p. 29; Höffkes, *Hitlers Politsche Generale*, pp. 309–311; M.H. Kater, *The Nazi Party: A Social Profile of Members and Leaders 1919–1945* (Oxford: Basil Blackwell, 1983), p. 170; Orlow, *The History of the Nazi Party*, p. 124. Furthermore, the size of Pomerania increased considerably with the break-up of the Border Province of Posen–West Prussia in 1938, when the entire northern portion, including the town of Schneidemühl, came under Pomeranian jurisdiction. See BA-LA, Ost-Dok. 8/645, pp. 4–8; Murawski, *Die Eroberung Pommerns*, p. 23.

81 Bessel, *Political Violence*, pp. 18–19, 58, 63–64. Höffkes, *Hitlers Politische Generale*, pp. 37–38.

82 Bessel, *Political Violence*, p. 91.

83 Ibid., p. 133.

84 Brückner probably became a political casualty because of the good relationship with Heines. The Silesian SS leader Udo von Woyrsch was also Brückner's enemy. Ostensibly, Brückner's dismissal arose from a further accusation of homosexuality, first levelled against him in 1928, and his apparent support for bisexuality. See Ibid., p. 145; Orlow, *The History of the Nazi Party*, p. 123; Siebel-Achenbach, *Lower Silesia*, pp. 18–19; Höffkes, *Hitlers Politische Generale*, p. 38.

85 D. Rebentisch, *Führerstaat und Verwaltung im Zweiten Weltkrieg: Verfassungsentwicklung und Verwaltungspolitik 1939–1945* (Stuttgart: Steiner, 1989), p. 197.

86 Siebel-Achenbach, *Lower Silesia*, p. 19; Höffkes, *Hitlers Politische Generale*, pp. 367–370; Rebentisch, *Führerstaat und Verwaltung*, p. 198. Following Rudolf Hess's flight to Britain on 10 May 1941, the Office of the Deputy *Führer* was named the Party Chancellery (12 May 1941) with Martin Bormann as its head. A. Nolzen, 'Charismatic Legislation and Bureaucratic Rule: The NSDAP in the Third Reich, 1933–1945', in *German History*, Volume 23, 2005, No. 4, pp. 494–518.

87 Rebentisch, *Führerstaat und Verwaltung*, p. 197; Siebel-Achenbach, *Lower Silesia*, pp.

19–20, Höffkes, *Hitlers Politische Generale*, pp. 369–370; Orlow, *The History of the Nazi Party*, pp. 270–271. Wagner was relieved of all duties by Hitler in front of a gathering of senior Party figures on 9 November 1941 and kicked out of the Party. Placed under surveillance by Himmler, Wagner was arrested by the Gestapo following the failure of the 20 July 1944 plot against Hitler. The Silesian Count Peter Yorck von Wartenburg, one of the leading conspirators, had advised Wagner during his period as Reich Price Commissioner during the late 1930s. Wagner was probably shot by the Berlin Gestapo on 22 April 1945.

88 Siebel-Achenbach, *Lower Silesia*, p. 27.

89 The Black *Reichswehr* was a reserve army financed, garrisoned and trained by the *Reichswehr* from 1923. Primarily it was formed to guard against a Polish attack. See G.A. Craig, *The Politics of the Prussian Army 1640–1945* (London: Oxford University Press, 1975), pp. 401–403.

90 Siebel-Achenbach, *Lower Silesia*, pp. 20–21; Orlow, *The History of the Nazi Party*, pp. 270–271; Kater, *The Nazi Party*, p. 382; Höffkes, *Hitlers Politische Generale*, pp. 120–123; R.G. Reuth, *Goebbels The Life of Joseph Goebbels The Mephistophellean Genius of Nazi Propaganda* (London: Constable, 1993), pp. 143, 174.

91 Siebel-Achenbach, *Lower Silesia*, p. 21; Reuth, *Goebbels*, p. 250; A. Speer, *Inside the Third Reich* (London: Phoenix edition, 1995), p. 244.

92 Rebentisch, *Führerstaat und Verwaltung*, p. 198; Siebel-Achenbach, *Lower Silesia*, p. 21; Orlow, *The History of the Nazi Party*, p. 271.

93 Orlow, *The History of the Nazi Party*, pp. 33, 36, 54, 109; Kater, *The Nazi Party*, p. 212.

94 Orlow, *The History of the Nazi Party*, p. 181; H. Heiber, 'Aus den Akten des Gauleiters Kube', *VfZ*, Volume 4, 1956, pp. 67–92. Kube was surprisingly rehabilitated and sent to Belorussia in 1941 to act as *Generalkommissar*. On 22 September 1943, he was blown to pieces when his Russian maid placed an anti-personnel mine in his bed. On Kube's complex views on the racial status of Belorussians and the extermination of Jews in his domain; he particularly opposed the killing of German Jews deported to Minsk, see Heiber, pp. 70–77; Orlow, p. 445; H. Höhne, *The Order of the Death's Head* (London: Classic Penguin edition, 2000), pp. 370–373.

95 On Stürtz see Höffkes, *Hitlers Politische Generale*, pp. 339–340; H. Eberle and M. Uhl (eds.), *The Hitler Book: The Secret Dossier Prepared for Stalin* (London: John Murray, 2005), p. 336.

96 Gause, *Die Geschichte der Stadt Königsberg*, p. 156.

97 *The Times*, 26 August 1939. Tents had been erected and loudspeakers and microphones installed at the Tannenberg site. Trains were also to provide accommodation for the visitors.

98 I. Kershaw, *Hitler 1936–1945: Nemesis* (London: Allen Lane, The Penguin Press, 2000), p. 197. As usual, the *Ostmesse* had been staged in Königsberg in August and Hitler's telegram to the organisers wished it 'further successes in its work of peaceful inter-State collaboration'. *The Times*, 21 August 1939.

Chapter 2 An Oasis of Tranquility? The German East, 1939–1944

1 The Germans suffered 50,000 casualties and lost 500 planes and over 1,000 armoured vehicles during the month-long Polish campaign.

2 I. Kershaw, 'How Effective was Nazi Propaganda?' in D. Welch ed., *Nazi Propaganda: The Power and the Limitation* (London: Croom Helm, 1983), pp. 180–205; D. Welch, 'Propaganda and Indoctrination in the Third Reich: Success or Failure?' *EHQ*, Volume 17, 1987, pp. 403–422.

3 M. Domarus, *Hitler: Speeches and Proclamations 1932–1945. Volume One, The Years 1932 to 1934* (London: I.B. Tauris and Co Ltd, 1990), p. 46. Speech by Hitler, 2 September 1933.

4 On views of the Soviet Union during the Nazi period see H.E. Volkmann (ed.), *Das Rußlandbild im Dritten Reich* (Cologne: Böhlau Verlag, 1994).

5 J. von Ribbentrop, *The Ribbentrop Memoirs* (London: Weidenfeld and Nicolson, 1954), p. 115; M. Balfour, *Propaganda in War 1939–1945: Organisations, Policies and Publics in Britain and Germany* (London: Routledge and Kegan Paul, 1979), p. 162; D. Welch, *The Third Reich: Politics and Propaganda* (London: Routledge, 1993), pp. 99–100.

6 Balfour, *Propaganda in War*, p. 163; Baird, *The Mythical World*, p. 147; D. Welch, *Propaganda and the German Cinema 1933–1945* (Oxford: Clarendon Press, 1983), p. 249.

7 Baird, *The Mythical World*, pp. 148–149.

8 Ibid., pp. 148–151; M. Steinert, *Hitler's War and the Germans: Public Mood and Attitude during the Second World War* (Athens, OH: University of Ohio Press, 1977), p. 97.

9 SD report for 8 May 1941 quoted in V.K. Bennet, 'Public Opinion and Propaganda in National Socialist Germany during the War against the Soviet Union.'(Unpublished Ph.D thesis, University of Washington, 1990), pp. 49–50. As well as information that the Germans were upgrading the naval base at Gdynia and repairing and improving roads, railways, bridges and aerodromes adjacent to their demarcation line in Poland with the Soviets, Polish intelligence reports reaching the British Special Operations Executive (SOE) reported that the constitution of two fortified lines was started by the Germans in the spring of 1940. One ran along the rivers Narew, Bug and San while the second line ran along the Vistula towards Warsaw through Deblin and Annopol. The building of fortifications and strongpoints continued throughout the year and into the spring of 1941. A Peplonski, 'Intelligence Behind the Eastern Front', in T. Stirling, D. Nalecz and T. Dubicki (eds.), *Intelligence Co-Operation Between Poland and Great Britain during World War II. Volume I. The Report of the Anglo-Polish Historical Committee* (London: Vallentine Mitchell, 2005), pp. 513–529; J.S. Ciechanowski (ed.), *Intelligence Co-operation between Poland and Great Britain during World War II. Volume II, Documents* (Warsaw: The Head Office of State Archives, 2005), pp. 742–745. SOE general appreciation of Polish intelligence reports on German preparations for an attack on the Soviet Union, 22 April 1941, also in TNA, HS 4/322.

10 On anti-Bolshevik propaganda in the *Wehrmacht* prior to Barbarossa see Militärgeschichtliches Forschungsamt (H. Boog, J. Förster, J. Hoffmann, E. Klink, R-D. Müller, G. Ueberschär, editors), *Germany and the Second World War. Part IV, The Attack on the Soviet Union* (Oxford: Clarendon Press, 1998), pp. 513–521.

11 The notion of Germany launching a preventive war has featured in V. Suvorov, *Icebreaker* (London: Hamish Hamilton, 1990); Hoffmann, *Stalins Vernichtungskrieg*; W. Maser, *Der Wortbruch. Hitler, Stalin und der Zweite Weltkrieg* (Munich: Olzog, 1994). For a review of these studies and other literature pertaining to the outbreak of the Russo-German conflict see K. Schmider, 'No Quiet on the Eastern Front: The Suvorov Debate in the 1990s', *Journal of Slavic Military Studies*, Volume 10, Number 2, June 1997, pp. 181–194. A dismissal of Suvorov's argument and a summary of the relevant literature can be found in J. Erickson, 'Barbarossa June 1941: Who attacked who?' *History Today*, June 2001, pp. 11–17.

12 On German press coverage see The Royal Institute of International Affairs, *Review of the Foreign Press 1939–1945. Series A. Volume V* (Munich: K.G. Saur, 1980), pp. 519–521, No. 84, 14 July 1941; pp. 539–542, No. 95, 21 July 1941.

13 J. Erickson, *The Road to Stalingrad: Stalin's War with Germany. Volume 1* (London: Weidenfeld and Nicolson, 1983), pp. 97–98.

14 I. Kershaw, *The Hitler Myth: Image and Reality in the Third Reich* (Oxford: Oxford University Press, 1987), p. 173; Baird, *The Mythical World*, pp. 148–151.

15 BAB, R22/3375, p. 85, 5 July 1941.

16 Ibid., p. 83, 23 June 1941.

17 Ibid.

18 Gause, *Die Geschichte der Stadt Königsberg*, p. 157.

19 BAB, R22/3375, pp. 85–86, 5 July 1941; GStA, NSDAP Gauarchiv Ostpreußen Rep. 240 D/119 contains an album of photographs of the damage and the dead in their coffins. Photographs of the damage in Königsberg and Gumbinnen are reproduced in Tilitzki, *Alltag in Ostpreußen*, pp. 85–86.

20 F. Taylor (ed.), *The Goebbels Diaries 1939–1941* (London: Hamish Hamilton, 1982), pp. 426–430, 23, 24 and 26 June 1941.

21 BAB, R22/3375, p. 86, 5 July 1941.

22 Murawski, *Die Eroberung Pommerns*, p. 21.

23 Tilitzki, *Alltag in Ostpreußen*, p. 8.

24 P. Hoffmann, *Hitler's Personal Security* (London: Macmillan, 1979), pp. 216–257; Dieckert and Großmann, *Der Kampf um Ostpreußen*, pp. 36–40; Kossert, *Ostpreussen*, pp. 304–305; *Das Ostpreußenblatt*, 27 March 1965.

25 Gause, *Die Geschichte der Stadt Königsberg*, p. 157. See, for instance, the plans for Pomerania discussed in BA-LA, Ost-Dok. 10/504.

26 Kossert, *Ostpreussen*, p. 301.

27 Racial categorisation came under the *Deutsche Volksliste* (DVL, German Ethnic Register). This was a method of racial selection administered by the SS on physical, racial and sociological grounds. By late 1942 the authorities in Zichenau claimed that their district was *judenrein*. This was mainly achieved by deportations to the *General Gouvernement*. Population figures for 1943 list 823,000 Poles, 21,500 *Reichsdeutsche*, 33,240 *Volksdeutsche* and 2,260 *Baltikdeutsche* (resettled Germans from the Baltic States). See J. Grabowski and Z.R. Grabowski, 'Germans in the Eyes of the Gestapo: The Ciechanow District, 1939–1945,' *Contemporary European History*, Volume 13, Number 1, 2004, pp. 21–43, p. 27 for these figures.

28 Tilitzki, *Alltag in Ostpreußen*, pp. 43–45. For photographs of this activity see GStA, NSDAP Gauarchiv Ostpreußen, Rep. 240D/110 Karton. See also E. Harvey, '"We Forgot All Jews and Poles": German Women and the "Ethnic Struggle" in Nazi-occupied Poland,' *Contemporary European History*, Volume 10, Number 3, 2001, pp. 447–461.

29 Greiser's rhetoric remained unchanged as the war turned decisively against Germany. At the annual conference of the *Volksbund für das Deutschtum im Ausland* held in Posen in January 1944, it was reported that '*Gauleiter* Greiser pledged himself to an uncompromising racial policy for the safeguarding of the regained German living-space.' TNA, FO 898/186, 31 January 1944, p. A5 quoting *Deutsches Nachrichten Bureau* report of 24 January 1944.

30 J. Noakes and G. Pridham (eds.), *Nazism 1919–1945: Volume 3, Foreign Policy, War and Racial Extermination* (Exeter: University of Exeter Press, 1991), p. 1055.

31 Tilitzki, *Alltag in Ostpreußen*, pp. 45–47. On conditions in Zichenau see also Grabowski and Grabowski, 'Germans in the Eyes of the Gestapo', pp. 21–43.

32 Ibid., pp. 48–50; <www.deathcamps.org/occupation/bialystok>, 12 May 2004.

33 BAB, Akte Koch, Lebenslauf, p. 3; p. 15, quoting *Völkischer Beobachter* (hereafter *VB*), 17 November 1941.
34 BAB, Akte Koch, Lebenslauf, p. 3.
35 BA-LA, Ost-Dok. 8/524, p. 6; Gause, *Die Geschichte der Stadt Königsberg*, p. 137; Kater, *The Nazi Party*, p. 210.
36 Kater, *The Nazi Party*, p. 225.
37 BA-LA, Ost-Dok. 8/524, pp. 6–7. Koch seized Tsuman because he required a forest for his guests to hunt when they came to Rowno. The sudden and brutal eviction of the local peasantry, camouflaged under the guise of an anti-partisan operation, is outlined in Reitlinger, *The House Built on Sand*, pp. 207–209.
38 Tilitzki, *Alltag in Ostpreußen*, pp. 48–49; Kossert, *Ostpreussen*, p. 302. Gerhard Pannenborg, *Landrat* of Mohrungen was Deputy *Reichskommissar*. Prominent East Prussian officials occupied three out of the ten *Generalkommissar* posts and many of the *Stadtkommissar* jobs. *Oberbürgermeister* Hellmuth Will of Königsberg was *Stadtkommissar* for Kiev.
39 See K. Sword (ed.), *The Soviet Takeover of the Polish Eastern Provinces 1939–41* (Basingstoke: Macmillan, 1991).
40 M. Burleigh, *Ethics and Extermination: Reflections on Nazi Genocide* (Cambridge: Cambridge University Press, 1997), p. 46.
41 Reitlinger, *The House Built on Sand*, p. 183.
42 Burleigh, *Ethics and Extermination*, p. 83; A. Bullock, *Hitler: A Study in Tyranny* (Harmondsworth, Middlesex: Pelican, 1963), p. 692.
43 Quoted in B. Krawchenk 'Soviet Ukraine under Nazi Occupation, 1941–4', in Y. Boshyk (ed.), *Ukraine during World War II History and its Aftermath* (Edmonton: Canadian Institute of Ukrainian Studies, 1986), p. 24.
44 G. Böddeker, *Die Vertreibung der Deutschen im Osten* (Munich: F.A. Herbig Verlagsbuchhandlung, 1980), p. 13.
45 Reitlinger, *The House Built on Sand*, pp. 194, 202, 205–206.
46 BAB, Akte Koch, Koch to Hitler, 6 July 1943; Burleigh, *Ethics and Extermination*, p. 83. See also Ciechanowski ed., *Intelligence Co-operation between Poland and Great Britain*, p. 840, Memorandum for the Record by the Chief of the Intelligence Department of the II Bureau of Polish General Staff, 17 January 1946 notes an American evaluation of a Polish report in January 1943: 'According to Koch, the 4000th train carrying food from Ukraine arrived in Germany in the beginning of January. He does not specify the amount of particular food items carried in [the] particular period of time.'
47 E. Fröhlich ed., *Die Tagebücher von Joseph Goebbels. Teil II Diktate 1941–1945. Band 11 Januar–März 1944* (Munich: K.G. Saur, 1994) (Hereinafter *TBJG 11*), p. 81, 13 January 1944; Speer, *Inside the Third Reich*, p. 329.
48 Prior to the launch of Barbarossa, Rosenberg had suggested Koch as the governor of a 'rump Russia' including Moscow and Leningrad. However, when the Nazi leadership met on Hitler's special train at Angerburg, East Prussia on 16 July 1941 to discuss the conduct of the war in the East, Rosenberg made clear his opposition to Koch governing either the Baltic States or Ukraine. Despite this objection, Hitler still decided to send Koch to the Ukraine. See Reitlinger, *The House Built on Sand*, pp. 136–137; 141–142.
49 BAB, Akte Koch, Rosenberg to Lammers (*Reichskanzlei*), 31 March 1943.
50 H. Heiber (ed.), *Hitlers Lagebesprechungen. Die Protokollfragmente seiner militärischen Konferenzen 1942–1945* (Stuttgart: Deutsche Verlags-Anstalt, 1962), p. 257. Reitlinger, *The House Built on Sand*, pp. 209–210.

51 Reitlinger, *The House Built on Sand*, p. 213.
52 W. Warlimont, *Im Hauptquartier der deutschen Wehrmacht 1939–1945. Grundlagen. Formen. Gestalten* (Munich: Bernard and Graefe Verlag, 1978 edition), p. 399, note 18; Speer, *Inside the Third Reich*, p. 371 note.
53 Burleigh, *Ethics and Extermination*, p. 80.
54 BAB, Akte Koch, Georg Elbrecht, *SS Gruppenführer und Generalleutnant der Polizei* Königsberg to Richard Hildebrandt, *SS Obergruppenführer und General der Polizei Danzig*, 26 May 1944.
55 TNA, FO 898/186, 10 January 1944, p. C1, quoting *Preussische Zeitung* (hereafter *PZ*), 20 December 1943.
56 Ibid., 31 January 1944, pp. A5–A6, quoting *Deutsche Ukraine–Zeitung*, 5 January 1944.
57 BA-LA, Ost-Dok. 8/645, pp. 4–8; Murawski, *Die Eroberung Pommerns*, pp. 23–24.
58 Murawski, *Die Eroberung Pommerns*, pp. 28–30.
59 P. Hüttenberger, *Die Gauleiter: Studie zum Wandel des Machtgefüges in der NSDAP* (Stuttgart: Deutsches Verlags-Anstalt, 1969), p. 176; Orlow, *History of the Nazi Party*, pp. 357–358.
60 Heiber ed., *Hitlers Lagebesprechungen*, p. 479, conference of 27 December 1943.
61 Hüttenberger, *Die Gauleiter*, p. 199. The job went to Paul Giesler, brother of Hitler's court architect, Hermann. Adolf Wagner died in April 1944, see *The Times*, 18 April 1944.
62 BAB, R22/13177, p. 190, Schwede-Coburg to Bormann, 23 October 1942 quoted in R.J. Evans, *Rituals of Retribution: Capital Punishment in Germany 1600–1987* (Oxford: Oxford University Press, 1996), p. 718.
63 Orlow, *The History of the Nazi Party*, p. 437.
64 Murawski, *Die Eroberung Pommerns*, p. 30.
65 TNA, FO 898/186, 25 October 1943, p. C2, quoting *Pommersche Zeitung* (hereafter *PomZ*), 15 October 1943.
66 BA-LA, Ost-Dok. 8/725, p. 2; 8/730, pp. 8–15; U. von Hassell, *The von Hassell Diaries 1938–1944* (London: Hamish Hamilton, 1948), pp. 179–180, 22 May 1941; Siebel-Achenbach, *Lower Silesia*, p. 21.
67 Speer, *Inside the Third Reich*, p. 306; Siebel-Achenbach, *Lower Silesia*, p. 21; Orlow, *The History of the Nazi Party*, p. 378. See Rebentisch, *Führerstaat und Verwaltung*, p. 356 for a summary of Sauckel's suitability for the job.
68 M. Domarus, *Hitler Reden und Proklamationen 1932–1945. Band II Untergang. Zweiter Halbband 1941–1945* (Munich: Suddeutscher Verlag, 1965), p. 1929.
69 *TBJG 11*, p. 391, 4 March 1944; p. 435, 8 March 1944; p. 442, 9 March 1944.
70 Hinrich Lohse, *Gauleiter* of Schleswig–Holstein and *Reichskommissar* Ostland (which largely consisted of the former Baltic States), 1941–1944.
71 Domarus, *Hitler Reden und Proklamationen*, pp. 2060–2062; E. Fröhlich (ed.), *Die Tagebücher von Joseph Goebbels. Teil II Diktate 1941–1945. Band 10 Oktober–Dezember 1943* (Munich: K.G Saur, 1994), p. 325, 20 November 1943; p. 334, 22 November 1943.
72 On Magda's illness which required her to undergo a complex operation on her jaw in Breslau in July 1944, the speech and the apparently favourable response to it see E. Fröhlich ed., *Die Tagebücher von Joseph Goebbels. Teil II Diktate 1941–1945. Band 13 Juli–September 1944* (Munich: K.G. Saur, 1995) (Hereinafter *TBJG 13*), p. 47, 3 July 1944; pp. 60–61, 7 July 1944; pp. 67–68, 8 July 1944; pp. 70, 79, 9 July 1944; p. 114, 14 July 1944. See also BAB, R22/3358, pp. 79–80, 1 August 1944; BAB, R55/601, pp. 39–40, 10 July 1944; Hanke married the wealthy society divorcee Freda Baroness von Fricks in November

1944. She had borne him a daughter the previous December. See D. Irving, *Goebbels: Mastermind of the Third Reich* (London: Focal Point Publications, 1996), pp. 467–468, 674 note 34.

Chapter 3 Enjoy the War, the Peace will be Dire

1 Schieder (ed.), *Expulsion Documents*, pp. 2, 6.

2 Noakes and Pridham (eds.), *Nazism 1919–1945. Volume 3,* p. 909; J. Noakes, 'Germany', in J. Noakes (ed.), *The Civilian in War: The Home Front in Europe, Japan and the United States in World War II* (Exeter: University of Exeter Press, 1992), pp. 35–61.

3 Hüttenberger, *Die Gauleiter*, p. 169.

4 O. Groehler, *Bombenkrieg gegen Deutschland* (Berlin: Akademie Verlag, 1990), pp. 264–265.

5 Hüttenberger, *Die Gauleiter*, pp. 169–170.

6 Around ten million air raid evacuees were scattered around Germany by the war's end. See Schieder (ed.), *Expulsion Documents*, p. 1.

7 Hüttenberger, *Die Gauleiter*, pp. 170–171.

8 Schieder (ed.), *Expulsion Documents*, p. 4.

9 Groehler, *Bombenkrieg gegen Deutschland*, pp. 135, 275. See also *The Times*, 11 October 1943. Nevertheless, the *Pommersche Zeitung* reported on 10 October 1943 that, 'As far as can be ascertained so far, none of the Stettin children evacuated to Anklam have been injured.' Quoted in TNA, FO 898/186, 25 October 1943, p. C6.

10 Tilitzki, *Alltag in Ostpreußen*, p. 91.

11 I. Kershaw, *Popular Opinion and Political Dissent in the Third Reich: Bavaria 1933–1945* (Oxford: Oxford University Press, 1983), p. 291.

12 BAB, R58/187, p. 7, report from Frankfurt an der Oder, 3 August 1943.

13 Ibid., p. 21, 5 August 1943.

14 BLHA, Pr. Br. Rep. 3B, I Pol. No. 1974, *Landrat* Königsberg/Neumark to *Regierungspräsident* Frankfurt an der Oder, 2 December 1943. By early January 1945, some 37,000 evacuees would be quartered in Königsberg/Neumark, 27,000 from Berlin alone. See January 1945, No. 1–22 *Landrat* Königsberg/Neumark to *Regierungspräsident* Frankfurt an der Oder, 4 January 1945.

15 BLHA, Pr. Br. Rep. 3B, I Pol. No. 1974, December 1943, p. 17, *Landrat* Züllichau to *Regierungspräsident* Frankfurt an der Oder, 10 December 1943.

16 Ibid., December 1943, p. 22, *Oberbürgermeister* Landsberg an der Warthe to *Regierungspräsident* Frankfurt an der Oder, 4 December 1943; January 1945, p. 22, *Oberbürgermeister* Landsberg an der Warthe to *Regierungspräsident* Frankfurt an der Oder, 3 January 1945.

17 Ibid., *Regierungsbezirk* Frankfurt an der Oder, December 1944.

18 BA-LA, Ost-Dok. 10/527, p. 47; 10/541, p. 27.

19 TNA, FO 371/34553, C 12217/G, reports of 28 September and 1 October 1943. Nevertheless, the somewhat basic conditions facing Hamburgers in Danzig–West Prussia were explained by *Gauleiter* Forster in the press. He admitted that, 'it is not easy for people from large towns to adapt themselves overnight to life in a lonely village' but added that 'especially in the liberated parts of our *Gau*, certain preconditions of civilisation such as are taken for granted in large towns are lacking owing to many years of Polish mismanagement.' TNA, FO 898/186, p. C8, report of 13 September 1943, quoting *Danziger Vorposten*, 22 August 1943.

20 BAB, NS6/411, pp. 63–64, 30 August 1943.

21 D. Irving, *The Destruction of Dresden* (London: Corgi Books edition, 1971), p. 75.
22 On new industry see BA-LA, Ost-Dok. 8/721, pp. 34–35; 8/729, p. 2; 8/731, p. 3; 8/734, pp. 3–4; 8/734b, p. 13; 10/607, p. 5; 10/624, p. 47; 10/633, p. 15; 10/634, Bauer testimony, p. 1; 10/644, p. 5; 10/652, p. 47; 10/659, p. 3; 10/670, p. 11; 10/677, p. 11.
23 BAB, R22/3358, p. 69, 27 September 1943; p. 71, 1 December 1943. Local newspapers in western Germany also had to advise their readers on the location of Lower Silesia. Many mothers in Cologne were said to be still blocking the evacuation of their children to Lower Silesia in January 1944 and were reminded that this was 'a *Gau* which, quite wrongly, is often regarded as being situated "almost in Poland"'. TNA, FO 898/186, 14–20 February 1944, p. C7 quoting *Westdeutscher Beobachter*, Cologne, 15 January 1944.
24 BA-LA, Ost-Dok. 10/677, p. 12. Even for locals, life amidst the harrowing war news and everyday shortages was only made more tolerable by the escapism provided by cinema. Pandemonium ensued when the first performances of new films were screened at Breslau's cinemas at weekends. Crowds pushed and jostled for tickets, adults argued, children screamed and some patrons tried to bribe attendants to gain entry. Young women were accused of going to see the same film on four occasions within a fortnight. TNA, FO 898/186, 20 December 1943, p. C7, quoting *ST*, 26 November 1943.
25 BA-LA, Ost-Dok. 10/633, p. 15. Following a visit by Werner Naumann, State Secretary at the Propaganda Ministry, to his native Silesia, Goebbels, somewhat biased as *Gauleiter* of Berlin, noted that Silesians preferred ten Berlin evacuees to one from Cologne. See Fröhlich ed., *TBJG 11*, pp. 220–221, 2 February 1944.
26 BA-LA, Ost-Dok. 10/633, p. 15. An article in the *Deutsche Allgemeine Zeitung* of 10 May 1944 covered the reception in Lower Silesia of expectant mothers and mothers with young children from Berlin. About 2,000 women had been involved so far and the 1,200th Berlin child to be born in the *Gau* was expected shortly. The same newspaper reported on 30 May 1944 that 8,000 Special Emergency Houses had been built in Lower Silesia and most had been offered to Berliners. A further 12,000 flats were also being built in the *Gau* and it was envisaged that most of these would go to evacuated Berliners too. See TNA, FO 898/187, 22 January 1945, p. C3.
27 BA-LA, Ost-Dok. 10/425. See endpaper for list of evacuated schools.
28 BA-LA, Ost-Dok. 10/375, p. 12; 10/377, p. 13; 10/402, p. 21; 10/414, testimony of Karl Wetzel, p. 3.
29 BAB, R22/3386, p. 56, 29 September 1943.
30 BAB, R22/3375, pp. 224–225, 28 September 1943.
31 Ibid., p. 225.
32 Ibid.
33 BAB, R22/3375, p. 230, 29 November 1943. However, even Party members in East Prussia were failing to use the Hitler salute. *Kreisleiter* Ernst Wagner of Königsberg was quoted in the *Preussische Zeitung* on 7 March 1944: 'The Heil Hitler salute must be considered a profession of faith and an obligation – Party members must be fighters, just as in the *Kampfzeit*.' See TNA, FO 898/186, 20 March 1944, p. C4, quoting *PZ*, 7 March 1944.
34 Königsberg radio said on 24 December 1943 that more farmers would be called up in 1944 but insisted that 'our many visitors from the bomb-damaged districts have in the meantime settled in nicely, and no women will refuse to help if the future of the Fatherland is at stake.' TNA, FO 898/186, 20–26 December 1943, p. A3.
35 BAB, R22/3375, p. 239, 26 January 1944; R58/189, pp. 43–48, 10 October 1943.
36 TNA, FO 898/186, 1 May 1944, p. C9 quoting *KAZ*, 15 April 1944.

37 BAB, R58/188, p. 7, 9 September 1943.
38 Ibid., pp. 7–8.
39 TNA, FO 898/186, 3 October 1943, p. C5.
40 BAB, R58/188, p. 9, 9 September 1943.
41 BLHA, Pr. Br. Rep. 55I, No. 2643.
42 Ibid., reports dated 10 January, 3 February 1944.
43 Ibid.
44 Ibid., 3 February 1944.
45 Ibid., 5 April 1944.
46 BAB, R58/188, pp. 122–126, 20 September 1943.
47 BA-LA, Ost-Dok. 10/529, p. 23.
48 BAB, R58/188, p. 127, 20 September 1943.
49 BAB, R58/192, pp. 141–150, 6 January 1944.
50 BLHA, Pr. Br. Rep. 551, No. 2643, 10 January 1944. TNA, FO 898/186, 20 December 1943, p. C10, quoting *PomZ*, 30 November 1943. Stettiners were reported to have returned to their home city in late 1943 for the distribution of special food rations and because insufficient coal for heating was available in rural districts. The *Pommersche Zeitung* carried the banner headline 'Urgent appeal. Take Evacuation Seriously'.
51 BLHA, Pr. Br. Rep. 551, No. 2643, 5 April 1944.
52 BAB, R58/190, p. 33, 29 November 1943.
53 Ibid., p. 136, 11 November, 1943.
54 Ibid. A few months later it was reported that evacuees from Breslau were particularly keen on taking any stores of potatoes with them to the countryside as they could purchase no more at their new residences because their ration card was already exhausted. TNA, FO 898/186, 28 March 1944, p. C11.
55 BAB, R22/3358, p. 70, 1 December 1943. Report by the OLG President Breslau. In February 1944 Breslau's restaurants had their allocation of potatoes cut and rye bread replaced potatoes in standard meals. See TNA, FO 898/186, 6 March 1944, p. A11, quoting *Breslauer Neueste Nachrichten*, 10 February 1944, 14 February 1944.
56 BA-LA, Ost-Dok. 8/694, p. 2.
57 BAB, R22/3386, p. 56, 29 September 1943.
58 BAB, R58/190, p. 138, 11 November 1943.
59 BAB, R22/3375, p. 243, 26 January 1944. *Landesbauernführer* Spickschen of East Prussia had already warned in the *Preussische Zeitung* on 3 October 1943 that 'The diet must increasingly be directed to vegetable foods.' TNA, FO 898/186, report of 18 October 1943, p. C5.
60 BAB, R22/3375, p. 244, 26 January 1944.
61 TNA, FO 898/186, 14–20 February 1944, p. C4, quoting *Ostsee Zeitung, Stettiner General Anzeiger*, 2 February 1944.
62 H. Gerhardi, *Helga* (Aylesbury: Virona, 1993), pp. 149–151.
63 See BA-LA, Ost-Dok. 8/694, p. 2 for instances of this in Schönlanke, Pomerania.
64 For a concise summary of the debate considering the motivations for the brutal treatment of forced labour see U. Herbert, 'Labour and Extermination: Economic Interest and the Primacy of *Weltanschauung* in National Socialism', *Past and Present,* Number 138, 1993, pp. 144–195. A fuller treatment is provided by U. Herbert, *Hitler's Foreign Workers: Enforced Labour in Germany Under the Third Reich* (Cambridge: Cambridge University Press, 1997). In comparison the British and American death rate in German captivity was 3.5%.

However, correspondingly horrendous is the fact that of 3,155,000 Germans captured by the Soviets, 1,185,000 (37.5%) died in captivity.

65 Herbert, 'Labour and Extermination', *Past and Present*, pp. 180–181.
66 BA-LA, Ost-Dok. 8/716, p. 7; 10/539, p. 21; 8/702, p. 10.
67 C. von Krockow, *Hour of the Women* (London: Faber and Faber, 1992), p. 9.
68 BA-LA, Ost-Dok. 10/415, p. 30.
69 BA-LA, Ost-Dok. 10/375, pp. 11–12.
70 BA-LA, Ost-Dok. 10/633, p. 15; 10/562, p. 47.
71 BA-LA, Ost-Dok. 10/607, testimony of Erich Bleul, p. 5.
72 BA-LA, Ost-Dok. 10/629, pp. 33–35.
73 BA-LA, Ost-Dok. 8/731, p. 3.
74 BA-LA, Ost-Dok. 8/735, p. 2.
75 BA-LA, Ost-Dok. 10/652, p. 47; BAB, R22/3358, p. 70, 1 December 1943.
76 BAB, R22/3358, p. 75, 3 April 1944; p. 77, 27 May 1944.
77 BAB, R22/3386, p. 56, 29 September 1943.
78 Ibid., pp. 70–71, 1 December 1943. See also Herbert, *Hitler's Foreign Workers*, p. 269.
79 BAB, R22/3386, p. 80, 1 August 1944.
80 BAB, R22/3375, pp. 211–212, 29 May 1943. Over 4,400 Polish officers were executed by the NKVD and buried at Katyn near Smolensk in April 1940. In total more than 20,000 Polish servicemen were murdered by the NKVD in 1940 and their bodies were dumped in mass graves in Russia and Ukraine. See FCO Historians, *FCO History Note No 16 Katyn: British Reactions to the Katyn Massacre 1943–2003* (London; FCO Historians, 2003).
81 GStA, Rep. 240 52a, pp. 46–51 and 52c for funeral photographs; Tilitzki, *Alltag in Ostpreußen*, p. 63. Polish bands and units of the Home Army were also active on the fringes of Pomerania. See BAB, R22/3386, p. 58, 31 January 1944; pp. 59–60, 30 May 1944; BA-LA, Ost-Dok. 8/648, p. 2.
82 BAB, R22/3375, pp. 253–254, 29 March 1944.
83 Ibid., p. 218, 27 June 1943; p. 228, 28 September 1943. From the early part of the war official rhetoric had urged caution in dealing with Western POWs. Dr Fritz Stumpf of Nuremberg had written in the *Württembergische Wirtschafts-Zeitschrift* on 12 August 1940 that in dealing with POWs 'strictness and justice, caution and reserve must be observed'. He added that the POW while in confinement 'remains Germany's enemy' and 'to disregard him is the best way of dealing with him. He who seeks association with prisoners of war or even cultivates it, is giving offence and loses honor (sic) and respect.' See TNA, FO 916/34.
84 BAB, R22/3375, pp. 239–240, 26 January 1944.
85 Ibid., p. 240, 26 January 1944.
86 Herbert, *Hitler's Foreign Workers*, pp. 131–132, 190, 269.
87 BAB, R22/3375, p. 241, 26 January 1944.
88 BAB, R55/600, pp. 171–172 Wagner (RPA Königsberg) to RMVuP, 19 May 1944; p. 173, Schäffer (RMVuP) to RPA Königsberg, 1 July 1944.
89 BAB, R58/188, pp. 81–86, 2 September 1943.
90 Ibid., p. 86.
91 BAB, R58/193, p. 14, 6 April 1944.
92 BAB, R22/3375, p. 241, 26 January 1944.
93 BAB, R58/189, p. 76, 7 October 1943.

94 BAB, R58/192, p. 124, 21 February 1944.
95 Royal Institute of International Affairs, *Review of the Foreign Press 1939–1945. Series A. Volume IX. Enemy Countries: Axis – controlled Europe* (Munich: K.G. Saur, 1980), Memorandum No. 253, p. 4, 28 November 1944.
96 BAB, NS6/352, pp. 25–26, 11 October 1944.
97 J. Stephenson, 'Triangle: Foreign Workers, German Civilians, and the Nazi Regime. War and Society in Württemberg, 1939–1945', *German Studies Review*, Volume 15, 1992, pp. 339–359.
98 See chapter two.
99 On the bombing of Breslau see BAB, NS1/579, pp. 290, 293, 297, 302; TNA, HW1/221, Instructions to *Luftflotte IV* following surprise daylight air raids by the Soviets on Breslau and Warsaw, dated 16 November 1941; Siebel-Achenbach, *Lower Silesia*, p. 23, incorrectly attributes the attack to the British. Eight bombs were dropped on Breslau on the morning of 13 October 1941. Ten inhabitants were killed and 30 were wounded but property damage was minor. For a summary of Soviet raids during 1941–1942 see Groehler, *Bombenkrieg gegen Deutschland*, pp. 161–166. A lone Soviet plane had dropped bombs on Ratshof railway station in the north of Königsberg in November 1941 and there were similar small raids on Königsberg in July, August and September 1942. BAB, NS1/579, pp. 296, 299, messages of Deputy *Gauleiter* Großherr, 14 November 1941. *The Times*, 21 July 1942; 23 July 1942; 27 July 1942; 20 August 1942; 28 August 1942; 31 August 1942; 11 September 1942; 15 September 1942. Tilitzki, *Alltag in Ostpreußen*, p. 215, quoting OLG President Dräger's report of 3 September 1942.
100 Groehler, *Bombenkrieg gegen Deutschland*, p. 167.
101 BAB, NS1/274, p. 195; R22/3375, p. 210, 29 May 1943; BA-MA, RW20-1/14, p. 11; K. Mehner (ed.), *Die Geheimen Tagesberichte der Deutschen Wehrmachtführung im Zweiten Weltkrieg 1939–1945. Band 6. 1. Dezember 1942–31. Mai 1943* (Osnabrück: Biblio Verlag, 1989), p. 326. For photographs of the damage see GStA, Rep. 240ED No.116 box.
102 BAB, NS1/274, p. 185; BA-MA, RW20-1/14, p. 11; BAB, R22/3375, p. 210, 29 May 1943; BA-LA, Ost-Dok. 8/583, pp. 2–3; 8/585, p. 4; Mehner ed., *Die Geheimen Tagesberichte. Band* 6, p. 347; Tilitzki, *Alltag in Ostpreußen*, pp. 89–90.
103 BAB, R22/3375, p. 210, 29 May 1943.
104 Groehler, *Bombenkrieg gegen Deutschland*, p. 167.
105 BAB, R22/3375, p. 210, 29 May 1943.
106 RAF reconnaissance over eastern Germany was particularly interested in shipbuilding and U-Boat activity at Stettin, Danzig, Gotenhafen (Gdynia) and Elbing in West Prussia. A high level of activity was always observed at the Schichau Werft in Elbing, a construction yard for destroyers, but this potential target was never attacked by Bomber Command. The RAF photographed Königsberg on 3 March 1942 when 'very extensive workshops' undertaking repairs and refits were observed at the Schichau shipyard. See TNA, AIR 34/611, Interpretation Report A77, 3 March 1942. Further reconnaissance in early 1944 noted the presence of the cruisers *Seydlitz* and *Köln* in Königsberg harbour but further reporting also came to the misleading conclusion that the photographs provided 'further evidence of the abandonment of the German U-Boat building programme'. See AIR 34/611, Interpretation Report No. 5910, 22 February 1944; Interpretation Report No. 6136, 17 April 1944. U-Boat deliveries actually peaked in December 1944. The Schichau yard at Danzig became a major centre for the production of the new Type XXI vessel in the autumn of 1944 and submarine activities became an air attack priority for the

Americans in November 1944. On information provided by Polish underground intelligence on German ports, shipyards and naval movements in the eastern provinces see A. Peplonski, T. Dubicki and R. Majzner, 'Naval Intelligence: Movement of Ships, Surveillance of Ports and Shipyards', in T. Stirling, D. Nalecz and T. Dubicki (eds.), *Intelligence Co-Operation Between Poland and Great Britain during World War II: Volume I: The Report of the Anglo-Polish Historical Committee* (London: Vallentine Mitchell, 2005), pp. 490–500.

107 C. Webster and N. Frankland, *The Strategic Air Offensive Against Germany. Volume 1* (London: HMSO, 1961), p. 444; M. Middlebrook and C. Everitt, *The Bomber Command War Diaries: An Operational Reference Book 1939–1945* (London: Penguin Books edition, 1990), p. 285; C. Tighe, *Gdansk: National Identity in the Polish-German Borderlands* (London: Pluto Press, 1990), pp. 178–179.

108 Middlebrook and Everitt, *The Bomber Command War Diaries*, p. 303. Launched at Kiel in 1938, the *Graf Zeppelin* never saw service as an aircraft carrier. Scuttled off Stettin in shallow water in 1945, it was re-floated by the Soviets and used to carry looted factory equipment back to Russia. In 1947, it was used as target practice for Red Air Force dive bombers and went to the bottom of the Baltic off Leba (Gulf of Gdansk). The wreck was only discovered by divers in 2006. See also TNA, AIR 34/612; *The Times*, 27 July 2006. No. 5 Group of Bomber Command also attacked Gotenhafen on the evening of 18–19 December 1944 with 236 Lancasters (four lost). There was damage to shipping, installations and housing in the port area, Middlebrook and Everitt, *The Bomber Command War Diaries*, p. 634.

109 Middlebrook and Everitt, *The Bomber Command War Diaries*, pp. 204–207. See also *The Times*, 6 September 1940; 4 October 1940; 16 October 1940; 20 November 1940; 14 August 1941.

110 BAB, NS1/274, p. 187; BAB, NS1/585, p. 8 initial reports submitted to the Party authorities in Munich. BA-LA, Ost-Dok. 8/636, pp. 1–15 the post-war report of the Police President of Stettin. BA-MA, RW 20-2/4, p. 16; BA-MA, RW 20-2/6, pp. 24–25; BA-MA, RW 21-56/1, p. 16; BA-MA, RW 21-56/2, p. 5 detail the damage in the armaments inspection and armaments command war diaries. Mehner ed., *Die Geheimen Tagesberichte. Band* 6, p. 347; *Band* 9, p. 176. Webster and Frankland, *The Strategic Air Offensive. Volume II. Endeavour. Part* 4, pp. 133, 200; Middlebrook and Everitt, *The Bomber Command War Diaries*, pp. 380, 464.

111 BA-MA, RW 20-2/4, p. 16.

112 BA-MA, RW 21-56/1, pp. 25–26. Similarly, a report sent to the German Air Attaché in Bucharest on 21 April 1943, which was intercepted by British codebreakers, noted: 'Concentrated attack on Stettin: no damage to the important industries. Considerable damage to dwelling houses.' TNA, HW 1/1628.

113 TNA, AIR 14/3779, Headquarters Bomber Command, Stettin: Immediate Assessment of Results (Collation of information received up to 19.1.44).

114 Ibid.

115 BA-LA, Ost-Dok. 8/636, pp. 12–13.

116 BA-MA, RW 21-56/2, p. 5; Mehner ed., *Die Geheimen Tagesberichte. Band* 9, p. 176.

117 BA-MA, RW 20-2/6, pp. 24–25.

118 Ibid.; Mehner (ed.), *Die Geheimen Tagesberichte. Band* 9, p. 176. British reports mention that 358 aircraft were despatched and 332 claimed to have participated in the attack. They dropped 1,100 tons of bombs on Stettin on the night of 5–6 January 1944. Some 20% or

224 tons fell on the heavily built-up administrative areas with the heaviest density falling on the area south of the city centre. About 6% of the city's buildings were badly damaged, including 4% of industrial premises. The impact on industry was said to be equivalent to the loss of labour of 40,000 workers for one month. The damage extended across to the West and East basins of the dock area where quayside warehouses were gutted. The main railway station was said to be '75% gutted' and the Baltischen Rubenzucker-Fabriken sugar refinery and the cement warehouses of the Pommerscher Industrie-Verein were heavily damaged. See TNA, AIR 14/3779, Immediate Interpretation Report No. K.1845, 16 January 1944; Interpretation Report No. K.1845, 19 January 1944; Ministry of Home Security, Research and Experiments Department, Preliminary Attack Assessment – Stettin, Attack of 5/6 January 1944. Bomber Command's assessment noted that 'it was the town itself that received most of the damage' and the impact on the business and commercial centre would have 'the greatest effect in throwing out of gear the civic life of the town'. The assessment stressed Stettin's continued importance as a port and mentioned that there had been little reduction in the tonnage of shipping. Further raids were likely in view of the city's significance and the 'relatively light damage it had received so far'. See AIR 14/3779, Headquarters Bomber Command, Stettin: Immediate Assessment of Results (Collation of information received up to 19.1.44).

119 BfZ, SSt Feldpost 1944/1, Senior Womens Leader E.S., 7 January 1944.

120 BAB, R22/3386, p. 58, 31 January 1944.

121 Ibid., pp. 54–55, 31 May 1943.

122 Ibid., p. 58, 31 January 1944. Police President Grundey was also quoted in the *Pommersche Zeitung* on 22 February 1944 announcing that, 'There is reason to urge all those who have salvaged or received articles belonging to other people since the last attack to surrender them immediately.' TNA, FO 898/186, 6 March 1944, p. C5.

123 BA-LA, Ost-Dok. 8/636, pp. 15–16. Reconnaissance reports highlighted the damage to the Stettiner Vulcan-Werft shipbuilders and to buildings at the Admiralty Base, as well as some damage to shipping caused by the 11 April 1944 raid. See TNA, AIR 14/3779, Immediate Interpretation Report No. K.2013, 14 April 1944; Interpretation Report No. K.2013, 17 April 1944. Excellent quality prints of the 13 May raid showed damage to buildings, workshops and storage sheds at the Vulcan-Werft as well as some damage to the Oderwerke, the naval base and to oil storage installations on the Dunzig waterfront. See AIR 14/3779, Immediate Interpretation Report No. K.2216, 23 May 1944.

124 BAB, R22/3386, p. 59, 30 May 1944.

125 BfZ, SSt Feldpost 1944/4, R.S., 19 April 1944.

126 BAB, NS1/274, p. 79; NS1/585, pp. 46–47; Mehner (ed.), *Die Geheimen Tagesberichte. Band 8*, p. 214; *Band 10*, pp. 112, 238; Groehler, *Bombenkrieg gegen Deutschland*, pp. 134, 227; *The Times*, 29 May 1944. American planes also sunk the submarine hunter *UJ 1210* at its moorings in Gotenhafen's Alte Werft shipyard on 9 October 1943. See Peplonski, Dubicki and Majzner, 'Naval Intelligence' in Stirling, Nalecz and Dubicki (eds.), *Intelligence Co-Operation Between Poland and Great Britain during World War II: Volume I*, p. 497. The Marienburg Focke-Wulf assembly plant is the subject of Interpretation Report No. 5910 L/41 of 19 February 1944 and Interpretation Report No. KS 1570 of 18 December 1944 in TNA, AIR 34/612. In the latter report it was observed that, 'Of the intense activity seen at the plant, scarcely any seems to have been devoted to the reconstruction of buildings.' The sheer number of planes observed was highlighted: 'Great activity connected with FW 190 production is being maintained here. At least 76 FW 190s are visible, and the

apron outside the largest serviceable hangar is crowded with fighters. Groups of aircraft can also be seen outside several of the remaining buildings.'

127 BAB, NS1/585, p. 80, 22 June 1944. American shuttle bombing of Germany began on 2 June 1944. Bombers flew across Europe to the Soviet Union and back to the 15th Air Force bases in southern Italy. See also chapter four, footnote 16.

128 D. Welch, 'Goebbels, *Götterdämmerung* and the *Deutschen Wochenschauen*', in K.R.M. Short and S. Dolezel (eds.), *Hitler's Fall: The Newsreel Witness* (London: Croom Helm, 1988), pp. 88–89.

129 BAB, R58/188, p. 2, 2 September 1943.

130 BAB, NS6/411, p. 39, 22 July 1943.

131 Ibid., p. 84, 30 September 1943.

132 BAB, R58/189, p. 7, 14 October 1943.

133 BAB, NS6/411, p. 123, 17 December 1943.

134 BAB, NS6/411, p. 127, 14 January 1944.

135 Ibid., p. 145, 18 February 1944; R58/192, p. 17, 17 February 1944. There were frequent reports from returning soldiers on the concentration of strong forces in the Lemberg area and an enormous Panzer Army being on standby.

136 BAB, R58/193, p. 22, 20 April 1944.

137 BAB, NS6/411, p. 140, 11 February 1944; R22/3375, p. 249, 29 March 1944.

138 C. Bielenberg, *The Past is Myself* (London: Chatto and Windus, 1968), p. 117.

139 BfZ, SSt Feldpost, 1944/2, Sdf. W.B., 9 February 1944. While this threat of territorial losses would increase the will to resist, the fact that the Allies might soon have the power to carry out such plans was not to be stressed, TNA, FO 898/186, 17 January 1944, p. A9; 21–27 February 1944, p. A8. Nazi propagandists played down the threat. The *Pommersche Zeitung* noted in January 1944 the Soviets' 'generous' offer of East Prussia and Silesia to the Poles but maintained that such 'marginal events . . . have a purely theoretical value' and 'do not worry us'. TNA, FO 898/186, 31 January 1944, p. C1 quoting Buschmann, military correspondent of the *PomZ*, 16 January 1944. However, as late as the summer of 1944 there seemed to be a lack of understanding of the looming disaster among educated eastern German circles. This is relayed in the story told by Field Marshal von Manstein's adjutant, who recalled that his superior, dismissed by Hitler as commander of Army Group South on 30 March 1944, was searching for an estate in eastern Pomerania later that summer. Manstein, who had been exposed to the gravity of the military situation in the East, dismissed his adjutant's mutterings about the 'westward shift of Poland' with the retort, 'If Pomerania were lost, we were all lost'. Moreover, the adjutant noted that 'only failing enterprises were available, the owners of flourishing farms were not thinking of selling'. See A. Stahlberg, *Bounden Duty: The Memoirs of a German Officer 1932–1945* (London: Brassey's, 1990), pp. 368–369.

140 BAB, R58/187, p. 71, 26 August 1943.

141 BAB, R58/188, p. 30, 2 September 1943.

142 BAB, R58/192, p. 41, 13 January 1944, quoting *PomZ*, 5 January 1944.

143 BAB, R58/192, p. 63, 27 January 1944.

144 BAB, NS6/411, p. 145, 18 February 1944.

145 Ibid., p. 94, 24 February 1944. Buschmann, the military correspondent of the *Pommersche Zeitung* even admitted that terms such as 'retreat according to plan' and 'orderly evacuations' tended to 'get on many people's nerves in the long run'. TNA, FO 898/186, 18 October 1943, p. C2, quoting *PomZ*, 3 October 1943.

146 BAB, R58/188, p. 2, 2 September 1943.

147 Ibid., pp. 3–4, 6 September 1943. Problems behind German lines are detailed in R58/190, p. 6, 11 November 1943; p. 32, 29 November 1943; R58/192, p. 18, 17 February 1944.

148 BAB, R58/189, p. 5, 17 October 1943; R58/190, p. 32, 29 November 1943. German field post intercepted by the underground Polish Home Army was analysed by them and in September 1943 the *Wehrmacht* on the Eastern Front was said to display a 'complete lack of hope linked to this year's campaign in the East'. A.G. Dabrowski, 'Information on the Morale of the German Forces and the Civilian Population in Germany' in Stirling, Nalecz and Dubicki (eds.), *Intelligence Co-Operation Between Poland and Great Britain during World War II: Volume I*, pp. 532–534.

149 BAB, R58/190, pp. 4–6, 11 November 1943.

150 BAB, R22/3375, p. 249, 29 March 1944.

151 BAB, R58/193, p. 23, 20 April 1944. In early 1944, one letter from the Eastern Front intercepted by the Polish Home Army, claimed that '90% of the German Army does not believe in victory – but wants peace at any price'. Dabrowski, 'Information on the Morale', p. 533. The spirit of soldiers on the Eastern Front was also sapped by news from home of heavy air raids on German cities leading to fears about the fate of family and friends back in the Reich.

152 BAB, NS6/411, p. 63, 30 August 1943.

153 BAB, R58/190, p. 6, 11 November 1943.

154 BAB, R58/188, p. 26, 30 September 1943.

155 BAB, R58/192, p. 85, 17 February 1944.

156 BAB, R58/187, p. 74, 30 August 1943.

157 BAB, NS6/411, p. 95, 22 October 1943.

158 BAB, NS6/411, p. 103, 15 October 1943.

159 Ibid., p. 107, 4 November 1943. The view that the Soviets were exerting 'continuous pressure' on Germany was expounded by Buschmann, the military correspondent of the *Pommersche Zeitung*. Buschmann said of the Soviet enemy, 'He is suffering enormous losses, and we are always reading that his attacks have slackened for days, but a few days later they flare up again in full force.' TNA, FO 898/186, 31 January 1944, pp. C2–3, quoting *PomZ*, 16 January 1944.

160 BAB, R58/189, p. 8, 14 October 1943.

161 BAB, NS6/411, p. 117, 3 December 1943.

162 BAB, R22/3375, p. 250, 29 March 1944; R58/193, p. 12, 6 April 1944.

163 BA-LA, Ost-Dok. 8/734b, p. 13.

164 BAB, R22/3358, p. 69, 28 September 1943. Breslau was viewed as dull by the visiting Foreign Ministry official Marie 'Missie' Vassiltchikov in March 1944: 'I found it a dreary town, although thus far it has been spared . . . [I] cast a rapid glance at the market-place and the cathedral, and then tried to have a bite at a local restaurant, but the fare was so poor that I gulped down some nondescript soup and sped back to the station.' M. Vassiltchikov, *The Berlin Diaries 1940–1945* (London: Pimlico edition, 1999), pp. 152–153, entry for 13 March 1944.

165 BAB, R22/3358, p. 76, 27 May 1944.

166 BAB, R22/3375, pp. 217–218, 27 July 1943; p. 224, 28 September 1943; NS6/411, p. 86, 1 October 1943.

167 The spectre of fighting in Germany itself was even raised by the military commentator of the *Pommersche Zeitung* in November 1943 in an attempt to counter weakening German

resolve: 'Much more territory may be lost in future, but, even if the war must be waged on German soil and even if ever so many towns were ruined and the scourge of war afflicted us ever so mercilessly, there cannot and must not arise the slightest thought of weakness.' TNA, FO 898/186, 15 November 1943, p. C1, quoting Buschmann in the *PomZ*, 9 November 1943.

168 Steinert, *Hitler's War*, pp. 194–195; Noakes, *Government, Party and People in Nazi Germany*, p. 30. To an accompanying propaganda fanfare, Total War was proclaimed by Goebbels at a mass rally in the Berlin Sportspalast on 18 February 1943. On impressions of this event 60 years later see *Der Spiegel*, 17 February 2003.

169 BAB, NS6/411, p. 108, SD report to Martin Bormann, 4 November 1943.

170 BAB, R22/3375, p. 210, 29 May 1943. See TNA, FO 898/186, report for 20–26 December 1943, pp. C2–C3. This mentions 'the opinion that Party members are shirkers' and cites the counter-blast by Nazi propaganda in the *Danziger Vorposten*, 10 December 1943, and the *Völkischer Beobachter*, 24 December 1943 denouncing accusations that young men were evading military service because of Party connections and instead claiming that casualties were actually higher in leading Party circles.

171 BAB, R58/188, p. 36, 9 September 1943; p. 50, 16 September 1943. For instance the death sentence passed on *Regierungsrat* Korselt of Rostock for defeatist talk and rumour-mongering reported in the German press at the beginning of September 1943. As the *Danziger Vorposten* proclaimed on 5 September: 'The Korselt sentence is a warning to men of ill will.' TNA, FO 898/186, report of 20 September 1943, p. C4.

172 TNA, FO 898/186, 13 March 1944, p. C1, quoting *PZ*, 21 February 1944.

173 Ibid., 13 March 1944, p. C1, quoting *ST*, 23 February 1944.

174 BAB, R22/3386, p. 55, 31 May 1943.

175 TNA, FO 898/186, 20 December 1943, p. C4, quoting *PomZ*, 4 December 1943.

176 Siebel-Achenbach, *Lower Silesia*, p. 25.

177 BAB, R58/192, p. 24, 3 January 1944.

178 TNA, FO 898/186, 8 May 1944, p. C6, quoting *PomZ*, 22 April 1944.

179 Ibid., 22 May 1944, quoting *PomZ*, 3 May 1944

180 D. Peukert, *Inside Nazi Germany: Conformity, Opposition and Racism in Everyday Life* (Harmondsworth, Middlesex: Penguin Books edition , 1989), p. 153. In Lauban, Lower Silesia, youngsters were accused of a whole array of offences. These included 'the continual burglaries, the numerous thefts of rabbits etc, the molestation of women during the black-out and the unauthorised closing of level-crossing gates'. According to this report they were also responsible for breaking windows, removing manhole covers and setting fire to wooden houses. See TNA, FO 898/186, 31 January 1944, p. C5, quoting *Breslauer Neueste Nachrichten*, 19 January 1944.

181 Gause, *Die Geschichte der Stadt Königsberg*, p. 158; Gerhardi, *Helga*, p. 162f; G. Gunter, *Last Laurels: The German Defence of Upper Silesia January-May 1945* (Solihull, West Midlands: Helion and Company, 2002), pp. 1–4.

182 BAB, R22/3386, pp. 68–69, 30 November 1944. There was also significant anti-Nazi resistance in Pomerania. These groups were mainly Communist led and included POWs in their numbers. They concentrated on undertaking sabotage operations against centres of war production in or around Stettin. Following a spate of arrests in November and December 1944, seven ringleaders were tried by the Special Court and shot on 9 February 1945. See BAB, R22/3386, p. 78, 10 February 1945; K.H. Jahnke, *Hitlers letztes Aufgebot Deutsche Jugend im Sechsten Kriegsjahr 1944/45* (Essen: Klartext Verlag, 1993), pp. 104–105; Murawski, *Die Eroberung Pommerns*, p. 50.

183 Tilitzki, *Alltag in Ostpreußen*, pp. 53–54. Figures were even higher for the incorporated district of Zichanau in south East Prussia. For instance, in the first six months of 1942 while 9% of cases before the Königsberg Special Court resulted in the passing of the death sentence, in Zichenau this was the sentence imposed in over 40% of cases. See Grabowski and Grabowski, 'Germans in the Eyes of the Gestapo', p. 23.

184 Kershaw, *Hitler: Nemesis*, p. 261

185 Noakes and Pridham (eds.), *Nazism 1919–1945: Volume 3*, p. 1054.

186 Ibid., pp. 1057–1058.

187 Siebel-Achenbach, *Lower Silesia*, pp. 23–24. According to the census of 16 June 1933 there were 20,202 Jews in Breslau, see TNA, FO 1046/36. Prior to the war reports submitted by the British Embassy in Berlin and the Vice-Consulate in Breslau to the Foreign Office in London told of the impact of Nazi legislation and terror on the Jews of Silesia. See for instance, TNA, FO 371/18861, p. 217, report of Vice-Consul Bashford from Breslau, 20 May 1935; despatch from Mr Newton, British Embassy, Berlin to Sir Samuel Hoare, Foreign Secretary, 17 July 1935; FO 371/21635, pp. 57–60, despatch from Mr Bashford, Breslau, 6 May 1938; pp. 187–189, despatch from Mr Bashford, 14 July 1938.

188 Davies and Moorhouse, *Microcosm*, pp. 365–370, 392–395; Siebel-Achenbach, *Lower Silesia*, pp. 23–24; G. Elze, *Breslau: Biographie einer deutschen Stadt* (Leer: Verlag Gerhard Rautenberg, 1993), p. 113. The extermination camps established in the *General Gouvernement* were Treblinka, Belzec, Majdanek and Sobibor.

189 Lucas-Busemann, *So fielen Königsberg und Breslau*, pp. 129–133.

190 Davies and Moorhouse, *Microcosm*, 399. Only three escapees, a Dutchman and two Norwegians managed to reach Britain. This event has been immortalised, less than accurately, in the feature film *The Great Escape*.

191 Ibid., pp. 390–391; Siebel-Achenbach, *Lower Silesia*, p. 24.

192 Tighe, *Gdansk*, pp. 168–171, 195. Both Stutthof and Groß-Rosen were particularly active, and ridden with epidemics and starvation, during the winter of 1944–1945. This was because of the influx of prisoners following the suppression of the Warsaw Rising and the evacuation of eastern camps.

Chapter 4 A Deep Anxiety over the Fate of East Prussia

1 Böddeker, *Die Flüchtlinge*, p. 11. Similar sentiments are found in Lass, *Die Flucht*, p. 11.

2 D.M. Glantz and J.M. House, *When Titans Clashed: How the Red Army Stopped Hitler* (Lawrence KA: University Press of Kansas, 1995), p. 196.

3 G. Niepold, *Battle for White Russia: The Destruction of Army Group Centre June 1944* (London: Brassey's Defence Publishers, 1987), p .15. On 30 May the recently installed Commander of Army Group Centre, Field Marshal Busch, was forced to relinquish control of the Fifty-sixth Panzer Corps to Field Marshal Model's Army Group North Ukraine. The frontage of Army Group Centre was shortened by 6%, but at the loss of 15% of its divisions, 82% of its tanks and half of its self-propelled anti-tank guns.

4 D. Thomas, 'Foreign Armies East and German Military Intelligence in Russia 1941–1945', *JCH*, Volume 22, 1987, pp. 261–310; Niepold, *Battle for White Russia*, p. 12; P. Carell, *Hitler's War on Russia. Volume 2. Scorched Earth* (London: Corgi Books edition, 1971), p. 530. In Brigadier-General Gehlen's memoirs he admits that it was only in June that he believed the Soviet offensive would fall on Army Group Centre. On 13 June, he warned that the Red Army had started to strengthen their forces facing the Army Group. Gehlen suggested that the attack would commence between 15 and 20 June but cautioned

that Soviet security was so good they had never successfully pinpointed the actual date and hour of a Red Army offensive. R. Gehlen, *The Gehlen Memoirs* (London: Collins, 1972), pp. 111–112.

5 P. Adair, *Hitler's Greatest Defeat: The Collapse of Army Group Centre, June 1944* (London: Brockhampton Press edition, 1998), p. 67. Niepold, *Battle for White Russia*, p. 14. However, Busch's active service was not complete. In April 1945, Hitler appointed him commander of German armies in north-west Germany.

6 BAB, R22/3375, p. 250, 29 March 1944.

7 TNA, FO 898/186, 26 June 1944, p. C6, quoting *PZ*, 12 June 1944. Other sources have mentioned a planned rising by Polish workers in East Prussia at this time. A letter from Memel, dated 11 June, said that following a denunciation by a Frenchman some 500 Poles were arrested. See FO 898/187, 11 September 1944, p. C8.

8 BAB, NS1/544, p. 33, 7 August 1944. Similarly, on 21 June 1944, Hitler Youth and youth representatives from throughout German occupied Europe gathered at the historic Marienburg in West Prussia to celebrate the summer solstice and the third anniversary of the attack on Russia. Speakers, such as Reich Youth Leader Artur Axmann, emphasised the danger that Jewish-Bolshevism posed to the European continent. See *Rheinische Landeszeitung*, 23 June 1944, quoted in Jahnke, *Hitlers letztes Aufgebot*, pp. 52–53.

9 G. Sereny, *Albert Speer: His Battle with Truth* (London: Picador, 1996), p. 434.

10 TNA, FO 898/186, 26 June 1944, p. A7 quoting German military communiqué, 23 June 1944.

11 Adair, *Hitler's Greatest Defeat*, p. 163.

12 Carell, *Scorched Earth*, p. 549; Gunter, *Last Laurels*, p. 7.

13 J. Erickson, *The Road to Berlin* (London: Weidenfeld and Nicolson, 1983), p. 228.

14 BAB, NS6/411, p. 202, 28 June 1944.

15 Ibid., pp. 210–211, 28 June 1944.

16 Ibid., pp. 202–203, 210–211, 28 June 1944; p. 198, 29 June 1944. Shuttle bombing had a bumpy history. The Soviets were suspicious hosts. The Poltava raid by the *Luftwaffe* on the night of 21–22 June 1944 destroyed 43 American bombers, 15 Mustang fighters and damaged a further 26 aircraft. Two million tons of fuel was also destroyed. On the Poltava raid see M.J. Conversino, *Fighting with the Soviets: The failure of Operation FRANTIC 1944–45* (Lawrence, KA: University Press of Kansas, 1997), pp. 85–95.

17 BAB, NS6/411, pp. 215, 224, 7 July 1944. The editor of the *Danziger Neueste Nachrichten* pointed out on 9 July that 'Here in the eastern corner of the Reich the present dramatisation of the situation has again made super-clever map-students visible and audible.' See TNA, FO 898/186, 24 July 1944, p. C7.

18 BAB, R55/601, pp. 33–35, 10 July 1944.

19 Ibid., p. 233, 6 July 1944; R55/601, p. 35, 10 July 1944.

20 BAB, NS1/544, p. 39, 13 July 1944; R55/601, pp. 35–36, 10 July 1944; p. 45, 17 July 1944.

21 BAB, NS6/411, p. 270, 21 July 1944.

22 BAB, NS1/544, p. 36, 13 July 1944. German broadcasts tried to console listeners by emphasising Soviet losses. The military commentator Dittmar argued on 27 June 1944 that, 'the successes gained so far by the Soviets are out of all proportion to the price they have paid'. TNA, FO 898/186, 3 July 1944, p. A3.

23 TNA, FO 898/1863, 31 July 1944, p. A7.

24 BAB, NS6/411, p. 266, 21 July 1944.

25 BAB, NS1/544, p. 39, 13 July 1944.
26 BAB, NS6/411, p. 269, 21 July 1944.
27 BAB, R55/601, p. 45, 12 July 1944, Mark Brandenburg; NS6/411, p. 269, 21 July 1944.
28 BAB, NS6/411, pp. 236, 239, 14 July 1944.
29 Ibid., p. 270, 21 July 1944.
30 von Lehndorff, *East Prussian Diary*, p. 36.
31 Gause, *Die Geschichte der Stadt Königsberg*, p. 158.
32 IfZ, MZ 235/4, *Das Reich*, 16 July 1944.
33 These treasures included the famed Amber Room from the Catherine Palace at Pushkin (Tsarskoe Selo) outside Leningrad which had been dismantled and displayed in Königsberg Castle since April 1942. Koch appears to have finally taken this idea seriously in November 1944 when he sent representatives to Saxony to find possible secure locations for artworks. See Scott-Clark and Levy, *The Amber Room*, p. 103. Some treasures, including icons looted from Kiev, were transferred to Count von Schwerin's home at Wildenhoff, Preußisch Eylau, 25 miles south west of Königsberg. Koch had pledged to the family that space would be made available on trains for the collections if evacuation was ordered. This did not transpire. After the family fled in January 1945, a Ukrainian art historian billeted at the house set herself and the whole place, including the artworks, alight. Wildenhoff was engulfed by the flames. See M. Hastings, *Armageddon: The Battle for Germany 1944–45* (London: Pan Books, 2005), pp. 320–322.
34 BAB, NS19/2606, pp. 6–11, 12 July 1944.
35 Ibid., pp. 12–19, 12 July 1944.
36 BA-LA, Ost-Dok. 8/510, p. 5; Dieckert and Großmann, *Der Kampf um Ostpreussen*, p. 28.
37 BAB, NS1/544, pp. 31–34, 7 August 1944.
38 Ibid., p. 34; TNA, FO 898/187, 14 August 1944, p. C7.
39 Grabowski and Grabowski, 'Germans in the Eyes of the Gestapo', p. 33. Information reaching the British Political Warfare Executive from East Prussia in mid-July claimed that East Prussians felt that the Russians had 'no desire to annihilate Germany'. They had not heavily bombed German cities and their propaganda was appealing. A Russian occupation was viewed as likely to be purely military and temporary whereas a Polish annexation would be designed to last. Similarly, East Prussian agricultural labourers were also apparently ready to welcome the Red Army. They were said to hope that the Junkers would be driven out and they would be able to divide up the great estates among themselves. See TNA, FO 898/187, 14 August 1944, pp. C7–C8. Meanwhile, the *Danziger Neueste Nachrichten* was most critical of the 'little armchair politicians who fancy that Stalin's march into Germany would not have such bad consequences at all'. FO 898/187, 21 August 1944, p. C4, quoting *Danziger Neueste Nachrichten*, 8 August 1944.
40 Lehndorff, *East Prussian Diary*, pp. 74–75. The author recalled shooting with his cousin Heinrich von Lehndorff in the latter's wood by the Mauersee in the winter of 1943–1944, 'picturing to ourselves what it would be like to live there together as "partisans" after the catastrophe'. Heinrich von Lehndorff was executed for his part in the 20 July plot against Hitler.
41 A. Seaton, *The Russo-German War 1941–1945* (London, 1971), p. 442; Colonel General H. Guderian, *Panzer Leader* (London: Michael Joseph, 1970), p. 338. Koch claimed that East Prussian soldiers wrote him letters requesting transfers to this sector of the front, see IfZ, MZ 235/4, *Das Reich*, 27 August 1944.
42 BfZ, SSt Feldpost 1944 /7, Uffz. W.F., 14 July 1944.

43 Ibid., H.R., 17 July 1944.
44 BAB, NS6/791, pp. 15–16, 6 July 1944.
45 *TBJG 13*, p. 86, 11 July 1944.
46 BA-LA, Ost-Dok. 8/510, p. 5; BAB, R55/616, p. 111, 17 July 1944.
47 E.F. Ziemke, *Stalingrad to Berlin: The German Defeat in the East* (Washington D.C.: Office of the Chief of Military History United States Army, 1968), p. 340. On Reinhardt's order to detain Russians near his Vitebsk headquarters in the late summer of 1943 and their transportation with their families to concentration camps in the *General Gouvernement* see Reitlinger, *The House Built on Sand*, pp. 278–279. Reinhardt was sentenced to 15 years imprisonment by the American tribunal at Nuremberg but was released in 1952.
48 BA-LA, Ost-Dok. 10/888, p. 100.
49 *Soviet War News*, 22 August 1944 quoted in Zeidler, *Kriegsende im Osten*, p. 217.
50 TNA FO 898/187, 14 August 1944, p. A9, quoting Lutz Koch interview with Model, 8 August 1944.
51 BAB, R55/616, p. 1, 13 July 1944. *Wehrmacht* military hospital provision is discussed in BAB, R55/426, p. 21, 11 July 1944; General F. Hoßbach, *Die Schlacht um Ostpreußen* (Überlingen: Otto Dikreiter Verlag, 1951), pp. 19–20.
52 Great Britain, Foreign Office, *Weekly Political Intelligence Summaries, Volume 10, July–December 1944* (London: Kraus, 1983), no. 250, 19 July 1944.
53 *TBJG 13*, p. 85, 11 July 1944; p. 90, 12 July 1944.
54 Ibid., p. 85, 11 July 1944; p. 106, 13 July 1944.
55 BAB, R55/616, p. 106, 13 July 1944; *TBJG 13*, p. 108, 13 July 1944.
56 *TBJG 13*, p. 113, 14 July 1944.
57 BAB, NS6/791, p. 31, 14 July 1944. During the following weeks almost all evacuees left the province. By early September, Erich Post, the East Prussian NSV Leader, reported that 159,586 evacuees had left East Prussia – 119,586 by special trains and around 40,000 by timetabled trains. IfZ, MA-736, report by Erich Post, 5 September 1944.
58 BAB, R43II/684, pp. 60, 63, 13 July 1944.
59 TNA, FO 898/187, 11 September 1944, p. C8.
60 BAB, R55/616, p. 107, 14 July 1944; p. 109, 15 July 1944.
61 Ibid., p. 110, 17 July 1944; Steinert, *Hitler's War*, p. 263. At Sondermann's prompting Maertins was forced to concede that the strong criticism of the behaviour of the Berliners was a temporary phenomenon and that he already had the general impression that the subject was no longer spoken about in the province. See BAB, R55/426, pp. 36–37, Sondermann to Goebbels, 18 July 1944.
62 BAB, R55/616, pp. 76, 86–88, 10 July 1944.
63 Ibid., pp. 77–78, 10 July 1944; pp. 86–88, 10 July 1944; p. 102, 11 July 1944.
64 Ibid., p. 102, 11 July 1944; p. 104, 12 July 1944. Koch had hoped that a Reich-wide travel ban would apply from the morning of 13 July. Special restrictions on railway travel in East Prussia from 11 July were announced in the *Königsberger Allgemeine Zeitung* on the following day to apply from 17 July. Special restrictions in Danzig-West Prussia were announced on 9 August. See TNA, FO 898/187, 14 August 1944, p. C6.
65 H. Jung, *Die Ardennes Offensive 1944/45* (Zurich and Frankfurt: Musterschmidt, Göttingen, 1971), p. 75.
66 Ibid., p. 109, 15 July 1944; p. 111, 17 July 1944.
67 TNA, FO 898/187, 14 August 1944, p. C7, quoting *PZ*, 28 July 1944.
68 Ibid., quoting *PZ*, 2 August 1944.

69 The first half of 1944 had been marked by the westward movement of German-friendly elements from the east. Facing this unregulated mass influx of easterners into the Reich, the German authorities were keen on developing mechanisms to screen those deemed reliable from the main refugee body. They were worried about the impact of 'Bolshevik agents and vacillating elements' among the refugees. See BA-MA, RW4-906, Behandlung von Flüchtlingen aus den besetzten Ostgebiete 1944.
70 BAB, NS6/791, pp. 34–35, 37.
71 BAB, R55/616, p. 93, 10 July 1944; p. 95, 11 July 1944.
72 BAB, R55/426, pp. 20–21, 23, 11 July 1944.
73 Ibid., pp. 22–23, 11 July 1944.
74 BLHA, Pr. Br. Rep. 3B 1 Pol Nr. 1973, pp. 37–39.
75 Ibid.; BAB, R55/426, p. 23, 11 July 1944. The German media later claimed that 'tens of thousands' of boys and girls from the East had joined up as *Luftwaffe* auxiliaries. See TNA, FO 898/187, 25 September 1944, p. A2 quoting *Deutsches Nachrichten Bureau*, 23 September 1944. Some 28,117 children and adolescents were seized according to reports in October 1944 but some 3,700 were girls and 6,700 were sent to the bomb blasted factories in the Ruhr. Reitlinger, *The House Built on Sand*, pp. 281–282.
76 BAB, NS1/544, p. 78, 29 August 1944.
77 J. Steinhoff, P. Pechel, D. Showalter (eds.), *Voices from the Third Reich: An Oral History* (Washington DC: Regnery Gateway, 1989), p. 420, testimony of Andreas Meyer-Landruth.
78 BAB, R55/426, p. 24, 11 July 1944.
79 The Kaminsky Brigade was a force of ex-Russian POWs commanded by the White Russian *SS-Brigadeführer* Bronislav Kaminsky. Kaminsky was shot on the order of *SS-Obergruppenführer* von dem Bach-Zelewski who wished to obscure German atrocities in Warsaw. The Brigade's indiscipline and violent behaviour in the Ratibor area of Upper Silesia was later reported in detail to the central authorities in Berlin. See BAB, R22/3372, pp. 167–168, 6 October 1944.
80 Lieutenant-General Andrei Vlasov, the commander of the Soviet Second Shock Army, was captured by the Germans in 1942. In German captivity and with limited assistance he established the anti-Stalinist 'Russian Liberation Army'.
81 BfZ, SSt Feldpost 1944/7, A.E., 10 July 1944. The Party newspaper, the *Preußische Zeitung*, detected this panic and on 16 July printed an article with the heading 'Eiskalte Ruhe' (Ice-cold calm). This warned that Germany's enemies 'are deliberately waging war against our nerves and intend to provoke rash reactions' but East Prussians 'must make sure that our nerves do not get the better of us'. It went on to warn that, 'Should any unfavourable event occur, even if it seems to threaten a certain home space, we must remember the calm and firm words of the *Führer* that no difficulty will make us capitulate.' TNA, FO 898/186, 31 July 1944, p. C3 quoting *PZ*, 16 July 1944.
82 BAB, R55/616, pp. 97–99, 11 July 1944. Wilfred von Oven's Political Review broadcast on 14 July echoed this theme: 'We Germans are conscious that both our Bolshevik and Capitalist enemies have only one war aim, to exterminate the German people, lock, stock and barrel. This is why with the approach of the danger, our firm resolve is growing to defend ourselves to the last breath with all means at our command.' TNA, FO 898/186, 17 July 1944, p. A1. Von Oven was Goebbels' press officer.
83 Ibid., pp. 100–101, 11 July 1944.
84 Ibid., p. 109, 15 July 1944; BAB, R55/426, pp. 32–33, 15 July 1944.

85 *TBJG 13*, p. 115, 14 July 1944; p. 123, 15 July 1944; p. 131, 16 July 1944.
86 TNA, FO 898/186, 17 July 1944, p. A8.
87 Ibid., 31 July 1944, p. A7.
88 Ibid., 7 August 1944, p. A6, quoting Hans Fritzsche broadcast of 5 August 1944.
89 BAB, R55/616, pp. 68–69, 10 July 1944. Goebbels had received storms of applause from his Breslau audience when he emphasised his belief in victory at this decisive stage of the war and when he turned to the *Vergeltungsthema* (theme of revenge weapons). See *TBJG 13*, pp. 67–68, 8 July 1944; p. 70, 9 July 1944. Measures compelling all women up to 50 to register at labour exchanges for work were enacted in late July, see TNA FO 898/186, 31 July 1944, p. A5.
90 BAB, R55/616, p. 71, 10 July 1944.
91 Ibid., p. 107, 14 July 1944.
92 BAB, R55/426, pp. 34–35, 17 July 1944; R55/616, p. 111, 17 July 1944; *TBJG 13*, p. 123, 15 July 1944.
93 BAB, R55/426, pp. 34–35, 17 July 1944; R55/616, p. 111, 17 July 1944. Koch's speech was reported in the *Preußische Zeitung* on 17 July under the headline 'Unlimited faith of the *Führer* in the people of East Prussia – East Prussia's great historical hour'. The report admitted that rumours had been flying around Königsberg concerning events in Bialystok, Grodno and in the East Prussian frontier towns. The report went on to state: 'If these tales had been taken literally, faint-hearted people would have been only one step from panicking.' TNA, FO 898/186, 31 July 1944, pp. C3–C4.
94 TNA, FO 898/186, 7 August 1944, p. C5, quoting *PomZ*, 26 July 1944.
95 Ibid., p. C6, quoting *Oberschlesische Zeitung* (hereafter *OZ*), 26 July 1944.
96 TNA, FO 898/187, 14 August 1944, p. C4, quoting *ST*, 30 July 1944.
97 Ibid, p. C5, quoting *Danziger Vorposten*, 30 July 1944.
98 TNA, FO 898/186, 7 August 1944, p. C6, quoting *KAZ*, 16 July 1944.
99 BAB, R55/616, p. 117, 20 July 1944. The *Preußische Zeitung* also tried to defuse the rumours of panic in East Prussia which had spread across Germany. A Masurian town was described as 'a picture of the profoundest peace'. 'Foolish' letters from the west saying that the rural population were 'fleeing, frightened and uneasy' were said to have caused local residents to laugh heartily. TNA, FO 898/186, 31 July 1944, p. C5, quoting *PZ*, 22 July 1944.
100 TNA, FO 898/187, 4 September 1944, p. C5.
101 Numerous studies have examined the German resistance to Hitler and the events of 20 July. The most comprehensive English language source remains P. Hoffmann, *The History of the German Resistance 1933–1945* (London: Macdonald and Jane's Ltd, 1977). A good recent account is J. Fest, *Plotting Hitler's Death: The German Resistance to Hitler 1933–1945* (London: Phoenix Paperback edition, 1997). Stauffenberg planted the bomb at the *Wolfsschanze* and then returned to Berlin by plane to help co-ordinate the resistance effort in Germany and occupied Europe. However, when it became clear that Hitler had survived the blast and the plot had failed, Stauffenberg was doomed. The commander of the *Ersatzheer*, Colonel-General Friedrich Fromm, long aware of the conspiracy but keen on personal preservation, ordered Stauffenberg's execution. Stauffenberg and three of his closest co-conspirators were shot in the courtyard of the Bendlerstrasse headquarters of the *Ersatzheer* on the evening of 20 July.
102 The first trials before the People's Court in Berlin commenced on 7 August 1944 and those condemned were executed at the city's Plötzensee Prison that same afternoon.

103 BAB, R55/614, p. 12, 21 July 1944.
104 Steinert, *Hitler's War*, p. 267.
105 Ibid., p. 10. Despite his self-proclaimed skill at backing the winning side, Colonel-General Fromm was arrested on the evening of 20 July, later convicted on a trumped-up charge of cowardice and shot in Brandenburg in March 1945.
106 Ibid., p. 8.
107 Steinert, *Hitler's War*, p. 266.
108 BAB, R55/614, p. 10, 21 July 1944.
109 Ibid., p. 49, 24 July 1944. The *Schlesische Tageszeitung* reported on 24 July that Koch-Erpach had been ordered by the conspirators to arrest Hanke but instead had taken counsel with him. TNA, FO 898/186, 31 July 1944, p. C8.
110 BAB, R55/614, p. 145, 23 August 1944. Ley told this mass meeting: 'From the *Gau* I take back with me to the Reich the certainty that its people have firm confidence and absolute faith in Germany's cause.' TNA, FO 898/186, 7 August 1944, p. C8.
111 BAB, R22/3358, p. 79, 1 August 1944.
112 BAB, R22/3386, p. 62, 10 August 1944. Nevertheless, newspapers still felt the need to justify the summary judicial process which indicates that the authorities detected some degree of criticism. The *Ostsee-Zeitung, Stettiner General-Anzeiger*, commented on 10 August: 'The trial before, and sentence of, the People's Court was so clear that no judicial hair-splitting is necessary at the hour of this atonement to explain why the accused were pronounced guilty.' TNA, FO 898/187, 21 August 1944, p. C1. Around 200 soldiers and civilians are estimated to have perished as a direct result of the regime's revenge for 20 July.
113 The SD reports on the assassination attempt have been criticised for giving the impression to the political leadership that all Germans were Hitler fanatics. It has been noted that in local SD reports that there were signs that many Germans would have favourably greeted a successful attempt, while other informants spoke of the quietness of the population. See *Der Spiegel*, 35/2004, interview with Ian Kershaw.
114 BAB, R55/601, pp. 57–58, 63, 24 July 1944; NS6/411, pp. 281, 284–285, 28 July 1944.
115 Kershaw, *The Hitler Myth*, p. 218.
116 BfZ, SSt Feldpost 1944/7, Oberst O.M., 20 July 1944.
117 Ibid., *Hauptmaidenführerin* E.S., 24 July 1944.
118 Ibid., Fr. K., 31 July 1944. At the same time, the Party's *Preußische Zeitung* quoted a remark which it attributed to an old woman in Masuria: 'The *Führer* will not leave us Masurians in the lurch, because we backed him up loyally in the years of the *Kampfzeit*.' See TNA, FO 898/186, 7 August 1944, p. C6 quoting *PZ*, 24 July 1944.
119 O. Bartov, *Hitler's Army: Soldiers, Nazis and War in the Third Reich* (New York: Oxford University Press, 1992), p. 172.
120 H-A Jacobsen (ed.), *Spiegelbild einer Verschwörung. Die Opposition gegen Hitler und der Staatsreich vom 20 Juli 1944 in der SD-Berichterstattung. Geheime Dokumente aus dem ehemaligen Reichssicherheitshauptamt. Erster Band* (Stuttgart: Biblio Verlag, 1984), pp. 1–11.
121 Ibid., p. 5, 21 July 1944; p. 7, 22 July 1944.
122 BAB, NS6/411, p .282, 28 July 1944; Jacobsen (ed.), *Spiegelbild einer Verschwörung*, p. 9, 24 July 1944.
123 *TBJG 13*, pp. 162–163, 25 July 1944.
124 Jacobsen (ed.), *Spiegelbild einer Verschwörung*, p. 10, 24 July 1944.
125 BAB, R55/601, p. 58, 24 July 1944; NS6/411, p. 282, 28 July 1944.

126 Jacobsen (ed.), *Spiegelbild einer Verschwörung*, pp. 10–11, 24 July 1944.

127 BAB, NS6/411, p. 286, 28 July 1944; Jacobsen (ed.), *Spiegelbild einer Verschwörung*, pp. 2, 5, 21 July 1944.

128 Fest, *Plotting Hitler's Death*, p. 398. Tresckow killed himself with a grenade on the Eastern Front in Poland after he heard of the failure of the assassination attempt.

129 For a summary of the appeal see Erickson, *The Road to Berlin*, pp. 229–230; K.P. Schoenhals, *The Free Germany Movement. A Case of Patriotism or Treason* (London: Greenwood Press, 1989), p. 106.

130 *TBJG 13*, p. 96, 12 July 1944; p. 206, 3 August 1944.

131 Ibid., p. 205, 3 August 1944; Jacobsen (ed.), *Spiegelbild einer Verschwörung. Zweiter Band*, pp. 631–632, Bormann to *Gauleiter* Eggeling, 8 September 1944. On Koch's view that NKFD agents were active in Army Group Centre see BA-LA, Ost-Dok. 8/594.

132 Schoenhals, *The Free Germany Movement*, p. 107.

133 TNA, FO 898/187, 21 August 1944, p. A6, quoting German radio broadcast, 18 August 1944, of *Das Reich* article.

134 BAB, NS19/2606, p. 25, 20 September 1944.

135 Ibid., pp. 26–27, 20 September 1944. The danger emanating from the traitorous deeds of these so-called *Seydlitz-Leute* were regularly stressed in German propaganda, orders and reports until the war's end. In reality, their number remained miniscule, but their existence was utilised by the Nazi regime to justify ever more ruthless measures in the combat zones and to explain continued battlefield reversals. General Walther von Seydlitz-Kurzbach had commanded the 51st Corps at Stalingrad. After the surrender he was persuaded by his Soviet captors to be at the forefront of the BDO (*Bund Deutscher Offiziere*, League of German Officers) from September 1943. Much of the organisation's activity was directed at encouraging German troops to cross over to Soviet lines. Their leaflets and pamphlets were rarely successful in attaining this goal. Nevertheless, Seydlitz was secretly sentenced to death *in absentia* by a German military court on 26 April 1944. See Schoenhals, *The Free Germany Movement*, p. 98.

136 *TBJG 13*, p. 157, 24 July 1944.

137 See R.L. Quinnett, 'The German Army Confronts the NSFO', *Journal of Contemporary History*, Volume 13, 1978, pp. 53–64.

138 IfZ, Fa.88, Stück 151 Ostpreußen, p. 22, Koch to *Kreisleiter*, 4 October 1944. Carl Gördeler, the likely Chancellor in a new administration was a former Deputy Lord Mayor in Königsberg. Gördeler fled into hiding following the plot's failure but was betrayed and arrested in August 1944. He was executed in 1945.

139 Siebel Achenbach, *Lower Silesia*, p. 25; Fest, *Plotting Hitler's Death*, p. 320.

140 Kershaw, *The Hitler Myth*, p. 219.

141 Hoffmann, *The History of the German Resistance*, pp. 441–444, 448–450.

Chapter 5 A Unique, Improvised Exertion: *Ostwallbau*, 1944

1 Schieder (ed.), *Expulsion Documents*, p. 9.

2 Lasch, *So fiel Königsberg*, pp. 12–16; Baedeker, *Germany: A Handbook*, p. 132.

3 Baedeker, *Germany*, p. 121.

4 BA-LA, Ost-Dok. 8/533, p. 2; Dieckert and Grossmann, *Der Kampf um Ostpreussen*, p. 20.

5 J.E. Kaufmann and R.M. Jurga, *Fortress Europe: European Fortifications of World War II* (Cambridge, MA: Da Capo Press, 2002), p. 60; ostwall.com website, 15 January 2003.

6 BA-LA, Ost-Dok. 8/533, pp. 4–7; Dieckert and Großmann, *Der Kampf um Ostpreussen*, pp. 17–20; Kaufmann and Jurga, *Fortress Europe*, pp. 60–63.

7 BA-LA, Ost-Dok. 8/702, p. 1; 8/712, p. 2; 8/715, pp. 2–4; 8/717, pp. 4–5.
8 Kaufmann and Jurga, *Fortress Europe*, pp. 64–65.
9 BA-LA, Ost-Dok. 8/533, pp. 5–6.
10 ostwall.com website, 15 January 2003.
11 On the *Westwall* which was built along the Reich's western frontier in 1938 see J.D. Heyl, 'The Construction of the *Westwall*, 1938: An Examplar for National Socialist Policymaking', *Central European History*, 14 (1981), pp. 63–78. By October 1938 some 342,000 men were involved in the building of the *Westwall*, 'a position of generally light defences with great depth and formidable obstacles.' Kaufmann and Jurga, *Fortress Europe*, pp. 66, 76.
12 Kaufmann and Jurga, *Fortress Europe*, pp. 65–66; ostwall.com website, 15 January 2003.
13 Kaufmann and Jurga, *Fortress Europe*, pp. 62–73. On pre-war defences in Pomerania see H. Lindenblatt, *Pommern 1945* (Leer: Verlag Gerhard Rautenberg, 1993), pp. 9–10; Murawski, *Die Eroberung Pommerns*, p. 100 comments that the *Pommernstellung* of 1939 consisted of 'only a chain of concrete bunkers of various types' to provide support in the case of a clash with Poland.
14 BA-LA, Ost-Dok. 8/694, p. 3; 10/375, p. 10.
15 Board of Editors, *Documents on German Foreign Policy 1918–1945, Series D, Volume VII* (London: HMSO, 1956), p. 40, meeting between Hitler and Count Ciano, 12 August 1939.
16 BA-LA, Ost-Dok. 8/666, p. 2; 8/712, pp. 2–3; Lindenblatt, *Pommern 1945*, p. 9.
17 Orlow, *The History of the Nazi Party 1933–1945*, p. 444.
18 BAB, R58/188, p. 29, 2 September 1943.
19 Erickson, *The Road to Berlin*, p. 122. Hitler's decision of 11 August 1943.
20 Speer, *Inside the Third Reich*, pp. 370–371, 727.
21 Guderian, *Panzer Leader*, pp. 325–326.
22 BAB, R58/193, p. 12, 6 April 1944.
23 *TBJG 13*, p. 95, 12 July 1944.
24 See BAB, NS6/351, pp. 34–37, 13 July 1944; pp. 78–81, 19 September 1944.
25 W. Warlimont, *Im Hauptquartier der deutschen Wehrmacht 1939–1945* (Bonn and Frankfurt: Athenäum Verlag, 1964), p. 399; Speer, *Inside the Third Reich*, p. 371.
26 For Keitel's order dated 27 July 1944, demanding effective co-operation between the military and civilian authorities and outlining areas of responsibility for the defence of the Reich, in a similar vein to his directive of 19 July 1944, see BAB, NS6/763, pp. 2–3. For Guderian's guidelines for the building of eastern defences, see NS6/792, pp. 17–20, 28 July 1944.
27 For instance, on 24 August 1944 Hitler issued his *Befehl über den Ausbau der deutschen Weststellung*. By 10 September some 211,000 women, elderly and young diggers were deployed reconditioning the *Westwall*, as well as 137 RAD units and numerous HJ formations. See Author Collective led by W. Schumann and O. Groehler, *Deutschland im zweiten Weltkrieg. Band 6. Die Zerschlagung des Hitlerfaschismus und die Befreiung des deutschen Volkes. Juni 1944 bis zum 8. Mai 1945* (Cologne: Pahl Rugenstein Verlag, 1985), p. 236.
28 Towns and cities in the east declared fortresses included Königsberg, Lötzen and Pillau (East Prussia); Stettin, Schneidemühl, Kolberg and Köslin (Pomerania); Breslau, Glogau, Oppeln and Ratibor (Silesia); Küstrin, Frankfurt an der Oder and Guben (Brandenburg); Danzig, Bromberg, Thorn, Graudenz, Elbing and Marienburg (Danzig–West Prussia); Posen (Warthegau) and Warsaw (General Gouvernement).

29 BAB, NS6/792, pp. 17–20, 28 July 1944.

30 Ibid.

31 Guderian, *Panzer Leader*, pp. 360–361. Guderian had authorised the formation of 100 fortress infantry battalions and the same number of artillery batteries, largely consisting of a variety of captured heavy guns. These men had been deemed by the military to be fit for only limited duties and Guderian hoped that they would occupy key sectors of the fortified areas in the German rear and guard against sudden armoured thrusts or airborne assaults. Unfortunately for Guderian, these units were denied to the eastern theatre as his hard pressed contemporaries in the west demanded reinforcements. As a result, Hitler ordered the transfer of the battalions to the *Westwall* on 2 September. See D K Yelton '"Ein Volk Steht Auf": The German *Volkssturm* and Nazi Strategy, 1944–45', *Journal of Military History*, Volume 64, Number 4, 2000, pp. 1061–1083, particularly pp. 1064–1065.

32 See J. Noakes (ed.), *Nazism 1919–1945. Volume 4: The German Home Front in World War II* (Exeter: University of Exeter Press, 1998), pp. 63–80.

33 On the private war between Frank and Koch see BA-LA, Ost-Dok. 8/584, p. 3; 8/591, p. 14.

34 BAB, NS6/448, p. 105, Hitler Directive 12/44, 1 September 1944.

35 Dieckert and Großmann, *Der Kampf um Ostpreussen*, p. 41.

36 BAB, R55/601, pp. 33–35, 10 July 1944.

37 Ibid., p. 58, 24 July 1944.

38 BA-LA, Ost-Dok. 8/593, p. 3; *TBJG 13*, p. 86, 11 July 1944.

39 Steinert, *Hitler's War*, pp. 263–264.

40 Author Collective led by W. Schumann and O. Groehler, *Deutschland im zweiten Weltkrieg. Band* 6, pp. 233–237.

41 F.W. Seidler, *Deutscher Volkssturm: Das letzte Aufgebot* (Munich: F.A. Herbig), p. 32.

42 BAB, R55/616, p. 108, 14 July 1944; R55/426, pp. 28–30, 15 July 1944.

43 BLHA, Pr. Br. Rep. 55 I Nr. 1479, pp. 1–2, 6–9.

44 BAB, R55/616, p. 118, 20 July 1944; pp. 119–124, 21 July 1944.

45 Ibid.

46 L. Dobroszycki, *Reptile Journalism: The Official Polish-Language Press under the Nazis 1939–1945* (London: Yale University Press, 1994), p. 145. The German authorities said that around 250,000 Polish 'volunteers' had helped dig fortifications in the *General Gouvernement*. TNA, FO 898/187, 30 October 1944, p. A7.

47 IfZ, MZ9/112, *VB*, 8 August 1944; MA-737, *KAZ*, 8 August 1944.

48 Ibid.; MA-736, NSDAP Hauptarchiv Gau Ostpreußen. Semester report by the *Gaustudentenführer* East Prussia for the months June–September 1944.

49 TNA, FO 898/187, 9 October 1944, p. C3, quoting *PZ*, 27 September 1944.

50 IfZ, MZ 9/112, *VB*, 8 August 1944; MA-737, *KAZ,* 8 August 1944.

51 IfZ MZ 9/112, *VB*, 15 August 1944; TNA, FO 898/186, 7 August 1944, pp. A6–A7. Similarly, a photograph of an anti-tank ditch on the East Prussian frontier featured on the front page of the 20 August edition of *Das Reich* with the caption 'East Prussia's castle wall'. See FO 898/187, 4 September 1944, p. A10.

52 TNA, FO 898/187, 14 August 1944, p.A9 quoting *Deutsches Nachrichten Bureau*, 7 August 1944.

53 IfZ MZ 9/112, *VB*, 8 August 1944.

54 IfZ, MA-737, *PZ*, 8 August 1944; MZ 9/112, *VB,* 27 August 1944; IfZ, Fa88 Stück 151 Ostpreußen, pp. 21–29, speech to *Kreisleiter*, 4 October 1944; Seidler, *Deutscher Volkssturm*, p. 297.

55 IfZ, Fa.88 Stück 151 Ostpreußen, pp. 21–29.
56 TNA, FO 898/186, 31 July 1944, p. C4, quoting *PZ*, 17 July 1944.
57 Ibid., pp. 23–24.
58 *TBJG 13*, p. 159, 24 July 1944; p. 167, 25 July 1944.
59 Eyewitnesses described one briefing by Guderian for Hitler in the *Wolfsschanze* at this time (probably 15 August 1944) when Koch and Model 'exchanged poisonous looks' when the situation on the East Prussian frontier was discussed. Koch suddenly interrupted, 'The *Wehrmacht* is not helping me build defences on the border. Mr Model seems little interested.' Model shouted back that Koch did as he pleased and was not content to use pioneer companies to prepare defences. Both flung tasteless insults at each other and Hitler struggled to restore order. Eberle and Uhl (eds.), *The Hitler Book*, pp. 165–166.
60 IfZ, Fa.88 Stück 151 Ostpreußen, p. 24.
61 TNA, FO 898/187, 21 August 1944, pp. C5–C6. Koch had made similar remarks in a *Preußische Zeitung* interview on 8 August when he had stressed that troops were not available to help and *Organisation Todt* units were only available in small numbers.
62 BAB, R55/602, p. 103, 7 November 1944.
63 TNA, FO 898/187, 28 August 1944, pp. A8–A9, quoting *Deutsches Nachrichten Bureau*, 24 August 1944.
64 Ibid.
65 IfZ, MA-737, *PZ*, 25 August 1944; MZ 235/4, *Das Reich*, 27 August 1944.
66 IfZ, MA-737, *PZ*, 6 September 1944.
67 IfZ, Fa.88 Stück 151 Ostpreußen, p. 23.
68 IfZ, MA-737, *PZ*, 10/11 August 1944; *KAZ*, 10/11 August 1944. Deputy *Gauleiter* Großherr of East Prussia was reported to have told boys attending a Flieger–HJ gliding competition in Rossitten in mid-July: 'While you have been preparing yourselves, tens of thousands of East Prussians have followed the *Gauleiter*'s appeal for special service at the hour of the greatest effort in the struggle for the Reich's future. Fifty thousand HJ boys have also been mobilised. When you return, many of you will follow.' TNA, FO 898/186, 31 July 1944, p. C4, quoting *PZ*, 17 July 1944.
69 TNA, FO 898/187, 4 September 1944, p. A1.
70 Gunter, *Last Laurels*, p. 15.
71 TNA, FO 898/187, 11 September 1944, p. C8 quoting *OZ*, 27 August 1944.
72 IfZ, MZ 9/112, *VB*, 27 August 1944. Koch's decree of 20 July, which covered the enlistment of emergency workers by the Party for 'special building measures', was the first to mention payment and allowances. After their period of special service workers were to return to their previous occupations at their former wage rates and were not to be held to have broken their contract. TNA, FO 898/186, 31 July 1944, p. C4, quoting *PZ*, 21 July 1944.
73 IfZ, MZ 235/4, *Das Reich*, 27 August 1944; MA-737, *PZ*, 25 August 1944.
74 Seidler, *Deutscher Volkssturm*, p. 34.
75 D. Schenk, *Hitlers Mann in Danzig. Gauleiter Forster und die NS Verbrechen in Danzig-Westpreußen* (Bonn: Verlag J.H.W. Dietz Nachfolger, 2000), p. 250.
76 IfZ, MZ 9/112, *VB*, 27 August 1944.
77 IfZ, MZ 235/4 *Das Reich*, 27 August 1944; MA-737, *PZ*, 25 August 1944.
78 IfZ, MZ9/112 *VB*, 27 August 1944.
79 IfZ, MZ 235/4, *Das Reich*, 27 August 1944; MA-737, *PZ*, 25 August 1944.
80 TNA, FO 898/187, 28 August 1944, p. A9, quoting Front Report, 21 August 1944.

81 TNA, FO 898/187, 18 September 1944, p. C7.
82 Soldiers were told that 'additional army' was digging defences 'from the Memel to the Oder'. TNA, FO 898/187, 21 August 1944, p. A5, quoting *Front und Heimat*, 18 August 1944.
83 BA-LA, Ost-Dok. 8/538, p. 4. Reinhardt replaced Model as commander of Army Group Centre on 16 August. Model assumed command of the retreating German forces in France.
84 BAB, R55/610, p. 147, 16 October 1944.
85 IfZ, MA-737, *PZ*, 21/22 October 1944.
86 BAB, NS6/411, p. 312, 20 August 1944.
87 *TBJG 13*, p. 199, 2 August 1944.
88 Ibid., p. 224, 4 August 1944.
89 Dieckert and Großmann, *Der Kampf um Ostpreussen*, p. 32.
90 IfZ, MA-736, report from *Kreisschulungsleiter* Goldap to NSDAP *Gauarchivamt* Königsberg, 30 August 1944.
91 IfZ, MA-736, report by Dr Kossow, 29 July 1944. See also the later testimony of the then East Prussian Doctors' leader Dr Schroeder who estimated that 200,000 men were called up and split between four major sectors, each divided into three or four sub-sections. He asserted that one-third of the labour force was foreign and they were mostly involved in the excavations on former Polish territory. BA-LA, Ost-Dok 8/596, p. 4.
92 IfZ, MA-248, Schwede-Coburg to *Reichsleiter* Rosenberg, October 1944. The first diggers from throughout Pomerania arrived by train on 10 August and were mostly deployed in the south of Friedeberg district and the environs of Deutsch Krone. One study notes that on many days 150,000 diggers were involved and they built defences 250 kilometres long. The military had insufficient reserves and formations undergoing training to man these positions. See Lindenblatt, *Pommern 1945*, pp. 10–16.
93 BA-LA, Ost-Dok. 8/638, p. 2.
94 von Krockow, *Hour of the Women*, p. 17.
95 Kaufmann and Jurga, *Fortress Europe*, p. 73.
96 BA-LA, Ost-Dok. 8/729, p. 5.
97 Siebel-Achenbach, *Lower Silesia*, p. 27; J. Kaps, *The Tragedy of Silesia 1945–46: A Documentary Account with a Special Survey of the Archdiocese of Breslau* (Munich: Christ Unterwegs, 1952/53), p. 44. The Lower Silesian *Gau* authorities also attempted to inspire the workforce engaged in *Unternehmen Bartold* by publishing a propaganda sheet *Der Schanzer* ('The Digger'). See BAB, R55/610, pp. 108–113 for copies of the editions for 12 August 1944, 15 August 1944 and 17 August 1944.
98 BA-LA, Ost-Dok. 8/735, p. 3.
99 TNA, FO 898/187, 28 August 1944, p. C7, quoting *ST*, 20 August 1944. Upper Silesian men and women were told at the end of July to register at labour offices to undertake work to assist in the defence of the Reich. Some ten days later the *Oberschlesische Zeitung* reported a speech made by *Gauleiter* Bracht to a Party audience in Kattowitz announcing that the Party would lead and organise this 'special service'. The report added that, 'The "special service" consists in the first place of constructing fortifications in Upper Silesia in readiness for any military eventuality.' TNA, FO 898/187, 28 August 1944, p. C7, quoting *OZ*, 30 July 1944, 9 August 1944.
100 BAB, R58/976, p. 8, 14 September 1944. Newspaper reports stressed the apparently harmonious working conditions, enthusiasm of the workforce and strength of the *Bartold* defences. IfZ, MZ 235/4, *Das Reich*, 19 November 1944.

101 BAB, R58/976, p. 8, 14 September 1944; Hornig, *Breslau 1945*, pp. 15–16.
102 On the *General Gouvernement* and Warthegau defences see Seidler, *Deutscher Volkssturm*, pp. 32, 299; Duffy, *Red Storm on the Reich*, pp. 377–378. In Danzig-West Prussia, 89,600 men and women 'including many Jews from the camps' were building defensive positions on 1 October 1944. Women between the ages of 17 and 55 were eligible for this work with some age variation arising from the number and age of children. See TNA, FO 898/187, 21 August 1944, p. C5, quoting *Danziger Neueste Nachrichten*, 6 August 1944; Schenk, *Hitlers Mann in Danzig*, p. 250. Digging was said to be 'completely under the direction of the Party'. See FO 898/187, 28 August 1944, p. C6, quoting *Danziger Vorposten*, 13 August 1944.
103 BA-LA, Ost-Dok 8/702, p. 2; 8/707, p. 2; 8/712, p. 3; 8/715, p. 4.
104 BLHA, Pr, Br, Rep. 55 I, No. 1479, p. 9, 2 August 1944; Pr. Br. Rep. 3B, I Pol. No. 1973, p. 44, 10 August 1944.
105 BA-LA, Ost-Dok. 8/514, p. 2; 8/518, p. 3; 8/569, pp. 2–3; 8/596, p. 12.
106 BAB, R55/601, p. 138, 25 September 1944; p. 149, 2 October 1944.
107 BAB, NS1/544, pp. 75–80, 29 August 1944; BA-LA, Ost-Dok. 8/569, p. 2.
108 IfZ, MA-736, report by the East Prussian NSV leader Erich Post, 5 September 1944. Some post-war accounts agree that the food was adequate. See BA-LA, Ost-Dok. 8/514, p. 2; 8/545, p. 2.
109 BAB, R55/601, p. 149, 2 October 1944; NS1/544, p. 78, 29 August 1944; pp. 86–87, 28 October 1944. On the feeding of daily diggers in Lower Silesia see BA-LA, Ost-Dok. 8/732, p. 3; 10/624, pp. 49, 51.
110 BAB, NS1/544 p. 78, 29 August 1944; p. 86, 28 October 1944.
111 BA-LA, Ost-Dok. 8/725, p. 3; 10/629, p. 35.
112 BfZ, SSt Feldpost 1944/8, R.T., 2 August 1944; Frau B., 8 August 1944; Feldpost 1944/9, R.T., 1 September 1944.
113 BA-LA, Ost-Dok. 8/721, p. 33.
114 BA-LA, Ost-Dok. 8/707. For the duties demanded of the BdM in a camp in Warthegau see M. Mackinnon, *The Naked Years: Growing Up in Nazi Germany* (London: Chatto and Windus, 1987), p. 159.
115 BA-LA, Ost-Dok. 8/721, p. 34.
116 IfZ, MA-248, Schwede-Coburg to Rosenberg, October 1944. Schwede-Coburg told the *Pommersche Zeitung* in late September that only a 'small number of men' were available for the work. Women of all ages, classes and professions, many of whom had 'never touched a spade before and had never before slept in camps on scanty palliasses'. He also claimed that thousands of women and girls had volunteered for a few more weeks of work at the *Pommernwall*. TNA, FO 898/187, 9 October 1944, pp. C2–C3, quoting *PomZ*, 28 September 1944.
117 BA-LA, Ost-Dok. 8/677, p. 2; 10/396, p. 13. The then East Prussian Doctor's leader Dr Schroeder maintained that there were fewer epidemics among diggers than had been expected. Dysentery and typhus were rare but lice and diarrhoea were commonplace. BA-LA, Ost-Dok. 8/596, pp. 14–15.
118 BA-LA, Ost-Dok. 8/596, pp. 3–4.
119 BAB, R55/601, p. 149, 2 October 1944.
120 BAB, NS1/544, p. 83, 28 October 1944.
121 BA-LA, Ost-Dok. 8/688, pp. 5–6.
122 TNA, FO 898/187, 21 August 1944, p. C8, quoting *ST*, 6 August 1944.

123 IfZ, MA-736, report by Dr Kossow, 29 July 1944. See also BA-LA, Ost-Dok. 8/596, pp. 5–7.

124 BAB, NS1/544, p. 88, 28 October 1944. Dr Schroeder disputed this and claimed that in East Prussia supplies of medicines and plentiful fuel stocks, the latter having been hitherto virtually unavailable for doctors, were found at the Action Koch. See BA-LA, Ost-Dok. 8/596, p. 7.

125 BA-LA, Ost-Dok. 8/734, pp. 4–5.

126 BAB, NS1/544, p. 87, 28 October 1944.

127 BA-LA, Ost-Dok. 10/375, p. 12.

128 BA-LA, Ost-Dok. 8/637, p. 4.

129 Ibid., pp. 3–4; 8/688, p. 6.

130 BA-LA, Ost-Dok. 8/637, p. 4.

131 TNA, FO 898/187, 18 September 1944, p. C6, quoting *PomZ*, 7 September 1944.

132 BA-LA, Ost-Dok. 8/593, p. 6; 8/514, p. 2.

133 BA-LA, Ost-Dok. 8/561, p. 2; 8/717, p. 5.

134 Royal Institute of Historical Affairs, *Review of the Foreign Press 1939–1945. Series A Volume IX, Enemy Countries; Axis-controlled Europe 4 January 1944–26 June 1945* (Munich: K G Saur, 1980), Memorandum 235, 10 October 1944. The German 'East Wall' through Poland.

135 BA-LA, Ost-Dok. 10/652, pp. 49–51.

136 BA-LA, Ost-Dok. 8/688, p. 8.

137 BA-LA, Ost-Dok. 8/533, pp. 10–11.

138 BA-LA, Ost-Dok. 8/596, p. 14.

139 BAB, NS1/544, pp. 77–78, 29 August 1944; Dobroszycki, *Reptile Journalism*, pp. 144–145. Polish peasants were also accused of ploughing over the new trenches and the *Krakauer Zeitung* warned on 6 September that, 'The fortifications must not be damaged either on purpose or through carelessness. In particular, no alteration must be embarked upon, the trenches must not be ploughed under or covered over, and the obstacles must not be removed.' TNA, FO 898/187, 23 October 1944, p. C10 quoting *Krakauer Zeitung*, 6 September 1944.

140 BA-LA, Ost-Dok. 8/645, p. 3.

141 BAB, R55/603, pp. 415–418, 3 September 1944.

142 BfZ, SSt Feldpost 1944/9, Frau P., 13 September 1944.

143 BA-LA, Ost-Dok. 8/662; 8/674, p. 2; 8/685, pp. 3–4; 10/407, p. 23.

144 K. Granzow, *Tagebuch eines Hitlerjungen: Kriegsjugend in Pommern 1943–1945* (Wiesbaden and Munich: Limes Verlag, 1986), p. 177.

145 *The Times*, 11 November 1944.

146 BA-LA, Ost-Dok. 8/688, pp. 6–7.

147 BAB, R22/3386, p. 64, GSA Stettin, 29 September 1944.

148 BAB, R55/603, pp. 427–430, no date. Nevertheless, the Pomeranian judicial authorities expressed concern at the high number of pregnancies among women diggers at the *Pommernwall*. This was deemed to be another sign of the slackening of the family unit during the war. See BAB, R22/3386, p. 71, 1 December 1944.

149 TNA, FO 898/187, 18 September 1944, p. C7 quoting *PomZ*, 4 September 1944.

150 TNA, FO 898/187, 11 September 1944, p. C8, quoting *ST*, 3 September 1944.

151 IfZ, MZ 235/4, *Das Reich,* 19 November 1944.

152 BAB, NS6/348, pp. 120–121, 28 September 1944; NS1/544, p. 84, 28 October 1944; R22/3386, p. 70, 1 December 1944.

153 BA-LA, Ost-Dok. 8/688, p. 7. On the deployment of the workforce during the winter months see Martin Bormann's order dated 19 November 1944 at BAB, NS6/352, pp. 57–58.
154 BLHA, Pr. Br. Rep. 3B, I Pol. No. 1973, p. 20, 6 December 1944.
155 BA-LA, Ost-Dok. 8/569, p. 3; Seidler, *Deutscher Volkssturm*, p. 30.
156 BA-LA, Ost-Dok. 8/688, pp. 7–8.
157 BAB, R22/3372, p. 272, GSA Kattowitz, 6 October 1944. See also Steinert, *Hitler's War*, p. 280.
158 BAB, R58/976, pp. 26–27, 21 November 1944. Large quantities of alcohol for the construction staff was mentioned in conjunction with the Red Army's incursion of October 1944 by *Landrat* Uschdraweit of Angerapp district in BA-LA, Ost-Dok. 8/577, p. 7. The behaviour of the OT was also criticised at the other end of the Reich. In Baden, the negative conduct of rear area troops and OT units had an adverse effect on the local population. The *Ortsgruppenleiter* of Eberbach, a small town 20 miles from Heidelberg noted that 'the OT men are seen to be wasting their time with the female sex'. They held wild parties in the local inn and drunken men had to be 'loaded into cars and carried away'. Locals were said to be considering a petition to the *Gauleiter* or the *Reichsführer-SS*. TNA, FO 898/187, 5 February 1945, 'Morale in Baden in Autumn 1944 through German official eyes', p. 2.
159 BA-LA, Ost-Dok. 8/524, p. 5. A BdM helper, assisting in the preparation of maps at a camp in the Warthegau, recalled similar activities at the base and the same philosophy governing the actions of the increasingly desperate German officers she encountered. See Mackinnon, *The Naked Years*, pp. 175–176.
160 BA-LA, Ost-Dok. 8/524, p. 5.
161 BA-LA, Ost-Dok. 8/735, p. 3.
162 BAB, NS1/544, pp. 89–90, 28 October 1944.
163 TNA, FO 898/187, 25 September 1944, pp. C8–C9.
164 TNA, FO 898/187, 28 August 1944, p. C7 quoting *KAZ*, 10 August 1944. Workers in Lower Silesia were warned that they required a discharge certificate when they left the digging duties in order to qualify for a ration card. See FO 898/187, 25 September 1944, p. C9, quoting *ST*, 9 September 1944.
165 TNA, FO 898/187, 28 August 1944, p. C8, quoting *PZ*, 13 August 1944.
166 BAB, NS1/544, p. 85, 28 October 1944.
167 BAB, R22/3358, p. 82, 26 September 1944; p. 85, 3 December 1944.
168 Steinert, *Hitler's War*, pp. 176, 180.
169 BAB, R55/601, pp. 117–118, Propaganda Activity Report, 11 September 1944. Buschmann, military commentator of the *Pommersche Zeitung* had admitted that, 'It is understandable that people should put one question, namely, how was the enemy ever able to penetrate the Atlantic Wall?' TNA FO 898/186, 26 June 1944, p. C3 quoting *PomZ*, 11 June 1944. The *Danziger Vorposten* even had the temerity to ask 'Is the Atlantic Wall a German Maginot Line?' TNA, FO 898/186, 17 July 1944, p. C1 quoting *Danziger Vorposten*, 24 June 1944.
170 On the *Ostwall* fortifications being unmanned in late summer and early autumn see BA-LA, Ost-Dok. 8/561, p. 2; 8/569, p. 3.
171 F.K.M. Hildebrand, *Underground Humour in Nazi Germany 1933–1945* (London: Routledge, 1995), p. 169.
172 TNA, FO 898/187, 2 October 1944, p. C8, quoting *PomZ*, 17 September 1944.
173 BAB, NS1/544, p. 103, 12 November 1944; von Krockow, *Hour of the Women*, p. 18; MacKinnon, *The Naked Years*, p. 159; Fenske, *Die Verwaltung Pommerns*, p. 164.

174 BA-LA, Ost-Dok. 8/674, p. 2. In contrast, a leading official in the more easterly Schlawe district considered that the mobilisation resulted in no general feeling of uneasiness in the population. He argued that they had 'simply no idea' of the seriousness of the situation and saw the building programme as a 'purely precautionary measure'. The reality of defending the province was not seriously contemplated. See BA-LA, Ost-Dok. 10/408.
175 BA-LA, Ost-Dok. 8/731, p. 3.
176 TNA, FO 898/187, 11 September 1944, p. C6, quoting *ST*, 3 September 1944.
177 A. M. De Zayas, 'Die Flucht', in F. Grube and G. Richter (ed.), *Flucht und Vertreibung: Deutschland zwischen 1944 und 1947* (Hamburg: Hoffmann und Campe, 1980), pp. 129–144; Seidler, *Deutscher Volkssturm*, p. 33.
178 Guderian, *Panzer Leader*, p. 361.
179 BA-LA, Ost-Dok. 8/677, p. 3.
180 BAB, R55/601, p. 138, Propaganda Activity Report, 25 September 1944.
181 National Archives of the United States (hereafter NA-US), Records of Headquarters German High Command, Microcopy, T-78, Roll, No. 304, pp. 6225710–6225714, 6 February 1945.
182 BA-LA, Ost-Dok. 8/524, p. 3.
183 BA-LA, Ost-Dok. 8/569, p. 2.
184 BA-LA, Ost-Dok. 8/670, p. 3.
185 BAB, NS1/544, pp. 95–96, 12 November 1944.
186 Ibid., pp. 97–98, 12 November 1944. In Lower Silesia *Bartold* inflicted dreadful damage on the landscape. On the right side of the Oder trenches were dug without prior consultation with the landowners and this inconsiderate action caused the destruction of drainage and other improvements to the land. See BA-LA, Ost-Dok. 8/718, p. 2; 8/725, p. 4; 10/607, p. 5; 10/629, p. 35.
187 TNA, FO 898/187, 9 October 1944, p. C4. Press reports emphasised that the *Pommernwall* was being built under professional military direction and senior officers had inspected the positions. See TNA, FO 898/187, 16 October 1944, p. C9, quoting *PomZ*, 4 October 1944 which mentioned Colonel General Strauss as responsible for the construction of this sector of the defences.
188 BAB, NS1/544, p. 103, 12 November 1944; BA-LA, Ost-Dok. 8/569, p. 2; Seidler, *Deutscher Volkssturm*, p. 33.
189 BAB, NS1/544, p. 103, 12 November 1944.
190 Duffy, *Red Storm on the Reich*, pp. 378–379.
191 BA-LA, Ost-Dok. 8/510, p. 6; 8/591, p. 15; Dieckert and Großmann, *Der Kampf um Ostpreussen*, p. 31; Lasch, *So fiel Königsberg*, p. 29.
192 BA-LA, Ost-Dok. 8/591, p. 15.
193 BA-LA, Ost-Dok. 10/154. Testimony of Karl Drengwitz, pp. 5–6.
194 BA-LA, Ost-Dok. 10/624, p. 49. When adverse weather caused the cancellation on a particular day, the scale of intrusion on local life was revealed. On 9 October, the *Schlesische Tageszeitung* carried the announcement, 'Emergency service for digging defence positions has been cancelled for Tuesday, October 10th, by order of the Reich Defence Commissioner on account of the weather conditions. All authorities and offices, all wholesale and retail businesses as well as all banks in towns contributing to this service will therefore be open to the public on this day.' TNA, FO 898/187, 30 October 1944, pp. C9–C10.
195 BA-LA, Ost-Dok. 8/645, p. 3; 8/670, p. 2; 8/679, p. 2; 8/688, pp. 2–3.

196 BA-LA, Ost-Dok. 10/415. Testimony of Willy Katzorke p. 4. On Schneidemühl's strategic importance and the planning and building of fortifications in late 1944 see Lindenblatt, *Pommern 1945*, pp. 14–16; Murawski, *Die Eroberung Pommerns*, pp. 113–114.
197 BAB, R22/3386, p. 63, 10 August 1944.
198 Ibid., p. 70, 3 December 1944.
199 VPLA, Rep. 76, No. 165, pp. 5, 26–27, President of the Stettin District Court to the OLG President, 23 November 1944.
200 BAB, R22/3358, p. 82, 26 September 1944.
201 Ibid., pp. 83–84, 3 December 1944.
202 See BA-LA, Ost-Dok. 8/513, p. 2; 10/645, p. 9 for this claim.
203 BA-LA, Ost-Dok. 10/888, p. 100; Dieckert and Großmann, *Der Kampf um Ostpreussen*, p. 31; Lass, *Die Flucht*, p. 12. The continued construction in East Prussia compounded the earlier disruption to agriculture at harvest time. *Landesbauernführer* Spickschen admitted on 2 October that, 'All East Prussian men able to carry arms or spades are conscripted for home defence, while women, invalids and old men are toiling to get the winter seed into the ground, although it will be late . . . Owing to the fortification work and conscription only very few men, not all of whom were fit for work, and women remained on the farms'. TNA, FO 898/187, 16 October 1944, p. C9, quoting *PZ*, 2 October 1944.
204 BA-LA, Ost-Dok. 8/657, p. 2; 8/670, pp. 2–3; 8/679, p. 2.
205 BA-MA, RW21-20/10.
206 BA-MA, RW21-37/11, pp. 26–27, 12 August 1944, 17 August 1944.
207 Ibid., pp. 34–35, 18 September 1944; p. 42, 26 September 1944.
208 BA-MA, RW 21-10/9, p. 34, 15 August 1944; p. 48, 4 September 1944; p. 50, 9 September 1944.
209 BA-MA, RW 20–8/29, pp. 40, 96, 103.
210 See BA-LA, Ost-Dok. 8/593, p. 7.
211 TNA, FO 898/187, 18 September 1944, p. C3 quoting *Westdeutscher Beobachter*, Cologne, 5 September 1944.
212 This theme was popular with scholars from the German Democratic Republic, for instance, K. Mammach, *Der Volkssturm: Das letzte Aufgebot 1944/45* (Cologne: Pahl Rugenstein Verlag edition, 1981), pp. 147–150.

Chapter 6 Confronting Catastrophe: The October Invasion of East Prussia and the Launch of the *Volkssturm*

1 TNA, FO 898/187, 28 August 1944, p. C8 quoting *Ostdeutscher Beobachter*, 15 August 1944. Two months later this same newspaper was still trying to reassure the anxious Germans of the Warthegau. On 15 October 1944, the *Ostdeutscher Beobachter* insisted that, in an emergency, women and children would be evacuated from the province while men would assist the *Wehrmacht* in the defence of the *Gau*. However, it was still maintained that 'the enemy will in all probability fail to reach the Wartheland' and the *Gau* was 'covered by a giant network of fortifications which is completely ready'. If evacuation came, the Party promised to ensure that the German and Polish populations would be 'evacuated to safer districts in orderly columns'. FO 898/187, 30 October 1944, p. C9.
2 Ibid., quoting *ST*, 14 August 1944.
3 Ibid., p. C4 quoting *Stockholm Social-Demokraten*, 25 August 1944.
4 Ibid., 11 September 1944, pp. C8–C9.
5 Ibid., p. C9.

6 Ibid., 4 September 1944, p. A2.
7 Ibid., 25 September 1944, quoting Söndermann, Propaganda Ministry, on *Deutsches Nachrichten Bureau*, 17 September 1944. The Battle of the Teutoburger Wald (AD 9) was between an alliance of Germanic tribes and the Roman Empire. The Battle of Liegnitz (1241) was between a combined German-Polish force and the invading Mongols. The Mongols were actually victorious on the battlefield.
8 A Red Army assault party crossed the border north of Schirwindt on 17 August but was swiftly repulsed. See Zeidler, *Kriegsende im Osten*, p. 67.
9 BA-LA, Ost-Dok. 8/510, p. 8.
10 BA-LA, Ost-Dok. 8/559, p. 1.
11 BA-LA, Ost-Dok. 8/557, p. 3.
12 Böddeker, *Die Flüchtlinge*, p. 15.
13 BA-LA, Ost-Dok. 8/542, p. 2; 8/552, p. 2.
14 BA-LA, Ost-Dok. 8/552, p. 3.
15 BA-LA, Ost-Dok. 8/570, p. 2.
16 BAB, R22/3375, pp. 264–265, report of GSA, 19 October 1944. See Chapter 4 for details of the evacuation of non-East Prussians from the province's borderlands in mid-July 1944.
17 Lass, *Die Flucht*, p. 13.
18 BA-LA, Ost-Dok. 8/530, p. 3.
19 Ibid.
20 BA-LA, Ost-Dok. 8/577, p. 3.
21 Hoßbach, *Die Schlacht um Ostpreußen*, p. 20.
22 Ibid., pp. 28–29.
23 de Zayas, 'Die Flucht', in Grube and Richter (eds.), *Flucht und Vertreibung*, p. 132.
24 BA-LA, Ost-Dok. 8/530, p. 3.
25 Schieder (ed.), *Dokumentation. Band 1/1*, pp. 9–10.
26 Ibid.
27 Early German reports claimed that the Soviets were using 'a stupendous mass of forces, comprising innumerable rifle divisions and a series of tank corps' but the recently dug defences were proving their worth as 'The Bolshevik attack on East Prussia has been checked by our newly created protecting positions.' TNA, FO 898/187, 16 October 1944, p. A7 quoting *Deutsches Nachrichten Bureau*, 8 October and 10 October 1944.
28 Ultimately renamed Army Group Courland on 25 January 1945, only limited elements were evacuated from this exposed outpost to fight elsewhere and most divisions remained there until the war's end when the survivors passed into Soviet captivity.
29 G. Sajer, *The Forgotten Soldier* (London: Orion Books edition, 1993), p. 498.
30 BA-LA, Ost-Dok. 8/552, p. 4; Glantz and House, *When Titans Clashed*, p. 228.
31 BAB, R22/3375, p. 262, 11 October 1944; p. 264, 19 October 1944.
32 BA-LA, Ost-Dok. 8/524, p. 3. German broadcasts did not initially reveal to the German public that *Volkssturm* battalions formed part of the Memel garrison although this was mentioned in reports for abroad. TNA, FO 898/187, 23 October 1944, p. A3 quoting Transocean news agency, 21 October 1944.
33 BA-LA, Ost-Dok. 8/552, p. 4.
34 BA-LA, Ost-Dok. 8/524, pp. 3–4; 8/542, p. 4.
35 BA-LA, Ost-Dok. 8/524, p. 4
36 Schieder (ed.), *Dokumentation*, pp. 1–4; Böddeker, *Die Flüchtlinge*, pp. 17–19; Dieckert and Großmann, *Der Kampf um Ostpreussen*, pp. 48–50; Lass, *Die Flucht*, pp. 23–36.

37 TNA, FO 898/187, 23 October 1944, p. A6 quoting Front Report, *Deutsches Nachrichten Bureau*, 19 October 1944.
38 BAB, R55/601, pp. 147–148, 2 October 1944.
39 Ibid., p. 181, 23 October 1944.
40 *The Times*, 25 October 1944.
41 Ibid., 26 October 1944.
42 E. Fröhlich (ed.), *Die Tagebücher von Joseph Goebbels: Im Auftrag des Instituts für Zeitgeschichte und mit Unterstützung des Staatlichen Archivdienstes Rußlands. Teil II. Diktate 1941–1945. Band 14 Oktober–Dezember 1944* (Munich, K.G. Saur, 1996) (Hereinafter *TBJG 14*), p. 108, 26 October 1944. On 22 October 1944 the *Wehrmachtberichte* had announced 'Eigene Absetzbewegung beiderseits Tilsit'. See BA-MA, RW4/v909.
43 IfZ, MZ 9/112, *VB*, 28/29 October 1944.
44 Ibid., 1 November 1944. This report also stressed the rudimentary qualities of the *Ostpreußenschutzstellung* and praised the native population for their weeks of tireless work. These deep defences had proved invaluable in halting a materially stronger foe. Hundreds of Soviet tanks were destroyed by only one Panzer division or by brave soldiers armed with *Panzerfäuste*, thus illustrating the contrast between 'the mass of steel and material against the heart of the individual fighter'. 'Every man a fortress' was said to be the slogan which had inspired the heroism of individual German soldiers. See TNA, FO 898/187, 6 November 1944, p. A4 quoting German Home Service broadcast, 3 November 1944.
45 IfZ, MA-737, *PZ*, 24 October 1944.
46 Ibid., *KAZ*, 27 October 1944.
47 Ibid., 28/29 October 1944.
48 Ibid., *PZ*, 30 October 1944.
49 Ibid., *KAZ*, 30 October 1944.
50 Ibid., *PZ*, 6 November 1944; MZ 9/112, *VB*, 7 November 1944.
51 BA-LA, Ost-Dok. 8/514b, p. 6.
52 Dieckert and Großmann, *Der Kampf um Ostpreussen*, pp. 70–71.
53 Ibid., p. 70.
54 BA-LA, Ost-Dok. 8/510, p. 9.
55 IfZ, MA-737, *KAZ*, 30 October 1944.
56 Ibid., *PZ*, 1 November 1944.
57 *TBJG 14*, p. 121, 30 October 1944; p. 126, 31 October 1944. The Political Review broadcast on German radio on 1 November 1944 claimed that, 'Moscow even considered it necessary to issue a lengthy statement to excuse the failure of the East Prussian offensive, which expresses Russian amazement at the effectiveness of the German defensive system and grudging admiration of the achievements of German soldiers, who are described as crack formations.' Moreover, the Soviets had 'dispatched a commission of experts to find out the secrets of the East Prussian fortifications'. TNA, FO 898/187, 6 November 1944, pp. A4–A5.
58 *TBJG 14*, p. 150, 4 November 1944. In the Arnhem–Nijmegen area of the Netherlands, the Germans had repulsed attempts by Allied paratroopers to seize three key bridges in late September 1944. The rising by the Polish Home Army in Warsaw was finally brought to a conclusion after more than two months of bitter fighting on 2 October 1944. The Germans then emptied the city and razed to the ground all remaining buildings. Ironically, rubble from the annexed western territories would later be transported to Warsaw to be

used in the post-war reconstruction of the Polish capital thus compounding the desolation in the former German lands.

59 BA-LA, Ost-Dok. 8/538, pp. 2–4.

60 BA-MA, RH20 4/551; Hoßbach, *Die Schlacht um Ostpreußen*, pp. 31–35; D. Irving, *Hitler's War 1942–1945* (London: Papermac, 1983), p. 731.

61 BA-LA, Ost-Dok. 8/544, pp. 3–7.

62 BA-LA, Ost-Dok. 8/560, p. 2.

63 BA-LA, Ost-Dok. 8/536, p. 3; 8/594, p. 3. Goebbels provided an even less plausible explanation for Koch's behaviour. He observed that extraordinary difficulties had arisen because evacuation orders were issued late and attributed this to Koch's great faith in the *Wehrmacht*'s powers of resistance. See *TBJG 14*, p. 100, 25 October 1944.

64 *Reichspropagandaleiter* Lemke, 24 October 1944, quoted in Schimitzek, *Truth or Conjecture*, pp. 254, 257.

65 *TBJG 14*, p. 100, 25 October 1944.

66 BAB, R55/601, p. 181, 23 October 1944; *Gaupropagandaleiter* Dierwege, 23 October 1944, quoted in Schimitzek, *Truth or Conjecture*, pp. 254–257.

67 Böddeker, *Die Flüchtlinge*, p. 20.

68 BA-LA, Ost-Dok. 8/577, pp. 1–8. Kaiser was accused of failing to prevent the flight and despite having one leg was assigned to the *Volkssturm*. Later he was released and undertook administrative tasks arising from the relocation of Angerapp refugees to Preußisch Holland (East Prussia).

69 Ibid., p. 8.

70 BA-LA, Ost-Dok. 8/558, pp. 2–3; Irving, *Hitler's War*, p. 725. Accounts of relatively smooth evacuations in late 1944 are contained in Ost-Dok. 8/513, pp. 2–3; 8/570, pp. 3–4.

71 BAB, NS19/2606, pp. 31–38, 9 November 1944.

72 BA-LA, Ost-Dok. 8/518, p. 3.

73 BA-LA, Ost-Dok. 8/509, p. 2; 8/517 p. 3; Schieder (ed.), *Dokumentation. Band 1/1*, p. 10.

74 BfZ, SSt Feldpost 1944/11, F.D., 5 November 1944.

75 Schieder (ed.), *Expulsion Documents*, pp. 12–13.

76 BAB, R55/602, p. 105, 7 November 1944. Maertins claimed that 779,000 people had been evacuated.

77 BAB, R55/601, p. 215, 16 November 1944.

78 BfZ, SSt Feldpost 1944/11, J.H., 21 November 1944.

79 BAB, R22/3375, p. 271, 24 November 1944.

80 von Lehndorff, *East Prussian Diary*, p. 2. Similar statements can be found in BA-LA, Ost-Dok. 8/524, p. 4; P. Bernecker, 'Flüchtlinge im Raum Heiligenbeil', in H. Reinoß (ed.), *Letzte Tage in Ostpreußen: Erinnerungen an Flucht und Vertreibung* (Frankfurt: Ullstein Sachbuch, 1985), pp. 50–51.

81 BA-LA, Ost-Dok. 8/515, p. 2.

82 BA-LA, Ost-Dok. 8/599, pp. 2–3; 10/154, p. 97; Schieder (ed.), *Dokumentation. Band 1/1*, pp. 12–13.

83 BA-LA, Ost-Dok. 8/577, p. 12.

84 Schieder (ed.), *Dokumentation. Band 1/1*, pp. 11–12.

85 Zeidler, *Kriegsende im Osten*, p. 74. On the propaganda exploitation of the East Prussians atrocities see, for instance, BAB, R55/793, pp. 7–9, 16 January 1945.

86 Lass, *Die Flucht*, pp. 43–50; Böddeker, *Die Flüchtlinge*, pp. 21–25; de Zayas, *Nemesis at Potsdam*, pp. 61–65.

87 Kreipe Diary in Jung, *Die Ardennes-Offensive*, p. 227; Irving, *Hitler's War*, p. 726.
88 Amberger quoted in Lass, *Die Flucht*, pp. 45–46; Böddeker, *Die Flüchtlinge*, p. 23; de Zayas, *Nemesis at Potsdam*, pp. 62–63.
89 Schieder (ed.), *Dokumentation. Band 1/1*, pp. 7–8; Lass, *Die Flucht*, pp. 44–45; Böddeker, *Die Flüchtlinge*, pp. 22–23; de Zayas, *Nemesis at Potsdam*, pp. 63–64.
90 Herminghaus quoted in Lass, *Die Flucht*, p. 47; Dieckert and Großmann, *Der Kampf um Ostpreussen*, pp. 48–49; de Zayas, *Nemesis at Potsdam*, p. 64.
91 BA-LA, Ost-Dok. 8/530, p. 4; Dethleffsen, quoted in Lass, *Die Flucht*, pp. 46–47; Böddeker, *Die Flüchtlinge*, p. 23; de Zayas, *Nemesis at Potsdam*, p. 62.
92 Hastings, *Armageddon*, p. 305.
93 Daily Slogan for 26 October 1944, quoted in Kirwin, 'Nazi Domestic Propaganda', p. 268. See also Steinert, *Hitler's War and the Germans*, p. 287.
94 Deutsche *Wochenschau* No.45/45 1944, quoted in D. Welch, 'Nazi Wartime Newsreel Propaganda', in K.R.M. Short (ed.), *Film and Radio Propaganda in World War Two* (London: Croom Helm, 1983), pp. 201–219.
95 TNA, FO 898/187, 30 October 1944, p. A5. The *Deutsches Nachrichten Bureau* also carried the headlines 'Soviet Beasts rage in East Prussian Border Area', 26 October and 'Beasts in Human Guise', 27 October.
96 Ibid., 6 November 1944, p. A3 quoting German Home Service broadcast, 30 October 1944.
97 Kossert, *Ostpreussen*, p. 319 shows a building in Sovetsk (Tilsit) with such a slogan.
98 IfZ, MZ 9/112, *VB*, 27 October 1944.
99 Ibid., 31 October 1944.
100 Ibid., 1 November 1944.
101 IfZ, MA-737, *PZ*, 6 November 1944; MZ 9/112, *VB*, 9 November 1944; *TBJG 14*, pp. 145–146, 3 November 1944.
102 IfZ, MZ 9/112, *VB*, 2 November 1944. The report of the International Medical Commission has been lost. See de Zayas, *Nemesis at Potsdam*, p. 200.
103 IfZ, MZ 9/112, *VB*, 9 November 1944; Böddeker, *Die Flüchtlinge*, p. 24.
104 von Krockow, *Hour of the Women*, p. 45.
105 Steinert, *Hitler's War*, p. 288.
106 In East Prussia the propagandists claimed that there was relief that the first reports were not too explicit as this allowed the population slowly to comprehend the monstrous details and ensured that [at this stage] a panic situation was avoided. See BAB, R55/601, pp. 198–199, 30 October 1944; p. 210, 7 November 1944. Likewise, the Nemmersdorf newsreel had made a deep impression on all Germans. The pictures provoked great sympathy, but according to official sources, had hardened the will to 'hold out'. See R55/601, p. 234, 21 November 1944.
107 BAB, R58/608, p. 29, *Mundpropagandaparole* 4, 7 November 1944. This is also quoted in Steinert, *Hitler's War*, p. 288.
108 BAB, R55/602, p. 105, 7 November 1944.
109 BA-LA, Ost-Dok. 8/530, p. 4; 8/560, p. 3.
110 Zeidler, *Kriegsende im Osten*, p. 67.
111 *The Times*, 25 October 1944.
112 Ibid., 27 October 1944.
113 BA-LA, Ost-Dok. 8/591, pp. 22–23.
114 Hoffmann, *Stalins Vernichtungskrieg*, p. 259.

115 Ibid.
116 Böddeker, *Die Flüchtlinge*, p. 18.
117 Schieder (ed.), *Expulsion Documents*, p. 49; de Zayas, *Nemesis at Potsdam*, p. 65; Hoffmann, *Stalins Vernichtungskrieg*, pp. 256–257. Streicher, the Jew-baiting *Gauleiter* of Franconia, was the founder of the wildly anti-Semitic weekly *Der Stürmer* in 1923. He was dismissed from his *Gauleiter* role in 1940 on grounds of corruption and was executed in 1946 following the Nuremberg trial.
118 Zeidler, *Kriegsende im Osten*, pp. 70–71.
119 BAB, R55/609, pp. 97–99, November 1944. Soviet reports on the discovery of the Majdanek death camp caused Allied and neutral states to take little notice of events in Nemmersdorf. See T. Charman, *The German Home Front 1939–1945* (London: Barrie and Jenkins, 1989), p. 186.
120 Seidler, *Deutscher Volkssturm*, p. 372.
121 Orlow, *The History of the Nazi Party 1933–1945*, p. 473.
122 H. Kissel, *Der Deutsche Volkssturm 1944/45 – Eine territoriale Miliz im Rahmen der Landesverteidigung* (Frankfurt: E.S. Mittler und Sohn, 1962); Orlow, *The History of the Nazi Party*, p. 528; Seidler, *Deutscher Volkssturm*, pp. 17–18.
123 Mammach, *Der Volkssturm*, pp. 147–150; Seidler, *Deutscher Volkssturm*, p. 18.
124 D. Yelton, *Hitler's Volkssturm: The Nazi Militia and the Fall of Germany, 1944–1945* (Lawrence: University Press of Kansas, 2002), pp. 19–23; Yelton, 'Ein Volk Steht Auf', pp. 1061–1070. See also G. Weinberg, *Germany, Hitler, and World War II* (Cambridge: Cambridge University Press, 1995), pp. 274–286 on German plans for victory during the final 18 months of the war.
125 Orlow, *The History of the Nazi Party*, p. 473. The personnel losses incurred by the *Wehrmacht* and *Waffen SS* were also huge. Between 1 June and 30 November 1944 they suffered around 1.5 million casualties and 106 divisions were destroyed or disbanded. German forces in the east dropped by 700,000 men, from 2,620,000 in June to 1,920,000 in October. The Replacement Army, administered at *Wehrkreis* level, could not fully compensate for this sudden shortfall, particularly as the quality of manpower at their disposal tended to consist of less healthy and older men. Moreover, some of their number were already serving in the army in the field or were engaged in important security tasks on the home front including the guarding of POWs. See Yelton, *Hitler's Volkssturm*, pp. 10–11.
126 Böddeker, *Die Flüchtlinge*, p. 19.
127 Orlow, *The History of the Nazi Party*, p. 473.
128 Hüttenberger, *Die Gauleiter*, p. 192; Yelton, *Hitler's Volkssturm*, p. 10.
129 Seidler, *Deutscher Volkssturm*, p. 55; Yelton, *Hitler's Volkssturm*, p. 9. Yelton notes that *Wehrkreis XXI* (covering the Warthegau military region) kept the scheme going in the face of local Party opposition until matters were overtaken with the formation of the *Volkssturm*.
130 J. Lucas, *Reich! World War II Through German Eyes* (London: Grafton Books paperback edition, 1989), p. 118. Small Party and SA units already existed within the *Stadtwacht* and *Landwacht*. Other auxiliary bodies, SA Special Purpose Units and Political Leader Squadrons were also available to quell internal unrest or to deal with emergency situations. These units had already participated in anti-partisan operations in East Prussia and Koch assigned them security duties at the new defensive positions. See Yelton, *Hitler's Volkssturm*, p. 15
131 Guderian, *Panzer Leader*, p. 362.

132 BAB, R55/616, p. 105, Lemke to Sondermann (RMVuP), 13 July 1944.
133 IfZ, Fa-88 Stück 151, pp. 7–8, Koch to Bormann, 18 September 1944.
134 BAB, NS6/98, pp. 2–3, 25 September 1944.
135 *The Times*, 13 November 1944.
136 BAB, NS6/98, p. 5; Circular 270/44, 26 September 1944. A full English translation is in H.R. Trevor-Roper (ed.), *The Bormann Letters: The Private Correspondence between Martin and Gerda Bormann* (London: Weidenfeld and Nicolson, 1954), p. 125.
137 B. Wright III, 'Army of Despair: The German Volkssturm 1944–1945.' (unpublished PhD thesis, Florida State University, 1982), pp. 113–114.
138 Lucas, *Reich!* pp. 121–122.
139 IfZ, Fa-88, Stück 151, p. 15, 2 October 1944.
140 Royal Institute of International Affairs, *Review of the Foreign Press 1939–1945. Series A. Volume IX*, Memorandum, No. 262, 12 December 1944, The German *Volkssturm*, p. 3. *Volkssturm* men were enlisted by the Party *Blockleiter* in Stettin using the information held in their household card register. Those wishing to enlist voluntarily could complete a registration form from the *Blockleiter*. Otherwise, they would be 'compulsory volunteered'. TNA, FO 898/187, 6 November 1944, p. C5, *PomZ*, 25 October 1944.
141 BAB, NS6/314, pp. 135–136, Koch to Bormann, 15 October 1944; Seidler, *Deutscher Volkssturm*, p. 127.
142 TNA, FO 898/187, 23 October 1944, p. A1.
143 BAB, R43 II/692a, pp. 31–32, *VB*, 19 October 1944; IfZ, MA-737, *PZ*, 19 October 1944; *KAZ*, 19 October 1944; *The Times*, 19 October 1944; Seidler, *Deutscher Volkssturm*, p. 127; Mammach, *Der Volkssturm*, p. 39; P. Padfield, *Himmler: Reichsführer SS* (London: Macmillan, 1990), pp. 540–541.
144 MA-737, *PZ*, 19 October 1944. It was thought in British circles that Koch's call for a final triple 'Sieg Heil' was not greeted with particular enthusiasm. TNA, FO 898/187, 23 October 1944, p. A1.
145 BAB, Akte Koch, S.O.285, Bormann to *Gauleiter*, Circular 369/44, 1 November 1944.
146 Ibid., Bormann to *Reichsleiter*, *Gauleiter*, *Verbändeführer*, Circular 353/44, 27 October 1944.
147 Rebentisch, *Führerstaat und Verwaltung*, p. 528.
148 IfZ, Fa-88 Stück 151, p. 63, note by Großherr to all *Kreisleitungen*, 13 October 1944.
149 Yelton, *Hitler's Volkssturm*, p. 66; Lucas, *Reich!*, p. 125.
150 IfZ, Fa-88, Stück 151, pp. 80–83, *Gau* directive for the swearing-in of the East Prussian *Volkssturm*, 4 November 1944.
151 BAB, NS6/312, pp. 6–7, *Der Politische Soldat*, 16 Special *Volkssturm* issue, 27 October 1944; pp. 56–57, *Der Dienstappell* (no date); BAB, Akte Koch S.O. 285, *Rustzeug für die Propaganda in der Ortsgruppe*, November 1944; Mammach, *Der Volkssturm*, p. 70.
152 R.D. Müller and G.R. Ueberschär, *Kriegsende 1945: Die Zerstörung des Deutschen Reiches* (Frankfurt: Fischer Taschenbuch Verlag, 1994), pp. 44–45. On *Kolberg* and the role of Goebbels see *TBJG 14* (all 1944), pp. 310–311, 1 December; p. 331, 2 December; p. 345, 3 December; p. 400, 12 December; p. 470, 23 December. R. Taylor, *Film Propaganda: Soviet Russia and Nazi Germany* (London: Croom Helm, 1979), pp. 216–219; Welch, *Propaganda and the German Cinema*, pp. 225–237.
153 BAB, R22/3375, p. 226, GSA Königsberg, 19 October 1944.
154 BAB, R55/601, pp. 184–185, 23 October 1944; p. 197, 30 October 1944; pp. 208–209, 7 November 1944; pp. 219–221, 14 November 1944; pp. 229–230, 21 November 1944.

155 Steinhoff, Pechel and Showalter (eds.), *Voices from the Third Reich*, p. 245; Hildebrand, *Underground Humour in Nazi Germany*, pp. 188–191.

156 Lehndorff, *East Prussian Diary*, p. 9.

157 *The Times*, 21 October 1944.

158 IfZ, Fa-88 Stück 151, p. 18, Erich Koch's order to all *Kreisleiter*, *Gaubefehl Nr 13/44*, 2 October 1944.

159 Yelton, *Hitler's Volkssturm*, p. 120.

160 Koch stressed that this was needed because of the size of the *Gau* and because the fortifications built under his auspices stretched from Windau to Warsaw. *Gruppe Nord* was commanded by *Kreisleiter* Ernst Wagner and *Gruppe Süd* was led by *Kreisleiter* Erich Matthes. Both were to report directly to Koch who described them as 'brave political leaders and soldiers' and emphasised to the Party Chancellery their service as officers in the current war. Despite reservations that this proposal seemed to create a new tier of the *Volkssturm* matters, Bormann and the Party Chancellery agreed to the suggestion so long as the province's other *Kreisleiter* would still be able to approach Koch directly on *Volkssturm* issues. BAB, NS6/313, p. 78, Hoegel to Bormann, 3 October 1944; Bormann to Koch, 7 October 1944.

161 IfZ, Fa-88 Stück 151, pp. 33–37, Koch to all *Kreisleitungen* (district Party offices) of the *Gau Ostpreußen*, 10 October 1944.

162 Ibid., pp. 74–77, Directive No. 16 from Koch to all *Kreisleitungen*, in *Gau Ostpreußen*, 29 October 1944. Party districts were told to requisition the uniforms of the German Red Cross, fire brigade, air raid protection service and the customs service. Party members with more than one uniform were to hand in the others.

163 BAB, Akte Koch S.O. 285, *Rustzeug für die Propaganda in der Ortsgruppe*, November 1944, p. 24.

164 Royal Institute of International Affairs, *Review of the Foreign Press 1939–1945. Series A. Volume IX*, Memorandum No. 262, 12 December 1944, p. 3.

165 BAB, NS6/314, pp. 46–47, Koch to Bormann, 25 October 1944; p. 67, Dargel to Bormann, 26 October 1944; Seidler, *Deutscher Volkssturm*, pp. 326–327. At first the Transocean news agency claimed that the battalions took up 'stations in the protective positions dug by the population . . . the battalions then took over those parts of the deeply echeloned defence positions which lie further back, with the double task of protecting them against enemy surprise thrusts and continuing the construction work.' TNA, FO 898/187, 23 October 1944, p. C3 quoting Transocean, 21 October 1944.

166 BAB, Akte Koch S.O. 285, *Rustzeug für die Propaganda in der Ortsgruppe*, November 1944, p. 24.

167 BAB, R55/608, p. 30, *Mundpropagandaparole* No. 5, 8 November 1944. A *Völkischer Beobachter* article quoted by the Transocean news agency on 10 November maintained that three factors had cooperated in blocking the Red Army: the *Wehrmacht* in the field, the fortifications and 'finally the *Volkssturm*'. TNA, FO 898/187, 13 November 1944, p. A4.

168 BAB, R55/602, pp. 103–105, 7 November 1944; R55/1394, pp. 43–44, 7 November 1944. A German news agency report on 29 October noted that the *Volkssturm* initially guarded bridges, railway lines and roads and extended the defences. They were also to safeguard the evacuation of local people, cattle and valuable goods. However, 'the hard days of struggle on the Rominten Heath also brought them their first combat service shoulder to shoulder with the front-line troops. When the Bolshevik attack with superior forces had torn a gap in our positions and threatened the flank of a division, the men and boys of the

Volkssturm bolted off the enemy attack in an isthmus between lakes. The old soldiers and enthusiastic boys did their job.' TNA, FO 898/187, 30 October 1944, pp. C3–C4, quoting *Deutsches Nachrichten Bureau*, 29 October 1944. Similarly, a report broadcast on German radio on 2 November stressed that the East Prussian *Volkssturm* was soon returned to a less demanding and more auxiliary role: 'They have fought gallantly in the front line and, now that the Soviet mass offensive has temporarily been stopped, the men of the *Volkssturm*, with sappers and other technical troops, are building defence works . . . The *Volkssturm* men have also taken on other tasks, such as the evacuation of huge herds of cattle and the removal of valuable agricultural implements; they remove hay and other vital supplies and do important agricultural work immediately behind the main fighting line, thus freeing men for more important duties connected with military operations.' See FO 898/187, 6 November 1944, p. C8.

169 TNA, FO 898/187, 6 November 1944, p. A2, quoting *Front und Heimat*, 2 November 1944.

170 BAB, Ost-Dok. 8/538, p. 4; 8/591, pp. 17, 19.

171 IfZ, Fa-88 Stück 151, p. 54, Schörner to Koch, 19 October 1944; MZ 9/112, *VB*, 27 October 1944.

172 BAB, Ost-Dok. 8/591, pp. 17–18.

173 BAB, NS6/764, pp. 309–310, Koch to Bormann, 21 November 1944, Dieckert and Großmann, *Der Kampf um Ostpreussen*, p. 64; Mammach, *Der Volkssturm*, p. 51. Waldemar Magunia, the veteran East Prussian Nazi, estimated that 120 battalions were established in the province incorporating around 67,000 men. BA-LA, Ost-Dok. 8/592, p. 2.

174 BAB, R22/3375, p. 274, 30 November 1944. Many patently unfit men were also to be found in the ranks of the East Prussian *Volkssturm*. The local *Kreisleiter* in Treuburg called up large numbers of invalids in an effort to boost numbers and impress Koch. See Yelton, *Hitler's Volkssturm*, p. 61. The *Gau* authorities in Upper Silesia reported to Berlin on 22 October that over 100 battalions had been formed. Similarly, *Gau* Danzig–West Prussia advised on 24 October that 432 companies were already set up, comprising 77,818 officers and men. Mammach, *Der Volkssturm*, p. 51.

175 The loss of key personnel and the corresponding disruption to rural trade and the orderly feeding and care of dairy cattle was reflected in an SD report comparing dairy production between 20 and 26 November 1944 and the same period the previous year. Milk production had fallen by 45% and butter and cheese production had dropped by more than half. Furthermore, for the ration period 11 December 1944 to 7 January 1945 the East Prussian butter ration was reduced from 800 to 500 grams, the cheese ration from 400 to 200 grams and the margarine ration from 250 to 125 grams. Additional strain was placed on this sector by the need to accumulate supplies for the Königsberg fortress authorities. See BAB, R58/976, pp. 79–81, 7 December 1944. An SS officer also complained that the *Volkssturm* was ineffectively deployed in the agrarian sector because units were led by men unfamiliar with the running of the rural economy. He added that the *Volkssturm* was preoccupied with its military role and neglected its pressing duties on the land. See BAB, NS19/2606, p. 38, 9 November 1944. Similarly, the drafting of *Volkssturm* in Ortelsburg and their absence on account of training in Lyck was reported to have caused great disruption to economic life in the district. BA-LA, Ost-Dok. 8/571, p. 4.

176 BAB, NS6/314, p. 67, Dargel to Bormann, 26 October 1944; de Zayas, 'Die Flucht', in Grube and Richter (ed.), *Flucht und Vertreibung*, p. 133. See also Kissel, *Der Deutsche Volkssturm*, p. 62.

177 BAB, NS6/314, p. 67, Dargel to Bormann, 26 October 1944. An East Prussian *Volkssturm* man, interviewed on German radio, said that he was called up on 19 October and saw action on the following day while manning a position. Asked by the interviewer if the *Volkssturm* was 'really well prepared for action', he responded 'No, we weren't. Some of the men had never had anything to do with weapons.' Any success was due to the experienced veterans of the First World War. TNA, FO 898/187, 13 November 1944, p. C6 quoting German home broadcast, 9 November 1944.

178 BfZ, SSt Feldpost 1944/10, G.M., 23 October 1944.

179 BA-LA, Ost-Dok. 8/510, p. 9.

180 BA-LA, Ost-Dok. 8/577, p. 11; 10/111, pp. 1–3. Companies comprising the Angerapp battalions had around 100 men. About 12 of the men were only given a *Panzerfaust*. More than 30 men in each company had no weapon at all. Ammunition was dispensed in very small quantities and Belgian ammunition was sometimes provided for Italian rifles. Battalion commanders assured their men that weapons in sufficient numbers would soon be available and the *Volkssturm* would be placed in defences behind the fighting front so they would see no action for the time being. However some units were placed in forward defences and soon came under enemy shell and machine gun fire. Lacking orders and direction an unavoidable retreat soon turned into disorderly flight.

181 Sajer, *The Forgotten Soldier*, p. 476.

182 BA-LA, Ost-Dok. 8/591, p. 14.

183 Hoßbach, *Die Schlacht um Ostpreußen*, pp. 49–50.

184 BA-LA, Ost-Dok. 8/553, p. 3. Colonel-General Erhard Raus, commander of the Third Panzer Army later remarked on the transformation brought about by *Wehrmacht* training: 'Months of continuous instruction raised their standard of training to such a degree that a number of *Volkssturm* battalions actually managed to carry out limited combat missions.' S. H. Newton, *Panzer Operations: The Eastern Front Memoir of General Raus, 1941–1945* (Cambridge, MA: Da Capo Press, 2005), p. 307.

185 BA-LA, Ost-Dok. 8/557, p. 7; Hoßbach, *Die Schlacht um Ostpreußen*, p. 50. Other testimonies state that sometimes the relationship was better. A member of the Goldap *Volkssturm* later recalled receiving valuable training from the *Wehrmacht* at the infantry barracks in Braunsberg where the accommodation, food and level of cooperation was excellent. Later, during the lull between the Red Army's October and January offensives, the *Wehrmacht* and Goldap *Volkssturm* trained alongside each other and a good working relationship was forged. See BA-LA, Ost-Dok. 8/514b, p. 4.

186 IfZ, Fa-88 Stück 151, p. 27. Speech by Koch to his *Kreisleiter*, 4 October 1944. Raus recalled that during the bitter fighting for East Prussia in the second half of January 1945 the Third Panzer Army had no jurisdiction over the *Volkssturm* battalions. The army command called for the battalions to be disbanded and the remaining men to be put into regular divisions but these repeated requests were rejected by the Party authorities. Newton, *Panzer Operations*, p. 307.

187 Dieckert and Großmann, *Der Kampf um Ostpreussen*, p. 65.

188 BA-LA, Ost-Dok. 8/524, p. 3.

189 Even reports describing men of the *Volkssturm* in Himmler's audience at Bartenstein on 18 October admitted that they were 'all equipped with rifles of various types'. TNA, FO 898/187, 23 October 1944, p. C7 quoting *Deutsches Nachrichten Bureau* report, 19 October 1944.

190 One historian notes that the *Volkssturm* was clad in an array of *Wehrmacht*, Party, Fire

Brigade, Red Cross and Air Raid warden uniforms. See Hüttenberger, *Die Gauleiter*, p. 193.

191 BA-LA, Ost-Dok. 8/592, p. 2. After the October fighting in East Prussia, the *Deutsches Nachrichten Bureau* reported that 'most of the men of the East Prussian *Volkssturm* have asked for permanent employment among the fighting troops.' TNA, FO 898/187, 30 October 1944, p. C4 quoting *Deutsches Nachrichten Bureau*, 29 October 1944.

192 Seidler, *Deutscher Volkssturm*, pp. 212–213; Mammach, *Der Volkssturm*, pp. 68–69; Yelton, *Hitler's Volkssturm*, pp. 108–109.

193 Seidler, *Deutscher Volkssturm*, p. 203.

194 BAB, R22/3375, p. 226, 19 October 1944.

195 IfZ, Fa-88, Stück 151, p. 66. RVK to all *Kreisleitungen*, 23 October 1944.

196 Ibid., pp. 17–18, 2 October 1944. According to a Transocean news agency report, the East Prussian *Volkssturm* was trained in the use of their new weapons in a concentrated course led by officers and men with combat experience. TNA, FO 898/187, 13 November 1944, p. C7, quoting Transocean news agency, 10 November 1944.

197 BAB, NS6/764, pp. 309–310, Koch to Bormann, 21 November 1944.

198 Ibid., pp. 311–313. Special *Volkssturm* courts were formed in February and March 1945 and the code of discipline was less tough than that applied in the *Wehrmacht*. However, as is illustrated in Part III the Party, police, SS and military would frequently consider instances of desertion or dereliction of duty by individual members of the *Volkssturm* to be worthy of the supreme penalty. See Yelton, *Hitler's Volkssturm*, p. 96.

199 BAB, R58/976, pp. 89, 14 September 1944.

200 BAB, R43 II/607, pp. 72–78, Dr Funk to Hanke, 29 September 1944. See also the earlier circular issued on 26 September 1944 by Dr Funk to all RVKs on the increasingly frequent encroachments into the production process and requisitions at regional level. See BAB, R43 II/607, pp. 69–70.

201 Ibid., p. 79. In November 1944, Speer's Armaments Ministry found out that Hanke had been requisitioning rayon staple without permission. Letter from Speer to Hanke, 11 November 1944 quoted in Hüttenberger, *Die Gauleiter*, p. 186.

202 BAB, NS6/314, p. 93, Hanke to Dorsch, 30 October 1944. See also Seidler, *Deutscher Volkssturm*, p. 209. The fraught relationship between Hanke and Bormann was once more to the fore, this time over Hanke's nominations for Lower Silesian *Volkssturm Gaustabsführer* (*Gau Volkssturm* Chief of Staff). See BAB, NS6/313 (all 1944), p. 69, Hanke to Bormann, 2 October; p. 95, Bormann to Hanke, 11 October; NS6/314, p. 137, Hanke to Bormann, 17 October; p. 141, Bormann to Hanke, 19 October. Hanke's first nomination, *SS-Obergruppenführer* Schmidt, was dismissed by Bormann because he had only fought in the First World War and thus lacked the necessary knowledge of modern military leadership. Schmidt also lacked awareness of the personnel and political circumstances of Lower Silesia and Bormann demanded that Hanke submit the name of a suitable Party member. When he did, he nominated *Kreisleiter* Paul Kubsch of Frankenstein. Kubsch had served on the Eastern Front for 14 months and with a small force had fought his way through to German lines after the Stalingrad encirclement. Kubsch was experienced in tank fighting and had been released from service because of wounds. Since then Kubsch had commanded a sector of the fortifications programme. Bormann was still unimpressed. Kubsch was deemed to have served on the Eastern Front for barely a year and was said to lack the necessary soldierly skills to be Chief of Staff for the *Gauleiter*. Again Hanke was ordered to submit another Party member for the post.

203 Seidler, *Deutscher Volkssturm*, p. 209.

204 BAB, NS6/314, p. 94, Bracht to Bormann, 30 October 1944. In a speech, reported by the *Oberschlesische Zeitung* on 22 October 1944, Bracht admitted that, 'for a certain time the equipment and arms of the *Volkssturm* would leave much to be desired'. TNA, FO 898/187, 6 November 1944, p. C7.
205 BAB, R22/3372, pp. 261–262, 26 December 1944.
206 BAB, R55/602, p. 111, Dr Schulz to Dr Naumann (RMVuP), 20 October 1944.
207 BA-LA, Ost-Dok. 10/562, p. 51.
208 BA-LA, Ost-Dok.10/636, p. 1.
209 BA-LA, Ost-Dok. 8/731, p. 4; 10/636, p. 3.
210 BA-LA, Ost-Dok. 8/725, p. 4. Similarly, the 600 men of the Breslau district battalion No 3 received 100 rifles of mixed origin and 15 cartridges for each of the weapons. Mammach, *Der Volkssturm*, p. 68.
211 BA-LA, Ost-Dok. 8/729, p. 5; 10/655, p. 9.
212 TNA, FO 898/187, 23 October 1944, p. C3 quoting Mirror of the Times, 21 October 1944.
213 Ibid.
214 Ibid. An article on *Volkssturm* training in the Upper Silesian defences did admit that 'some of the members were pronounced irreplaceable and were compelled to leave their comrades with regret and to go back'. See FO 898/187, 27 November 1944, p. C6 quoting *OZ*, 11 November 1944.
215 Kissel, *Der Deutsche Volkssturm*, p. 57; Seidler, *Deutscher Volkssturm*, pp. 314–315.
216 Siebel-Achenbach, *Lower Silesia*, p. 28.
217 BA-LA, Ost-Dok. 8/705, p. 2.
218 BA-LA, Ost-Dok. 8/702, pp. 6, 10. Sick men with medical certification were still called up for the East Prussian *Volkssturm* by the Party authorities. See Ost-Dok. 8/518, p. 3.
219 BA-LA, Ost-Dok. 8/708, p. 4; 10/543, p. 13.
220 BA-LA, Ost-Dok. 8/703, p. 3.
221 Murawski, *Die Eroberung Pommerns*, pp. 33–34.
222 BA-LA, Ost-Dok. 10/424, p. 1.
223 BA-LA, Ost-Dok. 8/639, p. 2; 8/670, p. 3. The shortage of clothing, footwear and other equipment was addressed by *Kreisleiter* Kieckhöfer of Stettin in an appeal published in the *Pommersche Zeitung* on 25 October 1944. Parts of uniforms were wanted – Party uniforms, as well as those of customs officials, tram conductors, policemen, firemen and foresters were deemed suitable. Compasses, maps, haversacks, field glasses, mess tins and water bottles together with boots and shoes of all types were also requested in the appeal. TNA, FO 898/187, 6 November 1944, p. C8.
224 BA-LA, Ost-Dok. 8/694, p. 5.
225 BA-LA, Ost-Dok. 8/674, p. 3. Schwede-Coburg had fewer difficulties than Hanke in his nomination for *Gaustabsführer*. He plumped for *Regierungspräsident* Paul Eckardt, an old Party member and *SS-Brigadeführer*. Eckardt had front-line experience in two world wars and deemed suitable for battalion command. With over 10 years of political experience in Pomerania he was well known in Party circles and among the general population. BAB, NS6/763, p. 48, Schwede-Coburg to Bormann, 30 September 1944.
226 BA-LA, Ost-Dok. 8/670, p. 4.
227 BA-LA, Ost-Dok. 8/637, p. 5.
228 BA-LA, Ost-Dok. 8/674, p. 3; 8/639, p. 2; 8/657, p. 2.
229 BA-LA, Ost-Dok. 8/648, p. 3.

230 BA-LA, Ost-Dok. 10/406. Testimony of Hans Dobrzinsky.
231 BAB, NS6/763, p. 105, Schwede-Coburg to Bormann, 6 October 1944.
232 BA-LA, Ost-Dok. 10/406, testimony of Fritz Voss; 10/410, p. 1.
233 BA-LA, Ost-Dok. 10/424, p. 4.
234 BA-LA, Ost-Dok. 8/657, p. 2; 8/666, p. 3; 10/406, testimony of Fritz Voss; 10/410, p. 3.
235 BA-LA, Ost-Dok. 8/670, p. 4.
236 BA-LA, Ost-Dok. 8/638, p. 4.
237 BAB, NS6/764, p. 327, Schwede-Coburg to Bormann, 18 December 1944.
238 BA-LA, Ost-Dok. 10/424, p. 2.
239 Ibid., pp. 4–5.
240 BAB, R55/622, p. 172, 8 February 1945; Müller and Ueberschär, *Kriegsende 1945*, p. 46.
241 BAB, R55/622, p. 172, 8 February 1945; R22/243, p. 136, 7 February 1945; Mammach, *Der Volkssturm*, p. 98.
242 Mammach, *Der Volkssturm*, p. 98.
243 Seidler, *Deutscher Volkssturm*, p. 373.

Chapter 7 A Stay of Execution

1 *The Times*, 27 July 1944; 28 July 1944.
2 BAB, NS1/585, pp. 111, 113; Mehner (ed.), *Die Geheimen Tagesberichte. Band 10: 1. März 1944 –31. August 1944*, pp. 382, 385.
3 BAB, NS1/585, p. 111; Mehner (ed.), *Die Geheimen Tagesberichte. Band 10*, p. 382.
4 Dieckert and Großmann, *Der Kampf um Ostpreussen*, p. 29.
5 BAB, NS1/585, p. 157.
6 IfZ, MA-736, report by the East Prussian NSV leader Erich Post, 5 September 1944.
7 BfZ, SSt Feldpost 1944/7, E.S., 28 July 1944.
8 Ibid., 1944/8, E.S., 2 August 1944.
9 BA-LA, Ost-Dok., 8/583, pp. 4–5; 8/585, p. 5.
10 BA-LA, Ost-Dok. 8/583, p. 5.
11 BA-LA, Ost-Dok. 8/585, pp. 4–5; 10/247, p. 4.
12 BA-LA, Ost-Dok. 8/583, p. 3.
13 See BA-LA, Ost-Dok. 8/583, p. 6 where a figure of 7,000 to 8,000 people remaining in Tilsit on 18 October is mentioned, whereas Ost-Dok. 8/585, p. 5 put the figure at around 12,000.
14 On the significance of Insterburg as a transportation centre see BA-LA, Ost-Dok.10/154, report by Arthur Roeseler, p. 6.
15 Mehner (ed.), *Die Geheimen Tagesberichte. Band 10*, p. 385.
16 BA-LA, Ost-Dok. 8/551, p. 4.
17 BA-LA, Ost-Dok. 10/154. Testimony of Karl Drengwitz, p. 5.
18 BA-LA, Ost-Dok. 8/551, pp. 4–5.
19 See BA-LA, Ost-Dok. 10/154, reports by *Bürgermeister* Dr Wander, pp. 14–15; Arthur Roeseler, p. 5. See also Schieder (ed.), *Dokumentation. Band 1/1*, testimony of Dr Wander, pp. 9–14. The 'loosening up' measures enacted in Insterburg during November and December 1944 resulted in the population dropping to 8,000 to 10,000 from a 1939 figure of 49,000.
20 BA-LA, Ost-Dok. 8/526, p. 2; Schieder (ed.), *Dokumentation. Band 1/1*, pp. 118–119.
21 BA-LA, Ost- Dok. 8/526, pp. 2–3; *Manchester Guardian*, 18 October 1944.
22 Siebel-Achenbach, *Lower Silesia*, p. 29.

23 Mehner (ed.), *Die Geheime Tagesberichte. Band 11: 1. September–31. Dezember 1944*, p. 108.
24 BAB, R22/3358, p. 85, 3 December 1944.
25 BfZ, SSt Feldpost 1944/7, Oberst O.M., 20 July 1944; 1944/10, E.S., 15 October 1944.
26 BA-MA, RW20-1/8, p. 18; Mehner (ed.), *Die Geheimen Tagesberichte. Band 10*, p. 112; Middlebrook and Everitt, *The Bomber Command War Diaries*, p. 493. Some 103 Lancaster bombers from No. 1 and No. 5 Bomber Groups of RAF Bomber Command embarked on this minelaying operation in the Baltic off Danzig, Gdynia and Pillau. Losses were considerable and nine Lancasters failed to return. The operation against Pillau was an attempt to block the 17.5 mile-long sea channel from Pillau to Königsberg harbour. The mission was only reported in *The Times* three months later on 6 July 1944 when it was claimed that all the crews involved in minelaying in the Königsberg sea canal had made it home. The report noted: 'Later it was learned that no traffic was able to get from Königsberg to the sea for 15 days.'
27 *The Times*, 18 August 1944, 31 August 1944; Webster and Frankland, *The Strategic Air Offensive. Volume III Victory, Part V*, pp. 176–180; Middlebrook and Everitt, *The Bomber Command War Diaries*, pp. 569, 575; A. Verrier, *The Bomber Offensive* (London: B.T. Batsford Ltd, 1968), p. 297. After the breakout from Normandy and the victories in France, in which Bomber Command was heavily involved, the period in late August and early September 1944 has been described as one of 'strategic hiatus' by one historian when airmen were 'astonishingly free to pursue their personal inclinations. M. Hastings, *Bomber Command* (London: Pan Books edition, 1999), p. 302. The future deployment of Bomber Command was discussed at the highest level but its commander Air Marshal Arthur Harris was concerned that the delay and the use of the force in tactical support tasks gave the German homeland an invaluable respite. From mid-August 1944, the Americans recommenced bombing German synthetic fuel facilities while Bomber Command, exploiting the weakness of Germany's fighter defences in the late summer of 1944, revisited Germany's cities. F. Taylor, *Dresden: Tuesday 13 February 1945* (London: Bloomsbury, 2004), p. 198.
28 BAB, NS1/585, p. 143, 18 August 1944.
29 BA-LA, Ost-Dok. 8/636, pp. 23–24.
30 Ibid.; BAB, NS1/585, p. 143, 18 August 1944.
31 BAB, R22/3386, p. 64, 29 September 1944.
32 BA-LA, Ost-Dok. 8/636, pp. 23–24.
33 BAB, NS1/585, p. 143, 18 August 1944.
34 Ibid., p. 160, 31 August 1944.
35 Ibid., p. 143, 18 August 1944. RAF reconnaissance quickly appraised the damage arising from the 16/17 August raid. Even although there was heavy cloud cover, considerable damage was observed across the city stretching east from the Kaiser-Wilhelm Platz in the city centre across to the River Oder. Many of the public buildings located in this area were gutted. TNA, AIR 14/3779, Immediate Interpretation Report No. K.3029, 19 August 1944. The reconnaissance highlighted the damage to industrial targets. The impact on the shipbuilding and machine shops of the Stettiner Oder-Werke, the heavy damage to the sugar refinery, 'every building is damaged and most of them are destroyed', and to the Admiralty fitting out yard featured in reports. AIR 14/3779, Supplement to Immediate Interpretation Report No. K.3029, 20 August 1944. On damage to dockside installations and warehouses see also Second Supplement to Immediate Interpretation Report No. K.3029, 21 August 1944. As well as stressing the damage to the eastern part of the city,

reports also claimed that the main railway station, gutted on 5/6 January 1944, had been hit again and the police headquarters were extensively damaged. See Interpretation Report No. K.3029, 25 August 1944. The Preliminary Attack Assessment estimated that 48%, or 660 tons, of the 1,373 tons of bombs reported over the target fell on the administrative area containing buildings and 21% of all buildings were seriously damaged, including 11% of industrial buildings. This equated to the loss of labour of 178,000 industrial workers for one month. Ministry of Home Security Research and Experiments Department, Preliminary Attack Assessment – Stettin, Attack of 16/17 August 1944.

36 BA-LA, Ost-Dok. 8/636, pp. 23–24.

37 BAB, NS1/585, p. 143, 18 August 1944.

38 Ibid., p. 160, 31 August 1944; BA-LA, Ost-Dok. 8/626, pp. 24–25; Middlebrook and Everitt, *The Bomber Command War Diaries*, p. 575. Webster and Frankland, *The Strategic Air Offensive. Volume III Victory, Part V*, p. 180 notes that three merchant ships were sunk. The intercept material can be found at TNA, HW1/3202; HW1/3208.

Initial British reconnaissance reported that most of the damage in the centre and north of the city had been caused by fire. TNA, AIR 14/3779, Immediate Interpretation Report No. K.3103, 4 September 1944. Initial assessments indicated that of the bomb load over the target, 1,243 tons, 340 tons or 27% of the bombs dropped fell on the administrative area containing buildings and about 9% of the city's buildings were destroyed, including 2% of the industrial facilities, Ministry of Home Security Research and Experiments Department, Preliminary Attack Assessment – Stettin, Attack of 29/30 August 1944. The rather limited impact of this raid on the German war economy was noted in later British reporting which, in contrast to accounts on the ground, indicated that the Stettiner Oder-Werke had not been severely affected. British reconnaissance seemed to show that 'the greater damage is to business and residential property west of the port area' and only pointed specifically to a badly damaged gas works and half gutted telegraph office. Interpretation Report No. K.3103, 9 September 1944.

39 *TBJG 13*, (all 1944), p. 257, 18 August; p. 275, 20 August; p. 297, 23 August; p. 363, 30 August.

40 *The Times*, 18 August 1944.

41 *TBJG 13*, pp. 365, 373, 31 August 1944.

42 BAB, R22/3386, pp. 64–65, 29 September 1944.

43 *The Times*, 28 August 1944, 31 August 1944; Webster and Frankland, *The Strategic Air Offensive. Volume III Victory, Part V*, pp. 176–181; Middlebrook and Everitt, *The Bomber Command War Diaries*, pp. 573, 575; Verrier, *The Bomber Offensive*, pp. 297, 299; D. Irving, *The Destruction of Dresden* (London: Corgi Books edition, 1971), pp. 61–62. On the Königsberg raids see A. Noble, 'A Most Distant Target: The Bombing of Königsberg, August 1944, *War & Society*, Volume 25, Number 1, May 2006, pp. 55–75. Königsberg was important as a shipping, administrative and transportation centre. Only 10.6% of the city's inhabitants were industrial workers, a lower percentage than Berlin, Dresden or Stettin and the city accounted for a mere 0.28% of the Reich's total industrial production. See US Strategic Bombing Survey, Studies Division Report (European Report 31), Volume II, 17a.

44 Mehner (ed.), *Die Geheimen Tagesberichte. Band 10*, p. 481.

45 On flying over Sweden see Mehner (ed.), *Die Geheimen Tagesberichte. Band 10*, p. 481; *TBJG 13*, p. 373, 31 August 1944; Webster and Frankland, *The Strategic Air Offensive. Volume III Victory, Part V*, Map 4 Night Operations 29th–30th August 1944. The attack on Stettin

on the same evening also involved the violation of Swedish airspace. On overestimates of RAF bomber numbers participating in the second raid on Königsberg see BA-LA, Ost-Dok. 8/588, p. 6, *Oberbürgermeister* Will, 'around 600 bombers'; Dieckert and Großmann, *Der Kampf um Ostpreussen*, p. 34, 'around 600 bombers'; Lass, *Die Flucht*, p. 20, 'the British attacked with 600 machines'; Lasch, *So fiel Königsberg*, p. 25, 'On 29/30 there followed a renewed attack by the British air force with around 660 planes'; *Das Ostpreußenblatt*, 30 August 1969, 'over 500 bombers'; Gause, *Die Geschichte der Stadt Königsberg*, p. 159, '600 aeroplanes'. M. Wieck, *Zeugnis vom Untergang Königsbergs. Ein 'Geltungsjude' berichtet* (Heidelberg: Heidelberger Verlagsanstalt, 1990), p. 144, 'Two bombing attacks by more than 800 British heavy bombers in total.'

46 BA-LA, Ost-Dok. 8/588, p. 6; Lasch, *So fiel Königsberg*, p. 25; Lass, *Die Flucht,* p. 20; *Das Ostpreußenblatt*, 30 August 1969.

47 BfZ, SSt Feldpost 1944/8, A.E., 27 August 1944.

48 Wieck, *Zeugnis vom Untergang Königsbergs*, p. 151. RAF reporting on the first Königsberg raid is limited. Reconnaissance carried out on the morning of 27 August produced 'excellent quality prints marred by smoke' and it was deduced that '[t]he weight of the attack fell across the Eastern side of the town where fires are still raging'. Fires were still burning at the Devau barracks where 20 buildings were said to have been damaged. Seven buildings, 'probably warehouses', along the banks of the River Pregel were destroyed, as were grandstands at the racecourse. TNA, AIR 34/611, Immediate Interpretation Report No. K.3094, 27 August 1944. Some interpretations have concluded that this attack was 'unsuccessful' as the clusters of J-bombs (incendiaries) were as ineffective in Königsberg as they had been in Stuttgart in July and Darmstadt on 25 August. See Irving, *The Destruction of Dresden*, pp. 61–62. The failure of the Darmstadt raid of 25 August was attributed to a series of misfortunes on the night. These led to a mere four or five crews hitting the target according to the official history, Webster and Frankland, *The Strategic Air Offensive. Volume Three Victory, Part V*, p. 179.

49 IfZ, MA-737, *PZ*, 28 August 1944.

50 Ibid.

51 Ibid.

52 Webster and Frankland, *The Strategic Air Offensive. Volume III Victory, Part V*, p. 180.

53 *The Times*, 31 August 1944.

54 Irving, *The Destruction of Dresden*, p. 61.

55 von Lehndorff, *East Prussian Diary*, p. 36.

56 On the same night 1,243 tons of bombs were reported to have been dropped on Bomber Command's other major target, Stettin. See Middlebrook and Everitt, *The Bomber Command War Diaries*, p. 575; *The Times*, 31 August 1944. See also Webster and Frankland, *The Strategic Air Offensive. Volume III Victory, Part V*, p. 180. The official history underlined the potency of the strike and the advances made by Bomber Command: 'Results of this kind against so distant a target would hardly have been achieved a year earlier by 1,000 bombers. Such was the developing power of air attack produced by greater marking and bomber accuracy. Major results could now be achieved by minor forces.'

57 Losses were also high in the Stettin raid that same evening. The loss of 23 planes from an attacking force of 403 machines equated to 5.7%. However, the raids on both targets earlier in the month produced losses which were significantly lower than the August 1944 average. Four planes were lost out of the 175 attackers in the 26–27 August raid on Königsberg, 2.3% of the force, while the five planes lost from the 461 bombers sent against

Stettin on the night of 16–17 August was 1.1% of the force. See Webster and Frankland, *The Strategic Air Offensive. Volume III Victory, Part V*, pp. 176–177.

58 Mehner (ed.), *Die Geheimen Tagesberichte. Band 10*, p. 490.

59 *TBJG 13*, pp. 365, 373, 31 August 1944.

60 Ibid., p. 389, 2 September 1944.

61 TNA, AIR 14/3773, Immediate Interpretation Report No. K.3104, 4 September 1944.

62 Ibid.

63 Ibid.

64 Ibid., Air Staff Intelligence, Immediate Assessment of Results, 5 September 1944.

65 Ibid.

66 Webster and Frankland, *The Strategic Air Offensive. Volume III Victory, Part V*, p. 180.

67 TNA, AIR 14/3773, Ministry of Home Security, Research and Experiments Department Preliminary Attack Assessment, based on cover of 2 September 1944.

68 TNA, AIR 14/3773, Interpretation Report No. 3104, 24 September 1944.

69 BAB, R22/3375, p. 258, 9 September 1944.

70 IfZ, MA-736, report by the East Prussian NSV leader Erich Post, 5 September 1944.

71 BAB, R22/3375, p. 273, 30 October 1944.

72 Gause, *Die Geschichte der Stadt Königsberg*, p. 159.

73 BA-LA, Ost-Dok. 8/588, p. 6; Dieckert and Großmann, *Der Kampf um Ostpreussen*, pp. 34–35; Lasch, *So fiel Königsberg*, pp. 25–26; Lass, *Die Flucht*, pp. 20–21.

74 BAB, R22/3375, p. 258, 9 September 1944; Baedeker, *Germany*, pp. 131–133; H. Gerhardi, *Helga* (Aylesbury: Virona, 1993) p. 160.

75 BA-LA, Ost-Dok. 8/588, p. 6; Dieckert and Großmann, *Der Kampf um Ostpreussen*, p. 35.

76 Gerhardi, *Helga*, p. 158.

77 von Lehndorff, *East Prussian Diary*, pp. 36–37.

78 Wieck, *Zeugnis vom Untergang Königsbergs*, p. 151.

79 BA-LA, Ost-Dok. 8/518, p. 4.

80 Diary of the Königsberg writer Wilhelm Matull in Bundesminister für Vertriebene, Flüchtlinge und Kriegsgeschädigte (ed.), *Dokumente Deutscher Kriegsschäden. Evakuirte. Kriegssachgeschädigte. Währungsgeschädigte. Die geschichtliche und rechtliche Entwicklung. 1 Beiheft Aus den Tagen des Luftkrieges und des Wiederaufbaues Erlebnis- und Erfahrungsberichte* (Bonn: Bundesministerium für Vertriebene, Flüchtlinge und Kriegsgeschädigte, 1960), pp. 355–356.

81 Gerhardi, *Helga*, p. 159; Wieck, *Zeugnis vom Untergang Königsbergs*, p. 152.

82 Wieck, *Zeugnis vom Untergang Königsbergs*, p. 152.

83 Lass, *Die Flucht*, p. 21.

84 TNA, AIR 14/3773, Immediate Assessment of Results, 5 September 1944.

85 See for instance Sebald, *On the Natural History of Destruction*, p. 14.

86 *Das Ostpreußenblatt*, 30 August 1969; Gerhardi, *Helga*, p. 160.

87 Gause, *Die Geschichte der Stadt Königsberg*, p. 165.

88 IfZ, MA-737, *Notstands-Ausgabe* no. 2, 1 September 1944.

89 Hastings, *Armageddon*, p. 305.

90 IfZ, MA-737, *PZ*, 5 September 1944.

91 Ibid., 11 September 1944.

92 IfZ, MA-736, report by the East Prussian NSV leader Erich Post, 5 September 1944.

93 Wieck, *Zeugnis vom Untergang Königsbergs*, p. 153.

94 BfZ, Archiv N 94.8, *Die Lebensgeschichte der Herry Schröder*.

95 Gerhardi, *Helga*, p. 159.
96 IfZ, MZ 9/112, *VB*, 28/29 October 1944.
97 IfZ, MA-737, *PZ*, 7 November 1944.
98 Gerhardi, *Helga*, p. 163.
99 BA-LA, Ost-Dok. 8/598, p. 14.
100 BAB, R22/3375, p. 265, 13 October 1944.
101 BAB, R55/600, pp. 316–317 Maertins, 14 November 1944; reply by Schäffer (RMVuP), 24 November 1944.
102 Gause, *Die Geschichte der Stadt Königsberg*, p. 160.
103 *Das Ostpreußenblatt*, 26 September 1964. One memoir account also mentions a raid on Ratshof, a northern suburb of Königsberg, in November 1944. A number of hospitals were said to have been hit – these were opposite military barracks deemed by the author to be the intended targets. The author was trapped in an air raid shelter for a few hours and there were 63 deaths from suffocation and in the stampede which followed rescuers breaking down the entrance door. Unfortunately, I have been unable to fully substantiate this account or to find any other mention of it in archival or published sources. The identity of the raiders is unclear. See Gerhardi, *Helga*, pp. 176–180.
104 *Das Ostpreußenblatt*, 30 August 1969. The RAF never bombed Breslau although it was considered as a target for a devastating blow during the closing months of 1944. The Red Army's rapid advance to the environs of Breslau in January 1945 removed the city from Bomber Command's attention, which was soon to focus squarely on Dresden. However, information and reconnaissance on Breslau was gathered. See TNA, AIR 40/1941, Target Information Sheet for the Linke-Hoffmann works and other targets, 14 August 1944; AIR 40/1943 for photographs of the Breslau–Brockau railway yards in December 1944.
105 TNA, AIR 34/611, Interpretation Report No 6892 Eastern Germany, 17 September 1944.
106 There were major attacks on Pölitz on 29 May 1944, 20 June 1944, 25 August 1944, 7 October 1944, 21 December 1944, 21 December 1944, 13 January 1945, 8 February 1945. See BAB, NS1/585, pp. 47, 77, 156, 251. BA-LA, Ost-Dok. 8/636, pp. 15–21; 8/652, pp. 3–5. See also Mehner (ed.), *Die Geheimen Tagesberichte. Band 10*, pp. 238, 283, 481; *Band 11*, pp. 104–105, 310. The Eighth Air Force attacked Stettin on 6 October 1944 aiming at the Stettiner Stowerwerke AG and the Pommersche Motorenbau GmbH. Later reconnaissance indicated that any damage to the targets was quickly repaired. See TNA, AIR 14/3779, Immediate Interpretation Report No K.3445, 23 December 1944. Details of the attacks in late 1944 by the American Fifteenth Air Force on Upper Silesia and on the territories added to the province following the defeat of Poland in 1939: 7 July, 7 August, 20 August, 22 August, 27 August, 29 August, 13 September, 13 October, 14 October, 17 October, 17 November, 20 November, 2–3 December, 17–19 December, 21 December and 26 December. See NS1/585, pp. 94, 127, 129, 146, 150, 158, 160, 191–192, 276, 341, 348, 381, 418. See also Mehner (ed.), *Die Geheimen Tagesberichte. Band 10*, pp. 325, 421, 460, 467, 484; *Band 11*, pp. 34, 123, 126, 135, 215, 224, 259, 286, 299, 302, 305, 310, 324. The air attacks on Upper Silesia were also mentioned in the OLG President Kattowitz reports dated 16 August 1944 and 20 December 1944 and in the GSA's report dated 6 October 1944, see BAB, R22/3372, pp. 261–263, 264–266, 267–273. See also Gunter, *Last Laurels*, pp. 1–4, 12–13.
107 G, Kirwin, 'Allied Bombing and Nazi Domestic Propaganda', *EHQ*, Volume 15, 1985, pp. 341–362.
108 Schieder (ed.), *Expulsion Documents*, pp. 2–3.

109 BA-LA, Ost-Dok. 8/652, p. 5. See also Granzow, *Tagebuch eines Hitlerjugend*, p. 184. The sight of waves of American bombers flying unchalleged over the Pomeranian coast towards Danzig led to an animated discussion between a visitor from the Ruhr and the author's father on Pomerania's likely fate. The former argued that his evacuated wife could not remain in Pomerania to fall into Soviet hands. The author's father indignantly replied that the Bolsheviks would never set foot in Pomerania.
110 IfZ, MZ 9/112, *VB*, 10 November 1944.
111 IfZ, MZ 235/4, *Das Reich*, 5 November 1944.
112 Ibid., 19 November 1944; MZ 9/112 *VB*, 20 December 1944.
113 BAB, R55/608, p. 30, *Mundpropagandaparole* 5, 8 November 1944.
114 IfZ, MA 737, *PZ*, 7 November 1944.
115 Ibid., 8 November 1944.
116 IfZ, MA 737, *KAZ*, 30 November 1944.
117 Schieder (ed.), *Dokumentation. Band 1/1*, p. 13.
118 Siebel-Achenbach, *Lower Silesia*, pp. 29–30.
119 TNA, FO 898/187, 11 December 1944, p. A6.
120 BA-LA, Ost-Dok. 8/571, p. 4.
121 BA-LA, Ost-Dok. 8/513, p. 4. When the Red Army winter offensive commenced on 12 January, part of the Army Group's staff was in Wartenburg, some still remained in Ortelsburg and others were in transit.
122 BAB, R55/793, p. 25, 1 December 1944.
123 *TBJG 14*, p. 146, 3 November 1944; p. 184, 9 November 1944; p. 223, 17 November 1944; p. 167, 24 November 1944; pp. 455–456, 21 December 1944.
124 BAB, R55/793, p. 25, 1 December 1944.
125 *TBJG 14*, p. 486, 29 December 1944.
126 BAB, R55/793, p. 13, 2 January 1945.
127 TNA, FO 898/187, 4 December 1944, p. A7, quoting *Nachtausgabe*, 25 November 1944.
128 *TBJG 14*, p. 88, 23 October 1944.
129 Ibid., pp. 230–231, 18 November 1944; pp. 354–355, 5 December 1944; E. Fröhlich (ed.), *Die Tagebücher von Joseph Goebbels. Im Auftrag des Instituts für Zeitgeschichte und mit Unterstützung des Staatlichen Archivdienstes Rußlands. Teil II Diktate 1941–1945. Band 15. Januar–April 1945* (Munich: K.G. Saur, 1995) (Hereinafter *TBJG 15*), p. 104, 11 January 1945.
130 *TBJG 14*, p. 492, 30 December 1944.
131 Ibid., pp. 165–166, 6 November 1944; pp. 179, 184, 9 November; pp. 422, 427, 16 December; p. 440, 19 December; pp. 455–456, 21 December; p. 464, 23 December; pp. 473–474, 24 December; pp. 486–487, 29 December; p. 492, 30 December; *TBJG 15*, p. 33, 1 January 1945; p. 38, 2 January; pp. 42–43, 3 January; p. 76, 6 January; p. 84, 8 January; pp. 106–107, 11 January.
132 *TBJG 14*, p. 230, 18 November 1944.
133 Ibid., pp. 455–456, 21 December 1944.
134 R. Semmler, *Goebbels: The Man Next to Hitler* (London: Westhouse, 1947), p. 173.
135 Ibid., pp. 173–174.
136 BAB, R55/601, p. 237, 5 December 1944.
137 Ibid., p. 264, 28 December 1944.
138 Ibid., p. 257, 19 December 1944
139 BA-LA, Ost-Dok. 8/591, p. 21; Schieder (ed.), *Dokumentation. Band 1/1*, pp. 13–14.

140 BfZ, SSt Feldpost 1944/11, J.H., 21 November 1944; BA-LA, Ost-Dok. 8/510, p. 14.
141 IfZ, MA-737, *PZ,* 30 November 1944; BA-LA, Ost-Dok. 8/591, p. 27.
142 F. H. Hinsley (ed.), *British Intelligence in the Second World War. Volume Three. Part II* (London: HMSO, 1988), p. 285, quoting *Luftwaffe* message of 14 October 1944.
143 Ibid., quoting message from Admiral Eastern Baltic, 29 November 1944.
144 BfZ, SSt Feldpost 1944/11, E.W., 12 November 1944.
145 Ibid., W.M. 29 November 1944.
146 BfZ, Archiv N94.9/1. Account of Heinz Künzler, p. 15.
147 H. Linck, *Königsberg 1945–1948* (Leer: Verlag Rautenberg und Möckel, 1948), p. 12.
148 BAB, R22/3375, p. 262, 11 October 1944.
149 Ibid., p. 271, 24 November 1944.
150 BAB, NS19/2606, pp. 39–41, 9 December 1944.
151 Ibid., p. 43, 28 December 1944.
152 BAB, R22/3375, p. 267, 19 October 1944.
153 BA-LA, Ost-Dok. 8/556.
154 BA-LA, Ost-Dok. 8/540, pp. 1–2.
155 BA-LA, Ost-Dok. 8/519, pp. 1–3. However, this assertion is somewhat weakened by Bredow's claim that most Germans were forced into this activity, received little training and were left to their fate by the Soviets after being dropped.
156 Ibid.
157 Dieckert and Großmann, *Der Kampf um Ostpreussen*, p. 78.
158 TNA, FO 898/187, 4 December 1944, p. A6 quoting *Deutsche Nachrichten Bureau* Europe, 30 November 1944.
159 Stahlberg, *Bounden Duty*, p. 372.
160 Irving, *Hitler's War*, p. 715.
161 Trevor-Roper (ed.), *The Bormann Letters,* pp. 139, 142. Field Marshal Wilhelm Keitel agreed that the presence of the FHQ in East Prussia had 'a very soothing effect on the population'. In a letter to his wife on 24 October he added, 'The Russians certainly won't dream that we are still here, which is an added safeguard for us. There are more than enough troops around to protect us.' W. Gorlitz (ed.), *The Memoirs of Field Marshal Wilhelm Keitel* (New York: Cooper Square Press, 2000 edition), pp. 190–191.
162 *TBJG 14*, p. 160, 5 November 1944; pp. 216–217, 16 November 1944.
163 Hoßbach, *Die Schlacht um Ostpreußen,* p. 30.
164 Irving, *Hitler's War*, p. 726.
165 Around 2,000 *Organisation Todt* labourers were still working to reinforce the Wolf's Lair on 20 November 1944 when Hitler left.
166 Dieckert and Großmann, *Der Kampf um Ostpreussen*, p. 73.
167 BA-LA, Ost-Dok. 8/591, p. 29.
168 BAB, R22/3375, p. 261, 11 October 1944.
169 Ibid., p. 274, 30 October 1944.
170 Ibid., p. 271, 24 November 1944. Similarly, a former official in Deutsch Krone (Pomerania) recalled that the Königsberg *Luftwaffe* command had started to look for alternative quarters in his district and in neighbouring Netzekreis from November 1944. They had no sooner moved into their new quarters before the Soviet advance swept them away. See BA-LA, Ost-Dok. 8/666, p. 6.
171 BAB, R22/3386, p. 70, 1 December 1944. One group which did not seem to want to stay in Pomerania were the school children of Bochum. Despite the city's proximity to the

Western Front and the terrible damage it had suffered from bombing, the desire to stay in the west is revealed in the pages of the *Westfälische Landeszeitung, Rote Erde* in late 1944. Influential figures in Westphalia and Pomerania called for the return of children to schools in their Pomeranian reception districts. TNA, FO 898/187, 22 January 1945, p. C6, quoting *Westfälische Landeszeitung, Rote Erde*, 13 November 1944, 30 December 1944. This desire to go home could be attributed to homesickness, from an unwillingness to participate in Party projects such as digging duties at the *Pommernwall* or as a result of the influence of parents terrified that their offspring would fall into Soviet hands.

172 BA-LA, Ost-Dok. 8/645, pp. 9–10.

173 BAB, R22/3386, p. 70, 1 December 1944.

174 BA-LA, Ost-Dok. 8/645, pp. 10–12.

175 BAB, R22/3386, p. 71, 1 December 1944.

176 BAB, R22/3358, p. 83, 3 December 1944.

177 Ibid., pp. 83–84. The worrying events on the Eastern Front also led to the Armaments authorities in Breslau identifying a so-called evacuation area in the eastern fringes of Lower Silesia – the districts of Brieg and Oels. Preparations were made for the immobilisation of plant and the salvaging of material. Businesses in these districts were only to accumulate supplies necessary for 14 days of production and finished goods were to be transported out straightaway. BA-MA, RW 20 –8/29, p. 68.

178 Grieger, *Wie Breslau fiel*, p. 5. See also chapter 6, footnote 7.

179 *TBJG 14*, p. 502, 31 December 1944; Reuth, *Goebbels*, p. 342 mentions Hanke's claim that, 'he would defend Breslau against the Soviets to the last drop of blood'.

180 BA-LA, Ost-Dok 8/730, p. 8; Siebel-Achenbach, *Lower Silesia*, p. 30.

181 IfZ, MA-737, *PZ*, 9 November 1944.

182 *The Times*, 16 December 1944.

183 TNA, FO 898/187, 18 December 1944, p. A2, quoting broadcast by Hans Fritzsche, 16 December 1944.

184 Ibid. Hitler's New Year Order of the Day to the *Wehrmacht* on 1 January 1945 mentioned the Allies' intention to give 'Soviet Poland' East Prussia, Danzig, Pomerania and Silesia. This order was broadcast, published in the press and quoted by military commentators. See H. Michaelis and E. Schraepler (eds.), *Ursachen und Folgen. Vom deutschen Zusammenbruch 1918 und 1945 bis zur staatlichen Neuordnung Deutschlands in der Gegenwart. Band 22* (Berlin: Dokumenten-Verlag Dr. Herbert Wendler & Co, 1975), p. 327; TNA, FO 898/187, 8 January 1945, p. A2.

185 BAB, R58/976, pp. 94–98, 28 December 1944.

186 BAB, R55/612, pp. 35–37 State Secretary Sondermann (RMVuP) to all RPA, 4 January 1945.

187 *TBJG 15*, p. 70, 5 January 1945.

188 BAB, R55/612, p. 80, 1 January 1945. The Ardennes offensive was launched on 16 December 1944. The spearhead of the attack was the Sixth SS Panzer Army which was given the ambitious objective of recapturing the port of Antwerp despite the paucity of tank fuel. After bitter fighting and initial German gains, in the days prior to Christmas the weather cleared and the air forces of the western Allies took command of the skies over the battlefield, resistance stiffened and the attack fizzled out with heavy and irreplaceable German losses.

189 Ibid., p. 51.

190 Ibid., p. 95.

191 Guderian, *Panzer Leader*, p. 387.

192 Ibid., p. 386; Irving, *Hitler's War*, pp. 752–753.

193 von Ahlfen and Niehoff, *So kämpfte Breslau*, pp. 8–12; Siebel-Achenbach, *Lower Silesia,* p. 57.

194 Dieckert and Großmann, *Der Kampf um Ostpreussen*, p. 72.

195 Guderian, *Panzer Leader*, p. 386.

196 BA-LA, Ost-Dok. 8/591, p. 27.

197 Hoßbach, *Die Schlacht um Ostpreußen*, p. 40.

198 J. Thorwald, *Es begann an der Weichsel* (Munich: Knaur edition, 1995), pp. 17–18.

199 Dieckert and Großmann, *Der Kampf um Ostpreussen*, pp. 73–74; Lasch, *So fiel Königsberg,* p. 28. As the Germans clung on to this corner of Latvia the propagandists claimed the bitter defence had a valid purpose: 'In Kurland [Couland], too, we fight for East Prussia'. TNA, FO 898/187, 4 December 1944, p. A6 quoting Front Report, 30 November 1944.

200 BA-LA, Ost-Dok. 8/591, p. 17.

201 Dieckert and Großmann, *Der Kampf um Ostpreussen*, p. 75.

202 Lasch, *So fiel Königsberg*, p. 28. This episode is also recalled in the memoirs of Colonel-General Raus. According to Raus, Koch was impressed by the gravity of the situation when they spoke in Königsberg in early December. Koch then visited Hitler who initially agreed to transfer reinforcements from Courland to the Third Panzer Army. But Hitler then changed his mind after consulting with Schörner at Army Group North, concluding that the forces in Courland could attack in a southerly direction into the Soviet rear if the Red Army tried to cross the River Memel. See Newton, *Panzer Operations,* p. 302.

203 Lasch, *So fiel Königsberg*, p. 26.

204 Dieckert and Großmann, *Der Kampf um Ostpreussen*, p. 75.

205 Guderian, *Panzer Leader*, p. 388. Guderian added that 'The army groups' operational zones remained limited to narrow strips of territory extending to a depth of six miles behind the front. The heavy artillery batteries were actually stationed in the so-called "Home Area", which was subordinate to the Gauleiters and where no strong point might be built, no tree felled, without such action causing an immediate quarrel with the civil administration – that is to say with the Party.' See *Panzer Leader*, pp. 389–399.

206 Lasch, *So fiel Königsberg*, p. 27.

207 BA-LA, Ost-Dok. 8/591, p. 26; Dieckert and Großmann, *Der Kampf um Ostpreussen*, p. 76. The Germans also appreciated that the Kurisches Haff on the East Prussian coast would freeze over in winter and the thick ice cover could carry troops and vehicles. Around 150 wooden bunkers for three to five men, with heating facilities and mounted on rafts with sled runners were constructed and towed out to the frozen lagoon. They were reinforced with blocks of ice and camouflaged by snow. Colonel-General Raus recalled that it was hoped to prepare a brigade of ice-boats and motor-sleighs to move up reserves to reinforce the soldiers in the bunkers but the necessary boats and sleighs were not available on time and the plan had to be abandoned. Newton, *Panzer Operations*, p. 304.

208 BA-MA, RH20-4/615, file note 30 December 1944.

209 BA-LA, Ost-Dok. 8/510, pp. 10–11.

210 BA-LA, Ost-Dok. 8/530, pp. 4–5. Hoßbach gave Koch a final warning when he visited Fourth Army headquarters in late December.

211 Lieutenant Colonel P.G. Tsouras (ed.), *The Anvil of War* (London: Greenhill Books, 1994), p. 165.

212 BA-LA, Ost-Dok. 8/591, p. 27. See also Newton, *Panzer Operations*, pp. 301–317. Raus

confirmed in his memoirs that he did receive daily aerial reconnaissance from the *Luftwaffe* which showed the Red Army's concentration of forces and material. But on the eve of the offensive Soviet preparations followed the usual format and the Red Air Force fighters made a determined effort to force the *Luftwaffe* reconnaissance planes from the skies.

213 TNA, FO 898/187, 22 January 1945, p. C1
214 Hastings, *Armageddon*, pp. 305–306.
215 BA-LA, Ost-Dok. 8/591, p. 12.
216 BA-LA, Ost-Dok. 8/583, p. 7.
217 BA-LA, Ost-Dok. 8/570, p. 4; 8/591, p. 12.
218 W. Jegutzki, 'Bericht aus schwerer Zeit', in Reinoß (ed.), *Letzte Tage in Ostpreußen*, p. 238.
219 BA-LA, Ost-Dok. 8/591, pp. 15–16.
220 Hastings, *Armageddon*, p. 305.
221 Dieckert and Großmann, *Der Kampf um Ostpreussen*, p. 76.
222 Von Krockow, *Hour of the Women*, p. 25.
223 Knopp, *Die große Flucht*, pp. 55–57.
224 BA-LA, Ost-Dok. 8/591, pp. 29–30.
225 Knopp, *Die große Flucht*, p. 56.
226 BAB, R58/976, p. 94, 28 December 1944.
227 BA-LA, Ost-Dok. 8/521, p. 2.
228 Gerhardi, *Helga*, p. 190.
229 *The Annual Register 1944* (London: Longmans, Green and Co, 1945), pp. 194–195; *Manchester Guardian*, 22 September 1944, 6 October 1944. Often additional rations of meat were provided in place of fats, dairy products or bread. This was the result of the large-scale slaughter of cattle evacuated from regions occupied by the Red Army. The meat ration was increased to 750 grams in place of 125 grams of butter in East Prussia between 14 and 27 August. In December, the *Oberschlesische Zeitung* was quite candid with its admission that extra meat allowances arose from the slaughter of cattle from areas threatened by the enemy: 'The additional East Prussian cattle has so enriched the stocks of the Upper Silesian slaughterhouses and butcheries that they are now better supplied than was planned by the Economic Cattle Association of Upper Silesia.' TNA, FO 898/187, 15 January 1945, pp. C7–C8, quoting *OZ*, 3 December 1944.
230 TNA, FO 898/187, 21 August 1944, p. A6.
231 Rebentisch, *Führerstaat und Verwaltung*, pp. 523–524.
232 Ibid., pp. 527–528.
233 Ibid., p. 529.
234 Wieck, *Zeugnis vom Untergang Königsbergs*, p. 165.
235 U. and S. Goerges, 'Unser-und nicht nur unser-grausamer Abschied', in Reinoß (ed.), *Letzte Tage in Ostpreußen,* pp. 218–219.
236 BA-LA, Ost-Dok. 8/598, p. 13.
237 P. Peikert, *'Festung Breslau' in den Berichten eines Pfarrers, 22. Januar bis 6. Mai 1945* (East Berlin: Union Verlag, 1968) (K. Jonca and A. Konieczny (eds.)), p. 23.
238 TNA, FO 898/187, 22 January 1945, p. C1 quoting *Danziger Vorposten*, 4 January 1945.
239 TNA, FO 898/187, 22 January 1945, p. C1, quoting *Danziger Vorposten*, 5 January 1945.
240 Böddeker, *Die Flüchtlinge,* p. 174.
241 Dieckert and Großmann, *Der Kampf um Ostpreussen*, p. 77.
242 TNA, FO 898/187, 22 January 1945, p. A2, quoting *Krakauer Zeitung*, 10 January 1945.

243 Knopp, *Die große Flucht*, p. 55.

244 *TBJG 15*, p. 61, 4 January 1945. But Goebbels should have known better. Among the 70 divisions of Army Groups Centre and A there were only five armoured divisions. The Germans realised that the Soviet offensive would be a far grander affair. British codebreake noted in late December from German decrypts that assessments issued by *Fremde Heere West*, the Japanese Naval Mission in Berlin and the Third Panzer Army pointed to co-ordinated Soviet blows against Courland, East Prussia and the Vistula front as soon as stable weather conditions allowed. Hinsley (ed.), *British Intelligence in the Second World War. Volume Three. Part II*, p. 643.

245 Schieder (ed.), *Dokumentation Band 1/1*, p. 345, testimony of General Walter Petzel, Posen; Thorwald, *Es began an der Weichsel*, pp. 41–44.

Chapter 8 The Deluge

1 The instrument signalling the unconditional surrender of Germany was signed by General Alfred Jodl at Rheims on 7 May 1945. The surrender document was ratified by Field Marshal Keitel, Marshal Zhukov and Air Marshal Tedder in Berlin on the following day.

2 Erickson, *The Road to Berlin*, pp. 447–449.

3 Ibid., pp. 448–449. A Front Report from East Prussia broadcast on the German Home Service on 18 January 1945 highlighted German anxiety at the dominance of the Red Air Force: 'A cold blizzard sweeps the winter sky and hurls ice needles into our soldiers' faces. At present, however, they prefer this to a clear winter sky, for as soon as the cloud-cover bursts open, the Soviet Air Force appears.' TNA, FO 898/187, 22 January 1945, p. A4.

4 General Hoßbach was accused of taking an independent decision and surrendering the strongest bulwark in East Prussia without a fight. See Guderian, *Panzer Leader*, p. 400. Hoßbach actually acted in accordance with Colonel-General Reinhardt's instructions. Hoßbach later stressed that no provision had been made against an attack on Lötzen from the north, south or west and described the garrison and their weaponry as 'completely insufficient'. Hoßbach, *Die Schlacht um Ostpreußen,* pp. 47–48. Hoßbach has also been attacked for planning to give up East Prussia, retreat behind the Vistula and leave the East Prussian civilians to their fate. This argument maintains that Hoßbach's 1951 memoirs developed the myth that the aim of this plan was to rescue the entire East Prussian population from annihilation. In reality he insisted that civilians remain behind as the fleeing masses threatened to hinder the breakthrough to the West and even ordered treks on the roads to be run down. See H. Schwendemann in *Spiegel Special. Die Flucht der Deutschen*, 2/2002, pp. 42–47

5 Irving, *Hitler's War,* p. 761.

6 BA-LA, Ost-Dok. 8/529, p. 13; 8/530, p. 7.

7 TNA, FO 898/187, 29 January 1945, p. A5, quoting Front Report, 24 January 1945.

8 Colonel General L. Rendulic, *Gekämpft, Gesiegt, Geschlagen* (Wels-Heidelberg: Verlag Welsermühl, 1950), pp. 335–341.

9 Lasch, *So fiel Königsberg,* pp. 68–75.

10 Marshal Vasilevsky later claimed that 'over 93,000 enemy officers and soldiers were killed and 46,000 were taken prisoner.' See A.M. Vasilevsky, *A Lifelong Cause* (Moscow: Progress Publishers, 1981), p. 411.

11 On the planning and execution of the Königsberg operation from the standpoint of a leading Soviet participant, see Ibid., pp. 399–423; Marshal I. Bagramyan, 'The Storming

of Königsberg' in J. Erickson, *Main Front: Soviet Leaders Look Back on World War II* (London: Brassey's Defence Publishers, 1987), pp. 221–243.

12 Vasilevsky, *A Lifelong Cause*, p. 417 asserted that the Red Army took some 92,000 prisoners in Königsberg and its suburbs.

13 Lasch, *So fiel Königsberg*, pp. 81–114; Dieckert and Großmann, *Der Kampf um Ostpreussen*, pp. 143–205; Thorwald, *Es begann an der Weichsel*, pp. 173–193; Erickson, *The Road to Berlin*, pp. 542–546; Duffy, *Red Storm on the Reich*, pp. 203–219. Reports from Army Command East Prussia indicated that the further deployment of a strong *Kriegsmarine* battle group to support Pillau's defenders had not taken place because of the shortage of fuel. NA-US, Microcopy T-78, Roll No 304, p. 6255171, Army Command East Prussia report, 17 April 1945.

14 The daily German military communique failed to mention the loss of specific Upper Silesian cities, except Oppeln on 25 January. TNA, FO 898/187, 5 February 1945, p. A4.

15 Marshal V.I. Chuikov, *The Fall of Berlin* (New York: Ballantine Books, 1969), pp. 113–117; Marshal G.I. Zhukov, *Marshal Zhukov's Greatest Battles* (London: Macdonald, 1969) (H.E. Salisbury (ed.)), pp. 264–281. This 'furious controversy' of the mid and late 1960s is examined in J. Erickson, '*Poslednii Shturm*: The Soviet Drive to Berlin, 1945' in G. Bennett (ed.), *The End of the War in Europe 1945* (London: HMSO, 1996), pp. 15–40.

16 Chuikov, *The Fall of Berlin*, p. 117.

17 Beevor, *Berlin*, p. 63.

18 Chuikov, *The Fall of Berlin*, p. 113.

19 Ibid., p. 116. Chuikov's version of events was challenged on grounds of authenticity by an irate Zhukov and contradicted by his own verbal statements to prominent historians. Chuikov told the British historian John Erickson in 1963: 'My opinion is that *if* our communications had not been so spread out, in February, we *could* have struck out for Berlin.' But he recounted to Erickson that ammunition and fuel were in short supply and pontoons were needed to bridge the Oder and the nearby network of canals. Erickson, *Poslednii Shturm*, p. 15. At the same time, the Red Army had overran supplies and support and fuel lagged behind the lead units. The thaw turned roads to rivers and Soviet engineers were faced with the European gauge on remaining railway tracks.

20 At the same time, Zhukov, despite having advocated a drive towards Berlin in February, later evoked precedent to justify patience and also to have a poke at Stalin's past as a Political Commissar during the Soviet–Polish War: 'History shows us that risks should be taken but not blindly. A useful lesson in this is offered by the Red Army's drive against Warsaw in 1920 when a reckless, unsecured advance turned success into a serious defeat.' Salisbury (ed.), *Marshal Zhukov's Greatest Battles*, p. 277.

21 Ibid., pp. 278–279.

22 BAB, NS6/354, pp. 30–31, Circular 21/45 g.Rs., 23 January 1945; Duffy, *Red Storm on the Reich*, p. 177.

23 *TBJG 15*, pp. 456, 459, 9 March 1945; Ziemke, *Stalingrad to Berlin*, pp. 432–433; Padfield, *Himmler*, pp. 562–563. On innocents suffering this fate see, BA-LA, Ost-Dok. 10/644, testimony of Karl Littmann, p. 1; H. von Luck, *Panzer Commander: The Memoirs of Colonel Hans von Luck* (London: Praeger, 1989), pp. 199–200.

24 See L. Degrelle, *Campaign in Russia: The Waffen SS on the Eastern Front* (Torrance, California: Institute for Historical Review, 1985), pp. 305–306.

25 H. Michaelis and E. Schraepler (eds.),*Ursachen und Folgen. Vom deutschen Zusammenbruch 1918 und 1945 bis zur staatlichen Neuordnung Deutschlands in der Gegenwart. Band 23. Das*

militärische Zusammenbruch und das Ende des Dritten Reiches (Berlin: Dokumenten-Verlag Dr. Herbert Wendler & Co, 1976), p. 24.

26 Schenk, *Hitlers Mann in Danzig*, pp. 256–257; R.D. Müller and G.R. Ueberschär, *Kriegsende 1945: Die Zerstörung des Deutschen Reiches* (Frankfurt: Fischer Taschenbuch Verlag, 1994), pp. 156–158; Lindenblatt, *Pommern 1945*, p. 166; Steinert, *Hitler's War*, pp. 300–301.

27 O. Skorzeny, *Skorzeny's Special Missions* (London: Robert Hale Limited, 1957), p. 186. TNA, FO 898/187, 12 February 1945, p. C5, quoting German Home Service broadcast, 9 February 1945.

28 NA-US, Microcopy T-78, Roll No. 304, pp. 6255774–6255775, Himmler to Guderian, 1 February 1945.

29 BAB, NS19/2721, pp. 2–3, 19 February 1945. The Avars were a people of unknown origin in eastern Europe from the Sixth to the early Ninth centuries defeated by Charlemagne around 800.

30 According to a Front Report on 13 February, the German garrison of Posen consisted of 'The Cadets of the Infantry, an SS Cadet Detachment, railwaymen, *Volkssturm*, *Luftwaffe*, men of the commissariat [and] dispersed troops who happened to be in Posen.' TNA, FO 898/187, 18 February 1945, p. A3. They put up a stout defence of the city until its surrender on 23 February. On the evening of 22 February the commandant, Major General Ernst Gonell, draped in a swastika flag , shot himself. The reduction of Posen had involved a large part of General Chuikov's Eighth Guards Army. Gonell's report of 11 February 1945 had illustrated the plight of *Festung* Posen. The garrison was gradually being squeezed into an ever smaller area as the vastly superior Soviet forces bombarded them with heavy weapons of all calibre. The troops were war weary and had suffered heavy losses in house-to-house fighting. These losses had gravely affected the garrison's fighting potential. The deteriorating military situation and no prospect of relief meant that the mood of the troops was inclining towards apathy. Gonell claimed that only now, through bearing the fighting spirit of the *Führer*, could the ever weakening defensive struggle go on. NA-US, Microcopy T-78, Roll No 304, p. 6255677, report from Posen, 11 February 1945. Schneidemühl was defended by a garrison comprising 6,000 *Volkssturmmänner*, teenagers from the local officers cadet school and a small number of regular *Wehrmacht* troops. The town was surrounded at the end of January and the Red Army soon captured the air strip. Despite an energetic defence, by 22 February it was clear that Schneidemühl could no longer be held. The fortress commander, Colonel Remlinger defied orders and told his men to breakout that day. Remlinger was captured by the Red Army on 25 February and died in Soviet captivity. See Hastings, *Armageddon*, pp. 516–517.

31 An estimated 10 million men – one-third of German manpower were under arms at the end of 1944. However, more than two million were deployed in other theatres away from the key Rhine and Vistula fronts – 400,000 in Courland, 400,000 in Norway, 600,000 in Austria and Hungary, 400,000 in Yugoslavia and 400,000 in Italy. See Müller and Ueberschär, *Kriegsende 1945*, pp. 58–59.

32 See Erickson, *The Road to Berlin*, p. 520. Returning from Hitler's evening briefing on 17 February, Wenck, the Deputy Chief of the General Staff, took over the wheel of his staff car from his tired driver and collided with a bridge parapet. Wenck would ultimately die from injuries sustained in a car accident at Bad Rotherfelde in 1982.

33 On the campaign in East Pomerania, see Murawski, *Die Eroberung Pommerns*; Lindenblatt, *Pommern 1945*.

34 Duffy, *Red Storm on the Reich*, pp. 230–231. Swedish newspapers had remarked on the tense atmosphere in Danzig from mid-January. Thousands of Baltic refugees were trying to move away from the front but the *Gau* authorities wanted them to assist the *Volkssturm* in digging trenches. TNA, FO 898/187, 22 January 1945, p. C3, quoting *Svenska Morgenbladet*, 20 January 1945.

35 Goebbels ordered that the loss of Kolberg on 18 March should not be mentioned in the *Wehrmacht* report as this would have a detrimental impact on the effectiveness of the *Kolberg* film. *TBJG 15*, p. 542, 19 March 1945.

36 TNA, HW1/3572. A German report of 6 March, intercepted by the British, noted that the situation at Swinemünde–Stettin was becoming serious. Preparations were being made to withdraw civilian shipping and the Stettin E-Boat base was being wound up.

37 *Die Pommersche Zeitung,* 22 April 1995; 13 May 1995; Duffy, *Red Storm on the Reich*, pp. 236–238.

38 Erickson, *The Road to Berlin*, pp. 523–524; T. Le Tissier, *Durchbruch an der Oder* (Augsburg: Bechtermünz Verlag, 1997), p. 120. On Küstrin's significance, defences and eventual capture see Chuikov, *The End of the Third Reich*, pp. 105, 111, 118–119, 126–132.

39 C. Ryan, *The Last Battle Berlin 1945* (London: Collins, 1966), p. 171.

40 Le Tissier, *Durchbruch an der Oder*, p. 141.

41 Thorwald, *Es begann an der Weichsel*, p. 99. The last group of German troops left Oels on the morning of 23 January and rows of *Luftwaffe* planes were left standing on the airfield. Duffy, *Red Storm on the Reich*, p. 96.

42 The *Wehrmacht* report stressed on 3 April 1945 that during six weeks of fighting the Glogau garrison had barred the enemy from the important Oder crossing point, engaged strong enemy forces and had fought to the last bullet. BA-MA, RW4/v142b, *Wehrmacht* report, 3 April 1945.

43 Siebel-Achenbach, *Lower Silesia*, p. 76.

44 According to German messages intercepted by the British, the *Luftwaffe* attempted to provide besieged Breslau with ammunition and was able to take out more than 6,000 wounded. The operation was made more difficult by orders issued on 23 February 1945 cancelling both night-fighter operations over Breslau and the flights to protect the air supply bridge. See TNA, HW1/3539, 23 February 1945.

45 BA-MA, RW4/v142b, *Wehrmacht* reports, 2, 3 April 1945.

46 Ibid., *Wehrmacht* report, 6 April 1945.

47 NA-US, Microcopy T-78, Roll No. 304, pp. 6255167, 6255170, 6255172, OKH War Diary, 16, 17, 18 April 1945. See also the daily reports on the Breslau sector for Army Group Centre for the period 10–12, 16–25 April 1945, pp. 6255121, 6255094, 6255080, 6255068, 6255051, 6255036, 6255422, 6255410, 6255396, 6255365, 6255351, 6255332, 6255316, 6255303, 62555287, 6255272, 6255263, 6255256, 6255244-45, 6255237, 6255231, 6255224, 6255200, 6255189, 6255188. German reports repeatedly claimed that localised breakthroughs were sealed off. On 18 April, it was admitted that the garrison had suffered heavy losses, the last reserves had been used to shore up the western front and the situation on the eve of the expected major attack by the Red Army was becoming critical. No heavy fighting was reported on 23 April but the following day the Red Army assault recommenced and a one kilometre deep breakthrough was reported, although the 17th Army claimed it was contained.

48 On operations in Silesia and the siege of Breslau see, for instance, von Ahlfen and Niehoff, *So kämpfte Breslau;* Thorwald, *Es begann an der Weichsel,* pp. 91–100, 113–122; Thorwald,

Das Ende an der Elbe (Munich: Knaur edition, 1995), pp. 271–278; Duffy, *Red Storm on the Reich*, pp. 87–97, 127–147, 252–267; Siebel-Achenbach, *Lower Silesia,* pp. 56–82. Schörner advised Guderian on 9 February 1945 that in case of encirclement, Breslau could be defended by 25,000 men, including 8,800 *Volkssturm*, NA-US, Microcopy T-78, Roll No. 304, p. 6255605. On 17 February 1945 the *Wehrmacht* admitted that there were 153,000 people in Breslau, of whom 37,000 were under arms. The difference between both figures was largely comprised of women and children, see Microcopy T-78, Roll No. 304, pp. 6255683–6255685. Soviet sources later estimated that Breslau was defended by 43,000 men on 1 April 1945, see Erickson, '*Poslednii Shturm*', p. 40

49 Duffy, *Red Storm on the Reich*, pp. 114–115. Other published accounts quote casualty figures of 600,000. E. McCarthy 'The Course of the Battle', in J.F. Dunnigan (ed.), *The Russian Front: Germany's War in the East 1941–1945* (London: Arms and Armour Press, 1978), p. 65.

50 Brigadier-General Reinhard Gehlen, the head of FHO, later claimed that he raised the prospect of destroying the Vistula bridges at Cracow, Deblin, Warsaw or Thorn with the *Luftwaffe* and the SS during the final week of March 1945. The bridges at Warsaw and Thorn were seen as crucial for the supply of the Red Army on the Oder and Neisse fronts. However, the fuel, aircraft and personnel were never found to undertake either an aerial or sabotage operation. R. Gehlen, *The Gehlen Memoirs* (London: Collins, 1972), p. 121

51 Schimitzek, *Truth or Conjecture*, p. 226.

52 Wiskemann, *Germany's Eastern Neighbours*, p. 87.

53 A. Surminski, 'Der Schrecken hatte viele Namen', in Grube and Richter (ed.), *Flucht und Vertreibung*, pp. 65–72. The debate on the triggers of flight is summarised in de Zayas, *Nemesis at Potsdam*, pp. 70–71.

54 A series of Propaganda Ministry reports on the direction of the evacuation has survived for the period 26 January to 22 March 1945. Entitled 'Lage der Evakuierungen' or 'Lage in der Evakuierung' they can be found within BAB, R55/616, pp. 140–251.

55 BA-LA, Ost-Dok. 10/656, p. 7.

56 TNA, FO 898/187, 29 January 1945, p. C5.

57 Ibid., 5 February 1945, p. C6, quoting German Home Broadcast, 1 February 1945.

58 Schwendemann in *Spiegel Special, Die Flucht der Deutschen, 2/2002*, p. 43.

59 *Das Ostpreussenblatt*, 5 March 1951, quoted in Bundesministerium für Vertriebene, Flüchtlinge und Kriegsgeschädigte (ed.), *Dokumente Deutscher Kriegssschäden: Evakuierte, Kriegssachgeschädigte, Währungsgeschädigte. Die geschichtliche und rechtliche Entwicklung. 1. Beiheft. Aus den Tagen des Luftkrieges und des Wiederaufbaues Erlebnis – und Erfahrungsberichte* (Bonn: Bundesministerium für Vertriebene, Flüchtlinge und Kriegsgeschädigte, 1960), p. 350. In regional broadcasts, Koch ordered local Party leaders, village mayors and the police to clear the East Prussian roads of snow. Treks were forbidden from using the roads. See TNA, FO 898/187, 29 January 1945, p. C6 quoting Königsberg broadcast, 26 January 1945.

60 Schieder (ed.), *Expulsion Documents*, pp. 133–143. An SS report noted that 1.4 million East Prussians were on the move in early February. The Frisches Nehrung was clogged with vehicles and despite the efforts of the Party and the *Wehrmacht* the mood of the refugees was said to be 'apathetic'. See BAB, NS19/2606, pp. 52–53, 12 February 1945.

61 See C. Bekker, *Flucht übers Meer: Ostsee-Deutsches Schicksal 1945* (Frankfurt: Ullstein Zeitgeschichte, 1995), p. 277; Müller and Ueberschär, *Kriegsende 1945*, p. 116.

62 *Die Pommersche Zeitung*, 11 March 1995; *Spiegel Special. Als Feuer von Himmel fiel. Der Bombenkrieg gegen die Deutschen*, 1/2003.

63 Swedish reports described the hurried evacuation of Litzmannstadt where German civilians were carried to safety on tanks and cited instances where tank crews had agreed to tow carts and wagons. TNA, FO 898/187, 29 January 1945, p. C5.
64 BA-LA, Ost-Dok. 10/624, pp. 51–55.
65 Schieder (ed.), *Dokumentation. Band 1/1*, p. 414.
66 BA-LA, Ost-Dok. 8/735, pp. 4–5; 10/655, pp. 3–11. On overcrowding and shortages in Lower Silesian reception districts see BAB, R55/616, pp. 164–165, 5 February 1945; Peikert, *'Festung Breslau'*, p. 36.
67 Already from 14 January 1945 some west German and Berliner evacuees had been sent out of Breslau by rail. Gleiss, *Breslauer Apokalypse, Band I Januar*, p. 64D.
68 Peikert *'Festung Breslau'*, p. 24; Hornig, *Breslau 1945*, pp. 15–16. This was the first attack on Breslau since the 7 October 1944 raid, although there had been an alarm on 24 December 1944.
69 Gleiss, *Breslauer Apokalypse, Band I, Januar*, p. 64D; Grieger, *Wie Breslau fiel*, p. 10.
70 Hornig, *Breslau 1945*, pp. 18–19.
71 Gleiss, *Breslauer Apokalypse. Band 1. Januar*, p. 215.
72 BA-LA, Ost-Dok. 8/734, p. 5.
73 Peikert, *'Festung Breslau'*, p. 26. A German Home Service broadcast on 25 January mentioned 'long treks of the peasant population and the inhabitants of the threatened towns'. TNA, FO 898/187, 29 January 1945, p. C4.
74 Hornig, *Breslau 1945*, p. 17; Peikert, *'Festung Breslau'*, p. 25.
75 Hornig, *Breslau 1945*, p. 20. Von Ahlfen and Niehoff, *So kämpfte Breslau*, p. 24.
76 Imperial War Museum, London, 95/4/1, Fritz N.
77 Duffy, *Red Storm on the Reich*, p. 138.
78 A. Speer, *Inside the Third Reich* (London: Phoenix, 1995), p. 566; Sereny, *Albert Speer: His Battle with Truth*, p. 509.
79 Speer, *Inside the Third Reich*, p. 566. Originally designed by Schinkel, the *Gauleitung* building was located at Eichbornstrasse 2. There were 97 *Ortsgruppen* (local groups) in Breslau in May 1944, Peikert, *'Festung Breslau'*, p. 29.
80 IfZ, Z1129, *ST*, 22 January 1945. The German Home Service reported on 25 January that the HJ, who were originally involved in the orderly evacuation of women and children, 'had been called away for *Volkssturm* service'. TNA, FO 898/187, 29 January 1945, p. C5.
81 The German Transocean news agency reported on 24 January that 'hundreds of trains have left the metropolis on the Oder during the last few days'. Nevertheless, most accounts highlighted those departing on foot. Open carts and lorries carried women and children but there was insufficient straw to keep them warm and only a few had covered their vehicles with tarpaulins or boards. On the railways women and children huddled together in cattle trucks or open goods wagons. TNA, FO 898/187, 29 January 1945, p. C4.
82 TNA, FO 898/187, 29 January 1945, p. C4.
83 Peikert, *'Festung Breslau'*, p. 30. Similarly, Knopp, *Die große Flucht*, p. 158 quotes evidence of 24 children being trampled underfoot in the panic at the city's Freiburger Station.
84 *ST*, 22 January 1945 reproduced in Gleiss, *Breslauer Apokalypse. Band 1. Januar*, p. 214.
85 G. Elze, *Breslau: Biographe einer deutschen Stadt* (Leer: Verlag Gerhard Rautenberg, 1993), p. 114.
86 Siebel-Achenbach, *Lower Silesia*, p. 60; Schimitzek, *Truth or Conjecture*, p. 289. According to a radio broadcast on 25 January, 'When trains and prepared transport were not sufficient, women and children marched in columns towards safety, despite the strong frost.'

TNA, FO 898/187, 29 January 1945, p. C5, quoting German Home Services broadcast, 25 January 1945.

87 Thorwald, *Es begann an der Weichsel*, pp. 95–99.

88 See chapter 7; Hornig, *Breslau 1945*, p. 18; Böddeker, *Die Flüchtlinge*, p. 176.

89 Gleiss, *Breslauer Apokalypse. Band 1. Januar*, p. 100D.

90 Hornig, *Breslau 1945*, p. 21.

91 Thorwald, *Es begann an der Weichsel*, p. 99.

92 Hornig, *Breslau 1945*, p. 18.

93 Thorwald, *Es begann an der Weichsel*, p. 100.

94 Grieger, *Wie Breslau fiel*, p. 12.

95 The SS seemingly threatened German women with rape if they remained. Despite these brutal orders to empty the city, one opponent of the regime admitted that he could find no instance where physical violence had been used to achieve this objective. See Peikert, *'Festung Breslau'*, pp. 29–30, 34–35.

96 TNA, FO 898/187, 12 February 1945, pp. C6–C7, quoting Breslau broadcast, 7 February 1945.

97 Grieger, *Wie Breslau fiel*, p. 9.

98 Ibid., p. 10.

99 Beevor, *Berlin*, p. 48. Ilse Braun had arrived by train at Berlin's Schlesischer station.

100 Gleiss, *Breslauer Apokalypse, Band I, Januar,* p. 100D

101 Böddeker, *Die Flüchtlinge*, p. 177.

102 Hornig, *Breslau 1945*, p. 35.

103 Grieger, *Wie Breslau fiel*, pp. 10–11.

104 Schörner was promoted to Field Marshal on 5 April 1945. Army Group A was renamed Army Group Centre on 25 January 1945.

105 S. Knappe with T. Brusaw, *Soldat: Reflections of a German Soldier, 1936–1949* (New York: Dell, 1992), pp. 300–301.

106 Ibid., pp. 303–304.

107 H.G.W. Gleiss, *Breslauer Apokalyse 1945. Band 2. Februar* (Wedel, Holstein: Natura et Patria Verlag, 1986–1997), p. 328. Regarding numbers in Breslau, different figures between 80,000 and 235,000 are suggested. See also Hornig, *Breslau 1945*, p. 23. On 17 February 1945, the *Wehrmacht* claimed that 116,000 people who were not under arms remained in Breslau, mainly women and children, see NA-US, Microcopy T-78, Roll 304, pp. 6255683–6255685. Another source notes that at the beginning of the siege there were between 150,000–180,000 civilians in the city, half of whom were evacuees, and 45,000–50,000 armed men, Siebel-Achenbach, *Lower Silesia*, pp. 72–73. An intercepted *Wehrmacht* signal mentioned 140,000 civilians as late as 27 April 1945, see TNA, HW1/3744.

108 Grieger, *Wie Breslau fiel*, p. 12

109 BAB, R55/616, p. 141, 26 January 1945; p. 158, 30 January 1945.

110 Thorwald, *Es begann an der Weichsel*, pp. 74–76.

111 *TBJG 15*, p. 205, 24 January 1945.

112 BA-LA, Ost-Dok. 10/535, p. 35. Goebbels vilified Greiser's conduct thereafter and wanted him put before the People's Court where the appropriate [death] sentence would be passed. See *TBJG 15*, p. 223, 25 January 1945. Jürgen Thorwald argued that Greiser was a pawn in the power struggle between Bormann and Himmler. He suggested that the original order for Greiser to leave Posen was a malicious manoeuvre by Bormann to discredit

Himmler through the actions of one of his minions. However, according to this account, Himmler rejected Greiser's seemingly serious offer to shoot Bormann. See Thorwald, *Es begann an der Weichsel*, pp. 77–78.

113 BA-LA, Ost-Dok. 8/709, p. 3; 10/531, p. 10.

114 BA-LA, Ost-Dok. 8/713, p. 1.

115 *TBJG 15*, pp. 280, 283, 31 January 1945.

116 BA-LA, Ost-Dok. 8/702, pp. 3–6.

117 *Die Pommersche Zeitung*, 7 January 1995.

118 Böddeker, *Die Flüchtlinge*, pp. 91–92.

119 von Krockow, *Hour of the Women*, pp. 30–31.

120 BA-LA, Ost-Dok. 8/643, p. 3.

121 M. von Dönhoff, 'Ritt durch Pommern', in K. Granzow (ed.), *Meine Heimat Pommern. Die Letzten Tage. Erinnerungen an Flucht und Vertreibung* (Augsburg: Weltbild Verlag, 1990), pp. 15–19.

122 TNA, FO 898/187, 12 February 1945, p. C8, quoting *Pommersche Zeitung*, 23 January 1945.

123 Ibid., 18 February 1945, p. C7, quoting *Pommersche Zeitung*, 30 January 1945.

124 Murawski, *Die Eroberung Pommerns*, p. 26.

125 BA-LA, Ost-Dok. 8/638, p. 3; 8/645, pp. 12–13; Murawski, *Die Eroberung Pommerns*, pp. 43–44.

126 BA-LA,Ost-Dok. 8/645, p. 13.

127 Murawski, *Die Eroberung Pommerns*, p. 42.

128 BA-LA, Ost-Dok. 10/407, p. 27.

129 BA-LA, Ost-Dok. 8/645, pp. 22–26.

130 One source maintained that Schwede-Coburg was upbeat after speaking with the *Reichsführer-SS* and had concluded that Himmler's intervention would result in the danger being overcome. See BA-LA, Ost-Dok. 8/645, pp. 25–26.

131 BA-LA, Ost-Dok. 8/658, p. 2.

132 BA-LA, Ost-Dok 8/677, p. 2; *Die Pommersche Zeitung*, 28 January 1995; Murawski, *Die Eroberung Pommerns*, p. 30; Böddeker, *Die Flüchtlinge*, p. 94.

133 *TBJG 15*, p. 283, 31 January 1945; p. 290, 1 February 1945; p. 324, 6 February 1945.

134 Murawski, *Die Eroberung Pommerns*, pp. 42–43.

135 Böddeker, *Die Flüchtlinge*, pp. 92–93. A contemporary report said that between 900,000 and one million Pomeranians and refugees from provinces further east had fallen into Soviet hands. See BAB, R55/616, p. 249, 22 March 1945.

136 VPLA, Rep.76, No. 165, p. 110, Schwede-Coburg to all Pomeranian Administrative Leaders, *Kreisleiter* and Organisation Leaders, 8 February 1945.

137 BA-LA, Ost-Dok. 8/677, p. 3; 8/658, p. 2. See chapter seven for evidence from late 1944 showing that many families from Bochum preferred their children to remain in the west.

138 BA-LA, Ost-Dok. 10/415, pp. 31–32. Testimony of *Oberbürgermeister* Friedrich Rogausch.

139 BA-LA, Ost-Dok. 10/397. Testimony of Herman Pahl.

140 BA-LA, Ost-Dok. 8/643, p. 2.

141 BA-LA, Ost-Dok. 8/685, p. 5.

142 Murawski, *Die Eroberung Pommerns*, pp. 27–28.

143 It has been argued that the German defence of Pyritz stopped the Soviet advance on Stettin and thereby allowed thousands of German refugees to cross the Oder bridges and reach the security of the river's west- bank. See, for example, *Die Pommersche Zeitung*, 29 April 1995.

144 BA-LA, Ost-Dok. 8/649, p. 2.
145 Ibid., p. 8.
146 BA-LA, Ost-Dok. 8/657, p. 5. For contemporary criticism of the Party and *Wehrmacht* leadership at national level see, for example, BAB, R55/622, pp. 181–183, *Briefübersicht* 10, 9 March 1945.
147 BA-LA, Ost-Dok. 8/566, pp. 2–3.
148 BA-LA, Ost-Dok. 8/565, p. 3.
149 BA-LA, Ost-Dok. 8/513, p. 6.
150 BA-LA, Ost-Dok. 8/512, p. 2.
151 Steinhoff, Pechel and Showalter (eds.), *Voices from the Third Reich*, p. 417.
152 Dräger was sentenced to death by the People's Court on 29 March 1945 for undermining the war effort and desertion. He was hanged at Brandenburg/Havel prison on 20 April 1945. Szelinski hanged himself in Moabit (Berlin) prison. BA-LA, Ost-Dok. 8/580, p. 3; 8/588, p. 10; Gause, *Die Geschichte der Stadt Königsberg*, p. 166; Tilitzki, *Alltag in Ostpreußen*, pp. 310–311.
153 BA-LA, Ost-Dok. 8/524, p. 3; 8/592, p. 3.
154 U. and S. Goerges, 'Unser-und nicht nur unser-grausamer Abschied', in Reinoß (ed.), *Letzte Tage in Ostpreußen*, pp. 222–224.
155 BA-MA, RH53-1/27, war diary of *Wehrkreis* I General Staff doctor, Dr. Zillmer, 21 January to 22 February 1945.
156 von Lehndorff, *East Prussian Diary*, p. 13.
157 BAB, NS19/2068, 'Meldungen aus dem Ostraum', p. 7, 17 February 1945.
158 von Lehndorff, *East Prussian Diary*, p. 22.
159 BA-LA, Ost-Dok. 8/588, p. 9.
160 Koch even arranged for Küssner's mother and grandmother to be collected by a Party car and they were taken to an airfield and put on a flight to Breslau. Hastings, *Armageddon*, pp. 322–323.
161 Schieder (ed.), *Dokumentation. Band 1/1*, p. 147. The British intercepted a *Kriegsmarine* directive on 24 January which ordered the evacuation of their vessels from Königsberg and stated that all shipping at Danzig requiring prolonged attention was to be towed away. TNA, HW 1/3479.
162 Lasch, *So fiel Königsberg*, pp. 36–37.
163 BA-LA, Ost-Dok. 8/510 p. 16; 8/580, p. 3; 8/588, p. 4; 10/890, p. 38; Ibid., pp. 56–57.
164 Makowka said that the worst time was 22–25 January. BA-LA, Ost-Dok. 8/602, p. 5. Others claim that the following days were more serious. One witness noted on 23 January when Red Army spearheads had broken the Deime Line that, 'The town has so far taken no notice of the fact. The trams are running as usual, people are getting their hair cut and going to the cinema.' This account did mention drunkenness and the looting of hospital supplies on 29 January. See von Lehndorff, *East Prussian Diary*, pp. 11, 18.
165 BA-LA, Ost-Dok. 8/580, p. 3. For other examples of vandalism and theft by German soldiers from empty houses during the fortress period in Königsberg and Breslau see Linck, *Königsberg 1945–1948*, pp. 12–13; Peikert, *'Festung Breslau'*, p. 202.
166 BA-LA, Ost-Dok. 8/602, p. 3. Lieutenant-Colonel Dr Sauvant remarked that only in particularly crass cases of cowardice and desertion were death sentences passed and Lasch weighed this necessary duty against his responsibility for the fate of around 300,000 people in the fortress area. See Lasch, *So fiel Königsberg*, pp. 58–59. A report on the shooting of two deserters at the north railway station appeared in the *Festung Königsberg*, 2 February

1945. See BfZ, Archiv N, the testimony of Werner Shorl contained in his book, *Von Chemnitz bis Balga: Ein Bericht* (Frankfurt, 1992), p. 170.

167 On the creation and equipping of new units see BA-LA, Ost-Dok. 8/586, p. 2; Lasch, *So fiel Königsberg*, pp. 57–60.

168 According to Lasch, Koch first returned to Königsberg on 5 February and made his final visit on 4 April. See Lasch, *So fiel Königsberg*, pp. 123–125. Despite Koch's claims to the contrary, his wife and the wife of the *Reichsbahn* President had already left the province for Bavaria in a special train on 20 January. See BA-LA, Ost-Dok. 8/510, p. 17. However, an Army Group North report of 2 February 1945 suggested that Koch's flight from Königsberg to Heiligenbeil in a little Fieseler Storch plane was overdue. Meanwhile, the accompanying Storch carrying Paul Dargel had landed in enemy occupied territory but the pilot was able to take off again and had flown back to Königsberg. NA-US, Microcopy T-78, Roll No. 304, p. 6255767, Army Group North report, 2 February 1945. It seems that on Koch's final visit to Königsberg on 4 April 1945, he reprimanded Dr Alfred Rohde, Director of the Königsberg Castle museum, for failing to arrange the evacuation of the crates containing the dismantled Amber Room. See Scott-Clark and Levy, *The Amber Room*, p. 87. Rohde remained in the city with his wife and two children. He was interrogated by Soviet investigators about the whereabouts of the Amber Room and other cultural treasures but he and his wife died in mysterious circumstances in the city later in 1945.

169 BA-LA, Ost-Dok. 8/584, p. 5.

170 *TBJG 15*, p. 285, 31 January 1945; pp. 304–305, 2 February 1945. Only Government President Hoffmann, Finance President Zehran and *Oberbürgermeister* Dr Will remained in Königsberg.

171 IfZ, MCI Zusammenbruch IV-8 Königsberg, Paul Franzek, p. 7.

172 BAB, NS19/2068, pp. 62–63, 14 March 1945.

173 Thorwald, *Es begann an der Weichsel*, p. 149.

174 BA-LA, Ost-Dok. 8/594, pp. 5–6.

175 IfZ, MCI Zusammenbruch, Franzek, p. 12.

176 Goebbels correctly considered Koch's figures for Soviet losses to be excessive. See *TBJG 15*, p. 592, 25 March 1945. The Red Army's own figures admitted 126,464 Soviet deaths in East Prussia between 13 January and 25 April 1945 and 458,314 medical casualties. See J. Erickson, 'Soviet War Losses: Calculations and Controversies' in J. Erickson and D. Dilks (eds.), *Barbarossa: The Axis and the Allies* (Edinburgh: Edinburgh University Press, 1994), p. 266.

177 BA-LA, Ost-Dok. 8/602, p. 8.

178 IfZ, MCI Zusammenbruch, Franzek, p. 9.

179 Deputy *Gauleiter* Großherr had flown out of Königsberg with Koch after the latter's visit on 5 February. BA-LA, Ost-Dok. 8/580, p. 4.

180 Lasch, *So fiel Königsberg*, p. 65.

181 IfZ, MCI Zusammenbruch, Franzek, pp. 9–10; Lasch, *So fiel Königsberg*, p. 44.

182 BA-LA, Ost-Dok. 8/591, p. 46.

183 IfZ, MZ9/57, *VB*, 2 March 1945. Heysing later claimed that 'a General and a *Kreisleiter*' had overcome the first great crisis confronting Königsberg in late January and early February. See *VB*, 3 April 1945.

184 BAB, NS6/135, pp. 157–159; TNA, FO 898/187, 5 March 1945, p. A5.

185 BA-LA, Ost-Dok. 8/591, p. 55.

186 IfZ, MCI Zusammenbruch, Franzek, p. 10; Lasch, *So fiel Königsberg*, p. 77. Koch utilised

the opportunity provided by the cutting of the telephone cable with Berlin to act against *Wehrmacht* and Party liaison officers who had endorsed Wagner and advised Berlin of the *Gauleiter*'s failings. Major Ibsen and Lieutenant Schelsky were sentenced to short terms of imprisonment and transferred from the province. See BA-LA, Ost-Dok. 10/888, p. 31.

187 Thorwald, *Es begann an der Weichsel*, pp. 170–171. Likewise, the commander of the East Prussian *Volkssturm*, Senior Area Leader Knuth, was outspoken in his criticism of *Wehrmacht* failures and disorganisation when in conversation with Heysing. See BA-LA, Ost-Dok. 8/591, pp. 36–37.

188 BA-LA, Ost-Dok 8/523, p. 3.

189 *TBJG 15*, p. 592, 25 March 1945.

190 Ibid., p. 674, 4 April 1945.

191 BA-LA, Ost-Dok. 8/591, p. 59; Michaelis and Schraepler (eds.), *Ursachen und Folgen. Band 23*, p. 235, *Wehrmacht* report, 12 April 1945.

192 The *Aschwöhnestellung*, a tank trap dug by local civilian labourers in Gerdauen, East Prussia, was never occupied or defended by German troops. See BA-LA, Ost-Dok. 8/588, p. 2. An extensive system of anti-tank ditches were dug along the southern boundary of Ortelsburg district in East Prussia but these proved to be futile when the Red Army attacked from the west through the forest from Neidenburg. See Ost-Dok. 8/571, p. 4.

193 NA-US, Microcopy T-78, Roll No. 304, pp. 6225710–6225714, 6 February 1945.

194 ostwall.com website, 15 January 2003.

195 Guderian, *Panzer Leader*, p. 360. However, Yelton does note that in late 1944 Guderian was faced with no real obstacles from eastern *Gauleiter* when he obtained authorisation to use the *Volkssturm* in large scale rear area security operations in the east of the Reich. Yelton, *Hitler's Volkssturm*, p. 121.

196 Skorzeny, *Skorzeny's Special Missions*, pp. 181–182.

197 Gleiss, *Breslauer Apokalypse Band I Januar*, p. 64D, 'Aufrufungsbefehl für den gesamten Deutschen *Volkssturm* im Osten'. Yelton, *Hitler's Volkssturm*, p. 121. Reporters broadcast stories of the Upper Silesian *Volkssturm* being rushed from schools, offices, workshops and mines to the trenches on the frontier: 'There they lay in their snow-covered positions, most of them wearing the same clothes in which only a few hours ago they had been working.' The cold was 'between 15–20 degrees below freezing point, and aggravated by an icy hurricane'. TNA, FO 898/187, 22 January 1945, p. A3, quoting Front Report from Silesia, 19 January 1945.

198 Yelton, *Hitler's Volksssturm*, p. 131.

199 Seidler, *Deutscher Volkssturm*, p. 206

200 BA-LA, Ost-Dok.8/646, p. 4; von Krockow, *Hour of the Women*, pp. 33–34.

201 Yelton, *Hitler's Volkssturm*, pp. 121–122.

202 BA-LA, Ost-Dok. 8/546, p. 3; Ost-Dok. 8/592, p. 3.

203 Kissel, *Der Deutsche Volkssturm*, p. 58.

204 Yelton, *Hitler's Volkssturm*, p. 121.

205 Seidler, *Deutscher Volkssturm*, pp. 329–331. Michaelis and Schraepler (eds.), *Ursachen und Folgen. Band 22*, p. 356. Hitler's directive of 28 January 1945 acknowledged that experiences on the Eastern Front had shown that *Volkssturm*, emergency and reserve units had little fighting value when left to themselves. He ordered that forthwith these units were to be formed into mixed battle-groups with regular units, H. Trevor-Roper, *Hitler's War Directives 1939–1945* (Edinburgh: Birlinn Books edition, 2004), pp. 290–291.

206 Skorzeny, *Skorzeny's Special Measures*, p. 183

207 BAB, NS19/2068, pp. 65–66, 15 March 1945. A Swedish observer reportedly passed through 20 *Feldgendarmerie* checkpoints between Küstrin and Berlin at this point. See Beevor, *Berlin*, p. 132.
208 Mammach, *Der Volkssturm*, pp. 114–115.
209 Yelton, *Hitler's Volkssturm*, p. 123.
210 Michaelis and Schraepler (eds.), *Ursachen und Folgen. Band 22*, pp. 350–351, proclamation by *Kreisleiter* Wagner, 5 February 1945.
211 BA-LA, Ost-Dok. 8/592, p. 2. See also J. Lucas, *The Last Days of the Reich* (London: Arms and Armour, 1986), pp. 28–29.
212 Mammach, *Der Volkssturm*, p. 117.
213 Yelton, *Hitler's Volkssturm*, p. 124.
214 Hitler decorated Pomeranian and Silesian HJ in Berlin and Goebbels performed similar duties in Lauban, Lower Silesia during March 1945. See *TBJG 15*, pp. 457–461, 9 March 1945; Jahnke, *Hitlers letztes Aufgebot*, pp. 155–157.
215 G. Knopp, *Hitler's Children* (Stroud: Sutton, 2002), pp. 249–250. See also NA-US, Microcopy T-78, Roll No 304, p. 6255422. In Army Group Centre's daily report for 16 April 1945, the role of the *Volkssturm* and HJ in the defence of Fortress Breslau was described as particularly excellent.
216 Hastings, *Armageddon*, p. 516, von Hase interview.
217 Yelton, *Hitler's Volkssturm*, p. 114. On the heavy Soviet tank losses during the fighting for Danzig, frequently the result of attacks by HJ armed with *Panzerfäuste* and Molotov Cocktails, see Hastings, *Armageddon*, p. 520.
218 TNA, FO 898/187, 5 February 1945, p. C7, quoting Silesian local broadcast, 1 February 1945.
219 On the defence of Kolberg see, BA-LA, Ost-Dok. 8/640; Lindenblatt, *Pommern 1945*, pp. 275–287; Unbekannter Offizier, 'Kampf um Kolberg', in K. Granzow (ed.), *Meine Heimat Pommern*, pp. 86–95; Böddeker, *Die Flüchtlinge*, pp. 110–120; Seidler, *Deutscher Volkssturm*, p. 333. The *Volkssturm* endured nearly 60% casualties in the defence of Kolberg. Yelton, *Hitler's Volkssturm*, p. 124.
220 See for instance BAB, R138 II/7, reports on the evacuation from the Warthegau compiled February–March 1945, pp. 14, 55. Similarly, an account from District Propaganda Leader Friedrich in Bromberg advised that the *Volkssturm* had 'almost completely failed' and had no leadership or weapons, BAB, R55/616, p. 145, 26 January 1945.
221 BA-LA, Ost-Dok. 8/637, p. 7.
222 BA-LA, Ost-Dok. 8/708, p. 3; 10/543, p. 13
223 BA-LA, Ost-Dok. 8/712, pp. 3–4.
224 Seidler, *Deutscher Volkssturm*, pp. 331–332.
225 G. Roos, 'Die Problematik ständiger Befestigungen im Licht der Erfahrungen des II Weltkrieges', *Wehrwissenschaftliche Rundschau*, Volume 3, Number 10, 1953, pp. 485–486, quoted in BA-LA, Ost-Dok. 10/520. Kissel, *Der Deutsche Volkssturm*, pp. 66–67.
226 Chuikov, *The End of the Third Reich*, p. 103.
227 BAB, R55/603, p. 107, 28 January 1945.
228 BAB, NS19/2068, p. 6, 16 February 1945.
229 *TBJG 15*, pp. 441–442, 7 March 1945.
230 BAB, R55/616, p. 47, *Kreisleitung* Liebenwerda (Saxony) to *Gauleitung* Saxony, 22 February 1945.
231 BAB, R22/243, p. 136, Senior Judge Cosel to Reich Ministry of Justice, 7 February 1945.

232 TNA, FO 898/187, 18 February 1945, p. C8, quoting DNB, 15 February 1945.

Chapter 9 Our Brave Fortresses in the East

1 BAB, NS19/2068, p. 13, 18 February 1945. See also Peikert, *'Festung Breslau'*, pp. 60–65, 133–135, 234–239; Siebel-Achenbach, *Lower Silesia*, pp. 68–70 and reproductions in Gleiss, *Breslauer Apokalypse*. A selection of Soviet leaflets dropped on Lower Silesia which repudiated Nazi 'atrocity' propaganda and told ordinary Germans they need not fear the Red Army is reproduced in Grau, *Silesian Inferno*, pp. 157–187.

2 Numerous editions are reproduced in Gleiss, *Breslauer Apokalypse*. See, for instance, *Band 2. Februar*, pp. 461–463, 661–663.

3 Lehndorff, *East Prussian Diary*, pp. 43–45.

4 Böddeker, *Die Flüchtlinge*, p. 82. For Königsberg see also BAB, NS19/2068, p. 62, 14 March 1945; p. 65, 15 March 1945; p. 84, 22 March 1945; von Lehndorff, *East Prussian Diary*, p. 43. For a selection of the leaflets dropped on Stettin see BA-LA, Ost-Dok. 8/636, pp. 90, 93–98.

5 BAB, R55/608, pp. 35–36, 17 February 1945. On *Wehrmacht* oral propaganda during the last months of the war see V.R. Berghahn, 'Meinungsforschung im "Dritten Reich": Die Mundpropaganda-Aktion der Wehrmacht im letzten Kriegshalbjahr', *Militärgeschichtliche Mitteilungen*, 1, 1967, pp. 83–109.

6 Steinert, *Hitler's War*, p. 297.

7 Kirwin, 'Nazi Domestic Propaganda', pp. 296–297.

8 Steinert, *Hitler's War*, p. 300.

9 TNA, FO 898/187, 29 January 1945, p. C1, quoting *PomZ*, 15 January 1945.

10 Ibid., p. C2, quoting *Ostdeutscher Beobachter*, 18 January 1945.

11 IfZ, MZ9/57, *VB*, 24 January 1945.

12 Ibid., 26 January 1945.

13 Ibid., 30 January 1945.

14 Ibid., 31 January 1945.

15 Ibid., 3 April 1945. See also TNA, FO 898/187, 2 April 1945, p. A5. This mentions a broadcast of 31 March 1945 by a tearful Front Reporter just back from Königsberg. He stressed that the Fortress was an example for all Germany. The reporter did not mention *Gauleiter* Koch.

16 *TBJG 15*, p. 375, 13 February 1945.

17 Proclamation by *Kreisleiter* Wagner to the Königsberg *Volkssturm*, 5 February 1945, quoted in Lasch, *So fiel Königsberg*, pp. 139–140.

18 BA-LA, Ost-Dok. 8/602, p. 10.

19 von Lehndorff, *East Prussian Diary*, p. 33.

20 BA-LA, Ost-Dok. 8/588, p. 4; Lasch, *So fiel Königsberg*, pp. 84–85.

21 BAB, NS19/2068, p. 60, 12 March 1945; BA-LA, Ost-Dok. 8/602, p. 10.

22 BA-LA, Ost-Dok. 10/890, p. 43. Testimony of Werner Kernsies.

23 BAB, NS19/2068, pp. 18–19, 21 February 1945; p. 34, 27 February 1945; BA-LA, Ost-Dok. 8/591, p. 50.

24 BA-LA, Ost-Dok. 10/890, p. 148, Wegener testimony; Gause, *Die Geschichte der Stadt Königsberg*, p. 166.

25 BA-LA, Ost-Dok. 10/890, pp. 144–145; Gause, *Die Geschichte der Stadt Königsberg*, p. 165.

26 BA-LA, Ost-Dok. 10/890, p. 44. Testimony of Werner Kernsies. See also von Lehndorff, *East Prussian Diary*, p. 33.

27 von Lehndorff, *East Prussian Diary*, p. 38.
28 Thorwald, *Es begann an der Weichsel*, p. 175.
29 BAB, R55/1394, p. 204, 19 March 1945.
30 *ST*, 25 January 1945, reproduced in Gleiss, *Breslauer Apokalypse 1945. Band 1. Januar*, p. 444.
31 Ibid., pp. 570–571. *ST*, 29 January 1945.
32 *Deutsche Allgemeine Zeitung*, 28 January 1945, reproduced in Gleiss, *Breslauer Apokalypse. Band 1*, p. 513. The 'Kanth Death March' is covered in chapter 8.
33 Knappe, *Soldat*, p. 307.
34 *TBJG 15*, p. 277, 30 January 1945. Hanke advised Goebbels that he was planning a mass rally in the Jahrhunderthalle on 30 January to celebrate the 12th anniversary of the Nazi assumption of power.
35 Hornig, *Breslau 1945*, p. 26.
36 Knappe, *Soldat*, p. 310.
37 Grieger, *Wie Breslau fiel*, p. 14.
38 IfZ, MZ 9/57, *VB*, 6 March 1945.
39 IfZ, MZ 235/4, *Das Reich*, 11 March 1945.
40 *Deutsche Allgemeine Zeitung*, 18 March 1945 reproduced in Gleiss, *Breslauer Apokalypse Band 3 März*, pp. 543–544.
41 Domarus, *Hitler: Reden und Proklamationen 1932–1945. Band II*, p. 2207; H. Heiber, *Hitlers Lagebesprechungen. Die Prokollfragmente seiner militärischen Konferenzen 1942–1945* (Stuttgart: Deutsche Verlags-Anstalt, 1962), p. 890.
42 TNA, FO 898/187, 2 April 1945, p. A5.
43 IfZ, MZ 9/57, *VB*, 13 April 1945. Domarus, *Hitler: Reden und Proklamationen 1932–1945. Band II*, p. 2219. Only *Reichsarbeitsführer* Hierl was more decorated. He received the Golden Cross of the German Order with swords and oak leaves on 24 February 1945. See also *TBJG 15*, pp. 692–693, 9 April 1945.
44 *TBJG 15*, p. 620, 28 March 1945. The spirit of heroic last ditch resistance was captured by the Nazi adaptation of the actions of the garrison and citizens of the Baltic port of Kolberg, encircled by French forces in 1807. The full colour film *Kolberg* emphasised that the resistance to the French came from the people and not from the military. In contrast with the determined Nettlebeck, Kolberg's *Bürgermeister*, the elderly commandant Colonel Lucadou, was seen calling for the town's surrender. The film was premiered on 30 January 1945 and this lavish piece of escapism was screened in the fortress cities. The capture of Kolberg by the Red Army on 18 March 1945 was not mentioned in the daily *Wehrmacht* report as it was believed that this news would lessen the impact of the film. See Taylor, *Film Propaganda: Soviet Russia and Nazi Germany*, pp. 216–229; Welch, *Propaganda and the German Cinema 1933–1945*, pp. 224–237.
45 For critical comment on Greiser's departure from Warthegau see, for example, *TBJG 15* (all 1945 entries), p. 209, 24 January; p. 232, 26 January; pp. 364–365, 12 February; p. 416, 4 March; p. 442, 7 March; p. 555, 21 March; p. 620, 28 March; pp. 639–640, 31 March; pp. 692–693, 9 April. Goebbels was particularly angry for although Greiser had departed, 'our Berlin *Volkssturm* battalions' had been sent to defend Posen. *TBJG 15*, p. 230, 26 January 1945.
46 Sereny, *Albert Speer: His Battle with Truth*, pp. 509–511. See also Speer, *Inside the Third Reich*, p. 566. Clearly by the late 1960s, Speer, probably disappointed that his old comrade had not died the expected hero's death, was more critical of Hanke and remarked on his

brutality in Breslau and his flight from the city. This view appears to be confirmed by Speer's letter to the Polish historian Professor Karol Jonca of 5 March 1975. He said that he now viewed Hanke as a 'brutal force' responsible for the futile destruction of human lives and culturally important buildings. See Gleiss, *Breslauer Apokalypse Band 1. Januar*, p. 284A. However, Speer's criticism was factually wrong on two points. Hanke had Deputy Mayor Spielhagen shot and not hanged, and Hanke escaped from Breslau in a small plane and not in a prototype helicopter.

47 BAB, R55/603, p. 530, RPA Mark Brandenburg to RMVuP, 15 March 1945.

48 Peikert, *'Festung Breslau'*, pp. 110–111, 118–119.

49 Ibid., pp. 99–100.

50 *ST*, 3 March 1945, reproduced in Gleiss, *Breslauer Apokalypse. Band 3. März*, p. 101.

51 Knappe, *Soldat*, p. 312.

52 Duffy, *Red Storm on the Reich*, p. 261.

53 Hornig, *Breslau 1945*, p. 35.

54 Peikert, *'Festung Breslau'*, pp. 78–81.

55 Knappe, *Soldat*, p. 311. The supply operation suffered heavy losses. An SS report on 20 March noted that over the previous three days, 10 *Junkers-52s* out of 24 had been lost. BAB, NS 19/2068, 20 March 1945. Siebel-Achenbach noted that on a typical day, 22 March, 40 Ju-52s and 25 Heinkel 111s dodged the intensified Soviet anti-aircraft activity to deliver 44.45 tons of supplies to Gandau. Siebel-Achenbach, *Lower Silesia*, p. 73.

56 Duffy, *Red Storm on the Reich*, p. 258.

57 von Ahlfen and Niehoff, *So kämpfte Breslau*, pp. 49–62; Duffy, *Red Storm on the Reich*, pp. 258–261; Siebel-Achenbach, *Lower Silesia*, p. 74; Thorwald, *Es begann an der Weichsel*, pp. 112–119. Schörner's warning was no idle threat. A sentence of death by hanging (in absentsia) and the detention of his family on account of his actions was the widely publicised fate of General Otto Lasch, the commandant of Königsberg, who surrendered the city on 9 April 1945. See *Wehrmacht* report of 12 April 1945, reproduced in *Ursachen und Folgen, Band 23*, p. 235. On 14 April, the repeated Red Army artillery salvoes fired at his Liebigs Hill headquarters resulted in Niehoff opting to join Hanke under Breslau's university library. See Duffy, *Red Storm on the Reich*, p. 263.

58 *TBJG 15*, p. 458, 9 March 1945; Kaps, *The Tragedy of Silesia*, pp. 121–122; Hornig, *Breslau 1945*, pp. 104–105; Siebel-Achenbach, *Lower Silesia*, p. 74; Thorwald, *Es begann an der Weichsel*, pp. 118–119.

59 Siebel-Achenbach, *Lower Silesia*, p. 74; Duffy, *Red Storm on the Reich*, p. 141.

60 See Böddeker, *Die Flüchtlinge*, p. 179. A discussion of this incident is contained in Gleiss, *Breslauer Apokalypse. Band 3. März*, pp. 34–35.

61 Schörner's final mention of his intention to break the siege of Breslau was contained in a report to Hitler on 30 March 1945. This report is reproduced in Gleiss, *Breslauer Apokalypse. Band 3. März*, pp. 940–941.

62 Gleiss, *Breslauer Apokalypse. Band 3. März*, pp. 940–941.

63 Kaps, *The Tragedy of Silesia*, p. 122.

64 Gleiss, *Breslauer Apokalypse. Band 4. April*, pp. 694–695.

65 Ibid., pp. 880–881.

66 Grieger, *Wie Breslau fiel*, p. 28.

67 BAB, R55/794, p. 33, *Mundpropagandaparole* 15, 17 February 1945.

68 Ibid., p. 35, *Mundpropagandaparole* 16, 27 February 1945.

69 Michaelis and Straepler (eds.), *Ursachen und Folgen. Band 22*, p. 343.

70 Böddeker, *Die Flüchtlinge*, p. 79; Hoffmann, *Stalins Vernichtungskrieg*, pp. 254–255. For a recent summary of the contents of proclamations issued to the Red Army in 1945 see Zeidler, *Kriegsende im Osten*, pp. 125–134.
71 TNA, FO 898/187, p. A6, 12 February 1945, quoting DNB broadcast, 8 February 1945.
72 Michaelis and Straepler (eds.), *Ursachen und Folgen Band 22*, pp. 391–393.
73 Müller and Ueberschär, *Kriegsende 1945*, p. 113.
74 Ibid., p. 114.
75 Beevor, *Berlin*, pp. 169–170.
76 On German planning to poison alcohol stocks and Soviet losses from drinking contaminated schnapps and from drinking unmarked industrial stores of methanol see P. Biddiscombe, *The Last Nazis: SS Werewolf Guerrilla Resistance in Europe* (Stroud: Tempus Publishing Ltd, 2005), pp. 81–84. In Schneidemühl, 120 Red Army soldiers were poisoned by methanol. See also Beevor, *Berlin*, p. 31.
77 BA-LA, Ost-Dok. 10/890, pp. 41–42, 144. Wagner also highlighted the Red Army's excesses at Labiau and Tannenwalde, on top of their crimes at Nemmersdorf, in his proclamation to the Königsberg *Volkssturm* on 5 February 1945. Michaelis and Straepler (eds.), *Ursachen und Folgen. Band 22*, pp. 350–351.
78 Lasch, *So fiel Königsberg*, pp. 74–75.
79 BAB, NS19/2068, p. 18, 21 February 1945.
80 BA-LA, Ost-Dok. 8/591, p. 48.
81 Böddeker, *Die Flüchtlinge*, pp. 79–80.
82 A. Werth, *Russia at War 1941–1945* (London: E.P. Dutton, 1964), p. 966.
83 Beevor, *Berlin*, p. 30.
84 von Lehndorff, *East Prussian Diary*, p. 29.
85 TNA, FO 898/187, 5 March 1945, p. A3.
86 A. Beevor and L. Vinogradova (eds.), *A Writer at War: Vasily Grossman with the Red Army* (London: Pimlico, 2006), p. 328.
87 Ibid.
88 Ibid., pp. 323–324. The anarchist Nestor Makhno had operated in Ukraine during the Russian Civil War.
89 Werth, *Russia at War*, p. 964. In Poland the actions of the Red Army were observed by RAF Sargeant John Ward, who had escaped from German captivity and had spent four years with the Polish resistance. 'On arrival they proceeded to act as though they were Masters of the earth . . . within a few days the Russians had raped every female in the district over fourteen years of age' and 'appeared to beat Polish men without provocation and some were shot'. TNA, HS 4/256, Sargeant John Ward, Interrogation Report.
90 Beevor, *Berlin*, p. 29
91 M. Djilas, *Conversations with Stalin* (Harmondsworth, Middlesex: Pelican edition, 1969), p. 76.
92 Gleiss, *Breslauer Apokalypse. Band 2. Februar*, pp. 318–319; Siebel-Achenbach, *Lower Silesia*, pp. 65–66. Earlier German deportations of Ukrainians and Belorussians to undertake forced labour in the Reich is mentioned in chapters 2–4.
93 IfZ, MZ9/57, *VB*, 11 March 1945.
94 BAB, NS6/135, pp. 98–101, no date.
95 BA-LA, Ost-Dok. 10/601, p. 11.
96 Grau, *Silesian Inferno*, pp. 82–83; Böddeker, *Die Flüchtlinge*, p. 136; Beever, *Berlin*, p. 127.
97 *Braunschweiger Zeitung*, 14 March 1945, quoted in Grau, *Silesian Inferno*, p. 83.

98 Beevor and Vinogradova (eds.), *A Writer at War*, p. 327.

99 Beevor, *Berlin*, p. 121.

100 Beevor and Vinogradova (eds.), *A Writer at War*, p. 327.

101 Great Britain, Foreign Office, *Weekly Political Intelligence Summaries Volume 11 January–June 1945* (London: Kraus International Publications, 1983), No 289, 18 April 1945, p. 6; Werth, *Russia at War 1941–1945*, pp. 966–968. Ehrenburg was also attacked for suggesting in articles that the Germans were letting the Allies into western Germany unhindered. Rather the Nazis were trying a 'provocational military and political trick' to induce dissension among the Allies. However, other interpretations have commented that Ehrenburg continued his 'Kill the Germans' theme unabated even after this warning and Stalin quite consciously closed his eyes to it. See Ryan, *The Last Battle*, p. 34.

102 *TBJG 15*, pp. 457–461, 9 March 1945.

103 IfZ, MZ9/57, *VB*, 11 March 1945.

104 Welch, 'Goebbels, Götterdämmerung, and the Deutsche Wochenschauen', in Short and Dolezel (ed.), *Hitler's Fall: The Newsreel Witness*, p. 94.

105 IfZ, MZ 9/57, *VB*, 11 March 1945; Beevor, *Berlin*, p. 127. Hitler also made a widely publicised visit to the Oder front in early March 1945. The propagandists claimed that Hitler's appearance signalled an imminent German counter-offensive and eastern refugees were said to be particularly optimistic about this development. See BAB, R55/794, p. 36, *Mundpropagandaparole* 20, 21 March 1945; R55/601, p. 299, propaganda activity report, 21 March 1945.

106 TNA, FO 898/187, p. A5, 12 February 1945, quoting DNB Europe broadcast, 9 February 1945.

107 *The Times*, 12 March 1945.

108 Beevor, *Berlin*, pp. 173–176. Prützmann committed suicide in May 1945. On Koch's strained relationship with Prützmann see Tilitzki, *Alltag in Ostpreußen*, p. 57. In his interesting study of the *Werwolf* Perry Biddiscombe points to six *Werwolf* Special *Kommando* detachments operating behind the lines of the Third Belorussian Front in late 1944. One nine-man Special *Kommando* worked in the Rominter Heath area during October and November. It reported back to Königsberg by radio and advised that the Soviets were most effective in evacuating almost all German men and most women from areas adjacent to the front. This tactic made partisan activity extremely difficult and the *Kommando* was eliminated by the Red Army in mid-November. Biddiscombe, *The Last Nazis,* pp. 178–191.

109 Krockow, *Hour of the Women*, p. 75.

110 Beevor, *Berlin*, p. 102.

111 L. Falk, *Ich blieb in Königsberg. Tagebücher aus dunklen Nachkriegssjahren* (Munich: Gräfe und Unzer Verlag, 1965), p. 45. On German boys interned at Labiau in late April 1945 and the continued Soviet searches for youths in East Prussia after this see Biddiscombe, *The Last Nazis*, p. 249.

112 IfZ, MZ9/57, *VB*, 11 February 1945.

113 BAB, NS19/2068, p. 66, 15 March 1945.

114 BAB, NS6/135, pp. 161–198, *Kreisleiter* Körner to Bormann, 5 April 1945.

115 BA-LA, Ost-Dok. 8/602, p. 10.

116 BfZ, S.St. Feldpost 1945/2, E.W., 23 February 1945.

117 Falk, *Ich bieb in Königsberg,* p. 5.

118 NA-US, Microcopy T-78, Roll No. 477, p. 6459653, 7 April 1945.

119 BA-LA, Ost-Dok. 8/518, p. 6; Falk, *Ich blieb in Königsberg*, p. 6; Lasch, *So fiel Königsberg*, p. 103.

120 See BAB, NS6/354, Circular 47/45g, 1 February 1945. BAB, NS19/2068, p. 62, 14 March 1945; p. 65, 15 March 1945; p. 84, 22 March 1945. See also BA-LA, Ost-Dok. 8/591, pp. 53–54; 10/888, p. 32; 10/890, pp. 43–44; Lasch, *So fiel Königsberg*, pp. 85–86; Bagramyan, 'The Storming of Königsberg', p. 235.
121 Bagramyan, 'The Storming of Königsberg', pp. 235, 241.
122 BAB, NS19/2068, p. 71, 17 March 1945. The anguish in Peyse was reported to *Kreisleiter* Wagner who visited the town and dismissed the complaints as trivial. Wagner was apparently furious at the nursing sister whose complaints had led to his journey, went for his revolver and but for the presence of others would have shot her in cold blood. See BA-LA, Ost-Dok. 8/602, p. 9.
123 BA-LA, Ost-Dok. 8/506, p. 4.
124 *Das Ostpreussenblatt*, 5 March 1951, quoted in Bundesministerium für Vertriebene, Flüchtlinge und Kriegsgeschädigte (ed.), *Dokumente Deutscher Kriegsssschäden: Evakuierte, Kriegssachgeschädigte, Währungsgeschädigte. Die geschichtliche und rechtliche Entwicklung. 1. Beiheft.*, p. 354.
125 BA-LA, Ost-Dok. 8/588, p. 9.
126 BA-LA, Ost-Dok. 8/591, pp. 57–58.
127 Schieder (ed.), *Dokumentation. Band 1/1*, pp. 145–146, 149–151.
128 Steinert, *Hitler's War*, p. 295.
129 BA-LA, Ost-Dok. 8/602, p. 7.
130 BA-LA, Ost-Dok. 8/591, pp. 46, 51.
131 BAB, NS19/2068, p. 71, 17 March 1945.
132 BA-LA, Ost-Dok. 10/890, p. 144; Lasch, *So fiel Königsberg*, p. 65; Gause, *Die Geschichte der Stadt Königsberg*, p. 162. Concurrently, in Pomerania the shortage of coal and other materials led to a further decrease in production in those armaments factories still in operation. In most plants only a 48-hour week or less could be worked. See BAB, NS19/2068, p. 74, 18 March 1945.
133 Sereny, *Albert Speer: His Battle With Truth*, p. 509 described Breslau in April 1945 as a 'burning and now starving city'. Only the first part of this statement is correct.
134 von Ahlfen and Niehoff, *So kämpfte Breslau*, pp. 37, 91; Kaps, *The Tragedy of Silesia*, p. 121.
135 Siebel-Achenbach, *Lower Silesia*, p. 75.
136 Thorwald, *Das Ende an der Elbe*, p. 273.
137 Grieger, *Wie Breslau fiel*, p. 19.
138 Peikert, *'Festung Breslau'*, p. 32.
139 Siebel-Achenbach, *Lower Silesia*, p. 307 points to the vastly differing figures quoted for the number of wounded flown out from Breslau. These range from 3,282 to 6,600 men.
140 Grieger, *Wie Breslau fiel*, pp. 15–16.
141 Böddeker, *Die Flüchtlinge*, p. 77; Lasch, *So fiel Königsberg*, pp. 59–60.
142 BA-LA, Ost-Dok. 8/591, pp. 44–45; Duffy, *Red Storm on the Reich*, p. 256.
143 BAB, NS19/2068, p. 71, 17 March 1945.
144 Ibid., p. 74, 19 March 1945; p. 84, 22 March 1945.
145 Duffy, *Red Storm on the Reich*, pp. 255–256; von Ahlfen and Niehoff, *So kämpfte Breslau*, pp. 90–95.
146 BAB, NS19/2068, p. 8, 17 February 1945.
147 According to post-war Polish accounts Glogau (Glogow) was 95% destroyed. See Rutkiewicz, *The Odra*, p. 19.
148 H. Hartung, *Schlesien 1944/45* (Munich, 1976), p. 79 quoted in Duffy, *Red Storm on the Reich*, p. 263.

149 Steinert, *Hitler's War*, p. 298.
150 von Lehndorff, *East Prussian Diary*, p. 16.
151 BA-LA, Ost-Dok. 10/888, p. 31.
152 BA-LA, Ost-Dok. 8/602, p. 6.
153 Hornig, *Breslau 1945*, p. 21.
154 Peikert, *'Festung Breslau'*, p. 37.
155 Ibid. p. 157.
156 Kaps, *The Tragedy of Silesia*, p. 49.
157 Hornig, *Breslau 1945*, pp. 28–29.
158 BA-LA, Ost-Dok. 10/408, p. 5.
159 W. Görlitz, 'Das große Sterben des pommerschen Adels', in Granzow (ed.), *Meine Heimat Pommern: Die Letzten Tage*, pp. 253–256. See also Krockow, *Hour of the Women*, pp. 44–45, 83.
160 Schimitzek, *Truth or Conjecture*, p. 249.
161 Beevor, Berlin, p. 122.
162 von Lehndorff, *East Prussian Diary*, p. 14.
163 Gause, *Die Geschichte der Stadt Königsberg*, p. 162.
164 BAB, NS19/2068, p. 62, 13 March 1945.
165 Ibid., p. 76, 20 March 1945, '7,300 foreign workers' from an SS source; Siebel-Achenbach, *Lower Silesia*, p. 75, 'more than 3,000' foreigners; Gleiss, *Breslauer Apokaypse. Band 2. Februar*, p. 328, 'more than 4,000 foreigners' from NSDAP statistics.
166 *ST*, 3 February 1945, reproduced in Gleiss, *Breslauer Apokalypse. Band 2. Februar*, p. 52. According to the security police the contents of letters found on their person made it clear that they sought to further the enemy cause.
167 *ST*, 8 February, 10 February 1945, reproduced in Ibid., pp. 198, 248.
168 BAB, NS19/2068, p. 18, 21 February 1945.
169 See R. Gellately, *Backing Hitler: Consent and Coercion in Nazi Germany* (Oxford: Oxford University Press, 2002), p. 252.
170 Ibid., p. 247; von Stahlberg, *Bounden Duty*, p. 387.
171 N. Wachsmann, *Hitler's Prisons: Legal Terror in Nazi Germany* (London: Yale University Press, 2004), p. 328.
172 Davies and Moorhouse, *Microcosm*, pp. 15, 536
173 Peikert, *'Festung Breslau'*, pp. 50–51.
174 BAB, R22/3386, pp. 74–78, 10 February 1945.
175 Wachsmann, *Hitler's Prisons*, pp. 325, 332–333.
176 On 13 January 1945, Hitler ordered all-half Jews to be sent to work at the Theresienstadt camp in the Sudetenland. Wieck, *Zeugnis vom Untergang Königsbergs*, p. 179. See also the account of Victor Klemperer, a Jewish academic resident in Dresden spared the death camps by virtue of being married to an Aryan. He reported that hitherto exempt Jews deemed capable of work were to be transported to Theresienstadt on 16 February 1945 but evaded this likely death sentence when Allied bombs engulfed Dresden on 13–14 February causing the breakdown of the Nazi administrative structure. V. Klemperer, *To the Bitter End: The Diaries of Victor Klemperer 1942–45* (London: Weidenfeld & Nicolson, 1999), pp. 387–396.
177 IfZ, MCI Zusammenbruch IV-8 Königsberg, Heinz Strittmatter, p. 1. Robert Gellately also mentions the evacuation of 1,500 Jews from the Stutthof subcamp at Seerappen north-west of Königsberg from 20 January. He adds that they were soon joined by prisoners from

other camps so that there was a total of 7,000 prisoners (6,000 women and 1,000 men). After a 10-day forced march, which cost around 700 lives, on 31 January the remaining prisoners were driven into the frozen Baltic Sea near Palmnicken on the Samland coast and machine gunned to death. See Gellately, *Backing Hitler*, p. 247. Miraculously there were 13 survivors and one, Celina Manielewicz, was quoted at the Imperial War Museum's Holocaust exhibition in 2000, 'The whole coast as far as I could see, was covered in corpses, and I too was lying on such a mountain of corpses which slowly sunk deeper and deeper.' See also the recollections of *Landrat* Klaus von der Groeben of Kreis Königsberg quoted in Moeller, *War Stories*, p. 75. He described how 'many of the hundreds in the processions died from exhaustion, hunger, and maltreatment and remained unburied in the snow drifts, while the rest were driven . . . into the sea or shot by the guards who were among [Germany's] foreign allies.'

178 Peikert, *'Festung Breslau'*, pp. 111, 152, 158.

179 BA-LA, Ost-Dok 10/943, pp. 1–3; Peikert, *'Festung Breslau'*, pp. 58–59.

180 *ST*, 7 March 1945 reproduced in Gleiss, *Breslauer Apokalypse. Band 3. März*, p. 230; Schimitzek, *Truth or Conjecture*, pp. 289–290. For an example of a man who did not register, was apprehended, placed before a drumhead court martial and shot see *ST*, 15 March 1945 quoted in Peikert, *'Festung Breslau'*, p. 143.

181 The runway was eventually around two kilometres long and between 200 and 400 metres broad. BA-LA, Ost-Dok. 10/943, p. 2; Peikert, *'Festung Breslau'*, pp. 199–200; Siebel-Achenbach, *Lower Silesia*, p. 75; Böddeker, *Die Flüchtlinge*, pp. 179–180.

182 Siebel-Achenbach, *Lower Silesia*, p. 75. The identity of the bombers appears to be unknown.

183 BA-LA, Ost-Dok 8/591, p. 49; 8/602, p. 6.

184 Lasch, *So fiel Königsberg*, p. 78. Other commentators are more critical of the role of Lasch and the *Wehrmacht* in demolitions and the construction of the Königsberg runway. See Lucas-Busemann, *So fielen Königsberg und Breslau*, p. 57.

185 IfZ, MCI Zusammenbruch IV-8 Königsberg, Fritz Schulz, pp. 1–2. The Party also called up women and girls to dig defences around Stolp and Stargard, Pomerania in February. BA-LA, Ost-Dok. 8/643, p. 3; 8/671, p. 9.

186 Gleiss, *Breslauer Apokalypse. Band 1. Januar*, pp. 574–575; Hornig, *Breslau 1945*, pp. 30–31; Siebel-Achenbach, *Lower Silesia*, p. 61.

187 Knopp, *Die große Flucht*, p. 164; <www.DerTodinEhren.htm>, 9 September 2002.

188 Among the other senior officials executed for leaving their posts were the *Bürgermeister* of Brockau, Bruno Kurzbach, the *Bürgermeister* of Klettendorf, Eugen Pfanz, and a Breslau company director. BA-LA, Ost-Dok. 10/601, pp. 14–15; Gleiss, *Breslauer Apokalypse. Band 2. Februar*, pp. 25–26, 99, 168, 454; Hornig, *Breslau 1945*, pp. 31–32.

189 BAB, NS6/354, pp. 137–138, 15 February 1945; *ST*, 17 February 1945 reproduced in Gleiss, *Breslauer Apokalypse. Band 2. Februar*, p. 434.

190 Hornig, *Breslau 1945*, pp. 32–33.

191 BfZ, SSt Feldpost 1945/2, W., 7 February 1945.

192 Davies and Moorhouse, *Microcosm*, p. 33. See also TNA, HW1/3744. German military signals reported open civilian revolt in Breslau on 27 April. Some 14,000 fighting men were said to be in the fortress, 140,000 civilians, mainly women and children and 7,000 wounded. A decision on the city's future was deemed urgent with a breakout and concurrent push by the 17th Army viewed as promising success.

193 Peikert, *'Festung Breslau'*, p. 38; Siebel-Achenbach, *Lower Silesia*, p. 75.

194 IfZ, MCI Zusammenbruch, Franzek, p. 12. Koch also took the opportunity to send the

East Prussian NSV leader Erich Post into Königsberg realising that this was tantamount to a death sentence for his former close colleague. Post maintained that on Koch's instructions he had left Pillau on 31 January to assist in relief measures for East Prussian refugees in the Reich. Due to a longer than anticipated voyage to Swinemünde, Post's whereabouts were unknown for a few days and it was suspected that he was with his wife who had already been evacuated to Saxony. Koch later denied that Post had been given this assignment. When Post finally returned to Pillau on 22 February he was stripped of Party rank. See BAB, R55/616, pp. 166–167, 8 February 1945; pp. 174–179, 10–11 February 1945; pp. 227–233, 11–22 February 1945; BA-LA, Ost-Dok. 8/584, pp. 5–6.

195 IfZ, MCI Zusammenbruch IV-8 Königsberg, Georg Strasas, p. 1.

196 Beevor, *Berlin*, p. 127.

197 These executions appear to have taken place in late February and early March. BA-LA, Ost-Dok. 8/643, p. 3; Schimitzek, *Truth or Conjecture*, p. 249.

198 Krockow, *Hour of the Women*, pp. 51–54.

199 Gause, *Die Geschichte der Stadt Königsberg*, pp. 162, 169. The 'Fire-Brigade General' Fiedler was prevented from entering Lasch's headquarters on 9 April in a bid to shoot Russian intermediaries arranging the surrender. As Fiedler attempted to escape he drowned in a sewer.

200 Reitlinger, *The House Built on Sand,* pp. 225–226.

201 IfZ, MCI, Zusammenbruch IV-8 Königsberg, Friedrich Henschel; *The Times*, 17 November 1986; *Das Ostpreußenblatt*, 29 November 1986.

202 Höffkes, *Hitlers Politische Generale*, p. 340.

203 BAB, NS19/2068, p. 84, 21 March 1945.

204 Murawski, *Die Eroberung Pommerns*, pp. 29–31. *Die Pommersche Zeitung*, 5 November 1960.

205 On Hanke's flight, his likely demise but persistent reports of post-war sightings, see BA-LA, Ost-Dok. 8/734, p. 9; Gleiss, *Breslauer Apokalypse. Band 5. Mai*, pp. 283–318; Siebel-Achenbach, *Lower Silesia*, p. 80; Böddeker, *Die Flüchtlinge*, pp. 182–183. It has been claimed that a Junkers-52 landed on the Kaisersstrasse runway and took out 22 wounded on 10 April 1945, see Davies *Microcosm*, pp. 31, 537.

206 *TBJG 15*, p. 209, 24 January 1945.

207 Höffkes, *Hitlers Politische Generale*, p. 35.

208 Thorwald, *Es begann an der Weichsel*, pp. 77–78; *The Times*, 22 July 1946.

209 See Schenk, *Hitlers Mann in Danzig*, pp. 260–290 for the circumstances of Forster's captivity and execution.

Conclusion

1 During the final months of the war Himmler was involved in clandestine peace negotiations with Count Folke Bernadotte, vice-chairman of the Swedish Red Cross. Himmler hoped to conclude a deal with the British and Americans. Meanwhile his subordinate *SS-Obergruppenführer* Karl Wolff was trying to arrange an armistice in Italy in order that German forces in that theatre could be withdrawn and sent against the Red Army.

Bibliography

PRIMARY SOURCES

Archives

BIBLIOTHEK FÜR ZEITGESCHICHTE ARCHIVALISCHE SAMMLUNGEN (STUTTGART)

Sammlung Sterz Feldpost 1. Januar 1944–30. April 1945.

Lebensdokumentensammlung

Archiv N94.2/1 Herta Boy. Ostpreußen 1943–1945.

Archiv N94.9/1 Heinz Künzler, Luftwaffe. Ostpreußen 1944.

Archiv N94.8 Die Lebensgeschichte der Herry Schröder. Ostpreußen 1944–1945.

Archiv N Ewald Festag. 'Aus eigenem Leben'. Ostpreußen 1945.

Archiv N Oberzahlmeister Kurt Gebhard. Briefe von ihm 1944–1945. General Gouvernement und Westpreußen 1944–1945.

Archiv N Leutnant Werner Shorl. 4. Armee. Ostpreußen 1944–1945.

BRANDENBURGISCHES LANDESHAUPTARCHIV (POTSDAM)

Preußen Brandenburg Repositur 3B Regierung Frankfurt an der Oder

Pr.Br.Rep.3B I Pol. 1973 Unterbringung der Flüchtlinge aus östlichen und westlichen Gebieten. 1944–1945.

Pr.Br.Rep.3B I Pol. 1974 Unterbringung von Bombenschädigten. 1943–1945.

Pr.Br.Rep.3B I Mil. 359 Personenschädenverordnung vom 1. September 1939 und darauf ergangene Bestimmungen. 1939–1944.

Pr.Br.Rep.3B I Mil. 360 Allgemeine Richtlinien über die Durchführung von Evakuierungsmaßnahmen, Umquartierung und Überweisung Bombengeschädigter. 1940–1944.

Pr.Br.Rep.3B I Mil. 365–366 Kriegsschäden durch Bombenangriffe im Regierungsbezirk und ihre Bezahlung durch den Staat. 1940–1944.

Preußen Brandenburg Repositur 55 Provinzialverband

Pr.Br.Rep.55 I 1479 Notdienstverplichtungen für die Notschanzarbeiten im Osten und Potsdam. 1944–1945.

Pr.Br.Rep.55 I 2643 Die Monatsberichte über die Preis- und Versorgungslage wichtiger Verbrauchsgüter in Pommern. 1942–1944.

Bundesarchiv Berlin

R22 Reichsjustizministerium

R22/243 Berichterstattung der Generalstaatanwälte und OLG Präsidenten über die allgemeine Lage in den Bezirken ('Lageberichte').

Lageberichte der Oberlandesgerichtspräsidenten und der Generalstaatanwälte 1934–1945:

R22/3358 Breslau 1940–1945.

R22/3372 Kattowitz 1940–1945.

R22/3375 Königsberg 1940–1945.

R22/3386 Stettin 1940–1945.

R43 II Reichskanzlei

R43II/522b Erlaß über den Grenzeinsatz der HJ. September 1944.

R43II/607 Eingriffe in die Produktionslenkung von Gauleiter Hanke. September 1944.

R43II/684 Räumungsmaßnahmen in Ostpreußen. Juli 1944.

R43II/690a Reichskommissariat Ostland. Band 3. 1941–1944.

R43II/692 Erfassung und Behandlungen deutscher und fremdvölkischer Flüchtlinge. 1944.

R43II/692a Deutscher Volkssturm.

R55 Reichsministerium für Volksaufklärung und Propaganda

R55/426 Einzelne Propagandaaktionen, propagandawichtige Meldungen, Stimmungsberichte der RPÄ. Ostpreußen. Juli 1944.

R55/600 Gau eigene antibolschewistische Propaganda – Aktion des RPA Ostpreußen. 1944.

R55/601 Wöchentliche Tätigkeitsberichte des Leiters der Abteilung Propaganda. Juli 1944–März 1945.

R55/602 Einzelne Propagandaaktionen, propagandawichtige Meldungen, Stimmungsberichte der RPÄ. 1944–1945.

R55/603 Einzelne Propagandaaktionen, propagandawichtige Meldungen, Stimmungsberichte der RPÄ. 1943–1945.

R55/608 Propagandaparolen.

R55/609 Einzelne Propagandaaktionen, propagandawichtige Meldungen, Stimmungsberichte der RPÄ. 1944–1945.

R55/610 Einzelne Propagandaaktionen, propagandawichtige Meldungen, Stimmungsberichte der RPÄ. 1943–1945.

R55/611 Einzelne Propagandaaktionen, propagandawichtige Meldungen, Stimmungsberichte der RPÄ. 1943–1944.

R55/612 Aufnahme der Führer und Goebbelsrede zu Sylvester 1944/45 bei der Bevölkerung, Meldungen der RPÄ und Ministervorlage.

R55/613 Einzelne Propagandaaktionen, propagandawichtige Meldungen, Stimmungsberichte der RPÄ. 1943–1945.

R55/614 'Treukundgebungen' nach dem 20. Juli 1944, insbesondere Berichte über einzelne Veranstaltungen und Stimmung nach dem Attentat. Juli 1944–August 1944.

R55/616 Ostpreußen Juli 1944. Evakuierung 1945.

R55/619 Einzelne Propagandaaktionen, propagandawichtige Meldungen, Stimmungsberichte der RPÄ. 1944–1945.

R55/620 Einzelne Propagandaaktionen, propagandawichtige Meldungen, Stimmungsberichte der RPÄ. 1943–1945.

R55/621 Einzelne Propagandaaktionen, propagandawichtige Meldungen, Stimmungsberichte der RPÄ. 1943–1945.

R55/622 Einzelne Propagandaaktionen, propagandawichtige Meldungen, Stimmungsberichte der RPÄ. 1944–1945.

R55/793 'Material für Propagandisten'. November 1944–Februar 1945.

R55/794 Mundpropaganda. 1944–1945.

R55/821 Inspektionsbesuche bei RPÄ. (Königsberg, Stettin, Brandenburg).

R55/946 Einzelne Propagandaaktionen, propagandawichtige Meldungen, Stimmungsberichte der RPÄ. 1943–1945.

R55/1212 Inspektionsbesuche bei RPÄ. (Kattowitz, Breslau).

R55/1263 Die Lage in der Sowjetunion. August 1944–März 1945.

R55/1267 Politische Sonderberichte. 2. November 1943–20. Dezember 1944.

R55/1394 Einzelne Propagandaaktionen, propagandawichtige Meldungen, Stimmungsberichte der RPÄ. 1944–1945.

R55/1438 Denkschrift von Ministerialrat Dr Taubert zur Lage der Ostpolitik. September 1944.

R58 Reichssicherheitshauptamt

SD-Berichte zu Inlandsfragen:

R58/187 August 1943.

R58/188 September 1943.

R58/189 Oktober 1943.

R58/190 November 1943.

R58/191 Dezember 1943.

R58/192 Januar–Februar 1944.

R58/193 März–April 1944.

R58/194 Mai–Juni 1944.

R58/397 Stimmung unter Kriegsgefangen und Fremdarbeitern in Gebiet Breslau-Sommerfeld. Bericht eines V-Mannes. 10. Januar 1945.

R58/976 Lage in Grenzgebieten. 1944–1945.

R58/1044 Kriegstagebuch der Dienststelle Schlesiersee/Kreis Glogau des Amtes VII des Chefs der Sicherheitspolizei und des SD. 20. Januar 1945–10. Februar 1945.

NS1 Reichsschatzmeister der NSDAP

NS1/274 Meldungen der Gauleitung über Bombenabwurfe und Fliegerschäden. 22. April 1942–Dezember 1943.

NS1/544 Meldungen des SD zu Einzelfragen. 1944.

NS1/579 Meldungen der Gauleitung über Bombenabwurfe und Fliegerschäden. November 1941.

NS1/585 Meldungen der Gauleitung über Bombenabwurfe und Fliegerschäden. Januar–Dezember 1944.

NS6 Partei-Kanzlei

NS6/78 Verfügungen, Anordnungen, Erlasse des Führers der NSDAP. 1942–1945.

NS6/98 Deutscher Volkssturm – Anordnungen, Verfügungen, Rundschreiben. Band 1. 18. September 1944–29. Dezember 1944.

NS6/99 Deutscher Volkssturm – Anordnungen, Verfügungen, Rundschreiben. Band 2. 5. Januar 1945–8. April 1945.

NS6/135 Meldungen, Erfahrungs – und Stimmungsberichte über die Haltung der Wehrmacht und der Bevölkerung angesichts der Verschlechterung der Kriegslage. 1944–1945.

NS6/153 Stimmung in der Bevölkerung insbesondere auch im Zusammenhang mit den Ereignissen des 20. Juli 1944.

NS6/167 Heranziehung der Partei, ihrer Gliederungen und angeschlossenen Verbände zum Kriegseinsatz. 1942–1944.

NS6/168 Bildung und Einsatz des Deutschen Volkssturms. 1944–1945.

NS6/312 Deutscher Volkssturm – Propaganda. 1944–1945.

NS6/313–314 Deutscher Volkssturm – Übereinstimmung mit Gauleiter usf. 1944–1945.

NS6/347–349, 351–352, 354 Anordnungen, Verfügungen und Rundschreiben. 1944–1945.

NS6/411 Meldungen aus den SD – (Leit) Abschnittsbereichen (Zusammenstellungen des RSHA für die Partei-Kanzlei) insbesondere zur Stimmung und Haltung der Bevölkerung und zur Entwicklung der öffentlichen Meinungsbildung. Juni 1943–August 1944.

NS6/412 Lage- und Stimmungsberichte des SD im Reichsgau Wartheland für die Zeit vom 16. April bis 17. August 1944.

NS6/763–764 Deutscher Volkssturm – Übereinstimmung mit Gauleiter usf. 1944–1945.

NS6/791 Mitwirkung von Parteidienststellen bei der Rückverlegung von Wehrmachtversorgungseinrichtungen und Rückführung von Flüchtlingen im Osten. Juli 1944.

NS19 Persönlicher Stab Reichsführer-SS

NS19/2068 'Meldungen aus dem Ostraum' insbesondere über Kampfhandlungen an den Ostfront. 15. Februar–22. März 1945.

NS19/2606 Berichterstattungen über Auflösungserscheinungen an der deutschen Ostfront durch Fluchtbewegungen der Truppen sowie über Evakuierung der Zivilbevölkerung aus den deutschen Ostgebieten. 1944–1945.

NS19/2721 Befehle der Heeresgruppe Weichsel, insbesondere zur Stärkung des Kampfgeistes, sowie Bergung zurückgelassener Güter in den geräumten Gebieten. 1945.

Akte Koch Erich Koch, Gauleiter Ostpreußen 1928–1945.

BUNDESARCHIV – LASTENAUSGLEICHSARCHIV (BAYREUTH)

Ost-Dokumentation

Ost-Dok. 8 *Berichte von Persönlichkeiten des öffentlichen Lebens aus Ostpreußen, Pommern, Ostbrandenburg und Niederschlesien zum Zeitgeschehen 1919–1945.*

East Prussia:

Ost-Dok. 8/506 O. Horn, Oberlandwirtschaftsrat der Landesbauernschaft Ostpreußen.

Ost-Dok. 8/507 Kurt Jacobi, Ministerialdirigent, Reichsinnenministerium.

Ost-Dok. 8/509 von Jaraczewski, Landwirt in Elkinehmen, Kreis Darkehmen (Angerapp).
Ost-Dok. 8/510 Major Kurt Dieckert, Verbindungsoffizier zwischen Zivilverwaltung und 3. Panzerarmee.
Ost-Dok. 8/512 Dr Grosse-Beilage, Oberregierungsrat, Regierung Allenstein.
Ost-Dok. 8/513 Horst G. Benkmann, Regierungsassessor, Landratsamt Allenstein.
Ost-Dok. 8/514 Georg Bobrowski, Regierungsoberinspektor, Landratsamt Goldap.
Ost-Dok. 8/515 Otto Bahl, Regierungsoberinspektor, Landratsamt Braunsberg.
Ost-Dok. 8/518 Dr Karl Brenke, Stadtverwaltung Königsberg.
Ost-Dok. 8/519 Oberst Hans Leberecht von Bredow, Gendarmerie.
Ost-Dok. 8/521 Dr von Bredow, Landrat Kreis Schloßberg.
Ost-Dok. 8/523 Generalleutnant Kurt Chill.
Ost-Dok. 8/524 Paul Gerber, Stadtverwaltung Memel.
Ost-Dok. 8/526 Otto Gerbauer, Gumbinnen.
Ost-Dok. 8/529 Generalmajor Erich Dethleffsen, Chef des Generalstabes, 4. Armee.
Ost-Dok. 8/530 Generalmajor Erich Dethleffsen, Chef des Generalstabes, 4. Armee.
Ost-Dok. 8/531 Klaus von der Groeben, Landrat, Kreis Samland.
Ost-Dok. 8/532 Generalmajor Dr Walther Grosse.
Ost-Dok. 8/533 Generalmajor Dr Walther Grosse.
Ost-Dok. 8/536 Dr Paul Hoffmann, Regierungspräsident, Oberpräsidium Königsberg.
Ost-Dok. 8/538 Oberleutnant Günther Heysing, Kriegsberichter, *Völkischer Beobachter*.
Ost-Dok. 8/540 Hartwig, Forstmeister, Memelwalde.
Ost-Dok. 8/542 Kurt Gutknecht, Heydekrug.
Ost-Dok. 8/544 Köhler, Leitender Regierungsdirektor, Leiter des Landwirtschaftamtes und des Führungsstabes Wirtschaft.
Ost-Dok. 8/545 Eduard Knuth, Kreisoberinspektor, Landratsamt Labiau.
Ost-Dok. 8/546 Eduard Knuth, Kreisoberinspektor, Landratsamt Labiau.
Ost-Dok. 8/551 Paul Kindt, Leiter der Feuerschutzpolizei, Insterburg.
Ost-Dok. 8/552 Arthur Kausch, Kreisbauernführer, Kreis Heydekrug.
Ost-Dok. 8/553 Oberst Ernst-August Lassen, Chef des Generalstabes, 28. Armee Korps.
Ost-Dok. 8/556 H. Kramer, Oberforstmeister, Elchwald.
Ost-Dok. 8/557 Generalmajor Burkhart Müller-Hillebrand, Chef des Generalstabes, 3. Panzerarmee.
Ost-Dok. 8/558 Albert Möller, Kreisburodirektor, Landratsamt, Gerdauen.
Ost-Dok. 8/559 Oberst Mendryk, Oberquartiermeister, 3. Panzerarmee.
Ost-Dok. 8/560 Walter Marquardt, Oberregierungsrat, Oberpräsidium Königsberg.
Ost-Dok. 8/561 Heinrich Lindner, Regierungsrat, Unterabteilungsleiter beim RVK.
Ost-Dok. 8/563 Generalleutnant O. von Natzmer, Chef des Generalstabes der Heeresgruppe Mitte (Nord).
Ost-Dok. 8/564 Paul Schmolski, Polizeimeister, Burdungen, Kreis Neidenburg.
Ost-Dok. 8/569 Artur Salecker, Kreisbaumeister, Kreis Samland.
Ost-Dok. 8/570 Helene Poweleit, NSV, Ebenrode.
Ost-Dok. 8/571 Dr Victor von Poser, Landrat, Kreis Ortelsburg.
Ost-Dok. 8/575 Brink, Regierungsamtmann, Regierung Gumbinnen.
Ost-Dok. 8/577 Paul Uschraweit, Landrat, Kreis Angerapp.
Ost-Dok. 8/580 Erich Zehran, Oberfinanzpräsident, Königsberg.
Ost-Dok. 8/582 Zander, Oberregierungsrat, stellvertretender Leiter des Landwirtschaftamtes Ostpreußen.
Ost-Dok. 8/583 Roderich Walther, stellvertretender Polizeidirektor in Tilsit.

Ost-Dok. 8/584 Wenzel, Oberregierungsrat, Referent beim RVK.
Ost-Dok. 8/585 Fritz Nieckau, Oberbürgermeister, Tilsit.
Ost-Dok. 8/586 Dr Victor Werbke, Stabsoffizier beim Festungskommandanten von Königsberg.
Ost-Dok. 8/587 Dr Wander, Bürgermeister, Insterburg.
Ost-Dok. 8/588 Dr Helmuth Will, Oberbürgermeister, Königsberg.
Ost-Dok. 8/590 Dr Werner Schmidt, Regierungsrat, Reichsinnenministerium.
Ost-Dok. 8/591 Oberleutnant Günther Heysing, Kriegsberichter, *Völkischer Beobachter*.
Ost-Dok. 8/592 Waldemar Magunia, Präsident der Handwerkskammer, Königsberg.
Ost-Dok. 8/593 Waldemar Magunia, Präsident der Handwerkskammer, Königsberg.
Ost-Dok. 8/594 Waldemar Magunia, Präsident der Handwerkskammer, Königsberg.
Ost-Dok 8/596 Dr Schroeder, Obermedizinalrat, Mitarbeiter der Gauarztkammer, Königsberg.
Ost-Dok. 8/598 Adolf Klein, Angestellter beim Oberforstamt Elchwald.
Ost-Dok. 8/599 Dr Schultz, Oberstudiendirektor, Hindenburg-Oberschule, Insterburg.
Ost-Dok. 8/602 G. Makowka, Bürgermeister, Königsberg.
Ost-Dok. 8/609 Klaus von der Groeben, Landrat, Kreis Königsberg.

Pomerania:
Ost-Dok. 8/636 C. Grundey, Polizeipräsident in Stettin.
Ost-Dok. 8/637 Siegfried Schug, Kreisleiter, Kreis Stargard-Saatzig.
Ost-Dok. 8/638 Helmut Meyer, Regierungsamtmann, Kreis Lauenburg.
Ost-Dok. 8/639 Erich Zahnow, Oberstudienrat Stettin.
Ost-Dok. 8/640 Fritz Wachholz, Stadtamtmann, stellvertretender Oberbürgermeister von Kolberg.
Ost-Dok. 8/643 F. Bachmann, Regierungsoberinspektor, Landratsamt Stolp.
Ost-Dok. 8/645 E.G. von Etzel, Landrat, Kreis Schlochau.
Ost-Dok. 8/646 Dr Eich, Obermedizinalrat, Amtsarzt, Kreis Stolp.
Ost-Dok. 8/648 Ludwig Förster, Landrat, Kreis Bütow.
Ost-Dok. 8/649 Otto Floret, Bürgermeister, Pyritz.
Ost-Dok. 8/652 Dr Alfred Heinrichs, Stadtkämmerer, Stettin.
Ost-Dok. 8/657 Max La Ramee, Regierungsoberdirektor, Landratsamt Pyritz.
Ost-Dok. 8/658 Hugo Krause, Polizeirat, Netzekreis.
Ost-Dok. 8/662 Hugo Rehbein, Lehrer in Gollnow.
Ost-Dok. 8/666 Otto Schmitz, Stadtdirektor, Bürodirektor, Landratsamtes Deutsch Krone.
Ost-Dok. 8/670 Walter Stark, Landwirt, Kreis Naugard.
Ost-Dok. 8/671 Gustav Wolffermann, Stadtbauinspektor und stellvertretender Kreisfeuerwehrführer in Stargard.
Ost-Dok. 8/674 Paul Windels, Landrat, Kreis Saatzig.
Ost-Dok. 8/677 von Wuthenau, Landrat des Netzekreises der Kreise Arnswalde und Friedeberg.
Ost-Dok. 8/678 Dr Zäschmar, Regierungsrat, Schneidemühl.
Ost-Dok. 8/679 Georg Werner von Zitewitz, Landwirt, Kreis Stolp.
Ost-Dok. 8/685 Hans Joachim Schmelzer, Landwirtschaftsrat, Köslin.
Ost-Dok. 8/687 General Werner Kienitz, Befehlshaber, Wehrkreis II, Stettin.
Ost-Dok. 8/688 Dr Gerhard Bode, Regierungsdirektor, Stettin.
Ost-Dok. 8/694 Gerhard Hohenhaus, Regierungsoberinspektor, Landratsamt, Schönlanke.
Ost-Dok. 8/701 Carl Wenzel, Inhaber der Firma Tetzloff und Wenzel KG Hamburg (Stettin). Carl Axt, Architekt, Stettin.

East Brandenburg:

Ost-Dok. 8/702 A. Hauk, Landrat und Kreisleiter, Kreis Züllichau–Schwiebus.
Ost-Dok. 8/703 Refardt, Regierungspräsident, Regierungsbezirk, Frankfurt an der Oder.
Ost-Dok. 8/704 Dr Munde, Landwirtschaftrat, Landsberg an der Warthe.
Ost-Dok. 8/707 Hans Pophen, Hitlerjugendführer, Berlin.
Ost-Dok. 8/708 C. Walter, Bürgermeister, Züllichau.
Ost-Dok. 8/712 Oberleutnant Kahl, Gendarmerie, Frankfurt an der Oder.
Ost-Dok. 8/712 W. Pahl, Amtvorsteher, Kreis Küstrin.
Ost-Dok. 8/715 Generalmajor Günther Meinhold.
Ost-Dok. 8/716 Richard Schultze, stellvertretender Kreisbauernführer, Kreis Königsberg/Neumark.
Ost-Dok. 8/717 Oberst Höhlbaum, Schwerin an der Warthe.

Lower Silesia:

Ost-Dok. 8/718 Dr Hans-Friedrich von Saint-Paul, Landrat, Kreis Militsch-Trachenberg.
Ost-Dok. 8/720 Professor Herbert Doms, Universitätsdozent, Breslau.
Ost-Dok. 8/721 Dr Walter Hübner, Kreis Reichenbach.
Ost-Dok. 8/725 Detlev von Reinersdorff-Paczenski, Landrat, Kreis Groß Wartenberg.
Ost-Dok. 8/729 Dr Ernst Heinrich, Landrat, Kreis Namslau.
Ost-Dok. 8/730 Professor Dr Günther Grundmann, Provinzialkonservator. Dr Herbert Dienwiebel, Archivrat, Stadtarchiv, Breslau.
Ost-Dok. 8/731 Dr Otto Fiebrantz, Landrat, Kreis Landeshut.
Ost-Dok. 8/734 Margarette Loose, Regierungsangestellte, Sekretärin des Regierungspräsidenten von Breslau.
Ost-Dok. 8/734b Oberleutnant Curt Neumann, Schutzpolizei, Breslau.
Ost-Dok. 8/735 Johannes Przybilla, Bankdirektor, Namslau.
Ost-Dok. 8/845 Wilhelm Adam, Landrat, Kreis Schweidnitz.

Ost-Dok. 10 *Berichte über Verwaltung und Wirtschaft in Ostpreußen, Pommern, Ostbrandenburg und Niederschlesien. 1930–1945.*

East Prussia:

Ost-Dok. 10/72 Dr Kerschensteiner, Präsident des Landesarbeitsamtes in Königsberg.
Ost-Dok. 10/111 Constanz Jaraczewski, Mitglied des Kreisausschusses, Kreis Darkehmen (Angerapp).
Ost-Dok. 10/139 Otto Buskies und Otto Lepenies. Der Volkssturm des Kreises Elchniederung.
Ost-Dok. 10/154 Dr Wander, Bürgermeister, Insterburg. Arthur Roeseler, Verwaltungsangestellter, Insterburg. Dr Liebnitz, Tierarzt, Insterburg. Karl Drengwitz, Fabrikant, Insterburg.
Ost-Dok. 10/247 Alfred Bannik, Stadtoberinspektor, Tilsit. Roderich Walther, Vertreter des Polizeidirektors Tilsit.
Ost-Dok. 10/888 Einsatz der 1 Ostpreußischen Infanterie Division insbesondere vom 15. August 1944 bis Mitte April 1945 in Ostpreußen (12 Berichte).
Ost-Dok. 10/890 Die Einschließung und Belagerung von Königsberg (35 Berichte).

Pomerania:

Ost-Dok. 10/375	Ludwig Förster, Landrat, Kreis Bütow.
Ost-Dok. 10/377	Otto Kanitz, Oberinspektor, Stadtverwaltung Bütow.
Ost-Dok. 10/385	Dr Friedrich Ackmann, Landrat, Kreis Flatow.
Ost-Dok. 10/388	Hans-Heinrich von Holstein, Landrat, Kreis Greifenberg.
Ost-Dok. 10/390	Emil Binder, Oberbürgermeister, Köslin.
Ost-Dok. 10/396	von Wuthenau, Landrat, Netzekreis.
Ost-Dok. 10/397	Herman Pahl, Ernst Molzahn, leitende Bürobeamte der Kreisverwaltung Neustettin.
Ost-Dok. 10/400	Otto Floret, Bürgermeister, Pyritz.
Ost-Dok. 10/402	Richard Spreemann, Regierungsdirektor, Kreis Regenwalde.
Ost-Dok. 10/406	Fritz Voss, Führer des Volkssturms bataillons Kreis Rummelsburg.
Ost-Dok. 10/407	Paul Windels, Landrat, Kreis Saatzig.
Ost-Dok. 10/408	Karl Ruschke, Kreisoberinspektor, Kreis Schlawe.
Ost-Dok. 10/410	Walter Poepel, Adjutant des Volkssturms bataillons 2, Kreis Schlawe.
Ost-Dok. 10/411	Udo von Alvensleben, Landrat, Kreis Schlochau.
Ost-Dok. 10/414	Karl Wetzel, Bürgermeister, Schlochau.
Ost-Dok. 10/415	Friedrich Rogausch, Oberbürgermeister, Schneidemühl.
Ost-Dok. 10/422	Dr M. Fabricius, Stadtrat, Stolp.
Ost-Dok. 10/424	General Werner Kienitz, Befehlshaber, Wehrkreis II, Stettin. Hans-Heinrich Staudinger, Leiter des Stabes der Wehrmachtinspektion, Stettin.
Ost-Dok. 10/425	Dr Otto Kleinschmidt, Leiter der Abteilung für höhes Schulweisen in Oberpräsidium der Provinz Pommern.
Ost-Dok. 10/504	Dr Adolf Leckzyck, Geschäftsführer der Industrie-und Handelskammer in Stettin.

East Brandenburg:

Ost-Dok. 10/520	Hans Voigt, Kampfkommandant, Arnswalde.
Ost-Dok. 10/523	von Wuthenau, Landrat, Kreise Arnswalde und Friedeberg/Neumark.
Ost-Dok. 10/524	Wilhelm Fürst, Kreisbürodirektor, Kreis Guben.
Ost-Dok. 10/525	Erik Schmiedicke, Oberbürgermeister, Guben.
Ost-Dok. 10/527	Dr Hans Faust, Landrat, Landsberg an der Warthe (12 Berichten).
Ost-Dok. 10/529	Dr Faust, Landrat und Klemm, Bürgermeister, Landsberg an der Warthe.
Ost-Dok. 10/531	Willy Hagemann, Oberinspektor, Kreis Meseritz.
Ost-Dok. 10/533	Krause, Kreisoberinspektor, Kreis Ost-Sternberg.
Ost-Dok. 10/535	O.C. Niemeyer, Landrat, Kreis Schwerin an der Warthe.
Ost-Dok. 10/537	Friedrich von Helmigk-Pinnow, Volkssturm 1945.
Ost-Dok. 10/539	Fritz Wüttig, Geschäftsführender Beamter, Kreis West-Sternberg.
Ost-Dok. 10/541	Wilhelm Hoeth, ständiger Vertreter des Landrats Kreis Züllichau–Schwiebus.
Ost-Dok. 10/542	Kampf, stellvertretender Landrat, Kreis Züllichau–Schwiebus.
Ost-Dok. 10/543	M. Leissnig, Beigeordneter, Züllichau.

Lower Silesia:

Ost-Dok. 10/586	Dr Bochalli, Regierungspräsident, Regierungsbezirk Liegnitz.
Ost-Dok. 10/601	W. Köhler, stellvertretender Leiter des Landwirtschaftsamtes Breslau.

Ost-Dok. 10/606 Karl Kapelle, Stadtoberamtmann, Breslau.
Ost-Dok. 10/607 Dr Erich Bleul, Mitglied des Kreistages und Kreisausschußmitglied in Breslau.
Ost-Dok. 10/624 Dr Hoffmann-Rothe, Oberbürgermeister, Glogau.
Ost-Dok. 10/625 Johannes Rohne, Landrat, Kreis Görlitz.
Ost-Dok. 10/629 Detlev von Reinersdorff-Paczenski, Landrat, Kreis Groß Wartenberg.
Ost-Dok. 10/633 Richard Spreu, Landrat, Kreis Habelschwerdt.
Ost-Dok. 10/634 Dr Alois Weiß, Bürgermeister, Habelschwerdt.
Ost-Dok. 10/636 Paul Flegel, Führer des Volkssturms bataillons Kreis Habelschwerdt.
Ost-Dok. 10/641 Dr Otto Fiebrantz, Landrat, Kreis Landeshut.
Ost-Dok. 10/643 Adolf Klenner, Polizei-Obersekretär und Standesbeamter, Liebau, Kreis Landeshut.
Ost-Dok. 10/644 Vieregge, Landrat, Kreis Lauban.
Ost-Dok. 10/645 Erich Pietzner, Kreisoberinspektor, Kreis Liegnitz.
Ost-Dok. 10/652 Johannes Anders, Kreisoberinspeketor, Kreis Militsch–Trachenberg.
Ost-Dok. 10/655 Dr Ernst Heinrich, Landrat, Kreis Namslau.
Ost-Dok. 10/656 Martin Frommer, Stadt und Kreis Namslau.
Ost-Dok. 10/657 Walter Deutscher, Bürodirektor, Kreis Oels.
Ost-Dok. 10/659 Erich Neugebauer, Kreisoberinspektor, Albert Scholz, Kreissekretär und Rudolf Gleiß, Konkretor, Kreisverwaltung Ohlau.
Ost-Dok. 10/660 Hans Quester, Der Volkssturm des Kreises Ohlau.
Ost-Dok. 10/665 Georg Trenk, Oberbürgermeister, Schweidnitz.
Ost-Dok. 10/670 Fritz Ferdinand, Leiter der Kreis-Kommunalverwaltung, Kreis Strehlen.
Ost-Dok. 10/672 Rudolf Kettner, Kreislandwirtschaftsrat, Kreis Trebnitz.
Ost-Dok. 10/675 Eberhard Kordetzky, Geschäftsführer der Kreishandwerkerschaft, Kreis Wohlau.
Ost-Dok. 10/677 Hermann Trautmann, Stadtoberinspektor, Wohlau.
Ost-Dok. 10/943 Durchschrift einer Aktennotiz über Besprechungen in russischen und polnischen Dienststellen in Breslau am 1. und 16. August über die Ruckführung von Flüchtlingen aus Sachsen nach Breslau mit Schilderungen über Kriegszerstörungen der Stadt Breslau und dortige Lebensverhältnisse.
Ost-Dok. 10/1394 Ernst von Schaubert. Der Volkssturm in Obernigk.

Bundesarchiv-Militärarchiv (Freiburg)
RH19 Heeresgruppe Mitte

RH19II-343K Der Kampf um Königsberg – Skizzen. Januar–April 1945.

RH20 4. Armee
RH20-4/551 Die Grenzschlacht um Ostpreußen 1944.
RH20-4/611 Tagesmeldungen, Berichte, Richtlinien. 7. Mai 1944–26. Januar 1945.
RH20-4/615 Unternehmen 'Winterreise'. 11. Dezember 1944–23. Dezember 1944.
RH20-4/616 Unternehmen 'Ingeborg' und 'Wildsau'. 29. Dezember 1944–4. Januar 1945.

RH53 Wehrkreis I Königsberg

RH53-1 27	Wehrkreisarzt I. Kriegstagebuch des Wehrkreisarztes I, Generalstabarzt Dr Zillmer. 22. Januar 1945–22. Februar 1945.

RW4 Wehrmachtführungsstab – Abteilung Wehrmacht Propaganda

RW4-24	Anweisungen für die Wehrmacht Propaganda.
RW4-142b	Wehrmachtberichte 1945.
RW4-704	Vorbereitungen der Verteidigungsfähigkeit der Ostfestungen. 1944–1945.
RW4-906	Behandlung von Flüchtlingen aus den besetzten Ostgebieten. 1944.
RW9-909	Auswertung und Gegenüberstellung der Wehrmachtberichte für alle Frontbereiche. 1. Oktober 1944–31. Dezember 1944.

RW20 Rüstungsinspektion

RW20-1/14	Kriegstagebuch der Rüstungsinspektion I (Königsberg). 1. April 1943–30. Juni 1943.
RW20-1/18	Kriegstagebuch der Rüstungsinspektion I (Königsberg). 1. April 1944–30. Juni 1944.
RW20-2/4	Kriegstagebuch der Rüstungsinspektion II (Stettin). 1. April 1943–30. Juni 1943.
RW20-2/6	Kriegstagebuch der Rüstungsinspektion II (Stettin). 1. Januar 1944–31. März 1944.
RW20-8/29	Kriegstagebuch der Rüstungsinspektion VIIIa (Breslau). 1. Juli 1944–30. September 1944.

RW21 Rüstungskommandos im Reichsgebiet

RW21-10/9	Kriegstagebuch des Rüstungskommandos Breslau. Band 9. 1. Juli 1944–30. September 1944.
RW21-20/10	Kriegstagebuch des Rüstungskommandos Frankfurt an der Oder. Band 9. 1. Juli 1944–30. September 1944.
RW21-23/5	Kriegstagebuch des Rüstungskommandos Gleiwitz. Band 5. 1. Juli 1944–30. September 1944.
RW21-37/11	Kriegstagebuch des Rüstungskommandos Liegnitz. Band 11. 1. Juli 1944–30. September 1944.
RW21-56/1	Kriegstagebuch des Rüstungskommandos Stettin. 1. April 1943–30. Juni 1943.
RW21-56/2	Kriegstagebuch des Rüstungskommandos Stettin. 1. Januar 1944–31. März 1944.

Geheimes Staatsarchiv Preußischer Kulturbesitz (Berlin-Dahlem)

Repositur 240	NSDAP-Gauarchiv Ostpreußen.

Institut für Zeitgeschichte (Munich)

Fa-88, Fasz.151	Deutscher Volkssturm. Ostpreußen.
MA-736	NSDAP Hauptarchiv. Gau Ostpreußen. Januar 1929–Dezember 1944.
MA-737	NSDAP Hauptarchiv. Gau Ostpreußen. (Zeitungsausschnitte) August 1944–November 1944.

MC-1 Zusammenbruch Königsberg. Spruchkammerakten Erich Koch.
MA-3/6 Zusammenbruch III.
MA-248 Zusammenbruch IV – 3 Osten. 27. September 1944–17. Dezember 1944.
MZ9/112 *Völkischer Beobachter* Münchener und Suddeutsche Ausgabe. 3. Juli 1944–31. Dezember 1944.
MZ9/57 *Völkischer Beobachter* Berliner Ausgabe 1945.
MZ 235/4 *Das Reich*. 1944–1945.
Z/1129 *Schlesische Tageszeitung*. Festung Breslau 1945.

National Archives of the United States, Washington DC (microfilm)

Records of Headquarters German High Command: Microcopy T-78 Roll No 304; T-78 Roll No 477; T-78 Roll No 488; T-78 Roll No 490

The National Archives, Kew

AIR 14 Air Ministry: Bomber Command; Registered Files
AIR 34 Air Ministry: Central Interpretation Unit, predecessors and related bodies; Reports and Photographs
AIR 40 Air Ministry: Directorate of Intelligence and Related Bodies; Intelligence Reports and Papers
FO 371 Foreign Office: Political Departments; General Correspondence from 1906
FO 898 Foreign Office: Political Warfare Executive
HW1 GCHQ: Government Code and Cypher School and Government Communications Headquarters Signals Intelligence Passed to the Prime Ministers
WO 208 War Office: Directorate of Military Operations and Intelligence, and Directorate of Military Intelligence; Ministry of Defence, Defence Intelligence Staff, files
WO 309 War Office: Judge Advocate General's Office, British Army of the Rhine War Crimes Group (North West Europe) and predecessors: Registered Files (BAOR and other series)

Vorpommersches Landesarchiv (Greifswald)

Repositur 60g Provinzialverband von Pommern

Rep.60g/145 Ostpropaganda. 1934–1945.
Rep.60g/175 Verlagerung von Kunst- und Kulturgut sowie Dienststellen im Rahmen der Luftschutzmaßnahmen. 1943–1945.
Rep.60g/790 Vorschläge zur Unterbringung aller kulturellen Einrichtungen des Provinzialverbandes in einem Gebäude. 1944.

Repositur 75 Oberlandesgericht Stettin

Rep.75/15 Landgericht Greifswald. Schriftwechsel betreffenden Ruckgeführte aus dem OLG-Bezirk Danzig und Königsberg. 1945.
Rep.75/136 Oberlandesgericht Stettin. Tägliche Notizen betreffend OLG Königsberg. 1945.
Rep.75/386 Bericht des Landgerichtspräsidenten des Bezirks Stargard Grassow über die Kriegsereignisse in Stargard. März 1945.

Repositur 76 Landgericht Stettin
Rep.76/165 Wehrmacht in auswärtige Angelegenheit. 1944–1945.

PRINTED PRIMARY SOURCES

Documents

Board of Editors, *Documents on German Foreign Policy 1918–1945. Series D. Volume VII. The Last Days of Peace, August 9–September 3, 1939* (London: HMSO, 1956).

Boberach, Heinz (ed.), *Meldungen aus dem Reich: Die geheimen Lageberichte des Sicherheitsdienstes des SS 1938–1945. Band 1–17* (Herrsching: Manfred Pawlak Verlag, 1984).

Bundesministerium für Vertriebene, Flüchtlinge und Kriegsgeschädigte (ed.), *Dokumente Deutscher Kriegsschäden: Evakuierte, Kriegssachgeschädigte, Währungsgeschädigte. Die geschichtliche und rechtliche Entwicklung. 1 Beiheft. Aus den Tagen des Luftkrieges und des Wiederaufbaues Erlebnis – und Erfahrungsberichte* (Bonn: Bundesministerium für Vertriebene, Flüchtlinge und Kriegsgeschädigte, 1960).

Butler, Rohan and Bury J.P.T. (eds.), *Documents on British Foreign Policy 1919–1939. First Series. Volume IX. German Affairs 1920* (London: HMSO, 1960).

Butler, Rohan and Bury J.P.T. (eds.), *Documents on British Foreign Policy 1919–1939. First Series. Volume X. German Affairs and Plebiscite Problems 1920* (London: HMSO, 1960).

Butler, Rohan and Bury J.P.T. (eds.), *Documents on British Foreign Policy 1919–1939. First Series. Volume XI. Upper Silesia, Poland and the Baltic States January 1920–March 1921* (London: HMSO, 1961).

Butler, Rohan and Pelly, Margaret (eds.), *Documents on British Policy Overseas, Series I, Volume I, The Conference at Potsdam July–September 1945* (London: HMSO, 1984).

Ciechanowski, Jan S, *Intelligence Co-operation between Poland and Great Britain during World War II. Volume II, Documents* (Warsaw: The Head Office of State Archives, 2005).

Domarus, Max, *Hitler Reden und Proklamationen 1932–1945, Band II Untergang. Zweiter Halbband 1941–1945* (Munich: Suddeutscher Verlag, 1965).

Domarus, Max, *Hitler: Speeches and Proclamations 1932–1945. Volume One. The Years 1932 to 1934* (London: I.B. Tauris and Co Ltd, 1990).

Federal Ministry for Expellees, Refugees and War Victims, *Facts Concerning the Problem of the German Expellees and Refugees* (Bonn: Federal Ministry for Expellees, Refugees and War Victims, 1960).

Heiber, Helmut (ed.), *Hitlers Lagebesprechungen: Die Protokollfragmente seiner militärischen Konferenzen 1942–1945* (Stuttgart: Deutsche Verlags-Anstalt, 1962).

Jacobsen, Hans-Adolf (ed.), *Spiegelbild einer Verschwörung: Die Opposition gegen Hitler und der Staatsreich vom 20. Juli 1944 in der SD-Berichterstattung. Geheime Dokumente aus dem ehemaligen Reichssicherheitshauptamt* (Stuttgart: Seewald Verlag, 1984).

Jahnke, Karl Heinz, *Hitlers letztes Aufgebot: Deutsche Jugend im sechsten Kriegsjahr 1944/45* (Essen: Klartext Verlag, 1993).

Mehner, Kurt (ed.), *Die Geheimen Tagesberichte der Deutschen Wehrmachtführung im Zweiten Weltkrieg 1939–1945.*

Band 6. 1. Dezember 1942–31. Mai 1943.
Band 7. 1. Juni 1943–31. August 1943.
Band 8. 1. September 1943–30. November 1943.
Band 9. 1. Dezember 1943–29. Februar 1944.
Band 10. 1. März 1944–31. August 1944.
Band 11. 1. September 1944–31. Dezember 1944.

Band 12. 1. Januar 1945–9. Mai 1945.
(Osnabrück: Biblio Verlag, 1984–1989).

Michaelis, Herbert and Schraepler, Ernst (eds.), *Ursachen und Folgen. Vom deutschen Zusammenbruch 1918 und 1945 bis zur staatlichen Neuordnung Deutschlands in der Gegenwart. Band 22* (Berlin: Dokumenten-Verlag Dr. Herbert Wendler & Co, 1975).

Michaelis, Herbert and Schraepler, Ernst (eds.), *Ursachen und Folgen. Vom deutschen Zusammenbruch 1918 und 1945 bis zur staatlichen Neuordnung Deutschlands in der Gegenwart. Band 23. Das militärische Zusammenbruch und das Ende des Dritten Reiches* (Berlin: Dokumenten-Verlag Dr. Herbert Wendler & Co, 1976).

Noakes, Jeremy and Pridham, Geoffrey (eds.), *Nazism 1919–1945. Volume 1. The Rise to Power 1919–1934. A Documentary Reader* (Exeter: University of Exeter Press, 1991).

Noakes, Jeremy and Pridham, Geoffrey (eds.), *Nazism 1919–1945. Volume 2. State, Economy and Society 1933–1939. A Documentary Reader* (Exeter: University of Exeter Press, 1991).

Noakes, Jeremy and Pridham, Geoffrey (eds.), *Nazism 1919–1945. Volume 3. Foreign Policy, War and Racial Extermination. A Documentary Reader* (Exeter: University of Exeter Press, 1991).

Noakes, Jeremy (ed.), *Nazism 1919–1945. Volume 4. The German Home Front in World War II. A Documentary Reader* (Exeter: University of Exeter Press, 1998).

Noakes, Jeremy and Pridham, Geoffrey (eds.), *Documents on Nazism 1919–1945* (London: Jonathan Cape, 1974).

Press and Information Office of the Federal Government, *Germany Reports* (Wiesbaden: Franz Steiner Verlag, 1961).

Royal Institute of International Affairs, *Review of the Foreign Press 1939–1945. Series A. Volume V. Enemy Countries: Axis-controlled Europe 7 July 1941–22 December 1941. Volume IX. Enemy Countries: Axis-controlled Europe 4 January 1944–26 June 1945* (Munich: K.G. Saur, 1980).

Schieder, Theodor (ed.), *Dokumentation der Vertreibung der Deutschen aus Ost-Mitteleuropa. Band 1/1. Die Vertreibung der Deutschen Bevölkerung aus den Gebieten östlich der Oder–Neisse* (Bonn: Bundesministerium für Vertriebene, 1953).

Schieder, Theodor (ed.), *Documents on the Expulsion of the Germans from Eastern-Central Europe. Volume 1. The Expulsion of the German Population from the Territories East of the Oder–Neisse Line* (Bonn: Federal Ministry for Expellees, Refugees and War Victims, 1958).

Trevor-Roper, H.R., *Hitler's War Directives 1939–1945* (Edinburgh: Birlinn Books edition, 2004).

Diaries, Memoirs, Autobiographies, Collections of Letters

Ahlfen, General Hans von, und Niehoff, General Hermann, *So kämpfte Breslau 1945: Verteidigung und Untergang von Schlesiens Hauptstadt* (Stuttgart: Motorbuch Verlag edition, 1994).

Beevor, Antony and Vinogradova, Luba (eds.), *A Writer at War: Vasily Grossman, with the Red Army* (London: Pimlico, 2006).

Bielenberg, Christabel, *The Past is Myself* (London: Chatto and Windus, 1968).

Chuikov, Marshal Vasili, *The Fall of Berlin* (New York: Ballantine Books, 1969).

Degrelle, Leon, *Campaign in Russia: The Waffen SS on the Eastern Front* (Torrance, California: Institute for Historical Review, 1985).

Dieckert, Major Kurt und Großmann, General Horst, *Der Kampf um Ostpreussen: Der Umfassende Dokumentarbericht über das Kriegsgeschehen in Ostpreussen* (Stuttgart: Motorbuch Verlag edition, 1995).

Djilas, Milovan, *Conversations with Stalin* (Harmondsworth, Middlesex: Pelican edition, 1969).

Falk, Lucy, *Ich blieb in Königsberg: Tagebücher aus dunklen Nachkriegssjahren* (Munich: Gräfe und Unzer Verlag, 1965).

Fröhlich, Elke (ed.), *Die Tagebücher von Joseph Goebbels. Im Auftrag des Instituts für Zeitgeschichte und mit Unterstützung des Staatlichen Archivdienstes Rußlands. Teil II Diktate 1941 –1945* (Munich: K.G. Saur, 1995–1996).

Gerhardi, Helga, *Helga: The true story of a young woman's flight as a refugee and how she re-united her war-scattered family* (Aylesbury: Virona, 1993).

Gorlitz, Walter (ed.), *The Memoirs of Field Marshal Wilhelm Keitel* (New York: Cooper Square Press, 2000 edition).

Granzow, Klaus, *Tagebuch eines Hitlerjungen: Kriegsjugend in Pommern 1943–1945* (Wiesbaden and Munich: Limes Verlag, 1986).

Granzow, Klaus (ed.), *Meine Heimat Pommern. Die Letzten Tage. Erinnerungen an Flucht und Vertreibung* (Augsburg: Weltbild Verlag, 1990).

Guderian, Colonel General Heinz, *Panzer Leader* (London: Michael Joseph, 1970).

Hassell, Ulrich von, *The von Hassell Diaries 1938–1944* (London: Hamish Hamilton, 1948).

Hindenburg, Marshal Paul von, *Out of My Life* (London: Cassell and Company, 1920).

Hornig, Ernst, *Breslau 1945: Erlebnisse in der eingeschlossen Stadt* (Würzburg: Bergstadtverlag Wilhelm Gottlieb Korn, 1986).

Hoßbach, General Friedrich, *Die Schlacht um Ostpreußen: Aus den Kämpfen der deutschen 4. Armee um Ostpreußen in der Zeit vom 19.7.1944–30.1.1945* (Überlingen: Otto Dikreiter Verlag, 1951).

Klemperer, Victor, *To the Bitter End: The Diaries of Victor Klemperer 1942–45* (London: Weidenfeld & Nicolson, 1999).

Knappe, Siegfried with Brusaw, Ted, *Soldat: Reflections of a German Soldier, 1936–1949* (New York: Dell, 1992).

Krockow, Christian von, *Hour of the Women* (London: Faber and Faber, 1992).

Lasch, General Otto, *So fiel Königsberg* (Stuttgart: Motorbuch Verlag edition, 1994).

Lehndorff, Count Hans von, *East Prussian Diary. A Journal of Faith 1945–1947* (London: Oswald Woolf, 1963).

Linck, Hugo, *Königsberg 1945–1948* (Leer: Verlag Rautenberg und Möckel, 1952).

Luck, Colonel Hans von, *Panzer Commander: The Memoirs of Hans von Luck* (London: Praeger, 1989).

Mackinnon, Marianne, *The Naked Years: Growing Up in Nazi Germany* (London: Chatto and Windus, 1987).

Newton, Steven H., *Panzer Operations: The Eastern Front Memoir of General Raus, 1941–1945* (Cambridge, MA: DeCapo, 2005).

Niepold, Lieutenant Colonel Gerd, *Battle for White Russia: The Destruction of Army Group Centre June 1944* (London: Brassey's Defence Publishers, 1987).

Norman, Käthe von, *Ein Tagebuch aus Pommern 1945/46* (Munich: Deutscher Taschenbuch Verlag, 1962).

Peikert, Paul, *'Festung Breslau' in den Berichten eines Pfarrers: 22. Januar bis 6. Mai 1945* (edited by Karol Jonca and Alfred Konieczny) (East Berlin: Union Verlag, 1968).

Reinoß, Heinrich (ed.), *Letzte Tage in Ostpreußen. Erinnerungen an Flucht und Vertreibung* (Frankfurt: Ullstein Sachbuch, 1985).

Rendulic, Colonel General Lothar, *Gekämpft Gesiegt Geschlagen* (Wels-Heidelberg: Verlag Welsermühl, 1950).

Ribbentrop, Joachim von, *The Ribbentrop Memoirs* (London: Weidenfeld and Nicolson, 1954).

Sajer, Guy, *The Forgotten Soldier* (London: Orion Books edition, 1993).

Skorzeny, Otto, *Skorzeny's Special Missions* (London: Robert Hale Limited, 1957).

Speer, Albert, *Inside the Third Reich* (London: Phoenix edition, 1995).
Stahlberg, Major Alexander, *Bounden Duty: The Memoirs of a German Officer 1932–1945* (London: Brassey's, 1990).
Steinhoff, Johannes, Pechel, Peter and Showalter, Dennis (eds.), *Voices from the Third Reich: An Oral History* (Washington D C: Regnery Gateway, 1989).
Taylor, Fred (ed.), *The Goebbels Diaries 1939–1941* (London: Hamish Hamilton, 1982).
Trevor-Roper, H.R. (ed.), *The Bormann Letters: The Private Correspondence Between Martin Bormann and his Wife from January 1943 to April 1945* (London: Weidenfeld and Nicolson, 1954).
Trevor-Roper, H.R. (ed.), *The Goebbels Diaries: The Last Days* (London: Book Club Associates, 1978).
Vasilevsky, Marshal A. M., *A Lifelong Cause* (Moscow: Progress Publishers, 1981).
Vassiltchikov, Marie, *The Berlin Diaries 1940–1945 of Marie 'Missie' Vassiltchikov* (London: Chatto and Windus, 1985).
Warlimont, General Walter, *Im Hauptquartier der deutschen Wehrmacht 1939–1945. Grundlagen. Formen. Gestalten* (Bonn and Frankfurt: Athenäum Verlag, 1964).
Werth, Alexander, *Russia at War 1941–1945* (London: E.P. Dutton, 1964).
Wieck, Michael, *Zeugnis vom Untergang Königsbergs. Ein 'Geltungsjude' berichtet* (Heidelberg: Heidelberger Verlagsanstalt, 1990).
Zhukov, Marshal Georgi, *Marshal Zhukov's Greatest Battles* (Introduction and Explanatory Comments by Harrison E. Salisbury) (London: Macdonald, 1969).

SECONDARY SOURCES

Books

Absolon, Rudolf, *Die Wehrmacht im Dritten Reich. Band VI. 19. Dezember 1941 bis 9. Mai 1945* (Boppard: Harald Boldt Verlag, 1995).
Adair, Paul, *Hitler's Greatest Defeat: The Collapse of Army Group Centre, June 1944* (London: Brockhampton Press edition, 1998).
Ash, Timothy Garton, *In Europe's Name: Germany and the Divided Continent* (London: Vintage, 1994).
Aust, Stefan and Burgdorff, Stephan (eds.), *Die Flucht: Über die Vertreibung der Deutschen aus dem Osten* (Munich: DTV, 2002).
Author Collective led by Wolfgang Schumann and Olaf Groehler, *Deutschland im zweiten Weltkrieg. Band 6. Der Zerschlagung der Hitlerfaschismus und die Befreiung des deutschen Volkes. Juni 1944 bis zum 8. Mai 1945* (Cologne: Pahl Rugenstein Verlag, 1985).
Baedeker, Karl, *Germany: A Handbook for railway travellers and motorists* (Leipzig: Karl Baedeker publishers, 1936).
Baird, Jay W., *The Mythical World of Nazi War Propaganda 1939–1945* (Minneapolis, MN: University of Minnesota Press, 1974).
Balfour, Michael, *Propaganda in War 1939–1945. Policies and Publics in Britain and Germany* (London: Routledge and Kegan Paul, 1979).
Bartov, Omer, *Hitler's Army: Soldiers, Nazis and War in the Third Reich* (New York: Oxford University Press, 1992).
Bartov, Omer, *Murder in Our Midst. The Holocaust, Industrial Killing and Representation* (Oxford: Oxford University Press, 1996).
Bartov, Omer, *The Eastern Front 1941–1945: German Troops and the Barbarisation of Warfare* (Basingstoke: Macmillan, 1985).

Beevor, Antony, *Berlin: The Downfall 1945* (London: Viking, 2002).

Bekker, Cajus, *Flucht übers Meer: Ostsee – Deutsches Schicksal 1945* (Frankfurt: Ullstein Zeitgeschichte, 1995).

Bennett, Gill (ed.), *The End of the War in Europe 1945* (London: HMSO, 1996).

Benz, Wolfgang (ed.), *Die Vertreibung der Deutschen aus dem Osten. Ursachen, Ereignisse, Folgen* (Frankfurt: Fischer Taschenbuch Verlag, 1985).

Berthold, Will, *Der Große Treck: Die Vertreibung aus den deutschen Ostgebieten* (Munich: Wilhelm Heyne Verlag, 1980).

Bessel, Richard, *Political Violence and the Rise of Nazism: The Storm Troopers in Eastern Germany 1925–1934* (London: Yale University Press, 1984).

Biddiscombe, Perry, *The Last Nazis: SS Werewolf Guerrilla Resistance in Europe 1944–1947* (Stroud: Tempus, 2005).

Board of Directors of the Western Institute, *Polish Western Territories* (Poznan, 1959).

Böddeker, Günter, *Die Flüchtlinge: Die Vertreibung der Deutschen im Osten* (Munich: F.A. Herbig Verlagsbuchhandlung, 1980).

Botwinick, Rita S., *Winzig, Germany, 1933–1946* (Westport, CN: Praeger, 1992).

Braithwaite, Rodric, *Across the Moscow River: The World Turned Upside Down* (London: Yale University Press, 2002).

Bramsted, Ernest K, *Goebbels and National Socialist Propaganda 1925–1945* (East Lansing, MI: University of Michigan Press, 1965).

Braun, Freiherr Joachim von, *Germany's Eastern Territories. A Manual and Book of Reference dealing with the regions East of the Oder and the Neisse* (Göttingen: Göttingen Research Committee, 1957).

Bruce, George, *The Warsaw Uprising 1 August–2 October 1944* (London: Granada Publishing Limited, 1972).

Bullock, Alan, *Hitler: A Study in Tyranny* (Harmondsworth, Middlesex: Pelican, 1963).

Burleigh, Michael, *Ethics and Extermination: Reflections on Nazi Genocide* (Cambridge: Cambridge University Press, 1997).

Burleigh, Michael, *Germany Turns Eastwards* (London: Pan Macmillan edition, 2002).

Carell, Paul, *Hitler's War on Russia. Volume 2. Scorched Earth* (London: Corgi Books edition, 1971).

Charman, Terry, *The German Home Front 1939–1945* (London: Barrie and Jenkins, 1989).

Clark, Alan, *Barbarossa: The Russian-German Conflict 1941–1945* (London: Macmillan Papermac edition, 1985).

Conversino, Mark J., *Fighting with the Soviets: The failure of Operation FRANTIC 1944–45* (Lawrence, KA: University Press of Kansas, 1997).

Craig, Gordon A., *The Politics of the Prussian Army 1640–1945* (London: Oxford University Press, 1975).

Davies, Norman, *God's Playground: A History of Poland. Volume II. 1795 to the Present* (Oxford: Oxford University Press, 1981).

Davies, Norman, *Rising '44 'The Battle for Warsaw'* (London: Macmillan, 2003).

Davies, Norman and Moorhouse, Roger *Microcosm: Portrait of a Central European City* (London: Jonathan Cape, 2002).

Donald, Sir Robert, *The Polish Corridor and the Consequences* (London: Thornton Butterworth Ltd, 1929).

Duffy, Christopher, *Red Storm on the Reich: The Soviet March on Germany 1945* (London: Routledge, 1991).

Dunnigan, J.F. (ed.), *The Russian Front 1941–1945* (London: Arms and Armour Press, 1978).

Elze, Günter, *Breslau. Biographie einer deutschen Stadt* (Leer: Verlag Gerhard Rautenberg, 1993).

Eberle, Henrik and Uhl, Matthias (eds.), *The Hitler Book: The Secret Dossier Prepared for Stalin* (London: John Murray, 2005).

Erickson, John, *The Road to Stalingrad: Stalin's War with Germany. Volume 1* (London: Weidenfeld and Nicolson paperback edition, 1983).

Erickson, John, *The Road to Berlin: Stalin's War with Germany. Volume 2* (London: Weidenfeld and Nicolson, 1983).

Erickson, John (ed.), *Main Front: Soviet Leaders Look Back on World War II* (London: Brassey's Defence Publishers, 1987).

Erickson, John and Dilks, David (eds.), *Barbarossa: The Axis and the Allies* (Edinburgh: Edinburgh University Press, 1994).

Evans, Richard J., *In Hitler's Shadow: West German Historians and the Attempt to Escape from the Nazi Past* (London: I B Tauris and Co Ltd, 1989).

Evans, Richard J., *Rituals of Retribution: Capital Punishment in Germany 1600–1987* (Oxford: Oxford University Press, 1996).

Fenske, Hans, *Die Verwaltung Pommerns 1918–1945* (Cologne: Böhlau, 1993).

Fest, Joachim, *Plotting Hitler's Death: The German Resistance to Hitler 1933–1945* (London: Phoenix Paperback edition, 1997).

Foreign and Commonwealth Office Historians, *FCO History Note No 16 Katyn: British Reactions to the Katyn Massacre 1943–2003* (London: FCO Historians, 2003).

Franzen, K. Erik, *Die Vertriebenen: Hitlers letzte Opfer* (Munich: Propyläen Verlag, 2001).

Friedrich, Jörg, *Der Brand – Deutschland im Bombenkrieg 1940–1945* (Berlin: List Verlag edition, 2004).

Gause, Fritz, *Die Russen in Ostpreußen 1914/15* (Königsberg: Gräfe und Unzer Verlag, 1931).

Gause, Fritz, *Die Geschichte der Stadt Königsberg in Preußen. Band III. Vom Ersten Weltkrieg bis zum Untergang Königsbergs* (Cologne: Böhlau, 1996).

Gehlen, Reinhard, *The Gehlen Memoirs: The first full edition of the Memoirs of General Reinhard Gehlen 1942–1971* (London: Collins, 1972).

Gellately, Robert, *Backing Hitler: Consent and Coercion in Nazi Germany* (Oxford: Oxford University Press, 2002).

Glantz, David M. and House, Jonathan M., *When Titans Clashed: How the Red Army Stopped Hitler* (Lawrence, KA: University Press of Kansas, 1995).

Gleiss, Horst G.W., *Breslauer Apokalypse 1945. Bände 1–5* (Wedel, Holstein, 1986–1997).

Göttingen Research Committee (ed.), *Eastern Germany. A Handbook: Volume II History* (Würzburg: Holzner Verlag, 1963).

Grass, Günter, *Crabwalk* (London: Faber and Faber, 2003).

Grau, Karl Friedrich, *Silesian Inferno: War Crimes of the Red Army on its March into Silesia in 1945* (Cologne: Centre of Information and Documentary Evidence, West, 1970).

Grieger, Friedrich. *Wie Breslau fiel* (Stuttgart, 1948).

Groehler, Olaf, *Bombenkrieg gegen Deutschland* (Berlin: Akademie Verlag, 1990).

Grube, Frank und Richter, Gerhard (eds.), *Flucht und Vertreibung: Deutschland zwischen 1944 und 1947* (Hamburg: Hoffmann und Campe, 1980).

Gudden-Lüddeke, Isle (ed.), *Chronik der Stadt Stettin* (Leer: Verlag Gerhard Rautenberg, 1993).

Gunter, Georg, *Last Laurels: The German Defence of Upper Silesia, January–May 1945* (Solihull, West Midlands: Hellion, 2002).

Habermas, Jürgen, *The New Conservatism: Cultural Criticism and the Historians' Debate* (Cambridge: Polity Press, 1989).

Hancock, Eleanor, *National Socialist Leadership and Total War 1941–1945* (New York: St. Martin's Press, 1991).

Hanson, J.K.M., *The Civilian Population and the Warsaw Uprising of 1944* (Cambridge: Cambridge University Press, 1982).

Hastings, Max, *Bomber Command* (London: Pan Books edition, 1999).

Hastings, Max, *Armageddon: The Battle for Germany 1944–45* (London: Pan Books, 2005).

Herbert, Ulrich, *Hitler's Foreign Workers: Enforced Foreign Labour in Germany Under the Third Reich* (Cambridge: Cambridge University Press, 1997).

Herzstein, Robert Edward, *The War That Hitler Won: The Most Infamous Propaganda Campaign in History* (London: Hamish Hamilton, 1979).

Hildebrand, F.K.M., *Underground Humour in Nazi Germany 1933–1945* (London: Routledge, 1995).

Hillgruber, Andreas, *Zweierlei Untergang: Die Zerschlagung des Deutschen Reiches und das Ende des europäischen Judentums* (Berlin: Seidler, 1986).

Hinsley, F.H. (ed.), *British Intelligence in the Second World War. Volume Three. Part II* (London: HMSO, 1985).

Höffkes, Karl, *Hitlers Politische Generale. Die Gauleiter des Dritten Reiches – Ein biographisches Nachschlagewerk* (Tübingen: Grabert Verlag, 1986).

Hoffmann, Joachim, *Stalins Vernichtungskrieg 1941–1945* (Munich: Verlag für Wehrwissenschaften, 1995).

Hoffmann, Peter, *The History of the German Resistance 1933–1945* (London: Macdonald and Jane's Ltd, 1977).

Hoffmann, Peter, *Hitler's Personal Security* (London: Macmillan, 1979).

Höhne, Heinz, *The Order of the Death's Head* (London: Classic Penguin edition, 2000).

Hornig, Ernst, *Die Bekennende Kirche in Schlesien 1933–1945: Geschichte und Dokumente* (Göttingen: Vandenhoeck und Ruprecht, 1977).

Hüttenberger, Peter, *Die Gauleiter. Studie zum Wandel des Machtgefüges in der NSDAP* (Stuttgart: Deutsche Verlags-Anstalt, 1969).

Irving, David, *The Destruction of Dresden* (London: Corgi Books edition, 1971).

Irving, David, *Hitler's War 1942–1945* (London: Papermac edition, 1977).

Irving, David, *Goebbels: Mastermind of the Third Reich* (London: Focal Point Publications, 1996).

Jung, Hermann, *Die Ardennes-Offensive 1944/45* (Göttingen: Musterschmidt, 1971).

Kaps, Dr Johannes (ed.), *The Tragedy of Silesia 1945–46. A Documentary Account with a Special Survey of the Archdiocese of Breslau* (Munich: Christ Unterwegs, 1952–1953).

Kaps, Dr Johannes, *The Martyrdom and Heroism of the Women of East Germany. An Excerpt from the Silesian Passion 1945–1946* (Munich: Christ Unterwegs, 1955).

Kater, Michael H., *The Nazi Party: A Social Profile of Members and Leaders 1919–1945* (Oxford: Basil Blackwell, 1983).

Kaufmann, J.E. and Jurga, Robert M., *Fortress Europe: European Fortifications of World War II* (Cambridge, MA: Da Capo Press, 2002).

Kershaw, Ian, *Popular Opinion and Political Dissent in the Third Reich: Bavaria 1933–1945* (Oxford: Oxford University Press, 1983).

Kershaw, Ian, *The Hitler Myth: Image and Reality in the Third Reich* (Oxford: Oxford University Press, 1987).

Kershaw, Ian, *The Nazi Dictatorship: Problems and Perspectives of Interpretation. Third Edition* (London: Edward Arnold, 1993).

Kershaw, Ian, *The Nazi Dictatorship: Problems and Perspectives of Interpretation. Second Edition* (London: Edward Arnold, 1989).

Kershaw, Ian, *Hitler 1889–1936: Hubris* (London: Allen Lane, The Penguin Press, 1998).

Kershaw, Ian, *Hitler 1936–1945: Nemesis* (London: Allen Lane, The Penguin Press, 2000).

Kissel, Hans, *Der Deutsche Volkssturm 1944/45: Eine territoriale Miliz im Rahmen der Landesverteidigung* (Frankfurt: E.S. Mittler und Sohn, 1962).

Kitchen, Martin, *Nazi Germany at War* (London: Longman, 1995).

Koburger, Charles W. Jnr., *Steel Ships, Iron Crosses and Refugees: The German Navy in the Baltic 1939–1945* (Westport, CN: Praeger Publications, 1989).

Kossert, Andreas, *Ostpreussen: Geschichte und Mythos* (Munich: Siedler, 2005).

Knopp, Guido, *Die große Flucht: Das Schicksal der Vertriebenen* (Munich: Ullstein Taschenverlag, 2002).

Knopp, Guido, *Hitler's Children* (Stroud: Sutton, 2002).

Krockow, Christian Graf von, *Die Reise nach Pommern: Bericht aus einem verschweigenen Land* (Munich: Deutscher Taschenbuch Verlag, 1995).

Krockow, Christian Graf von, *Begegnung mit Ostpreußen* (Munich: Deutscher Taschenbuch Verlag 1995).

Lass, Edgar Günther, *Die Flucht: Ostpreussen 1944/45* (Dorheim: Podzun Pallas Verlag, 1964).

Lesniewski, Andrzej, *Western Frontier of Poland. Documents, Statements, Opinions* (Warsaw, 1965).

Le Tissier, Tony, *Durchbruch an der Oder: Der Vormarsch der Roten Armee 1945* (Augsburg: Bechtermünz Verlag, 1997).

Lindenblatt, Helmut, *Pommern 1945: Eines der letzten Kapitel in der Geschichte vom Untergang des Dritten Reiches* (Leer: Verlag Gerhard Rautenberg, 1993).

Lucas, James, *The Last Days of the Reich: The Collapse of Nazi Germany. May 1945* (London: Arms and Armour Press, 1986).

Lucas, James, *Reich! World War II Through German Eyes* (London: Grafton Books paperback edition, 1989).

Lucas-Busemann, Erhard, *So fielen Königsberg und Breslau: Nachdenken über eine Katastrophe ein halbes Jahrhundert danach* (Berlin: Aufbau Taschenbuch Verlag, 1994).

Maier, Charles S., *The Unmasterable Past. History, Holocaust, and German National Identity* (London: Harvard University Press, 1988).

Majewski, Ryszard and Sozanska, Teresa, *Die Schlacht um Breslau Januar–Mai 1945* (East Berlin: Union Verlag, 1979).

Mammach, Klaus, *Der Volkssturm: Das letzte Aufgebot 1944/45* (Cologne: Pahl Rugenstein Verlag, 1981).

Meyhöfer, Max, *Der Kreis Lötzen: Ein ostpreußisches Heimatbuch* (Würzburg: Holzner Verlag, 1961).

Middlebrook, Martin and Everitt, Chris, *The Bomber Command War Diaries: An Operational Reference Book 1939–1945* (London: Penguin Books edition, 1990).

Mierzejewski, Alfred C., *The Collapse of the German War Economy 1944–45: Allied Air Power and the German National Railway* (London: University of North Carolina Press, 1988).

Militärgeschichtliches Forschungsamt (Horst Boog, Jürgen Forster, Joachim Hoffmann, Ernst Klink, Rolf-Dieter Müller and Gerd R. Ueberschär) *Germany and the Second World War, Volume IX, The Attack on the Soviet Union* (Oxford: Clarendon Press, 1998).

Moeller, Robert G., *War Stories: The Search for a Usable Past in the Federal Republic of Germany* (London: University of California Press, 2003).

Morrow, Ian F.D., *The Peace Settlement in the German Polish Borderlands: A Study of Conditions Today In The Pre-War Prussian Provinces of East And West Prussia* (London: Oxford University Press, 1936).

Müller, Rolf-Dieter and Ueberschär, Gerd R., *Kriegsende 1945: Die Zerstörung des Deutschen Reiches* (Frankfurt: Fischer Taschenbuch Verlag, 1994).

Müller, Rolf-Dieter and Ueberschär, Gerd R., *Hitler's War in the East 1941–1945: A Critical Assessment* (Oxford: Berghahn Books, 1997).

Murawski, Erich, *Die Eroberung Pommerns durch die Rote Armee* (Boppard: Harald Boldt Verlag, 1969).

Naimark, Norman M., *The Russians in Germany: A History of the Soviet Zone of Occupation 1945–1949* (London: Harvard University Press, 1996).

Noakes, Jeremy (ed.), *Government, Party and People in Nazi Germany* (Exeter: University of Exeter Press, 1980).

Orlow, Dietrich, *The History of the Nazi Party 1933–1945* (London: University of Pittsburgh Press, 1973).

Padfield, Peter, *Himmler: Reichsführer SS* (London: Macmillan, 1990).

Pagel, Karl ed., *The German East* (Berlin: Konrad Lemmer Verlag, 1954).

Peukert, Detlev J.K., *Inside Nazi Germany: Conformity, Opposition and Racism in Everyday Life* (Harmondsworth: Penguin books edition, 1989).

Rebentisch, Dieter, *Führerstaat und Verwaltung im Zweiten Weltkrieg: Verfassungsentwicklung und Verwaltungspolitik 1939–1945* (Stuttgart: Steiner, 1989).

Reitlinger, Gerald, *The House Built on Sand* (London: Weidenfeld and Nicolson, 1960).

Reuth, Ralf Georg, *Goebbels: The Life of Joseph Goebbels: The Mephistophellean Genius of Nazi Propaganda* (London: Constable, 1993).

Rutkiewicz, Ignacy, *The Odra* (Warsaw: Interpress Publishers, 1977).

Ryan, Cornelius, *The Last Battle: Berlin 1945* (London: Collins, 1966).

Scharloff, Willi, *Königsberg. Damals und Heute* (Leer: Verlag Gerhard Rautenberg, third edition, 1990).

Schenk, Dieter, *Hitlers Mann in Danzig. Gauleiter Forster und die NS-Verbrechen in Danzig-Westpreußen* (Bonn: Verlag J.H.W. Dietz Nachfolger, 2000).

Schimitzek, Stanislaw, *Truth or Conjecture? German Civilian War Losses in the East* (Warsaw: Western Press Agency, 1966).

Schoenhals, Kai P., *The Free Germany Movement A Case of Patriotism or Treason?* (London: Greenwood Press, 1989).

Scholz, Albert A., *Silesia Yesterday and Today* (The Hague: Martinus Nijhoff, 1964).

Schulz, Wolfgang, *Stettin: Früher und Heute* (Berlin: Stiftung Deutschlandhaus Berlin, 1996).

Scott-Clark, Catherine, and Levy, Adrian, *The Amber Room* (London: Atlantic Books, 2004).

Seaton, Albert, *The Russo-German War 1941–1945* (London: Arthur Barker Ltd, 1971).

Sebald, W.G., *On the Natural History of Destruction* (London: Hamish Hamilton, 2003).

Seidler, Franz W., *Deutscher Volkssturm: Das Letzte Aufgebot* (Munich: F.A. Herbig, 1989).

Semmler, Rudolf, *Goebbels: The Man Next to Hitler* (London: Westhouse, 1947).

Seraphim, Peter-Heinz, *Die Deutschen Ostgebiete: Ein Handbuch. Band 1. Die Wirtschaft Ostdeutschlands vor und nach dem Zweiten Weltkrieg* (Stuttgart: Brentano-Verlag, 1952).

Sereny, Gitta, *Albert Speer: His Battle with Truth* (London: Picador, 1996).

Showalter, Dennis E., *Tannenberg: Clash of Empires* (Hamden, CN: Archon Books, 1991).

Siebel-Achenbach, Sebastian, *Lower Silesia from Nazi Germany to Communist Poland 1942–1949* (Basingstoke: Basingstoke, 1994).

Solzhenitsyn, Alexander, *August 1914* (Harmondsworth, Middlesex: Penguin, 1974).

Steinert, Marlis G., *Hitler's War and the Germans: Public Mood and Attitude During the Second World War* (Athens, OH: University of Ohio Press, 1977).

Stirling, Tessa, Nalecz, Daria and Dubicki, Tadeusz (eds.), *Intelligence Co-operation between Poland and Great Britain during World War II. Volume I. The Report of the Anglo-Polish Historical Committee* (London: Vallentine Mitchell, 2005).

Stone, Norman, *The Eastern Front 1914–1917* (London: Hodder and Stoughton, 1975).

Suvorov, Viktor, *Icebreaker: Who Started the Second World War?* (London: Hamish Hamilton, 1990).

Sword, Keith (ed.), *The Soviet Takeover of the Polish Eastern Provinces 1939–1941* (Basingstoke: Macmillan, 1991).

Taylor, Frederick, *Dresden: Tuesday 13 February 1945* (London: Bloomsbury, 2004).

Taylor, Richard, *Film Propaganda: Soviet Russia and Nazi Germany* (London: Croom Helm, 1979).

Thorwald, Jürgen, *Es begann an der Weichsel: Flucht und Vertreibung der Deutschen aus dem Osten* (Munich: Knaur edition, 1995).

Thorwald, Jürgen, *Das Ende an der Elbe: Die letzten Monate des Zweiten Weltkriegs im Osten* (Munich; Knaur edition, 1995).

Tighe, Carl, *Gdansk: National Identity in the Polish-German Borderlands* (London: Pluto Press, 1990).

Tilitzki, Christian, *Alltag in Ostpreußen 1940–1945: Die geheimen Lageberichte der Königsberger Justiz 1940–1945* (Leer: Verlag Gerhard Rautenberg, 1991).

Tsoraus, Peter G. (ed.), *The Anvil of War. German Generalship in Defence on the Eastern Front* (London: Greenhill Books, 1994).

Ulrich, Gerhard (ed.), *Ostpreussen in 144 Bildern* (Leer: Verlag Gerhard Rautenberg, 1987).

Verrier, Anthony, *The Bomber Offensive* (London: B.T. Batsford Ltd, 1968).

Volkmann, Hans E. (ed.), *Das Rußlandbild im Dritten Reich* (Cologne: Böhlau Verlag, 1994).

Wachsmann, Nikolaus, *Hitler's Prisons: Legal Terror in Nazi Germany* (London: Yale University Press, 2004).

Webster, Sir Charles and Frankland, Noble, *The Strategic Air Offensive Against Germany 1939–1945. Volumes I–III* (London: HMSO, 1961).

Welch, David, *The Third Reich: Politics and Propaganda* (London: Routledge, 1993).

Welch, David, *Propaganda and the German Cinema 1933–1945* (Oxford: Clarendon Press, 1983).

Wheeler-Bennett, John W., *Hindenburg: The Wooden Titan* (London: Macmillan, 1967 edition).

Wiewiora, Boleslaw, *Polish-German Frontier from the Standpoint of International Law* (Poznan and Warsaw: Western Press Agency, 1959).

Wiskemann, Elizabeth, *Germany's Eastern Neighbours: Problems relating to the Oder-Neisse line and the Czech Frontier Regions* (London: Oxford University Press, 1956).

Yelton, David K., *Hitler's Volkssturm: The Nazi Militia and the Fall of Germany 1944–1945* (Lawrence, KA: University Press of Kansas, 2002).

Zayas, Alfred Maurice de, *Nemesis at Potsdam: The Anglo-Americans and the Expulsion of the Germans Revised Edition* (London: Routledge and Kegan Paul Paperback, 1979).

Zayas, Alfred Maurice de, *The German Expellees: Victims in War and Peace* (New York: St. Martin's Press, 1993).

Zeidler, Manfred, *Kriegsende im Osten: Die Rote Armee und die Besetzung Deutschlands östlich von Oder und Neiße 1944/45* (Munich and Vienna: R Oldenbourg Verlag, 1996).

Ziemke, Earl F., *Stalingrad to Berlin: The German Defeat in the East* (Washington DC: Office of the Chief of Military History United States Army, 1968).

Articles

Baranowski, Shelley, 'Continuity and contingency: agrarian elites, conservative institutions and

East Elbia in modern German history', *SH*, Volume 12, 1987, pp. 285–308.

Baranowski, Shelley, 'The Sanctity of Rural Life: Protestantism, Agrarian Politics, and Nazism in Pomerania during the Weimar Republic', *GH*, Volume 9, 1991, pp. 1–22.

Beer, Mathias, 'Im Spannungsfeld von Politik und Zeitgeschichte – Das Großforschungsprojekt "Dokumentation der Vertreibung der Deutschen aus Ost-Mitteleuropa"', *VfZ*, Volume 46, 1998, pp. 345–389.

Berghahn, Volker R, 'Meinungsforschung im "Dritten Reich": Die Mundpropaganda-Aktion der Wehrmacht im letzten Kriegshalbjahr', *Militärgeschichtliche Mitteilungen*, 1, 1967, pp. 83–119.

Bessel, Richard, 'Eastern Germany as a structural problem in the Weimar Republic', *SH*, Volume 3, 1978, pp. 199–218.

Blanke, Richard, 'The German Minority in Inter-war Poland and German Foreign Policy – Some Reconsiderations', *JCH*, Volume 25, 1990, pp. 87–102.

Broszat, Martin, 'Massendokumentation als Methode Zeitgeschichtlicher Forschung', *VfZ*, Volume 2, 1954, pp. 202–213.

Erickson, John, 'Barbarossa June 1941: Who attacked who?' *History Today*, June 2001, pp. 11–17.

Evans, Richard J., 'Review Article. The New Nationalism and the Old History: Perspectives on the West German *Historikerstreit*', *JMH*, Volume 59, 1987, pp. 761–797.

Grabowski, Jan and Grabowski Zbigniew R., 'Germans in the Eyes of the Gestapo: The Ciechanow District, 1939–1945,' *Contemporary European History*, Volume 13, Number 1, 2004, pp. 21–43.

Harvey, Elizabeth, '"We Forgot All Jews and Poles": German Women and the "Ethnic Struggle" in Nazi-occupied Poland,' *Contemporary European History*, Volume 10, Number 3, 2001, pp. 447–461.

Heiber, Helmut, 'Aus den Akten des Gauleiters Kube', *VfZ*, Volume 4, 1956, pp. 67–92.

Herbert, Ulrich, 'Labour and Extermination: Economic Interest and the Primacy of *Weltanschauung* in National Socialism', *Past and Present*, Number 138, 1993, pp. 144–195.

Heyl, John D.,'The Construction of the *Westwall*, 1938: An Exemplar for National Socialist Policymaking', *Central European History*, Volume 14, 1981, pp. 63–78.

Kershaw, Ian, 'Ideology, Propaganda and the Rise of the Nazi Party', in Peter D. Stachura (ed.), *The Nazi Machtergreifung* (London: George Allen and Unwin, 1983), pp. 162–181.

Kershaw, Ian, 'How Effective was Nazi Propaganda?' in David Welch (ed.), *Nazi Propaganda: Power and Limitations* (London: Croom Helm, 1983), pp. 180–205.

Kirwin, Gerald, 'Waiting for Retaliation – A Study in Nazi Propaganda Behaviour and German Civilian Morale', *JCH*, Volume 16, 1981, pp. 565–583.

Kirwin, Gerald, 'Allied Bombing and Nazi Domestic Propaganda', *EHQ*, Volume 15, 1985, pp. 341–362.

Konrad, Joachim, 'Das Ende von Breslau', *VfZ*, Volume 4, 1956, pp. 587–590.

Krawchenk, Bohden, 'Soviet Ukraine under Nazi Occupation, 1941–4', in Yun Boshyk (ed.), *Ukraine during World War II History and its Aftermath* (Edmonton: Canadian Institute of Ukrainian Studies, 1986), pp. 15–37.

Leslie, R.F., 'Germano-Polish Relations in the Light of Current Propaganda in the English Language', *German Life and Letters*, Volume XV, 1961–1962, pp. 129–139.

Merkl, Peter H., 'The German Search for Identity', in Gordon Smith, William E. Paterson and Peter H. Merkl (eds.), *Developments in West German Politics* (Basingstoke: Macmillan, 1989), pp. 6–21.

Mühlberger, Detlef, 'The Occupational and Social Structure of the NSDAP in the Border Province Posen–West Prussia in the early 1930s', *EHQ*, Volume 15, 1985, pp. 281–311.

Nicholls, A. J., 'The Post-War Problems of the Germans', *EHQ*, Volume 17, 1987, pp. 101–107.

Noakes, Jeremy, 'Germany', in Jeremy Noakes (ed.), *The Civilian in War: The Home Front in Europe, Japan and the United States in World War II* (Exeter: University of Exeter Press, 1992), pp. 35–61.

Noakes, Jeremy, '"Viceroys of the Reich?" Gauleiters 1928–45', in Anthony McElligott and Tim Kirk (eds.), *Working Towards the Führer: Essays in Honour of Sir Ian Kershaw* (Manchester: Manchester University Press, 2003), pp. 118–152.

Noble, Alastair, 'The Phantom Barrier: Ostwallbau 1944–1945', *War in History*, Volume 8, Number 4, November 2001, pp. 442–467.

Noble, Alastair, 'The Volkssturm and Popular Mobilisation in Eastern Germany 1944–45', *The Journal of Strategic Studies*, Volume 24, Number 1, March 2001, pp. 165–187.

Noble, Alastair, ''A Most Distant Target: The Bombing of Königsberg, August 1944', *War & Society*, Volume 25, Number 1, May 2006, pp. 55–75.

Noble, Alastair, 'The First Frontgau: East Prussia, July 1944', *War in History*, Volume 13, Number 2, 2006, pp. 200–216.

Nolzen, Armin, 'Charismatic Legislation and Bureaucratic Rule: The NSDAP in the Third Reich', in *German History*, Volume 23, 2005, No. 4, pp. 494–518.

Schieder, Theodor, 'Die Vertreibung der Deutschen aus dem Osten als Wissenschaftliches Problem', *VfZ*, Volume 8, 1960, pp. 1–16.

Schmider, Klaus, 'Review Article. No Quiet on the Eastern Front: The Suvorov Debate in the 1990s', *Journal of Slavic Military Studies*, Volume 10, 1997, pp. 181–194.

Selvage, Douglas E., 'The Treaty of Warsaw: The Warsaw Pact Context' in David C. Geyer and Bernd Schäfer (eds.), *American Détente and Ostpolitik, 1969–1972*, German Historical Institute Washington DC, Supplement 1 (2003), pp. 67–79.

Showalter, Dennis E., 'Even Generals Wet Their Pants: The First Three Weeks in East Prussia, August 1914', *W&S*, Volume 2, Number 2, September 1984, pp. 60–86.

Stephenson, Jill, 'Triangle: Foreign Workers, German Civilians and the Nazi Regime. War and Society in Württemberg 1939–1945', *German Studies Review*, Volume 15, 1992, pp. 339–359.

Ther, Philipp, 'The Integration of Expellees in Germany and Poland after World War II: A Historical Reassessment', *Slavic Review*, Volume 55, Number 4, 1996, pp. 779–805.

Thomas, David, 'Foreign Armies East and German Military Intelligence in Russia 1941–45', *JCH*, Volume 22, 1987, pp. 261–301.

Welch, David, 'Nazi Wartime Newsreel Propaganda', in K.R.M. Short (ed.), *Film and Radio Propaganda in World War Two* (London: Croom Helm, 1983), pp. 201–219.

Welch, David, 'Propaganda and Indoctrination in the Third Reich: Success or Failure?' *EHQ*, Volume 17, 1987, pp. 403–422.

Welch, David, 'Goebbels, Götterdämmerung and the Deutsche Wochenschauen', in K.R.M. Short and Stephen Dolezel (eds.), *Hitler's Fall: The Newsreel Witness* (London: Croom Helm, 1988), pp. 80–99.

Yelton, David K., '"Ein Volk Steht Auf": The German Volkssturm and Nazi Strategy, 1944–45' *Journal of Military History*, Volume 14, Number 4 (October 2000), pp. 261–283.

Zayas, Alfred Maurice de, 'The Legality of Mass Population Transfers: The German Experience 1945–1948', *East European Quarterly*, Volume XII, 1978, pp. 1–23, 143–160.

Dissertations

Bennet, Victor K., 'Public Opinion and Propaganda in National Socialist Germany during the War against the Soviet Union.' (unpublished doctoral thesis, University of Washington, 1990).

Falk, Hans Joachim, 'Die Flucht und die Ausweisungen aus dem deutschen Osten dargestellt an einem pommerschen Landkreis.' (unpublished doctoral thesis, University of Hamburg, 1952).

Kirwin, Gerald, 'Nazi Domestic Propaganda and Popular Response 1943–1945.' (unpublished doctoral thesis, University of Reading, 1979).

Wright, Burton III, 'Army of Despair; The German Volkssturm 1944–1945.' (unpublished doctoral thesis, Florida State University, 1982).

Newspapers and Magazines

Daily Telegraph.

Das Ostpreußenblatt (Vertriebenzeitung – expellee newspaper).

Das Reich (NSDAP weekly newspaper).

Der Spiegel.

Die Pommersche Zeitung (Vertriebenzeitung – expellee newspaper).

Financial Times.

Independent.

Independent on Sunday.

International Herald Tribune.

Königsberger Allgemeine Zeitung.

Manchester Guardian (later *Guardian*).

New York Times.

Preußische Zeitung (NSDAP Königsberg).

Schlesische Tageszeitung (NSDAP Breslau).

Stern.

Sunday Telegraph.

Sunday Times.

Time.

The Times.

The Times Higher Education Supplement.

Völkischer Beobachter (NSDAP national daily newspaper).

Other Publications

The Annual Register 1944 (London: Longmans, Green and Co, 1945).

Damals, Flucht und Vertreibung, November 2002.

Spiegel Special, Die Flucht der Deutschen, 2/2002.

Spiegel Special, Als Feuer vom Himmel fiel, 1/2003.

Spiegel Special, Die Ur-Katastrophe des 20. Jahrhunderts, 1/2004.

Index

Aachen
evacuees from *Gau* Köln–Aachen, 45
captured by Americans, 73
Werwolf murder of *Oberbürgermeister*, 230
Adenauer, Konrad, Dr, Federal German Chancellor, 3
AEG, 47
Ahlfen von, Hans, Major-General, 204, 222, 224, 248n
Air Ministry, Berlin, 40
Albert Commission, 84
Alexandrov, G. F., 229
Allenstein, East Prussia
Berlin evacuees, 49
evacuation, 1945, 208
HQ Army Group Centre, 175
manpower mobilisation, 76
plebiscite, 1920, 18, 252
Alsace, 178, 195, 201
Alsatian, 131
Alt-Wüsterwitz, East Prussia, 138,140
Altdamm, Pomerania, 194
Alte Kämpfer, 26, 42
Alte Werft shipyard, Gotenhafen, 268n
Amber Room, Königsberg castle, 250n, 274n, 320n
Amberger, Heinrich, Dr, 140, 292n
American Journal of International Law, 5
Amt für Agrarpolitik (AfA), 28
Angerapp, East Prussia
departure of *Kreisleiter*, 1945, 208
evacuation, 1944, 136, 137, 138, 139, 291n
fighting, 1944, 133
Ostwall, 114, 286n
Volkssturm, 152, 153, 154, 297n
Angerapp, River, 20, 132, 133, 137, 140
Angerburg, East Prussia
anti-partisan measures, 178
birthplace of Andreas Hillgruber, 6
'loosening up' measures, 1944, 138
site of Hitler's special train, 260n
Anklam, Pomerania, 46, 48, 61, 262n
Annopol, Poland, 258n
Antwerp, Belgium, 308n
Arado, 46, 47, 61
Ardennes offensive (1944), 179, 181, 182, 183, 196, 308n
Arlt, Eva, Karl Hanke's secretary, 203
Armaments Command, Breslau, 119
Armaments Command, Frankfurt an der Oder, 119
Armaments Command, Liegnitz, 119
Armaments Inspectorate, Breslau, 119, 138n
Armaments Staff Italy, 155
Armenians, Turkish massacres (1915), 1
Armistice
Armistice, 1918, 78
sought by Finland and Romania, 1944, 73
sought by German forces in Italy, 1945, 331n
Arnhem, Netherlands, 135, 290n
Arnswalde, Pomerania, 196
Arys, East Prussia, 37
Aschwöhnestellung, East Prussia, 321n
Atlantic Wall, 69, 73 98, 115, 126, 127, 142, 174, 286n
Augustow, East Prussia, 89
Auschwitz extermination camp, 38, 68
Austria
Austrian Poland, 252n
Benes Decrees, 9
birthplace, Erhard Raus, 184
birthplace, Lothar Rendulic, 192
evacuation destination, 45
German troops, 1945, 313n
Volkssturm, 213
AVIATIK cigarette factory, Breslau, 233
Avars, 195, 313n
Axmann, Artur, *Reichsjugendführer*, 273n

B1, B2 defences, 116, 212
Baarova, Lida, Czech actress, 30
Bach-Zelewski, Erich von dem, *SS-Gruppenführer*, 27, 276n
Bad Landeck, Silesia, 46
Bad Rothenfelde, Osnabrück, Lower Saxony, 313n

Bad Wiessee, Bavaria, 29
Baden, 44, 286n
Baden, *Gau*, 46, 146
Bagramyan, Ivan, Marshal, 232, 311–312n
Bagration, Operation (1944), 73
Balkan Wars (1912–1913), 1
Balkans 1, 37, 172
Baltic Germans, 1, 30, 34, 40, 85, 259n, 260n, 261n, 314n
Baltic Red Banner Fleet, 9
Baltic Sea, 8, 10, 18, 19, 35, 37, 48, 74, 75, 101, 106, 131, 133, 161, 164, 172, 177, 179, 183, 194, 196, 200, 267n, 301n, 330n
Baltic States, 25, 37, 73, 80, 100, 185
Baltischen Rubenzucker Fabriken, Stettin, 268n
Baltiysk, *see* Pillau, East Prussia
Baranowicze (Baranovichi), Poland, 74
Barbarossa, Operation (1941), 35, 45, 67, 133, 258n, 260n
Barczewo, *see* Wartenburg, East Prussia
Bartenstein, East Prussia, 149, 297n
Bartold, *see Unternehmen Bartold*
Bashford, Roderick F O'N, British Vice-Consul, Breslau, 272n
Batocki, Adolph von, *Oberpräsident*, 21, 254n
Bavaria, 5, 9, 28, 29, 41, 45, 46, 49, 50, 181, 241, 320n
Bavarian *Landtag*, 28
BBC, 68
BDO, *see Bund Deutscher Offiziere*
Beevor, Antony, 7, 249n
Belgium, 22, 237
Belka, Marek, Polish Prime Minister, 11
Belorussia, 62, 73, 74, 75–76, 93, 99, 130, 257n, 326n
Belzec extermination camp, 272n
Bendlerstrasse, Berlin, 277n
Benes, Eduard, President and Benes decrees (1945), 8, 9
Berchtesgaden, Bavaria, 86
Berezina, River, 75
Bergen-Belsen concentration camp, 5
Berger, Rolf, *see* Erich Koch
Beria, Lavrenty P., Head, NKVD, 228
Berichte zu Inlandsfragen, 12
Berlin, 10, 11, 18, 19, 22, 27, 29, 30, 31, 40, 45, 46, 55, 56, 60, 67, 68, 73, 78, 79, 84, 86, 87, 88, 90, 92, 96, 98, 101, 102, 109, 111, 138, 158, 162, 168, 171, 173, 176, 197, 203, 204, 208, 210, 211, 223, 224, 226, 229, 237, 239, 241, 248n, 250n, 253n, 257n, 271n, 272n, 276n, 277n, 296n, 311n, 312n, 313n, 317n, 319n, 320–321n, 322n
Berlin by Antony Beevor, 7, 249n
Berlin air raids, 58, 61, 64, 66, 77, 302n
Berlin evacuees, 47, 48–49, 50, 80, 81–84, 89, 100, 137, 262n, 263n, 275n, 316n
Berlin, *Gau*, 148, 179, 263n, 324n
Berlin Olympics (1936), 31
Berlin Philharmonic Orchestra, 175
Bernadotte, Folke, Count, Swedish diplomat, 223, 331n
Bessarabia, 34
Bessel, Richard, Professor, 17, 24, 251n
Bevin, Ernest, Foreign Secretary, 245n
Bialystok, Poland, 38, 55, 74, 75, 78–79, 80, 101, 178, 277n
Bibliothek für Zeitgeschichte, Stuttgart, 13
Biddiscombe, Perry, Professor, 326n, 327n
Bielefeld, Westphalia, 240
Bielenberg, Christabel, 62
Bischofswalde, Breslau, 239
Bismarck family, 205
Bismarck, Otto von, Chancellor, 34
Bismarck, Sibylle, Countess, 236
Bitburg military cemetery, 5
Black *Reichswehr*, 30, 257n
Black Sea, 37, 101
Blechhammer, Silesia, 66
Blitzkrieg, 243
Blockhaus Line, East Prussia, 96
Bobruisk, Belorussia, 62, 74
Bochum, Westphalia, 48, 207, 307–308n, 318n
Boer, 199
Bohemia–Moravia, Protectorate, 67, 237
Bolsheviks
  anti-Bolshevik Nazi propaganda, 33–34, 35, 39, 55, 56, 81, 86, 97, 103, 104, 114, 128, 133, 134, 146, 150, 166, 170, 174, 175, 184, 187–188, 195, 211, 214, 219, 258n, 273n, 276n, 289n, 295–296n
  anti-Polish sentiments, 2
  Bolshevik Revolution (1917), 176
  Bolshevik Russia, 19
  collapse of Communism, 2, 9
  Communist Polish claims, 5, 8, 245n
  espionage, 93, 276n
  Federal German anti-Communism, 3
  German fears of, 63, 64, 99, 101, 103, 106, 126, 133, 176, 216, 306n
  losses (Red Army), 143, 144, 176
  Nazi murders of, 251n
  pre-1933 Bolshevik threat, 25, 27, 29, 33–34
  sympathisers, 55, 56, 58, 144, 180, 218, 271n
Bomber Command, *see* Royal Air Force Bomber Command
Bonaparte, Napoleon, German resistance to, 147, 204
Bonn, 3, 5
Bormann, Martin, *Reichsleiter*, Head, Party Chancellery
  evacuation of Wolf's Lair, 179

Bormann, Martin, *Reichsleiter*, Head, Party Chancellery *(continued)*
Head, Nazi Party Chancellery, 12, 29, 186, 232, 242, 256n
Ostwall, 286n
relationship with Hanke, 31, 42, 298n
relationship with Schwede-Coburg, 41
siege of Breslau, 224
siege of Küstrin, 231
Volkssturm, 145, 146–147, 148, 149, 150, 152, 154, 156, 159, 160, 192, 295n
Wehrmacht, 93
Borsig, 47
Boyen, fort, Lötzen, East Prussia, 96
Bracht, Fritz, *Gauleiter*, Upper Silesia
appointed *Gauleiter*, 29, 30
defences, 116, 283n
heart attack, later suicide, 241
Ostwall, 286n
Volkssturm, 156–157, 299n
Brackmann, Albert, Professor, 253n
Brandenburg
administration and *Gauleiter*, 19, 25, 31, 240
air raids, 61, 64
defences and *Ostwall*, 95, 96, 97–98, 101, 102, 107, 108, 109
evacuees, 45, 46–47, 50, 51
fighting and evacuation, 1945, 193, 195, 200, 204–205, 215–216, 223, 240, 278n, 319n
foreign workers and POWs, 53–54
fortresses, 280n
post-1945, 11, 245n, 246n
rationing, 51
Volkssturm, 151, 158, 213, 215
Wehrkreis III, 84
see also Einsatz Zielenzig; Meseritz fortified zone; Oder–Warthe fortified area; *Tirschtiegel Riegel*
Brandt, Willy, Federal German Chancellor, 3
Braun, Eva, 203
Braun, Ilse, 203, 317n
Braunsberg, East Prussia, 97, 139, 297n
Bredow, Hans von, Colonel, East Prussian Gendarmerie, 178, 307n
Breslau, Silesia
air raid, November 1941, 58, 266n
air raid, October 1944, 161, 164, 172–173
air raid protection measures, 64
arrival of Bach-Zelewski, 1935, 27
birthplace of Rudi Pawelka, 11
defence preparations, 82, 96, 108, 110, 118, 119, 174, 180, 280n, 308n
Deutscher Bismarckbund, 31
evacuation, 1944, 64, 187, 264n
executions, 68, 239
expulsion of Germans, 1945, 245n
Festung Breslau, 1945, 7, 197–198, 201–204, 211, 212, 214, 221–225, 233–236, 238–239, 241, 242–243, 248–249n, 314n, 315n, 316n, 317n, 324–325n, 328n, 329n, 330n, 331n
foreign workers and POWs, 53, 54, 55, 57, 236–237
Jewish community, 67–68, 272n
lack of goods, 50, 51, 264n
Lower Silesia *Gau*, 30
mood in city, 47, 129, 180, 182, 187, 201, 263n, 270n
Nacht und Nebel trials, 68
Oberpräsidium, 29–30
RAF target, 305
SD reports, 50, 52, 57
Soviet advance, 193, 197, 201
Soviet propaganda, 218, 226, 323n
suicides, 1945, 235–236
trade fair, 19, 37
Treukundgebungen, July 1944, 90–91
visits by Nazi leaders, 42, 87, 261n, 277n
Volkssturm, 156–157, 201, 213, 214, 299n, 322n
Wehrmacht regrouping, 1945, 220
Wroclaw, post-1945, 7
Breslau–Brockau, 164, 201, 305n, 330n
Breslau–Markstadt, 156
Breslau, University of, 204, 224, 241, 247n, 325n
Breslauer Neueste Nachrichten, 264n, 271n
Brezhnev, Leonid, General Secretary, Soviet Communist Party, 250n
Brieg, Silesia
evacuation preparation, 1945, 308n
evacuees, 51
prisoners, 237
Volkssturm, 157
British Embassy, Berlin, 272n
Bromberg (Bydgoszcz), West Prussia
evacuation, 1945, 185
Fortress, 280n
Hamburg evacuees, 47
Volkssturm, 322n
Broszat, Martin, Professor, 246n
Brücker, Helmut, *Gauleiter*, 29, 256n
Brunswick, Lower Saxony, 167
Buch, Frau, 31
Buch, Walter, *Reichsleiter*, 31
Bucharest, Romania, 267n
Buchenwald concentration camp, 237
Bug, River, 99, 100, 258n
Bukovina, 34
Bund der Vertriebenen, 10, 250n
Bundesarchiv Lastenausgleichsarchiv, Bayreuth, 4

Bund Deutscher Mädel
assisting *Volksdeutsche*, 37
assisting *Wehrmacht*, 284n, 286n
Einsatz Zielenzig, 108
role in evacuation, 1945, 202
Unternehmen Bartold, 108, 109–110
Bund Deutscher Offiziere (BDO), 218, 279n
Bundestag, 6, 8
Bundeswehr, 145
Burgsdorff, Eleonore, 185
Busch, Ernst, Field-Marshal, 74–75, 80, 272n, 273n
Buschmann, *Pommersche Zeitung*, 88, 205, 206, 219, 269n, 270n, 271n, 286n
Busse, Theodor, General, 97
Bütow, Pomerania, 54, 109
Byrnes, James, US Secretary of State, 245n

Cairo, Egypt, 64
Carlowitz, Breslau, 239
Carlsbad Sudetengau, 204, 223
Carpathians, 74
Catholic Action resistance group, 30
Catholicism, 24, 29, 65, 66, 255n
Caucasian, units in *Wehrmacht*, 85
CDU, *see* Christian Democratic Union
Centre Against Expulsion, Berlin, 10
Charlemagne, Emperor, 313n
Charter of the German Expellees, 2
Cherkassy, Ukraine, 62
Chernyakovsky, Ivan, General, 135, 191, 192, 226
Christburg position, East Prussia, 97
Christian Democratic Union (CDU), 5, 9, 10
Christian Social Union, Bavaria (CSU), 5, 9
Chuikov, Vasily, Lieutenant-General, 193–194, 215, 227, 312n, 313n
Churchill, Winston, Prime Minister, 168, 181, 245n
Ciano, Galeazzo, Count, Italian Foreign Minister, 98
Coburg, Bavaria, 28–29, 41, 240–241
Cohn, Willy Israel, Breslau Jew, 67
Cold War, 2, 10
Cologne, 45, 68, 223, 254n, 263n
see also Aachen
Comintern Congress, 34
Communists, *see* Bolsheviks
Conze, Werner, Professor, 246n, 247n
Cosel, Silesia, 216
Cossacks
in World War I, 22, 253n, 254n
serving with *Wehrmacht*, 85
Cottbus, Brandenburg, 203
Courland 79, 131, 183, 191, 196, 309n, 311n, 313n
Cracow, Poland, 37–38, 84, 315n
Cranz, East Prussia, 187, 208
Crossen, Brandenburg, 97
CSU, *see* Christian Social Union
Czartorisky, Prince, 39
Czechoslovakia, 3, 8, 9, 241, 245n
Czech Republic, 9, 10, 11
Czestochowa, Poland, 111, 116

DAF, *see Deutsche Arbeitsfront*
Damals, 8
Dante's Inferno, 169
Danzig
air raids, 59, 161, 164, 167, 172–173, 266–267n, 301n, 306n
birthplace of Günter Grass, 7–8
condition in 1954, 246n
evacuation, 1945, 199, 200, 208, 241, 314n, 319n
fighting, 1945, 191, 194, 196, 218, 234, 322n
fortress status, 280n
Free City, 4, 18, 19, 32
German expellees after 1945, 1, 4
Naumann speech, September 1944, 129
offered to Poles, 181, 308n
'relief army', 1945, 221
Soviet threat, 76, 135, 142
Volkssturm, 151, 187
Danzig–West Prussia, *Gau*
annexed to Reich, 37, 67
anti-German partisans, 178
evacuation, 1945, 198
evacuees, 1943–1944, 47, 84, 136–137, 262n
Ostwall, 95, 101, 105–106, 111, 284n
travel restrictions, 83, 275n
Volkssturm, 296n
see also Warthegau
Danziger Neueste Nachrichten, 273n, 274n, 284n
Danziger-Vorposten, 88, 262n, 271n, 284n, 286n
Dargel, Paul, *Gauamtsleiter* East Prussia
evacuation, 136, 137, 143, 187, 208, 209
Ostwall, 101
plane landed in enemy territory, 1945, 320n
service in Ukraine, 39
Volkssturm, 152
Wehrmacht in Bialystok, 1944, 78
Darmstadt, Hesse, 167, 358n
Darre, Walther, *Reichsminister*, 28
Das Reich, 78, 174, 222, 274n, 279n, 281n
Davies, Norman, Professor, 7, 237, 247n
DDP, *see Deutsche Demokratische Partei*
DDR, *see* German Democratic Republic
Deblin, Poland, 258n, 315n
Degrelle, Leon, *SS-Standartenführer*, 194
Deime Line, 116, 209, 319n

Deime, River, 96, 97
Denmark, 200, 240
Der Dienstappell, 150
Der Politische Soldat, 150
Der Schanzer, 283n
Dethleffsen, Erich, Major-General, 130–131, 140, 184
Deutsch Krone, Pomerania
dead German children, 205
Himmler's train, 206
Königsberg *Luftwaffe* Command visit, 307n
Pommernwall, 283n
Schneidemühl evacuation, 207
Deutsche Arbeitsfront (DAF), 12
Deutsche Demokratische Partei (DDP), 24
Deutsche Volksliste, 259n
Deutsche Volkspartei (DVP), 24
Deutscher Bismarckbund, 31
Deutsches Nachrichten Bureau (DNB), 216n, 259n, 276n, 289n, 292n, 295–296n, 297n, 298n
Deutschheide, East Prussia, 89
Deutschlandsender radio frequency, 224
Deutschnationale Volkspartei (DNVP), 24, 25, 27, 31
Devau Barracks, Königsberg, 303n
Die Flucht, *Der Spiegel* book, 8
Die große Flucht by Guido Knopp, 8
Die Vertriebenen by K Erich Franzen, 8
Dickmann, Ernst, *Kreisleiter*, Neumarkt, Silesia, 237
Dieckert, Kurt, Major
bombing of Königsberg, 169
East Prussian fighting, 1944, 135, 184
German retreat, 1944, 79
impressions of Goldap, 134
Volkssturm, 154
Diestelkamp, Adolf, Dr, 247n
Dietl, Eduard, General, 92
Dievenow, Pomerania, 196
Dirschau, West Prussia, 179
Dittmar, Kurt, Lieutenant-General, 273n
Djilas, Milovan, 228
Dnieper, River, 63, 69
DNVP, *see Deutschnationale Volkspartei*
Dokumentation der Vertreibung der Deutschen aus Ost-Mitteleuropa, 3–4, 246n
Dönhoff, Marion von, Countess, 205, 247n
Dorsch, Xaver, Head, OT, 156
Dräger, Dr Max, *Oberlandesgerichtspräsident*
air raid protection, 64
air raids on Königsberg, 168
departure from East Prussia, 208
evacuees, 49
fears of Red Army advance, 63, 74, 179
POWs, 55
Soviet air raids, 1941, 35
trial and execution, 319n
visiting evacuated districts, 1944, 139
visiting Suwalki, June 1941, 35
Dragon's Teeth, 98
Drahlfunk (public loudspeaker system), 202
Dramburg, Pomerania, 206
Dresden, Saxony, 167, 170, 172, 200, 204, 302n, 305n, 329n
Duffy, Christopher, Dr, 224, 248n
Dünaburg (Daugavpils), Latvia, 75
Dunzig waterfront, Stettin, 268n
DVP, *see Deutsche Volkspartei*
Dyhernfurth, Silesia, 237

East Berlin, 2
East Germany, *see* German Democratic Republic
East Hanover, *Gau*, 146
East Prussia
air raids, 1941, 58
air raids, 1943, 59
air raids, 1944, 161–164, 165–172
Communist sympathies, 56–57, 274n
East Prussian expellees, 240
East Prussian Front, late 1944, 175–176, 177, 178–179, 183, 188, 309n, 311n
economy, 18, 251n
emigration, 17, 251n
Erich Koch, trial, imprisonment, 240
evacuation of Berliners, 1944, 81–85, 274n, 289n
evacuation, October–November 1944, 136–139, 177, 180, 184, 291n
evacuation, 1945, 198, 199, 205, 206, 208–210, 232, 311n, 315n
evacuees, 45–46, 48–50
executions, 1945, 239
fate of Jews, 237–238
First World War, 20–23, 34, 252n, 253–254n
foreign workers and POWs, 53, 55–56, 74, 273n
invasion of Soviet Union, 35–36
lack of goods, 50–52, 264n, 296n, 309n
July crisis, 1944, 76–81, 289n
Nazi support, 25–26, 41
Ostwall and defences, 95–97, 99–107, 108–109, 110, 111, 112, 113–116, 117, 119, 126–127, 212, 280n, 281n, 282n, 283n, 284n, 285n, 288n, 290n, 321n
partisan activity, 55, 178
post-20 July 1944, 89–94
post-war fate, 62, 181, 245n, 246n, 250n, 269n, 308n
pre-war administration, 26–28, 256n
propaganda, July 1944, 85–89, 275n, 276n, 277n

rumoured relief army, 1945, 220–221
Soviet atrocities, October 1944, 140–145, 292n
Soviet invasion, October 1944, 128, 129–136, 175
Soviet invasion, January 1945, 191–192, 193, 198, 218, 220, 311n, 320n
Soviet propaganda, 144, 226
Special Court, 66–67, 272n
Tannenberg ceremonials, 23, 32
territorial losses, 1919–1923, 18–20
Volkssturm, 145, 147, 149–159, 173–174, 185, 212–213, 232, 296n, 297n, 298n, 321n
wartime administration, 40–41
wartime mood, 62–65, 73, 74, 75–76, 176–177, 179–180, 181–182, 184–187, 263n, 274n, 307n
wartime significance, 36–37, 260n
wartime territorial acquisitions, 37–39
Werwolf, 230, 327n
Ebenrode, East Prussia, 36, 82, 87, 129, 130, 132, 133, 136, 138, 161, 191
Eberbach, Baden-Württemberg, 286n
Eckardt, Paul, *Regierungspräsident*, Pomerania, 206n, 299n
Ehrenburg, Ilya, 144, 226, 229, 327n
Einsatz Zielenzig, Brandenburg, 102, 108
see also Ostwall
Einsatzbereitschaft, East Prussian *Volkssturm*, 152
Elbe, River, 209
Elberfeld, Westphalia, 26
Elbing, West Prussia, 39, 83, 192, 266n, 280n
Elbing Nazi Party premises, Breslau, 238
Elbrecht, Georg, *SS-Gruppenführer*, 40
Elchniederung, East Prussia
evacuees from the Memelland, 132
evacuees from the West, 46
'loosening up' measures, 1944, 138
Endsieg (final victory), 40–41, 47, 61, 68, 115, 126, 128, 244
Erben, East Prussia, 185, 186
Ermland, East Prussia, 255n
Ermland, Bishop of, 150
Ernst, *Bürgermeister*, Bromberg, 195
Ersatzheer, 89–90, 93–94, 148, 155, 183, 277n, 293n
Essen, Westphalia, 68
Estonia, 80
Estonian evacuees, 84, 142
EU, *see* European Union
European Court of Human Rights, 11
European Union (EU), 9, 10
Evacuation
authority, 99–100, 104, 255n
Berlin, 46, 47, 48–49, 263n
Breslau, 1944, 64
East Prussia, 1941, 35, 36, 41
East Prussia, July 1944, 76–77, 78, 81–85, 87, 88–89, 129–132, 162–163, 289n
East Prussia, October, November, 1944, 128, 132–133, 136–139, 140, 141, 142–143, 153, 161, 163, 177, 179, 184, 185–186, 274n, 291n, 295–296n, 310n
eastern Germany, 1945, 5, 187–188, 195, 196, 198–209, 215, 216, 221, 231, 37, 239, 244, 315n, 316n, 319n, 320n, 322n, 327n, 331n
Hamburg, 44, 47, 49
Königsberg, 1944, 168, 171, 172
prisoners, 237–238, 272n, 329–330n
Silesia, 1944, 128–129, 180–181, 187, 308n
Stettin, 46, 60, 262n, 264n
Ukraine, 1943–44, 62, 289n
Warthegau, 1944, 128, 288n
western Gemany, 44–46, 48, 50, 263n, 306n
Eydtkau, East Prussia, 87, 132, 133

Fahrzeug und Motorenwerke (FAMO), Breslau, 53, 234
Falkenburg, Pomerania, 206
FAMO, *see* Fahrzeug und Motorenwerke
Federal Ministry for Expellees (later Federal Ministry for Expellees, Refugees and War Victims), 3, 246n, 247n
Federal Republic of Germany, 1–4, 9, 11
Feldman, *Kreisleiter*, Memel, 146
FHO, *see Fremde Heere Ost*
Fiedler, 'Fire Brigade General', East Prussia, 117, 211, 331n
Fifteenth Air Force, American, 269n, 305n
Finland, 73
First World War
fighting, East Prussia, 1914–1915, 20–23
German hopes for stalemate, 1944, 146
Marne and Somme battles, 78
veterans in *Volkssturm*, 149, 151, 153, 158, 213, 220, 297n, 298n
veterans overseeing *Ostwall*, 106, 116
Fischer, *Kreisleiter* Namslau, Silesia, 200
Fischhausen, East Prussia, 232
Flakhelfer, 66
Flatow, Pomerania, 188
Floret, Otto, *Bürgermeister*, Pyritz, Pomerania, 208
Flöter, Kurt, *Kreisleiter*, Königsberg/Neumark, 195
Flying Fortress, US bomber, 66
Focke-Wulf
Marienburg works, 61, 268n
Posen works, 61, 64
Sorau works, 50, 61, 64
Forced Paths exhibition, Berlin, 2006, 10

Forst, Brandenburg, 47
Forster, Albert, *Gauleiter*, Danzig–West Prussia
East Prussian evacuees, 136–137
escape from Danzig, 1945, 241
evacuation of Bromberg, 1945, 195
Hamburg evacuees, 262n
Ostwall, 106
treatment of Poles, 37
trial and execution, 241, 331n
Volkssturm, 187
Förster, Otto, General, 97
Fourth U-Boat Flotilla, German 165
France, 23, 30, 34, 35, 44–45, 78, 115, 199, 237n, 283n, 301n
see also Normandy
Frank, Hans, *Generalgoverneur*
Ostwall, 101, 281n
position on Jews, 38
refugees from east, 84
Frankenstein, Silesia, 298n
Frankfurt an der Main, 67, 254n
Frankfurt an der Oder
Berlin evacuees, 47
defences, 98
Einsatz Zielenzig, 113, 119
execution of German troops, 1945, 194–195
fighting, 1945, 197, 215, 216, 231
fortress, 280n
Gau Brandenburg area, 31
Greiser's arrival, 1945, 204
impact of Allied bombing, 46, 61
rationing, 51, 52
treatment of prisoners, 1945, 237
Volkssturm, 158
Franzen, K Erich, Dr, 8
Frederick the Great, 219, 229
Frederick William III, King of Prussia, statue, Breslau, 239
Free Germany Committee, *see Nationalkomitee Freies Deutschland*
Freiburger Station, Breslau, 316n
Freiheitskämpfer, Der (newspaper of Communist Freedom Movement, Breslau), 218
Freikorps, 24, 25
Fremde Heere Ost (FHO), 74, 315n
Fremde Heere West, 311n
French campaign (1940), 30, 31, 34, 35, 45, 199
French workers and POWs, 54–55, 57, 111, 140, 142, 169, 236, 237, 273n
see also Nacht und Nebel
Frick, Wilhelm, *Reichsminister*, Interior, 30
Fricks, Freda von, Baroness, 261n
Friedeberg, Pomerania, 282n
Friedrich, Jörg, 7
Friedrich, *Kreispropagandaleiter*, Bromberg, Warthegau, 322n
Friesenweise, Breslau, 224
Frisches Haff, 97, 191, 199, 208, 210, 232
Frisches Nehrung, East Prussia, 199, 210, 232, 315n
Frisching Canal Position, 116
Frisching, River, 97
Fritzsche, Hans, *Ministerialdirektor*, Propaganda Ministry, 93, 181
Fromm, Friedrich, Colonel-General, 90, 277n, 278n
Front und Heimat, 153
Führer, *see* Adolf Hitler
Führerhauptquartier
Adlerhorst, Bad Nauheim, 182
Reich Chancellery, 211, 224, 241
Wolfsschanze, Rastenburg, 38, 87, 89–90, 137–138, 149, 179, 277n, 282n
Führerprinzip, 40
Funk, Walther, Dr *Reichsminister*
dispute with Hanke, 156, 298n;
visits Königsberg, 78;
Volksopfer, 160

Gandau, Silesia, 197, 224–225, 233, 325n
Ganzenmüller, Albert, Dr, State Secretary, Transport Ministry, 82
Gause, Fritz, Professor, biographer of Königsberg, 168–169, 172, 236, 303n, 331n
GDR, *see* German Democratic Republic
Gdynia, *see* Gotenhafen
Gehlen, Reinhard, Brigadier-General, 272–273n, 315n
Gehrke, Otto, Pastor, 205
General Gouvernement
concentration camps, 275n
dumping ground, 37, 67, 259n
evacuation and treks, 200, 201, 205
extermination camps, 67–68, 272n
fortresses, 280n
German forces, 62, 85
goods sent to the Reich, 51
loss of territory, 1944, 77
mood of German soldiers, 79
Ostwall, 95, 103, 108, 111, 112, 187, 281n, 284n
Red Army Vistula bridgeheads, 184
treatment of prisoners, 1944, 237
see also Warthegau
Geneva, Switzerland, 10
Geneva Courier, 142
Genscher, Hans Dietrich, Federal German Foreign Minister, 8
Gerdauen, East Prussia, 137, 138, 178, 321n
German Democratic Republic (GDR), 2, 3, 8, 101, 145, 288n
German greeting, 49, 94, 114

German Labour Front, *see Deutsche Arbeitsfront*
German–Polish Non-Aggression Pact (1934), 19
Gestapo, 27, 28, 49, 57, 68, 80, 238, 242, 257n
Gettysburg, Pennsylvania, USA, 23
Giesler, Hermann, 261n
Giesler, Paul, *Gauleiter*, Upper Bavaria, 261n
Glatz, Silesia, 237
Gleiss, Horst, 201
Glogau, Silesia
  birthplace of Wilhelm Kube, 51
  evacuation, 200
  fighting, 1945, 197, 234, 314n, 328n
  fortress, 96, 180, 280n
  Unternehmen Bartold, 115, 117–118
Glowitz, Pomerania, 54, 185
Gneisenau, August Wilhelm Antonius Graf Neidhardt von, Field-Marshal, 211
Gneisenau Party premises, Breslau, 238
Goebbels, Magda,
  friendship with Hanke, 30–31, 42
  operation, July 1944, 261n
Goebbels, Dr Paul Joseph, *Reichsminister*, Propaganda
  air raids on eastern provinces, 36, 165, 167, 171–172
  anti-Bolshevik propaganda, 34, 93
  Breslau speech, July 1944, 42, 87, 277n
  Gauleiter of Berlin, 42, 82–83, 111, 179, 263n
  Görlitz speech, March 1945, 229–230
  New Year 1945 radio address, 182
  Ostwall, 107, 111
  post-20 July 1944, 92, 93
  propaganda effectiveness, 242, 244, 314n
  propaganda reports, 12
  Reich Plenipotentiary for the Mobilisation of Total War, 91, 92, 118, 186
  relationship with Arthur Greiser, 223, 317–318n, 324n
  relationship with Karl Hanke, 30–31, 42, 181, 222, 223, 308n, 324n
  relationship with Adolf Hitler, 31, 86, 179, 187, 223
  relationship with Erich Koch, 27, 40, 80–81, 82, 83, 100, 104, 210, 211, 291n, 320n
  remarks on Fritz Bracht, 241
  remarks on Emil Stürtz, 205
  SD reports, 12
  state of German forces, 1945, 216, 220, 222, 224, 311n
  Total War speech, March 1943, 271n
  views on General Vlasov, 175, 216
  views on Soviets, 1944–1945, 135, 175, 176
  visits to Eastern Front, 1945, 194–195, 214, 229, 322n
  Volkssturm, 148, 150, 160, 324n
  Wehrmacht reporting, 133
  Werwolf, 230
Goerdeler, Carl, Price Commissioner, 279n
Goldap, East Prussia
  defensive preparations, 1944–1945, 184
  evacuation, 136, 137, 138
  evacuation of Berliners, 82, 83
  fighting, 1944, 132, 134
  mood, July 1944, 89
  Ostwall, 107
  Soviet atrocities, 138, 140
  Volkssturm, 152, 154, 297n
Golden Pheasant, 79
Goltz, Colmar, General Freiherr von der, 96
Gomulka, Wladyslaw, General Secretary, Polish United Workers' Party, 2
Gonell, Ernst, Major-General, 313n
Göring, Hermann, *Reichsmarshall*
  close to *Führerhauptquartier*, 36
  critical of Koch, 40
  German Greeting, 94
  patron of Joseph Wagner, 29, 30
  Prussian Interior Minister, 28, 256n
  rumours about Schwede-Coburg, 165
Görlitz, Silesia
  evacuees and rationing, 1945, 233, 239
  Goebbels speech, March 1945, 229
Görlitz Agreement (1950), 2
Gotenhafen (Gdynia), West Prussia
  bombing, 1942–1944, 59, 267n, 268n
  Polish intelligence, 258n
  RAF reconnaissance and mine-laying, 266n, 301n
  Red Army conduct, 1945, 229
  Soviet advance and capture, 194, 196
Göttingen Research Committee, 2–3
Goya, German freighter, 200
Graf Zeppelin, German aircraft carrier, 59, 267n
Grass, Günter, 7–8
Grau, *Kreisleiter*, Memel, 116
Graudenz, West Prussia
  aircraft factory, 62
  fortress and fighting, 1945, 96, 195, 196, 231, 234, 280n
Greece, 1
Greifenberg, Pomerania, 111
Greiser, Arthur, *Gauleiter*, Warthegau
  criticism from Goebbels, 223, 317n, 324n
  departure from Warthegau, 188, 204, 317–318n
  execution, 1946, 241
  expels Poles, 37
  forbids evacuation, 1944, 123
  Litzmannstadt ghetto, 38
  murder of asylum patients, 67
  Naumann speech, January 1945, 187–188
  racial policies, 259n

Greiser, Arthur, *Gauleiter*, Warthegau *(continued)*
  Volkssturm, 147
Grodno, Poland, 75, 89, 277n
Groeben, Klaus von der, *Landrat*, Kreis Königsberg, 330n
Grolmann Aktion, 147
Großherr, Ferdinand, Deputy *Gauleiter*, East Prussia
  bombing of Königsberg, 170, 266n
  death, 320n
  Fortress Königsberg, 210, 211, 320n
  speech to HJ, 282n
  Volkssturm, 150
  warning foreign workers, 74
Grossman, Vasily, *Red Star* correspondent, 227, 229
Großwaltersdorf, East Prussia, 138
Groß Friedrichsburg, East Prussia, Koch's residence, 39, 170, 209
Groß Rosen concentration camp, Silesia, 68, 237, 272n
Groß Wartenberg, Silesia
  Unternehmen Bartold, 109
  Volkssturm, 157
Groß Zeidel, Silesia, 105
Grundey, Police President, Pomerania, 60, 164, 268n
Gruppe Nord, East Prussian *Volkssturm*, 295n
Gruppe Süd, East Prussian *Volkssturm*, 295n
Guben, Brandenburg
  birthplace of Wilhelm Pieck, 2
  evacuees, 47
  fortress, 280n
Guderian, Heinz, Colonel-General
  critical of Koch, 194, 309n
  defences in Russia, 99
  Eastern Front, 1945, 182, 183, 196, 197
  Ostwall, 100, 105, 116, 212, 280n, 292n
  Red Army offensive, 1945, 87
  relationship with Himmler, 195
  Soviet atrocities, 226
  Volkssturm, 147, 149, 291n, 321n
Gulf of Danzig, 191, 200
Gulf of Gdansk, 267n
Gumbinnen, East Prussia
  evacuation, 137, 138
  evacuation of Berliners, 1944, 82–83
  fighting, 1944, 132–133, 135, 136, 138, 177
  Russian administration, 1914, 253n
  Soviet air raid, 1941, 35–36, 259n
  Soviet air raids, 1944, 132, 161, 163, 173
  Soviet atrocities, 140–145
  Volkssturm, 152–153
Gustav Drengwitz chemical factory, Insterburg, East Prussia, 117, 163
Gut Neudeck, East Prussia, 20, 23
Habelschwerdt, Silesia, 48, 157
Habermas, Jürgen, Professor, 247n
Hain, Riesengebirge, 203
Halle, 60
Halle-Merseburg, *Gau*, 82, 83
Haltung, 12
Hamburg
  269 Infantry Division, 201
  bombing, 46, 64
  evacuation, 45, 47
  flak defences, 66
  Hamburger evacuees, 47, 48, 49, 51, 262n
  Koch found nearby, 240
  Volkssturm, 213
Hanke, Karl, *Gauleiter*, Lower Silesia
  appointed *Gauleiter*, 30
  appointed *Reichsführer-SS*, 223
  departure from Breslau, 1945, 241, 325n, 331n
  early life, 30
  evacuation from Breslau, 1944, 64, 187
  evacuation from Breslau, 1945, 202–203, 209
  Fortress Breslau, 202, 204, 211, 221, 222, 223, 224, 233, 239, 241, 242, 325n
  likely death, 1945, 241
  post-20 July 1944, 90–91, 278n
  private life, 261–262n
  propaganda, 1944, 181
  relationship with Adolf Hitler, 31, 42, 187, 222, 223
  relationship with Albert Speer, 30, 42, 223, 324–325n
  relationship with Heinrich Himmler, 31
  relationship with Joseph Goebbels, 30–31, 42, 82, 181, 222, 223, 308n, 324n
  relationship with Martin Bormann, 31, 42, 224, 298n
  Soviet invasion, 1945, 202
  Unternehmen Bartold, 108, 115, 156
  Volkssturm, 156–157, 298n, 299n
  wartime administration, 42
  Wehrmacht service, 31
Hannibal, Operation (1945), 219
Hanover, 254n
Hanseatic, 168
Hanssen, Kurt Walter, Chief Public Prosecutor, Brandenburg, 237
Harlan, Veit, film director, 150
Harpe, Josef, Colonel-General, 174, 182–183, 193
Harris, Arthur, Sir, Air Marshal, 301n
Hartwig, *Forstmeister*, Memelwalde, 178
Hase, Karl Günther von, Major, 214
Hassenstein, von, Colonel, 195
Hauk, *Landrat* and *Kreisleiter*, Schwiebus–Züllichau, 158, 205

Havel, Vaclav, Dr, Czech President, 9
Heidelberg, Baden–Württemberg, 286n
Heilbronn, Baden–Württemberg, 167
Heiligenbeil, East Prussia, fighting, 1945, 192, 210, 220, 232, 234, 320n
Heilsberg, East Prussia, 97
Heilsberg–Deime Position, East Prussia, 116
Heilsberger Dreieck, East Prussia, 96–97
Heimat, 2, 85, 126, 134, 147, 149, 153, 203
Heimatschutz, 156
Heines, Edmund, Silesian SA Leader, 29, 256n
Heinkel aircraft factory, Rostock, 29
Heinrich, Ernst, Dr, *Landrat*, Namslau, Silesia, 157
Heinrichswalde, East Prussia, 152
Heinrici, Gotthard, Colonel-General
  Army Group Vistula commander, 197
  Fourth Army commander, 135
Hela, West Prussia, 191, 196
Herbert, Ulrich, Professor, 53, 264–265
Hermann Göring Panzer Corps, *see Luftwaffe*
Herminghaus, Emil, Captain, 140
Herrenvolk, 53, 191
Herzog, Otto, *SS-Obergruppenführer*, 214, 241
Herzog, Roman, Federal German President, 249n
Hess, Rudolf, Deputy *Führer*, 29–30, 256n
Hesse-Nassau, *Gau*, 146
Heuer, *Kreisleiter*, Angerapp, East Prussia, 114, 208
Heusinger, Adolf, Major-General, 147
Heydebruck, Silesia, 66
Heydekrug, East Prussia
  capture by Red Army, 1944, 132
  departure of Berlin evacuees, 82
  evacuation, 138
Heysing, Gunther, *Völkischer Beobachter*
  Christmas 1944, 186
  German weakness, 1944, 177, 179
  impression of Tilsit, 185
  interview with Reinhardt, 106, 135, 153
  Königsberg reports, 1945, 220, 226, 227
  Ostwall, 117
  Pillau, 1945, 232
  Volkssturm, 154, 321n
  Wagner and Lasch, 211, 320n
Hierl, Konstantin, *Reichsarbeitsführer*, 324n
Hillgruber, Andreas, Professor, 6, 247n
Himmler, Heinrich, *Reichsführer-SS*
  commander, Army Group Vistula, 194–195, 197, 206, 242
  commander, *Ersatzheer*, 90, 91, 93–94, 148, 183–184
  evacuation in East Prussia, 137, 143
  evacuation of Groß Rosen, 237
  forbidding evacuation, 1945, 207
  headquarters, East Prussia, 36
  Interior Minister, 65
  peace negotiations, 223, 331n
  prominent role, late 1944, 182
  relationship with Erich Koch, 27, 184
  relationship with Franz Schwede-Coburg, 41, 318n
  relationship with Karl Hanke, 31
  rumours of Himmler Army, 1945, 220
  support for Fritz Bracht, 29
  support for Arthur Greiser, 37, 204, 317–318n
  support for Karl Otto Saur, 42
  surveillance of Joseph Wagner, 257n
  Volkssturm, 146, 148, 149, 157, 158, 160, 297n
  Werwolf, 230
Hindenburg, Paul von Beneckendorff und, Field-Marshal
  evacuation of coffins, 1945, 179, 219
  freedom of Königsberg, 1914, 22
  German commander, East Prussia, 1914–1915, 20–23, 254n
  German President, 1925–1934, 20, 24, 255n
  Gut Neudeck estate, 20
  Tannenberg celebrations, 1924, 23
  Tannenberg monument and burial, 23, 254n
  use in Nazi propaganda, 1944–1945, 185
Hindenburg, Silesia, 214
Hindenburgstände, 97
Hirsch, Herbert, Breslau HJ Leader, 214
Hirschberg, Silesia, 197, 204, 237
Historikerstreit (Historians' Dispute), 6, 247n
Hitler, Adolf, *Führer*
  20 July 1944 putsch, 89–93, 277n, 278n
  birthday, 20 April, 59, 225
  criminal policies, 250n, 329n
  Eva and Ilse Braun, 203
  evacuation measures, 45
  fear of puppet Soviet regime, 232
  foreign workers views of, 57
  Germans and Hitler, 13, 25, 61, 65, 76, 80, 86, 88, 94, 185, 222, 239, 243, 244, 276n, 277n, 278n
  headquarters, 36, 89, 99, 179, 282n
  military commander, 41, 64, 74–75, 80, 94, 97–98, 99, 100, 101, 104, 105, 108, 126, 133, 135, 182–183, 185, 191–192, 193, 194, 195, 196, 214, 220, 224, 225, 244, 269n, 273n, 280n, 281n, 282n, 321n, 322n, 325n, 327n
  Nacht und Nebel decree, 68
  New Year address, 1945, 182, 308n
  Night of the Long Knives, 26, 27, 29
  population movements, 1
  pre-war *Führer*, 25, 26, 27, 257n

Hitler, Adolf, *Führer (continued)*
relations with Poland, 19
relationship with Alfred Rosenberg, 40, 260n
relationship with Arthur Greiser, 204
relationship with Erich Koch, 27, 28, 39, 40, 41, 82, 86, 100, 183–184, 256n, 260n, 309n
relationship with Franz Schwede-Coburg, 40
relationship with Karl Hanke, 30, 31, 42, 187, 222, 223
relationship with Joseph Goebbels, 31, 86, 187
relationship with Joseph Wagner, 29–30, 257n
relationship with Wilhelm Kube, 31
road to power, 25–26, 255n
Soviet attacks on, 143, 158, 229
Sudeten Germans, 8
suicide, 241
Tannenberg ceremonials, 23, 32
views on Communism, 33, 35
Vlasov movement, 175
Volkssturm, 146, 147–150, 152, 158, 160
Hitlerjugend (HJ)
evacuation, 1945, 202, 208, 316n
Marienburg summer solstice, 1944, 273n
mood, 66, 219
Ostwall, 105, 108, 109, 110, 112, 173, 280n, 282n
Volkssturm service, 148, 214, 215, 220, 222, 229, 322n
wartime evacuation, 1940–1944, 45, 48, 49
Hiwis (Russian auxiliaries), 78, 79
HJ, *see Hitlerjugend*
Hoare, Samuel, Sir, 272n
Hofer, Andreas, 147
Hoffmann, Joachim, Dr, 6–7
Hoffmann, Paul, Dr, *Regierungspräsident*, Königsberg, 136
Hoffmann-Rothe, Dr, *Oberbürgermeister*, Glogau, Silesia, 117–118, 200
Hohenstein, East Prussia, 21
Hohenstein Position, East Prussia, 97
Holocaust Exhibition, Imperial War Museum, London, 380n
Holocaust Memorial, Berlin, 10
Holtei Hill, Breslau, 234
Hong Kong, 10
Hornig, Ernst, Pastor, 234
Hoßbach, Friedrich, General, 130–131, 135, 154–155, 181, 183, 184, 191–192, 309n, 311n
House of Commons, 181
Hoyerswerda, Saxony, 203
Hubertus Line, 183
Hundsfelder Bridge, Breslau, 201
Hungary, 3, 174, 179, 183, 196, 245n, 313n
Hupka, Herbert, Chairman, *Landmannschaft Schlesien*, 8
Hüttenberger, Peter, Dr, 46

Ibsen, Major, 321n
IG Farben, 237
Im Krebsgang by Günter Grass, 7–8
India, 1
Information Age, 2
Insterburg, East Prussia
defensive preparations, late 1944, 177
evacuation, 131, 136, 138, 139, 300n
foreign workers and POWs, 55
military hospitals, 51, 87
mood, July 1944, 87, 129
nearby partisan threat, 178
Ostwall, 117
post-evacuation impressions, 185
rumours of *Wehrmacht* regrouping, 1945, 221
Russian administration, 1914, 253n
Soviet air raids, 1944, 161, 163
Soviet atrocities, 140
Soviet leaflet drops, 89
Volkssturm, 153, 174
von Lehndorff's impressions, 139, 167
Inter-Allied Military Control Commission, 96
Interior Ministry, 30, 45, 65, 82–84, 143, 208
Internet, 2
Iron Curtain, 2
Irving, David, 137
Italy
20th anniversary 'March on Rome', 42
Allied air bases, 66, 161, 269n
Cossacks in northern Italy, 85
fall of Mussolini's regime, 99
German troops, 196, 313n, 331n
Italian weapons for *Volkssturm*, 154, 155, 158, 212, 297n
place in *Wehrmacht* report, 77

Jacob, General, 99
Jahr Null, 1945, 2
Jahrhunderthalle, Breslau
Goebbels speech, July 1944, 42
Hitler speech, November 1943, 42
planned rally, January 1945, 324n
SS defenders, 1945, 241
Japanese Naval Mission, Berlin, 311n
Jehovah's Witness, 156
Jews
death marches, 1945, 237–238, 329–330n
deaths in extermination camps, 38, 68
deaths through forced labour, 57
East Prussian Jews, 28, 186, 240
eastern German accounts, 4, 67
Einsatzgruppen, 251n

expelled from annexed territories, 37–38, 67
Hillgruber on the Holocaust, 6
Holocaust, 1
Nazi propaganda, 25, 33–34, 39, 93, 141, 148, 214, 273n
Ostwall in Danzig–West Prussia, 284n
Pomeranian Jews, 41, 67
Silesian Jews, 67–68, 272n
Unternehmen Bartold, 111
treatment of Jews in Belorussia, 257n
treatment of Jews in Ukraine, 40
Jodl, Alfred, General, 311n
Johann-Gottfried-Herder Research Council, Marburg, 3
Johannisburg, East Prussia
evacuation, 82, 187
Polish partisans, 55
Jonca, Karol, Professor, 325n
Josef Stalin tank 133
Judenrein, 67, 259n
Junkers, 24, 236, 253–254n, 274n
Junkers Ju-52, 325n, 331n

Kaczynski, Jaroslaw, Polish Prime Minister, 11, 251n
Kaczynski, Lech, Polish President, 251n
Kahl, Lieutenant-Colonel, Gendarmerie commander, Frankfurt an der Oder, 215
Kaiser, Deputy *Kreisleiter*, Angerapp, East Prussia, 137, 291n
Kaiser Wilhelm Platz, Stettin, 301n
Kaiserreich (1871–1918), 96
Kaiserstrasse runway, Breslau, 238, 241, 242
Kalinin, Mikhail, President of the Soviet Union, 9
Kaliningrad, *see* Königsberg
Kaltenkirchen, near Hamburg, 240
Kaminsky Brigade, 85, 276n
Kaminsky, Bronislav, *SS-Brigadeführer*, 276n
Kampfzeit, 29, 33, 263n, 278n
Kant, Immanuel, 10
Kanth, Silesia, 202–203, 242, 324n
Karpenstein, Wilhelm, *Gauleiter*, Pomerania, 28
Kattowitz (Katowice), Silesia
defences, 283n
evacuation of prisoners 237
fear of shuttle bombing, 76
new *Gau*, 30
Soviet threat, 88
Katyn massacre (1940), 55, 265n
Kaufmann, Karl, *Gauleiter*, Hamburg, 213
Kaunas (Kovno), Lithuania, 75
Keitel, Wilhelm, Field-Marshal, 100, 149, 280n, 307n, 311n
Kershaw, Ian, Sir, Professor, 6, 46, 67, 94
Kharkov, Ukraine, 62
Khrushchev, Nikita S, Chairman of the Soviet Council of Ministers, 250n
Kieckhöfer, *Kreisleiter*, Stettin, 299n
Kienitz, Werner, General, commander *Wehrkreis* II, 159
Kiev, Ukraine, 39, 40, 175, 260n, 274n
Kinderlandverschickung, 45
Kissel, Hans, General, 145, 215
Kleinschmidt, Otto, Dr, Pomeranian official, 48
Klemperer, Victor, Professor, 329n
Kletschkaustrasse prison, Breslau, 68, 239
Klettendorf, Silesia, 330n
Knappe, Siegfried, Major, 222, 223
Kneiphof Island, Königsberg, 169–170
Knopp, Guido, 8
Knuth, East Prussian *Volkssturm* commander, 321n
Koch, Erich, *Gauleiter*, East Prussia
air raids, 166–167, 170
annexed Polish territories, 37, 38
appointed *Gauleiter*, 27, 255n
brutality, 28, 239
capture, 1949, 240
departure from East Prussia, 240
departure from Königsberg, 209–211, 320n, 323n
early life, 26–27
Erich Koch Stiftung, 28, 210, 256n
evacuation, 129–133, 136–140, 163, 184, 209, 210, 274n, 309n, 315n
evacuation of Berliners, 81–83
fighting, 1945, 192, 238
July 1944 crisis, 78, 80–81, 274n
Königsberg University anniversary, 78
murder of asylum patients, 67
named a war criminal, 100
Night of the Long Knives, 27, 255–256
'Oberpräsidentkrise' (1935), 27
Ostwall, 100–105, 106–107, 112, 116, 117, 282n
post-20 July 1944, 91, 94, 279n
pre-war administration, 27–28
propaganda, 85–86, 88, 181–182, 184, 277n
refugees, 1944, 84
Reichskommissar Ostland, 154
Reichskommissar Ukraine, 38–41, 42, 62, 100, 104, 260n
relationship with Adolf Hitler, 27, 28, 39, 40, 41, 82, 86, 100, 183–184, 256n, 260n, 309n
relationship with Alfred Rosenberg, 40, 260n
relationship with Erich Bach-Zelewski, 27
relationship with Ferdinand Schörner, 153–154
relationship with Hans Frank, 281n
relationship with Hans-Adolf Prützmann, 230, 327n

Koch, Erich, *Gauleiter*, East Prussia *(continued)*
relationship with Heinrich Himmler, 27, 184
relationship with Heinz Guderian, 184
relationship with Hermann Göring, 40
relationship with Joseph Goebbels, 27, 40, 80–81, 82, 83, 100, 104, 210, 211, 291n, 320n
relationship with Walther Darre, 28
relationship with Walther Model, 87, 104, 282n
Soviet atrocities, 150, 226
Soviet attacks on, 144, 210, 226
SS views of, 40
travel ban, July 1944, 83, 275n
treatment of subordinates, 1945, 208, 209, 211, 319n, 320n, 330–331n
trial and imprisonment, 240
Volkssturm, 147, 149–154, 155–156, 174, 192, 293n, 294n, 295n, 296n, 297n
wartime administration, 49–50
Koch Line, 107
see also Ostpreußenschutzstellung; *Ostwall*
Koch Pots (Töpfe), 117
Koch-Erpach, Rudolf, General, 82, 90, 91, 278n
Kohl, Helmut, Dr, Federal German Chancellor, 5, 8, 249n
Kolberg, Pomerania
defence, 1807, 145, 147, 223
fighting, 1945, 196
fortress, 280n
propaganda significance, 314n
Volkssturm, 215, 322n
Kolberg, film (1945), 150, 211, 221, 294n, 314n, 324n
Köln, German cruiser, 266n
Kommunistische Partei Deutschlands (KPD), 24, 25, 33, 34
Konev, Ivan, Marshal, 191, 193, 194, 201–202, 226, 228
Königsberg, East Prussia,
administration, 27–28, 39, 40–41
anti-Communist propaganda, 56, 78, 227
conditions, 1918, 253–254n
defences, 96, 97, 99
evacuation of city, 83, 173, 179, 208, 209, 307n, 319n
evacuees, 48–49, 50, 177
executions, 66–67, 238, 239, 272n, 319–320n
Festung Königsberg, 7, 209–211, 212, 220, 221, 231–232, 233, 234, 238–239, 240, 280n, 296n, 311–312n, 320n, 323n, 325n, 330n, 331n
foreign workers and POWs, 55–56, 236
Kaliningrad, 8, 9–10, 249n, 250n
lack of goods, 50, 52, 186
looting, 209, 319n
Luftwaffenhelfer, 66
mood, 186–187, 237, 263n
Ostwall, 102, 103, 104–105, 106, 110, 113, 114, 116
post-20 July 1944, 91, 92
RAF raids, 36, 161, 162, 164, 165–172, 173, 266–267n, 301n, 302–304n
Red Air Force raids, 35, 58–59, 164, 259n, 266n, 303n
rumoured relief army, 220–221
Soviet advance, 63, 74, 76, 85, 133, 135, 179, 191, 192, 277n
Soviet atrocities, 226–227, 326n
Soviet propaganda, 210, 218–219, 221
suicides, 235
Volkssturm, 140, 152, 213, 214, 220, 326n
Königsberg Castle (Schloß), 96, 167, 169, 209, 250n, 274n, 320n
Königsberg Castle Church (Schloßkirche), 169
Königsberg cathedral (Dom), 169
Königsberg Circle, 27
Königsberg, University of (Albertina)
400th anniversary, 77–78
air raid damage, 1943, 59
air raid damage, August 1944, 169
departure of medical faculty, 1945, 209
honorary doctorate for Hindenburg, 22
honorary doctorate for Ludendorff, 23
prominent academics, 247n, 253n
Racial Biology Institute, 56
service in First World War, 252–253n
student service at *Ostwall*, 102, 103, 110
Königsberg/Neumark, Brandenburg, 25, 46, 195, 213, 262n
Königsberger Allgemeine Zeitung (*KAZ*), 88, 134, 253n, 275n
Koppe, Wilhelm, *SS-Obergruppenführer*, 187
Körner, *Kreisleiter*, Küstrin, 231
Korselt, *Regierungsrat*, Rostock, 271n
Köslin, Pomerania, 196, 207, 280n
Kossar, Dr, East Prussia, 283n
KPD, *see Kommunistische Partei Deutschlands*
Krakauer Zeitung, 184, 285n
Kramer, *Oberforstmeister*, Elchwald, 178
Krause, Johannes, Major-General 187, 204, 224
Kreipe, Werner, General, 140
Kreisau Circle, 94
Kreuzburg, Silesia, 200
Kriegsmarine, 6, 28, 177, 183, 196, 200, 212, 312n, 319n
Krockow, Christian von, Count, 247n
Krupp, 47, 156
Kube, Wilhelm, *Gauleiter*, 25, 31, 257n
Kubsch, Paul, *Kreisleiter*, Frankenstein, Silesia, 298n
Kühn, *Regierungspräsident*, Bromberg, 195

Kulm, West Prussia, 96
Kulmhof (Chelmo), Warthegau, 68
Kurisches Haff, 97, 132, 309n
Kurland, *see* Courland
Kurmark, 31
Kursk offensive (1943), 61, 62, 98, 99
Kurzbach, Bruno, *Bürgermeister* Brockau, 330n
Küssner, Lise-Lotte, Erich Koch's secretary, 209, 319n
Küstenwacht, 55
Küstrin, Brandenburg
condition in 1954
diversionary air raids, 61
evacuation, 205
fighting, 1945, 196–197, 216, 231, 234
fortress, 96, 193, 280n, 314n
pre-1933 NSDAP meetings, 25
Stürtz visit, 1945, 223, 246n
Volkssturm, 213, 322n

Labiau, East Prussia, 97, 132, 208, 212, 326n, 327n
Lammers, Hans, Dr, Head Reich Chancellery, 36, 156
Lancaster bomber, 59, 165, 167, 267n, 301n
Landeshut, Silesia, 54, 157, 201
Landmannschaft Schlesien, 11
Landsberg an der Warthe, Brandenburg
evacuees, 47
Greiser stayed, 1945, 204
Volkssturm, 158
Landsturm, 20, 147, 149
Landwacht, 55, 85, 293n
Landwehr, 20
Lasch, Otto, General
bombing of Königsberg, 169, 303n
commandant, *Festung* Königsberg, 192, 209–211, 220, 231–232, 238–239, 248n, 319–320n, 330n, 331n
commander, *Wehrkreis* I, 183
death sentence, 1945, 211, 325n
relationship with Erich Koch, 183–184
Lass, Edgar, 169, 303n
Lassen, Ernst-August, Colonel, 155
Latvia, 131, 192, 309n
Latvian evacuees, 84, 142
Latvian workers, 60
Lauban, Silesia
German counter-attack, 1945, 197, 224
Goebbels visit, March, 1945, 229, 322n
Soviet atrocities, 226, 228
Volkssturm, 157, 201
wartime behaviour of youths, 271n
Lauenburg, Pomerania
Party meeting, 1943, 65
Pommernwall, 108
suicides, 236
Volkssturm, 159
League of Nations, 18
Leba, Pomerania, 267n
Lebensraum, 31
Lehndorff, Hans von, Count, 139, 169, 218, 227, 236, 246n, 274n, 319n
Lehndorff, Heinrich von, 274n
Leipzig, Battle of (1813), 148, 149
Lemberg (Lwow, Lvov, Lviv), Poland, 269n
Lemke, Propaganda Ministry, 147
Leningrad, 37, 145, 195, 226, 260n, 274n
Ley, Robert, Dr, 12, 91, 92, 103, 205, 207, 278n
Leyser, Ernst, *Generalkommissar*, Zhitomir, 40
Libau (Liepaja), Latvia, 183
Lichterfelde barracks, Berlin, 27
Liebigs Hill, Breslau, 224, 325n
Liegnitz, Silesia, 52, 119, 197, 237
Liegnitz, Battle of (1241), 129, 181
see also Wahlstatt, Battle of
Linke–Hoffmann–Busch locomotive works, Breslau, 53, 203, 239, 305n
Lithuania
evacuees, 84
fortifications 82, 101, 103, 107, 111, 115, 117, 163
German retreat, 79
joined EU, 10
Lithuanians in Kaliningrad, 249n
Memelland, 18
Red Army conduct, 143;
shooting of Breslau Jews, 67
Litzmannstadt (Lodz), Warthegau
capture by Red Army, 193
evacuation forbidden, 1944, 128
evacuation, 1945, 316n
Jewish ghetto, 38
Volksdeutsche settlement, 74
Volkssturm, 154
Lohbrück, Silesia, 203
Lohse, Hinrich, *Gauleiter*, Schleswig–Holstein, *Reichskommissar Ostland*, 42, 261n
Lomza, Zichenau, East Prussia, 111
London, 45, 272n
Lötzen, East Prussia
evacuation of Berliners, 82
Ostwall, 107
partial evacuation, 1944, 138
Patenschaft, 1915–1922, 254n
Lötzen fortified area, East Prussia
defences, 96, 97
fortress 280n
lost by Germans 192, 311n
Soviet partisans 178
Lower Bavaria, 29

Lower Silesia
economy, 18
evacuation, 180–181, 200–204, 308n, 316n
evacuees, 45, 47–48, 49, 51, 263n
fighting, 1945, 193, 195, 197–198, 221–225, 230, 232–234
foreign workers and POWs, 54, 57, 68, 236–237
formation of *Gau*, 29–30
German propagsnda, 229–230
Jews, 275n
lack of goods, 51, 52
mood, 64, 65–66, 88, 180, 271n
Nazi crimes, 237, 238
Nazi support, 26
Polish administration, 1945, 245n
post-20 July 1944, 90–91
Soviet advance, 128, 181
Soviet atrocities, 228–229
Soviet propaganda, 158, 323n
suicides, 235–236
Unternehmen Bartold, 108–110, 111, 113, 114, 115, 118, 119, 156, 180, 201, 203, 283–284n, 286n, 287n
Volkssturm, 156–157, 158, 213–215, 298n
wartime administration, 42
see also Breslau; Karl Hanke; Silesia; Upper Silesia
Lublin, Poland, 67, 144
Lucadou, Ludwig Moritz von, Colonel, Kolberg, 1807, 324n
Lucas-Busemann, Erhard, Professor, 7, 330n
Ludendorff, Erich von, Field-Marshal, 20, 22, 23, 185
Luftschutzkeller Deutschlands, 66
Luftwaffe
attacks on London, 1940, 45
combing out of personnel, 1945, 198, 212
East Prussian theatre, 1944–1945, 161, 167, 178, 307n
Festung Breslau, 197, 314n
Frankfurt an der Oder, 1945, 231
Hermann Göring Panzer Corps, 135, 140
Luftflotte Four, 266n
Luftflotte Six, 177
Luftwaffenhelfer, 66, 84, 276n
Poltava, Mirgorod raids, 1944, 76, 273n
Posen, 1945, 313n
Trekundgebungen, 1944, 90
weakness, 1944–1945, 173, 177, 307n, 310n, 314n, 315n
Werner Kreipe, Nemmersdorf, 1944, 140
Lukaschek, Hans, *Oberpräsident*, Silesia, 94
Luneburg, Lower Saxony, 213
Lütsk (Luck), Poland, 62
Lyck, East Prussia
conduct of German military, 81, 87
evacuation, 82, 138
evacuees, 48
First World War, 21, 254n
foreign workers and POWs, 55
mood, 89, 181, 187
Soviet air raids, 36
Volkssturm, 296n

Mackensen, August von, Field-Marshal, 23
Maertins, *Gaupropagandaleiter*, East Prussia
Berlin evacuees, 83, 275n
evacuation of East Prussians, 138, 143, 291n
Hitler's New Year 1945 speech, 182
impact of Königsberg bombing, 171–172
propaganda and mood, July 1944, 85, 87–90
Ostwall, 102, 107
Volkssturm, 153
Maginot Line, 97, 286n
Magnuszew, Poland, 193
Magunia, Waldemar, *Gauwirtschaftberater,* East Prussia, 39, 213–214, 246n
Majdanek extermination camp, 144, 272n, 293n
Makhno, Nestor, 227, 326n
Makinn, Karl, *Kreisleiter*, 208, 213
Makowka, Gustav, *Bürgermeister*, Königsberg, 209, 235, 319n
Mammach, Klaus, Dr, 145–146
Mandrel Screen, 167
Manielewicz, Celina, Holocaust survivor, 330n
Manstein, Erich von, Field-Marshal, 269n
Marienburg, West Prussia
description, 1929, 19
fighting, 1945, 192, 195, 196
Focke-Wulf plant, 61, 268n
fortress status, 1944, 280n
history of town, 96
HJ festival, 1944, 273n
Mariensee estate, Wathegau, 187–188
Marienwerder plebiscite, 1920, 18, 252n
Markinkiewitz, Kazimierz, Mayor of Warsaw, 250n
Marne, Battle of the (1914), 78
Marwitz Barracks, Bartenstein, East Prussia, 149
Masurian Canal, East Prussia, 113
Masuren Kanal Position, East Prussia, 97
Masurian Lakes, East Prussia, 96, 131
Masurian Lakes, Battle of the (1914), 20–21
Matthes, Erich, *Kreisleiter,* 295n
Mauersee, East Prussia, 274n
Mehlsack, East Prussia, 192
Meldungen aus dem Reich, SD reports, 12
Memel, 28, 35, 45, 49, 50, 82, 83, 101, 114, 116, 129, 131, 132, 138, 143, 144, 151, 152, 155, 156, 273n, 289n

Memel, River, 59, 131, 132, 162, 163, 185, 283n, 309n
Memelland, 18, 28, 37, 129, 130, 131, 132, 185
Memelstellung, 152
Memelwalde, 178
Mendrzyk, Colonel, Third Panzer Army, 129
Merkel, Angela, Federal German Chancellor, 10
Mertinett, Walter, SS reporter, 220
Meseritz, Brandenburg, 30, 97, 108, 109, 113, 216
Meseritz fortified zone, 158, 193, 215
see also Oder–Warthe Bend fortified area; Tirschtiegel Riegel
Metgethen, East Prussia, 117, 213, 226–227
Metz, Lorraine, 96
Meyer, Alfred, *Gauleiter*, North Westphalia, 30
Middle East, 35
Militsch–Trachenberg, Silesia, 111
Miller, Leszek, Polish Prime Minister, 10
Minsk, Belorussia, 74, 75, 76, 93, 257n
Mirgorod, Ukraine, 76
Mittenheide, East Prussia, 55
Model, Walther, Field-Marshal
addressing troops, 81, 275n
appointed commander Army Group Centre, 75
clash with Koch, 87, 282n
commander of Army Group North Ukraine, 272n
praise for *Ostwall*, 104
succeeded by Reinhardt, 106, 283n
Mogilev, Belorussia, 74
Mohr, Major, Breslau 1945, 197
Mohrungen, East Prussia, 139, 260n
Mokotow prison, Warsaw, 240, 241
Moltke, Helmuth James, Count von, 94
Molochnaya, River, 99
Mongols/Mongolians, 79, 108, 181, 195, 222, 289n
Monster, building Kaliningrad, 250n
Moorhouse, Roger, 7
Morgenthau Plan (1944), 219
Moscow, 2, 4, 10, 33–34, 39, 40, 53, 82, 134, 135, 143, 163, 175, 176, 181, 196, 227, 228, 249n, 260n, 290n
see also Russia; Soviet Union
Mueller, Ludwig, Reich Bishop, 255–256n
Müller, Friedrich-Wilhelm, General, 192, 220
Müller-Hillebrand, Burkhart, Major-General 129, 130, 132
Munich, 29, 41, 240, 255n
Munich Putsch (1923), 25, 150
Murawski, Erich, Dr, 36, 41
Mussolini, Benito, Duce, 195

Nacht und Nebel, 68, 237
Namslau, Silesia
evacuation, 200–201
treatment of Poles, 54
Soviet invasion, 193
Unternehmen Bartold, 108, 114
Volkssturm, 157
Narew Army (Imperial Russian Army), 20
Narew front, 1944, 175
Narew, River, 183, 258n
Nationalkomitee Freies Deutschland (NKFD)
appeal signed by German generals, 93, 279n
propaganda, Breslau, 218
propaganda broadcasts, 1944, 82
propaganda Königsberg, 232
Nationalsozialistische Frauenschaft (NSF), 45, 88, 105, 110, 111
Nationalsozialistische Kraftfahr-Korps (NSKK), 45, 79, 148
Nationalsozialistische Volkswohlfahrt (NSV), 35, 45, 46, 48, 51, 84, 105, 109, 137, 138, 162, 166, 168, 171, 180, 185, 198, 201, 205, 275n, 331n
Nationalsozialistischer Führungs-Offizieren (NSFO), 94, 135, 220
Nationalsozialistisches Deutsche Arbeiterpartei (NSDAP)
20 July 1944 putsch, 89–94
air raid protection, 64–65
crimes against foreigners, 236–238, 272n
crimes against Germans, 238–240, 244
eastern Germany, pre-1933, 24–32, 243, 255n
eastern Germany, 1933–1939, 30, 31, 242, 256n
evacuation, 5, 35, 44–53, 81–85, 99, 132, 134, 136–139, 162, 185–186, 187, 1 99–210, 216, 244n, 288n, 315n
GDR view, 2
Hindenburg's funeral, 1934, 23
interference with military, 94, 100, 101, 115–116, 210–211, 215–216, 309n
murder of Jews, 67–68, 237–238
Nazi 'justice', 66–67, 279n
Ostwall and defences, 95, 96, 98–112, 114, 118–119, 126–127, 135, 282n, 283n, 284n, 308n, 330n
Polish view, 5
propaganda, 12–13, 33–34, 75, 82, 85–89, 95, 101, 104, 105, 140–145, 166, 170, 172, 174–175, 181, 219, 220, 222, 234, 235, 255n, 269n, 276n, 278n
racial hierarchy, 53–58, 251n, 272n
Reichsparteitag, 34
Volkssturm, 143, 145–149, 150–160, 212–215, 293n, 294n, 295n, 297n, 298n, 299n

Nationalsozialistisches Deutsche Arbeiterpartei (NSDAP) *(continued)*
wartime view of the Party, 65–66, 79, 88, 126, 180–181, 184, 186, 218, 241, 242, 263n, 271n
Werwolf, 230
West German views, 5–7
see also Night of the Long Knives
Naumann, Werner, Dr, State Secretary, Propaganda Ministry
Danzig speech, September 1944, 129
Posen speech, January 1945, 187–188
Silesian visit, January 1944, 263n
Nazi–Soviet Pact (1939), 1, 33–35, 37, 39
Nehring, Walther, Colonel-General, 224
Neidenburg, East Prussia, 208, 254n, 255n, 321n
Nemmersdorf, East Prussia
damage by German troops, 182
fighting 1944, 133–134
Soviet atrocities, 138, 140–143, 292n
Volkssturm, 150, 154
Netherlands, 237, 290n
Nettlebeck Uwe, *Bürgermeister*, Kolberg, 211, 324n
Netze, River, 97, 98, 206
Netzekreis, 110, 307n
Neuhausen airfield, Königsberg, 213
Neumarkt, Silesia, 237
Neustettin, Pomerania
evacuation, 207
Pommernwall, 112, 113, 118
possible Polish rising, 1944, 57
Neutief, East Prussia, 210, 232
Newton, Basil C, Minister, British Embassy, Berlin, 272n
Niehoff, Hermann, Lieutenant-General, 224, 225, 241, 248n, 325n
Niemen Army (Imperial Russian Army), 20
Night of the Long Knives (30 June 1934), 26, 27, 146
Nijmegen, Netherlands, 290n
NKFD, *see Nationalkomitee Freies Deutschland*
NKVD, 38, 39, 175, 228, 230, 244, 265n
Nogat, River 96, 99, 192, 196
Nolte, Ernst, Professor, 247n
Nordenburg, East Prussia, 178
Norman, Käthe von, 246n
Normandy, 73, 74, 301n
North Westphalia, 30
Norway, 192, 196, 313n
Nowak, Günther, HJ Hindenburg, Upper Silesia, 214
NSF, *see Nationalsozialistische Frauenschaft*
NSFO, *see Nationalsozialistischer Führungs-Offizieren*
NSKK, *see Nationalsozialistische Kraftfahr-Korps*
NSV, *see Nationalsozialistische Volkswohlfahrt*
Nuremberg, 34, 265n
Nuremberg Laws (1935), 67
Nuremberg trials (1945–1948), 42, 140, 226, 275n, 293n

Oberkommando des Heeres (OKH), 74, 99
Obersalzberg, Berchtesgaden, Bavaria, 86, 98
Oberschlesische Zeitung, 105, 283n, 299n, 310n
Obra, River, 97, 216
Oder Front (1945), 85, 213, 327n
Oder Line, 96, 98
Oder Position, 96, 98
Oder, River, 1, 3, 4, 5, 8, 13, 17, 24, 26, 28, 31, 47, 61, 67, 96, 97, 158, 165, 180, 181, 191, 193, 194, 195, 196, 198, 200, 201, 206, 207, 213, 215, 216, 218, 227, 230, 234, 235–236, 239, 242, 243, 245n, 247n, 255n, 287n, 301n, 312n, 314n, 315n, 316n, 318n
Oder–Neisse Line, 2, 3, 4, 8, 249n
Oder–Warthe Bend fortified area, 96, 97, 98, 193, 212, 215
see also Meseritz fortified zone; Tirschtiegel Riegel
Oderwerke, Stettin, *see* Stettiner Oder-Werke
Oels, Silesia
evacuation preparations, 308n
German slave labour, 1945, 228
Luftwaffe, 314n
Red Army, 197
Soviet POWs, 57
Unternehmen Bartold, 115
Ohlendorf, Otto, *SS-Gruppenführer*, 12, 251n
OKH, *see Oberkommando des Heeres*
Oldershausen, Libussa von, Countess, 54, 185, 205, 240
Oppeln, Silesia, 68, 116, 254n, 280n, 312n
Oppenhoff, Franz, *Oberbürgermeister*, Aachen, 230
Opperau, Silesia, 202
Oppermann, Ewald, Head, National Socialist Flying Corps, East Prussia, 150
Orel, Ukraine, 62
Organisation Todt (OT) 36, 99, 156, 282n, 307n
Orlow, Dietrich, Professor, 28
Orsha, Belorussia, 74
Ortelsburg, East Prussia, 81, 136, 175, 185, 208, 296n, 306n
Ortelsburger Position, East Prussia, 97, 321n
Ost-Dokumentation, 4, 12, 13
Ostdeutscher Beobachter, 219, 288n
Ostenburg, Zichenau, East Prussia, 177
Osterode, East Prussia, 22, 132, 137
Ostforschung, 253n
Ostheer, 20, 198
Osthilfe, 24, 255n

Ostland, 100, 154, 261n
Ostland factory, Königsberg, 234
Ostmark, 31
Ostmesse, Königsberg, 28, 37, 257n
Ostministerium (Ministry of the Occupied Eastern Territories), 40, 75, 84, 175
Ostpolitik, 3, 5
Ostpreußen icebreaker, 240
Ostpreußen und sein Hindenburg film (1917), 22–23
Ostpreußenschutzstellung, 102, 107, 290n
  see also Koch Line; *Ostwall*
Ostpreußischen Kriegshefte, 253n
Ostsee Zeitung-Stettin General-Anzeiger, 278n
Ostwall, 36, 76, 95–119, 126–127, 137, 153, 174, 211–212, 242, 243, 244, 280–288n, 321n
  see also Einsatz Zielenzig, Ostpreußenschutzstellung, Pommernwall, Unternehmen Bartold
OT, *see Organisation Todt*
Oven, Wilfred von, 194–195, 276n

Pakistan, 1
Palatinate, 29, 44
Palmnicken, East Prussia, 320n
Panzerfaust, 153, 154, 155, 157, 158, 159, 173, 185, 210, 214, 230, 231, 290n, 297n, 322n
Panzerschreck, 153
Panzerwerke, 98
Papen, Franz von, German Chancellor, 25
Paradeplatz runway, Königsberg, 238
Paris, 73
Park Hotel, Königsberg, East Prussia, 210
Partisans, in Belorussia, 75
Parisans, Czech, 241
Partisans, in East Prussia, 80, 117, 178, 274n, 293n
Partisans, German, 230, 327n
Partisans, Polish, 36, 38, 68, 76, 156
Partisans, Soviet, 36
Partisans, in Ukraine, 38, 40, 175, 260n
Patenschaft, 22, 254n
Patten, Chris, EU Commissioner, 250n
Pawelka, Rudi, founder Prussian Trust, 11
Peikert, Paul, Father, 235, 317n, 330n
People's Court, 94, 277n, 278n, 317n, 319n
Peter the Great, Tsar, 250n
Peyse, East Prussia, 232, 234, 328n
Pfafferott, Dr, 78–79
Pfanz, Eugen, *Bürgermeister* Klettendorf, Silesia, 330n
Piast dynasty, 5
Pieck, Wilhelm, President of the GDR, 2
Pillau, East Prussia
  air raids, 164, 301n
  Baltiysk, 9
  fighting and evacuation, 1945, 200, 208, 209, 210, 220, 221, 232, 234, 239, 312n, 331
  fortress, 280n
  sea defences, 96
  troops disembarking, 1939, 27
  visit by Koch, 1934, 27
Plötzensee Prison, Berlin, 277n
Poland, 1–5, 8, 10–11, 18–19, 20, 28, 31, 32, 33, 37–38, 47, 49, 62, 73, 79, 96, 97, 108, 178, 181, 183, 187, 188, 191, 193, 212, 241, 243, 245n, 246n, 247n, 248n, 251n, 252n, 258n, 263n, 269n, 279n, 280n, 308n, 326n
Poles, ill-treatment of, 29, 37–38, 53, 56, 68, 78, 80, 128, 236, 259n, 265n, 285n
Polish Corridor, 18, 19–20, 32, 37, 220
Polish Home Army, 265n, 270n, 290–291n
Polish Intelligence, 258n, 260n, 266–267n, 268n
Polish Question, 181
Polish workers and POWs, 29, 44, 54, 55, 56, 57, 84, 95, 103, 108, 111, 112, 162, 236–237, 240, 273n, 281n, 285n
Political Warfare Executive, 13, 128–129, 274n
Politz, Pomerania, bombing of synthetic oil plant, 59, 60, 161, 172, 305n
Poltava, Ukraine, 61, 76, 273n
Pomerania
  administration and *Gauleiter*, 17–18, 26, 28–29, 41, 241, 251n, 256n, 328n
  air raids, 46, 59–61, 164–165, 172, 173, 200
  Catholic Church, 65, 66
  defences and *Pommernwall*, 95, 96, 98, 101, 107–108, 110–113, 115, 116, 117, 118–119, 280n, 283n, 285n, 330n
  evacuees, 45–46, 48, 132, 138, 180, 185
  fighting and evacuation, 1945, 193–198, 200, 205–207, 213, 237, 246n, 247n, 307–308n, 318n
  foreign workers and POWs, 54, 57
  fortresses, 280n
  German executions, 1945, 194–195, 240
  impact of war, 36, 62, 269n
  Jews, 67
  lack of goods, 50–52
  mood, 65, 180, 182, 205–206, 306n
  opposition, 66, 271n
  post-20 July 1944, 90, 91, 92
  post-1945, 3, 245n, 308n
  Soviet propaganda, 226
  Soviet terror, 1945, 236, 240
  suicides, 1945, 236
  Volkssturm, 158–160, 213, 215, 299n
  Wehrkreis II, 84, 158, 159, 207
Pommernstellung, 96, 98, 280n

Pommernwall
conditions, 110–111, 111–113, 284n, 285n, 287n
evacuation from eastern disricts, 206, 207, 208
fears arising from construction, 115, 208n
inception, 107–108, 283n
labour force, 108, 283n
manning, 159, 283n
Schwede-Coburg's directives, 116
Pommersche Motorenbau GmbH, 305n
Pommersche Zeitung (*PomZ*), 62, 66, 88, 111, 113, 115, 165, 205, 219, 262n, 264n, 268n, 269n, 270n, 270–271n, 284n, 286n, 287n, 294n, 299n, 318n
Pommerscher Industrie-Verein, Stettin, 268n
Pöpelwitz station, Breslau, 214
Popp, *Gaupropagandaleiter*, Pomerania, 182
Popular Fronts, 34
Posen, Warthegau
fifth anniversary of Warthegau, 1944, 184
fighting, 1945, 193, 194, 195, 231, 234, 313n, 324n
Focke-Wulf works, 61, 64
fortress, 280n
Germans abroad conference, 1944, 259n
Greiser's flight, 204, 223, 241, 317–318n, 324n
Naumann speech, January 1945, 187–188
post-1918, 18, 19
propaganda, 1945, 219
Warthegau, 37
Posen–West Prussia border province, 18, 26, 31, 251n, 256n
Poser, Victor von, Dr, *Landrat*, Ortelsburg, East Prussia, 175
Post, Erich, East Prussian NSV leader
air raids on Königsberg, 168
departure of Berlin evacuees, 275n
final months and probable death, 331n
Ostwall, 109, 284n
Potrek, Karl, Königsberg *Volkssturm*, 140
Potsdam, Brandenburg, 31
Potsdam conference (1945), 1, 2, 4, 245n
Pregel, River, 168, 169, 170, 172, 220, 303n
Preußisch Eylau, East Prussia, 83, 185, 274n
Preußisch Holland, East Prussia, 291n
Preußische Zeitung (*PZ*), Königsberg, 104, 105, 134, 141, 166, 170, 221, 226, 263n, 273n, 276n, 277n, 278n, 282n, 288n
Prussian Interior Ministry, 28, 256n
Prussian State Archive, Stettin, 247n
Prussian Trust, 11
Prützmann, Hans-Adolf, *SS-Obergruppenführer*, 230, 327n
Pulawy, Poland, 193
Pushkin (Tsarskoe Selo), Russia, 274n
Putin, Vladimir, President, Russian Federation, 10
Pyritz, Pomerania
fighting, 1945, 196, 208, 213, 318n
Kreisleiter Schug, 110

Rächer, Die, 66
RAD, *see Reichsarbeitdienst*
Radio Moscow, 68, 163, 196
Radziwill family, 39
RAF, *see* Royal Air Force
Ragnit, East Prussia, 139, 162, 177
Rampf, *Kreisleiter*, Bromberg, 195
Rassow, Peter, Professor, 247n
Rastenburg, East Prussia
Hitler's HQ, 36, 86, 99, 179
impression, 1944, 185
interwar reconstruction, 254n
late evacuation, 208
Ratibor, Silesia, 276n, 280n
Ratshof, Königsberg air raids, 1941, 1944, 266n, 305n
Rau, Johannes, Federal German President, 250n
Raus, Erhard, Colonel-General, 184, 297n, 309n, 310n
Rauschen, East Prussia, 232
Reagan, Ronald, US President, 5
Rebentisch, Dieter, Professor,186
Red Air Force
raids on Breslau, 1941–1945, 58, 164, 201
raids on East Prussia, 1941–1944, 36, 58–59, 161–164
superiority, 80, 108, 177, 196, 231, 232, 238, 310n, 311n
target practice, *Graf Zeppelin*, 267n
Red Army
First Baltic Front, 232
First Belorussian Front, 191, 193, 194, 195, 196
Second Belorussian Front, 191, 193, 196, 230
Third Belorussian Front, 132, 135, 144, 191, 192, 226, 327n
First Ukrainian Front, 193, 194, 197, 201–202
Second Shock Army, 276n
Eighth Guards Army, 193, 313n
Sixty-Second Army, 193
Twelfth Guards Tank Corps, 213
Red Cross, 52, 166, 208, 295n, 298n, 331n
Red Star, 143, 227, 330
Refardt, *Regierungspräsident*, Frankfurt an der Oder 113, 158
Reich Chancellery, Berlin, 156, 203, 241, 256n
Reich Food Estate, 28
Reich Railways, *see Reichsbahn*

Reichsarbeitdienst (RAD), 54, 60, 92, 280n
Reichsbahn, 66, 82, 102, 136, 198, 320n
Reichsdeutsche, 259n
Reichskristallnacht, 67
Reichsparteitag, 34
Reichssicherheitshauptamt (RSHA), 56, 67
Reichstag, 24, 25, 26, 27, 29, 31, 255n
Reichswehr, 23, 25, 26, 257n
Reinefarth, Heinz Friedrich, *SS-Gruppenführer*, 197, 223
Reinersdorff-Paczenski, Detlev von, *Landrat*, Groß Wartenberg, Silesia
  Unternehmen Bartold, 109
  Volkssturm, 157
Reinhardt, Georg-Hans, Colonel-General
  commander, Third Panzer Army, 81
  commander, Army Group Centre, 106, 283n
  dismissal, 1945, 192, 311n
  Soviet threat, 135, 183, 184
  Volkssturm, 153, 174
  war crimes, 275n
Remlinger, Colonel, 313n
Rendulic, Lothar, Dr, Colonel-General
  commander, Army Group North, 192
  ideological reliability, 194, 242
Rennenkampf, Pavel K. von, General, 20
Replacement Army, *see Ersatzheer*
Reval (Tallinn), Estonia, 40
Rheims, France, 311n
Rhine Front, 313n
Rhine, River, 8
Rhineland, 45, 48, 139
Rhode, Dr, *Regierungspräsident* Gumbinnen, East Prussia, 136, 143
Ribbentrop, Joachim von, 34, 36, 135
Riesengebirge, 47, 203
Riga, Latvia, 40, 75, 154
Rohde, Alfred, Dr, Curator, Königsberg Castle Museum, 320n
Röhm, Ernst, SA Chief of Staff, 26, 27, 28, 29, 31, 146
Rokossovsky, Konstantin, Marshal, 191, 193, 195, 196, 226, 227
Romania, 3, 73, 74, 225, 245n
Rome, 42, 73, 219
Rominte Position, 154
Rominte, River, 140
Rominten Heide, East Prussia, 133, 295–296n, 327n
Rommel, Erwin, General, 31, 202
Roosevelt, Franklin D, US President, 181
Rosenberg, Alfred, *Reichsleiter*, 30, 40, 175, 226, 260n
Rossitten, East Prussia, 282n
Rostock, Mecklenburg, 29, 60, 271n
Rothfels, Hans, Professor, 246n, 247n
Rowno, Ukraine, 39, 40, 62, 78, 260n
Royal Air Force Bomber Command
  Berlin raids, 45
  Danzig raids, 59, 161, 266n, 301n
  Dresden raids, 167, 170, 200, 305n
  Gotenhafen (Gdynia) raids, 59, 266n, 267n, 301n
  Hamburg raids, 46
  Königsberg raids, 161, 164, 165–172, 266n, 301n, 302–303n, 303–304n, 305n
  minelaying in the Baltic, 161, 164, 301n
  planning Breslau raid, 305n
  Stettin raids, 59–60, 161, 164–165, 266n, 268n, 301–302n, 302–303n, 303–304n
RSHA, *see Reichssicherheitshauptamt*
Rügen Island, Pomerania, 240
Ruhr, 18, 26, 146, 173, 198, 276n, 306n
Rummelsburg, Pomerania, 159
Rundstedt, Gerd von, Field-Marshal, 94
Russia, 2, 6, 8, 9–10, 19, 33–34, 35, 39, 61, 62, 63, 64, 73, 76, 77, 78, 79, 80, 81, 82, 85, 88, 92, 96, 98–99, 111, 114, 115, 128, 129, 133, 134, 140, 142, 144, 145, 147, 154, 158, 160, 162, 168, 175, 176, 177, 178, 179, 197, 198, 203, 204–205, 206, 208, 218, 220, 221, 224, 225–226, 228, 229, 236, 238, 248n, 249n, 251n, 252n, 257n, 260n, 265n, 267n, 274n, 275n, 290n, 307n, 326n, 331n
  see also Moscow; Soviet Union
Russian Civil War (1918–1920), 34, 326n
Russian Federation, 9–10
Russian invasion, 1914, 20–23, 96, 108, 179, 252n, 253n, 254n
Russian workers and POWs, 53, 54, 56–57, 58, 68, 89, 185, 203, 243
Russian Liberation Army, 85, 144, 198, 276n
Rust, Bernhard, *Reichsminister*, Education, 78
Rustzeug für die Propaganda in der Ortsgruppe, 150
Rüttgers plant, Breslau, 214
Rwanda, 1

SA, *see Sturmabteilung*
Saatzig, Pomerania, 110, 115, 159
Sagan, Silesia, 68
Sajer, Guy, 131, 154
Salisch von, *SS-Standartenführer*, 195
Samland, East Prussia, 96, 132, 192, 209, 210, 211, 213, 220, 232, 238, 330n
Sammlung Sterz, 13
Samsonov, Alexander V., General, 20
San, River, 258n
Sandkirche, Breslau, 234
Sandomierz, Poland, 188, 193
Sarajevo, Bosnia-Herzegovina, 10
Sattelberg, O, 111–112

Sauckel, Fritz, Reich Plenipotentiary for Labour Force Deployment, 40, 42, 226, 261n
Saur, Otto, *Hauptabteilungsleiter*, 42
Sauvant, Dr, Lieutenant-Colonel, 319n
Saxony, 45, 50, 132, 139, 168, 172, 203, 216, 274n, 331n
Scandinavians, in SS service, 198
Scharfenweise, Zichenau, East Prussia, 78
Schaubert, Klaus, Major, *Wehrkreis* II, 159
Scheibenweg, Breslau, 234
Scheitniger Stern, Breslau, 224
Schelsky, Lieutenant, 235, 321n
Schepmann, Wilhelm, SA Chief of Staff, *Volkssturm* Inspector-General, 147, 148, 151
Schichau shipbuilding yard, Danzig, 266n
Schichau shipbuilding yard, Elbing, 266n
Schichau shipbuilding yard, Königsberg, 53, 169, 172, 234, 237–238
Schieder, Theodor, Professor, 3, 247n, 289n
Schimitzek, Stanislaw, Dr, 198, 247n
Schirwindt, East Prussia, 133, 143
Schlawe, Pomerania
  Pommernwall, 108, 112, 287n
  suicides, 1945, 236
Schleicher, Kurt von, German Chancellor, 25–26
Schlesische Tageszeitung (*ST*), 65, 88, 108, 110, 113, 202, 203, 221, 223, 225, 236, 239, 248n, 263n, 278n, 286n, 287–288n, 316n, 330n
Schlesischer Station, Berlin, 317n
Schleswig-Holstein, 66–67, 146, 261n
'Schlittenfahrt' plan, 183
Schlochau, Pomerania, 98
Schloppe, Pomerania, 207
Schloßberg, East Prussia
  evacuation, 82, 136, 138, 186
  fighting, 1945, 191
  Third Panzer Army HQ, 81
Schloßplatz, Breslau, 91, 157
Schmidt, *SS-Obergruppenführer*, Lower Silesia, 298n
Schneidemühl, Pomerania
  air raids, 1944, 61
  deportation of Jews, 1940, 67
  evacuation, 206, 207, 237
  fighting, 1945, 195, 214, 226, 234, 313n
  fortress, 159, 280n, 288n
  poisoning of Red Army, 326n
  Pomeranian jurisdiction, 1938, 256n
  Pommernwall, 107, 118
  POWs, 54
  transfer of files from East Prussia, 180
  Volkssturm, 159
  Wehrmacht demands, 180
Scholtz-Klink, Gertrud, *Reichsfrauenschaftsführerin*, 111
Schönlanke, Pomerania, 52, 206–207, 236
Schörner, Ferdinand, General later Field-Marshal
  clash with Koch, 154
  commander, Army Group North, 153, 309n
  commander Army Group A then Centre, 193, 194, 204, 224, 225, 229, 241, 242, 315n, 317n, 325n
Schröder, Gerhard, Federal German Chancellor, 10, 11
Schroeder, Dr, East Prussia, 283n, 284n, 285n
Schug, Siegfried, *Kreisleiter*, Stargard, Pomerania
  critical of *Wehrmacht*, 215
  Pommernwall, 110, 111
  Volkssturm, 159
Schulenburg, Fritz Dietlof von der, 30
Schulz, *Gaupropagandaleiter*, Lower Silesia
  Hitler's New Year 1945 speech, 182
  Treukundgebungen, post-20 July, 90–91
  Volkssturm launch, 157
Schutzstaffeln (SS), 5, 10, 27, 29–30, 31, 40, 57, 68, 79, 84, 85, 93, 101, 108, 146–147, 148, 156, 159, 175, 177–178, 180, 183, 194, 198, 204, 210, 212, 216, 220, 221, 230, 231, 233, 234, 236–237, 238, 240, 241, 244, 248n, 250n, 259n, 296n, 298n, 313n, 315n, 317n, 325n, 329n
Schutzwallehrenzeichen, 105
Schwede-Coburg, Franz, *Gauleiter*, Pomerania
  appointed *Gauleiter*, Pomerania, 29
  bombing of Stettin, August 1944, 165
  departure from Stettin, 1945, 240
  early life, 28–18
  hatred of Jews, 41, 67
  later life, 240–241
  murder of asylum patients, 67
  Pommernwall, 108, 110, 112, 116, 284n
  private life, 41
  post-20 July 1944, 91
  Soviet invasion, 1945, 206–207, 208, 318n
  Volkssturm, 158–159, 299n
  wartime administration and prejudices, 41–42, 65
  western German evacuees, 48
Schwedt, Brandenburg, 195, 212
Schweidnitz, Silesia, 68, 94, 201
Schwendemann, Heinrich, Dr, 199, 311n
Schwerin an der Warthe, Brandenburg
  defences, 97
  Einsatz Zielenzig, 108, 113
  Red Army excesses, 1945, 227, 229
Schwerin, Count von, 185, 274n
Schwiebus, Brandenburg, 97, 158
SD *see Sicherheitsdienst*
Sealion, Operation (1940), 59
Sebald, W.G., Professor, 7, 249n
Second Revolution, 26

Seeckt, Hans von, General, 23
Seerappen, East Prussia, 329n
Seidler, Franz W, Professor, 145, 160, 215
Sensburg, East Prussia, 185
Seven Years War (1756–1763), 219
Seydlitz, German cruiser, 266n
Seydlitz Leute, 232, 279n
Seydlitz-Kurzbach, Walther von, General, 279n
Seym (Polish Parliament), 11
Showalter, Dennis, Professor, 23
Shtemenko, S. M., General, 193
Siberia, 38, 86, 141, 228
Sicherheitsdienst (SD), 12–13, 41, 46–47, 50, 51–52, 57, 61–62, 63–64, 65–66, 76, 77, 79, 84–85, 91, 92, 99, 107, 109, 110, 111, 114, 115–116, 137, 142, 181, 239, 278n, 296n
Siebenbürger Saxons, 225
Siemens, 47
Silesia
  emigration, 17
  expellees, 8, 11
  First World War, 20
  Gau, pre-1941, 29–30
  see also Lower Silesia; Upper Silesia
Silesian Military District, 82, 174
Simon, Paul, Deputy *Gauleiter*, Pomerania, 112–113
Skorzeny, Otto, *SS-Obersturmbannführer*, 195, 212, 213
Slutsk, Belorussia, 74
Smolensk, Russia, 86, 265n
Sobibor extermination camp, 272n
SOE, *see* Special Operations Executive
Soldau, East Prussia, 18–19, 83, 208
Somme, Battle of the (1916), 78
Sommer, Dr Felix, Head, Lower Silesian Agrarian Office, 239
Sondereinsatz-Ost, 118
Sondergericht (Special Court), 38, 66–67, 68, 115, 118, 131, 149, 156, 164, 271n, 272n
Sondermann, Heinrich, State Secretary, Propaganda Ministry, 83, 86, 275n
Sonnenberg Prison, Brandenburg, 237
Sonnenwende (Solstice), Operation (1945), 196
Sorau, Brandenburg
  air raids, 61, 64
  evacuated Focke-Wulf plant, 50
South Westphalia, *Gau*, 29, 31, 45
Sovetsk, *see* Tilsit
Soviet Baltic Fleet, 10, 133
Soviet Union (and Soviet), 1, 2, 3, 4, 6, 7, 8, 9, 10, 12, 13, 19, 33–35, 36, 37, 38, 39, 40, 44, 47, 55, 56, 57, 58–59, 61, 62, 63, 64, 69, 73, 74, 75, 76, 77, 79, 80, 81, 82, 85, 86–87, 88, 89, 93, 98, 100, 101, 105, 106, 107, 117, 119, 126, 128, 129, 130, 131, 132, 133, 134, 135, 136, 137, 138, 139, 140–145, 151, 153, 154, 155, 159, 159, 160, 161, 162, 163, 165, 168, 169, 171, 172, 173, 174, 175, 176, 177, 178, 179, 181, 183, 184, 187, 191, 192, 195, 196, 197, 198, 199, 200, 201, 203, 204, 206, 207, 208, 209, 210, 211, 212, 213–214, 215, 216, 218, 219, 220, 221, 222, 223, 224, 225–233, 234–241, 242, 243, 244, 245n, 249n, 250n, 258n, 265n, 266n, 267n, 269n, 270n, 272–273n, 279n, 289n, 290n, 292n, 293n, 296n, 306n, 307n, 308n, 309n, 310n, 311n, 312n, 313n, 315n, 318n, 320n, 322n, 323n, 325n, 326n, 327n
  see also Moscow; Russia
Sozialdemokratische Partei Deutschlands (SPD), 3, 24
Spanish Civil War, 34
SPD, *see Sozialdemokratische Partei Deutschlands*
Speer, Albert, *Reichsminister*
  Armaments Minister, 42
  defences, 99
  friendship with Hanke, 30, 42, 202, 223, 298n, 316n, 324–325n, 328n
  friendship with Stürtz, 31
  impressions of Ukraine, 40
  Volkssturm, 155
Spickschen, Erich, *Landesbauernführer*, East Prussia, 264n, 288n
Spiegel, Der, 8, 249n, 250n, 271n, 278n, 311n
Spielhagen, Wolfgang, Dr, *Bürgermeister*, Breslau, 239, 329n
Spreu, Richard, *Landrat*, Habelschwerdt, Silesia, 48
SS, *see Schutzstaffeln*
Stablack, East Prussia, 37
Stadtwacht, 55, 85, 293n
Stahl, Dr, SS officer, 138, 140
Stahlberg, Alexander, Major, von Manstein's adjutant, 269n
Stalag Luft III, POW camp, Sagan, Silesia, 68, 272n
Stalin, Josef, General Secretary, Soviet Communist Party
  German admiration of, 64, 92
  Goebbels' view of, 93, 176
  hate propaganda, 229, 327n
  Hitler's fears of, 232
  military commander, 193, 195, 312n
  Red Army excesses, 228, 248n, 274n
  resettlement, 249n
  territorial ambitions, 181
Stalingrad, battle of (1942–1943), 55, 75, 82, 193, 219, 226, 279n, 298n
Stalingrad by Anthony Beevor, 7
'Stalingrad mood', 62
Standbereitschaft, East Prussian *Volkssturm*, 152

Stargard, Pomerania
defences 330n
fighting, 1945, 196
Kreisleiter Schug, 10, 159, 215
prisoners, 237
Stauffenberg, Claus Schenk Count von, Colonel, 89–90, 277n
STAVKA Soviet High Command headquarters, 198
Steiermark, train of *Reichsführer-SS*, 206
Steinbach, Erika, President, *Bund der Vertriebenen*, 10, 250n
Steindamm, Königsberg, 169
Steinert, Marlis, Professor, 219
Stettin
criminality, 66
evacuation of city, 46, 173, 262n, 264n
evacuees, 48, 180
execution of deserters, 194
expulsion of Germans, 1945, 245n
foreign workers and POWs, 54, 57
fortress status, 280n
impact of war, 36
Jewish community, 67
lack of goods, 50, 51
mood, 41–42, 142, 173, 182
nearby concentration camp, 1933, 28
opposition groups, 66, 271n
Pommernwall, 11, 112, 118
possible Polish administration, 181
post-war Polish rule, 246n
Prussian State Archive, 247n
RAF raid, April 1943, 59–60, 267n
RAF raid, January 1944, 60, 267–268n
RAF raids, August 1944, 161, 164–165, 172, 301–302n, 303–304n
RAF reconnaissance, 226n
rumoured relief army, 221
Schwede-Coburg's departure, 240
scuttling of *Graf Zeppelin*, 267n
Soviet advance, 196, 206, 207, 208, 314n, 318n
Soviet propaganda, 323n
Treukundgebungen, July 1944, 90, 91, 92
US air raids, 1944, 60–61, 305n
Volkssturm, 149, 158, 294n, 299n
Stettiner Oder-Werke, 165, 268n, 301n, 302n
Stettiner Stowerwerke AG, 305n
Steuben, German transport ship, 200
Stimmung, 12
Stoiber, Edmund, Bavarian Prime Minister, 9
Stolp, Pomerania
Christmas 1944, 185
dead children, 205
defences, 330n
Drumhead courts martial, 240
evacuated East Prussian records, 180
evacuation, 207
fighting, 1945, 196
French POWs, 54
German suicides, 236
profiteering, 52
Pommernwall, 108, 112
rumoured relief army, 221
Stone, Norman, Professor, 252n
Strasbourg/Strasburg, Alsace, 10–11, 96
Strasser, Gregor, 25–26, 27
Strauss, Adolf, Colonel-General, 287n
Streicher, Julius, *Gauleiter*, Franconia, 30, 143
Strength through Joy, 200
Striegau, Silesia, 197, 224, 226, 228–229, 230
Stuckart, Wilhelm, Dr, Interior Ministry, 30, 143
Stumpf, Fritz, Dr, 265n
Sturmabteilung (SA), 25, 26, 27, 28, 29, 67, 110, 146, 147, 148, 152, 155, 158, 159, 215, 237, 243, 293n
Stürmer, Michael, Professor, 247n
Stürtz, Emil, *Gauleiter*, Brandenburg
Brandenburg appointment, 1936, 31
Einsatz Zielenzig, 102
evacuation, 204, 205
Küstrin, 1945, 223
likely fate, 240
Sonnenberg prison killings, 237
Volkssturm, 188
Stuttgart
air raids, 303
Bibliothek für Zeitgeschichte, 13
Stutthof concentration camp, Danzig–West Prussia, 68, 272n, 329n
Sudauen (Suwalki), East Prussia, 35, 36, 37, 55, 89, 107, 132, 182
Sudetengau evacuees, 45
Sudetenland, 9, 67, 82, 83, 204, 242, 241, 245n, 249n; 329n
Süd-Ost Messe, Breslau, 37
Surminski, Arno, 186, 198
Suvorov, Viktor, 258n
Swabia, *Gau*, 146
Swinemünde, Pomerania
Erich Post, 331n
evacuation, 1945, 314n
evacuees, 48
US bombing, 1945, 200
Szelinski, Fritz, GSA, East Prussia, 52, 59, 208, 319n

Tabun nerve agent, 237
Taganrog, Ukraine, 62
Tallinn, *see* Reval
Tannenberg (Grunwald), battle of (1410), 20

Tannenberg, battle of (1914), 20–23
Tannenberg, East Prussia legacy, 23, 32, 129, 185, 257n
Tannenberg, Group, East Prussian SA, 110
Tannenberg memorial, 23, 179, 219–220, 255n
Tannenwalde, East Prussia, 326n
Tapiau, East Prussia, 97, 250n
Tartars, 85, 195
Tass (Soviet news agency), 135
Tedder, Arthur, Air Marshal, 311
Teheran conference (November 1943), 64
Tendenzwende (after 1982), 5
Teutoburger Wald, Battle of (AD 9), 129, 289n
Teutonic Knights and Order, 10, 19, 20, 21, 96
The Great Escape, film (1963), 272n
The Hague Convention (1907), 151
The National Archives, Kew, 13
The Times, 135, 143, 165, 167, 175, 246n, 250n, 253n, 254n, 257n, 261n, 267n, 268n, 301n
Theresienstadt concentration camp, Sudetengau, 67, 329n
Thierack, Otto, Dr, *Reichsminister* for Justice, 239
Thirty Years War (1618–1648), 41, 79
Thorn (Torun), Danzig–West Prussia, 96, 212, 280n, 315n
Thuringia, *Gau*
  East Prussian evacuees, 138
  Gauleiter Fritz Sauckel, 42
Tiburzy, Ernst, Königsberg *Volkssturm*, 214
Tilitzki, Christian, 36
Tilsit, East Prussia
  departure of Berlin evacuees, 83
  escaped Soviet POWs, 89
  evacuation, 138–139
  fighting, October 1944, 132–133, 138, 300n
  fighting, 1945, 221
  images of Tilsit, late 1944, 139, 173, 177, 185
  returning Memellanders, 129
  Sovetsk, 292n
  Soviet air raids, 36, 59, 161–163
  Volkssturm, 152, 153
Tirschtiegel Riegel (barrier), Brandenburg, 97, 215
  see also Meseritz fortified zone; Oder–Warthe Bend fortified zone
Todt, Fritz, Dr, *Reichsminister*, 42, 92
Tolkemit, West Prussia, 191
Trakehnen, East Prussia, 133
Transoceon German news agency, 259n, 295n, 298n, 316n
Transport Ministry, 82, 84
Treblinka extermination camp, 38, 272n
Tresckow, Henning von, Brigadier-General, 93, 279n
Treuburg, East Prussia
  Berlin evacuees, 83
  evacuation, 1944, 136, 138, 185
  mood, 1944, 89
  Volkssturm, 152, 153, 296n
Treuekundgebungen (1944), 90–92
Truman, Harry S, US President, 245n
Tsarskoe Selo, *see* Pushkin
Tsuman, Ukraine, 39, 260n
Turkey, 1
Turks, 195
Tyrol, 147

U-Boat
  activity at Stettin, 165, 314n
  plans for a new fleet, 146, 266–267n
  production at Danzig, 59, 266–267n
  RAF reconnaissance, 266n
Ukraine
  American air bases, 61, 76
  German devastation, 145, 175
  German forces, 74, 100
  German loss of, 61–62, 63, 77, 101, 136, 145
  NKVD crimes, 265n
  partisan activity, 38, 40, 175, 260n
  refugees, 84
  Reichskommissar and *Reichskommissariat*, 38–41, 100, 104, 144, 211, 226, 230, 240, 260n
  Ukrainian labourers, 54, 237, 326n
  Ukrainians in Kaliningrad, 249n
  Volksdeutsche, 74
Ulbricht, Walter, Chairman, Socialist Unity Party of the GDR, 2
United States Army Air Force (USAAF), 46, 61, 64, 161, 172
Untermenschen, 34, 53
Unternehmen Bartold
  conditions, 109, 110, 113, 114, 203
  fears arising from construction, 115
  impact on economy, 118, 119, 156, 180
  impact on landscape, 287n
  inception, 108
  labour force, 108, 111, 228
  manning, 201
  propaganda, 283–284n
  see also Ostwall
Upper Austria, 45
Upper Bavaria, 45, 49, 181
Upper Palatinate, 29
Upper Silesia
  air raids, 66, 161, 172, 173, 305n
  Albert Commission (1944), 84
  annexed territories, 37, 67, 68, 178
  background, 17, 251n
  Catholic population, 24
  defences, 96, 98, 101, 105, 114, 116, 283n
  extra meat allowances (1944), 310n

Upper Silesia *(continued)*
fighting, 1945, 193, 198, 224, 241, 312n
indiscipline/looting, 216, 276n
Jews, 67
lower Nazi support, 25
mood, 64
new province (1940), 30
plebiscite (1921) and conflict, 18, 24, 25, 26
propaganda, 88, 184
Soviet advance, 88, 128, 184
Volkssturm, 156, 157, 214, 296n, 299n, 321n
USAAF, *see* United States Army Air Force
Uschdraweit, *Landrat*, Angerapp, East Prussia, 137, 286n

V-1, 77
Valkyrie, Operation, 57
Varzin, Pomerania, 205, 236
Vasilevsky, A.M., Marshal, 192, 232, 311n, 312n
Vassiltchikov, Marie 'Missie', 270n
Verdun, Battle of (1916), 23
Versailles, Treaty of (1919), 17, 18, 19, 25, 31, 37, 96, 243, 252n
Vertriebenenliteratur, 5
Vesuvius, Mount, 169
Vienna, 67
Vilnius (Vilna), Lithuania, 74, 75
Vistula Line, 99, 100, 103
Vistula–Oder, operation, 226
Vistula, River, 21, 68, 73, 76, 84, 88, 96, 100, 104, 115, 127, 128, 134, 135, 145, 179, 183, 184, 188, 191, 192, 193, 195, 196, 197, 198, 205, 216, 258n, 311n, 313n, 315n
Vitebsk, Belorussia, 74, 75, 76, 275n
Vlasov, Andrei, Lieutenant-General, 85, 144, 175, 198, 216, 221, 259n
Volga, River, 88, 145
Völkischer Beobachter, 38, 83, 103, 106, 133, 135, 141, 211, 220, 222, 228, 231, 271n, 295n, 320n
Volksbund für das Deutschtum im Ausland, Posen, 1944, 259n
Volksdeutsche, 37–38, 55, 74, 84, 108, 225, 259n
Volksgemeinschaft (People's Community), 33, 46, 91, 104, 126, 166, 170, 173, 207, 238, 242, 243
Volksgenossen, 13, 64, 76, 77, 91, 92, 94, 101, 133
Volksgerichtshof, *see* People's Court
Volksgrenadier divisions, 130, 134, 174, 176
Volkskrieg, 220
Volksopfer, 160
Volkssturm
combat deployment, 132, 145–146, 151–153, 154, 159, 192, 195, 196, 197, 201, 208, 212–215, 220, 240, 289n, 313n, 315n, 321n, 322n, 324n
discipline, 156, 160, 177, 180, 201, 213, 239, 298n
effectiveness, 145–146, 154–155, 159–160, 187, 192, 212, 215, 242–244, 297n, 322n
equipment, 148, 151, 152, 154, 155, 156, 157, 158, 159, 160, 212, 214–215, 297–298n, 299n
evacuation, 153, 155, 198–199, 202–203, 215, 316n
impressions of battlefield, 134, 140, 141, 234
launch/swearing-in, 107, 145, 148, 149–150, 151, 156–157, 297n
organisation, 126, 145, 148–152, 154, 155, 156–157, 158, 210, 294n, 295n, 296n, 298n, 299n
origins, 99, 145–148, 293n
propaganda, 143, 149–151, 153–154, 159–160, 174, 185, 214, 220, 221, 222, 229, 295–296n, 326n
rear deployment, 117, 145–146, 152–153, 154, 157–158, 159, 173, 180, 209, 222, 233, 295n, 299n, 314n, 321n
relationship with *Wehrmacht*, 153–154, 155, 297n, 298n, 321n
Soviet atrocities against, 151, 213–214
Soviet propaganda, 158, 230
training, 118, 152, 153, 154, 156, 157, 158, 159, 201, 297n, 298n
Volkssturm Night Attack Squadron, 150
Voronezh, Russia, 226
Vozhd, *see* Josef Stalin
Vulcan-Werft shipbuilders, Stettin, 268n

Waffen-SS, 31, 194, 204, 212, 293n
6th SS Panzer Army, 196, 308n
11th SS Panzer Army, 193, 313n
Großdeutschland division, 131, 154
Waggonfabrik Steinfurt AG, Königsberg, 168
Wagner, Adolf, *Gauleiter*, Upper Bavaria, 41, 261n
Wagner, Ernst, *Kreisleiter*, Königsberg
death, 240
faith in Hitler, 65, 263n
Festung Königsberg, 210–211, 213, 220, 320–321n
mass funeral, 170
Soviet atrocities, 226, 227, 326n
violent nature, 328n
Volkssturm commander, 210, 213, 220, 295n
Wagner, Joseph, *Gauleiter*, Silesia, 29–30, 257n
Wahlstatt, Battle of (1241), 181
Waldenburg, Silesia, 197, 204
Wander, Dr, *Bürgermeister*, Insterburg, 131, 136, 139, 177, 300n

War of Liberation (1813–1814), 147–148, 149, 157, 222
Ward, John, RAF Sargeant, 326n
Warsaw, 2, 5, 8, 11, 19, 74, 100, 101, 135, 176, 193, 220, 221, 240, 241, 245n, 258n, 266n, 280n, 295n, 312n, 315n
Warsaw Old Town, 3, 291n
Warsaw Pact, 2
Warsaw Rising (1944), 3, 11, 27, 57, 85, 128, 197, 250n, 272n, 276n, 290n
Wartenburg, East Prussia
Army Group Centre HQ, 175, 306n
evacuation, 208
Koch's death, 1986, 240
Wartenburg, Peter Yorck von, Count, 257n
Warthe, River, 97, 98, 193, 196, 216
Warthegau
air raids, 64
destination for evacuees, 45, 284n
eastern refugees, 85
evacuation and treks, 1945, 198, 200, 201, 205, 322n
expulsion of Poles, 37
extermination camp, 68
fifth anniversary, 1944, 184
fortresses, 212, 280n
general mood, 1944, 133
German propaganda, 1944–1945, 187, 188, 219, 288n
German resistance groups, 230
Greiser's crimes, 241
Greiser's departure 204, 324n
mood of German soldiers, 79, 286n
Ostwall, 95, 101, 108, 111, 284n
Red Army's Vistula bridgeheads, 184
Soviet agents, 178
travel restrictions, 83–84
treatment of Jews, 38, 67
Volkssturm, 147, 154, 215, 293n
see also Danzig–West Prussia, *Gau*; *General Gouvernement*
Wehlau, East Prussia, 186, 250n
Wehler, Hans-Ulrich, Professor, 246n
Wehrkamerad, 105
Wehrkreis
I East Prussia, 116, 183, 319n
II Pomerania, 84, 158, 159, 207
III Brandenburg, 84
VIII Silesia, 82, 84, 174
XXI Warthegau, 293n
organisational issues, 26, 100, 147, 212, 293n
Wehrmacht
Army Group A, 174, 182–183, 188, 191, 193, 194, 204, 317n
Army Group Centre
changes in command, 75, 106, 192, 283n
collapse, Belorussia, 1944, 73–76, 82, 83, 99, 100, 243, 272n, 279n
headquartered in East Prussia, 81
jurisdiction in East Prussia, 116
Ostwall, 105–106
readiness, autumn 1944, 130, 172
readiness, 1945, 175, 179, 183, 191
renamed Army Group North, 192
Silesia, 1945, 224, 314n, 317n, 322n
Soviet propaganda, 93
Army Group Courland, 192, 289n
Army Group North
Centre renamed North, 192
danger of being cut-off, 73–75, 131, 133, 183
fighting in East Prussia, 320n
outside Leningrad, 37
Schörner as commander, 153, 309n
supplies, 59, 161
Army Group North Ukraine, 74, 75, 272n
Army Group South, 40, 74, 100, 269n
Army Group South Ukraine, 75, 92
Army Group Vistula, 194–195, 206
Second Army, 81, 93, 135, 194, 196
Third Panzer Army, 74, 79, 81, 92, 129, 131, 132, 144, 184, 192, 194, 297n, 309n, 311n
Fourth Army
East Prussia, 1944–1945, 81, 130, 135, 179, 183, 184, 191–192, 220, 309n
losses in Belorussia, 1944, 75
Ninth Army, 194, 197, 215
Seventeenth Army, 202, 224, 314n, 330n
Twenty-Fourth Panzer Corps, 224
Twenty-Eighth Corps, 155
First East Prussian Infantry Division, 35, 81, 119, 132, 220
Fifth Panzer Division, 135
Twelfth Panzer Division, 80
609th Division, 222
Weimar Republic (1919–1933), 7, 17–20, 23–25, 96–97
Weiss, Walter, Colonel-General, 135
Welles, Sumner, US Under-Secretary of State, 245n
Wenck, Walther, General, 178, 196, 313n
Werkgruppen, 97–98
Werth, Alexander, *The Times* correspondent, Moscow, 175, 227
Werwolf, 230, 327n
West Germany, *see* Federal Republic of Germany
Western Allies, 4, 64, 73, 86, 115, 173, 181, 223, 230, 234, 237, 245n, 253–254n, 269n, 308n, 327n
Western Neisse, River, 1, 245n
Westfälische Landeszeitung, Rote Erde, 307–308
Westphalia, 29–30, 31, 45, 308n

Westwall, 97, 99, 100, 126, 280n
Whisper Propaganda, 219, 225
White Russia, *see* Belorussia
Wieck, Michael, Königsberg, 187, 237, 303n
Wildenhoff, East Prussia, 185, 247n
Wilhelm II, *Kaiser*, 20–21
Wilhelm Gustloff, liner, 8, 200
Will, Hellmuth, Dr, *Oberbürgermeister*, Königsberg, 169, 220, 260n, 303n, 320n
Willenberg, East Prussia, 253n
Windau (Ventspils), Latvia, 295n
Winkler, Dr, Silesian official, 156
Winter Battle in Masuria (1915), 20–21
Winter Relief Fund, 27
Wiskemann, Elizabeth, 198, 246n
Wolff, Karl, *SS-Obergruppenführer*, 331n
Wolff, Paul, Königsberg official, 27
Wolfsschanze (Wolf's Lair), *see Führerhauptquartier*
Wollin Island, Pomerania, 196
Woyrsch, Udo von, *SS-Obergruppenführer*, 29, 256n
Wprost, 10
Wroclaw, *see* Breslau
Württembergische Wirtschafts-Zeitschrift, 265n
Wuthenau von, Dr, *Landrat*, Netzekreis, Pomerania, 110, 139

Xylander, Wolfdietrich von, Lieutenant-General, 183

Yelton, David, Professor, 146, 155
Yugoslavia, 1, 3, 196, 245n, 313n

Zachodia Agencja Prasowa (Western Press Agency), 5, 247n
Zayas, Alfred Maurice de, 6, 144, 293n, 296n, 298n, 321n
ZDF, *see Zweites Deutsches Fernsehen*
Zehran, Erich, President, Finance Department, Königsberg, 209, 320n
Zeman, Milos, Czech Prime Minister, 9
Zentrum (Centre Party), 24
Zhukov, Georgi, Marshal, 191, 193–194, 195, 196, 225, 226, 311n, 314n
Zichenau, East Prussia
  annexed to East Prussia, 28, 37, 39
  death sentences, 272n
  deportation of Jews, 295n
  evacuation, 177
  German retreat, 1944, 78
  mood of German settlers, 63, 80
  Ostwall, 111
  Polish inhabitants, 55
Zillmer, Dr, *Wehrkreis* I, General Staff officer, 319n
Zimpel, Breslau, 239
Zitronenfalter (code word), 131
Züllichau, Brandenburg
  Berlin evacuees, 46–47
  defences, 97
  defences unmanned, 1945, 215
  Einsatz Zielenzig, 108, 113
  Volkssturm, 158
Zweites Deutsches Fernsehen (ZDF), 8